SUSTAINABLE URBANISM AND BEYOND

SUSTAINABLE URBANISM AND BEYOND

RETHINKING CITIES FOR THE FUTURE

EDITED BY
TIGRAN HAAS

Rizzoli
NEW YORK

New York · Paris · London · Milan

First published in the United States of America in 2012 by
Rizzoli International Publications, Inc.
300 Park Avenue South
New York, NY 10010
www.rizzoliusa.com

ISBN: 978-0-8478-3836-3
LCCN: 2011944834

Distributed to the U.S. trade by Random House, New York

Design: Abigail Sturges

Printed and bound in China

2012 2013 2014 2015 2016 / 10 9 8 7 6 5 4 3 2 1

CONTENTS

FIG. 1. Different Urbanism Ideals existing side by side in Graz, Austria.
Vito Acconci's Murinsel sits on the Mur river in Graz, Austria.

SUSTAINABLE URBANISM AND BEYOND

TIGRAN HAAS

We have modified our environment so radically
that we must now modify ourselves
to exist in this new environment.
— Norbert Wiener

"May you live in interesting times," and "Tell me, I forget. Show me, I remember. Involve me, I understand." These Chinese proverbs fit well with the complex reality of everyday life in the twenty-first century—a reality that is bestowed upon each and every one of us, and is characterized by seldom-seen natural and manmade structural change. Global climate change—with its social, economic, political, cultural, and ecological dimensions (and the impact on our spatial, physical, and planning patterns)—is one of the principal challenges facing humanity. The cities of today are the greatest assemblage of material resources, human capital, and goods and services the planet has ever seen, in which now more than half of the world population live and about three fourths of world resources are being consumed as we speak. Urbanization is the defining phenomenon and process of this century. The impact of rapid urbanization coupled with population growth will be felt most acutely in developing countries, where the built-up area is expected to increase threefold while the urban population doubles by 2030. From this troubling perspective, both city sustainability and the resilience of cities become the main issues at hand. The search for a more conventional and livable lifestyle in the city or in the countryside continues unabated for citizens and consumers globally, regardless of the realization and predictions of "dark ages ahead." Finding enthusiasm for giving up the car-centric, middle-class, consumerist lifestyle has not been easy; and moving from the wasteful life of suburban sprawl toward a tighter, more self-contained, enclosed neighborhood setting and a more connected public transit system will not be the only solution. Unlike established global centers like New York, London, Paris, Hong Kong or Tokyo, exploding megacities of more than ten million people—such as Mexico City, Cairo, Mumbai, Moscow, Beijing, Karachi, Calcutta, Dhaka, Seoul, São Paulo, Shanghai, Istanbul—or dense, sprawling, continuously rising metropolises like Los Angeles, Bangkok, Bogotá, Lima, Tehran, Dhaka, Kinshasa, and other supercharged growth places such as Dubai, Wuhan, Chittagong, Chennai, Tel Aviv, Santiago,

Atlanta, Hanoi, Melbourne, Austin will be (and are) both the problem and the solution for solving urban problems. And while explosions in growth present one type of problem, urban shrinkage presents another—as evidenced in the shrinking cities of the U.S. and Europe, where urban problems emerge in stagnant or slow-growing population levels, often coupled with very weak or crumbling economies.

As Dushko Bogunovich rightly points out, the "significance of cities in the global outlook picture is further underlined by the grim fact that they are simultaneously the main aggregate source of environmental degradation of the planet, and most likely the main victim of extreme weather events, global sea level rise, shortages of key supplies, and other environmental disturbances that are likely to affect the planet toward the middle of this century if cities remain as greedy as they are now." Sustainable Urbanism can be viewed as a new and emerging framework for interdisciplinary urban planning, design, and management of our regions, cities, towns, neighborhoods, and urban blocks. It explores sustainability and urban design in a rapidly changing and urbanizing world by focusing on the processes that shape the form and function of the built environment in its full complexity— the infrastructures, land developments, built landscapes, and facilities that collectively make up metropolitan regions. The synergy of multimodal transportation, sustainable economics, ecology and natural resource management, socio-cultural aspects, and physical-urban form become crucial for creating livable cities and communities of place that, together with their hinterlands, produce sustainable metropolitan-regional cities. This can be achieved only through a new prism—that of "sustainable (green) thinking and holistic regional design," through which comprehensive physical planning and sustainable urbanism become crucial. Unfortunately, in the last century we have, as citizens as well as professionals working with urban development and planning, developed a disconnection from nature that has contributed to the greatest crisis in the history of mankind and the greatest threat to the natural eco-balance of our planet and our built environment—to our cities. There is no doubt in the mind of any urbanist that, to avoid the looming environmental disaster, one of the greatest cultural and technological transformations that we (as citizens, not consumers) must undertake pertains to the way we plan, design, build, maintain, govern, and use our cities. The radical transformation of how cities work implies, for most urbanists, a radical change in the way they plan and design. At the same time, we cannot forget that the human aspects of urban form remain essential—maybe more now than ever before. We need to plan, design, and maintain various places—foremost through understanding their identity (individuality), structure (physical pattern), meaning (practical-emotional impact), and setting (relation to environment). The new paradigm of Landscape Urbanism is a commendable one, but one wonders if the fundamental part of urban and city planning doesn't lie in the arrangement of buildings, and thereby the human aspects of urban form, rather than the natural landscape upon which the buildings stand.

As urbanists, we find ourselves challenged by the rise of a new epoch. It is a period of uncertainty, risk, distress, and rapid change on multiple levels. As the reality of global climate change and fossil fuel dependency fully kicks in, there will be a growing feeling that almost every aspect of life and work will be touched and altered by new forces that are, at present, insufficiently understood. The task at hand is directly connected to the rebuilding and building of our planet's cities and their massive and complex infrastructures. How we engage in this task, and how we manage human development and planning, will determine the future path of global warming and the resilience of the earth's carrying capacity. Beyond the older sustainable and newer resilience-based methods of planning and designing, changes are needed at all levels of practice, not least in ways of addressing the infrastructure-transit lines. If (public) transportation systems in general are going to become more accessible, affordable, reliable, and more environmentally responsive, then coordination or multimodality between various means—buses, light railway, trains, cars, commuter vans, ships, and airplanes—is of the essence. Close systems networking and meticulous traffic information, as well as the usage of environmentally friendly and energy-saving materials and fuels, will be some of the solutions for global cities and mega-metropolitan regions experiencing exploding populations, changing economies, and continuing urbanization. Meeting the mobility requirements of people and goods, as well as creating pragmatic, affordable, and sustainable directions "to achieve a planet of cities, not a planet of slums" (to paraphrase Mike Davis) in the coming decades will dominate urbanism and require transformation on all levels. As Peter Calthorpe recently observed, "Such a transformation will require deep change, not just in energy sources, technology, and conservation measures but also in urban design, culture, and lifestyles. More than just deploying green technologies and adjusting our thermostats, it will involve rethinking the way we live and the underlying form of our communities." The good news, according to Calthorpe, is that our environmental, social, and economic challenges

have a shared solution in urbanism, which is "shaping regions that reduce oil dependence and simultaneously reduces carbon emissions, costs less for the average household, and creates healthy, integrated places for our seniors: one solution for multiple challenges." Sustainable Urbanism furthers the concepts, approaches, and methods of New Urbanism and becomes a sort of umbrella term and frame for architecture, urban planning, and urban design that takes into greater account the issues of sustainability, resilience, human health and safety, eco-system dependency, natural resource management, permaculture, green building and eco-tech design, environmental justice, accessibility and mobility, and green economic growth.

A tripartite vision of the future direction of urbanism—coinciding with the three main principles that should guide public policy, development practice, and urban planning and design (as set in the Charter of the New Urbanism)—needs to be centered around macro regional analysis (the region, metropolis, city and town), overall town planning questions (the neighborhood, the district, and the corridor), and analysis of urban and town planning and design on the micro level (the block, the street, and the building). Åke E. Andersson calls this micro, meso, and macro levels of built environment. The first component is the macro regional analysis; to understand these issues in a holistic and systematic way, the built environment has to be placed in a macro regional level. The overall town-planning issues should be oriented toward synthesis, planning, and policy questions—a meso analytical level. Closely related to these issues are environmental and urban design (sustainable urbanism) questions addressing the overall placement of the building, the urban setting, and the urban region in which that setting is located. Of importance are the causal and dependent issues of the type of built environment and infrastructure system (especially transportation) to be achieved, as well as other complex issues of building use. When we speak of the micro level, the area of interest (not just in practice, but also in education and research) should include the micro built level, namely taking in issues ranging from room analysis and use, to the building in which a person(s) is housed. Evaluating the use of the residential built environment is, however, just one component of the micro level; the focus should not be only be on housing but should also be directed strongly to other aspects of the built environment—for instance civic, cultural, leisure, industrial, and other uses and types. The third component of the tripartite approach necessitates a strong focus on the relation of the aforementioned components of the built environment to their surroundings, and all the psychological, social, political, economic, and environmental aspects that play a part in the overall town planning level. This component therefore deals with the complexity of issues at stake in the built environment, pointing toward a multidisciplinary approach. What is really needed within this new sustainable urbanism and holistic regionalism is a highly strategic, immediate, interdisciplinary, focused, doable, systemic vision for planning: retrofitting and preparing new and old urban regions for the troubled and uncertain times ahead. A one-sided belief in technology, green buildings, and recycling alone is not sufficient; the problem lies more in the manner in which our cities are planned and designed. Thinking in terms of grand master plans and city-branding architecture—artificial archipelagos of non-sustainable extravagant urban forms (as many of the global cities do) instead of plans of action (especially on the local level)—will hardly take us toward the desired goal of sustainability.

The Dark Ages provided a foundation for the Renaissance, a time when artists, master builders, writers, philosophers, and all other intellectuals proposed a new image of mankind and of the world to emerge, one based on empiricism, experimentation, and observation. If we imagine that we have stepped into this age now, and that the resurgence of learning based on classical sources and historical and natural laws that worked previously is being embedded in all of us, it is now time to sustain this effort. The Sustainable Urbanism idea must be one of an "Enlightenment" of sorts, whereby the ideas of this New Renaissance will continue to grow and become widespread. Specifically, this has to be a time when advancements in science and technology lead us to an emphasis on the power of human reasoning. Furthermore, we need to bring the world back (from and within our own fields and competences) to a harmonic and natural balance; not just a mechanical, informational, digital, virtual, and technological process that we see unfolding in front of our eyes, and not just by relying on the infrastructures of the network society. Major challenges facing urban development and planning (urbanism) can be viewed through multiple prisms, but the challenges that will seemingly dominate the coming decades include: Increased Urbanization (Conflicts over Natural Resources); "Hot, Flat, and Overcrowded" Territories (Rise and Increased Consumption of the Middle Class); Heightened Diversity (of People, Ideas, and Groups); Presence of the Information Technology and Network Society (New Places and Spaces); Dichotomy of Environmental Urban-Rural Sustainability (Land Use and Resource Allocation); Governance and Management (at Local, Regional, and National Levels); Disaster Planning and Resilience (Preventive and Contingency Risk Scenarios); Cross-disciplinary and Interdisciplinary Collaboration (Joint Work, Initiative, and Skills); Flexibility and Innovation of Institutions (Talented Cities, Adaptation, and Civil Society); Cities of Fear and Cities of Hope (Balancing the Just and Livable Communities); Urban Mobility and Multi-modality (Cars, Energy, and Commuting); Accessibility, Affordability, and Availability (Just and Equidistant Urbanism); Signature Cities and Place Marketing (Brands, Global Flows, and Media); and others.

Good urban design is essential for delivering places that are sustainable on all counts: places that create social, environmental, and economic value. But in order to do good urban design, we need to go back to the basics. We have become disconnected from nature in our modern, consumerist, industrialized, and network society. We talk about consumption, and how the driving force nowadays seems to be economy, *the economy*, and in accepting that we have lit-erally tapped out our planet's resources and now need to initiate a sweeping shift toward renewable energy. The Sustainable Urbanism ideas in this book constitute an attempt to provide a vision of the phenomena that are now transforming advanced societies and the urban centers of our modern civilizations—the phenomena of climate change and rapid and unstoppable hyper-urbanization on all levels—and the role that urbanism plays in addressing these challenges. Nations powered by alternative energy, carbon-neutral cities, and self-sustaining buildings already offer ideas for a new direction. In some instances, these things are happening, but they are far from being the only solutions. If a state of resilience, and cities of hope, are to be achieved in the long run, everyone must become involved to reverse the destruction and climate change—not just architects, urban planners, and designers. This task requires community participation and citizen input on all levels. As Andrés Duany noted recently, "While democracy doesn't need a great number of voters to function well, it does require a full cross-section to participate; that is the source of its collective intelligence."

Michael Sorkin calls for more "humane, equitable, sustainable, and beautiful cities . . . cities that need to supply their own food, energy, water, thermal behavior, air quality, movement systems, building and cultural and economic institutions. This urban self-sufficiency is a means to political autonomy and planetary responsibility." However noble this might seem and sound, in order to achieve it we need a moral, ethical, and cultural transformation—a reevaluation of all we do, as well as a major shift in the attitudes, values, and norms of urbanists. That notwithstanding, far too much is being put on the shoulders of architects, urban planners, and designers, who are expected to invent a kind of universal formula or "golden key" for solving most of the acute global problems we are faced with today. At the same time, urbanism has to attain some paragon state—a just society and equality for all, enhancing equity, diversity, and ultimately the survival of the planet in its capacity to support humanity. As a matter of fact, urbanism can support these noble goals and work toward providing a good quality of life for all—but urbanism alone is not and cannot be concerned with devising the means to do this. This is not its task; rather, it is the task of socio-technology, governance, and social policymaking.

Recently, there has been an ascendency of theories and discourses that criticize *dialogue democracy, cosmopolitan* democracy, *democratization of democracy*, etc. These have to do with the "utopian realist" third way in politics, with its belief in dialogue and deliberation. Some of the critics oppose the claim of what they call the "post-political perspective," a view that, in a new era, potential antagonisms will disappear. The opposing thesis is that "as far as international politics is concerned, we will be faced with the multiplicity of antagonisms." From the point of view of urban planning and design, these speculations—or futuristic deliberations—are rather irrelevant. Imposing such political approaches in cities—through regional/municipal/neighborhood talks, deliberations, and negotiations over urban problems between professionals, politicians, real estate developers, and the general public—would be superfluous and miss the point. If such an imposition were to occur, it would simply be done in a speculative out-of-context way, just to apply—*a priori* and *in abstracto*—those new (world) political theories to "real world issues" through matters of urban planning and design.

Another problem can be located in the pretense of postmodern, poststructuralist discourse that has to do with the suggestion of (re)inventing new concepts in urbanism. In the guise of a bulwark literary analysis, urban space, i.e., physical and even social/livable/behavioral realms, suddenly lose their basic meaning. The discussions are characterized by wordplay and hence are hardly translatable. Even more dangerous, such an approach is creating an illusion that with a change of terminology, concepts, and words (the conceptual framework) relating to social problems, issues of inequality, stigmatization, etc., will be improved. The proponents of such an outlook on urbanism advocate the change of our talk about reality and real concepts and suggest the invention of other concepts, words, and means (*something in between*) in order to change reality and our attitude toward that reality. They advocate that the changing of "formulas"—in most *cases words*—will change reality! As the world-renowned philosopher of science Mario Bunge observed, "The postmodern rejection of clarity, rationality, consistency, and objective truth (intellectual values of Enlightenment) implemented through literary criticism, cultural studies, and deconstructionism in general, is incoherent rambling with almost no shred of evidence for the extravagant claims it makes." According to proponents of postmodernism, concepts, names, meanings, and conceptual frameworks are prior to real life; language is prior to meaning; there is nothing outside the text. How we talk about and define urbanities, spaces, and places is not, however, the product of pure reason, abstractions, wishful thinking, literary analysis, and magic formulas produced through discourse, but rather more a complex process that goes on within and around urbanism. It is social, technological, cultural, economic, political, material, scientific—with all the multi-professional disciplines and various expertise involved. All of this changes and develops urban planning and design, thereby changing and developing conceptual frameworks and categories, adapting them, making them more appropriate and understandable.

The task ahead of us is enormous if we are to adapt and plug in our growing and emergent cities and our splintered urbanisms into urban regions and regional cities of resilience, sustainability, and hope. Dense or compact, sprawling or edgeless, fractured or splintered, iconic or exemplary, desolate or forgotten, decaying or shrinking, uncontrolled and squatted—all our global cities have urbanisms and urban forms that grow and exist side by side. As we now live in an age of unprecedented rapid change, brought about by the modern service economy, the network society (Internet being its main energy), and the transportation system, our urban forms need to respond to that challenge. A "one size fits all" approach will not work over the long haul, and each place

will have to have its own unique solution based in the most appropriate and sustainable design possible. *Sustainability* and *resilience* need to work parallel. Taken together, these two positions add up to a new vision of city and town planning that does not put a priority on either city life or suburban living; it rather focuses on resource protection, the creative use of natural infrastructure, and on systems thinking and seeing. As Peter Calthorpe soundly calls sustainable development, it is "a thoughtful combination of good urbanism with renewable energy sources, state-of-the-art- conservation techniques, new green technologies, and integrated services and utilities."

A balance must be made—being explicitly against density and vehemently pro-automobile will not work at all; sticking too much to all-classical and traditional ways of planning and building will not work everywhere; and designing and building sprawling high-tech, avant-garde post-urbanist Disneylands will not be sustainable anymore. We therefore need to start rethinking what "the good city" should be for all its citizens. Thinking that slums or poor neighborhoods are appropriate (dense or splintered) urban forms that make a contribution to ecological footprint and sustainability through resource allocation and recycling is a dangerous path to take. Implying that being poor is ecologically sound is simply wrong, because it is a matter of pure necessity—not of ecological awareness or choice—to live in a decent and healthy urban environment. For sustainability to fully take command on all levels, it must comply with the laws of the market (financial incentives) and it must become "easy to sell," "passively consumed," and "require very little involvement and engagement," as Cia Rinne reminds us. As we do find ourselves in "interesting times," in an interdependent age of networked society and globalization, there is a message for all of us here. It has to do with recovering forgotten values—a lost understanding of the holistic view of "nature as systemic processes"—and the realization that we are undergoing the deepest crises of humanity: a crisis of material actions, a crisis of ecology, a crisis of our cities and neighborhoods, of our built environment, and of our planet Earth.

Aim and Overview of This Book

The aim of *Sustainable Urbanism and Beyond: Rethinking Cities for the Future* is to provide a comprehensive, state-of-the-art overview of ideas and thoughts on urbanism—architecture, planning, and urban design—at a time of global climate change, energy crisis, and rapid urban development from some of the leading minds of today. The Sustainable Urbanism theme is taken as the leitmotif, trend, paradigm, and approach to planning and urban design that—through sustainability, resilience, human aspects of urban form, new technologies, natural resource management, landscape and nature, transportation, and other aspects of the built environment—raises the quality of life and standard of living through creating better urban places. As was the case with the preceding book in the series, *New Urbanism and Beyond*, this book also aims to offer a better understanding of how cities can thrive in a new, complex, and unpredictable modern era. The timeliness of this book goes in line with the current efforts toward sensitizing and establishing guidelines and tips for city leaders, community activists, business people, researchers, students, and regular citizens who seek to better understand and improve the status of their cities, communities, neighborhoods, and other urban places in response to climate change, economic changes, urban sprawl, peak oil, population growth, and the rise of the middle class.

This book (as part of a trilogy on urbanism) concentrates on the fundamental issues confronting contemporary urbanism and urban/town planning and design in the light of climate change and energy crises as well as crises of the built environment. It therefore focuses on key topics that will be of value to scholars, undergraduate and graduate students, and professionals and decision makers in this and all fields related to development and urban studies. The contributions come from more than seventy major theoreticians and practitioners in the field today. In line with *New Urbanism and Beyond*, the intention is to produce a first-class work of urban planning and design reference, with Sustainable Urbanism as the recurring theme. This advanced *primer-digest-engager* will be both an essential resource for practice and a useful aid in academic teaching: a solid, but also provocative, next step for wider exploration of the urbanism field and related subjects.

In the past three decades, urban design has emerged as an academic specialty akin to, but somewhat distinct from, traditional architecture and urban planning. Sustainable Urbanism, as a logical successor to the ideas and thoughts put forward by the New Urbanism movement, has attracted attention in the academic literature of several other disciplines and in popular literature, and has put forward and advanced new paradigms and outlooks on cities (Landscape Urbanism). All of that has been followed by a remarkable number of publications that have emerged from all sides which theorize or analyze the newest urban condition and propose (new and green) approaches to its design challenges.

This is yet another unique collection of essays, untarnished, in their raw form. The authors assembled here under the Sustainable Urbanism banner originate from an array of disciplines, including architecture, urban planning, urban design, landscape urbanism, and human geography, among others. The book is organized into ten topical sections with pertinent, contemporary themes including "Beyond New Urbanism," "Climate Change and Resilience," "Emerging Tools of Urban Design Sustainability," "Systemic Mobility and Structural Ecology and Urban Informatics," "Sustainable Communities," "Urban Theory and City Planning," "New Spatial Geographies and Regional Cities," "Just Environments and Structure of Places," "Urban Shifts," "New Networks and Geographies," and "The Future of Globalized Cities." More than sixty diverging, engaging, provocative, and highly dynamic essays cover issues within the fields in which urbanism operates: architecture, planning and urban design, landscape architecture, ecology, urban development,

and social and natural science in general. The essays are highly varied, representing modes of thinking that are consistent with the multidimensional complexity of our cities, with their many layers of social, political, environmental, cultural, economic, technological, legal, experiential, and aesthetic meanings. The papers address the aforementioned urban development and planning challenges in diverse, intriguing, and interesting ways which hint at the contours of an emerging, vast, complex, and intricately interconnected field of Sustainable Urbanism—a paradigm for rethinking our cities for the future and adopting new tools and paraphernalia for the complex age ahead of us.

The previous volume *New Urbanism and Beyond* was inspired by, not the result of, the "New Urbanism and Beyond" conference, debates, and summer course held in Stockholm, Sweden, in October 2004 at the Royal Institute of Technology (in fact, 90 percent of the papers were written especially for the book between 2005 and 2008). This was the largest ever gathering (after the famous conference "Exploring New Urbanism" at the Harvard Graduate School of Design in 1999) of what Professor Manuel Castells has called "some of the brightest urban minds of today." While New Urbanism showed the negative aspects of suburban sprawl, automobile dependency, edgeless city expansion, strip and shopping malls, generic and soulless subdivisions, rigid zoning, and failed public housing programs, it also offered an alternative in compact, walkable, dense, diverse communities and neighborhoods, with public transit nodes and the possibility of building a successful social housing program. Sustainable Urbanism in turn goes *one step beyond*— it debates and offers a next phase in the understanding of the complexity and the systemic nature of urbanism today and works toward a vision of urban planning and design for cities that will ultimately look for the best and most rewarding solutions for all the citizens of the world and, ultimately, for the future of our planet.

This book, *Sustainable Urbanism and Beyond: Rethinking Cities for the Future*, similarly started as being inspired by, not the result of, the Council for European Urbanism and Congress for New Urbanism Conference on Climate Change and Urban Design held in Oslo, Norway, in September 2008. Building on the ideas from its predecessor, the structure of the current work assembles yet another collection of some of the brightest urban minds of today. This is not an anticipatory work, a book of dreams, or a nostrum for the future design of cities and our communities. As noted in the preceding book in the series, it is also valid here to make the final observation that this is simply a solidly grounded collection of ideas and thoughts on our urban condition and beyond written by an exceptional group of individuals never assembled before. It is a homogenous series of proactive lessons on how the evolution of urbanism will alter the way we live, work, build, and communicate in our cities, communities, and neighborhoods—an unpretentious but coherent and balanced set of essays with a vision of contemporary and future urban form and its influence on everyday life patterns in our "brave, new twenty-first-century world."

PART 1: SUSTAINABLE URBANISM, CLIMATE CHANGE, AND RESILIENCE

1.1   URBANISM AND CLIMATE CHANGE

PETER CALTHORPE

The world's urban population has more than quadrupled since 1950, more than half of us live in urban environments for the first time, and the trend is accelerating. Like it or not, the globe has an urban future. The pressing question, then, is what type of urbanism will prevail. The answer will not only define the physical nature of our communities, but also will prescribe our environmental footprint, frame our social opportunities, and underwrite our economic future. Yet urbanism is often missing from the proposed remedies for climate change and environmental stress; it is the invisible wedge in the pie chart of green solutions.

To respond to the energy and climate change challenge, compounding layers of design must be integrated. Efficient, climate-responsive buildings are important but miss many community-scale opportunities. Individual communities, while offering more options for whole-systems design, cannot in themselves create robust alternatives to the car nor enact large-scale strategies for farmland preservation, habitat conservation, or economic revitalization. Transit Oriented Development begins to imply a regional framework of transit and intelligently located development but is ultimately just one dimension of a broad range of strategies needed to shape healthy regional growth. Over decades, I learned that each scale depends on the others and that only a whole systems approach, with each scale nesting into the other, can deliver the kind of transformation we now need to confront climate change.

Certainly cities are green. On a per capita basis, they require less land, less auto travel, and less energy, and they emit less carbon. But this message may well oversimplify the complex, multilayered urban and regional strategies that are key to our future. More than stand-alone "sustainable communities" or even "green cities," we now need "sustainable regions"—places that carefully blend a broad range of technologies, settlement patterns, and lifestyles. Only a regional plan can create a framework for communities of differing scales and intensities, for transportation choices that can significantly offset auto dependence, and for environmental

systems and green technologies that function at both the large and small scales. Whole systems design functions best at the regional scale.

Too often we see our environmental challenges in technical terms, within the domain of industrial efficiencies, renewable power generation sources, or green technologies. Instead, we need a vision of the future that sees climate change and energy through the lens of lifestyles, land use, urbanism, and, most significantly, design of the metropolitan region.

But it is not just the threat of climate change or the depletion of energy resources that will dramatically redirect our patterns of settlement. The lines of pressure are converging from many directions: limits of environmentally rich land and clean water are being felt throughout the world; shifts in family size and workforce are changing our social structure; issues of environmental and personal health are mounting; costs of capital and time are reordering investments; and, not least, a new search for identity, community, and a sense of place is motivating many peoples' lives. It is my thesis that a future that responds to all of these pressures will also best address the climate change crisis.

In fact, these wide-ranging environmental, social, and economic challenges should not, and realistically cannot, be resolved individually. I have always been suspicious of single-issue causes—no matter how worthy—mostly because they are often blind to both unintended consequences and important collateral benefits. Urbanism's effects reverberate well beyond carbon emissions, and that is exactly why it can become such a powerful solution to the climate change challenge: it is propelled by many other needs. The economics of urbanism reach from simple infrastructure and energy savings to public health, affordable housing, and land conservation. In addition, it involves more qualitative outcomes that relate to social capital, economic equity, and quality of life.

There are three interdependent approaches to these nested challenges: lifestyle, conservation, and clean energy. Lifestyle involves how we live—the way we get around, the size of our homes, the foods we eat, and the quantity of goods we consume. These depend in turn on the type of communities we build and the culture we inhabit—degrees of urbanism. Conservation revolves around technical efficiencies—in our buildings, cars, appliances, utilities, and industrial systems—as well as preserving the natural resources that support us all: our global forests, ocean ecologies, and farmlands. Conservation measures are simple, they save money, and they are possible now. The third fix, clean energy, is what we have been most focused on: new technologies for solar, wind, wave, geothermal, biomass, and even a new generation of nuclear power or fusion. These energy sources are sexy, they are relatively expensive, and they will be available sometime soon. All three approaches will be essential, but here I focus on the first two—lifestyle and conservation—because they are, in the end, our most cost effective and easily available tools.

The intersection of these two is urbanism. Consider that in the United States industry represents 29 percent of our greenhouse gas (GHG) emissions; agriculture and other non-energy-related activities, just 9 percent; and freight and planes, another 9 percent. This 47 percent total represents the GHG emissions of the products we buy, the food we eat, the embodied energy of all our possessions, and all the shipping involved in getting them to us. The remaining 53 percent depends on the nature of our buildings and personal transportation system—the realm of urbanism.[1] As a result, urbanism, along with a simple combination of transit and more efficient buildings and cars, can deliver much of our needed GHG reductions.

Perhaps just as important as greenhouse gas reductions and oil savings is the fact that urbanism generates a fortuitous web of co-benefits—it is our most potent weapon against climate change because it does so much more. Urbanism's compact forms lead to less land consumed and more farmland, parks, habitat, and open space preserved. A smaller urban footprint results in less development costs and fewer miles of roads, utilities, and services to build and maintain, which then leads to fewer impervious surfaces, less polluted storm runoff, and more water directed back into aquifers.

More compact development leads to lower housing costs as lower land and infrastructure costs affect sales prices and taxes. Urban development means a different mix of housing types—fewer large single-family lots, more bungalows and town houses in the U.S.—but in the end provides more housing choices for a more diverse population. It means less private space but more shared community places—more efficient and less expensive overall. Urbanism is more suited to an aging population, for whom driving and yard maintenance is a growing burden, as well as for working families seeking lower utility bills and less time spent commuting.

Urbanism leads to fewer miles driven, which then leads to less gas consumed—and less dependence on foreign oil supplies, less air pollution, less carbon emissions. Fewer miles also leads to less congestion, lower emissions, lower road construction and maintenance costs, and fewer auto accidents. This then leads to lower health costs because of fewer accidents and cleaner air, which is reinforced by more walk-ing, bicycling, and exercising, which contributes to lower obesity rates. And more walking leads to more people on the streets, safer neighborhoods, and perhaps stronger communities.

The feedback loops go on. More urban development means more compact buildings—less energy needed to heat and cool, lower utility bills, less irrigation water, and, once again, less carbon in the atmosphere. This then leads to lower demands on electric utilities and fewer new power plants, which again results in less carbon and less costs. As Buckminster Fuller exhorted us, urbanism is inherently "doing more with less."

Vision California

Measuring and understanding the feedback loops and co-benefits of urbanism is critical to judging the trade-offs. Few comprehensive studies have brought all of these variables together, so we typically cannot understand all the relationships and see all the implications. Fortunately, California's effort to implement its new greenhouse gas reduction laws has provided a comprehensive look at urbanism and its potential in relation to a range of conservation and clean energy policies. The Vision California study, developed for the California High-Speed Rail Authority and the California Strategic Growth Council, measured the results of several statewide land use futures coupled with conservation policies through the year 2050.[2] The results make concrete the choices before us, the feedback loops, and the scale of both benefits and costs.

California is projected to grow by 7 million new households and 20 million people, to a population of nearly 60 million, by 2050.[3] It is currently the seventh-largest economy in the world and therefore provides an important model of what is possible.

The study compared a "Trend" future dominated by the state's now typical low-density suburban growth and moderate conservation policies to a "Green Urban" alternative. This Green Urban alternative assumed that 35 percent of growth would be urban infill; 55 percent would be formed from a more compact, mixed-use, and walkable form of suburban expansion; and only 10 percent would be standard low-density development. In addition, the Green Urban alternative would push the auto fleet to an average 55 miles per gallon (MPG), its fuel would contain one third less carbon, and all new buildings would be 80 percent more efficient than today's norm. It does not represent a green utopia, but it is heading in that direction. The results of this comparison highlight just how much is at stake and what the costs will be.

Remarkably, the quantity of land needed to accommodate the next two generations was reduced 75 percent by the Green Urban scenario, from more than 5,600 square miles in the Trend future to only 1,500 square miles.[4] By comparison, the state's current developed area is 5,300 square miles. This difference would save vast areas of prime farmland in the Central Valley along with key open space and habitat in the coastal regions of the state. The more compact future means smaller yards to irrigate and fewer parking lots to landscape, saving an average of 3.4 million acre-feet of water per year—enough to fill the San Francisco Bay annually or to irrigate 6.5 million acres of farmland.[5] Less developed land also translates to fewer miles of infrastructure to build and maintain. The annual savings would be around $194 billion for the state, or $24,300 for each new household—not including the costs of ongoing maintenance. In addition, the Trend future would cost more in police and fire services as coverage areas increased.

Surprisingly, such a future did not dramatically change the range of housing choices available in the state. In fact, some would argue that the outcome would be more market responsive, providing a long overdue adjustment of housing types and prices. Specifically, while large single-family lots would decline from 40 percent of the total today to 30 percent in 2050, small-lot homes and bungalows would increase slightly and town houses would double to 16 percent. Multifamily condominiums and apartments would actually end up the same, at around a third of the market. Overall, detached single-family homes would drop from 62 percent of all homes today to just over half. Many would conclude that this a reasonable shift, one ultimately making the housing stock more diverse and affordable.

In the Green Urban future, auto dependence drops dramatically—in fact, average vehicle miles traveled throughout the state would be reduced 40 percent, to 18,000 miles per household from a Trend projection of 28,600. Closer destinations, better transit service, and more walkable neighborhoods all contribute to this significant shift. We would all still have cars, but they would be more efficient and we would use them less. The implication of this reduction in auto use is far-reaching. In terms of congestion, it is the equivalent of taking 18.6 million cars off the road.[6] There would be fewer roads and parking lots built, less land covered with impervious surface, and less runoff water to be cleaned and stored. The list of collateral benefits is long. In fact, the need for new freeways and highways is reduced by 4,700 miles, a savings of around $400 billion for the state.

Less driving means fewer accidents, in this scenario potentially saving around 3,100 lives and $5 billion in associated hospital costs per year.[7] Less driving means less air pollution and less respiratory diseases.[8] More walking means healthier bodies and less obesity, affecting diabetes rates and all of its associated health costs.[9] Most significantly, the Green Urban scenario reduces carbon emissions and comes very close to achieving the 12% Solution in the transportation sector of the economy.

When the savings in vehicle miles traveled are combined with low-carbon/high-MPG cars, emissions for transportation drop from more than 230 million metric tons to just 55. Moreover, we would consume 300 billion fewer gallons of fuel over the next forty years, for a savings of over $1.8 trillion. These numbers are almost too big to imagine, but by way of comparison, the proposed high-speed rail system running from San Diego to San Francisco is projected to cost $42 billion, just half the value of the potential annual gas savings. Put simply, at a projected $8 per gallon in 2050, these gas savings represent around $5,550 of savings per household.

There is more. The efficient and compact buildings of urban development use less energy, produce fewer greenhouse gases, and cost less to operate. The carbon reduction in the building sector is projected to be around 52 percent less. In total, the average household in the Green Urban future would save around $1,000 per year in utility payments. When this figure is combined with reduced auto ownership, maintenance, insurance, and gas costs, California households would save close to $11,000 per year in current dollars. With an interest rate of 5 percent, this could pay a mortgage of $200,000.

Urbanism Expanded

What is not to like in such a Green Urban future? For some, exactly the thing that makes most of these savings possible: a more urban life. For many people *urban* is a bad word that implies crime, congestion, poverty, and crowding. For them, it represents an environment that moves people away from a healthy connection with nature and the land. Its stereotype is the American ghetto, a crime-ridden concrete jungle that simultaneously destroys land, community, and human potential. The reaction to this stereotype has been a middle-class retreat into a closeted world of single-family lots and gated subdivisions in the suburbs. As a result, much of the last half century's planning has been directed toward depopulating cities, whether through the satellite towns of Europe or the suburbs of America.

But, for many others, the word urban represents economic opportunity, culture, vitality, innovation, and community. This positive reading is now manifest in the revitalized centers of many of our historic cities. In these core areas, the public domain—with its parks, streets, commercial centers, arts, and institutions—is once again becoming rich and vibrant, valued and desirable. There is new life in many city centers and their public places, from cafés and plazas to urban parks and museums—ultimately drawing people back to the city.

Traditional urbanism has three essential qualities: (1) a diverse population and range of activities, (2) a rich array of public spaces and institutions, and (3) walkable and human scale in its buildings, streets, and neighborhoods. Most of our built environment, from city to suburb, manifested these traits prior to World War II. Now, most suburbs succeed in contradicting each trait; public space is withering for lack of investment, people and activities are segregated by simplistic zoning, and human scale is sacrificed to a ubiquitous accommodation of the car.

None of these urban design principles are new. Jane Jacobs postulated a similar definition of urbanism in her landmark 1961 work *The Death and Life of Great American Cities*.

The difference here is that urban issues are also being considered in the context of climate change and environmental protection. In fact, one can arrive at the same design conclusions from the criteria of conservation, environmental quality, and energy efficiency that Jacobs located largely by social and cultural needs. By investigating the technologies and formal systems scaled for limited resources, climate change concerns add a new and critical element to Jacobs's rationale. If traditional urbanism and sustainable development can truly reduce our dependence on foreign oil, limit pollution and greenhouse gases, and create socially robust places, they not only will become desirable but will be inevitable.

To Jacobs's three traditional urban values of civic space, human scale, and diversity, the current environmental imperative adds two more: conservation and regionalism. Although the traditional city was by necessity energy and resource efficient, it commonly showed a destructive disregard for nature and habitat that would be inappropriate today. Bays were filled, wetlands drained, streams and rivers diverted, and key habitat destroyed. A green form of urbanism should protect those critical environmental assets while reducing overall resource demands.

Indeed, the simple attributes of urbanism are typically a more cost efficient environmental strategy than many renewable technologies. For example, in many climates, a party wall is more cost effective than a solar collector in reducing a home's heating needs. Well-placed windows and high ceilings offer better lighting than efficient fluorescents in the office. A walk or a bike ride is certainly less expensive and less carbon intensive than a hybrid car even at 50 miles per hour. A convenient transit line is a better investment than a "smart" highway system. A small co-generating electrical plant that reuses its waste heat locally could save more carbon per dollar invested than a distant wind farm. A combination of urbanism and green technology will be necessary, but the efficiency of urbanism should precede the costs of alternate technologies. As Amory Lovins of the Rocky Mountain Institute famously advocates, a "negawatt" of conservation is always more cost effective than a watt of new energy, renewable or not. Urban living in its many forms turns out to be the best type of conservation.

In addition, the idea of "conservation" in urban design applies to more than energy, carbon dioxide, and the environment; it also implies preserving and repairing culture and history as well as ecosystems and resources. Conserving historic buildings, institutions, neighborhoods, and cultures is as essential to a vital, living urbanism as is preserving its ecological foundations.

Regionalism sets city and community into the contemporary reality of our expanding metropolis. At this point in history, most of our key economic, social, and environmental networks extend well beyond individual neighborhoods, jurisdictions, or even cities. Our cultural identity, open space resources, transportation networks, social links, and economic opportunities all function at a regional scale—as do many of our most challenging problems, including crime, pollution, and congestion. Major public facilities, such as sports venues, universities, airports, and cultural institutions, shape the social geography of our regions as well as extend our local lives.

We all now lead regional lives, and our metropolitan forms and governance need to reflect that new reality. In fact, urbanism can thrive only within the construct of a healthy regional structure. The tradition of urbanism must be extended to an interconnected and interdependent regional network of places, creating polycentric regions rather than a metropolis dominated by the old city/suburb schism.

This last point is critical to understanding urbanism and the climate change challenge. City life is not the only environmental option; a regional solution can offer a range of lifestyles and community types without compromising our ecology. A well-designed region, when combined with aggressive conservation strategies, extensive transit systems, and new green technologies, can offer many types of sustainable lifestyles. New York City may have the smallest carbon footprint per capita, but to solve the climate change crisis we do not all have to live in the city.

Identifying an appropriate balance between technology, urban design, and regional systems in confronting climate change is now the critical challenge. As a greater percentage of the world's population increases its wealth, their definition of prosperity will become critical. If progress translates into the old American suburban lifestyle, we are all in trouble. If China and India adopt our development patterns—auto-oriented, low-density lifestyles or even a high-rise, high-density version of the same—we will truly need breakthrough technologies to accommodate the demands. If they develop an enlightened and indigenous form of urbanism, we all will have the opportunity to address climate change in a less heroic, more cost-effective and ultimately more humane way.

RESILIENT CITIES

PETER NEWMAN, TIMOTHY BEATLEY, AND HEATHER BOYER

Adapted from Resilient Cities: Responding to Peak Oil and Climate Change,
Peter Newman, Timothy Beatley, and Heather Boyer, Island Press (islandpress.org), 2009.

Resilience is increasingly being used as a way to describe human activities that are smart, secure, and sustainable. They are smart in that they are able to adapt to the new technologies of the twenty-first century, secure in that they have built-in systems that enable them to respond to extreme events as well as being built to last, and sustainable in that they are part of the solution to the big questions of sustainability such as how to minimize our impact or adapt to climate change, prepare for peak oil, and protect biodiversity. Resilience thinking has been applied mostly to regions and natural resource management systems,[1] but is increasingly being applied to cities.[2]

Characteristics of Resilient Cities

Globally, there are seven features of resilient cities that are emerging. These are described as seven archetypes:
- the renewable energy city
- the carbon-neutral city
- the distributed city
- the biophilic city
- the eco-efficient city
- the place-based city
- the sustainable transport city

These city types are overlapping in their approaches and outcomes. The challenge for urban professionals is to apply all of these approaches together to generate a sense of purpose through a combination of new technology, city design, and community-based innovation.

The Renewable Energy City

There are now a number of urban areas that are partly powered by renewable energy technologies, from the region to the building level. Renewable energy enables a city to reduce its ecological footprint, and, if using biological fuels, can be part of a city's enhanced ecological functions.

Renewable energy production can and should occur within cities, integrated into their land use and built form, and comprising a significant and important element of the urban economy. Cities are not simply consumers of energy but catalysts for more sustainable energy paths that can increasingly become a part of the earth's solar cycle.

New model cities that are 100 percent renewable are needed (see Masdar City in the United Arab Emirates), but retrofitting existing cities is just as important. In Europe, Freiburg and Hannover have become demonstrations on how to bring renewable energy into city planning.[3]

Along with planning strategies and incentives (financial and density bonuses), renewable cities recognize the need to set minimum regulatory standards (see Barcelona solar ordinance). Transport can also be a major part of the renewable energy challenge. The more public transport moves to electric power, the more it can be part of a renewable city (see Calgary Transit's "Ride the Wind" program). Renewable power enables cities to create healthy and livable environments while minimizing the use and impact of fossil fuels. But, by itself, this will not be enough to ensure resilient urban development.

The Carbon-neutral City

Many businesses, universities, local governments, and households are now committed to minimizing their carbon footprint and even becoming carbon neutral. But can it become a feature of whole neighborhoods and even complete cities? There are those who suggest it is essential if the world is to move to "post-carbon cities."[4]

Several initiatives focus on helping cities to reach these goals, including ICLEI-Local Governments for Sustainability Cities for Climate Change, Architecture 2030, the Clinton Foundation's C40 Cities climate change initiative, and UN-HABITAT's Cities and Climate Change Initiative (CCCI).

The U.K. government has decided that all urban development will be carbon neutral by 2016, and phasing-in began in 2009. The Beddington Zero Energy Development initiative (BedZED) is the first carbon-neutral community in the United Kingdom. It has extended the concept to include building materials and, as it is a social housing development, it has shown how to integrate the carbon neutral agenda with other sustainability goals, making it a more resilient demonstration.

Cities using carbon neutral as their planning strategy include Malmö and Växjö in Sweden; Adelaide, Sydney, and Fremantle in Australia; and Newcastle in the U.K. Vancouver's Winter Olympic Village was built as a model North American demonstration in carbon neutral urban development.

The link to the green agenda of a city is very direct with respect to the carbon neutral approach of bioregional tree planting schemes. By committing to be carbon neutral, cities can focus their offsets into bioregional tree planting as part of the biodiversity agenda as well as to address climate change.

Although there are many good tree-planting programs (see Australia's Green Fleet and Gondwana Links), none are committed yet to a comprehensive city-wide carbon-neutral approach that can link tree planting to a broader biodiversity cause. If this is done, cities can raise urban and regional reforestation to a new level and contribute to reducing the impact of climate change, simultaneously addressing local and regional green agenda issues.

The carbon-neutral city will receive a big boost when a global compact on carbon trading can be achieved, because this will enable the voluntary carbon trading market to become mainstream.

The Distributed City

The development of distributed power and water systems aims to achieve a shift from large centralized power and water systems to small-scale and neighborhood-based systems in cities. The distributed use of power and water can enable a city to reduce its ecological footprint because power and water can be more efficiently provided using the benefits of electronic control systems and community-oriented utility governance.

The distributed water system approach is often called "water sensitive urban design." It includes using the complete water cycle, i.e., using rain and local water sources like groundwater to feed into the system and then to recycle "gray" water locally and "black" water regionally, thus ensuring that there are significant reductions in water used and hence reductions in energy.[5]

A number of large cities including New York and London are moving to distributed energy generation through co-generation and tri-generation from natural gas as well as local solar and wind. This distributed generation offers a number of benefits, including energy savings, the ability to provide power without long distribution lines, better control of power production to meet demand, lower vul-

nerability, and greater resilience in the face of natural and human-made disaster (including terrorist attacks). Clever integration of these small systems into a grid can be achieved with new technology control systems that balance the whole system in its demand and supply from a range of sources as they rise and fall and link it to storage, especially vehicle batteries through vehicle-to-grid, or "V2G," technology.[6] A number of such small-scale energy systems are being developed to make cities more resilient in the future.

Distributed infrastructure needs compact, mixed-use urban development and new governance to go with new urban design. Examples of new local utilities are now appearing, as in Woking, Surrey.[7]

The Biophilic City

Biophilic cities are using natural processes as part of their infrastructure—green roofs, green walls, and integrated open space management—together with creative use of urban areas for food production.[8] One of the core reasons for cities moving down the biophilic path is to air-condition their city through the photosynthetic cooling effects of plants and water in the urban landscape as well as by using less heat-absorbing materials.

One of the most important potential biofuel sources of the future is blue-green algae that can be grown intensively on roof tops. Blue-green algae photosynthesize, so all that they require is sunlight, water, and nutrients. The output from blue-green algae is ten times greater than most other biomass sources, so it can be continuously cropped and fed into a process for producing biofuels or small-scale electricity. Most importantly, city buildings can all use their roofs to tap solar energy for local purposes without the distribution or transport losses so apparent in most cities today. This can become a solar ordinance set by town planners as part of local government policy. Chicago and Toronto are requiring green roofs in commercial development, and Singapore is moving to be Asia's first "Biophilic City."[9]

Progress in moving away from fossil fuels also requires serious localizing and local sourcing of food and building materials.[10] This, in turn, provides new opportunities to build more biophilic economies. The value of emphasizing the local is manyfold, with the primary benefit of dramatic reductions in the energy consumed mass producing and delivering products and food (see BedZED, for example). A biophilic approach can produce local textiles, which will mean an added reduction in fiber miles as well as potential to help regrow local bioregions.

The Eco-efficient City

In an effort to improve eco-efficiency, cities and regions are moving from linear to circular or closed-loop systems, where substantial amounts of their energy and material needs are provided from waste streams. Eco-efficient cities reduce their ecological footprint by reducing waste and resource requirements.

The eco-efficiency agenda has been taken up by the United Nations and the World Business Council for Sustainable Development, with a high target for industrialized countries of a ten-fold reduction in consumption of resources by 2040, along with rapid transfers of knowledge and technology to developing countries. While this eco-efficiency agenda is a huge challenge, it is important to remember that throughout the industrial revolution of the past two hundred years, human productivity has increased by 20,000 percent. The next wave of innovation has a lot of potential to create the kind of eco-efficiency gains that are required.[11]

The urban eco-efficiency agenda includes the "cradle to cradle" concept for the design of all new products and includes new systems like industrial ecology, where industries share resources and wastes like an ecosystem.[12] Good examples exist in Kalundborg, Denmark, and Kwinana, Australia.[13]

One extremely powerful example of how this eco-efficiency view can manifest in a new approach to urban design and building can be seen in the dense urban neighbourhood of Hammarby Sjöstad, Stockholm, which is connected to central Stockholm by a high-frequency light rail system. Here, from the beginning of the planning of this new district, an effort was made to think holistically, to understand the inputs, outputs, and resources that would be required and that would result. For instance, about 1,000 flats in Hammarby Sjöstad are equipped with stoves that use bio-gas extracted from wastewater generated in the community. Bio-gas also provides fuel for buses that serve the area. Organic waste from the community is returned to the neighborhood in the form of district heating and cooling. While not a perfect example, it represents a new and valuable way of seeing cities, requiring a degree of interdisciplinary and inter-sector collaboration in its planning system that is unusual in most cities.[14]

Eco-efficiency does not have to involve just new technology; it can also be introduced into cities through intensive use of human resources, as in Cairo's famous Zabaleen recycling system.[15] There are many other examples of how cities across the third world have integrated waste management into local industries, buildings, and food production.[16]

The Place-based City

The more place-oriented and locally self sufficient a city's economy is, the more it will reduce its ecological footprint and the more it will ensure that its valuable ecological features are enhanced. Place-based city concepts will increasingly be the people-oriented motivation for the infrastructure decisions that are made in each of the other city types.

Local economic development has many advantages in the context of sustainable development, including the ability of people to travel less as their work becomes local. Finding ways to help facilitate local enterprises becomes a major achievement for cities in moving toward a reduced ecological footprint. What the pioneers of local job creation initiatives have found, time and time again, is that place really matters. When people belong and have an identity in their town or city, they want to put down their roots and create local enterprise.

Local economic development is a first priority for most cities. As part of this, many cities are placing increasing emphasis on local place identity, as social capital has been found to be one of the best ways to predict wealth in a community.[17] Thus, when communities relate strongly to the local environment, the city's heritage and its unique culture, they develop a strong social capital of networks and trust that forms the basis of a robust urban economy.

This approach to economic development, which emphasizes place-based social capital, has many supporters, but very few relate this to the sustainability agenda in cities. For example, energy expenditures—by municipalities, companies, and individuals—represent a significant economic drain because they often leave the community and region. Producing power from solar, wind, or biomass in the locality or region is very much an economic development strategy that can generate local jobs and economic revenue from land (farmland) that might otherwise be economically marginal, in the process recirculating money, with an important economic multiplier effect. Energy efficiency can also be an economic development strategy. For example, research on renewable energy and the creation of related products have developed into a strong part of the economy in Freiburg, Germany.

Sense of place in a city requires paying attention to people and community development in the process of change—a major part of the urban planning agenda for many decades. This localized approach will be critical to creating a resilient city. It creates the necessary innovations as people dialogue through options to reduce their ecological footprint, which in turn creates social capital that is the basis for ongoing community life and economic development.[18] City dwellers in many countries increasingly want to know where their food is grown, where their wine comes from, where the materials that make up their furniture come from. In addition to a slow movement for local foods, a slow fiber and slow materials movement for local textile and building purposes can also help create a sense of place and make greater resilience.

The Sustainable Transport City

Transport is the most fundamental infrastructure for a city because it creates the primary form of the city.[19] Cities, neighborhoods, and regions are increasingly being designed to use energy sparingly by offering walkable, transit-oriented options, more recently supplemented by vehicles powered by renewable energy. Cities with more sustainable transport systems have been able to increase their resilience through reduced use of fossil fuels, reduced urban sprawl, and reduced dependence on car-based infrastructure.

The agenda for large sprawling cities now is to become a "polycentric city," where real cities in the suburbs are rapidly developed as local centers of jobs and services and the focus for bringing distributed infrastructure. This will significantly reduce car use and help cities face peak oil and the need to decarbonize—the first signs of which are now appearing in all U.S. and Australian cities as car use per capita declines and transit grows dramatically.[20]

Sustainable transport strategies will need to incorporate: (1) quality transit down each main corridor that is faster than traffic; (2) dense transit-oriented developments (TODs) built around each station; (3) pedestrian and bicycle strategies for each center and TOD, with cycle links across the city; (4) plug-in infrastructure for electric vehicles as they emerge; (5) cycling and pedestrian infrastructure as part of all street planning; and (6) a green wall growth boundary around the city preventing further urban encroachment.[21]

Conclusion

Resilience for the city of the future is becoming an agenda that cannot be neglected as global concerns accelerate over climate change, peak oil, water, waste, biodiversity, and urban quality of life. There will need to be infrastructure to support the seven city types outlined here if any city is to respond to these concerns. Examples have been provided of how each agenda is underway; however, no city has begun to work equally on all seven areas. Eventually this will be required. This is a challenge but it is also a great opportunity.

INTERROGATING URBAN RESILIENCE

LAWRENCE J. VALE

The Burgeoning of Resilience

In recent years, the term *resilience* has increasingly found favor in several fields. It has been embraced by planners and urbanists as a way to describe the ability of cities to respond to systemic threats, emerging as a more action-oriented alternative to perpetually elusive notions of "sustainability," "sustainable development," or "sustainable urbanism." Resilience also has an established resonance in fields ranging from engineering to ecology to psychology, and it is increasingly applied to business and economics, to information technology networks, and even to homeland security.[1]

Management analysts use resilience as a measure of an organization to recover from a disruption to a headquarters or to some key element in a supply chain and to return to "business as usual." Economists measure resilience with regard to the ability of a place to recover from the loss of an industry or key employer. IT professionals see resilience as a measure of how well a communications network can cope with the disruption of service, epitomized by a massive power failure. Homeland security personnel also see resilience in terms of large systems and seek new ways to ensure robust communications even after a massive disruption, whether caused by a hurricane or a terrorist.[2]

Psychologists have long used *resilience* to describe the capacity of certain kinds of individuals to withstand major traumatic events and to continue to function effectively. This leaves us with the engineers and the ecologists, who have tended to use the term *resilience* rather differently from one another, and in revealing ways. To engineers, and to materials scientists, resilience is a mechanical process of bouncing back from a perturbation, something inherent in the materiality of the disturbed object. Ecologists, concerned with the long-term viability and nature of ecosystems, are also concerned with resilience as a measure of how much a system can be restored to its original balance following a disruptive event, such as an oil spill. What seems different about the ecological approach to resilience, however, is not this property. Instead, it is the notion that there is a limit to ecological resilience and that once such systems pass this limit they collapse into a qualitatively different state, one that is controlled by a different set of processes.

Making Resilience Urban

When one attempts to link the concept of *resilience* to socio-spatial systems such as cities, one gets into the realm of planning and urbanism in two somewhat distinct ways. Resilience, in one sense, is an anticipatory venture. Planners and designers ask: What can we do now that will enable us to recover more quickly *if* a sudden perturbation should occur? Or, applied to cities and neighborhoods: What designs and policies can we implement now that will make communities more likely to be energy efficient, environmentally sensitive, broadly affordable, physically and socially attractive, and equipped to withstand climate change, security threats, and other likely disasters? This type of design and planning is resilience as a form of resistance, an effort to anticipate future problems and seek proactive solutions that enhance the quality of both public and private living spaces. More frequently, perhaps, planning and design also operate in a reactive mode. Planners and designers are brought in *after* a disaster has already occurred. Such disasters range from acute situations such as an earthquake, hurricane, or tsunami to more protracted challenges such as rampant slum conditions, lack of affordability, systemic neighborhood disinvestment, or uncontrolled sprawl. In this second sense, the urban design and planning challenges are centered on questions of retrofit and on strategies for recovery management. Both forms of urban resilience—proactive anticipatory design and planning, and reactive creative retrofit and management—underscore the urgency of urban recovery.

Urban resilience forces us to ask questions about the steady state, or status quo, that we want our society (our human ecosystem) to maintain or regain. Unfortunately, this pre-perturbation state that many idealize as the goal of "recovery" is often not a very just or equitable system. One always has to examine the self-interest that is ever present in efforts to speed and direct recovery of urban systems. In this sense, the chief advantage of the term *urban resilience* over *sustainable urbanism* is that *resilience* is somewhat more explicit in suggesting efforts to improve existing systems, whereas sustainability implies that it may be sufficient merely to sustain them. Nonetheless, *resilience* shares the same drawback as sustainability, since it is all too possible to "bounce back" into an untenable situation that is prone to further breakdown and inequity. Resilience is not always a good thing.

In the immediate aftermath of the 9/11 attacks of 2001, I directed the "Resilient City" project at MIT, which aimed at understanding the ways that people and places cope with a sudden traumatic disruption. We did not want to look only at the impact of 9/11 since it was too soon to tell, but instead sought to set the 9/11 attacks in a much broader historical context of other places facing instances of sudden destruction—whatever the cause—followed by difficult periods of recovery. Our goal, both in the initial colloquium and in the co-edited volume that followed, was to try to characterize what we called "The Resilient City" and to explain "how modern cities recover from disaster." In other words, rather than just tell the stories of various ways that traumatized cities and their people had exhibited resilience, we wanted to set out a proto-theory of urban resilience. Often, all of us ask questions that are both straightforward and remarkably vague: Has New Orleans recovered from Katrina? Will Port-au-Prince recover from the 2010 earthquake? Embedded in such questions is a triply contestable set of terms and assumptions: 1) has the entity that we call a "city" embarked on 2) something we can characterize as a "recovery" from 3) something we can understand to have been a "disaster"? For the concept of *urban resilience* to be useful, it needs to help us engage with this full set of complex embedded assumptions. Who counts as "the city"? (And *who* decides who counts as "the city"?) How do we measure *recovery* and whose measurements matter? Finally, how do we name and frame the disaster that has occurred, given that the way a *disaster* gets defined may well reflect its causality and thereby allocate blame?

Taking post-Katrina New Orleans as an example, it quickly becomes clear that judging recovery depends on where one looks, given that the city's repopulation has taken radically different forms from neighborhood to neighborhood in the years since the August 2005 disaster. Is "New Orleans" resilient even if some of its component neighborhoods remain half-empty? Has "the city" recovered even if many of its poorest former citizens have been able to return? Or, as is the view of some, is the city's "recovery" actually *dependent* on the departure of many of its most vulnerable residents? Does "New Orleans" recover when its public housing projects get rebuilt, and what does it mean that these new developments are now for mixed-income "workforce" housing, rather than the last-chance housing for the city's least economically advantaged? Whose New Orleans matters? Similarly, how should progress toward recovery be benchmarked? Is recovery to be measured by the number of cranes that rise above building sites? Is increased economic activity a sufficient proxy for recovery? If so, which economic activity matters most? Is it the restoration of the port, the resurgence of the tourists to the French Quarter, or the fate of those involved with the fishing and shellfish industries? Whose jobs matter most? Finally, is it even clear what kind of disaster New Orleans has faced? In 2005, Mississippi suffered a violent *hurricane*, but New Orleans chiefly suffered the inundation of a *flood*. This terminology matters because hurricanes are primarily forces of nature but contemporary floods are inextricable from the failures of levees and other infrastructure, put in place by well-meaning human beings. The effect of Katrina upon New Orleans cannot be measured, nor can responsibility be assigned, by terming the disaster a "hurricane." More generally, it has become commonplace to observe that few if any "natural disasters" are wholly natural in their origins.[3] Both the disaster itself and the risk and allocation of damage are deeply implicated in societal choices about infrastructure location, residential development patterns, and disaster recovery priorities. Because of the social and political complexities of disasters, it matters how we frame them and what we name them.

Urban resilience, as a concept, has the advantage of conveying both a process and an end-state goal. That said, taking a hard look at a broad range of efforts to recover from wildly divergent urban disasters around the world, it seems clear that most leaders of cities have rebuilt very stubbornly and done very little to acknowledge ecological limits and ongoing vulnerabilities when so doing. In most cases, the will to rebuild is rooted in efforts 1) to control the recovery storyline in ways that benefit dominant groups, 2) to rely on symbolic acts of rebuilding as a means to signal resolve, and 3) to support a highly politicized redevelopment agenda. Human-dominated social systems are different from ecological systems because of these three things: they rely on the power of human stories, the human capacity to invent powerful symbols to guide action, and the human ability to exercise political power. This is a triple willfulness that refuses to let an environment die. Often, the persistence of resilience is an admirable thing. Sometimes, however, the obduracy of resilience means "bouncing back" to the same undesirable state of affairs that prevailed before disaster struck. At other times, and often in an unacknowledged way, the engineering model of resilience—rooted in the concept of bounceback—may shift into the ecological model of resilience, which admits the possibility of paradigm shift. The system recovers in the sense that it is able to sustain some forms of life, but as the result of its shift it becomes a different system. In the new system, like the old one, some will fare better than others, but the costs and benefits will surely be distributed differently.

The Resilience of Resilience

As with other terms, like sustainability and development, the term resilience may also be headed for the meaninglessness that results from having too many meanings. For better or worse, as a word, resilience is itself becoming resilient. Rather than a cause for dismissal or despair, however, the malleability of resilience ought to encourage greater discipline and specificity. Because urban resilience is both a process and a product, it encodes what I call a *design politics*. This means that those who use the term need to interrogate it in a double way. It is not enough to judge the design products on the ground; one also must assess the power dynamic that permitted new forms of development to be implemented.

GREEN URBANISM

FORMULATING A SERIES OF HOLISTIC PRINCIPLES

STEFFEN LEHMANN

New Urbanism is an urban design movement which arose in the U.S. in the early 1980s, promoting walkable, mixed-use neighborhoods and transit-oriented development, seeking to end suburban sprawl and promote community. Characteristics include narrow streets, wide sidewalks, and higher densities. *Green Urbanism* is a conceptual model for zero-emission and zero-waste urban design, which arose in the 1990s, promoting compact, energy-efficient urban development, seeking to transform and reengineer existing city districts and regenerate the postindustrial city center. It promotes the development of socially and environmentally sustainable city districts.

Formulating the Principles of Green Urbanism

Green Urbanism is by definition interdisciplinary; it requires the collaboration of landscape architects, engineers, urban planners, ecologists, transport planners, physicists, psychologists, sociologists, economists, and other specialists, in addition to architects and urban designers. *Green Urbanism* makes every effort to minimize the use of energy, water, and materials at each stage of the city's or district's life cycle, including the embodied energy in the extraction and transportation of materials, their fabrication, their assembly into the buildings, and, ultimately, the ease and value of their recycling when an individual building's life is over.

Cities can and must become the most environmentally friendly model for inhabiting our earth. It is more important than ever to reconceptualize existing cities and their systems of infrastructure to be compact, mixed-use, and polycentric cities.

This text introduces the *Principles of Green Urbanism* as a conceptual model and as a framework for how we might be able to tackle the enormous challenge of transforming existing neighborhoods, districts, and communities, and how we can rethink the way we design, build, and operate in our future urban settlements. These principles are partly universal, but there is no one single formula that will always work.

To achieve more sustainable cities, urban designers must understand and apply the core principles of Green Urbanism in a systematic and adapted way. These principles can be effective in a wide variety of urban situations, but they almost always need to be adapted to the context and the project's scale, to the site's constraints and opportunities, adapting the principles to the particular climatic conditions, availability of technology, social conditions, project scale, client's brief, diverse stakeholder organizations, and so on. It is an approach to urban design that requires an optimization process and a solid understanding of the development's wider context and its many dimensions before the designer can produce an effective design outcome.[1]

The 15 Guiding *Principles of Green Urbanism* for Local Action and a More Integrated Approach to Urban Development

The following is a short list of the principles; for full discussion see my book *The Principles of Green Urbanism: Transforming the City for Sustainability* (2010). It must be noted, though, that in order to enable sustainable urban development and to ensure that eco-districts are successful on many levels, all urban design components need to work interactively and cannot be looked at separately. Understandably, it requires a holistic approach to put the principles in action, although they need to be adapted to the location, context, and scale of the urban development. It may be difficult at first to achieve some of the principles, but they can potentially reach early payback, improve livability, and increase opportunities for social interaction of residents. The 15 principles offer practical steps on the path to sustainable cities, harmonizing growth and usage of resources. The truly "carbon-neutral" city has not yet been built, but all eco-projects are important steps toward turning this vision into a reality.

With all this technological progress, we should not lose sight of the fact that a key component in any society's sustain-

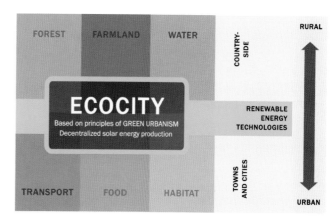

FIG. 1 The three pillars of Green Urbanism, and the interaction between these pillars.

FIG. 2 The holistic concept of Eco-City has again a balanced relationship between the urban (city) and the rural (countryside). Both diagrams by Steffen Lehmann, 2006.

ability is more than its carbon footprint. The future of our societies is not merely a technical matter of finding more eco-friendly energy solutions but a question of holistic social sustainability and healthy communities.

The sustainability matrix—the 15 *Principles of Green Urbanism*—consists of:

Principle 1.
Climate and context
The city based on its climatic conditions, with appropriate responses to location and site context. What are the unique site constraints, climatic conditions, and opportunities?

Every site or place has its own individual conditions in regard to orientation, solar radiation, rain, humidity, prevailing wind direction, topography, shading, lighting, noise, air pollution, and so on. Climatic conditions are seen as the fundamental influence for form-generation in the design of any project: understanding the site and its context, which is essential at the beginning of every design project; optimizing orientation and compactness to help reduce the city's heat gain or loss; achieving a city with minimized environmental footprint by working with the existing landscape, topography, and resources particular to the site, and the existing microclimate of the immediate surroundings. Maintaining complexity in the system is always desirable (be it biodiversity, ecosystem, or neighborhood layout), and a high degree of complexity is always beneficial for society. Enhancing the opportunities offered by topography and natural setting leads to a city well adapted to the local climate and its ecosystem. Due to the different characteristics of every location, each city district has to come up with its own methods and tailored strategies to reach sustainability and to capture

the spirit of the place. We will need to understand how to take full advantage of each location's potential and how to fine tune the design concept appropriate to its societal setting and contexts (cultural, historical, social, geographical, economical, environmental, and political).

Principle 2.
Renewable energy for zero CO2 emissions
The city as a self-sufficient, on-site energy producer, using decentralized district energy systems. How can energy be generated locally and supplied emission-free and in the most effective way?

The various aspects of this principle include energy supply systems and services, as well as energy efficient use and operation, promoting increased use of renewable power, and perhaps natural gas as a transition fuel in the energy mix, but moving quickly away from heavy fossil fuels such as coal and oil; and the transformation of the city from an energy consumer to an energy producer, with local solutions for renewables and the de-carbonizing of the energy supply. The supply of oil will last shorter than the life expectancy of most buildings. Energy-efficiency programs are not enough. Too often we find that savings from energy-efficiency programs are absorbed by a rise in energy use. The local availability of a renewable source of energy is the first selection criteria for deciding on energy generation. In general, a well-balanced combination of energy sources can sensibly secure future supply, with distributed decentralized systems. This will transform city districts into local power stations of renewable energy sources, which include solar photovoltaic (PV), solar thermal, wind, biomass, geothermal, and mini-hydro energy as well as other new technologies. Some of the most promising technologies are in building-integrated PV, urban wind turbines, micro-CHP (combined heat and power), and solar cooling. That is to say, there should be on-site electrical generation and energy storage in combination with a smart grid, which integrates local generation, utilizing energy-efficiency in all its forms. Solar hot water systems would be compulsory. Co-generation technology utilizes waste heat through combined-heat-and-power plants. Eco-districts will need to operate on renewable energy sources as close to 100 percent as possible; as a minimum, at least 50 percent of on-site renewable energy generation should be the aim of all urban planning. Optimizing the energy balance can be achieved by using exchange and cascading (exergy) principles.

Principle 3
Zero-waste city
The zero-waste city as a circular, closed-loop eco-system. How to avoid the creation of waste in the first place—changing behaviour of consumption?

Sustainable waste management means to turn waste into a resource. All cities should adopt nature's zero-waste management system. Zero-waste urban planning includes reducing consumption, recycling, and reusing and composting waste to produce energy. All material flows need to be examined and fully understood, and special attention needs to be given to industrial waste and e-waste treatment. We need to plan for recycling centers, for zero landfill and eliminating the idea of waste through better understanding of nutrient flows. Eco-districts are neighborhoods where we reuse and recycle materials and significantly reduce the volume of consumption and toxic chemical releases. All construction materials as well as the production of building components need to be healthy and fully recyclable. Waste prevention is always better than the treatment or cleaning-up after waste is formed. The remanufacturing of metals, glass, plastics, and paper into new products needs to be a routine (without downgrading the product); an "extended producer responsibility" clause is needed for all products. Essentially, we need to become (again) a "recycling society," where it is common that around 70 to 90 percent of all waste is recycled or composted, and materials and nutrients are recovered.

Principle 4
Water
The city with closed urban water management and a high water quality. What is the situation in regard to the sustainable supply of potable drinking water?

The various aspects of this principle include, in general, reducing water consumption, finding more efficient uses for water resources, ensuring good water quality, and the protection of aquatic habitats. The city can be used as a water catchment area by educating the population in water efficiency, promoting rainwater collection, and using waste-water recycling and storm water harvesting techniques.

Storm water and flood management concepts need to be adopted as part of the urban design, and this includes storm water run-offs and improved drainage systems and the treatment of wastewater. This includes such things as algae and biofiltration systems for gray water and improving the quality of our rivers and lakes so that they are fishable and swimmable again. An integrated urban water cycle planning and management system that includes a high-performance infrastructure for sewage recycling (gray and black water recycling; solar-powered desalination plants), storm water retention, and harvesting the substantial run-off through storage must be a routine in all design projects. On a household level we need to collect rainwater and use it sparingly, and install dual-water systems and low-flush toilets. On a food production level we need to investigate the development of crops that need less water and are more drought resistant.

Principle 5
Landscape, gardens, and urban biodiversity
The city that integrates landscapes, urban gardens, and green roofs to maximize biodiversity. Which strategies can be applied to protect and maximize biodiversity and to reintroduce landscape and garden ideas back in the city to ensure urban cooling?

A sustainable city takes pride in its many beautiful parks and public gardens. This pride is best formed through a strong focus on local biodiversity, habitat and urban ecology, wildlife rehabilitation, forest conservation, and the protection of regional characteristics. Ready access to these public parks, gardens, and public spaces, with opportunities for leisure and recreation, are essential components of a healthy city, as is arresting the loss of biodiversity by enhancing the natural environment and landscape and planning the city using ecological principles based on natural cycles (not on energy-intensive technology) and increasing urban vegetation. A city that preserves and maximizes its open spaces, natural landscapes, and recreational opportunities is a more healthy and resilient city. The sustainable city also needs to introduce inner-city gardens, urban agriculture, and green roofs in all its urban design projects (using the city for food supply). It needs to maximize the resilience of the ecosystem through urban landscapes that mitigate the "urban heat island" (UHI) effect, using plants for air-purification and urban cooling. Further, the narrowing of roads, which calms traffic and lowers the UHI effect, allows for more (all-important) tree planting. Preserving green space, gardens, and farmland creates a green belt around the city, and planting trees absorbs CO_2. Restoring stream and river banks maximizes species diversity. In all urban planning, we need to maintain and protect the existing ecosystem that stores carbon and plan for the creation of new carbon storage sinks by increasing the amount of tree planting. The increase in the percentage of green space as a share of total city land is to be performed in combination with any densification activities.

Principle 6
Sustainable transport and good public space: compact and polycentric cities
The city of eco-mobility, with a good public space network and an efficient low-impact public transport system for post-fossil-fuel mobility. How can we get people out of their cars, to walk, cycle, and use public transport?

Good access to basic transport services is crucial, as it helps to reduce automobile dependency, as does reducing the need to travel. We need to see integrated non-motorized transport, such as cycling or walking, and, consequently, bicycle/pedestrian-friendly environments, with safe bicycle ways, free rental bike schemes, and pleasant public spaces. It is important to identify the optimal transport mix that offers interconnections for public transport and the integration of private and public transport systems. Some ideas here include: eco-mobility concepts and smart infrastructure (electric vehicles); an integrated system of bus transit, light railway, bike stations; improved public space networks and connectivity; and a focus on transit-oriented development ("green TODs"). It is a fact that more and wider roads result in more traffic and CO_2 emissions, and also allows for sprawling development. The transport sector is responsible for causing significant greenhouse-gas emissions (over 20 percent). To combat this effect we need to change our lifestyles by taking public transport, or carpooling. Alternatively, we can ride a bike or walk, if the city district has been designed for it. Personal arrangements have the potential to reduce commuting and to boost community spirit. We want a city district that is well-connected for pedestrians, a city with streetscapes that encourage a healthy, active lifestyle and where residents travel less and less by car. Green TODs can create a range of medium-density housing typologies and provide a variety of transportation choices, achieving a mix of residences and employment.

Principle 7
Local and sustainable materials with less embodied energy
City construction using regional, local materials with less embodied energy and applying prefabricated modular systems. What kind of materials are locally available and appear in regional, vernacular architecture?

The various aspects of this principle include advanced materials technologies, using opportunities for shorter supply chains where all urban designs focus on local materials and technological know-how, such as regional timber in common use. Affordable housing can be achieved through modular prefabrication. Prefabrication has come and gone several times in modern architecture, but this time, with closer collaboration with manufacturers of construction systems and components in the design phase, the focus is on sustainability. We need to be aware of the embodied energy of materials and the flow of energy in closing life cycles. We need to emphasize green manufacturing and an economy of means, such as process-integrated technologies that lead to waste reduction. It is more environmentally friendly to use lightweight structures, enclosures, and local materials with less embodied energy, requiring minimal transport. This includes improved material and system specifications, supported by research in new materials and technological innovation, and by reduced material diversity in multicomponent products to help facilitate resource recovery, disassembly, value retention, and the possibility of reusing entire building components. Success in this area will increase the long-term durability of buildings, reduce waste, and minimize material consumption.

Principle 8
Density and retrofitting of existing districts
The city with retrofitted districts, urban infill, and densification/intensification strategies for existing neighborhoods. What are the opportunities to motivate people to move back to the city, closer to workplaces in the city center?

This principle includes: encouraging the densification of the city center through mixed-use urban infill, center regeneration, and green TODs; increasing density and compactness (compact building design means developing buildings vertically rather than horizontally); promoting business opportunities around green transit-oriented developments; retrofitting inefficient building stock; and systematically reducing the city's carbon footprint. Consideration will need to be given to better land-use planning to reduce the impact of urban areas on agricultural land and landscape and to increasing urban resilience by transforming city districts into more compact communities and designing flexible typologies for inner-city living and working. Special strategies for large metropolitan areas and fast-growing cities are required. Special strategies are also needed for small and medium-sized towns (due to their particular milieu), and for the particular vulnerabilities of Small Island States and coastal cities. Public space upgrading through urban renewal programs will bring people back to the city center, as will strategic thinking about how to reuse brownfield and grayfield developments and the adaptive reuse of existing buildings, remodeling, and re-energizing existing city centers. This can be achieved through mixed-use urban infill projects, building the "city above the city" by converting low-density districts into higher-density communities, and by revitalizing underutilized land for community benefit and affordable housing. In the compact city, every neighborhood is sustainable and self-sufficient and uses Energy Service Company (ESCO) principles for self-financing energy efficiency in all retrofitting programs.

Principle 9
Green buildings and districts, using passive design principles
The city that applies deep green building design strategies and offers solar access for all new buildings. How can we best apply sustainable design and passive design principles in all their forms and for all buildings?

The various aspects of this principle include: low-energy designs applying best practices for passive design principles for all buildings and groups of buildings; dramatically reducing energy use; introducing compact solar architecture; and retrofitting the entire building stock. New design typologies need to be developed at low cost, and we need to produce functionally more neutral buildings that last longer. This includes applying facade technology with responsive building skins for bio-climatic architecture, to take advantage of cooling breezes and natural cross-ventilation, and maximizing cross-ventilation, daylighting, and opportunities for night-flush cooling. We will focus on the low consumption of resources and materials, including the reuse of building elements (design for disassembly); mixed-use concepts for compact housing typologies; adaptive reuse projects that rejuvenate mature estates; and solar architecture that optimizes solar gain in winter and sun shading technology for summer, catching the low winter sun and avoiding too much heat gain in summer. It is important to renew the city with energy-efficient green architecture, creating more flexible buildings of long-term value and longevity (flexibility in plan leads to a longer life for buildings). Technical systems and services have a shorter life cycle. This means, first of all, applying technical aids sparingly and making the most of all passive means provided by the building fabric and natural conditions. Buildings that generate more energy than they consume, and collect and purify their own water, are totally achievable.

Principle 10
Livability, healthy communities, and mixed-use programs
The city with a special concern for affordable housing, mixed-use programs, and a healthy community. How does urban design recognize the particular need for affordable housing, to ensure a vibrant mix of society and multifunctional mixed-use programs?

Land use development patterns are the key to sustainability. A mixed-use (and mixed-income) city delivers more social inclusion and helps to repopulate the city center. Demographic changes, such as age, are a major issue for urban design. It is advantageous for any project to maximize the diversity of its users. Different sectors in the city can take on different roles over a twenty-four-hour cycle; for example, the typical central business district is used for more than just office work. In general we want connected, compact communities applying mixed-use concepts and strategies for housing affordability and offering different typologies for different housing needs. To this end we need affordable housing together with new flexible typologies for inner-city living. These mixed-use neighborhoods (of housing types, prices, and ownership forms) avoid gentrification and provide affordable housing in districts inclusive for the poor and the rich, young and old, and workers of all walks of life, and also provide secure tenure (ensuring "aging in place"). Housing typologies need to deal with demographical changes. We have to understand migration and diversity as both an opportunity and a

challenge. Mixed land use is particularly important as it helps reduce traffic. Master plans should require all private developments to contain around 40 percent of public (social) housing integrated with private housing. Higher densities will center on green TODs, with jobs, retail, housing, and a city campus being close by, and with IT and telecommuting from home helping significantly to reduce travel (motto: "Don't commute to compute"). By integrating a diverse range of economic and cultural activities, we avoid single-function projects, which generate a higher demand for mobility.

Principle 11
Local food and short supply chains
The city for local food supply, with high food security and urban agriculture.

Which strategies can be applied to grow food locally in gardens, on rooftops, and in small spaces in the city?

The various aspects of this principle include: local food production; regional supply; and an emphasis on urban farming and agriculture, including "eat local" and "slow food" initiatives. The sustainable city makes provision for adequate land for food production in the city, a return to the community and to the allotment gardens, where roof gardens can become an urban market garden. It is essential that we bridge the urban-rural disconnect and move cities toward models that deal in natural ecosystems and healthy food systems. The people of the eco-city will garden and farm locally, sharing food, creating compost with kitchen scraps and garden clippings, and growing community vegetables, buying and consuming locally. Such things as reusing paper bags and glass containers, paper recycling and the cost of food processing will need reconsideration. We will need to reduce our consumption of meat and other animal products, especially shipped-in beef, as the meat cycle is very intensive in terms of energy and water consumption, and herds create methane. As much as 50 percent of our food will need to be organically produced, without the use of fertilizers or pesticides made from oil, and grown in local allotments.

Principle 12
Cultural heritages, identity, and sense of place
The city of public health and cultural identity: a safe and healthy city, which is secure and just. How to maintain and enhance a city's, or region's, identity, unique character, and valued urban heritage, avoiding interchangeable design that makes all cities look the same?

All sustainable cities aim for high air quality and pollution reduction to foster resilient communities, strong public space networks, and modern community facilities. This is the nature of sustainable cities. However, each city has its own distinct environment, whether it be by the sea, a river, in a desert, a mountain; whether its climate is tropical, arid, temperate, etc.—each situation is unique. The design of the city will take all these factors better into consideration, including materials, history, and population desires. The essence of place is the up-swelling of grassroots strategies, the protection of its built heritage, and the maintenance of a distinct cultural identity, for example, by promoting locally owned businesses and supporting creativity and cultural development. New ideas require affordable and flexible studio space in historic buildings and warehouses. Cities will grow according to the unique qualities of localities, demographic qualities of the populace, and the creativity of the authorities and citizens. The aim of a city is to support the health, the activities, and the safety of its residents. It is, therefore, incumbent on city councils to protect the city by developing a master plan that balances heritage with conservation and development, fostering distinctive places with a strong sense of place, where densities are high enough to support basic public transit and walking-to retail services.

Principle 13
Urban governance, leadership, and best practices
The city applying best practices for urban governance and sustainable procurement methods. Which networks and skills can be activated and utilized through engaging the local community and key stakeholders to ensure sustainable outcomes?

Cities are a collective responsibility. Good urban governance is extremely important if we want to transform existing cities into sustainable compact communities. It has to provide efficient public transport, good public space, affordable housing, and high standards of urban management. Without political support, change will not happen. City councils need strong management and support for their urban visions to be realized. They need a strategic direction in order to manage sustainability through coherent combined management and governance approaches, which include evolutionary and adaptive policies linked to a balanced process of review, and to public authorities overcoming their own unsustainable consumption practices— changing their methods of urban decision-making. A city that leads and designs holistically, that implements change harmoniously, and where decision-making and responsibility is shared with the empowered citizenry is a city on the road to sustainable practices. In balancing community needs with development, public consultation exercises and grassroots participation are essential to ensuring people-sensitive urban design and to encouraging community participation. Enabling people to be actively involved in shaping their urban environment is one of the hallmarks of a democracy. As far as bureaucratic urban governance is concerned, authorities will consider the following: updating building codes and regulations; creating a database of best practice and policies for eco-planning; revising contracts for construction projects; raising public awareness; improving participation in planning and policy making; creating sustainable subdivisions and implementing anti-sprawl land-use and growth boundary poli-

cies; legislating for controls in density and supporting high-quality densification; arriving at a political decision to adopt the Principles of Green Urbanism; promoting measures to finance a low-to-no-carbon pathway; introducing a program of incentives, subsidies, and tax exemptions for sustainable projects that foster green jobs; eliminating fossil-fuel subsidies; developing mechanisms for incentives to accelerate renewable energy take-up; promoting sustainability assessment and certification of urban development projects.

Principle 14
Education, research, and knowledge
The city with education and training for all in sustainable urban development.

How to best raise awareness and change behavior?
This principle includes: technical training and up-skilling, exchange of experiences, and knowledge dissemination through publications about ecological city theory and sustainable design. Primary and secondary teaching programs need to be developed for students in such subjects as waste recycling, water efficiency, and sustainable behavior. Research in behavior change is necessary. The city is a hub of institutions, such as galleries, libraries, and universities, where knowledge can be shared. We must provide sufficient access to educational opportunities and training for the citizenry, thus increasing their chances of finding green jobs. Universities can act as "think tanks" for the transformation of their cities. We also need to redefine the education of architects, urban designers, planners, and landscape architects. Research centers for sustainable urban development policies and best practices in eco-city planning will be founded, where assessment tools to measure environmental performance are developed and local building capacity is studied.

Principle 15
Strategies for cities in developing countries
Particular sustainability strategies for cities in developing countries, harmonizing the impacts of rapid urbanization and globalization. What are the specific strategies and measurements we need to apply for basic low-cost solutions appropriate to cities in the developing world?

Developing and emerging countries have their own needs and require particular strategies, appropriate technology transfer, and funding mechanisms. Cities in the developing world cannot have the same strategies and debates as cities in the developed world. Similarly, particular strategies for emerging economies and fast-growing cities are required, as well as for the problem of informal settlements and urban slum upgrading. Low-cost building and mass housing typologies for rapid urbanization are required in cooperation with poverty reduction programs. It is essential that we train local people to empower communities, creating new jobs and diversifying job structures, so as not to focus on only one segment of the economy (e.g., tourism). Achieving more sustainable growth for developing metropolitan cities is necessary to combat climate change—which was mainly caused through emissions by industrialized nations and which is having its worst effect in poorer countries in Africa, Asia, and Latin America—is now a priority.

The problem of urban design is complex. Designing a city requires holistic, multidimensional approaches and the adaptation of strategies to each unique context.

Clearly, much of *Green Urbanism* is common-sense urbanism. In future, *Green Urbanism* has to become the norm for all urban developments. The *Principles of Green Urbanism* are practical and holistic, offering an integrated framework encompassing all the key aspects needed to establish sustainable development and encouraging best practice models. The replicability of models is hereby very important. The principles form a sustainability matrix, which will empower the urban designer—to use Richard Buckminster Fuller's words—"to be able to do more with less."

FROM RENEWABLE CITIES
TO REGENERATING REGIONS

FIRE, THE FIRST ELEMENT OF SUSTAINABLE URBANISM

PETER DROEGE

There can be no sustainable development while fossil and nuclear power prevail as the drivers of urban growth, the very definers of city culture. The by-product of fossil fuel burning is skyrocketing atmospheric CO_2 concentrations. These are now at 390 parts per million, a full third above the proven stable level of 280 ppm. Earth's climate may well be drifting toward that of Venus, from a balmy 20° Celsius to the lifeless inferno of 250° Celsius and raining sulphuric acid.[1]

While irresponsible talk in international climate negotiation circles still focuses on 450, 550, or even 650 ppm as "realistic targets," the outlook for escaping runaway climate change grows dimmer by the day. Meanwhile time runs out on avoiding global economic paroxysms brought on by rolling post-peak oil supply bottlenecks[2] striking the 95 percent fossil-fuel-based global transport system,[3] or the equally oil-dependent global food and industrial goods production machinery.

Most policymakers are confident that there is still time for successful action. But they are less certain about how to imagine a dramatic shift of current practice in the face of intransigence among the energy supply policy institutions and the standoffs that mark more than a dozen years of global climate negotiations. Still entirely absent from the global agenda is a broad and action-geared response. Lacking this, sustainable urbanism remains an idle idea, at best a marketing device, while the planet's climate may well already drift past the point of no return.[4]

To be credible, sustainable urbanism here and beyond requires principles like all normatively founded concepts. These principles must be structured in theory, manifest themselves in reality, and be testable in practical applications. They must be measurable.

Dating from pre-Socratic times and sometimes associated with the five Platonic solids, the five elements are fire, earth, water, air—and aether. In the Hindu and Buddhist tradition, we have the same elements. In Japan and Tibet, too, the same elements prevailed as traditional cosmologies, with aether also being connoted with heaven, sky, void, or space.[5] In seeking a whole, holistic, and systematic foundation of sustainable urbanism, it makes sense to choose fire, earth, water, and air as existential performance dimensions. And it is sensible to define the fifth, space, as the entirety of the cultural realm that comprises human existence in the miraculous, fragile, and rare realm of our biosphere that lies between the outside of the earth's crust and the central reaches of the atmosphere. The four elements of sustainable urbanism then are: air, water, earth, and fire—while the fifth, the meta-element, is our very existential space.

Across these elements, the reliance on true sustainability in resource flow is axiomatic: to avoid any economic activity that cannot take place without depleting any finite resource, whether this is fossil fuels or biological species. This axiom is based on the fundamental understanding that sustainable development must be founded on a practice of not depleting resources. The origin of this thinking is credited to the seminal work of Saxon mining chief Carl von Carlowitz (1645–1714) on sustainable forestry of the time, *Sylvicultura oeconomica*.[6] Not distinguishing ecology and economy, von Carlowitz witnessed the destruction of forests for mining construction and power generation, and wrote a primer for economical forestry, economical being synonymous with *sustainable*, i.e., based on regrowth, nurturing a sustained stream of healthy biomass and wood products without running down the stock. The prefix eco- is derived from *oikos*, the classical Greek term for the very nucleus of society, the family, and the autonomous farmstead.

Fire represents the essential conversion to a renewable base. It also stands for putting mobility on a fully renewable footing by taking on the gargantuan task of shifting a global disaster of 95 percent oil dependence in mechanized surface and air transport to a mode of renewable electricity—hydrogen. Earth represents humus build-up, bio-char use worldwide, and the introduction of biodiversity reserves for the protection of soil. Air represents the purity of the gaseous mix we breathe and the lowering of carbon dioxide emissions to a level of stability safeguarding human existence. Water represents sustainable protection, the respectful treatment of the liquid foundation of life.

The focus of this paper is on the first element of sustainable urbanism, fire, and fifth, cultural space.

Fire, the First Element, Calls for a World Fully Renewable—and Beyond

"Fully renewable" means zero fossil or nuclear fuel content in operational or embodied energy, either in stationary use or transport. "And beyond" means the urgent need to boost the absorption of greenhouse gas from the atmosphere by enhancing the ability of soils, forests, wetlands, and water bodies to sequester and manage carbon dioxide and other greenhouse gases. "Beyond" also means the need for cities and communities to improve efficiency, lower consumption, and increase renewable energy production to generate an excess of nonpolluting power for parts of the community and economy that need it to escape the fossil fuel trap. Above all, "beyond" means focus on poverty reduction, health, education, and social empowerment at the very base of the global society, without which the effectiveness of an energy transformation would at best be incomplete.

What are the ways of pursuing this aim?

An individual strategy:

Every city is different. While there are certain principles that apply generally, experience shows that each city and community must find its own path. For example, this individual path can be determined by:
- local resources
- climate and weather
- development history
- level of globalization or trade interdependence
- relation to and control over the surrounding region
- state of development and level of prosperity
- government form and strength; institutional capacity
- structure and level of community organization: civil society
- control over energy generation and distribution assets

A tiered response:

A tiered response depends on managing energy carefully locally, and in seeking a close to full supply with renewable energy as much as possible—using local resources and physical opportunities. Efficiency and demand reduction are widely understood as the first tier, yet parallel to the others (local renewable supply, and regional as well as continental renewable energy systems).

The technical tools to achieve energy autonomy are roof and facade surfaces for solar conversion into electricity and thermal energy, small wind power, heat pumps and deep geothermal, the tapping into sewage and exhaust waste flows, methane capture and use, biomass, distributed networks of renewable power sources, and a host of other means. These can be stand-alone islands or locally networked, both as electric grids and thermal distribution systems.

The next tier is provided by a national or supranational network—this could take the form of a "supergrid," or even supersmart grid, as promised by rising if highly controversial initiatives in Europe, the United States, and Australia. These are controversial due to the large costs involved and the very real question of whether they are indeed needed or are blatant attempts at seizing and centralizing control over renewable energy, an inherently decentralized and ubiquitous, even largely free, source, with all of the potential advantages this implies to local communities, including the repatriation of wealth now escaping the community.

Set a real 100 percent target:

Only an absolute and unequivocal renewable energy target can help in the guidance of urban strategies. Ideally, this will cover all electricity and thermal consumption and transport energy—which also includes consumed energy—embodied in the goods and services procured. Most fractional target setting exercises—say, a reduction of 20 percent by 2020—today are aimed at the direct use of emissions derived from operational energy only.

This approach is problematic because the targets are typically set arbitrarily and for political purposes; they are set too low, even when they are attached to a specific implementation commitment; and they cover only a small fraction of actual energy consumption. In Australian cities, for example, household energy embodied and consumed in goods and services comprises some 60 to 70 percent of total energy use, while the rest—direct and transport energy use—is typically elevated to represent the "total" energy use in municipal statistics.[7]

Address lifestyle and consumption:

Understanding and managing embodied and imported fossil energy or emissions is crucial in assigning responsibility to consumers and for initiating important lifestyle changes. Consumption-based energy and emissions are not difficult to understand, but their control is thought to go beyond some of the traditional activities of cities. Thinking through the full choices and tools available to cities—as described in the next section—helps enlarge the radius of capability enormously. Consumption-embodied fossil fuel and carbon emissions can be countered by a wide range of measures, from regionalization strategies that focus on local food supplies, information campaigns building consumer demand for carbon labels, and other ways of achieving reduced fossil-content consumption, to substituting local and regional for international recreational travel.

Build metropolitan carbon sinks:

The fostering of *climate-stabilizing regions* is the most advanced frontier of renewable city planning and development. Many industries pride themselves on fostering carbon sink projects in Amazonia and other distant places as short-term attempts at "offsetting" their fossil fuel sins—and the emerging emissions trading regime is based on this idea. In principle this aims at good and beneficial outcomes, although continued reliance on fossil fuel emissions makes it an unsustainable model.

What about our own regional and local ecosystems? How can they become "carbon negative"—capable of absorbing emissions? Land use planning, open space and waterway management, and forestry and agriculture practices are relevant to the carbon and nitrogen cycle, and usually involve methane, a powerful greenhouse gas. Only a radical transformation in cities' perception of their consumption habits and rural relations can help change this.

An urban world?:

Much is made of the fact that cities accommodate more than half of the world's population. Yet it is also important to realize that this growth prospect cannot be sustained in a world of declining fossil resources, and that, in any event, an increasing share of this growth takes place in the metro-slums and other large urban informal settlements of the South: the lion's share of all new growth takes place here.[8] To a large extent this results from trade and energy policies of the past twenty-five years.

Also, cities are not autonomous worlds: no city is an island. Cities depend not only on the globalized trade cherished so much as the putative bulwark of international stability and prosperity; they also entirely depend on regional and rural areas for resilience in times of need, and, even more profoundly, on the rapidly shrinking domains of undisturbed forests, wetlands and waters, sources of oxygen, and sinks for the tragically unmanaged and rising industrial waste streams of advanced urban civilization—including nitrogen, ammonia, methane, and carbon dioxide.

The institutional connection—overcoming the fossil fuel legacy:

Despite the great commitment and dedication devoted to this self-evidently critical cause, the effort has had disappointing results. Fossil energy use has risen faster than most efficiency measures, even in the most dedicated of communities. Nancy Carlisle of the National Renewable Energy Laboratory, at the U.S. Department of Energy, calls this a "planning gap," because it signals a widening chasm between what a community would need to do to become renewable-energy-based and what actually is being done. The paucity of bold government regulation aside, it has become clear that communities "*focus on short-term, incremental approaches instead of tackling the more challenging task of guiding the deeper transition to a 'renewable energy community.'*"[9]

The Urban Renewable Power Policy Toolbox

Cities and town governments have extraordinary powers of influence yet only use a small fraction of this potential. This central section lists all the major ways in which cities can act through their government and administrative apparatus—effectively, efficiently, and with persuasion.

Expanding from cues for public policy development, following Mark Schuster and his colleagues regarding cultural development (1997), cities can become extremely effective in implementing 100 percent renewable strategies, using seven different sets of devices:

1. Regulation, legislation, and standards

The making of rules is a basic and traditional role of cities, but it is not always applied with as much focus or conviction as possible, or as needed. Cities must move swiftly and boldly to issue building regulations, efficiency standards, and mandatory renewable energy provisions for new buildings. The phenomenal success of Spain's Solar Ordinance is a good start to consider as a guiding model: here renewable thermal and electric supply is made mandatory in all residential building works across many cities.[10] But today cities can and should go further, embracing full renewable energy supply as mandatory where climate, resource, and national pricing support mechanisms allow this. Regulations and standards can also be provided in cooperation with state and national governments where municipal discretion to regulate is restricted.

2. Incentives and disincentives

Incentives—rewards, or "carrots"—for taking efficiency measures and developing renewable energy installations, but also for the setting up of renewable energy service companies (RESCOs), can be provided through taxation and pricing policies. Free or highly affordable, well-reticulated public transport will induce better commuter behavior. Cities can also regulate access to parts of the city for electric vehicles propagation, provide production and market incentives for solar charging stations, and encourage solar car-share providers.

But strong disincentives work, too, and can be applied as "sticks." Development applications can be slowed, fees set higher, or licensing taxes doubled to discourage, say, motor vehicle ownership, or the operation of industrial facilities relying on inadequate energy support systems.

3. Corporate asset development and management

The facilities and stock owned, operated, managed, and/or controlled by the city—from the urban infrastructure apparatus to the development of municipal buildings to street lights, car fleets, and undeveloped or underused property— can be deployed as a readily available tool as well. Indeed, the public hand has a higher degree of accountability and responsibility—and hence an obligation—to do better than the private sector, and certainly no worse than the best of the private industry. It is also obliged to use its asset management and capital investment policy and practice to set a powerful example to the community.

Today, at this late stage of decline in the health of the biosphere, the stakes are too high for vague exhortations to "do better in saving energy" or to employ voluntary green building rating tools. Now all new buildings should be developed as energy-autonomous structures, gasoline powered car fleets should be eliminated and replaced with bus tickets or electrical vehicles, and unused land should be opened to urban gardening cooperatives or community solar farms. Doing anything less is failing our present communities, not to mention future generations.

But "assets" do not have to be made of bricks and mortar or steel and glass. Municipal assets also include institutional frameworks and organizations. For example, cities that own and operate power companies and other public utilities are fortunate: these are powerful tools in projecting renewable energy and efficiency policies, developing infrastructure, and engaging in farsighted autonomy measures of all kind. Where no public power assets exist, these sometimes can be acquired or won back and become an important asset in the fight against climate change and fossil fuel dependence.

• *The development of virtual utilities* as effective policy apparatuses in the absence of real public power companies is a real and practical option for large metropolitan areas or smaller cities in alliance with regional or state government. A good example is Delaware's Sustainable Energy Utility (SEU), a state institution issuing bonds to fund efficiency and renewable energy development and retiring these from the income or savings generated. The SEU concept is also an example for how to raise funds in the absence of a strong capital asset or tax base: the issuing of dedicated municipal bonds can support efficiency and renewable energy development finance.[11]

• *Renewable power asset investment:* Cities can and indeed should move to use bond finance, their own assets, public-private partnerships, contracting arrangements, or cooperatives to develop projects near or far. Useful examples include Copenhagen's participation in the Middelgrunden offshore wind cooperative, or Munich's investment in North Sea offshore wind assets, or Spanish solar thermal capacity. Small town examples abound: in 2008 the Bavarian village of Wildpoldsried developed wind and solar power assets that help them produce 380 percent of their own electricity demand in renewable power, generating millions of euros in income for the community thanks to Germany's renewable energy feed-in tariff, some version of which is now in use in over fifty countries around the world.[12]

• *Long-term renewable power-purchasing contracts*, as bulk purchasing for end-consumer use, are becoming increasingly popular, allowing cities to act as nonprofit agents to acquire renewable electricity at large-volume rates and passing the savings on to the community by distributing the power without price mark-up.

• *The conversion of all city buildings and associated new construction projects* as high-efficiency measures and comprehensive renewable energy supply infrastructure now provides the basis for theoretical long-term carbon negative practice by projecting practice to surrounding areas and acting as supplier of renewable energy.[13] The best example is the English town of Woking, which has combined this policy with a practice of distributed cogeneration units as emergency devices to rapidly cut the city's corporate emissions.

4. Institutional reform and improved strategic and general planning practice

Traditional city government is modeled after nineteenth- and twentieth-century realities, including energy practices. It is specialized in sectors—the famous guilds of bureaucracy. The modern world of energy- and emissions-conscious governance has no room for over-specialization. Now is a time for broadbanding of skills, outcome-oriented practice, and an institutional structure in which all departments are focused on energy autonomy.

Planning practice also changes dramatically. For cities geared toward energy autonomy the following rule is important: *Know Thy Assets.* Mapping renewable energy capacity, understanding energy flows, realizing what roof and open space assets are available for renewable electricity and thermal energy conversion—this knowledge is the basis for achieving renewable energy independence in a structured and purposeful manner.

By generating a full picture of all energy streams—both sources and sinks—we can build a foundation for successful strategies. By fully mapping the potential of the city—its physical "skill" to generate renewable power based on the very built form—the stage is set for an energy-autonomous city that maximizes its potential *intra muros* first.[14]

Traditional local physical planning practice is being reformed, too: urban planning now regularly designates certain "green development" zones or infrastructure; anticipates electric vehicle infrastructure needs; and engages renewable energy in public infrastructure in some systematic way, for street lighting, traffic lights, say, or other infrastructures.[15] The limitation of these piecemeal efforts and fractional target setting exercises has become all too clear.

5. Community action development, industry alliances, information, and education

Outreach is another very traditional municipal function, and yet it is also often not well used. Here is enormous potential that can be realized without owning assets or large capital investment. The examples of effective municipal agencies, activist support organizations, educational and information programs, and community aid entities focused on improved energy practice are legion. However, many have been far too timid at this stage, content with early Local Agenda 21 and CCP-style emissions estimation and target-setting exercises. The time has long come to squarely focus on 100 percent renewable as the only sensible goal remaining, regardless of climatic and cultural setting, level of development, or size of the city or community involved.

6. Fostering energy autonomy within

The large majority of case examples in this study encompass smaller cities and towns, even villages. And yet there is a great deal that can be learned from these—if only cities and their community organizations could be rallied to take up the energy-autonomy agenda neighborhood by neighborhood, precinct by precinct, and ward by ward. Some cities will be culturally more amenable to this agenda than others. The powerful community self-help organizations, and other "little town hall"-anchored local area institutions in Dutch cities; Japanese ku (ward) governments; Swiss town-, district-, and canton-level organisations; Chinese neighborhood assistance and regulatory structures, usually politically founded—these are all examples for the essential elements on which to base distributed, self-reliant renewable energy development strategies that can even serve as a trading base between communities. And physical assets abound. Just like parking lots and rooftops cry out to be developed as communal solar electric or thermal assets, port cities can use their shipping areas as new wind power generation hubs, as a growing number of seaside Dutch cities demonstrates: Rotterdam, Amsterdam, or Groningen serve as excellent examples.

7. Fostering energy autonomy and carbon sequestration practice

Methodical use of open space for garden and urban forest development, for wetland growth and surface water management, contributes to lowering a city's carbon footprint. This means the rebuilding of regional links, one of the most exciting and challenging but also most promising opportunities. From nurturing regional climate forests to re-localizing the food supply to seeking to recharge the regional agriculture through energy-active land uses to solar and wind farms: the reconnection of city and region promises to become the most powerful driver of geographically proximate partnerships among long-separated neighbors: city cores, suburban rings, and rural economies.

SHARING AN ELUSIVE GOAL

RAY GINDROZ

FIG. 1 Drawing by Doug Cooper of a street in a compact Pittsburgh hillside neighborhood showing its connection to other neighborhoods, the city center, jobs, and transit. *Pittsburgh, Scene 2,* 2010, 48 x 96 inches, charcoal on paper on board.

In September 2008, members of the Council for European Urbanism (CEU) gathered in Oslo for their annual congress. The subject was climate change and ways in which urbanism could move the world toward a zero carbon future.

An impressive array of papers were debated, ranging from ways of translating the arcane formulas of legislation into practical action to simple measures that had produced results easily and quickly. Most of the presentations dealt with very specific issues. They were like the individual dots of color in a pointillist painting, but the vision that this collection of dots was struggling to portray was less clear—even elusive.

Fortunately, Oslo and its region provided a model for that vision. Oslo is a polycentric region of compact, walkable communities linked by transit and set in a natural and agri-cultural landscape. Over the course of the last century, it has built the regional pattern that we usually only see in the idealized diagrams of conceptual regional plans.

To experience this "diagram" as reality was a revelation, especially for the American participants. High-speed rail quietly whisked us from the airport to the city center, quickly passing through orderly industrial areas around the airport, then through unspoiled natural conservation areas, and then, as we approached the city, through beautifully tended agricultural land. Once we crossed into the developed area, we quickly arrived at the central train station, located in the most densely populated and active part of the city. From there, we easily found our way via tram or bus to our destination in another part of the city center.

A relatively modern city, most of Oslo was developed in the last 120 years. The core of the city, planned by Camillo Sitte with picturesque, curving streets and squares, is immediately adjacent to the grand axes and parks of the monumental city, which in turn are within an easy walk to the garden city neighborhoods built in the early twentieth century. Each stop on the tram or metro line is a high-density destination with its own type of uses, some civic, some commercial, some recreational, but all of which have the residential, business, and retail uses that support walkable city life. The transit lines also link the city to smaller towns in the region.

The contrast with most American Cities was shocking. How far behind we seem to be on our side of the Atlantic!

And yet, American cities once had such regional structures. With the inevitable pendulum swing of history (and history writing), the urbanism of the Industrial Era was condemned for its polluted air, labor oppression, and lack of modern sanitary conditions, causing us to forget the positive aspects of early-twentieth-century urbanism.

Pittsburgh 1908 and 2008

The Pittsburgh region is a good example. Steel Mills were built alongside the rivers for water and access. Later, railroads were built next to mills on the floors of the river valleys. Workers were housed near the mills in towns that climbed up the hills. In that pre-automobile era, towns were no larger than the area a person could walk in ten minutes.

Within that diameter all the needs of daily life were provided: work, housing, shops, churches, schools, libraries, social clubs, and parks. Neighborhoods and towns were defined by topography, which served to reinforce their sense of community identity, thereby providing an environment that enabled residents to create social capital and the social sustainability for communities to weather hard times. These compact towns were set within an agricultural landscape that produced much of the food for the region. A network of streetcars connected the towns to each other and to Pittsburgh. Long-distance rail lines with terminals within easy access of the streetcar lines connected the region to the rest of the country.

It was the same diagram we experienced in Oslo: a polycentric region of compact, walkable communities linked by transit and set in an agricultural and natural landscape.

Unfortunately, unlike European cities, American cities did not maintain and refine this model. In the "Age of the Automobile," traditional town centers were abandoned by retailers in favor of highway-oriented shopping centers; traditional neighborhoods held less appeal for families than the sprawling subdivisions; schools were decentralized; streetcar lines stopped running and their tracks were abandoned and pulled up.

And then, in the 1980s, the American steel industry collapsed. But in spite of a long decline in the Pittsburgh region, the traditional pattern of compact settlements remained more or less intact along with a strong sense of community pride and will to succeed as a city and region. It has been named among the most liveable cities and

FIG. 2 Oslo, Norway.

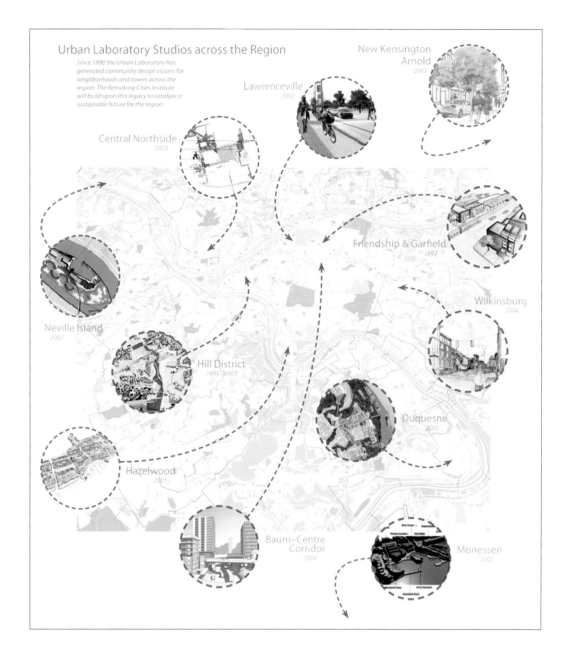

FIG. 3 Overview of projects conducted by the Urban Lab of the Remaking Cities Institute at Carnegie Mellon University, Pittsburgh, Pennsylvania.

regions many times in recent national surveys. Other legacies, including the philanthropic ones from Pittsburgh's industrial period, became stronger in the late twentieth century, especially the regions, universities, research institutes, and medical centers.

As a result, the Pittsburgh region transformed itself into a new kind of economy based on research, medical, and educational institutions. Its success was celebrated by President Obama when he chose it as the host city for the 2009 G-20 summit.

Although the city of Pittsburgh and most of its neighborhoods have prospered in this new economy, the region has a long way to go before it is a model of a sustainable region. Some neighborhoods within the city and nearby towns are struggling, especially along the river valleys once dominated by steel mills. Here traditional patterns are only partially intact, many badly deteriorated. Yet these areas, with their convenient locations and intact infrastructure, are the most

sustainable locations for development. Younger generations are discovering them, and many individual efforts are underway to bring them back to life.

But formidable obstacles remain. The scale of investment required to restore transit infrastructure and support revitalization is beyond the capacity of individuals or individual towns. Public funding priorities do not include rail and other transit investments; complex political jurisdictions make it nearly impossible to reach consensus across the region; and the national political climate remains hostile to large-scale public investments and interventions. Fresh ideas, new programs, and additional resources are needed.

International Vision and Local Need

Participants in the Oslo congress proposed a joint initiative with the American-based Congress for the New Urbanism to

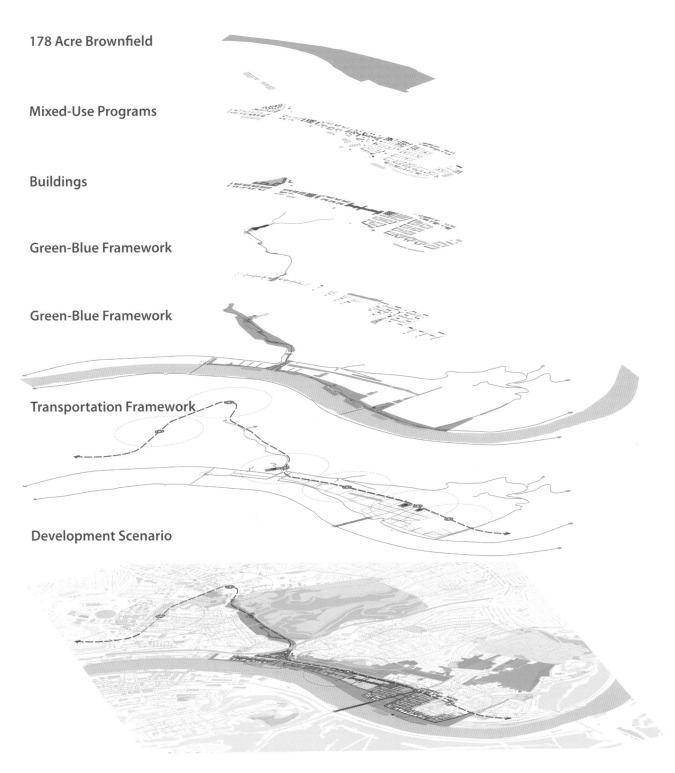

178 Acre Brownfield

Mixed-Use Programs

Buildings

Green-Blue Framework

Green-Blue Framework

Transportation Framework

Development Scenario

FIG. 4 Analyses of the urban structure of a
former industrial riverfront area in Pittsburgh,
prepared by students of the Urban Lab of the
Remaking Cities Institute.

The Matrix Illustrated

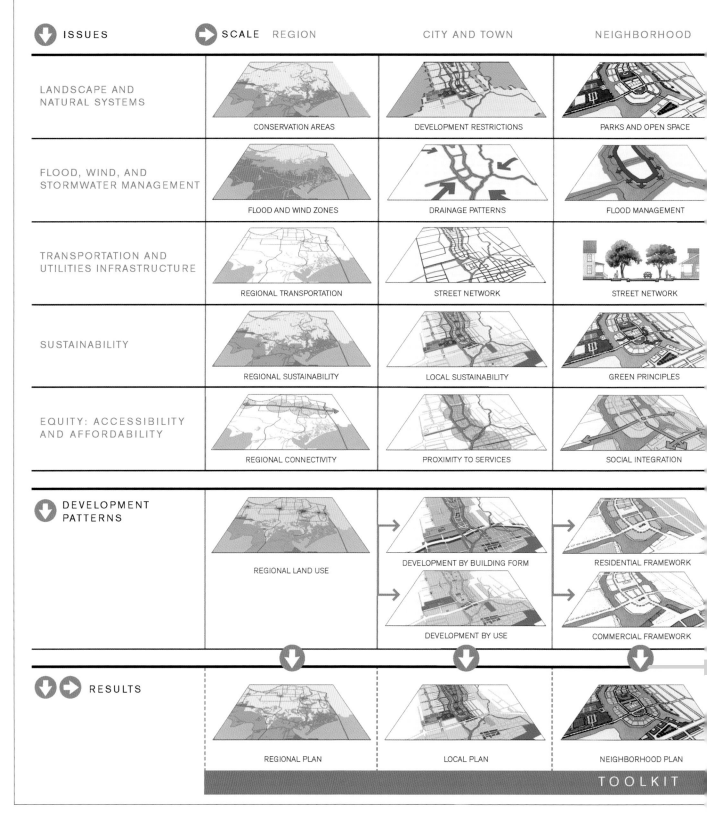

⬇ ISSUES	➡ SCALE REGION	CITY AND TOWN	NEIGHBORHOOD
LANDSCAPE AND NATURAL SYSTEMS	CONSERVATION AREAS	DEVELOPMENT RESTRICTIONS	PARKS AND OPEN SPACE
FLOOD, WIND, AND STORMWATER MANAGEMENT	FLOOD AND WIND ZONES	DRAINAGE PATTERNS	FLOOD MANAGEMENT
TRANSPORTATION AND UTILITIES INFRASTRUCTURE	REGIONAL TRANSPORTATION	STREET NETWORK	STREET NETWORK
SUSTAINABILITY	REGIONAL SUSTAINABILITY	LOCAL SUSTAINABILITY	GREEN PRINCIPLES
EQUITY: ACCESSIBILITY AND AFFORDABILITY	REGIONAL CONNECTIVITY	PROXIMITY TO SERVICES	SOCIAL INTEGRATION
⬇ DEVELOPMENT PATTERNS	REGIONAL LAND USE	DEVELOPMENT BY BUILDING FORM / DEVELOPMENT BY USE	RESIDENTIAL FRAMEWORK / COMMERCIAL FRAMEWORK
⬇➡ RESULTS	REGIONAL PLAN	LOCAL PLAN	NEIGHBORHOOD PLAN

TOOLKIT

FIG. 5 The Louisiana Speaks Planning Tool Kit: the Matrix is a visual table of contents for techniques for sustainable planning and design at all scales, from the region to the individual building. It is used by local planning agencies and communities throughout the State to gain information relevant to Louisiana's unique conditions.

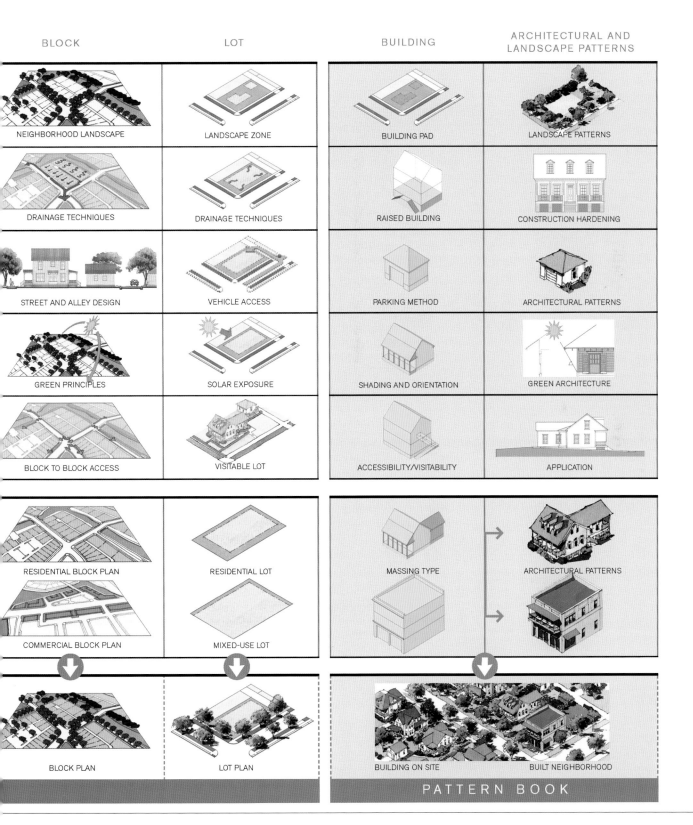

BLOCK	LOT	BUILDING	ARCHITECTURAL AND LANDSCAPE PATTERNS
NEIGHBORHOOD LANDSCAPE	LANDSCAPE ZONE	BUILDING PAD	LANDSCAPE PATTERNS
DRAINAGE TECHNIQUES	DRAINAGE TECHNIQUES	RAISED BUILDING	CONSTRUCTION HARDENING
STREET AND ALLEY DESIGN	VEHICLE ACCESS	PARKING METHOD	ARCHITECTURAL PATTERNS
GREEN PRINCIPLES	SOLAR EXPOSURE	SHADING AND ORIENTATION	GREEN ARCHITECTURE
BLOCK TO BLOCK ACCESS	VISITABLE LOT	ACCESSIBILITY/VISITABILITY	APPLICATION
RESIDENTIAL BLOCK PLAN	RESIDENTIAL LOT	MASSING TYPE	ARCHITECTURAL PATTERNS
COMMERCIAL BLOCK PLAN	MIXED-USE LOT		
BLOCK PLAN	LOT PLAN	BUILDING ON SITE	BUILT NEIGHBORHOOD

PATTERN BOOK

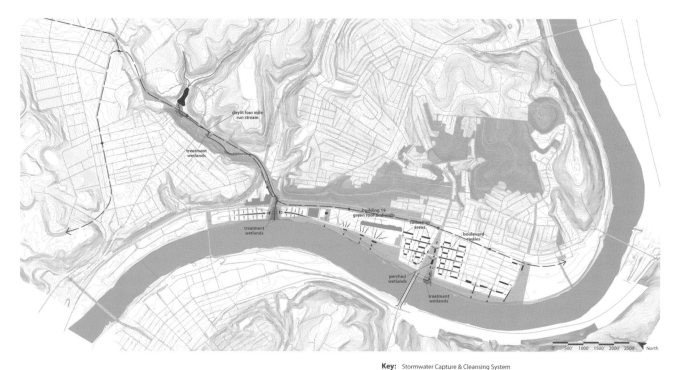

FIG. 6 Recommendations for former industrial sites and adjacent neighborhoods in Pittsburgh, prepared by students of the Urban Lab of the Remaking Cities Institute.

Key: Stormwater Capture & Cleansing System
- Stormwater Collection
- Stormwater Conveyance
- Boulevard Swales
- Treatment Wetlands
- Major Green Roof Collection
- Daylit Four Mile Run
- Permeable Ground

exchange information and experience all aspects of sustainable design. There is much to share: extraordinary technical advances in renewable energy, water management, waste disposal, and transportation hold great promise. Visionary Plans in the United States, Britain, France, China, Singapore, and the Middle East are often variations on this polycentric regional structure.

But how can these ideas be made available to local communities who need them? And how can they be applied? In countries with centralized governments, large-scale efforts can be accomplished with top-down planning processes. But Americans resist and even resent large-scale change and investment from   centralized government. When radical change has happened, it has often been the result of grassroots efforts such as the civil rights, preservation, and environmental movements.

In the past ten years, planning processes that engaged a broad range of local citizens have produced visions that call for polycentric, transit-based regions with growth management. Envision Utah, Envision Central Texas, and the Louisiana Speaks Regional Plan are examples led by Calthorpe Associates in collaboration with other New Urbanist firms.

For example, the Louisiana process was sponsored by the locally based Center for Planning Excellence (CPEX). Thousands of people participated in surveys and workshops and were able to reach a consensus on goals toward protection of the region from storms by preserving natural features and by managing growth. CPEX now provides support for local communities as they implement the plan, such as providing materials like the Planning Toolkit prepared by Urban

Design Associates, which documents key aspects of the plan and illustrates sustainable design principles.

Similar organizations in other countries and regions provide a bridge between progressive planning and local communities. Examples include the Knight Center for International Media at the University of Miami, The Prince's Foundation for the Built Environment in Great Britain, the Kresge Foundation in Detroit, and, in the Pittsburgh region, the Remaking Cities Institute (RCI), which grew out of the 1988 International Remaking Cities Conference. Jointly chaired by the Prince of Wales and David Lewis of Urban Design Associates, it set a precedent for bringing international professionals together with local leaders to develop proposals for reviving the industrial valleys of Pittsburgh.

Now based at Carnegie Mellon University, the RCI is one of two centers within the School of Architecture engaged in international research on energy-efficient buildings and sustainable development. Its Urban Laboratory program works with local communities to assess needs and identify potential solutions and, with a number of community based organizations, foundations, and public agencies, to assist local jurisdictions as they revitalize their communities and infrastructure for a sustainable region.

Organizations like these provide a means for local communities to share experiences from around the world and to bring state-of-the-art developments in technology and sustainable urbanism to local communities in a way that is responsive to their needs and aspirations. Building sustainable regions is a goal, however elusive it may seem, that we all share. An expanded network of such organizations would make the goal less elusive and more achievable.

A TRANSATLANTIC ENCOUNTER

THE COLLABORATIVE FUTURE OF URBANISM

HARALD KEGLER

FIG. I A former industrial site in Bochum, Germany.

Ten years ago I participated in a Congress for the New Urbanism for the first time, in Denver, in 1998. It was the sixth such congress, and I was mainly impressed by the atmosphere, the openness of the discussions, the diversity of the representatives from different camps and the clarity with which the main urbanistic problem, namely sprawl, was tackled. But I was also impressed by the self-critical debate. The "pitfalls" of New Urbanism were a topic of discussion, and they proved to be an accurate self-criticism. I had not experienced anything like that in Europe. On the contrary, here we move within our circles and cut ourselves off from the outside. Back then I already began to be interested in a network that also cultivates exactly this culture of cooperative dialog in Europe, or at least in Germany. Since then we

in Europe have made good progress in this area. We have gotten off to a good start with the Council for European Urbanism (CEU), founded in 2003. At that time I presented our projects for the conversion of old industrial regions, especially in East Germany, and put them in the context of the new era of post-industrial urbanism. More broadly, the CEU has addressed the increasingly urgent questions of demographic and climate change, social division throughout the world, and the necessary rebuilding of our urban regions.

Regarding that first encounter with the Congress for the New Urbanism, one thing in particular impressed me: It only appeared to be a matter of urban design at first glance. At its core, it was a matter of forming coalitions for a "new urban development" beyond sprawl and for regaining an

FIG. 2 German-American Charrette team.

FIG. 3 The Charrette-Team at work with the public.

urban culture in society. It sounded like an end to fighting between camps, between the "modernists" and the "traditionalists." I had great hope and flew back to Germany, strengthened, to the Bauhaus in Dessau, where I worked at that time. Today I teach and am involved in Urban Conversion, with a focus on the resilient, sustainable city. I have experienced the changes in the CNU over the past years from a primarily design-oriented network to a societal instance with international charisma that is now devoted to the comprehensive approach of a sustainable development—with its specific "anti-sprawl approach." However, I also noticed new deficits. Too much pragmatism and too little differentiated consideration of the international developments. In Europe there is not just the hardened faction of crude modernists, who oppose the lonely warriors of the Prince's Foundation. On the contrary, in Europe there is a broad field of activities that tend to favor New Urbanism. And there is a lot that can be learned in Europe. We have a tremendously better developed system of public transport, we have better regional urban regulation, and we have many practical projects in the energy and sustainability sector which are shining examples internationally.

And it is exactly the fact that there are a large number of initiatives that opens up a new chance for the CNU and the

CEU. The significance of the term "new urbanism," a truly new urbanism, can now be seen in the context of climate change. After being a member of the CNU for ten years, and as a cofounder of the CEU, I feel everything points in that direction. We are faced with major upheavals in urban development. This requires a New Urbanism that stands for a climate-oriented, socially balanced city, for the urbanism of the past is intertwined with the urbanism of the industrial age—even if many reforms have already been initiated. This should be discussed.

The "Oslo-Denver Initiative" (ODI) was an offer of cooperation. The initiative was born at the last CEU Congress, in September 2008 in Oslo. The initiative was very popular, and it was articulated in even more concrete terms at the CNU session in Denver, in 2009. The next upcoming session gives us the opportunity to discuss the initiative further, to question it from various angles, and to enrich or modify it with concrete ideas. Apparently, there is a need for transatlantic exchange in the question of how to deal with climate change from the perspective of urban development. This dimension of reducing effects and promoting prevention on an urban-regional level is underrepresented in the international debate among experts (e.g., in the Intergovernmental Panel on Climate Change). Here the cities, and in particular the metropolises, are mainly responsible for climate change and at the same time are the ones mainly affected—especially in coastal areas.

Nevertheless, the topic of climate change has arrived, and the discussions on taking climate-relevant statements into account in urban-regional planning are on the increase. However, on closer inspection, and on both sides of the Atlantic, it becomes apparent that this perspective is too narrow. It is primarily a matter of the use of regenerative energy (casually speaking, climate change can not be stopped with a few solar roofs). We know this. Everyone has realized this. There have been a number of promising achievements; however, in various areas there is still an infinite amount that must be done, and urgently regulated, so that the consequences of climate change can be weakened and the increase in climatic damage reduced. This is especially true in the U.S. The U.S. has a great deal of catching up to do, but it will benefit from its tradition of great resourcefulness—in some cases considerably more than in Europe. But the financial and economic crisis is slowing things down. That is also a transatlantic experience.

One could say the Council for European Urbanism has been an oracle—the congress in Oslo took place exactly at the time of the collapse of Lehman Brothers. For since September 15, 2009, the world has become a different place. The neoliberal model has begun to sway. Regulation and planning are becoming more important again in public debate. They are no longer obstacles to economic growth, but instead are once again becoming indispensable instruments for structuring beneficial, sustainable development. This should be an occasion for us to think about possibilities and initiatives together as to how we can join forces and focus these initiatives without having to "march in step." On the contrary, according to the Overseas Development Institute, creative forces should be combined to better meet this enormous challenge of climate change. But this will not happen by itself. After all, everyone has to deal with their own problems first. These problems are immediate and have also mostly grown out of the financial crisis. However, the advantage of this crisis is that it has become clear just how closely intertwined we are—especially across the Atlantic. So if we are united in the crisis, then we should also come together to tackle it. This congress and this session offer an excellent forum to do this. Here and now we will only be able to take one further step, but we will trigger an impulse that can be followed by further steps.

What must a "new urbanism" of the future—a new urbanism in the age of climate change—consist of? What we have already formulated in the charters of the CNU or the CEU is probably not sufficient. We have vague ideas of what the climate-friendly city should look like. It should be based on the model of the "European city." However, the question remains: How do we get there? And: What are the historically stable elements of urban design that are available to us on the road to a climate-friendly city? This should be worked on empirically. We are just beginning to prepare a project of this kind together with European partners. As an additional field of cooperation, the results should also be integrated with the training of urban and regional planners, of architects and engineers.

A contribution of New Urbanism as a movement is that it tests its propositions by actually building major projects. If they fail, they fail—sometimes embarrassingly. But an instructive example is the large city of Bochum, in the Ruhr region of Germany, where the intention is to build a residential project that meets international standards for sustainable urban development, simultaneously preventing the expansion of urban sprawl and giving an old industrial city a new

image with a future. If this is successful, then we have an ideal case of sustainable, climate-friendly urban development. In the planning process, methods and instruments of New Urbanism from the U.S. and from the German culture of urban development, which is closely aligned with the CEU, have been interlinked.

This was not foreseeable. It is an experiment that succeeded and should encourage others to travel the same route. Ultimately, the offices of urban development came from different "schools," i.e., the rational school of German urban development and that of New Urbanism with a Caribbean influence. I have purposely brought the two together, have mediated and oriented them, and have built bridges between the cultures as intended by the CEU. Both are committed to sustainability; however, its expression differs greatly. In the dialogue between the two and with the residents, all have learned a great deal and have not made any bad compromises. The results really are convincing and have been approved by the city parliament. This could be an incentive to build bridges as an offensive tactic. It is easy to induce "those of a kindred spirit" to work together. But it is more important to bring together different attitudes to really tap into the intellectual potential that results from working together. A surprising amount of agreement has resulted between those who appear to be so far apart. Both the "modernists" and the "traditionalists" have been able to learn from each other that a great deal of what separates us is only based on prejudices and misunderstandings. In view of the challenges we are faced with by climate change as planners and architects, we cannot afford to get sidetracked with discussions on questions of style. The example of Bochum has shown that it can work and that everyone can save face in the process—to the advantage of all and the city.

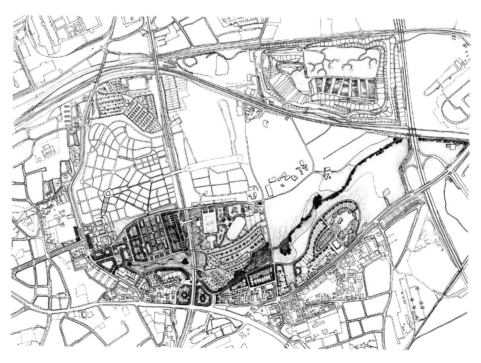

FIG. 4 Masterplan Bochum Urban Housing at the Green Edge 1:2500.

CLIMATE CHANGE AND THE DIFFERENTIAL EVIDENCE OF EUROPEAN URBANISM

MICHAEL MEHAFFY

FIG. 1 Oslo, Norway.

Climate change—at once the tip of a larger crisis of unsustainability, and in its own right a looming threat to human well-being on par at least with the Black Death of the thirteenth century—has changed everything, except our way of thinking. Our response to date has been characterized by a bizarre mix of paralysis, denial, and tokenism. We have hardly begun to change the titanic operating system that pulls us deeper into the crisis.

The built environment professions, whose work generally makes them aware of the seriousness of the issue, are now wrestling with their own professional responsibility. What can be done—must be done—to mitigate the onset? What can only be done as an adaptation to an irreversible reality? How will we prepare our settlements?

One such assessment occurred in Oslo in September 2008, at a conference dubbed "Climate Change and Urban

FIG. 2 This ordinary street in a traditional urban neighborhood of London shows a surprisingly complex series of layered zones of public and private, offering a diversity of perspectives and choices for dwelling, moving, and interacting within the city.

FIG. 3 An imaginative work of art—but what is the quality of public space? How well does it function as part of a larger sustainable urban fabric?

Design"—a review of the latest science, policy, education, and best practices in urban design as they apply to that seminal crisis. The assessment brought together a wide assortment of government research bodies, NGOs, universities, and practitioners from around the world. (This author, along with the two colleagues whose essays follow this one, helped to host the event for the Stockholm-based Council for European Urbanism.)

Amid all the discussion of the crisis and what is to be done about it, one salient fact stood out: the carbon footprint per person of Europeans is, by most measures, less than half that in the U.S. and other countries with more "modern" development patterns. Their use of other nonrenewable resources is equally low by comparison. Yet their standard of living, and their quality of life, are certainly not less than half. Indeed, by many measures they are notably higher.

To be clear, the European level is not a low enough level to mitigate the coming crisis, even if we could get the entire world to live like an average European. In fact, were we to do so we would still exceed our natural carrying capacity by several times. But it tells us that there is already an important contributing factor or factors at work in the change from a

European way of life to a U.S. one: quite possibly a structural change that may be key to the generation of this crisis, or to its excessive extent. And this factor appears to have very little role in delivering other real benefits for the quality of human life.

If we could isolate this factor, we might be able to put it to work as a key strategy in mitigating this crisis.

What is the factor that accounts for this disparity? It can't be a mere cultural difference—that, say, Europeans are somehow more moral or more frugal people. After all, it was Europeans who first settled the U.S., and those Europeans who move there today also generally increase their use of resources to match their new countrymen. Nor can it be simply the fact that Europe is a smaller landmass than the United States. Very few Americans drive across the continent on a regular basis.

What Americans certainly do is drive around in cities to perform their daily activities, generating demand for resources. The resources they use are a clear function of the way they move around (how much, what kind of vehicle, where to) and, closely related to that, the pattern and distribution of their homes and other facilities. The infrastructure required by this segregated operating system is itself a profligate consumer of resources in its construction, operation, and maintenance. It also destroys ecosystems and the low-carbon services they perform, like water purification and CO2 removal.

Moreover, if residents are dependent on this car-based pattern, they will very likely be equally dependent on car-based services, like high-consumption drive-through restaurants and the like. If they live in isolated, large-house subdivisions, they will likely be more dependent on the high-consumption amenities provided within those houses and the goods they can buy (often on credit) to stock them. This fuels ever more growth of the same consumption patterns. And it fuels ever more waste, as the geometries of neighborhoods and neighborhood activities expand—often along with the geometries of waistlines.

Conversely, the evidence from Europe suggests that if people live in settlements with more efficient distribution of amenities, and if they can avail themselves of a strong public realm, affording social interaction, walking, cycling, public transit, and recreational amenities close by, then they will use fewer resources in the immediate activities of getting around and passing time. Research suggests they may even use fewer resources in other activities like eating, consuming goods, and the like.

Cities are thus, in a real sense, the physical operating systems on which these quotidian activities are run—and it appears that the shape of cities plays a profound role in shaping the patterns of activity, use, and waste. Thus it matters a great deal how efficient the settlement is—how conducive it is to a high ratio of quality of life to expenditure of resources, while minimizing waste.

How can one achieve such an optimum? It is certainly a matter of changing design practice as well as the system of regulations and incentives. But it is also, to borrow a phrase from U.S. politics, "the economics, stupid." And it is a matter of cultivating the tools of self-organization and emergence.

These are not entirely new tools. Two centuries ago, settlement naturally followed the logic of pedestrian access to a mix of uses, because that was the generative rule by which neighborhood-scale systems evolved adaptively. Put simply, people and businesses followed common-sense adaptive rules to maintain access to goods and to markets in an age of relatively scarce energy.

As Jane Jacobs and other urban scholars have long noted, the apparently messy character of a lively street is actually an intricately ordered series of layered zones of public and private, offering a diversity of perspectives and choices for dwelling, moving, and interacting within the city.

FIG. 4 Rome's organic complexity is the result of centuries of small adaptive actions by legions of people—and the result is an exquisitely ordered, livable, biophilic city. It still functions today as a place for modern business activity—indeed, a prestigious one.

FIG. 5 A satellite image of New York, one of the regions of lowest carbon emissions per capita in the U.S., and closer to that of many European cities. Jane Jacobs wrote about its marvelous emergent order in *The Death and Life of Great American Cities.*

This urbanism evolves from the order that people create around them every day when they form social spaces, create small arrangements, solve small human problems.

From those small acts of ordering—and from only occasional, strategic top-down interventions—larger urban patterns have emerged and evolved, forming clusters of reusable information. This evolutionary process has produced cumulative intelligence about how to live well in cities.

Such clusters of reusable information are nothing other than the patterns of the traditional city. They are more than stylistic contrivances: they are evolutionary adaptations to the perennial biological and psychic needs of human beings. In Europe, these patterns were constantly harvested from the past, refined, adapted, and reinvented over centuries—until, that is, the historically recent obsession with (technologically propelled) novelty.

But there is reason to suppose these patterns—these resilient traditional types—may be reused usefully today, under the right adaptive conditions. Indeed, there is evidence to suggest they will be essential components of sustainability. For they are, in essence, nothing other than an evolutionary transmittal of learning from successes, and from mistakes.

But as Jacobs also noted, this has not been the dominant approach to city-making, or indeed to architecture, in the modern era. That era has been characterized by the concept of segregation—segregation of the functions of the city from one another, segregation of object-buildings from urban fabric, segregation of the present from the past, and segregation of art from life.

This segregation is in fact a kind of waste—a waste that has been used as fuel for the unsustainable economic growth that we now confront. This is in fact the modernist DNA of sprawl. Le Corbusier made very clear this intimate connection between industrial growth and profligate waste, in his Depression-era manifesto *The Radiant City* (1935):

The cities will be part of the country; I shall live 30 miles from my office in one direction, under a pine tree; my secretary will live 30 miles away from it too, in the other direction, under another pine tree. We shall both have our own car. We shall use up tires, wear out road surfaces and gears, consume oil and gasoline. All of which will necessitate a great deal of work . . . enough for all.

As Jacobs noted, Le Corbusier thought cities were like wonderful mechanical toys, and our acts of city-making ought to be as though we were assembling the machinery of industry: this function handled here, that function handled there, everything segregated and then recombined in a neat linear hierarchy. But he failed to understand the crucial qualities (and efficiencies) of complex networks and systems. These are the essentials of the new modernity: the capacity to adapt and self-organize, to evolve to become more efficient with time.

A new generation of avant-garde designers has now come along seeking to exploit the power (or at least the imagery) of networks, systems and organized complexity: the Parametricists, the Landscape Urbanists, and various others. They are finally taking cues from the half-century-old insights of Jane Jacobs, Christopher Alexander, and other pioneers of urban complexity. But have the new designers grasped the essential urban problems requiring complex adaptation and formulated an effective set of responses? Or are they still acting as specialized fine artists, simply draping the garb of complexity on the same old failing industrial paradigm?

In their ongoing debate with traditional urbanists and New Urbanists—who, at their best, still champion the deeper lessons from Jacobs and Alexander—turnabout is fair play for both. Now we must all ask, what does a deeper engagement with the lessons of biological complexity really imply, not only for the creation of novel aesthetic experiences but, crucially, for resilient, high-quality habitat? What robust new approaches can we develop, beyond the top-down methods of rational planners, or imaginative artists?

What does biophilia hold out for us? Evidence-based design? Integrated generative systems and generative codes? Can we develop a new approach to pattern languages, learning from the brilliant open-source progress of the software designers? Can we gain new design methods from the powerful insights of genetics, about the structure of biological wholes, and their transformation and growth?

At its heart, what new transformation awaits in the technology of design, as it merges with the technologies of living systems? Let me suggest that these frontiers, only dawning, point the way to the fearsome, exhilarating—and most necessary—revolution ahead.

PART 2: BEYOND NEW URBANISM

HOUSING FABRIC AS URBAN FORM

A NEW URBANIST ARGUMENT AGAINST THREE GENERATIONS OF ANTI-URBAN MODERNIST HOUSING

STEFANOS POLYZOIDES

They do not acknowledge it or even remember it anymore, but the modernist opposition to the New Urbanism practices its own Charter. It is called the Charter of Athens. It was framed during the Fourth Congress of CIAM, "The Functional City," which took place in Athens, Greece, and also on board the S.S. *Patris*, sailing through the Aegean Sea in 1933. The Charter of Athens was the critical instrument in establishing the ideology and the global urbanist domination of CIAM and the Modern Movement. It was written under the strong influence of Le Corbusier, who had, during the same year, published his radical treatise on modern planning called *The Radiant City (La Ville radieuse)*. Both through the Charter and in this book, Le Corbusier spelled out in absolute detail the theoretical underpinnings of the ideal city of the twentieth century, its formal principles, and the manner in which, applied through individual projects, it would come to transform the world.

Le Corbusier was a master polemicist and a keen observer of the traditional city. By the early 1930s, he had concluded that the dimensions of its blocks and the spacing of its intersections could not accommodate the speed of the automobile—in effect that the traditional urban infrastructure of 5,000 years of human development was not fit to become the formal root of the contemporary city. He made this point explicitly with reference to the shortcomings of the Champs Elysees in Paris in his seminal book *The City of Tomorrow (Urbanisme)* of 1925.

The CIAM founders and their followers interpreted the city, per a machine analogy, as operating under a limited number of standard building parts at maximum repetition and efficiency—the diametric opposite of the traditional city. He followed up with individual design projects absent of traditional blocks, streets, and familiar building types. His drastically overscaled urbanism of freeways, repeating, massive housing blocks, and isolated monumental buildings became the lingua franca of internationalist modernism's proponents.

Their theories knowingly rejected not only the structure of the European medieval city, but also the entire rationalist

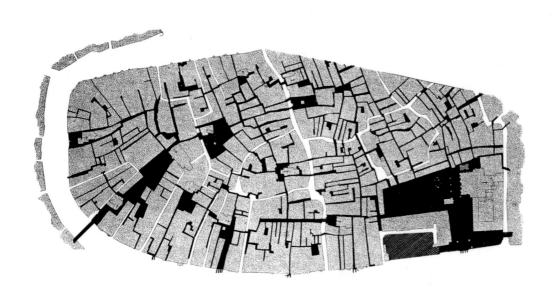

FIG. 1 "Venice is a great inducement for us to continue studying urban organization in a machine age civilization"—Le Corbusier, from *La Ville Radieuse*.

urban tradition from the Renaissance to the twentieth century. In their place, he proposed a "modern urban form": disaggregating streets from blocks and buildings, designing them all to the scale and needs of the automobile, and allowing them to each operate for their own benefit, separated from the others.

When analyzing Venice, Italy, in the *The Radiant City* (fig. 1), Le Corbusier observed admiringly that canals and streets were disconnected from each other. He thought this to be a highly desirable pattern because it allowed pedestrians and gondolas to operate each on their own speed and traffic volume terms. He proceeded to argue through his subsequent projects that all streets everywhere should be separated from each other, as should the other two key ingredients of urban form, blocks and buildings—all of this in the interest of optimizing the individual performance of each.

Buildings would be divorced from their blocks and right-of-ways by being designed at an enormous scale and in a mechanically repeated pattern that rendered them not as interrelated objects but rather as continuous and neutral infrastructure, separated from the ground and relieved of any relationship to other finite building fragments. Dwelling units were also limited in type and range and endlessly repeated in the interest of inexpensive production. Le Corbusier's project for a Suburb of Rome of 1934 was typical of this emerging formal strategy (fig. 2).

When Le Corbusier began to apply his ideas as large-scale additions to existing cities, as in the case of Antwerp in

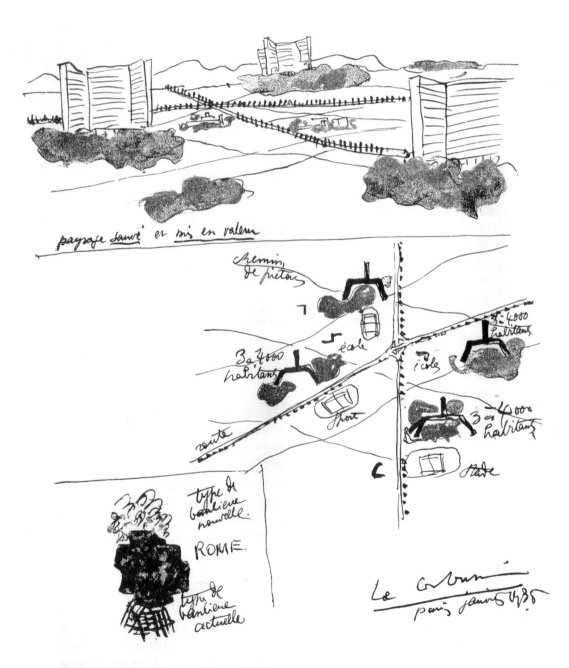

FIG. 2 Le Corbusier, Suburb of Rome, 1934, from *La Ville Radieuse*.

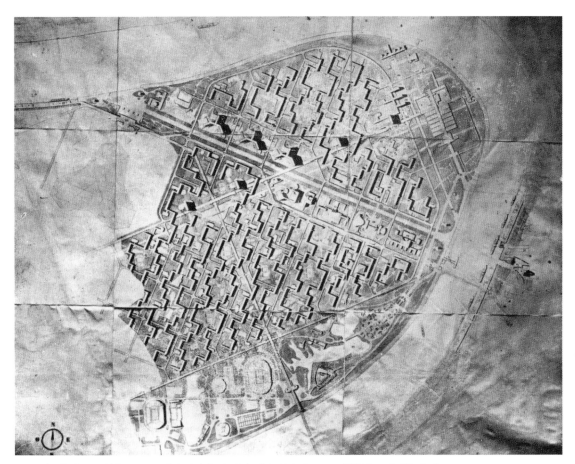

FIG. 3 Le Corbusier, Urbanization of the Left Bank of the Scheldt in Antwerp, 1933, from *La Ville Radieuse*.

1933 (fig. 3), the magnitude of the disparity between the physical scale of the proposed and the existing city fabric was cleverly disguised. The pattern of the new, modern urban growth seemed relatively tame because it was not possible to understand it or to see it in clear juxtaposition to the historic city. The conflict between the two began to emerge more clearly, when figure/field drawings of great European metropolitan centers were drawn side by side with Corbusian "Blocs en Redent" in *The Radiant City*, and in a scale where new and old could be readily compared (fig. 4). Eventually, more and more arrogant assertions of the merits of a housing-block-based, hypermonumental CIAM urbanism began to emerge in written and in architectural form. Le Corbusier had dedicated the Radiant City to "Authority." Not an odd choice, considering the ascendance of authoritarian, both fascist and communist, regimes at the time.

Before long, modernist architects began to test the ambitions of their potential totalitarian clients by envisioning new, grand, and often brutal urbanist transformations. The project for the renovation and extension of Barcelona in 1932 by GATEPAC, the Catalan branch of CIAM, was such an early project—and an ominous sign of international developments to come. The pattern and size of streets, the size of blocks, the repetition and immense scale of both new buildings and the urban space between them, the intended demolition of the Barrio Gotico, all rendered older, existing urban

neighborhoods, and the human life that they enabled, immediately obsolete (figs. 5, 6). This sense of an a priori dismissal of the existing city as irrelevant has been key to the urban culture of modernism from the beginning. Clearance became the engine of urban renewal in the second half of the twentieth century. Throughout the world, the lucky cities that were spared the fate of aerial bombardment during the Second World War were brutally demolished by the pickax of the modernist architect/planner.

After 1945, the urban pattern that was used to replace or to extend traditional cities became massively larger. Streets and blocks were increasingly scaled to the automobile and challenged the very presence of the pedestrian. Buildings emerged as autonomous objects of singular, monumental form, typically as large as the sites given to accommodate them. Housing buildings were conceived as typical blocks, their form reflecting the average density of the entitlement of each site. They were repeated mindlessly, under the pretense that their authors and sponsors were operating in line with the mass production ethic of a machine culture and with the discipline of machine production. This, of course, has never been the case. Dwellings for people to live in were renamed product.

Amazingly, the theory and practice of modernist housing design launched in 1933 have thrived independently of the political regime that sponsored them. Wanton urban destruc-

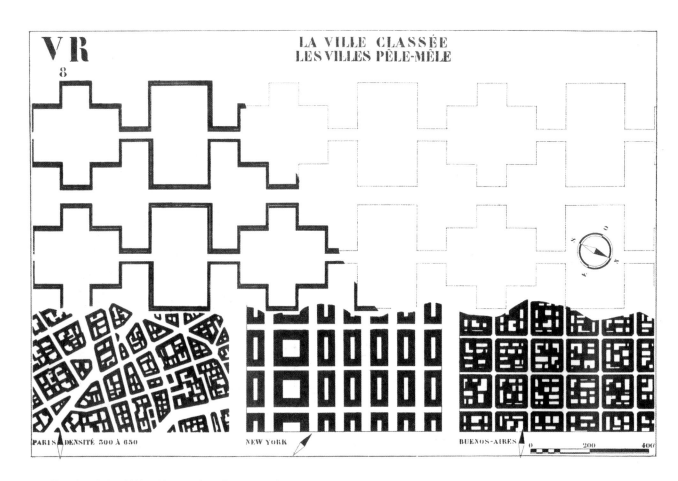

FIG. 4 "The New Scale of Urban Housing Units, Elimination of the Street, Elimination of the Courtyard," from *La Ville Radieuse*.

FIG. 5 Josep Lluís Sert, "Old and New Neighborhoods, Barcelona," from *Can our Cities Survive?*

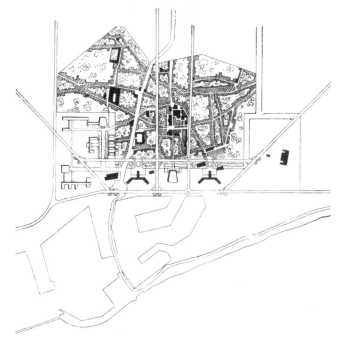

FIG. 6 Le Corbusier, the "Macia" plan for Barcelona, 1932, from *La Ville Radieuse*.

tion and stupefying suburbanization have been promoted by governments across the political spectrum, from capitalism to communism, from the public housing programs of New York and every other American metropolis to the Soviet reconstruction of Leningrad after World War Two. The pattern continues unabated in the breathtakingly rapid urban development of China since 1990.

There were, of course, severe reactions to this process of urban restructuring and "renewal," particularly in the United States. The traditional city proved to be too resilient, too vast a public investment and physical presence, too useful and beloved an object, too well defended by various citizen groups, and ultimately too expensive to change in a wholesale modernist fashion. And the availability of open land on the periphery of the American metropolis fueled a sprawl binge unprecedented in the history of the world that canceled the modernist dream of controlling urban growth by design.

Slowly but steadily, modernist projects in America began to falter in the marketplace. Their one-size-fits-all architecture in program, form, and style proved to be less desirable and less marketable than the traditional buildings these projects displaced. As it became increasingly invasive of neighborhoods, modernist housing began to have a worse effect of blight and disinvestment on its surroundings than the buildings it was ostensibly replacing. By the 1980s it was virtually impossible to build the isolated, dull, and repetitive buildings in the style of the pantheon of modern housing without massive negative popular reaction.

Yet, this kind of housing is still being perpetuated, decades later, by the continuing corrosive influence of zoning codes. Modernist codes in transportation, infrastructure, and planning institutionalized the failed vision of "a new urban order" at the same time as doctrinaire modernist housing projects were beginning to be understood as a hoax. The un-mixing of uses, excessive parking standards, elimination of a shared realm of public space, collapse in the diversity of building and dwelling types, and emergence of the megablock and house tracts were all purposefully packaged into codes, often copied from one municipality to another.

The principal ingredients of modern housing forms and their damaging urban consequences were cleverly camouflaged in the body of the seemingly innocuous verbal and numerical recipes of this Euclidean zoning. The drag effect continues unabated to our day: Small-scale modernist housing fragments are allowable by right. They are enabled by Floor Area Ratio (FAR) rules as opposed to traditionally sanctioned housing typologies. Without typological discipline, housing projects are rendered a priori monumental and incompatible with their surroundings. Continuous disorder and chaos-by-design are introduced incrementally, one building project at a time. The American municipal system of governance is converted into an ineffective circus, where much floor time is still taken by the micromanaging of planning and design issues, by people who know little about either subject, to ends that please no one and continuously undermine both the form and the quality of life for everone in the city.

FIG. 7 Queensbridge Houses, New York City, 1939, from Sert's *Can our Cities Survive?*

FIG. 8 Avtovo Residential Quarter, St. Petersburg, from *Leningrad, Amenagement et Construction, 1945–1957.*

The random, ugly, disconnected, and dense market housing projects recently built in your neighborhood may not look like a heroic fragment of the Ville Radieuse. They were drawn by lesser hands and minds, which were still schooled to believe that they had the talent and the undisputed authority of true masters. Their repetitive, banal housing designs obey the rules of the same theory and intellectual tradition as the heroic, mechanically repetitive designs of CIAM. Worse still, they are imposed by regulation from above, by a cynical and exhausted architectural avant-gardism that keeps on undermining the traditional city, one project at a time. Use-based zoning has now reached the end of its useful life, yet it continues to wreak havoc on the form of the American city.

After decades of negative consequences, we now know yet again that this theory of disaggregated urban design is grossly inadequate and misleading. For best functional and formal performance, cities depend both on the infinite variety, the diversity, and the total integration of their constituent parts. Streets of all types and all infrastructures operate best in interconnected networks. Urban spaces are best formed by the incremental construction of individual buildings that are designed with open-space formation in mind. Monument buildings depend for their visibility on the collective form of adjacent fabric buildings. The best fabric buildings are generated on integrated street networks. The list goes on.

The recent modernist mantra that contemporary cities are out of human control is a self-fulfilling prophecy. For half a century, the measures introduced by most architects to ameliorate perceived urban problems have wreaked a level of chaos-by-design worse than the problems that invited architectural mediation in the first place. The Venice/LeCorbusier virus of separation of buildings from their urban surroundings has been a devastating conceptual gap that has allowed architects in the twentieth century to destroy cities all over the world. In the process, the erosion of their physical character has measurably reduced the livability of urban settings worldwide as well.

It is clear that as a response to three generations of failed housing design, New Urbanist housing projects need to be realized under a theory and through a method that binds their architecture to a new urban and environmental protocol. The theory is based on the charter of the Congress for the New Urbanism and is principally connected to those articles that advocate housing design as an ingredient of neighborhood- and district-making. The method depends on the design of a regulating plan that includes permanently fixed rights-of-way and blocks and a range of development intensities. Blocks are divided into lots. Individual lots are then coded by building placement, building frontage, building height and profile, building use, and parking placement. Each lot is entitled with a range of building types. Diversity is guaranteed by architecture designed by various hands, while the underlying layers of urban structure and typological discipline produce a harmonious city unified in form to the degree desired by its sponsors, its designers, and its users.

FIG. 9 "A spaceship landed in my garden." Pasadena, California, ca. 1960.

What is clearly not spelled out by the theoretical toolbox of the New Urbanism is a specific set of issues that may assist in the design of particular housing projects—neighborhood and district fragments, conceived as a fabric of buildings and open space, and a pattern of landscape and infrastructure.

In our recent housing work, we have begun to practice on a set of New Urbanist housing principles and a checklist of accompanying questions. We have found these useful in framing the general content of our housing and urbanist projects, and in probing the particular architectural design of individual sites.

1. An individual project must be designed to an urban form that is larger than its specific site.

• Is the project site part of a neighborhood or district-wide regulating plan that distributes building intensity across multiple sites?

• Is the project designed to various specific densities as opposed to one average one?

• Does it contribute to the formation of a building fabric, an open space figure, a streetscape, and infrastructure pattern that are larger in size and scale than its site?

• Does it support a block structure, including building frontages and profiles that can generate a coherent public realm?

2. An individual project must engage and respond to the various forms of regional infrastructure that border or intersect its site.

Is the project connected to and scaled properly to large scale, including:

• natural elements, such as rivers, lakefronts, agricultural fields, major views, etc.?

• transportation elements, such as rail and transit lines, thoroughfares, freeways, canals, etc.?

• recreational elements such as parks, greenways, playing fields, etc.?

• sustainable water management systems and utility networks?

3. An individual project must offer a traffic/parking solution that serves both it and the neighborhood/district it is a part of; the denser and more mixed the setting, the greater the need to provide a parking framework that transcends the needs of each project.

- Does the project direct the points of car access into its site in a manner that supports the pedestrian qualities of surrounding thoroughfares?
- Do building(s) obscure or entirely suppress the visual presence of cars?
- Is parking provided conveniently to all the uses that it serves?
- Are project parking solutions of a pattern that is repeated by neighboring projects?
- Is the parking load of an individual project reduced by a neighborhood- or district-wide shared parking policy?

4. Buildings must be located and massed in a manner that promotes the incremental completion of a figure of shared public space.

- Are buildings designed into ensembles by pairing their front, side, and back facades?
- Are buildings serviced and parked in a manner that maintains their public facades car-free?
- Do blocks and buildings define a network of space types by reference to a spectrum of uses from public to private?
- Do buildings define a continuously accessible and pedestrian-scaled ground floor?

5. Buildings must be conceived in form proper, rather than in mechanical repetition.

- Does the project need to be composed of various building types?
- Do individual buildings contain a variety of dwelling types appropriately mixed?
- Is the project composed to express a scale other than that of repeating units?
- Is the project compatible with the form and details of adjacent buildings?
- Are buildings expressed in a variety of styles and related to the style interval of the urban setting they are inserted into?
- Are the color, texture, and materials of the project designed in response to its setting?

6. Buildings must respond to the natural conditions of their site and become part of a more general landscape and streetscape pattern beyond its boundaries.

- Are buildings properly configured for solar orientation, natural daylighting, and natural ventilation, depending on their location within a site plan?
- Are buildings climate-specific in terms of their thermal mass, apertures, and materials?
- Are buildings and gardens efficient in terms of water and energy consumption?
- Are buildings designed for permanence?
- Do buildings form climate-specific garden extensions to interior rooms?
- Does the project form gardens at various scales, e.g., patios, courtyards, quads, greens?
- Does the project complete the patterns of adjacent public landscape and streetscape larger than itself?

7. Buildings must be composed to respond to their particular setting.

- Is the project designed to stand out or fit in?
- Are buildings designed by reference to their city block location, e.g., corner vs. mid-block, A Street vs. B street vs. Alley?
- Are buildings designed to define routine or unique public space, to focus on axial views, and to promote the collective architectural fabric of the city?
- Is building detail and ornament visible to the pedestrian-proximate portions of the building?

This simple and evolving set of issues, and the questions that they generate, can become the inspiration for the design of an engaging New Urbanist housing fabric that is at the same time the foundation of traditional town form.

The secret to this New Urbanist housing design is abandoning the machine analogy—designing without reference to floor area ratios (FAR), average densities, deadening repetition, and one-size-fits-all recipes; recognizing that buildings leverage all other aspects of urban structure, open space, landscape, transportation, and utility infrastructure; and promoting the idea that through the variety, diversity and character inherent in time-honored building typologies—so that every single design can become a significant link in constructing towns and cities of harmonious overall form.

SUSTAINABLE URBANISM IN EVOLUTION

STEPHEN MARSHALL

Back in the 1920s, Le Corbusier famously envisioned cities of soaring crystalline skyscrapers and superhighways—visions that still look futuristic today.[1] But on closer inspection, Le Corbusier's imagery featured old-fashioned-looking automobiles chugging along the highways, and puny looking biplanes buzzing through the sky between the towers. By extension, we can imagine avant-garde apartments stocked with the latest typewriters, slide rules, and gramophones. If such a city had actually existed in the 1920s, would it have been "sustainable"?

The challenge of working out what is "sustainable" is particularly acute for urbanism because of the nature and timescale of urban change. For a short-term sustainability fix, we could easily imagine changing a single thing—say, the energy consumption of a light bulb—while assuming everything else stayed the same, to satisfy us that tomorrow's world is definitely, if only slightly, more "sustainable" than today's. In the very long term, say thousands or even millions of years, it could be sufficient to imagine that a "sustainable" planet is one still habitable by *Homo sapiens*, or successor species. But at the intermediate timescales which visionary planning is typically concerned with—years and decades—it is not so clear what, if anything, "sustainable" urbanism might mean.

How would we know which direction sustainability lay in, in the case of Le Corbusier's urbanism? Would it mean "sustaining" the towers and highways, the use of automobiles and biplanes—or sustaining the prevailing street-based steam- and horse-powered urbanism of its day? But more fundamentally, how can one "sustain" something like a city, which is inherently in constant flux?

To answer this, we need to understand the *nature* of urban change. This chapter argues that it is useful to understand urbanism in evolutionary terms, and this can help us better grapple with the challenges of sustainable urbanism.[2] Here, we first interpret the organic and evolutionary nature of cities, before suggesting implications for sustainability, planning, and urbanism.

A City Is Not an Organism

A city is often considered "organic" in that it sometimes seems to have a life of its own, one that is in a constant state of flux. But this does not mean it is an organism. A city is not corporate: it is not a finite, self-contained whole, constituted by parts that support the functioning of the whole such that that the purposes of the parts are subordinate to the purposes of the whole. Also, a city is not in equilibrium: it does not have an optimal "balanced" state that it must maintain in the face of change. Finally, a city is not developmental: it does not, like an organism, develop progressively from birth to maturity; it does not grow and unfold like a seed growing into a tree that, however unique and unpredictable in detail, has a typical and predictable, characteristic overall form. The three facets relating to corporate whole, state of equilibrium, and developmental process are interlinked, and these make sense together in the case of an organism but not, it is argued, for a city.

We can agree, then, with Christopher Alexander that "a city is not a tree."[3] Rather, a city may be likened to a forest, or, indeed, an ecosystem. A city, like an ecosystem, may appear to be a coherent whole in the sense of having a complex web of interrelationships in which all components are ultimately interdependent. But, significantly, the parts are not subordinate to the whole. The individual components have their own agendas: these may be to some extent in cooperation, but they are also partly in competition. A city, like an ecosystem, can change over time in an open-ended manner; the end result is unknowable. There is no particular optimum equilibrium state to which it "should" return in resistance to forces of change. There is no final mature form toward which change is precipitated. In effect, urban change over time tends to be not so much developmental—like the unfolding of a whole according to a pre-envisaged program—but may better be regarded as being *evolutionary*.

The Evolutionary Nature of Cities

A city is evolutionary in the sense that urban change is gradual and incremental, adaptive, and ultimately transformative. While there is some continuity over time, there is no particular direction of progress, and the long-term outcome is unforeseeable. A city may suddenly gain new extensions in new formats that are radical departures from what went before. There is no fixed functional or hierarchical order: a suburb may become the new center; a new town may outperform an old city.

In this evolutionary perspective, a city is not a unitary whole but a collection of many types of components—buildings, roads, land uses, institutions, and so on. Each of these kinds of components may be said to evolve.[4] Indeed, these all co-evolve together. Urban evolution, then, is the long-term aggregate effect of these co-evolving components.[5]

As with biological evolution, urban evolution can be seen as involving a combination of variation and selective retention. Urban plans and designs and codes and patterns are varied and copied and selected for further copying and variation. Unlike biological variation and natural selection, of course, in the urban context there will be deliberate purpose applied to individual instances of variation and selection. Nevertheless, the long-term adaptive effect is *emergent*: it cannot be anticipated from individual increments of design.[6] So, we make individual purposeful increments of intervention—to our buildings and vehicles and lightbulbs and so on—but these do not follow a predictable developmental program.

Significantly, urban evolution is a continuous process that applies as much today as in the past. That is, evolutionary urbanism is not some rudimentary historic process that was supplanted by modern town planning. From an evolutionary perspective, traditional "unplanned" urbanism, classical town planning, old modernism, and New Urbanism are all part of the same evolutionary game. They each, to different degrees, have some innovation or variation, and some selective retention or building on precedent.

The evolutionary perspective outlined here is not suggested because of any theoretical organic appeal but because it seems to work. It seems to fit urbanism much better than the sometimes contrived analogy between a city and an organism: the evolutionary perspective still allows cities to be interpreted as "organic" without this interpretation being burdened by the limitations of the city-as-organism metaphor.

The evolutionary perspective seems useful as it can relate directly to real-world concerns of cities: the realities of urban change, social cooperation, economic competition, environmental adaptation, technological innovation, and different kinds of planning and design intervention. "Urban evolution" although an abstract concept is something that everyone tangibly participates in, just as we participate in the abstract entity we call "'society" when conversing with a neighbor, or participate in "the economy" when shopping online, or participate in "the environment" when building our homes or tending our gardens.

Challenges for Sustainability

Were urban change simply developmental—like a growing organism—we could imagine that sustainability meant maintaining growth, or maintaining the organism in a healthy mature state. Or, sustainability could mean maintaining a "harmonious balance" between organism and environment. But to the extent that cities are evolutionary—or, like ecosystems, comprising co-evolving components—this begs questions about both what is being sustained and what would be a sustainable outcome.

A first problem is that there is no fixed status quo to be "sustained" into the future. This questions the meaningfulness of "sustaining" something that is undergoing evolutionary change. Sustained evolutionary change would seem to imply a sustained dynamic evolutionary trajectory, such as we could see with computers, evolving from room-sized plant to palm-held gadget. But this dynamic interpretation is the opposite of maintaining something in an existing state, which the term sustainability might otherwise imply. Would sustaining Le Corbusier's 1920s vision mean "sustaining" a consistent technological evolution from typewriter, slide rule, and gramophone to a modern PC or iPod? Or would it mean "sustaining" a society in which typewriters, slide rules, and gramophones are still in a harmonious "balance" in the technological environment of the 1920s? Hence long-term sustainability cannot be a simple extrapolation of the present. "What is to be sustained" will always be open to question and reinterpretation.

A second problem is whether there is such a thing as a target sustainable future state. This is partly because the future is inherently unpredictable, which in its most basic form could be said to affect everything from random motions of subatomic particles to the clunky caprice of political decisions that could result in a desirable strategy being reversed almost overnight. But over and above these kinds of unpredictability, evolutionary history teaches us that there is no single direction that is identifiable with progress; changes can go in any direction, according to context. There is an ever-changing environment where the goalposts are always moving. What is "good" is relative, contingent, and uncertain. We cannot necessarily say what is absolutely good or bad—wings or fins, two legs or four—since it all depends on context. So we can not be sure in advance what will be sustainable or not—as the extinction of once-successful species or obsolescence of once-viable technologies could testify.

And however we might imagine a future optimal sustainable state, evolutionary history reminds us that the path to sustainability in the long term must be built on viability in the short term. So without taking our eye off the longer-term goals, we need to work with things that are viable now. What is deemed "sustainable" today may not turn out to be "sustainable" tomorrow—and vice versa.[7]

In the end, evolution leaves an open verdict on what to do with the future. So the question of "sustainability" is not merely the question of how to get to some commonly imagined destination through technical solutions or effective policy delivery. What we do about the future becomes a political and philosophical question, as it concerns not only notions of the "good life" for individuals but notions of the good society, the purpose of life, and the future of humanity.

Challenges for Planning and Urbanism

The very notion of town planning was premised on the idea that towns and cities could and should be planned. It implies the ability to envisage an optimal future state in advance and steer policy and design interventions toward it. But the complexity and unpredictability of urban systems means that we can not guarantee that planning interventions will have the desired effect, or if their effect (if actually achieved) will be desirable.

Conventional master planning has typically involved the vision for what a future city should be like: a preconceived structure, perhaps with distinct neighborhoods or fixed types of zones in fixed locations. To the extent that plans for new towns and cities have diverged from more traditional urbanism, there was always a danger that they might be dysfunctional. Evolution teaches us that tomorrow's optimal is probably an adapted version of today's—that is, not exactly the same as today's, but still recognizably a progression from it. The monstrous novelties of modernism led to what we could call the problem of "Frankenstein" urbanism—the attempt to create new, artificial cities by bolting together from a bag of components urban features such as neighborhoods that arose naturally by other means. This is not just a matter of "good urban form" but also timing: by the time your planned Utopia is built, it might be out of date.

On the other hand, evolution is a combination of tradition and innovation; without innovation, there can be no evolution. Therefore it is not sufficient to base planning visions on outmoded concepts of what cities used to be like. Arguably, many of the new towns and planned cities, while superficially novel, were based on already-outmoded models of what cities were really like. Their rigid town plans ossified these structures. Therefore, traditional models of large-scale urban structure, whether monocentric cities or polycentric conurbations, may be useful starting points to build from, but are not sacrosanct as models for future long-term targets. Attempting to plan cities and city regions based on moribund models of what they used to be like would amount to a kind of "Neanderthal" urbanism. "Neanderthal" urbanism could be as dysfunctional as "Frankenstein" urbanism (although, at least in the "Neanderthal" case, this would be based on a model that at least was once viable).

An Evolutionary Urbanism

So how, then, to plan? The contention here is that urbanism is evolutionary whether we will it so or not—evolutionary urbanism is not a historic phase before modern planning, nor confined to some kind of incremental neo-traditional urban-

ism. Conventional planning and modernism are part of it too. So evolutionary urbansim is not something we need to proactively strive to achieve, but we should strive to realize an urbanism that is cognizant of the workings of evolution and in directing efforts toward generating good urbanism.

The idea of evolutionary urbanism might at first sight seem antithetical to the foresight and control associated with town planning. However, acknowledging the evolutionary nature of urbanism need not mean accepting "the law of the jungle" or a laissez-faire free-for-all; it does not mean we abandon attempts to intervene in the urban system for the common good. The point is to understand how best to intervene, informed by the evolutionary realities of urbanism. At least two broad kinds of mechanisms are possible, over and above conventional master planning, both of which have analogues in biological evolution: the first to do with generation, the second with selection.

In the first case, civic intervention takes the form of the proactive codes for generating urbanism. Codes can specify urban components—such as building type, land use, street type, block type, and so on—and how these may relate to one another. While the urban components and their relationships are organized in a preenvisioned manner, the overall outcome can be left open according to the needs of individual actors, such as developers in particular circumstances. The code may be set by the planning authority to ensure a basic compatibility and functionality, for the public good, but otherwise allowing individual freedom for incremental construction. A code-based approach could form the basis of a bottom-up "planning" system—like "genetic engineering" for urbanism.[8]

The second basic kind of intervention is a selective mechanism. Just as humans can intervene in biological evolution through artificial selection, public authorities can intervene in urban evolution through mechanisms such as development control to override the "natural selection" of the urban marketplace, where appropriate. This can act to counterbalance any danger that a wholly "generative" system could create emergent outcomes that were dysfunctional.

In addition to generation and selective development control, we can yet find a role for design. This is where we can usefully apply design to individual buildings, streets, blocks, and perhaps some larger urban features where an optimal form is foreseeable and realizable. So evolutionary urbanism becomes a matter of getting the right kind and degree of intervention, i.e., the right kind of codes, the right designs, and the right scale, and the right kind and degree of development control, at the right scale, to work together.

Conclusion

What then of "sustainable" urbanism? From an evolutionary perspective, it could imply nothing other than urbanism that is viable now. Sustainability may be something that cannot be predicted in advance but can be only judged in hindsight, like judgment on what can be considered a successful species.

This is not to deny the importance of vital, forward-looking design solutions like energy-efficient lightbulbs or zero-carbon buildings or resilient sea defenses. It's just that the label "sustainable" is not necessarily the most helpful way of defining or justifying them. Perhaps we need to go beyond the term "sustainability"; we can at least expect the meaning of the term to evolve.

In terms of future urbanism and planning, a suggestion for evolutionary urbanism has been made here, based on a combination of design interventions, codes, and development controls. This package embodies the mechanisms of generation and selection that can be part of an onward evolutionary process to create the functional complexity of viable urbanism. This could be what "planning" now needs to be about, rather than simply creating master plans or visions of target future states.

A potential handicap of evolutionary urbanism is that it has no definite vision of a future state: no stirring images of Corbusian cityscapes—nor, for that matter, today's futuristic eco-utopias. But this is because it accepts that the longer-term future is unknowable; predictive images are usually "wrong," and the optimizable sustainable city a chimera. That's not to say that Corbusian cityscapes or eco-utopias can't be part of the solution—it's just that we can't be sure which would ultimately be more "sustainable": a city of slide rules, typewriters, and gramophones in glass and concrete towers, or a city of bicycles and iPods and straw-bale terraces or vegetation-festooned eco-skyscrapers? In effect, we need to go beyond "sustainability" as a catch-all aspiration for urbanism and refocus our vision and energy on determining the best solutions that work now, whatever the future may hold.

LEED-NEIGHBORHOOD DEVELOPMENT

THE TWENTY-FIRST-CENTURY TOOL
FOR MAKING AMERICAN URBANISM SUSTAINABLE

DOUG FARR

You never change things by fighting the existing reality. To change
something, build a new model that makes the existing model obsolete.
— R. Buckminster Fuller

FIG. I This Green Line Corridor plan introduced transit-oriented development "ped shed" planning
to the Chicago region.

Precis

In the early 1990s, years before there was any public interest in the topic, I worked to build an architectural practice in the design of "environmental buildings." In so doing I learned how the creation of certification standards can create market demand. This insight, combined with an "aha moment," led me to campaign for the creation of LEED-Neighborhood Development as essential to creating demand for sustainable urbanism.

For most of that decade I was one of a core group of Chicago architects passionate about designing "environmental" buildings and seeking to build professional practices designing environmental buildings. To do so we had to educate ourselves on this emerging field and to build public awareness and interest in the design of environmental buildings. The AIA Committee on the Environment (COTE) was the centerpiece of our efforts.

In advance of the 1992 United Nations Earth Summit in Rio de Janeiro, the AIA COTE began to establish the intellectual agenda for the yet-to-be-named "green building" movement. This environmental building agenda was moved to center stage internationally in 1993 (coincidentally the founding year of both the Congress for the New Urbanism and the United States Green Building Council) when the national and global architects conferences were held jointly in Chicago. The conference theme of sustainability was supported by a keynote speech by William McDonough and expanded through an international sustainable design competition, which my firm entered.

The design competition was prepared jointly with the Center for Neighborhood Technology and used a controversy involving the Chicago Transit Authority's (CTA) Lake Street Elevated line as the focus for the design. Citing budget woes and deferred maintenance, earlier in 1993 the Chicago Transit Authority announced plans to dismantle the Lake Street Elevated public transit line connecting Chicago's Loop and neighborhoods with the suburb of Oak Park to the west. Our competition entry tried to improve this real world crisis by introducing the economic and social benefits of transit-oriented development (TOD) as a strategy to overturn the CTA's retrogressive decision. The big innovation in the competition entry was a "sustainable kit of parts" for transit-oriented development, or redevelopment in this case, created in a series of church basement meetings. The process of preparing the plan exposed me to the ideas and practice of New Urbanism. The resulting TOD plan, presented in 1994 at the second Congress for the New Urbanism, singlehandedly launched my TOD planning practice. Through the remainder of the 1990s, my office, Farr Associates, prepared neighborhood and TOD station area plans regionally and nationally.

Meanwhile, my group of Chicago architects were largely unsuccessful in finding clients wanting to build environmental buildings. It took the introduction in 1999 of the Leadership in Energy and Environmental Design (LEED) criteria to create a platform for building public awareness and client demand for environmental building design services. But the LEED tool by itself was not enough to make market demand; it took local government serving as an early-adopter client.

The visuals help explain that these strips are not built out, which might not otherwise be quite so obvious.

Need a reason for urgency? Here's one: Habits of suburban life that seemed routine at $30 or $40 per barrel of light sweet crude will seem completely unthinkable when it costs $300 or $400 per barrel, and that inevitable day is crashing toward us. Switching from an auto-only configuration to one that supports motoring but also walking, cycling, transit, and trip-shortening would seem to be one economical, convenient part of the solution.

Watching the Glacier

However sensible and popular it all sounds, when we first began drawing these corridor images we did not realize how long it would take to see the first projects mature. It turns out that watching a corridor evolve can be like observing a glacier retreat: experts assure us it is moving even though the motion is too slow to see with the naked eye. A series of impediments obstructed the corridor-makeover progress.

Largest among these (and thankfully in some jurisdictions, the first to fall) was the transpocracy.

Putting supersized, congested roads on a diet sounded counterintuitive at first to the folks in charge of the key agencies. Spending some of the public treasure habitually devoted to road-widening schemes on transit systems has also been a hard sell. Traffic engineering and transportation planning professionals just were not ready in the beginning for the idea of rebuilding these corridors to make them better habitats for pedestrians. It took a while for the old idea—that wider roads are better roads—to be replaced by the current ethos of multimodal, context-sensitive, networked road design.

Whether the transpocrats like hearing it or not, it is essential to corridor transformation to eventually rework the details of the roadway design. The width of the lanes, onstreet parking, street trees, "design speeds," and sidewalk configurations all determine whether the adjacent addresses can or cannot support the set-forward, street-oriented buildings that complete the scene. (This is not to say that the reformed corridor needs to sport a single, continu-

FIG. 1 The suburban strip transformed into a traffic-calmed urban arterial. High levels of vehicular capacity can be maintained while simultaneously unlocking valuable sites for pedestrian-friendly, street-oriented infill development.

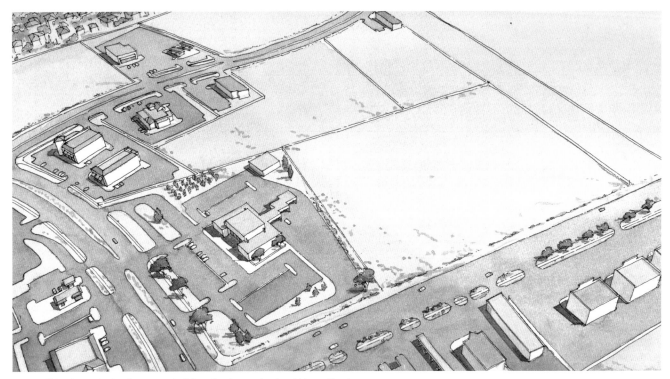

FIG. 2 Suburban strip development—buildings floating randomly within parking lots.

FIG. 3 Over time, street-oriented infill buildings can transform the strip into an interconnected series of well-defined public spaces.

ously similar, extruded cross section for its entire length; usually the road should be considered in a series of relatively short segments, only some of which are meant to be designed and intensified like main streets.) Naturally, the right things to do in the roadway redesign regularly contradict the standards manuals and habits, so that many corridor retrofit plans were stalled by public works departments and trans-

portation agencies. Some progress on this front has been made with publication of the new manual issued by the Congress for the New Urbanism and the Institute for Transportation Engineers (CNU/ITE) for walkable urban thoroughfares, which ostensibly gives entrenched transpocrats the permission to loosen up and allow intelligent redesigns (though the manual must be much more widely

FIG. 4 Suburban arterial intersections are typically hostile to pedestrians and often result in disinvestment in adjacent real estate.

FIG. 5 Rethinking major thoroughfares as signature public spaces forming great addresses helps to encourage new street-oriented infill development.

adopted). The lack of good standards meant the first generation of corridor retrofit plans was delayed for decades by this obstacle alone.

Compounding the effect of the delay, even where agencies can eventually be brought into agreement, corridor reconstruction plans and transit systems are shockingly expensive undertakings—and are therefore usually conceived decades in advance of funding. New Urbanists need to get our plans adopted and have them replace old, questionable highway schemes. Had more corridor makeovers been drawn up and agreed upon years ago, so much of the recent torrent of infrastructure funding might not have been wasted on dumb projects just because they were "shovel-ready."

FIG. 6 The suburban strip corridor may at first glance seem "built-out" but actually offers tremendous opportunity for improved livability through incremental infill development.

FIG. 7 Through thoughtful reconfiguration and street-oriented infill over time, what was once an auto-dominated strip corridor can become a livable, multimodal signature public space.

The Private Side of the Equation

Property owners have been hesitant to risk money building their piece of the new scene until they are sufficiently certain about what the government is going to do in the right-of-way (if anything) and what their neighbors and competitors are going to be allowed to build. With its zoned-in setbacks, parking requirements, and limited land uses, the old strip had a way of isolating the individual property owners' problems; when each development results in a stand-alone build-

ing poking out of parking lots, set far apart from other buildings, it is a sadly straightforward matter to predict what will come next and build accordingly.

The urban corridor makeover, however, gains its power from the synergy between components brought close together, from the efficient use of land, and from transforming both sides of the road until the street itself becomes a spatially defined place. As the master developer, only the local government can provide the necessary certainty to the individual investors via its budget choices, its policies, and its regulations. Local gov-

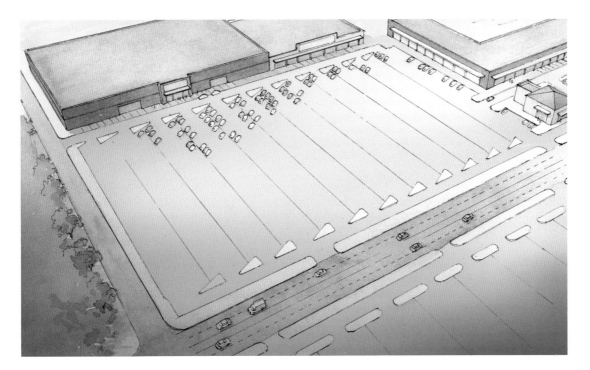

FIG. 8 With consolidated land ownership and fairly large contiguous parcel sizes, strip shopping malls can be attractive sites for walkable infill development.

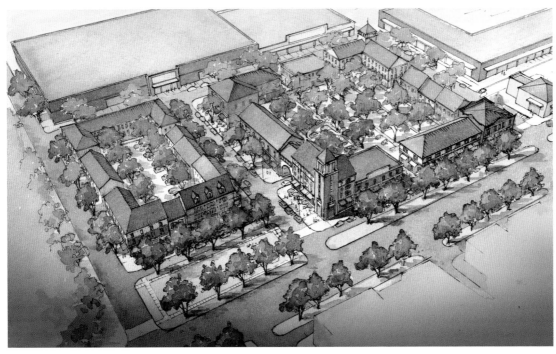

FIG. 9 New infill buildings gradually replace expanses of asphalt, forming an interconnected network of well-shaped public spaces.

ernment should correct zoning for the corridors with a meaningfully detailed, form-based code that regulates certain things strictly and trusts the marketplace with others.

The progress on fixing corridors will be minimal until all three of these—a form-based code, coupled with an adopted roadway redesign, plus a firm commitment to the public transit component—are in place.

Columbia Pike in Arlington, Virginia, is one corridor for which the three pieces are coming together, and it is among the farthest along in transformation. Arlington County adopted a

form-based code for the portions of the corridor in 2002, following thirty years of disinvestment and decline. Two years later, the county finalized public space standards that will control the reengineering of the Pike, and last year took over the road from the Virginia Department of Transportation. Five major private redevelopments have been completed, replacing low-slung stores, parking lots, and car dealerships with multi-story, mixed-use buildings incorporating housing, office space, and stores, including a full-size grocery store tucked within an urban block. The character of the corridor has changed rapidly

FIG. 10 The aging suburban strip—an unprotected, unshaded, uninteresting environment for pedestrians.

FIG. 11 Adding the basic hardware of great walkable streets—continuous wide sidewalks, street trees, on-street parking, pedestrian-scaled lighting, and engaging street-oriented buildings.

from despair to optimism. Most interestingly, the Columbia Pike Streetcar—just an idea during planning sessions in 2002—has progressed far through the approval and funding pipeline and is expected to be operational in 2015. Installing the streetcar will require reconstructing the street, following the new design. All of this progress on Columbia Pike can be attributed to elected officials and neighborhood leaders who got impatient and doggedly persisted until somebody listened.

The early-adopter developers of the first few new private buildings were made sufficiently confident by the county's commitments to get started, but if follow-through is stalled, private development will stall too. With the main street reconstruction still several years away, the redo of the Pike has not, thus far, acquired significant stretches of on-street parking. There are not yet any new buildings facing each other on opposite sides of the street to create the effect of two-sided street space. For these reasons, not even Columbia Pike can be called a 180-degree transformation of a strip corridor into a full-blown main street, at least not yet. On other corridors, like one spectacular boulevard in Cathedral City, California, local leaders have accomplished the reverse: the rebuilding of the roadway is complete but no substantial private construction faces it as planned.

Jeff Speck recently wrote that corridor-makeover illustrations should come with a disclaimer stamp, acknowledging "THIS RARELY HAPPENS."

Why Is It Taking So Long?

One reality is that in their heyday the strip commercial corridors cultivated a comfortable, complacent set of industries populated by experts in building, in their customary, generic, suburban way. The neighbors and city leaders may love the classy corridor-makeover idea, but to the owners and landlords of chain stores and fast food joints, switching to an urban format is a shock to the system and a blow to business as usual. We should not be surprised when the usual suspects expect to continue their usual habits. Delay is inevitable while some new investors are recruited and one has to wait for others to change their game to match the new expectations.

That obstacle is worsened somewhat by an old urban renewal mindset that assumes large-scale land assembly is required for redevelopment. This need not be the case under better planning and form-based codes, but old habits die hard. Parking is one of the reasons. When parking is treated solely as a private matter on private parcels, developers need sites large enough to lay out efficient lots and garages. In mature cities, parking is instead treated as part of public infrastructure, and small parcels can be relieved of ridiculously high minimum parking requirements. One hopes that once this stage is reached, the grain of redevelopment will grow to be less coarse.

Impatient Persistence

Not long ago a Manhattan journalist questioned the corridor/grayfield strategy for retrofitting suburbia, wondering what good can come from "creating islands of walkability" in the otherwise seamlessly automotive world of sprawl. We counter without apology that islands of walkability are better than no walkability at all! But clearly the experience of the last two decades of replanning corridors suggests that, at least for a long time, the segments of strips that do get transformed in an orderly way will stand within a discontinuous, evolving, disorderly context.

The visions for transformed corridors first emerged during a time period when the many other development prospects at hand seemed easier or richer: it was, at least for a while, easiest to build on cheap farmland. (One hopes the corner has been turned on that subject.) There is still a sizable supply of opportunities to fill in downtown parking lots, revitalize historic districts, and clean up waterfront industrial sites. Following the principle that the low-hanging fruit is always picked first, it was natural to let the strip corridors wait. But the era of the corridor makeover is coming. Plan for it. Accelerate it, like Arlington County did. Get impatient and be persistent.

BEST PRACTICES IN DOWNTOWN REVITALIZATION, NEW URBAN STYLE

JEFF SPECK

It is presumptuous for any planner to call his work "best practices," but I hope I might be forgiven for sharing a methodology for downtown planning that I have tremendous confidence in, and which I believe represents the culmination of decades of New Urban downtown work to this point. Needless to say, it is not my own invention, but rather the accumulated wisdom of some of the field's leading practitioners—most notably the form of Duany Plater-Zyberk—reorganized into a single-minded theoretical framework that makes it easier to sell and implement. For the sake of a better term, it all comes down to walkability.

There are many ways to measure the success of a city, but the hallmark of a vital downtown is pedestrian culture, also known as "street life." There is no better leading indicator—or contributor—to urban success. Fortunately, New Urban discourse has advanced to the point where I do not need to prove this claim. If you disagree, you may as well stop reading now.

But if you concur that generating pedestrianism is the central goal of a good downtown plan, then you can see the logic behind refining a General Theory of Walkability that explains why people make the choice to become pedestrians, and then creating a comprehensive planning technique centered on optimizing those influences. This is the approach that I have brought to five Walkability Studies conducted in American cities over the past few years, most recently to the Lowell (Massachusetts) Downtown Evolution Plan, completed in September 2010.

Part I: A General Theory of Walkability

The pedestrian is a delicate creature. While there are many harsh environments in which people are physically able to walk, there are few in which they actively choose to walk, especially when the option of driving is available. The following four sections provide a hierarchy of conditions that must be met if the average person is going to make that choice. Each is necessary but not alone sufficient. They are:

- a reason to walk
- a safe walk
- a comfortable walk
- an interesting walk

A Reason to Walk

As Jane Jacobs noted, "Almost nobody travels willingly from sameness to sameness . . . even if the physical effort required is trivial." For people to choose to walk, the walk must serve some purpose. In planning terms, that goal is achieved through mixed use, or, more accurately, placing the proper balance of the greatest number of uses all within walking distance of each other. In most downtowns, achieving this balance is only possible through the explicit identification of which uses are lacking or underrepresented so that policy can be directed toward fixing that problem. This effort must be coupled with an identification of key anchors, including parking lots, so that special attention can be paid to the paths between them.

A Safe Walk

While crime is always a concern, most people who avoid walking do so because the walk feels dangerous due to the very real threat of vehicles moving at high speed near the sidewalk. Statistically, automobiles are much more dangerous to pedestrians than crime, and the key to making a street safe is to keep automobiles at reasonable speeds and to protect pedestrians from them. This is achieved by meeting the following ten criteria:

- A network of many small streets. Generally, the most walkable cities are those with the smallest blocks, because many small blocks allow for many small streets. Because traffic is dispersed among so many streets, no one street is required to handle a great amount of traffic, and that traffic does not reach a volume or speed that is noxious to the pedestrian.
- Lanes of the proper width. Different-width traffic lanes correspond to different travel speeds. A typical urban lane width is 10 feet, which comfortably supports speeds of 30

miles per hour. A typical highway lane width is 13 feet, which comfortably supports speeds of 60 miles per hour or more. Drivers instinctively understand the correlation between lane width and driving speed, and speed up when presented with wider lanes, even in urban locations.

• Welcoming bikes. There are many reasons to institute a comprehensive downtown bicycle network, including pedestrian safety. Bikes help to slow cars down, and new bike lanes are a great way to use up excess road width currently dedicated to oversized driving lanes.

• Limiting use and length of turn lanes. Left-hand turn lanes, ubiquitous in many cities, should be used only at intersections where congestion is caused by cars turning left. When unnecessary (or over-long) left-hand turn lanes are provided, the extra pavement width encourages speeding, lengthens crossing distances, and eliminates valuable on-street parking. Right-hand turn lanes are only justified in those rare circumstances where pedestrian crowding on crosswalks excessively burdens through-traffic.

• Limiting curb cuts. Every time a driveway crosses a sidewalk, pedestrians are endangered. Front parking lots, drive-throughs, and porte cocheres are suburban solutions that do not belong in cities. Any parking lots or drive-throughs should be accessed off of rear alleys, and front drop-offs can be accomplished simply by reserving a few on-street parking spaces for that use.

• Two-way streets. Drivers tend to speed on multiple-lane one-way streets because there is less friction from opposing traffic and because of the temptation to jockey from lane to lane. Incidentally, one-way streets can also be detrimental to downtown businesses due to the way they distribute traffic peaks unevenly—and often at the wrong time of day.

• Continuous on-street parking. On-street parking provides a barrier of steel between the roadway and the sidewalk that is necessary if pedestrians are to feel fully at ease while walking. It also causes drivers to slow down out of concern for possible conflicts with cars parking or pulling out.

• Pedestrian-friendly signals. Cities that prioritize driving have long signal cycles and "dedicated" crossing regimes in which pedestrians are allowed to cross only when no cars are moving. Cities that prioritize walking have signal cycles of sixty seconds or less, and "concurrent" crossing regimes, in which pedestrians move with parallel traffic and turning cars must wait for the crosswalks to clear.

• Continuous street trees. In the context of pedestrian safety, street trees are similar to parked cars in the way that they protect the sidewalks from the cars moving beyond them. They also create a perceptual narrowing of the street that lowers driving speeds.

• Avoiding swooping geometries. Pedestrian-centric environments, particularly in cities, can be characterized by their rectilinear and angled geometries and tight curb radii. Wherever suburban swooping geometries are introduced into otherwise urban cities, cars speed up, and pedestrians feel unsafe.

The above ten criteria lead directly to the street reconfigurations described in Part 3.

A Comfortable Walk

Evolutionary biologists tell us how all animals seek two things: prospect and refuge. The first allows you to see your prey and predators. The second allows you to know that your flanks are protected from attack. That need for refuge, deep in our DNA from millennia of survival, has led us to feel most comfortable in spaces with well defined edges. This is accomplished in several ways:

• Streets shaped by buildings. The typical way in which cities shape streets is with the edges of buildings that pull up to the sidewalk. These buildings need to be of adequate height so that the 1:6 height-to-width rule is not violated, ideally approaching 1:1. Gaps between buildings should not be very wide, and missing teeth should be designated as priority sites.

• No exposed surface parking lots. City codes and private land-use practices must be reviewed in order to fundamentally alter the conditions that lead to the proliferation of surface parking. Among these are the on-site parking requirement, which must be replaced by practices that treat parking as a public good, provided strategically in the proper locations to encourage more productive land use.

• Avoiding object buildings. In the traditional walking city, buildings take rectangular or other nondescript shapes in order to give shape to the spaces they surround—the streets and squares. In the modernist city of the automobile, buildings stand apart as sculptural objects. As a result, the space between them—the public realm—becomes residual and poorly formed.

• Street trees. Already mentioned under A Safe Walk, trees are also essential to pedestrian comfort in a number of ways. They reduce ambient temperatures in warm weather, absorb rainwater and tailpipe emissions, provide UV protection, and reduce the effects of wind. Trees also improve the sense of enclosure by "necking down" the street space with their canopies.

An Interesting Walk

Finally, even if a walk is useful, safe, and comfortable, people will not choose to go on foot unless it is also at least moderately entertaining. There needs to be something interesting to look at.

Humans are among the social primates, and nothing interests us more than other people. The goal of all of the designers who make up the city must be to create urban environments that communicate the presence, or likely presence, of human activity. This is accomplished by placing "eyes on the street"—windows and doors that open—and avoiding all forms of blank walls. These include the edges of structured parking lots, which must be shielded by a minimum twenty-foot thickness of habitable building edge, at least at ground level. Cities that support walkability do not allow any new parking structures to break this rule.

This discussion of the Interesting Walk, combined with the four criteria of the Comfortable Walk above, lead directly

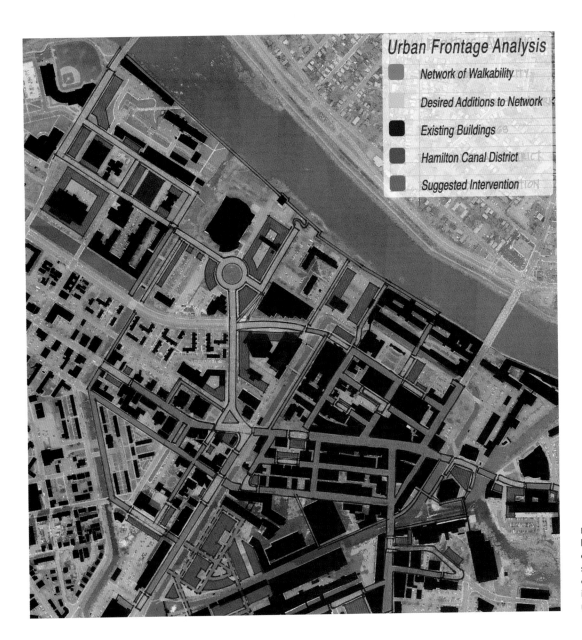

Urban Frontage Analysis
- Network of Walkability
- Desired Additions to Network
- Existing Buildings
- Hamilton Canal District
- Suggested Intervention

FIG. I The Urban Frontage Analysis documents where street spaces are most comfortable and most in need of improvement.

into the Urban Frontage Analysis and Urban Triage described in Part 2, and also inform the Specific Interventions described in Part 4.

Part 2: Urban Frontage Analysis and Urban Triage

Most mayors, city council members, municipal planners, and other public servants feel a responsibility to their entire city. This is proper, but it can be counterproductive, because by trying to be universally good, most cities end up universally mediocre. This is particularly the case when it comes to pedestrian activity. Every city has many areas that would benefit from concerted public investment, but there are two types of areas within the downtown where public investment will have a greater impact on walkability than in others.

First, only certain streets in the downtown are framed by buildings that have the potential to attract and sustain pedes-

trian life. There is little to be gained in livability by improving the sidewalks along a street that is lined by muffler shops and fast-food drive-throughs. Investments in walkability should be made first in those places where an improved public realm is given comfort and interest by an accommodating private realm—or a private realm that can be improved in short order.

Second, there are streets of lower quality than those above but which are essential pathways between downtown anchors, for example from a restaurant hub to a nearby entertainment venue. These streets may require greater investment to become walkable, but that investment is justified by their importance to the downtown pedestrian network.

By studying existing conditions, we can see where streets are most ready, or most needed, to support pedestrian life, and focus there. This technique of "urban triage"—a phrase coined by Andrés Duany—may seem mercenary and unfair, but it results in money being spent wisely.

Figure 2 shows is the Urban Frontage Analysis for downtown Lowell, Massachusetts. The axes marked in green comprise the current "network of walkability," in which streets (or paths) are fairly consistently shaped by buildings that render them comfortable. In contrast, the axes marked in yellow are street segments that are not currently comfortable, but are nonetheless important to walkability.

Finally, the objects shown in red are the new interventions that are needed to provide adequate spatial definition where it is lacking within the desired network. Every stretch of yellow requires a corresponding stretch of red. As these interventions are constructed, the network of walkability will become increasingly complete.

Please note that this analysis only addresses the quality of the buildings flanking the street and does not consider the traffic or safety characteristics of the thoroughfare. That said, this drawing has tremendous implications on thoroughfare design: only the streets marked in yellow or green are slated to receive public improvements. Dollars spent elsewhere will be dollars wasted, for the reasons already described.

Part 3: Fixing the Streets

The next step in the planning effort is straightforward: the judicious application of the ten street design criteria described above to the streets within the network of walkability. Unsurprisingly, this is achieved with the following ten techniques:

- Elimination of unnecessary travel lanes
- Resizing lanes to support appropriate driving speeds
- Insertion of bicycle lanes and sharrows
- Removing or shortening unnecessary or overlong turn lanes
- Elimination and consolidation of curb cuts wherever possible
- Conversion from one-way to two-way travel
- Insertion of missing on-street parking
- Recalibration of crossing signals
- Planting trees where they are missing
- Reconfiguration of swooping geometries

Making these changes to a dozen or more downtown streets is a lot more difficult to implement than it is to plan, but we are now able to point to a large number of cities, from West Palm Beach, Florida, to Vancouver, Washington, where such reconfigurations have been instituted with great success. It does not hurt that, of the ten items above, only the final two require anything more costly than paint.

The biggest challenge is necessarily political: convincing the people and their elected officials that traffic will not grind to a halt. That is one reason why the plan requires two relatively expensive things: an intensive public process—as yet unmentioned, but of course essential—and a computer-modeled traffic analysis from an established yet enlightened transportation planner.

The plan for Lowell, Massachusetts, includes thirteen reconfigured streets, nine of which require no reconstruction beyond the eventual addition of trees. A typical example, Central Street, is shown in Figure 2.

Part 4: The Specific Interventions

The final steps of the plan involve all of the red objects indicated on the Urban Frontage Analysis, the interventions that are needed if the network of walkability is to be not just safe but also comfortable and interesting. Each one of these sites becomes a specific intervention in the plan and is designed to a degree of detail that ensures its future contribution to the enfronting public realm.

In the Lowell plan, these interventions are grouped into three chapters—short-, mid-, and long-range projects—based upon their current momentum toward implementation. The plan contains five short-term interventions, all of which are anticipated to be completed within five years. It contains six long-term interventions, better described as "dreams," that have little momentum but are understood as the sort of exciting, big-picture thinking that is necessary if the city is to evolve over time. And it contains four mid-term interventions, which lack both momentum and impediments. In each case, these designs are not enticements to act as much as they are simply the pre-permitting of the right thing in the right place; not "build this now," but, "when you build something, put it here and make it like this."

I will use a mid-term project to demonstrate the technique employed in all fifteen interventions. Enfronting the Tsongas

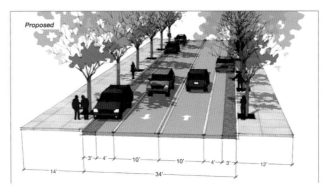

FIG. 2 Central Street, Lowell, Massachusetts: A typical reconfiguration shows conversion to two-way traffic and the addition of parking without moving any curbs.

FIG 3. Cox Circle now: well located but devoid of activity.

Center arena, Cox Circle is well positioned to be the next great public space and mixed-use office development in Lowell (fig. 3). It is the only downtown site that is flanked by a large, unused reserve of daytime parking spaces; it is adjacent to a large, successful office development; and it is a key connector in the network of walkability.

The proposal detailed in the plan enlarges the central green by right-sizing the two driving lanes that surround it (from an inexplicable 22 feet down to 12 feet each) and redesigns it as a true urban circle (fig. 4). The three empty lots surrounding Cox Circle are proposed for office and poten-

tial hotel use, with commercial space facing the sidewalk. Properly shaped, landscaped, and activated, Cox Circle is here transformed from a space to a place. This isn't rocket science, but just good, standard New Urban practice applied to a site that needs it.

In a break from most New Urban plans, the Lowell plan does not include a form-based code, or any code at all. Instead, given the limited number of recommended interventions, it simply designs every site. When it endorses the plan—anticipated in early 2011—the City Council will authorize its planning office to effectively transform the plan's proposals into as-of-right permissions for each property (fig. 5).

Part 5: A Word on Process

This article summarizes the approach as well as is possible in a few words but does not begin to communicate all of the theory, strategy, and proposals that characterize a thorough downtown plan. Also included in the Lowell plan are chapters on transit, parking, and other topics that are essential to Lowell but not central to the technique outlined here.

As already mentioned, this approach is not an invention, but merely a reconceptualization of the strategies and techniques that I have seen brought to bear on a wide range of successful New Urban downtown plans. I am hopeful that this article has made explicit—and replicable—some of the less-understood practices that have accounted for the positive and lasting impacts of this work.

FIG. 4 New buildings (in pink) surround a circle redesigned as a public square.

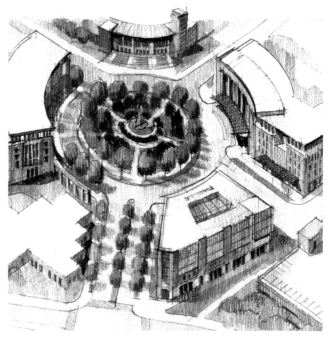

FIG. 5 Each intervention in the plan is also described in three dimensions, and thus loosely coded for future as-of-right construction.

THE LAST WORD

THE RELEVANCE OF NEW URBANISM

DHIRU A. THADANI

Globally, cities are changing, and most are becoming worse places to live. Many intersecting forces are responsible for this decline—among them, increasing populations, failing infrastructure, dependency on the automobile, outward-sprawling development, and an inability to provide adequate housing for lower- and middle-income residents.

Are there measures that would alleviate this accelerating decline? Why are some cities experiencing a renaissance or an improvement in quality of life while other cities are undergoing a noticeable decline?

Cities are the largest and most complex things that we humans make. Despite evidence to the contrary, knowledge of how to make them well and how to reverse their decline does exist. For the past eighteen years the Congress for the New Urbanism (CNU) has been aiding both the public and the private sectors with techniques to repair the urban fabric and improve the quality of life in cities. The following are some of the major principles that guide the CNU's efforts.

Streets Are For People

What makes a city memorable? For the most part, the answer is a well-defined public realm, in which public spaces are defined by buildings, helping to generate an engaging street life. A successful public realm is one that people can inhabit, experience, and enjoy as pedestrians.

Human mobility starts the day one learns to walk on his or her own, not the day a driver's license is obtained. This fundamental fact needs to be impressed on cities' departments of transportation, which generally concentrate on vehicular mobility at the expense of the pedestrian. The result of ignoring this understanding is environments where sidewalks are nonexistent or permanently in disrepair, often having been dug up for utility upgrading or littered with signs, poles, and utility boxes. Each city needs to create a department for pedestrians, an agency that would serve the interests of pedestrians and help equalize the imbalance.

Because their goal is to move vehicles efficiently, traffic engineers routinely ignore the real needs of pedestrians. For example, parallel parking, which is essential to protecting people on the sidewalk, is often eliminated to speed up traffic. Every aspect of the streetscape, including lane widths, curbs, sidewalks, trees, and lighting, can be designed to meet the needs of either vehicles or people—or it can be handled in a way that serves both.

In pedestrian-intensive areas, barriers (often fences) have sometimes been installed along the edges of streets, restricting movement and enclosing pedestrians like cattle. Pedestrians should always be allowed to cross streets at grade at all intersections. Whoever designed an elevated pedestrian crosswalk must have been in an automobile at the time. Overhead crosswalks do not work and never will. And you have only to walk through a below-grade street crossing once to realize that it, too, is a bad idea.

Specialist and Generalist

The city by definition is a general enterprise, and the specialist is the enemy of the city. Urban designers, architects, and engineers are not alone in their quest to shape the city around specialized needs. Experts generally ignore criteria that lie beyond their own profession. Cities need generalists to weigh the advice of specialists against the common good.

For instance, traffic engineers, in their quest to move traffic, propose grade-separated interchanges without considering what this decision does to the quality of life of local residents who have to look at, and live with, these noisy monstrosities.

While cities such as Mumbai and Shanghai have embarked on ludicrous and expensive construction of new inner-city highways, cities such as San Francisco, Milwaukee, Portland, and Seoul, to name a few, are demolishing inner-city highways so that they can provide a better quality of life to their residents.

Unenlightened departments of transportation propose widening existing roads to ease traffic generated by the very

FIG. I Mixed-use is an essential component that can support the daily needs of a community when located within walking distance of residences.

in their uses that they are occupied around the clock. Eating, shopping, working, socializing, and recreating—these activities are mutually reinforcing. They flourish in each other's presence.

The best parts of all cities have a diverse mix of uses. Neighborhoods are alive during the day, when some residents are away, because workplaces and retail in the neighborhood are active. By the same token, in the evening, when the offices and shops are closed, the residences keep the neighborhood vibrant and safe, and storefront windows provide visual interest. Moreover, many businesses, such as restaurants, general stores, and health clubs, rely on a combination of daytime and evening traffic to cover their rent. The key is to stop building single-use zones, particularly employment districts devoid of residents. These places are unsafe in the evening due to a lack of activity. Similarly, cities should stop approving residential enclaves, monocultures that eventually become residential ghettos.

Hide the Parking Lots

In most developing countries, the majority of city dwellers are pedestrians. The city is obligated to make the pedestrians feel safe, comfortable, and occasionally entertained. However, in these same countries there is a growing infatuation with automobiles and personal mobility. Consequently the need to store automobiles is a burgeoning problem. For a pedestrian, the experience of walking past a parking lot or a blank wall is most unsatisfying. Whether they are open-air or six stories tall, parking facilities must be banished along any street that is designated for pedestrian use.

In the hands of a skilled designer, parking lots are easy to hide. It takes only a 25-foot-thick wrapper of housing or offices to block an unsightly parking lot or garage from view. New parking structures can easily be built above street-level shops; cities worldwide are mandating this.

Small Is Beautiful

People are small when compared to automobiles, and most world-class walkable cities acknowledge this fact with small blocks, small streets, and small buildings, usually made with small increments of investment.

Historic districts in many cities owe much of their success to tiny blocks, which create a porous network of streets. Pedestrians like to crisscross through the fabric, intelligently looking for the shortest routes between two points. Unfortunately planning practices of the past sixty years ignored block dimensions. Obscenely large blocks were created, making many parts of the city impenetrable.

Aggravating the problem, many cities operate under building codes that prevent the remaking of their most desirable and memorable areas. Building setbacks and requirements for spaces between buildings prevent good urbanism and encour-

sprawl that such roads cause. Such an approach is wrong in a city. It is a proven fact that expanding the width and capacity of existing streets leads to the phenomenon known as *induced demand*: people are encouraged to drive more, resulting in more traffic. This in turn leads to an increase in automobile-related accidents, which cause further delays, nullifying the investment's goal.

The money earmarked for inner-city highways and grade-separated intersections should be diverted to developing or improving the train and bus network. As all world-class cities have come to realize, investing in public transportation is the only way to alleviate congestion. Imagine, ten years into the future, what will be on these streets when the price of petrol doubles or triples. There will be streetcars, buses, bicycles—and very few private cars.

Mix the Uses

Another key to active street life is the creation of a city that pulsates at all times of the day, with neighborhoods so diverse age high-rise buildings. However, building height is another place for smallness. Tall buildings place undue stress on small land parcels. By concentrating population at a single point within the city, overly tall buildings put pressure on all systems, including accessibility, parking, garbage removal, and water and utility supplies. In the long run, this creates an unhealthy, unsustainable living condition.

Preservation

How many buildings need to be torn down before a city learns its lesson? Every city deeply regrets the destruction of historic or heritage structures. Traditional societies pay homage to their elders, and preserving historic structures may be the best way to respect a place's ancestry. Preservation can also be justified on economic grounds. Economists suggest that differentiated products command a monetary premium. This is why cities like Savannah, Charleston, and Miami Beach can point to historic preservation as the key ingredient in their recent booms. It is not always easy to find a productive use for an empty old building, but tearing it down makes that outcome impossible.

Build Normal (Affordable) Housing

The shortage of affordable housing remains a crisis in most cities; the solution is not to build housing projects in the suburbs, which taxes the less fortunate residents by imposing

FIG. 2 Large parking lots should be located within the block, screened, and lined with active street frontage to create a satisfactory pedestrian experience.

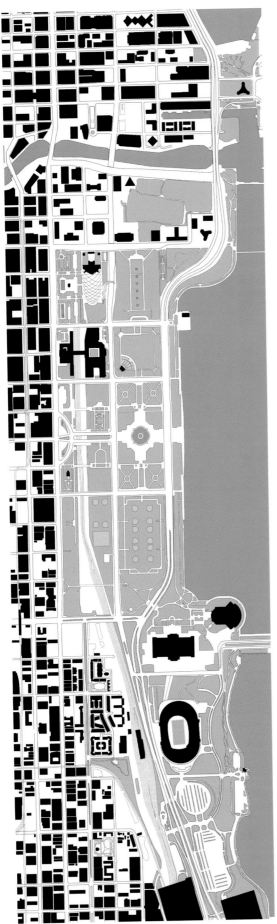

FIG. 3 The beautiful town of Sitges, Spain, has a population of 28,000 with a land area that would fit within Chicago's Grant Park.

FIG. 4 New construction can seamlessly integrate affordable housing with market rate housing as demonstrated in this redevelopment project in Washington, D.C.

long commutes on them. Rather, to be successful, affordable housing must have two traits: (1) it must be integrated with market-rate housing, and (2) it must look like market-rate housing.

In their efforts to provide affordable housing, architects should not be permitted to experiment on the poor or pioneer new design styles for the poor. Most housing projects built in recent years play geometric games that only their designers understand and appreciate. The rule should be: Experiment on the rich; they can always move out. The poor do not have a choice. Housing for the poor should provide smaller-than-standard apartments, but should be stylistically compatible with their neighbors and the context. There should be no visible stigma attached to living in subsidized housing.

Build Green/Grow Green

People have been talking about sustainable architecture for decades. Given their burgeoning populations, developing nations cannot afford to be anything but sustainable. History shows, however, that as a country becomes more affluent, it also becomes less concerned about conservation and more wasteful of its resources—recycling less, producing more solid waste, and increasing its dependence on artificial cooling and lighting. When resources are abundant, architects and developers get lazier, failing to design buildings that truly respond to the environmental conditions of place. Two to three generations ago, very few homes relied on air-conditioning for comfort because buildings were designed to passively keep their inhabitants at least moderately comfortable.

In hot climates, ceilings were higher, transom windows above doorways permitted air circulation, and windows had deep overhangs that shaded interior spaces while also providing protection from rain.

The city needs to mandate that all new buildings be smart by using less energy than their predecessors. An example: every dwelling in Israel must obtain the heating for its domestic hot water from roof-mounted solar panels. This is a viable technology that can easily be adapted worldwide.

There is also a proven correlation between tree cover and real estate value. The more green, the higher the value. Cities should encourage the planting of trees.

At the forefront of the green agenda is a movement that strives to reduce the travel distance of food from "farm to table." Agricultural urbanism encourages city dwellers to grow their own food no matter where they live. At the smallest scale, one can grow herbs in window boxes, or vegetables in kitchen gardens or in dedicated areas within the city limits. This grassroots movement is helping reduce consumption of processed foods while also educating households about seasonal fruits and vegetables.

Question Your Codes

The existing building codes that govern new development within the city are usually made up of incomprehensible statistics dealing with floor-area ratios, setbacks, and open space requirements, often ignoring the differences between pleasant and unbearable urbanism.

FIG. 5 The planned grouping of trees can create a memorable place within an urban fabric.

As mentioned earlier, codes often make the city's traditional urban form—the most loved elements of the city—illegal to emulate. To produce enjoyable, healthy cities, codes should be based instead on a picture of what is desired and not on statistical manipulations. Residents should envision what they want the city to be and then have planners write a code to achieve it.

Around the world a new generation of design ordinances is gaining favor among city planning officials. Referred to as form-based codes, these ordinances regulate what really matters: a building's height, disposition, location, relationship to the street, and placement of parking. In the twenty-first century, some cities are starting to replace their segregated zoning with form-based codes.

Don't Forget Beauty

Joe Riley, Charleston's mayor since 1968, reminds us that cities should be places that make the heart soar. For many citizens, especially those too poor or infirm to travel, the city is their entire world. Many cities make the mistake of routinely building to the lowest denominator, when it comes to constructing public schools, parks, and government buildings—the only investments that belong to all the citizens of the city. In the interest of short-term frugality, the city cheats itself out of having an honorable public realm and a noble legacy. This was not always the case, and it need not continue. The city should be proudly maintained. It should function properly and, more than that, it should also afford moments of beauty.

Cities are civilization's greatest achievement. Using the time-tested principles common to the most-loved cities, we must give new emphasis to the legacy of place making and civic art.

FIG. 6 The element of surprise and random insertions of beautiful object can help create a memorable experience.

PART 3: EMERGING TOOLS OF URBAN DESIGN SUSTAINABILITY

3.1 COMMUNITY DESIGN CHARRETTES

AN ESSENTIAL METHODOLOGY FOR CIVIC ENGAGEMENT IN THE COMMUNITY DESIGN PROCESS

CHARLES C. BOHL, ELIZABETH PLATER-ZYBERK, DAVID BRAIN, AND ANDREA GOLLIN

The methodology of the community design charrette has been advanced and refined through the New Urbanism as combination community design studio and town hall meeting. These intensive workshops have become an important public participation method in the United States and increasingly abroad, fostering the civic engagement of citizens and stakeholder groups in community planning and urban design. The University of Miami School of Architecture has incorporated the charrette as both a pedagogical tool and a community outreach method for nearly two decades (fig. 1).

At the University of Miami, the tradition of studio-based involvement in the community by students and faculty of the School of Architecture has been elaborated in the form of three distinct but complementary programs: the Center for Urban and Community Design (CUCD), formed in 1992; the Knight Program in Community Building (KPCB), founded in 2000 with a grant from the John S. and James L. Knight Foundation; and the master's program in Real Estate Development and Urbanism (MRED+U), created in 2008. The CUCD's outreach efforts have generally been focused on neighborhoods and communities within the region of South Florida, whereas the graduate programs have engaged graduate students, faculty, and mid-career professionals in communities throughout the United States.

All programs reflect the School of Architecture's commitment to the practice of civic art as stated in the School's mis-

sion statement that begins with "the faculty commitment to community and its focus on the city as a work of art and architecture." The School has also made an explicit commitment to the principles outlined in the Charter of the New Urbanism, emphasizing an understanding of design as an integrated (and integrative) practice that requires an ability to move skillfully and thoughtfully from the scale of the building to the scale of the region, and that engages issues beyond architectural form in a comprehensive, reflective, and pragmatic fashion. The principles of the School also emphasize environmental responsibility and the challenges of sustainability in terms of the valuable cultural and built legacies of real communities.

Such principles were given particularly compelling significance by the devastation brought to South Florida by Hurricane Andrew in 1992. The extent of the destructive impact of the storm, the scale and complexity of the urgent problems that had to be addressed in a very short time in the storm's aftermath, and the challenge of simultaneously rebuilding the physical fabric, restoring the social fabric, and reviving the economy of the region provided a powerful motivation for building a coherent, ongoing, and effective program of community outreach which resulted in the establishment of the CUCD.

The KPCB builds on the School's commitment to community building by extending the reach beyond the regional to the national level. In creating a fellowship program for mid-career professionals, the educational goal was conceived as a collaboration in which the fellows would learn the principles and practices of livable community design and community building from the School's faculty, experts in the field, and each other, while the School's students and faculty would benefit from interactions with leaders in community building fields. The KPCB program evolved into the MRED+U program, a graduate-level program that blends livable community design with real estate development. Full-time graduate students holding undergraduate degrees and work experience in a variety of fields take the place of the mid-career fellows and work with architecture and urban design students and

FIG. 1 University of Miami Charrette

faculty on community outreach projects. Instead of a thesis, the MRED+U adopts the Community Development and Design Workshop as the program's capstone.

In addition to foundational principles, the programs all share a common practice: the charrette. A charrette is an intensive, collaborative design process in which a multidisciplinary design team works closely with stakeholders in a compressed time period in order to move efficiently from clear articulation of a shared vision to specific and feasible plans and proposals in design, policy, and management areas related to the urban environment.

The charrette, as practiced by these programs, provides valuable opportunities for students to participate in real-world projects, to work side-by-side with faculty and professionals from different fields. The charrettes go beyond the usual academic studio experience and constitute an expansive conception of architectural practice, combining an inclusive engagement with the community and the ability to design collaboratively across professional disciplines. The charrettes transcend the limits of both a typical professional office and a conventional academic program. The projects are real and consequential; the relationships with the community are meaningful and durable; and the experience for participants is both pedagogically compelling and rich with opportunities for the production of knowledge grounded in an integrated practice of research and community-based practice.

Center for Urban and Community Design (CUCD)

The formation of the CUCD in 1992 emerged directly from the daunting task of mustering resources for rebuilding South Florida in the aftermath of Hurricane Andrew. The CUCD's first project, the New South Dade Planning Charrette (1992), was sponsored by We Will Rebuild, an organization formed by civic leaders to coordinate recovery efforts, government agencies, non-profits including local universities, and regional professional associations. A series of projects emerged from the initial South Dade charrette, including everything from plans to address regional issues like transportation and preservation of natural resources, to more specific issues of neighborhood rebuilding and revitalization. Since 1992, the CUCD's regional outreach has included zoning studies for Miami Beach, a master plan for West Coconut Grove, and vision plans for multiple South Florida neighborhoods.

The CUCD's work in Miami's West Coconut Grove exemplifies its approach and its successes. The "West Grove" is a neighborhood with a historic urban fabric and a cultural heritage that still reflects the early settlement of the area in the late nineteenth century by Bahamians. It is also a community that faces the economic hardships and social ills associated with pervasive poverty. Although the neighborhood has been relatively resistant to gentrification—as a result of significant homeownership rates, its stable ethnic character, its poverty and problems related to high crime rates—its future has long been in question.

FIG. 2 Vernacular home design, Coconut Grove, CUCD.

Between 1999 and 2003, the CUCD applied for and received funds from USHUD and the City of Miami to document the built legacy of the historic neighborhoods of Coconut Grove and to explore the potential for sustainable growth and long-term preservation. This unique opportunity for students to engage in detailed study of vernacular architecture as part of the living tradition of a neighborhood had the side effect of establishing relations of trust between the university and a community that might ordinarily regard such outside intervention with suspicion.

The CUCD's work in the West Grove was multidisciplinary and involved the university's Center for Family Studies (social and behavioral sciences), Institute for Public History (history), Center for the Advancement of Modern Media (communications), Department of Art and Art History, and the Center for Ethics and Public Service (community legal services). Almost three hundred university students and more than forty faculty from different disciplines collected oral histories, took photographs of people and places, produced a documentary film, drew maps, and developed drawings of the neighborhood's architecture—documenting, recognizing, and celebrating the people, cultural life, and architectural heritage of the West Grove.[1]

Projects have included designing and building affordable houses on infill sites, facilitating neighborhood planning, providing legal assistance for neighborhood residents, and creating a Community Resource Center that coordinates

FIG. 3 Vernacular home built, Coconut Grove, CUCD.

ongoing improvement efforts. The CUCD established a design/build studio in 1999, giving students the opportunity to participate in everything from design to permitting and construction for affordable housing in West Coconut Grove.

The major planning project was the Grand Avenue Vision Plan and Master Plan (started in 2002), the goal of which is to promote the social, economic, and physical renaissance of the West Grove neighborhood. The Grand Avenue plan led to other design projects, including a 2008 charrette for the renovation and revival of the historic Coconut Grove Playhouse. The Playhouse is a controversial project of historic preservation and renovation, on a challenging site bordering the West Grove and more affluent sections of Coconut Grove. The invitation to lead this project is indicative of CUCD's standing as a long-time and trusted community partner.

The Knight Program in Community Building

The mission of the KPCB was to advance the knowledge and practice of effective, collaborative community building through interdisciplinary initiatives, including charrettes, graduate assistantships, fellowships for mid-career professionals, symposia, workshops, executive education courses, publications, and study tours. The program was designed to help break down the barriers that have divided the design and urban policy fields into separate and often conflicting disciplines and to foster a holistic, integrative, collaborative approach to place making and community building.

From 2000 to 2007, the program awarded fellowships each year to twelve mid-career community development professionals from a wide range of fields. Fellows have come from community-based non-profits (e.g., housing, community development, the arts), journalism, real estate development, and city government, as well as planning, engineering, landscape architecture, and architecture. The fellows were convened six times per year for workshops focused at the intersection of community building and place making. The culmination of the fellowship year was an annual charrette. The KPCB charrette brought School of Architecture faculty, graduate students from the School's postprofessional urban design program, and KPCB fellows to a community seeking planning and design assistance. The charrette cities were chosen through a competitive process on the basis of applications reviewed by the fellows themselves. Part of their educational experience was selecting a community that is judged to be "charrette ready," places where there is a timely opportunity to make a difference and which might not otherwise obtain the type of design expertise provided by the program.

The charrette was a new method of civic engagement and community building for the majority of fellows, and the KPCB provided intensive training through the National Charrette Institute. At the charrettes, the fellows participated in organizing, facilitating, and documenting the stakeholder meetings. Fellows, faculty members, consultants, and

FIG. 4 University of Miami Charrette

students collaborated to produce a master plan, detailed urban design plans, and architecture proposals. The fellows also formulated recommendations in policy and management areas, linking questions of physical form with questions of social equity, economic viability, environmental sustainability, and cultural heritage. The themes of the charrettes were as diverse as the communities in which they took place, including downtown and neighborhood revitalization, historic preservation, affordable housing, infill and redevelopment, and repairing and retrofitting suburban patterns.

The Master of Real Estate Development + Urbanism

The MRED+U adopts the Community Development and Design Workshop as the program's capstone and builds on the interdisciplinary model developed in the KPCB program. The Workshop is a charrette that adds robust real estate development expertise to the mix of community design studio and town hall meeting. The capstone workshop occurs during the last semester of study for students in the MRED+U and Master of Urban Design (MUD) programs. The community identified by the program director brings a rich set of challenges that requires students to apply and synthesize the knowledge and analytical techniques they have gained throughout the coursework. Students and faculty work together in interdisciplinary teams to generate proposals that integrate economic, social, cultural, and environmental challenges and produce solutions that create and enhance good urban neighborhoods. Each team contributes unbiased, pragmatic advice on real estate, financing, market analysis, potential public-private partnerships and tools, and regulatory issues related to development that expand the architecture, community planning, and urban design capacities of the School's outreach programs.

Education and Publication

As part of their expansion of both professional and academic practice, both programs have coupled community outreach with programs of lectures, symposia, and publications that have extended the impact of their work. Since 2006, the work of the CUCD has included projects and partnerships with communities and universities in Caribbean and Latin American countries. In connection with its design work in Latin

America, CUCD has translated key urban design texts into Spanish, and held a symposium on the evolution of Havana's urban form. The CUCD hosted a 2007 symposium, "Under the Sun: Sustainable Innovations and Traditions," that was cosponsored with the University of Miami Center for Ethics and local chapters of the U.S. Green Building Council and the AIA. The event contributed to the regional discussion of green building techniques and practices, focusing on integrating approaches involving new technology, vernacular architecture, and sustainable urbanism.

The KPCB has organized a wide variety of events and initiatives in the U.S. and abroad, including an annual symposium, conferences and exhibitions with the Council for European Urbanism (CEU), and workshops to support the establishment of a design development center to assist in the rebuilding of the Mississippi Gulf Coast in the aftermath of Hurricane Katrina. Knight Fellows, faculty members, and students have collaborated on publications and research, often based on the individual fellowship research projects, including book projects such as *The Creative Community Builder's Handbook*[2] by Thomas Borrup, and *Greyfields into Goldfields: Dead Malls Become Living Neighborhoods*.[3]

Lessons for a Successful Design Center

One of the striking things about the CUCD is that it has had little dedicated funding. It emerged as an organizational identity for the ongoing involvement of faculty in the surrounding community rather than as a resource-dependent form of institutional support for faculty projects. This spirit of volunteerism reflects a consistent orientation toward outreach in teaching and research that has carried the CUCD from its inception. Faculty, students, and other consultants involved in projects have been paid modestly out of the fees associated with particular projects.

One key advantage of this arrangement is that there has been a strong sense of ownership by the faculty, which has used the CUCD as a conduit for community involvement not only as a source of studio projects but also as a source of opportunities for connections in the community necessary to build a professional practice. The downside of relying on faculty volunteerism is that the work of the CUCD has tended to wax and wane somewhat with the interest of particular faculty over time.

Although initially funded by a grant, the KPCB has also been accomplished with relatively little institutional overhead. The original grant provided for the fellowship program, an annual charrette, the director's salary, one administrative staff person, a part-time publications manager, and some publications support. The grant funding has been supplemented through partnerships organized for particular projects and events, and some additional fellowship sponsorships. The School's reputation and connection to an international network of multidisciplinary practitioners has also allowed it to leverage the resources of the program with outstanding speakers, community building experts, and supple-

mental charrette team members (consultants) who have participated at little or no cost. The MRED+U program extends the collaborative approach developed for the KPCB program through a tuition-based graduate program.

Conclusion

The School of Architecture's design center and interdisciplinary programs situate design as part of a comprehensive approach to community outreach that extends from the very local (West Coconut Grove), to state (MRED+U capstone workshops), to national (as in the Knight charrettes), to the global (CUCD and MRED+U partnerships in the Caribbean and Latin America and KPCB collaborations with the CEU).

University-based centers, institutes, and design studios often take up community problems in a way that reflects the narrower perspectives, training, and expertise of the professionals rather than the community's own understanding of its issues. The most profound contributions of design centers, however, involve moving beyond a conventional "service" model to a model of community-based engagement that simultaneously solves complex problems and contributes to community as well as academic understanding. The direct civic engagement and dialogue inherent in this model is not without risk—in fact, the model purposefully embraces community conflicts—and design skills must be supplemented with very specific training about the public process, facilitating community dialogue, managing conflicts, and negotiating solutions and compromises.

From the standpoint of a university-based program, the charrette offers a focused pedagogical opportunity, beginning with involvement in pre-charrette research and stakeholder education, and continuing through the charrette itself and extensive follow-up work. The ability of a charrette to engage complex community issues with a multidisciplinary team offers both the practical and pedagogical benefit of ensuring that design solutions are thoughtfully and carefully integrated with issues of policy. The unique contribution of the charrette method as employed by the School of Architecture is the ability to communicate complex strategies to citizens and decisionmakers through the use of the visual language of design. It also allows students to participate in a condensed experience that otherwise stretches beyond the academic calendar.

Post-charrette implementation represents a critical challenge for all design centers and often gets overlooked as either beyond the scope of the charrette or beyond the capacity of a design center. The limitations of design center staff and resources require a balance to be struck between providing direct design assistance to new client communities and the ongoing demands for post-charrette implementation assistance in support of past charrettes. Part of the solution is to seek more resources and staff for centers dedicated to implementation and ongoing assistance, recognizing that the expertise needed for implementation will include not only design but policy, finance, engineering, and other areas of expertise not commonly based in design centers or schools of architecture. Another part of the solution is to build local and regional capacity to support implementation by training more design practitioners and community building partners, assisting in the establishment of more local and regionally based design centers and programs, and institutionalizing the community design process in existing non-profit and local governmental agencies and organizations.

Some of the capacity building strategies include: the creation of stewardship committees consisting of community leaders, stakeholders, and citizen representatives who continuously prioritize, track, and renew local community design plans and strategies; the training of community staff and design professionals in dynamic planning processes (e.g., visioning, charrettes, neighborhood model block workshops), form-based coding, and LEED; the creation of a public officials' design institute modeled on the Mayor's Institute on City Design, such as the Florida Public Officials Design Institute that was created by a Knight Fellow; establishing a partnership network of professional design and development firms capable of refining and implementing plans and recommendations; working with partners such as the AIA and higher education institutions to help establish local and regional design centers; and providing training and advocating the establishment of city architects and professional urban design staff positions. These are initiatives that can be replicated nationally and internationally to build local community design capacity, sustain design center initiatives, and advance post-charrette implementation of plans and recommendations.

PLANNING IS CHOOSING, OR SHOULD BE

TORBJÖRN EINARSSON

A Lingering Paradigm—Time to Get On

Town planning is a tricky term. It can give the layman a misleading idea about the essence or quality of current everyday planning. The term has turned into a hoax! Today's planning praxis is still very much influenced, or dominated, by a ninety-year old modernism and its idea of zoning different functions into different enclaves. This means that it does not deal with real *town planning*, rather it continues the Corbusian formula for creating more *suburbia*, or non-town as Dan Solomon put it. The urban debate

has repeatedly dismissed the ongoing nature of the modernist paradigm, but so far it has survived, not so much because of its strength but more obviously because of inertia and lack of strong or clear alternatives. This article is another attempt to illustrate such an alternative.

The modernist form of "*planning*" struck the world by claiming that it would create a "new town for the new man," and by being so simple. Life was seen as a set of functions, each function was put in separate land use zones, with traffic in seven different speed zones—"*les 7v*"—all neat and tidy. It was green and sunny, but also very aggressive toward

FIG. 1 Participation needs tools. The Urban STEP method promotes round-table work with house or block models on ortophoto maps of the site in question. This has turned out to be more efficient and more creative than regular workshops, charrettes with pencil and sketching paper, and 3D modelling. People around the table can vary, professionals and laymen, neighbours and politicians.

FIG. 2 Mid Sweden University 1997, Arken architects, an example of the Urban Step method—built as a small town with gable roofs, glass and plaster facades, alleys and squares—a mix of modern and traditional building styles and concepts.

the existing towns; "*il faut tuer la rue corridor*," as Le Corbusier put it. It was, let's face it, with this "killing the corridor street," a recipe for killing existing towns.

After ninety years, we continue to see the dismal effect—"non-town eats town"—and the paradigm is still alluringly aggressive. The modernist newspeak prevails; critical remarks generate an ever more elaborate collection of statistics, buffer criteria, limits, and restrictions. And even worse: much of the sustainability debate seems to get trapped in the same pattern of just adding new "functions," new restrictions, and proposing larger buffer zones, on the assumption that if you make those inventories and processes ever more elaborate, you will avoid all disadvantages and then, at the end, get some sort of "sustainable town plan" falling out from the "process." It normally doesn't. Instead, this modernist thinking tends to give you modernist zoning, leading to ever more specialized and rebranded enclaves for living, working, and services. In spite of alluring marketing labels, such as eco-village, garden town, and office park, the enclaves are still enclaves. This is far from the real urbanity that people would normally expect, prefer, or demand when we talk about "*town planning*."

The Urban STEP—A Method for Changing the Paradigm

There is an alternative method—"planning by choosing"

This article suggests that we should move away from modernistic enclaves and its "restriction planning" and move toward "attraction planning" based on a broad evaluation of the town and village types that mankind has developed over the centuries.

The STEP method is empirical. Instead of modernism's notion of inventing the "new town for the new man," this method asks you to evaluate the performance of settlement types around us in the broadest way possible. It then urges you to choose: which types should we be inspired by and build more of, and which types should we avoid. Hence, *evaluating performance* forms the E in the STEP method. In sum, the key factors are:

Sustainability (achieved by using)
• Town types (and settlement patterns) with
• Evaluated and proven performance in
• Participatory processes.

There are several other important elements, of course, but "S," "T," "E," and "P" are cornerstones, or keys to this door into a paradigm of real planning for real towns and real villages.

Subjectivity—and dreaming your dreams

An evaluation of town and village types is, in many respects, subjective. And yes, subjectivity is a problem if plans are based on the subjectivity of one planner or one politician, whereas subjective evaluation is relevant if it sums up the subjectivities and dreams of a group or society. And that is the crux of the evaluation we propose—we have evolved a combination of an urban matrix and a "value rose" that help in assessing different settlements' sustainability in a broad sense, both the measurable and not so measurable aspects: ecological sustainability, of course, but also economic sustainability, social sustainability, and physical/technical sustainability.

Bringing the Charrette af Further Step

The STEP method can also be described as a development of charrettes and workshops—it makes planning more participatory and bottom-up, more hands-on, more based on and emerging from local settlement types and cultural context.

Laymen and professionals work hands-on with models representing blocks or houses, on top of aerial photos. Paper and pencils are not used—they tend to make the architects take over the procedure.

The method is an experience-based approach that not only underlines the qualities gathered in our built heritage but that also encourages people to trust their own experiences and dreams. The focus on settlement types, as opposed to discussing house types and restrictions, offers a vocabulary that makes STEP easily understood by people of all walks of life.

The method has been used for designing villages, towns, and regional patterns. The Urban STEP Method has proven to bring seemingly opposing parties closer in creative dialogue. The vocabulary and imagery makes the method an open arena for laymen and professionals of different trades. The tools encourage all to take part hands-on, in dialogue, and in shaping plans that bear the fingerprints of many.

STEP has often meant the end of receiving angry letters that "find faults" when plans are distributed for consultation. NIMBY-based deadlocks can often be dissolved. Real cooperation with real people tends to make the coauthors into ambassadors of a mutual future.

Three vital tools

The three vital tools are the *round table*, a *matrix* of town and village types, and a *value rose* that assesses sustainability in a broad sense, both for choosing settlement types and for comparing the layouts coming forth in the workshops.

Procedure: The Workshop Process Step by Step

The Urban STEP has been tested extensively in the Scandinavian context, once in Sri Lanka in an urban corridor proj-ect, and also in Australia. The tools are clear-cut but also open for adaptation to each project.

Step 1: Reminder of heritage—opening eyes

A STEP workshop starts with a display of the vast heritage of settlement types that have evolved over centuries in different cultures and subcultures—dense and sparse, beautiful and ugly, threatening and promising, elegant and bohemian, posh and humble, silly and sensible—locally and globally.

This display is there to work as a reminder that human settlement has many truths and myths, many experts claiming knowledge of what the people or the consumer likes or should like, can afford, or should be teased into.

Step 2: Imagining—thirty seconds for thirty years

An important next step is to get the participants to lean back and close their eyes using their imagination for the purpose of foreseeing a future trip to their children and grandchildren. Use, let's say, thirty seconds. Imagine a future, say thirty years from now, and visualize the town or village you wish for your loved ones. Ask the participants to describe their images to one another. The result is often creative—and a good input into the coming discussion.

Step 3: Distributing a matrix of town types

Ask participants to comment and improve a given matrix of town types by adding in their own images. Then ask the participants to circle those types they want to see more of, and cross out those types they want to see less of. The notion of town types is there to offer a vocabulary open to laymen and professionals of different trades. The vacant boxes of the matrix are there to urge people to come up with their own dreams and images—travel photos, memories, postcards, etc.

Step 4: Collecting the matrix sheets and making a summary

Make a summary of preferred and rejected types within the matrix. Ask participants to describe the suggestions they have advocated.

Step 5: Introducing the "value rose"—"what we want and what we should have"

Draw attention to the second matrix on the back of the matrix sheet, where the same town types are portrayed as maps, and also to the value roses indicated in the upper corner of each of the town types.

Introduce the value rose and how it is used to evaluate the quality and *performance* of town types. Clarify with examples. Introduce sustainability as a relevant means to measure urban *performance* if sustainability is given a broad spectrum of aspects.

Explain the four corners of STEP's broad four-legged sustainability, and the twelve spokes of different indicators. Ask people to consider adding spokes for aspects they find missing. Ask the participants to double-check if it turns out that they had chosen sustainable town types, or not so sustainable town types, in the previous poll. Ask the participants

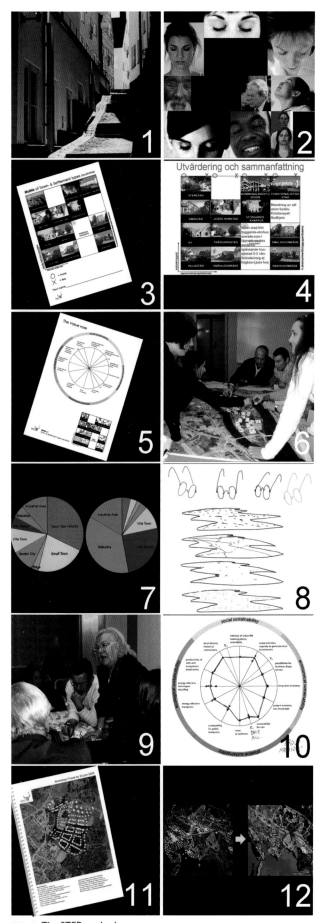

FIG. 3 The STEP method.

to contemplate the effects of street grids and cul-de-sacs and their correlation to sustainability aspects.

Ask the participants to make an evaluation of their own town or the district under discussion. This can be done by jointly filling in an empty value rose on the back of the matrix sheet, aspect by aspect, spoke by spoke.

Step 6: Gathering around the round table

The round table is a metaphor for the value rose but also the place where the participants of the workshop now gather for the hands-on work of creating their own plans and layouts. Aerial photos and plastic models are the work tools. Five to fifteen people around each round table form handy groups. The groups should be as mixed as possible—preferably representing as many of the spokes of the value rose as possible: neighbor, planner, developer, traffic engineer, economist, environmentalist, historian, politician, etc.

Different round tables can be given different themes, different amounts of model pieces representing "small, medium, large," etc. Ask the groups to create a first alternative, take a photo of it, and then quickly make new alternatives with other emphases and with timid participants having a say.

Step 7: Mixing a bouquet of town types— adding aspects of urban texture

The group work is interspersed with short lectures on subjects of interest by the workshop crew and by group members and invited stakeholders. A first topic and challenge is to ask the group to consider changing town types, testing different densities, and mixing different types into a richer bouquet of town types. A second topic and challenge could be to ask the group to improve the street grid for better conditions for workplaces and local services.

Step 8: The four glasses—adding aspects of regional pattern

If the task is a regional one, add the aspect of sustainable regional patterns. The tool presented here as "the four glasses" is suggested as a guide. Consider central, dispersed, polycentric, and linear alternatives. Imagine a situation with soaring prices of energy, food, etc., to check the robustness of different patterns.

Step 9: Switching the group mix

If a second workshop day is available, let the workshop groups get into a second phase where participants are free to switch to another round table. The choice pattern is observed in estimating which scenarios seem most tempting or successful.

Step 10: Creating and filling in your own value rose

Ask the groups to make an evaluation of their own result. They are asked to do this by yet again filling in the value rose on the back of the matrix sheet, aspect by aspect, spoke by spoke. They should discuss this outcome internally, and then make mutual presentations with the other workshop groups.

Step 11: Preliminary report—summing up and venturing conclusions

The finalizing discussion and photos of the proposals from the workshops are summarized in a preliminary report assembled by the workshop crew. A set of conclusions, common denominators, and one or two boiled-down alternatives are ventured. The report is distributed to the participants for comments and feedback.

Step 12: Professional summary

After feedback, a summarized plan, or a set of alternatives, is put together by a professional team of planners. Ideas are aligned within the legal and practical frameworks, aiming at including and refining as many of the participants' fingerprints as possible. The result is distributed to the participants and this time also to a wider circle of stakeholders for consultation. The plan and the feedback then goes to the political bodies for decision procedure.

Tools and Observations

Tool 1: Matrix of town types

A matrix of town types gives an overview. The notion of town types is chosen as this vocabulary represents a language that can be used by both laymen and professionals of different trades. This notion of town types offers a perspective of wholes, as opposed to focusing on house types, on street types, or on technical details such as dBA, FAR, VKT, or "minimum this" and "maximum that."

The matrix, shown in figure 4, has been used extensively in Scandinavian contexts. In other regions and countries, it has been—and should be—adjusted accordingly. Empty boxes in the matrix are kept open for alternatives that arise during discussions. The photos in the matrix (postcards, clippings, or private photos) can be placed randomly, or, as in this matrix, sorted vertically, indicating density, and horizontally, indicating the scale of ownerships and projects.

There are many "town types" and "village types" to gather inspiration from. The matrix works as a reminder of the great diversity of settlement types that have developed over generations, and that this urban heritage offers a broad reference as to which types work well and which do not. The matrix depicts this *urban performance* with a value rose in the upper left corner of each town type picture.

Using the matrix in a project in Sri Lanka with Sri Lankan town types gave similar evaluations. With the same X- and Y-axes used, it was found that good performances were generally on the left hand side of the matrix, in Sri Lanka as well as in Scandinavia. It will also be noticed that there is good, or even the best, performance among the traditional urban town types. Not for all but for most people.

The matrix works as a reminder that no town type is perfect. It illustrates how town types will have different sets of advantages and disadvantages. "Planning by choosing" means that while choosing advantages, you are also aware of, and prepared to take a stand for, the disadvantages that come with your choice.

The matrix has other benefits: it helps turn the attention to urban morphology. It helps the layman, politician, and planner to perceive and remember the qualities that come with scale, density, and street pattern. Thereby it reminds us that a town is more than the sum of its parts, and that the urban challenge, and the planner's task, is "life between buildings," as Jan Gehl has pointed out so eloquently.

Experience has shown that the town grids with even moderate density give quite good urban performance; they are sustainable. In contrast, areas that show "functions" segregated into different "zones" tend to produce weak urban performance also at high densities, i.e., they are poor in sustainability.

Tool 2: The value rose

The value rose is a tool for evaluating urban performance of town, village, and settlement types, measured as sustainability in a broad perspective. The four-legged, twelve-spoke value rose shown in figure 5 is chosen to give a reasonable summary of the hundreds of indicators involved in a sustainability analysis. Each indicator or issue is a spoke with 0, or "bad," in the center and 100, or "perfect," out at the edge.

Participants should feel welcome to add spokes they find dear or relevant to the project at hand. Hence the spokes marked x, y, and z. The value rose works as an efficient explanatory tool in the participation process. It offers a vocabulary that can be understood by both laymen and professionals of different trades.

An important part of planning is understanding that planning is choosing among *options with sets of advantages and disadvantages*. The value rose helps illustrate this and helps participants keep a broad set of aspects of indicators alive throughout a workshop. Hence the "E" in STEP emphasizes *evaluated* or *evidence-based* choices.

The value rose is also used to evaluate the proposals that come up during a workshop, or a charrette. The value rose can easily be retailored for a specific district, a town as a whole, or for different regions. The indicators chosen around the circle in this value rose are, as mentioned, subjective to some extent. However, we have found in our extensive use of this STEP method, that significant trends do occur, and that choice patterns in these workshops seem to favor sustainable settlement types. Luckily!

The indicators or spokes shown in our value rose here are:

Ecological Sustainability, for instance:
• local recycling
• green corridors for wildlife, animals, and plants
• green spaces for man's enjoyment and recreation
• capacity for local food cultivation "in your back yard"

Economical Sustainability, for instance:
• capacity to generate local economics (shops and businesses)
• long-term economy in a national or municipal perspective
• project economy for investor/developer/builder
• small investment thresholds

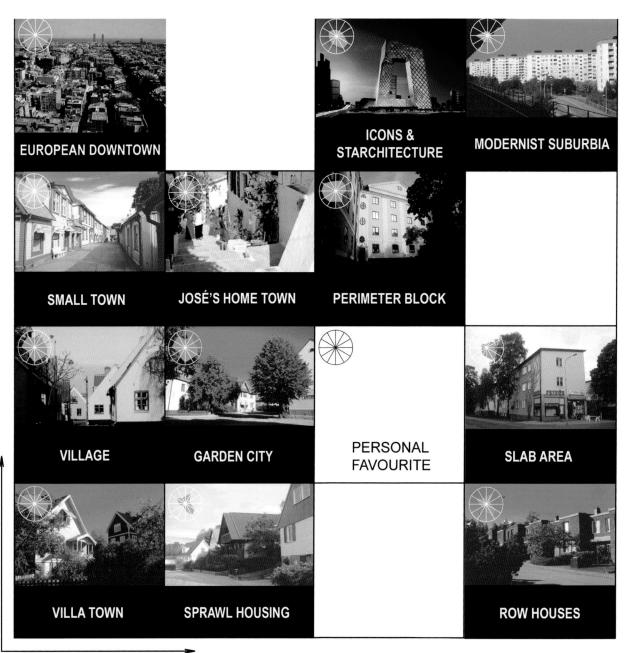

EUROPEAN DOWNTOWN

ICONS & STARCHITECTURE

MODERNIST SUBURBIA

SMALL TOWN

JOSÉ'S HOME TOWN

PERIMETER BLOCK

VILLAGE

GARDEN CITY

PERSONAL FAVOURITE

SLAB AREA

VILLA TOWN

SPRAWL HOUSING

ROW HOUSES

Plot size, project size

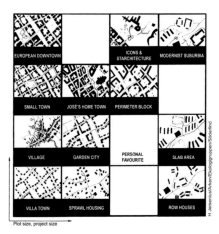

EUROPEAN DOWNTOWN

ICONS & STARCHITECTURE

MODERNIST SUBURBIA

SMALL TOWN

JOSÉ'S HOME TOWN

PERIMETER BLOCK

VILLAGE

GARDEN CITY

PERSONAL FAVOURITE

SLAB AREA

VILLA TOWN

SPRAWL HOUSING

ROW HOUSES

Plot size, project size

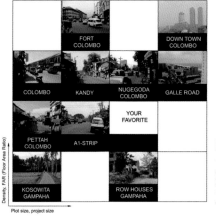

FORT COLOMBO

DOWN TOWN COLOMBO

COLOMBO

KANDY

NUGEGODA COLOMBO

GALLE ROAD

PETTAH COLOMBO

A1-STRIP

YOUR FAVORITE

KOSOWITA GAMPAHA

ROW HOUSES GAMPAHA

Density, FAR (Floor Area Ratio)

Plot size, project size

TOWN CENTRAL BLOCKS

CENTRAL BLOCKS

RESIDENTIAL

A1 STRIP

YOUR FAVORITE

RURAL

BEMULLA

Density, FAR (Floor Area Ratio)

Plot size, project size

FIG. 4 Matrix of town and village types—as photos and maps.

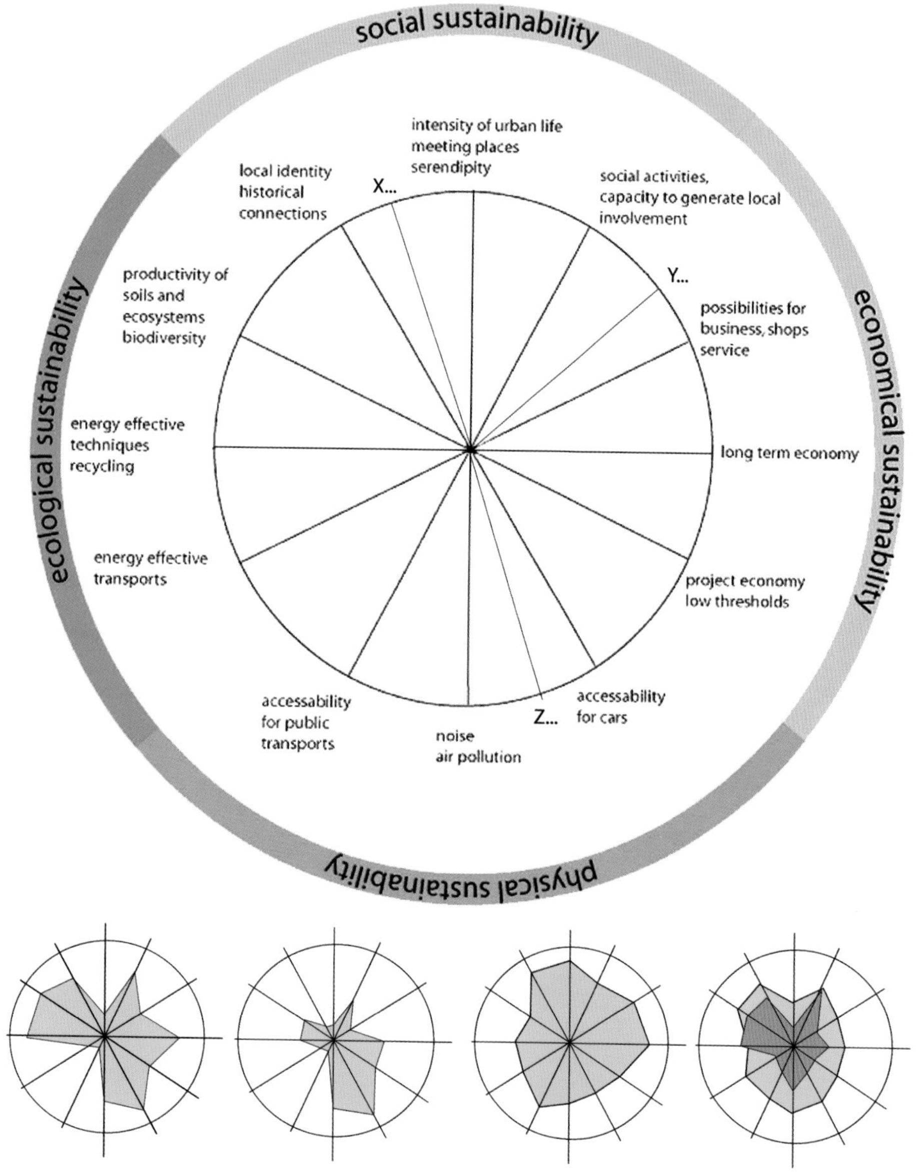

FIG. 5 Value-roses facilitate a transparent evaluation of different town and village types.

Social Sustainability, for instance:
- urban vitality, serendipity, performance as a meeting point
- local identity, as opposed to anonymity
- capacity to generate involvement, pride, and responsibility

Physical Sustainability, for instance:
- car accessibility
- public transport accessibility
- transport yield, as opposed to movement dependency
- security, safety
- noise and pollution levels

It turns out that the broadened sustainability perspective makes the value rose into a pedagogic tool. It shows that there exists a broad palette of sustainable town and village types at hand for complementing your town or village.

The value rose assessment clarifies other important observations:
- One quality is not necessarily detrimental to any of the others.
- Some town types offer a reasonable balance between qualities and demands.
- There is no town type or village type that has maximum yield on any of the spokes.
- There are well-balanced sustainable town types

at different densities.

- Grid plans perform better than cul-de-sac plans.
- Large-scale projects and large scale ownerships tend to give poorer performance.
- Sparse projects tend to give weaker performance.
- Over-emphasizing one aspect can lead to forgetting other aspects.

"Sustainability" is a relevant but by now also a commonly misused word, as indeed most buzz words tend to be. Nonetheless, the Urban STEP method maintains that *sustainability in this broadened sense* gives relevant criteria for a broad evaluation of our settlement types. And it reminds us to consider sustainability as *quality over time*.

Tool 3: Round table

The round table is the place in the workshop where the participants are coming together, the key forum of the process. This is the place at the heart of the discussion—choosing town types, adding evaluation criteria in the value rose, working with models, etc. The round table is the arena where bottom-up planning can materialize.

The round table can also be seen as a metaphor for the value rose. A good round table has the value rose indicators represented in a wide variety of participants—neighbor, builder, ecologist, traffic engineer, historian, politician, bus company, architect, economist, etc.

Here, the different stakeholders, lobbyists, and locals can face each other, hear new viewpoints, and, by listening to each other, find mutual qualities that will work over time. "The presence of all," the actual sitting at a roundtable, promotes openness, and openness promotes proper public behavior and the kind of responsibility that history and thinkers like Kant and Kirkegaard taught us.

Tool 4: Hands-on modeling

Laying out model houses or model blocks on aerial photos is something that people can understand and easily visualize. It is also quite fun and energizing. The method works well for both laymen and professionals of different trades. The "fingertip" contact through models is more realistic and creative than working with pencil and sketch paper where the architects tend to take over. Likewise, the fingertip work is more for realistic than "listing program points," which tend to end in noncommittal and wishful "request lists." Those "wish lists" seldom come to the point where the group has to contemplate making compromises and choices. Laying out models on aerial photos means that the participants can quickly illustrate different alternatives and observe how different sets of advantages—and disadvantages—occur.

Roundtable workshops, bringing together seemingly antagonistic stakeholders, have proven to be quite efficient in increasing mutual understanding. The round table means quick feedback. For the professional planner, the workshop process gives the basis not only for a well-grounded town plan but also a quick way of getting an abundance of knowledge and ideas that would otherwise not have come out.

OUT OF PLACE

CONTEXT-BASED CODES AND THE TRANSECT

SANDY SORLIEN AND EMILY TALEN

American towns and cities are eager to revise, augment, or entirely replace their conventional use-based zoning with codes that place more emphasis on the form of development. They want to promote forms and patterns that are compact, reasonably predictable, and composed of an array of livable, humane environments satisfying a range of human needs. The trend toward form-based codes reflects a growing understanding of this need. However, all scales of development must respond to context, or a form-based project can be as unsustainable as a single-use subdivision or commercial strip. The question for planners and designers is, what form goes where?

One innovative framework for context-based coding is the rural-to-urban Transect of the built environment.[1] Transect-based coding employs environmental methods usually intended for sampling of plant and animal habitats. In general terms, a transect is simply a path or cross-section through the environment. It guides the sampling of the human habitat, including its natural elements. More specifically, in terms of planning discourse, the rural-to-urban transect has been systematized into "Transect Zones," which are best understood as integrated ecological zones, rather than the monocultural separations of the past several decades of American zoning.

The transect is a context-based framework. Just as certain plants and animals thrive together in distinct habitats, the elements of the built environment support specific habitats for humans. A new element will not thrive if it is introduced without regard to context. A live oak will not survive in the northern plains. High-rise buildings in low-rise habitats and deep suburban setbacks in urban zones similarly disregard context. A zoning system based on the transect means that metropolitan areas can begin, over time, to organize in a way that strengthens the innate rural-to-urban gradients of their neighborhoods.

Using transect methodology requires calibration to local character. A normative template like the generalized six-zone Transect is possible because all walkable neighborhoods share certain basic attributes. Still, every place is

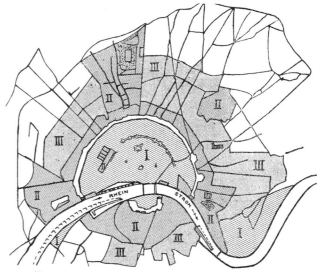

FIG. 1 The Zone System of Cologne, Germany. c. 1905.

unique. To customize a model code like the open source SmartCode, then, a local transect is sampled for each study area. Patterns are analyzed with a Synoptic Survey, an ecological technique. Urbanists extract the local DNA from this sampling and write it into the new zoning code to guide future development.

Municipal planning staffs sometimes ask, "Isn't this transect stuff experimental?" They know their current code is not producing the kind of development they want; at the same time, they are wary of change. Yet there is ample precedent for these ideas. When zoning first arrived on the scene in Germany in the 1870s, it was context-based—*what* was coded depended on *where* it was. Closer-in locations were allowed taller, attached buildings, while further-out locations were allowed smaller, detached buildings. It was a simple basis for rule-making, and it worked well. Transferred to the U.S., and through the course of the twentieth century, this spatial logic was lost. Zoning assignments seemed to have no underlying logic for the patterns being created, other than to separate uses or maximize commercial property.

Fortunately, with the advance of context-based codes, this situation is changing. This chapter reviews this changing regulatory landscape. We first present the historical basis of context-based codes—especially the ways in which a previous generation of coders tied rules to context. We then review a selection of Transect-based codes that comprise a toolkit for coding sustainable habitats.

Historical Overview

Zoning is really nothing more than building regulation adapted to location. Early planners thought that such laws that were not place-based were a serious problem: "building laws, apart from those applying to fire limits, treated all parts of the city alike whether inside or suburban, whether business centers or residential outskirts."[2] In fact, the original inventors of zoning, German planners, were specifically reacting against uniformly applied building regulations. Their whole premise was that different types of places needed to have different types of rules.[3]

The idea of "zoning," where rules vary by district, was an 1870s invention of German engineer Richard Baumeister. Germany called it "zoning" because of the way in which its cities were so clearly differentiated into zones of land value and intensity. This pattern was in part a function of walls. The business center was typically encircled by a line where the old walls had been, "within which the land was dearest." This "dear" land was concentrated into distinct zones.

The idea of changing building rules according to the intensity of these zones was vigorously implemented by Dr. Franz Adickes in 1884 in a suburb of Hamburg and later in 1891 in Frankfurt. Mannheim's 1904 ordinance had just three zones that varied rules by building intensity corresponding to central location: an inner zone where 60 percent of the lot could be built on, a surrounding zone with a 50 percent lot coverage limit, and a farther out zone with a 40 percent limit.[4] Residential buildings were limited in these zones to five, four, and three stories respectively. Other German cities, like Hannover, Frankfurt, and Munich, had similar types of spatially graded building ordinances. Such gradients can be seen today in standards of the SmartCode and other transect-based codes based on existing traditional cities.

Baumeister's concept of zoning was built on a well-developed spatial ideal of the city, which we would today call "sustainable": workers, housing, and services were to be in proximity in all areas, but the organization varied by level of intensity, depending on spatial location: on busier commercial streets, living quarters were above shops; on quieter streets, live/work units (the "shop/house") were the norm. German planners used zoning rules to maintain a pattern in which density resided at the urban center, leaving the periphery for lower-intensity buildings in the form of either larger estates or worker's cottages. The pattern was based on an intensity gradient, with detached buildings at the outskirts—not on a pattern of class segregation. It was form-based rather than use-based—there could be residential use in any area, but its form would change based on the character of the habitat.

American planners, at least initially, understood the German-based system of rules based on context, pattern, and spatial location. We have many written testaments verifying this. Frank Williams, an early zoning promoter, defined zoning in 1914 as "planning in recognition of the differences in different parts of the city . . . regulation, to be effective, must adapt itself to these differences." By analogy, wrote Williams, "clothes, in order to fit equally well, must be specially and differently made for the short and the tall, the fat and the thin."[5] Remarking on Dusseldorf's zoning code, Williams wrote: "The purpose of the zoning rules, in Dusseldorf as elsewhere, is to produce structures which in bulk and type are, so far as possible, suited to the part of the city in which they are to be situated."[6]

American planners used this sense of context to establish an essential relationship between use and form. A 1929 summary of zoning principles explained that "the districts having the greatest 'use' restrictions should correspond with the greatest restrictions on height and area, and the districts having the least 'use' restrictions should correspond with the least restrictions on height and area."[7] In modern parlance, these early rules were context-based. They recognized that each place has a particular intensity, character, and quality ranging from more urban to less urban. New York's 1916 zoning code, the first comprehensive zoning code in the U.S., was fundamentally context-based, where land use was regulated according to "intensity of building development." The intensity of each district depended upon "the character of occupa-

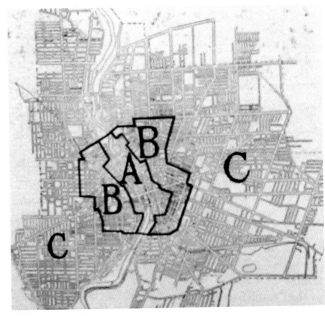

FIG. 2 Original simplicity of zoning in Rochester, New York, c. 1925.

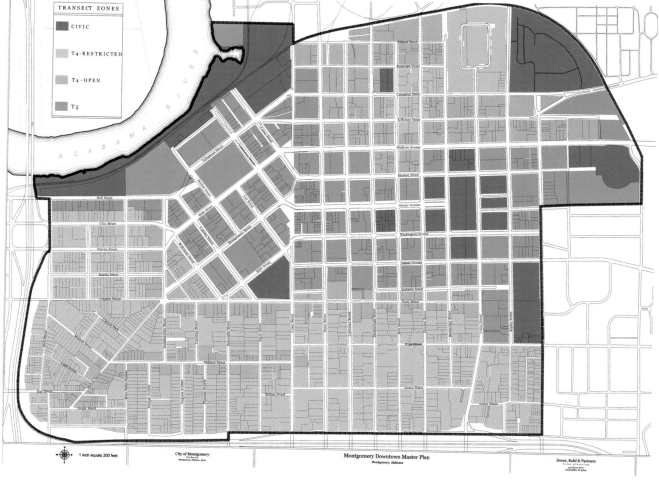

1 inch equals 200 feet

City of Montgomery
P.O. Box 1111
Montgomery, Alabama 36101

Montgomery Downtown Master Plan
Montgomery, Alabama

Dover, Kohl & Partners
1571 Sunset Drive
Coral Gables, FL 33143
town planning

FIG. 3 The 2006 transect-based regulating plan for downtown Montgomery, Alabama. The area regulated by the SmartCode has since expanded to several other Montgomery neighborhoods. It resembles the simple early codes illustrated previously.

tion and use in that particular district."[8] In keeping with these principles, planners argued that "small-lot districts" should be "closer to the center of activity of the community." In Philadelphia's first zoning code (1933), some rules were not only context-based but generative; for example, a thoroughfare's width generated the standard for the height of its enfronting buildings, expressed in the code as a multiplier. This helped form a well-proportioned "outdoor room."

What happened to these initial impulses? Changes to zoning ordinances over the course of the twentieth century can be seen as a gradual wearing down of this connection between place, character, and rule, to the point that zoning now is a seemingly random, ad hoc distribution. Herbert Hoover's commission that produced the Standard Planning and Zoning Acts of the 1920s discussed separation apart from any kind of spatial logic—in other words, apart from a *plan*. (A signal innovation of the SmartCode is that it codes for planning and zoning together.) Although they did discuss the need for "access to local shopping centers in each residence neighborhood," and that "the ideal arrangement would permit a citizen to walk to his work," this was not worked out in a codified, spatially explicit way. If it had

been, they would have seen that there was a fundamental conflict being created with another common goal at the time: that "open spaces should increase proportionately" with population density.[9]

Absent a meaningful and enforceable plan, the spatial logic of city-building—that rule about "what" should depend on "where"—dissolved. A significant problem was that the relationship between where people lived and the things they needed to go about their daily lives was being undermined by city rules that were oblivious to these pattern effects.

By the 1950s, the loss of context-based coding was complete. One prominent planner at the time, New York's director of the Department of City Planning, recommended that zones requiring "plenty of open space around a house" should be located in areas "relatively close in, so that those who want this type of living will not necessarily have to travel several hours a day to and from work."[10] With these kinds of views, it is sometimes hard to argue against the view that zoning boiled down to a system that sought "the greatest good for the fewest and richest in number," assuring more light and air for higher-income people no matter where they lived, and leaving the lower classes to share homes with manufacturing and commercial uses.[11]

What changed? As sprawl and pollution worsened over the last half of the twentieth century, it became obvious that these disconnected patterns were unsustainable. They created monocultures meant for only one income level or use. Today it is critical to understand zoning as the allocation of complex habitat zones. Within the pedestrian shed of a sustainable neighborhood, there must be a diversity of distinct habitats, with choice in housing and multimodal access to different environments.

Transect-based Tools for Habitat in Context

The technical tools represented in this section have been created by planners, engineers, ecologists, architects, urban designers, landscape architects, land use attorneys, and zoning code writers. The following section headings represent those disciplines that have emerged as climate change imperatives over the last decade, providing urgent topics for discussion and implementation in forward-looking communities and academic programs. Each is accompanied by some of the code modules available as open-source downloads from the nonprofit Center for Applied Transect Studies.[12]

As we have discussed, lack of attention to context has been a fundamental weakness of conventional zoning codes. Perhaps surprisingly, it is also a weakness of many cutting-edge urban design proposals. In response, the authors of these modules seek to counter one-size-fits-all solutions that may undermine the immersive qualities of each human habitat, whether it is essentially rural, sub-urban, or urban. The modules are correlated to the articles, sections, and tables of the model SmartCode. However, they may plug into any codes that employ Transect Zones or other context zones at the neighborhood scale.

Green Infrastructure

Dangers of one-size-fits-all:

Green Infrastructure (GI), discussed in detail elsewhere in this volume, is a sustainable approach to stormwater management. For example, the city of Philadelphia is implementing GI to replace their aged Combined Sewer Overflow (CSO) system.[13] Many citizens love this because such plans show abundant new green space in their city. Others fear a "Chia Tech" approach, where their beloved historic streets and buildings may be covered over by random acts of greenery. A balance must be struck. Biophilia is real and powerful,[14] and the problems of CSOs are also real.[15] However, without precise attention to context, GI may result in a sub-urbanizing of urban places. It may include lot-scale drainage requirements without regard for the urban context of the lot. Landscaping solutions for natural drainage, an important goal generally, may require deeper setbacks, which reduce density and affect the spatial definition of the urban "outdoor room."[16] These consequences may significantly degrade "utility" walkability, which should be a primary goal of sustainable urban design.

Transect-based solutions:

- Landscape (Susan Henderson, PlaceMakers, with Paul Westhelle)
- Light Imprint (Tom Low, Duany Plater-Zyberk & Co.)
- Natural Drainage (Mary Vogel, PlanGreen)
- Regional Watersheds (Paul Crabtree, Crabtree Group, Inc.)
- Riparian and Wetland Buffers (Duany Plater-Zyberk & Co.)
- Stormwater Management (Leslie Oberholtzer, Doug Farr, Farr Associates)

FIG. 4 A model transect from the Agrarian Urbanism module, which incorporates food production into a declension of human habitats.

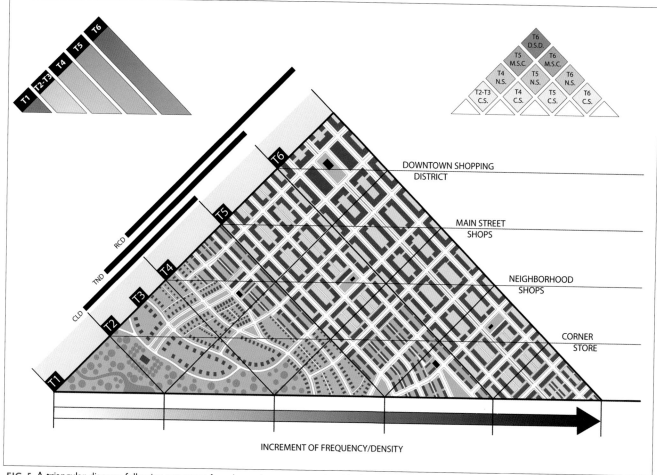

FIG. 5 A triangular diagram following a transect from less urban to more urban blocks, densities, and retail types within a typical traditional neighborhood structure. This is a table in *Retail: Sustainable Commerce, a SmartCode Module* by Seth Harry & Associates.

Landscape Urbanism

Dangers of one-size-fits-all:

The dangers are the same as those for Green Infrastructure, as Landscape Urbanism depends on GI, or at least the appearance of it, to accomplish its designs. (To date, most Landscape Urbanism designs exist only on the drawing board.[17]) And there is another danger, the danger of disconnected creativity. Within a transect-based framework there is ample room for creative solutions to design problems. Yet without such a framework there is the real possibility of the Corbusian "tower in the park" effect, where visually spectacular and enjoyable projects are nevertheless quite removed from the rest of the community.

Transect-based solutions:

The above six modules for Green Infrastructure listed under "Transect—by Sed Solutions," plus:
- Agrarian Urbanism (Christina Miller, Andrés Duany, Duany Plater-Zyberk & Co.)
- Renewable Resources (Jaime Correa, Correa and Associates)

Sustainability

Dangers of one-size-fits-all:

The dangers are different for each of the categories below. Here are three examples. First, sustainable building orientation is more easily accomplished in lower Transect Zones where there are larger lots and detached dwellings. Different strategies are necessary in more urban contexts where there are blocks of attached buildings. Second, public darkness standards cannot be the same in every habitat, as denizens of busier, more mixed-use habitats require and enjoy more lighting and more kinds of lighting. Third, tree canopy standards cannot be the same in every habitat because zones with larger lots and deeper setbacks can accommodate more trees, and more different types of trees, than urban zones where setbacks may be zero, streets may be narrow, and shopfronts should be visible. A map of the Providence, Rhode Island, tree canopy clearly shows the rural-to-urban transect of the canopy, which will be reinforced in its Trees 2020 plan.[18]

Transect-based solutions:

The above eight modules listed under Green Intrastructure and Landscape Urbanism, plus these sections of the Sustainable Urbanism Module by Farr Associates:

- Building Orientation
- Food Production
- Public Darkness
- Shading of Glazing
- Solar Energy
- Stormwater Management
- Surface-to-Volume Ratio
- Tree Canopy Cover
- Wind Power
- Zero Net Energy Buildings

Suburban Retrofit

Dangers of one-size-fits-all:

The first danger comes in painting all "suburban" areas with the same brush. Not every suburban place is autocentric, separated-use sprawl in the form of isolated residential subdivisions and commercial strips. Even today many of the prewar streetcar and rail suburbs of major American cities maintain their walkable form and a distinct rural-to-urban transect, or at least, a less-urban to more-urban transect. One of the innovations of the latest version of the SmartCode is the addition of a G-5 Regional Sector for mapping existing sprawl apart from the G-4 Sector for existing walkable urbanism. Strategies for these patterns are different, and must also be differentiated within each sector according to the type of community or open space desired.

Transect-based solutions:

- Neighborhood Conservation Code (Sandy Sorlien; infill/retrofit code redacted from the model SmartCode, Duany Plater-Zyberk & Co.)
- Sprawl Repair (GalinaTachieva, Duany Plater-Zyberk & Co.)

VMT Reduction

Dangers of one-size-fits-all:

Approaches to reducing vehicle miles traveled range from employer incentives to walkable neighborhood design. The former need not be dependent on context, but may be, while the latter must be. Transportation alternatives to the private car are the means to the goal, but a common error of transit-

oriented development is that it may be a small pod of very high density on a rail line, surrounded by unwalkable areas. This approach results in a monoculture of apartment dwellers. Its application without a surrounding neighborhood structure may undermine its long-term health. If a planned transit line never materializes, or existing service is curtailed, the habitat may become isolated and once again car-dependent.

Transect-based solutions:

- Bicycling (Mike Lydon with Zachary Adelson and Tony Garcia)
- Transit (Hank Dittmar and Laura Pinzon, Prince's Foundation for the Built Environment)
- Vehicle Miles Traveled (Farr Associates)

Complete Streets

Dangers of one-size-fits-all:

The Complete Streets movement has made progress in the promotion of multimodal design. Bike lanes, at-grade transit, street trees, attractive shopfronts, and well-marked crosswalks are shown in appealing renderings.[19] But unilaterally applied multimodal design can create wide thoroughfares in the wrong parts of the neighborhood. They may present a psychological barrier for pedestrians to cross, thus undermining two-sided retail and neighborhood connectivity while dissipating the spatial definition of the outdoor room. Transect-based planning recognizes that a "street" is merely one type of thoroughfare, along with roads, boulevards, alleys, etc. Contextual design matters. If streets all have the same curb type and radius, lane width, tree species, lighting type, and parking arrangements, the results are homogeneity and, worse, inappropriate target speeds for cars. Bikeways should also be transect-based. In urban areas with narrow thoroughfares, where the actual vehicle speed is 25 miles per hour or slower, cyclists are arguably (and the argument continues) safer riding along with car traffic than they are in a bike lane alongside parallel parking where they may be doored. The codes below call for land use first, thoroughfares second—in context with the purpose of the habitat zone.

Transect-based solutions:

- Bicycling and Transit as above plus:
- Canal Urbanism (Dan Bartman)
- Complete Thoroughfares (Rick Hall, Hall Planning & Engineering; Peter Swift; Rick Chellman; Duany Plater-Zyberk & Co.)
- SmartCode (Duany Plater-Zyberk & Co.)

DESIGN CHARRETTES
FOR SUSTAINABLE COMMUNITIES

PATRICK CONDON AND JACQUELINE TEED

FIG. I The City of North Vancouver 100 Year Sustainability plan looks similar to the existing city pattern, but performs more sustainably when measured against the targets used to guide the charrette process that generated this plan.

Introduction

Charrettes have many competing definitions, but for our purposes let us say that a design charrette is: a *time-limited multiparty design event organized to generate a collaboratively produced plan.* In the past two decades, design charrettes have emerged as a powerful tool for planning, in no small measure from the sustained and pio-

neering efforts of American urbanists. As their use spread, they have been employed to produce everything from business management software to plans for entire metropolitan regions. However, there is very little understanding in the public mind about them, no professional discipline to regulate them, and no accepted methodology by which they are conducted. Thus there are many who promote and practice charrettes without a clear basis in practice and theory for their actions. In this piece we attempt to briefly provide a theory basis for charrettes, explaining why they are needed, and then provide a framework for charrettes that is rigorous enough to withstand empirical scrutiny.

Sustainability

First it must be admitted that in our own work and the work of our Design Centre for Sustainability at the University of British Columbia, we specialize in charrettes for *sustainable communities*. We think that charrettes, as a method, and sustainability, as an objective, are intimately related. Sustainability, as most of us now know, derives from the concept that the actions of this generation should not inhibit the potential health, safety, and welfare of future generations. In short, we have to leave the planet as we found it, if not better. Most of us also know that sustainability is a three-legged stool, where decisions aimed at preserving the integrity of the planet must rest on the three legs of ecology, economy, and equity. Any decision that favors the one over the other is thus not sustainable.

We are Handcuffed by Our Methods

While sustainability is a simple concept, it is difficult to put into practice. Sadly, we do not have highly developed methodologies for dealing with complex systems. But when simultaneously thinking about how ecology, economy, and equity connect, we are thinking about the most complex system imaginable. This is, of course, the opposite of the way we are trained to think. We are taught that the solution to a problem is found through narrowing it down to the fewest number of variables possible, preferably to only one. You can then play with that variable to measure its influence over the phenomenon under scrutiny. Repeat the procedure and, if the result is the same, voila! Truth! This is, of course, the "scientific method" so widely used in academia, but it is also influential in the everyday practices of planners and engineers.

We are also taught that if and when we are unlucky enough to confront a real-world problem where, try as we will, we cannot winnow the variables down to only one, we must somehow analyze them such that the effects of one variable can be isolated while all others are held to be equal. This method is statistical regression analysis, commonly used within the social sciences but also used by large planning and engineering firms.

The "Problem" of the Sustainability Problem

The problem is that sustainability problems cannot be "solved" with either method. Sustainability, by definition, is distinguished by its inclusion, not its exclusion, of variables. It has emerged as a powerful drive in global culture precisely in response to what we are all beginning to see as the limits

FIG. 2 Achieving a sustainable community design means addressing multiple design variables, such as mobility and green networks, jobs, and housing, etc., that cannot be analyzed independently but instead require an integrative design approach.

FIG. 3 A good design solution responds not only to factual targets, such as achieving more density to create sustainable neigbourhoods, but also the practical considerations of those exposed to the results, such as careful attention to building form to maintain the character of those neighborhoods.

of our scientific or statistical problem-solving tools. These limits are limits of method, or methodology; but they are also limits that have a cultural, political, economic, and ecological dimension. The failures of these methods, and the way in which these methods cause us to view the globe as no more than materials to be extracted for the infinite extension of economic growth—a growth that presumably continues until the planet is exhausted—are distressingly obvious.

The Design Part of the Charrette— Design as Method

Against this background the value of the charrette method can be understood. A charrette is a decision-making method that accepts complexity while still being able to provide credible solutions to multivariate problems. This is because the charrette method is not a scientific method, or a statistical method. It is a *design* method. Even the simplest of design problems has many variables (scale, color, materials, style, budget, environmental systems, and so forth). Designers are constantly ingesting variables by the dozens and operating in complex contexts influenced by budget, politics, and a multitude of technical considerations. Early modernists tried for a time to escape this reality, claiming that function was in truth the only variable, and that function could be deter-

mined mechanistically and precisely. Initial enthusiasm for this position collapsed in the 1960s, a collapse marked by the failure and subsequent demolition of the Pruitt-Igoe housing project in St. Louis (the design for which closely followed the form-follows-function principle, and indeed the exact design parti, embodied in Le Corbusier's Radiant City schemes).

It seems then that the design process is fundamentally different than the scientific method or statistical processes. At the heart of the design process is a capacity to integrate all of the variables that might influence a place and, impelled by a design goal (in our case sustainability), to then produce an integrative design proposal. Design charrettes use the power of human intuition (in this context the capacity to integrate many variables through a gestalt process as opposed to a linear or mechanical process) to formulate a "good" solution. The choice of the word "good" is here intentional. In design, different in this respect from both science and statistics, the quest is seldom for the one and only correct calculation, or the "truth" in other words. Rather the quest is for the "good" solution. And while the good solution may not be perfect, the use of the word "good" is significant. It signifies that the design operates within a primarily moral rather than a primarily factual evaluative frame. A good design is one that is judged not only against a factual yardstick but against a combination of the practical considerations that occur in the world and the judgments rendered by the many

Energy Demand Per Unit

30 GJ / Unit per Year

75 GJ / Unit Per Year

150 GJ / Unit Per Year

2050 Charrette Plan

FIG. 4 (above) and FIG. 5 (opoosite) These energy demand maps illustrate the result of mapping a charrette concept plan against an indicator, in this case reduction in energy use and related greenhouse gas emissions. The 100 Year Vision (darker green) is much more energy efficient and emits fewer GHGs than existing conditions (lighter green).

subjects who are, in one way or another, exposed to the work. This does not imply a skepticism toward metrics as a basis for sustainable design. As discussed below, metrics provide the final validation of the intuition-driven charrette processes. Our point here is only to suggest that charrettes are important insofar as they facilitate solutions to problems that are far too complex for purely scientific or statistical methods to handle.

The Charrette Part of the Design

So in this very brief essay, having explained the design part of the charrette, we turn to the charrette part of the design. Why do charrettes? Why bring people together? Why not just let the designers, with their integrative powers, do the job? For community design charrettes, the answer is that the conventional process of building cities is broken, and charrettes offer a way to fix it. As North American regions have sprawled across vast landscapes, a regulatory system has emerged that seems only capable of replicating the madness. Efforts to curb sprawl and create complete communities are thwarted by a regulatory environment that focuses almost exclusively on the narrow details of the urban machinery (the

width of a particular intersection, the number of sprinkler heads in a closet, the number of feet that a house may encroach on a neighbor and so forth). And while these details in and of themselves are often laudable, the net result of all these individually rational details are regions and localities that are unsustainable.

The diagnosis of this pathology is the same. The same limits on thinking that hamper us from thinking about sustainability questions in general prevent us from executing sustainability plans in our communities. Decisions are commonly made on very narrow criteria (a required intersection geometry based on single variable research for example), while ignoring the linkage of any incremental decision to the sustainability of the whole (the gradual increase in average driver speeds consequent to consistently widening intersections, and the resultant loss of life). Ways must be found to bring all of the players together, players who collectively make decisions about the city (the stakeholders, in the unlovely parlance of convention) and provide them with the opportunity to think, not individually about the single item they are typically responsible for, but about all of them. Thus the following charrette framework provides a structure that is intentionally designed to create such an environment, an environment

Energy Demand Per Unit

30 GJ / Unit per Year

75 GJ / Unit Per Year

150 GJ / Unit Per Year

Current Conditions

where empathy with others, and a mutual desire to save the planet, can emerge. The result is, always in our experience, a sustainable design.

Framework

In this context, our Design Centre uses a charrette framework that provides a structure to integrate stakeholder values across a range of sustainability variables, or themes, including energy, water, natural habitat, local economic development, mobility, and so on. Based on well-known strategic planning frameworks, the charrette framework links a sustainable community design vision through principles, goals, and objectives to design indicators and targets that provide a measure of success, and to specific strategies and actions for achieving the vision. The framework provides a roadmap to a sustainable community design that is primarily aligned with stakeholder values but also responds to existing policy and regulation and allows for a performance-based approach to evaluating different design options. In this way, the framework allows for the complexities of planning and design to be examined and communicated in a clear, systematic, and comprehensive way.

The framework is the primary content of the design brief that guides a charrette team's decision-making at a charrette event. We work with stakeholders and with existing policy and regulation to generate the content of the framework, ensuring charrette outputs reflect community aspirations and current best practices. Many communities have made inroads to sustainable design and often have an existing vision and other high-level language describing sustainability intentions for the community. In a workshop format, stakeholders together create a refined vision composed of principles, goals, and objectives that speak specifically of both their values and the context of the design problem. Facilitated by our team, stakeholders then prioritize design-specific indicators—which reveal the magnitude of attributes explicitly linked to physical community design variables—and set targets for each indicator as the performance of charrette-generated design options are compared against each other and the intentions embodied in the framework. There is at least one indicator for each objective identified by the stakeholders, and such indicators express in clear and precise terms how performance will be measured, while the targets provide a guide for what kind of performance is expected. Together, the elements of the framework provide a collective foundation on which the charrette team can build design strategies.

As an evaluative tool, the framework provides a means to consider the sustainability of different design alternatives holistically and across scales or time. Importantly, the framework also links visual charrette outputs to empirical evaluation, enabling differentiation between design alternatives that *look sustainable* but may not *perform sustainably* from those that *perform sustainably* but *look less sustainable*. It links community intentions and policies for sustainability to the processes of making and implementing community planning and design decisions in a way that is accessible to decision-makers. Used within the decision-making process of a charrette, the framework can provide an input to planning and design choices rather than purely evaluate outcomes. In this way, the framework strengthens the role of design in informing the generation of public policy.

Conclusion

In the end, then, we can simplify the *theory* and *framework* for sustainable community design charrettes as follows. In *theory*, charrettes provide the only way conceivable to break through the urban development paralysis that afflicts our urban regions. It does this in two ways: first by providing a decision-making method that can handle complexity and, second, by recognizing the need to influence the culture of decision-making in urban regions by deeply involving stakeholder communities. The design charrette *framework*, on the other hand, provides a grounding in reality for this deeply intuitive and collaborative process, ensuring that results are both grounded in existing policy and that the built results will ultimately perform in a way that meets community-generated sustainability goals.

thus requires postoccupancy user surveys. An area may also become run-down and criminalized over time. We are reminded how sustainability is not something that can be delivered once and for all, but must be assessed continually with the users as the experts.

Historical Roots

The Value Map builds on important precedents from various disciplines. In the nineteenth century, Frédéric Le Play developed the triad of *organism-function-environment* to analyze the relationships between living organisms and their ecosystems. Around 1910, the famous Scottish biologist and planner Patrick Geddes developed this into the triad of *folk-work-place*, which he used extensively in city planning. Geddes inspired influential planners such as Lewis Mumford, in America, and Erik Lorange, in Norway. These early holistic approaches were both conceptual models as well as concrete working tools.

Models with a threefold, holistic structure thus existed long before the 1987 Brundtland Report on sustainable development. In more recent times, we have seen varying versions of this, such as *society-technology-nature*, often depicted as overlapping circles. Since 1980 I have used the triad *ecology-economy-ecosophy*, corresponding loosely to *head*, *hands*, and *heart*: head (*logos*) refers to what we know about ecosystems, hands (*nomos*) refers to the way we manage them, while heart or wisdom (*sofos*) refers to our ethics and values. Though most people now use the triad

ecology-economy-society, a few have added a fourth dimension. For example, Joachim Spangenberg (United Nations) proposes a fourth area, the *institutional*, in the sustainability circle. But the institutional is part of economy (*oikos* + *nomos* = management, housekeeping). Economics is all the structures, institutions, and processes with which we manage society. The money system is just one part of this (but today's *money system* is largely incompatible with sustainability). Hence economics corresponds to Le Play's *function*, and to Geddes's *work*.

Applications

The Value Map is now being applied in many ways and at many *levels*, from a product to a service, a building or a region. In its basic form, it provides a powerful working method, a checklist and framework for designers and participants in a planning process, illustrating the whole picture and how every choice impacts other parts. In its detailed form, with all parameters benchmarked, it can provide a very complete picture of the sustainability of a project or community.

Sustainability is about *time*. Many designers see the world in a static way: when our product is delivered, that is the end of our job. But sustainability is a dynamic reality: the life of a building, a town, a community. Change and decay are parts of that reality. A successful district may go into decline. A low-energy house may have a high-energy use from day one if users misunderstand or misuse it. Sustainability is

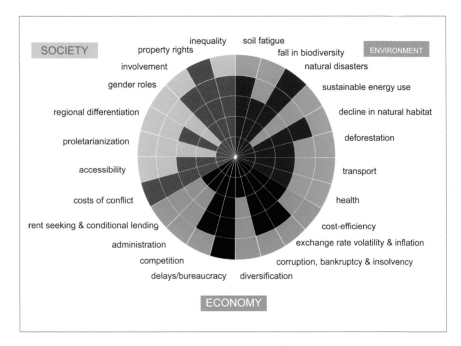

FIG. 5 Risk Assessment, Developing Countries
One especially interesting application has been evaluation of project proposals in developing countries—such as dams or irrigation schemes. The parameters commonly incorporated into risk and impact assessments, by bodies such as the World Bank, fit well into the Value Map framework—providing an improved and more holistic perspective. Factors such as risk to water tables, gender implications, etc, may otherwise be underrated in the very specialised planning processes involved.

thus not something which can be *delivered*. It is a condition which must be evaluated—and sustained—over time. The Value Map is extremely useful for postoccupancy evaluation and for feedback processes, such as annual community sustainability audits.

In general, users should be asked to draw up their own parameters and priorities. This makes users develop their own understanding of what sustainability means for them.

An interesting application has been in evaluating projects in developing countries—such as dams or agricultural schemes. Factors such as cultural appropriateness, risk to local biodiversity, gender implications, etc., have often been overlooked because the planning is complex and is done by specialists instead of in collaboration with the local communities. The Value Map gives far greater clarity to risk and impact assessments—especially for ecological and cultural factors—providing an improved and more holistic approach than is often the case with major development institutions.

Conclusions

The design and assessment method of the Sustainability Value Map addresses the goal that all architecture, urbanism, and other production should fulfill the three conditions of sustainability. It has a broad range of applications. It functions equally well with expert groups and with lay users and can be applied in both simple and detailed form. It is important that the "horizon" clearly shows the high level of ambition needed, corresponding roughly to what we can conceive of today as "fully sustainable." The Value Map visualizes sustainability in a comprehensive way that is immediately and easily readable.

There is little incentive for holistic thinking in our specialized world, yet this is the very key to achieving sustainability. We must broaden our focus from environmental to full sustainability, from eco-technology to the complete picture. We thus need tools that foster thinking and seeing holistically. The Value Map provides a practical method of working with sustainability in its full sense.

FROM EVALUATION TO DESIGN OF THE URBAN FORM THROUGH ASSESSMENT OF ENVIRONMENTAL INDICATORS

EUGENIO MORELLO AND CARLO RATTI

Assessing the Environmental Performance of the Urban Form

Policy makers today show an increasing interest in cities as the correct level of investigation and the main drivers toward achieving effective environmental sustainability. For example, work on future scenarios for cities is not concerned with social and behavioral policies alone but also the spatial configuration of our built environment. In fact, the city is intended here as a physical and spatial entity, the result of planning strategies, whereby the construction of the space plays a fundamental role toward the improvement of the Urban Environmental Quality (UEQ).

Moreover, the performance of the urban form is not just the sum performance of the single layers that compose the city, for example buildings or infrastructures, but also the synthesis of more complex relationships. These multifaceted emerging patterns represent the field of exploration and the challenges of the discipline of urban design, which aims to combine the multiple aspects of the built environment. In fact, the way built forms (geometry and urban density) and road networks (size and connectivity of mobility infrastructures) are related greatly affect the behavior of people in space, thus determining the degree of environmental, economic, and social sustainability of cities.

While at the scale of architecture, large-scale improvements toward more sustainable and energy efficient design solutions have been proposed in recent years, the answers offered in response to environmental questions at the even larger scale of the city are still inadequate, and only a few tools are available to support urban designers in the decision-making process. Moreover, the analysis and evaluation of design strategies often require a vast amount of data (environmental and statistical information primarily), which makes the investigation more time-consuming and less related to physical aspects of the urban form.

However, urban designers are mainly interested in understanding the consequences of their actions on the urban environment, as opposed to designers, who consider first of all the shape and arrangement of the built volumes and the layout of the street network and open spaces. Hence, the fundamental question arising is: Does the planning of a site affect the environmental and energy performance of our cities, and how is this contribution quantified? For this reason a technique has been developed to use the urban form as the principal variable of investigation, thus allowing designers to become more aware of their actions. The main aim of the proposed technique is to provide tools to analyze and design the urban form. The technique should be fast and accurate enough to give guidelines at the neighborhood level, making use of the least amount of input information as possible.

Therefore, the use of 3-D city models is the main source of information (in some applications the only source) to run the analyses. The convenience of the technique relies on the fact that just by using the same urban model, we can run different simulations and investigate multiple aspects such as solar accessibility, energy consumption, urban visibility, and natural ventilation. The use of 3-D data has dramatically increased in recent years. Today we can easily acquire digital city models, which are becoming cheaper and more diffused. We can make use of official city models provided by governmental institutions (top-down data) or user-generated models available on open-source geobrowsers (bottom-up data). Among the different types of city models, a special type of data derived from remote sensing imagery, i.e., the Light Detection and Ranging (LIDAR) data, represents a powerful source for the technique described here. In this case the reconstruction of the digital model does not require CAD, and the model itself can reach a high level of detail since it includes vegetation and superstructures (like roof superstructures, urban furniture, unauthorized and informal parts of buildings, and all the small objects that are not included in the official cartography).

In past years, numerous applications of the technique in various urban contexts (including Geneva, Glasgow, Lisbon, Milano, New York, and Tripoli, among others) advanced the improvement of the tools and implementation of new ones. The diffusion of the tools among students provided the opportunity to improve the user interface and to introduce young professionals to a quantitative approach to urban design using mathematical software. The analysis of the urban form and the quantification of UEQ indicators reveals itself to be fundamental from an educational point of view: students better understand the significance of the urban design level for determining environmental strategies; at the same time, students begin to interpret the city as a complex system based on built volumes and open spaces that have to be considered together in order to reach an adequate environmental quality balance between indoor and outdoor requirements. The increasing need to consider environmental issues in city planning make the tools suitable for valid final design choices not only among students but also among professionals.

The proposed tools are used particularly for comparative studies to make the different performances evident; for instance, alternative design schemes can be evaluated and the discrepancies of specific UEQ indicators assessed. By conducting this type of analysis we notice that the further step to a new urban design approach is very short, because the tools can easily be applied as a trial-and-error procedure, thus affecting the design process so that the scheme is improved through a continuous validation and refinement of the urban form in order to assure the best environmental performance.

Automated Tools Based on the Digital Image Processing 2.5-D Urban Models and Applications

Tools for the analysis and evaluation of the urban texture were implemented at the University of Cambridge in the 1990s by Nick Baker, Carlo Ratti, Paul Richens, and Koen Steemers,[1] and further developed at the SENSEable City Laboratory at the Massachusetts Institute of Technology.[2] This research stream is rooted in the studies conducted during the 1970s at the Martin Centre for Architectural and Urban Studies at the University of Cambridge, founded in 1972 by Leslie Martin and Lionel March, who were pioneers in research on the environmental and energy performance of the urban form. Martin and March began a systematic study focused on various aspects of the physical structure of the city, using modeling to define relationships and extract sound environmental design principles.

The introduction of digital city models, which made possible the implementation of a new approach, is based on the Digital Image Processing (DIP) of simple raster images of the urban form. For instance, 3-D city models are translated into Digital Elevation Models (DEMs) or 2.5-D Urban Models (2.5 DUMs), which are de facto raster images, where the intensity value of each pixel contains the information about the height of the pixel itself.

Once the model is constructed (if we use LIDAR data, a process of enhancement of the original model is required) it is uploaded into a series of codes developed in a mathematical environment (MatLab for instance). Numerous applications of the technique range from the computation of morphological and accessibility indicators to the environmental and energy analysis of the urban form. Depending on the code used, we can obtain different outcomes. Results can be both numerical and visual. An aim of this work is also to give back to the end user a quantification of indicators, because this permits the comparison of results and evaluation of design schemes. Visual maps are produced in order to communicate and interpret results on the urban layout directly. Even if we work at the scale of the neighborhood, where the level of detail does not include building components, nevertheless it is possible to estimate the energy demand of the urban form, in particular for the heating and artificial lighting needs of buildings.[3] Another promising topic is solar accessibility, which covers the computation of the shadowing conditions of urban spaces (fig. 1), the calculation of solar envelopes,[4] the solar irradiation on urban surfaces (both facades and roofs), and consequently the determination of the potential renewable energy that can be produced using pho-

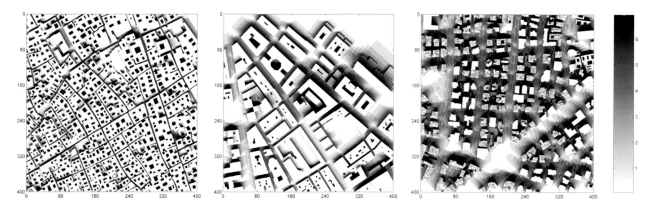

FIG. I The comparative analysis of the mean shadow densities during the winter solstice on three different urban structures in Tripoli, Libya.

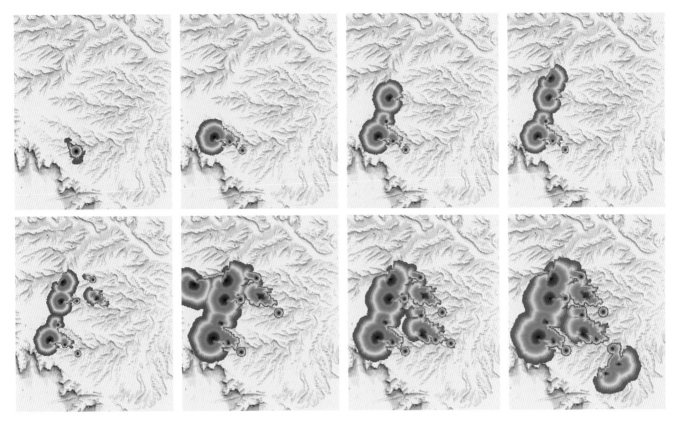

FIG. 2 Cellular automatons exploring a site to evaluate environmental resources and travel cost in terms of slopes and accessibility.

tovoltaic panels.[5] A completely different subject is urban visibility analysis,[6] which investigates the visual perception of open spaces by city users through the measurement of isovists, i.e., the visible space around the observer. For instance, the shape of open spaces greatly affects the behavior of people in the urban environment and is an almost unexplored research topic at the city scale.

Toward an Automated Morphogenesis of the Urban Form

We can go beyond the use of the tools described here for the analysis and evaluation of the environmental performance alone and, instead of simply using these as support for the concept design through a trial-and-error procedure, we can directly use the environmental mapping of the city as the generator of the new urban form. In other words, we can reverse the process and begin to use the environmental resources on site to generate the urban form according to sustainability principles. This innovative declination of the technique is based on cellular automatons that explore the site and its environmental indicators through an automated process (fig. 2).

The idea is to derive a new approach to city design that proposes an organic growth of the urban form according to actual needs and constraints dictated by the availability of local resources. We are facing a new era of design in which the complex issues to be considered in a city plan cannot be

integrated and translated into the final city design scheme using traditional approaches to planning. We can learn from the past, when the process of the construction of the city followed informal rules and the emerging urban forms were the result of long-term processes of transformation and adaptation to the local environmental conditions aimed at optimizing the environmental performance. Obviously, this long process of adaptation in time, which seems to mimic an organic growth of the city, is no longer practicable in the contemporary urban planning praxis.

For example, we can work at different levels: at the large territorial scale, i.e., the level of site layout planning, we can explore the best locations to establish human settlements according to environmental conditions; at the micro-level we can automate the process of land titling and the definition of urban morphology features (urban density, building types) in order to optimize the environmental performance of the city layout.

This approach can support the urban designer by giving her/him guidance in the construction of the city plan. This can happen through a dialectic process whereby the assumptions of the algorithm are continuously discussed, verified, and adapted in order to drive the simulations to the final layout that best suits the specific brief. In any case, as complex as the algorithm and the variables taken into account by the model might be, the model will never substitute the sensibility and complexity that the designer can contribute to the project.

PART 4: SYSTEMIC MOBILITY, STRUCTURAL ECOLOGY, AND INFORMATICS

4.1

URBANISM IN THE ANTHROPOCENE

ECO-EMERGENCY, RESOURCE SECURITIZATION, AND PREMIUM ECOLOGICAL ENCLAVES

STEPHEN GRAHAM AND SIMON MARVIN

Introduction

Earth scientists now argue that the current geological era should be renamed the anthropocene to better reflect the impact of humans in reshaping planetary ecology. Global urbanism encompasses the social, economic, and political processes most closely linked to the rapid transformation of habitats, destruction of ecologies, overuse of materials and resources, and the production of pollutants and carbon emissions that threaten planetary terracide. Consequently, the key concern for twenty-first-century global urbanism is to critically understand the wider societal and material implications of strategic responses to the pressures of climate change, resource constraint, and their interrelationships with the global economic crisis. The aim of this short chapter is to explore this question drawing upon our mutual interests in security, ecology, and the politics of contemporary urbanism.[1]

Consequently we discuss the following three themes: first, conceptualizing and placing "eco-emergency" by exploring what gets privileged as a result of eco-emergency and how this is shaping strategies for twenty-first-century urbanism; Second, reviewing the extension of the role of markets in the provision of networked ecologies, the emergence of resource "grabs," and the extension of the national state into the political and military security of ecological resources; third, looking at the emergence of ecological enclaves and neo-liberal utopias and the way in which eco-cities, eco-towns, eco-city-states, floating cities, and the like represent ecologically secure premium enclaves that bypass existing infrastructure and build internalized ecological resource flows that attempt to guarantee strategic protection and further economic reproduction. Finally we speculate on the potential challenges and alternatives to this new style of emergency urbanism.

Conceptualizing "Eco-emergency"

Geologists are now collectively agreed that there are enough measurable and definite physical markers in the global environment—carbon emissions, other pollutants, and wastes, etc.—that the current period of geological development should be now renamed the anthropocene.[2] The concept of the anthropocene is final recognition that the dominant processes reshaping the constitution of planetary global ecology are the product of human induced socioeconomic change. Critical to these processes in the early eighteenth century were the coal-based industrialization and rapid urbanization of economic activity and population.[3] Even organizations like the UN now rather uncontroversially recognize that global capitalism and processes of planetary urbanization are the critical factors in shaping global ecological change through ecosystems change and damage as well as climate change and critical resource constraints.

Global urbanism—both the majority of the world's population living in cities and the critical role of global cities as key command and control centers for political and economic power—has critical ecological consequences and implications. Global cities are quite literally ecological transformers in two important senses. The first is as the center of complex metalogistical systems composed of food, water, waste, energy, and material, human, and informational flows. As Tim Luke argues, these "metalogistical" systems quite literally span the global economy seeking out, collecting, and directing critical resources, which are transformed and consumed in large cities and their wastes treated and emitted.[4] Consequently it is not surprising that large cities may be responsible for up to 70 percent of global energy use and possibly according to some estimates 78 percent of carbon emissions. Global urbanism as a social and political process then quite literally is responsible for planetary global ecological change as well as controlling many of the critical flows of resources through political and economic centers as well as being a critical node in logistic and transportation flows. We can conceptualize these metalogistical flows as being primarily in the service and control of large global cities.

Of course the ultimate paradox of this shift in the reshaping role of urbanization is that cities have quite literally reshaped the planetary ecological context in which they must attempt to ensure their continued economic and social reproduction. Tim Luke, again quite brilliantly, captures the tensions involved in this relational shift by conceptualizing the new, much more uncertain global ecological context with which cities must deal as the new "urbanaturra."[5] This contemporary period is characterized by a much more politically uncertain ecological context as cities have to prepare to deal with the consequences of the anthropocene.

Consequently what becomes critical for cities attempting to ensure their longer-term material as well as social reproduction becomes centrally connected with their abilities to be able to anticipate and manage issues like: variability in rainfall and flooding; other extreme weather conditions such as high temperatures or prolonged drought; questions around the longer-term security and reliability of resource flows in particular food, energy, materials, and water; the ability to continue disposing effectively of wastes; and overlaid over all of this the need to more effectively manage carbon emissions and undertake purposive low carbon transition as well as adapting built environment infrastructure and urban society to climate change. We know there are significant differences between cities in their resource consumption as well as even more significant differences between which populations within cities get access to which resources. Added to this are questions regarding which cities have the knowledge, expertise, capacity, and capability to purposively manage the responses needed to attempt to ensure continued reproduction. Overall this represents a pretty tall order as cities become much more sensitive to the increasingly uncertain global ecological conditions and their implications for urban infrastructure and resource flows within and between cities.

Securitization and Marketization of Ecological Resources

Yet what do these challenges mean for a new style of urbanism? Does it generate the potential for a lighter, greener, more progressive form of ecological urbanism in which ecological and distributional questions reshape urban metabolisms? Or alternatively, does it signal the intensification of the securitization and marketization of cities in which guaranteeing access to ecological resources becomes another new indicator in the competition between global cities? Our concern is that we are talking more about the latter rather the new progressive style of green urbanism we might hope for.

Critically, how does the national state respond to these new ecological pressures that may unevenly and differentially shape the ability of governments to guarantee their economic and material reproduction? Central to understanding the implication of this turn are the lenses through which the national state views these changed ecological issues and how these are then translated into action—through which policy arenas. Our critical concern is that ecological pressures are being primarily viewed through two dominant and exemplary state functions: ensuring global economic competitiveness and guaranteeing political and military security in an international context.

Global ecological issues are also being viewed through a discourse of economic competitiveness and military security. What this represents is a fundamental narrowing of sustainability discourse as wider questions about the implication for civil society and the interconnection between ecology and participative and democratic processes are squeezed out by refocusing on techno-economic and securitized responses. We can see that the national state is increasingly focused on five aspects of these changes. First, the increasing involvement of economic departments and the wider security apparatus in developing new knowledge and expertise designed to understand the national implications of resource constraint and climate change. Second, the commissioning of research on the effects of climatic change on national economic and security space; for example, where are critical threats and implications—flooding, uncertain weather incidents, resource consequences, energy security, water security, food security? Third, an increasingly military and security-led analysis of the effects of climate change on populations including potential threats—migration, unrest, and political disturbance. Fourth, the reinterpretation of ecological challenges as economic opportunity for green-growth jobs, new technologies, and the further marketization of resources and carbon regulation. Finally, such responses increasingly prioritize securitized techno-economic dimensions with a consequent weakening of societal and democratic dimensions of change.

Attempts to make the ecological a strategic issue produces contradictory effects. Our concern though is that this is less about recognition of climate change and economic crisis stimulating a new form of ecologically modernised capitalism that seeks to live within ecological limits and more about responses that extend the role of the market into ecologies and low-carbon and green technologies that seek to commodify, securitize, and transcend ecological constraint. What is produced, then, are particular types of marketized and securitized responses: First, the desire to create marketized and commoditized approaches to carbon regulation. Second, a shift to responses that seek securitization of resource flows through resource land grabs. Third, local approaches to securitization through relocalization and increasing autonomy of resource flows. Fourth, trying to create alternative resource flows and infrastructure such as biofuels and hydrogen that have contradictory and uncertain consequences. Finally, seeking to create markets for low-carbon technologies to try to use ecology to further a new round of economic accumulation through productionist responses that may increase resource efficiency but not reduce absolute consumption. These responses raise critical questions about how ecological dimensions—in very selective ways—inform economic and security governance of resource flows at many different scales. But where does the urban sit in this shift?

Cities are emerging as critical sites through which questions of economic and securitized approaches to ecological flows are newly visible. Clearly this is not the only scale, but for three reasons the city has emerged as a critically important site for experimentation and strategic responses to marketized and securitized resource flows. Large cities are particularly intensified sites of economic growth, critical sites of consumption of ecological resources, and prioritized in protection and security strategies. Consequently, national states take a marketized and securitized approach to ecological questions, state prioritization of large cities, and new priorities around ecological security as passed down through the sub-national governance architecture on to large cities. This becomes manifest in a number of ways. First, critical strategies around national resource security—food, water, and energy increasingly have an urban dimension and are translated into cities' priorities. Second, targets for carbon regulation, energy transitions, and fortressing infrastructure are increasingly passed on to cities. Third, city leaders are increasingly required to develop understanding of the pressures of climate change and resource security as well as develop response strategies around adaptation and protection. Fourth, critical security strategies and infrastructure protection are increasingly taking on ecological dimensions. Finally, concepts of low-carbon transitions increasingly have an urban dimension. Next we consider how emerging styles of urbanism are responding to these new pressures and targets.

Ecological Enclaves and Neo-liberal Utopias

We are interested in how the transformation of ecological concerns into marketization and securitization is underway and what it means for contemporary urbanism. Our critical concern is that emerging styles of ecological urbanism largely represent ecologically secure premium enclaves that bypass existing infrastructure and build internalized ecological resource flows that attempt to guarantee strategic protection and further economic reproduction. This represents the coincidence of secure premium enclaves with new bounded and divisible ecologically secure zones and infrastructure that contribute little toward the building of more inclusive collective planetary security.

What we see happening is the way in which ecological issues and strategies are being layered over existing security and economic priorities in an attempt to create premium secure ecological environments. At a variety of different levels—eco-buildings, eco-towns, eco-blocks, eco-cities, eco-islands, and eco-regions—attempts are being made to construct re-bundled ecologies that reduce reliance on extensive and external infrastructure as they seek to re-localize and internalize resource flows. The autonomous building is being rescaled upward as efforts are made to construct premium developments that re-internalize and securitize resource flows. There are numerous examples of attempts to construct these premium spaces, which are basically attempts to allow

development to proceed when normal ecological limits would prevent development in ways which seek to ensure greater autonomy and self-reliance. Such attempts to rescale securitization of infrastructure and resource flows upward are even emerging at the enlarged metropolitan scale as efforts are made to secure resource flows for world cities and metropolitan areas. In this way, ecological questions are being layered carefully over creation of gated communities and premium ecological enclaves in order to attempt to ensure their continued reproduction.

At a strategic level, city managers are developing the knowledge and expertise to better understand how climate change is reshaping the ecological context within which they ensure their strategic protection. Critically, resources and expertise are being developed in the leading world cities to more effectively understand how different climate change scenarios may produce more unpredictable weather and flooding events. In a number of contexts, assessments are being made of the longer-term implications—over the course of fifty to one hundred years—of projected sea level rise to work through the investment required to strategically protect premium cities and to engage national states as sponsors of multibillion dollar investments. This then raises questions about which cities and even which parts of cities will receive critical protection, whose infrastructure and flood defences will be armored, and whose will be abandoned or subjected to greater risks and threats.

Conclusion

Our critical concern, then, is that the interweaving and interpenetration of selected ecological questions together with national state priorities is producing a style of ecological urbanism that places a premium on the ability of new sociotechnical configurations to transcend ecological constraint, to attempt to guarantee ecological security that can predict and survive a more unstable urbanaturra, and to develop such fixes into commercial products that can be replicated and reproduced in different ecological contexts. We argue that ecological politics will be increasingly focused on marketization and securitization as selected aspects of ecology—protection from climate change impacts, carbon regulation, and questions around resource security become critical to securing and guaranteeing urban reproduction. We hope that such exclusionary and bounded responses are contested and questioned. In place of bounded techno-economic approaches to ecology are alternatives reemphasizing social and ecological justice; cultural and societal change can develop an alternative logic and experiments that question the increasingly narrowing policies of urban ecological discourse and practices.

THE ROLE OF TRANSIT IN THE DEVELOPMENT OF URBAN AREAS OF THE UNITED STATES

WILLIAM R. BLACK AND BRADLEY W. LANE

A Brief History of Accessibility and Development

Today the level of mobility in most urban areas of the United States is very highly related to the level of automobile ownership. This was not always the case. In the late 1800s and early 1900s, cities in the U.S. began to add transit in the form of streetcars to provide transport along various corridors into the center city. It is important to understand that the objective of these operations was to provide a relatively dispersed population with access to a single area: the central business district. Therefore, one can question the level of mobility provided to the entire urban system.

There can be little doubt that this transit mode was influential in guiding where development would take place. To a certain extent this has led to the perception that transit may indeed be used to guide or at least focus where future development will take place. How correct is this perception?

There should be little doubt that the early streetcar lines were located along the major corridors that already existed in urban areas. Perhaps they were extended beyond the existing limits of that corridor development, but were they extended beyond the limits that were sought by developers? Probably not. In other words, the transit lines were looking at the proposed developments in existing corridors, and these were dictating the placement of the streetcar lines.

Today we are interested in the extent to which urban development can be influenced by the placement of transit lines. The premise today is that such lines can influence future urban development. This has led to the research area of "transit-oriented development." But are we absolutely certain that we can control the development of urban areas by the placement of transit lines? After all, this is not what the earlier transit development indicated, it is what planners of late perceived it indicated.

In most cases the corridors that received streetcars were formed by the placement of early roads for horse and wagon transport. Transit, in the form of stagecoaches, later used these roads and, within urban areas, omnibus transit was found there as well. Still later, these corridors became the logical location for the placement of intercity rail lines.[1] By and large each of these modes filled a niche in the total transport/travel demand world. While there was some temporal overlap in the availability of these modes, one cannot say that there was much competition between them; each served a different part of the market.

Contemporary Transit and Development

Today the number of modes available to the urban traveler has multiplied, with many of these competing for the same passengers. These include standard bus transit, rapid bus transit, rail transit (including subways), commuter rail service, light rail lines, and a host of personal travel modes ranging from walking to the private automobile. Additionally, the central business district is no longer the major focus of urban trips, as origins and destinations have been dispersed more evenly across the urban area.

It is the purpose of this paper to examine each of the various transit modes and assess to what extent they are capable of influencing the development of urban areas. The modes of interest here are primarily the transit modes noted above. We begin with some generalizations about the different modes and then follow this with some examples from around the U.S.

At the outset we can make some general statements. First, it seems apparent that the transit mode most influential in terms of development is going to be one that represents a substantial investment of public funds in a set location. The most obvious example of such an investment is a rail transit or metro type of system. Such an investment is recognized as something that is going to remain in place for many decades to come. It is not easy to change the placement of track or guideways for such systems.

A second general statement is the opposite of this case. If the public investment is still substantial but not fixed in terms of its location, then entrepreneurs will be cautious terms of its location, then entrepreneurs will be cautious about investment in land development along such routes, recognizing that the mode can very quickly be shifted to another location. It is for this reason that bus transit is often not very influential in terms of determining the location of future development. Even if the transit agency has every intention of keeping the route in place, financial concerns brought on by increases in costs or decreases in revenues may lead to the removal or relocation of parts of the route.

This is not meant to imply that bus transit offers no incentive and has no role for development. If the bus transit is located in such a way to act as a feeder to something like the various stations of a rail transit system, then its presence can be very influential simply because it generates a substantial amount of activity at these locations. This activity may be very attractive for the placement of retail development. Similarly, if the bus route guideway can become both grade-separated from street traffic and fixed, the effect of permanence on development is also possible. This is seen in such places as Curitiba, Brazil, and Mexico City, which have extensive and well-used fixed-route transit systems that operate on rubber tire instead of rail.

Although the mode discussed above is traditional bus transit, these statements also apply to rapid bus transit for the same reasons noted: the routes are too easily shifted to influence development.

The Potential Exception of Light Rail

The transit mode that doesn't quite fit in the previous discussion is light rail. Although it often does represent a substantial public investment (usually in excess of twenty million dollars a mile) for the urban area, it is not located in areas on the urban fringe. Indeed, its major function in most urban areas is to relieve congestion in the central area and in some cases provide an alternative to the automobile or walking in areas contiguous to the central city and just beyond such areas. Since it does cut down on automobile travel it is also viewed as a more sustainable travel mode, and this has also led to its adoption in numerous urban areas.[2]

Another purpose served by light rail has been to help reinvigorate central city economic activity by instigating new development around rail stations. The success of this component has been less clear. Rail transit was once the dominant for-profit form of transportation in American cities, but by the late 1950s almost all the transit companies had gone out of business and the rail systems had been removed, replaced with private automotive transportation and some limited bus service. These replacements were complemented with federal policies providing incentives for single-family home ownership and the development of the interstate highway system. This facilitated the rapid and complete adoption of the automobile as the mode of choice in the U.S. and the transition of development to single-use and low-densities of housing and employment.

Over time, concerns related to congestion, development,

and negative externalities of car use led to the renaissance of rail transit in the U.S., beginning with new heavy rail systems constructed in San Francisco, Atlanta, and Washington, D.C., in the 1960s and 1970s. These systems were costly and did not meet expectations of ridership performance or improvements to surrounding development. This contributed to the adoption of light rail in subsequent new projects in Portland, Buffalo, Pittsburgh, Baltimore, and San Diego in the 1970s and 1980s. These systems were more successful, and light rail became the preferred mode in using transit to alleviate congestion and stimulate central city redevelopment elsewhere in the U.S.[3] By 2010, there were light rail systems in thirty-three cities, with commuter/heavy rail systems in twenty-two cities, and new systems planned or under construction in several cities as well.[4]

Light rail has become politically popular due to a variety of factors. One is the image associated with the development that occurs around light rail stations of busy pedestrian environments in economically thriving urban areas. This is politically attractive and useful for drawing economic development into dense, walkable environments. Such developments represent a contemporary or modern appeal for the city to broadcast and for outsiders to identify with in many cases.

The application of light rail is also highly flexible. It can encompass short-distance, slow-moving streetcars as well as trains with car lengths of up to a half dozen on lines between 20 and 30 miles long, moving at speeds over 65 miles per hour. This flexibility has allowed cities to introduce light rail "starter" lines that are small enough in scope and cost so that the project can overcome potentially strong local political opposition. The success of these initial lines often leads to large expansions of the system. Light rail usually operates at grade, which increases the street presence of the system while also keeping costs down. Smaller vehicles, shorter distances, and smaller station footprints also contribute to the initial cost appeal. In addition to the permanence of stations and routes mentioned earlier, light rail has advantages over bus systems for higher quality-of-service characteristics (speed, comfort, noise, etc.) that tend to appeal to the coveted "choice rider" market, and features priority in traffic that is absent with most buses.

The Effects of Light Rail
on Travel and Development

This brings us to a discussion of the type of development related to transit modes. A key component of transport sustainability is reducing auto travel and replacing it with modes that have less (or very little) impact on the environment. The primary motivation for transit-oriented development is instigating a change in travel behavior away from driving and toward trips that involve transit, walking, or biking. These trips are more likely in a built environment of higher densities, mixed land uses, shorter distances, and separated networks for each mode.

An obvious question is the efficacy of light rail at achieving these changes in travel mode choice. Significant research attention has been drawn to this in the U.S. There is evidence indicating such an effect on travel behavior within the development area around stations and along the rail line. Trips around station areas have been found to be reduced in length, and modal shifts away from the automobile to other modes in denser, mixed-use, and transit-oriented developments have been observed.[5] Small, urban-wide effects are apparent on work trips in U.S. cities as well, with changes occurring both in areas of the city immediately around stations and in areas on the urban periphery, where people appear to access the system by car for commutes into the central city.[6]

However, light rail can be inconsistent in influencing development. This is partly because the lines often fail to provide a significant improvement in accessibility.[7] Lines have often been located along abandoned rail corridors or other places where right-of-way was available or cheap within the city, and not necessarily located where they may be the most effective in attracting riders and influencing development.[8] The limited extent of systems in urban areas has also inhibited the influence of light rail on the development market. The impact on urban travel, even where significant, can be minuscule compared to the normal trends of travel and development elsewhere in the urban area. This leads to a disconnect between the objective to affect trips through urban design and the reality that most origins and destinations lie outside the transit-oriented development.[9]

Wither Rail Transit and Development?

The primary conflict between transit investment and effects on development rests with the expectation that light rail directly drives development. When this does not occur on its own, light rail is criticized as failing to meet its objectives. In reality, no mode of transport drives development without complementing policies and market incentives tailoring development to that mode. The adoption of the automobile as the dominant mode of transport in the U.S. is often attributed to some internal characteristic of Americans relating to freedom, individuality, and a love of the "open road," when in fact there were several major changes to the structure of the relationship between transport and development:

1. An enormous federal financing of interstate infrastructure through the 1956 Interstate Highway Act

2. A rewriting of tax code to encourage low-density, single-family homeownership beginning with the National Housing Act of 1934

3. The widespread adoption of single-use zoning codes as standard practice in urban cities, forbidding mixed uses and separating origins and destinations in the urban travel network

4. The purchase and disassembly of major urban streetcar lines by oil companies and automakers in the 1950s and 1960s and their replacement with lower-quality bus service

5. Massive amounts of advertising by major automobile companies

Neither light rail nor any other form of transit has been the beneficiary of such a comprehensive set of policies and incentives. The revival of interest in transit, beginning with the Urban Mass Transportation acts of the 1960s and 1970s and the reform in transit funding beginning with the Intermodal Surface Transportation Efficiency Act of 1991, pales in comparison. The evidence suggests that light rail, if not directly or solely responsible for instigating new development, does play a significant role in focusing it and speeding it up, and has played a role in reversing long-term trends of declining transit use and its relevance in urban development. That residential and commercial property redeveloped at higher densities around transit stations sells at a premium price indicates pent-up demand for this form of urban design. This occurs despite the U.S. being "the developed world's most unfavorable public transport environment," characterized by wide roads, little pedestrian access, and the mandate of most transit agencies not to influence development or grow ridership but to maintain a social service and operate within budget.[10] When light rail projects are coupled with supportive zoning exemptions and development incentives around stations (and in rare cases limits on the automobile), they serve the purpose of transitioning travel behavior in surrounding environs to more sustainable forms.

In the end, the question is not necessarily can or should transit influence development. We can set the playing field to encourage any kind of development around any mode of transportation we desire as a society. The question is how we want to use transportation to influence the travel behavior and built environment of society. Since the early to mid-twentieth century, the answer has been a singular focus on single-occupant automobiles and low density, single-use development. These forms are clearly not sustainable, and it is no longer obvious if they are desirable. Properly incentivized and structured, light rail transit and development can be coordinated to induce changes in travel behavior that meet current needs for travel and economic development while also allowing future generations to meet those same needs.

GREEN TODs

ROBERT CERVERO AND CATHERINE SULLIVAN

Abstract

Green TODs, or Transit-Oriented Development, shrink environmental footprints by reducing Vehicle Kilometers Traveled (VKT) and incorporating green urbanism and architecture in community designs. Synergies from combining TOD and green urbanism derive from: increased densities, which promote transit usage and conserve heating/cooling expenses; mixed land uses, which promote non-motorized transportation and limited-range electric vehicles; reduced impervious parking services matched by increased open space and community gardens; and opportunities for generating solar power from photovoltaics atop rail-stop canopies. The carbon footprints of Green TODs can be 35 percent less than those of conventional development. Experiences with Green TODs are reviewed for urban regeneration projects in Sweden and Germany. The paper concludes with ideas on moving Green TODs from theory to practice.

The Idea of Green TODs

TOD has gained popularity worldwide as a sustainable form of urbanism.[1] It typically features compact and mixed-use activities configured around light or heavy rail stations, interlaced by pedestrian amenities. TODs are one of the more promising tools for breaking the vicious cycle of sprawl and car dependence feeding off each other, replacing it with a virtuous cycle where increased transit usage reduces traffic snarls and compact station-area development helps to curb sprawl.

A new ultra-environmentally friendly version of TOD—what I am calling "Green TOD"—is taking form in several European cities. Green TOD is a marriage of TOD and Green Urbanism (table 1). The combination can create synergies that yield environmental benefits beyond the sum of what TODs and Green Urbanism offer individually. TOD works on the VKT-reduction side of shrinking a city's environmental footprint—i.e., reducing Vehicle Kilometers Trav-

eled, a direct correlate of energy consumption and tailpipe emissions. VKT declines not only from rail travel by those living and working in TODs but also by converting trips that would be by car to off-site destinations with on-site walking and cycling. Green Urbanism reduces emissions and waste from stationary sources in the form of green architecture and sustainable community designs.[2] With Green Urbanism, pocket parks and community gardens replace surface parking. Renewable energy might come from solar and wind as well bio-fuels created from organic waste and wastewater sludge. Recycling and reuse of materials, insulation, triple-glazed windows, bioswales, and low-impact building materials further shrink the footprint of Green TODs. In combination, the co-benefits of TOD and Green Urbanism can deliver energy self-sufficiency, zero-waste living, and sustainable mobility.

Synergies that accrue from combining TOD and Green Urbanism could occur in several ways:

1. Higher Densities

The higher community densities needed to fill the trains and buses that serve TODs simultaneously reduce heating and cooling expenses from the embedded energy savings of shared-wall construction. The financial savings from lower energy bills and reduced transportation costs create higher market demand for compact living in green TOD buildings.

2. Mixed Land Uses

The intermixing of housing, shops, restaurants, workplaces, libraries, day care centers, and other activities place many destinations close together, thus inviting more walking and bicycling—not only to access rail stops but also for neighborhood shopping and socializing. Green TODs might also help to grow infant-industries like the development of lithium-ion electric vehicles (EVs). Limited range EVs can serve a large share of trips in mixed-use settings, not unlike golf-cart communities. One could imagine a future of hydrogen-fueling and electric-battery swap depots in a green community wrapped around a central rail station.

3. Reduced Surface Parking and Impervious Surfaces

Surface parking, which can consume half the land of many suburban multifamily dwelling complexes,[3] is replaced by more green space for play, socializing, and interacting with neighbors. Shrinking parking's footprint reduces heat-island effects and water pollution from oil-stained run-off into streams. Less impervious surfaces of concrete and asphalt help recharge groundwater and replenish urban aquifers, thereby allowing greener and healthier gardens.

4. Solar Energy Production at Stations

With TODs, station areas are often community hubs, places not only to get on and off of trains and buses, but also to congregate, socialize, and take in community life.[4] Surface train and bus depots often feature overhead canopies that provide shade and weather protection. Photovoltaic panels and even small wind turbines can be placed atop caponies at stops to generate electricity that is piped into surrounding homes and businesses through a smart grid. Solar energy can also power light-rail cars and recharge batteries of plug-in hybrids at car-sharing depots and electric buses stopped during low demand periods (as currently done with Tindo solar-electric buses in Adelaide, Australia).

As noted, the environmental benefits of TOD by itself, even absent green urbanism and architecture, comes from per capita VKT reductions, courtesy of more transit trips to out-of-neighborhood destinations and more non-motorized travel within.[5] However, benefits also accrue from policy initiatives like bike-sharing and car-sharing, which research shows prompt residents to shed private cars.[6] In TOD settings, bike-sharing can solve "the first and last mile problem"—getting to and from stations from origins and destinations that are beyond an easy walk. Sharing bikes becomes all the more attractive when extensive networks of cycleways and paths exist, as borne out by experiences in cities like Copenhagen and Stockholm, where more than 30 percent of access trips to suburban rail stations are by bicycle, even in inclement weather.[7] Car-sharing also plays a pivotal role in Green TODs. By making the marginal cost of using a car more evident, car-sharing prompts "judicious automobility"—members tend to use cars more selectively and when it has clear advantages over alternative modes (e.g., grocery shopping, weekend excursions to the countryside)—and accordingly end up significantly reducing their VKT. The combined effects of substituting car trips for transit, walking, and cycling trips can reduce the VKT per capita of those residing in Green TODs relative to conventional suburban development by an estimated 40 percent to 50 percent on the mobility side of the environmental and carbon equation.[8] Green buildings and green urbanism further reduce energy consumption and carbon emissions from stationary sources relative to conventional development by even higher shares—in the range of 50 percent to 60 percent, based on some of the experiences reviewed later in this paper. The synergies of pursuing TOD and green urbanism in combination shrink environmental footprints even more. Back-of-the-envelope calculations suggest reductions in annual CO_2 emissions equivalent per capita among those residing in Green TODs relative to conventional development patterns fall in the 29 to 35 percent range.[9]

Not many TODs have been consciously designed as "Green TODs," certainly not in the United States. More typical are sustainable communities that promote renewable energy and recycle waste that also have very good transit services. Similarly, many places that bill themselves as eco-communities do not always embrace and showcase public transit to the degree they could. Unlike some of the most successful TODs, where the station and its immediate surroundings are often the centerpiece of a community,[10] the stations of eco-neighborhoods are sometimes found on the community's edge.

The next section reviews several case experiences where transit forms the backbone of eco-communities. In these instances, synergies abound from bundling TOD designs with green architecture and green urbanism. In addition to describing the built forms and Green TOD attributes of these places, evidence on environmental benefits is reviewed. The paper concludes with suggestions for moving Green TOD from theory to reality.

Case Experiences with Green TODs

The cases reviewed in this section—Hammarby Sjostad in Stockholm, Sweden, and the Rieselfeld and Vauban districts of Freiburg, Gemany—come as close to the ideal of a Green TOD as can be found today. Since descriptions and background details of these projects can easily be found on the Internet, the focus here is on isolating elements that make them Green TODs.

TABLE 1. ENVIRONMENTAL FEATURES OF GREEN TODs

TOD	GREEN URBANISM
Mobile Sources	Stationary Sources
• Transit Design: World-class transit (trunk & distribution); Station as hub; Transit spine • Non-Motorized access: Bike paths; Pedestrian-ways; Bikesharing/Carsharing • Minimal Parking: Reduced land consumption, building massing and impervious surfaces • Compact, Development of mix of uses	• Energy Self-Sufficient: Renewably powered—solar, wind; organic waste converted to biogas; Energy efficiency: District heating/cooling; Combined heat and power • Zero-waste: Recycle; re-use; Methane digesters; Rainwater collection for irrigation and gray-water use; bio-swales • Community Gardens & Open Space: Composting; tree canopies; water-table recharging • Buildings: Green roofs; Orientation (optimal temperatures); Insulation; glazing; Air-tight construction; Low-impact and recycled materials

TABLE 2. GREEN TOD ATTRIBUTES OF HAMMARBY SJÖSTAD

| | GREEN TRANSPORTATION | | GREEN URBANISM | |
Built Environment	Infrastructure	Programs and Policies	Energy	Open Space, Water and Stormwater
• Brownfield • Infill • Former Army Barracks • High density along light rail boulevard (8 stories) • TOD: Mixed use with ground-floor retail-wide range of goods and services	• "Tvärbanan" light rail line: 3 stops in District ▪ 5 minutes to major station ▪ 10–30 minutes to all parts of Center City ▪ 7-minute peak headway • 2 Bus lines • Ferry • Bike lanes and bike and pedestrian bridges • Ample bike parking at every building • Car-sharing: 3 companies, 37 vehicles • Near congestion toll boundary • Pedestrian-friendly design/complete streets	• Transit-Boulevard is focus of activity • Grid streets increase connectivity/calm traffic • Convenient bike parking/ storage at every building	• Waste converted to energy ▪ Food waste and waste water sludge converted to biogas and used for heating ▪ Combustible waste burned for energy and heat ▪ Paper recycled • Heat recaptured for reuse • Combined heat and power plant • Low-energy construction and energy saving measures ▪ Efficient appliances ▪ Maximum insulation and triple glazed windows	• Stormwater treatment ▪ Rainwater collection ▪ Maximum permeable surfaces ▪ Purify run-off through soil filtration • Ample open space: ▪ Inner courtyards ▪ Parks ▪ Playgrounds ▪ Green medians ▪ Borders large nature reserve with ski slopes • Preservation of existing trees and open space • Reduced water flow faucets and low-flush toilets

Hammarby Sjöstad: Stockholm, Sweden

Hammarby, a brownfield redevelopment in the city of Stockholm, is an example *par excellence* of marrying TOD and green urbanism. The combination of railway services, car-sharing, and bike-sharing has dramatically reduced vehicle-kilometers traveled of Hammarby's residents and correspondingly greenhouse gas emissions and energy consumption. And the design of an energy self-sufficient and low-waste community has shrunk the project's environmental footprint. Today, residents of Hammarby Sjöstad produce 50 percent of the power they need by turning recycled wastewater and domestic waste into heating, cooling, and electricity.

The development of Hammarby Sjöstad marked an abrupt shift in Stockholm's urban planning practice. After decades of building new towns on peripheral Greenfield sites, Hammarby Sjöstad is one of several "new towns–in town" created following Stockholm's 1999 City Plan that set forth a vision to "build the city inwards." Consisting of some 160 hectares of brownfield redevelopment, Hammarby Sjöstad today stands as Stockholm's largest urban regeneration project to date. Table 2 outlines Hammarby Sjöstad's Green TOD features.

Green Transportation

A tramway ("Tvärbanan") runs through the heart of the community along a 3-kilometer boulevard (Hammarby Allé and Lugnets Allé). Taller buildings (mostly six to eight stories) cluster along the transit spine, and building heights taper with distance from the rail-served corridor. Trams run every seven minutes at peak periods and provide five-minute connections to Stockholm's underground metro network and commuter trains. Rail stations are well designed, are fully weather protected, and provide real-time arrival information. Hammarby Sjöstad's buses, moreover, run on bio-gas produced by local wastewater processing.

Parks, walkways, and green spaces are also prominent throughout Hammarby Sjöstad. Where possible, the natural landscape has been preserved. Bike lanes run along major boulevards, ample bike parking can be found at every building, and bike and pedestrian bridges span waterways. Design features that are integral to TOD, such as buildings that go up to the sidewalk line (i.e., no setbacks), offer comfortable and secure walking corridors with clear sight lines. As in the case of Hammarby Sjöstad, they also bring destinations together and through side friction end up slowing traffic.

The presence of three car-sharing companies that together provide access to thirty-seven low-emission vehicles has further reduced the need for owning a car in Hammarby Sjöstad. Also, the project was designed at just 0.25 parking spaces per dwelling unit, though this rate has inched up some in recent years. All commercial parking, moreover, is available for a fee, and rates discourage long-term parking. The neighborhood also sits just outside

Stockholm's congestion toll boundary, which adds a further incentive to use public transport, walk, or bike when heading to the central city.

Green Urbanism

Hammarby Sjöstad's green urbanism is found in energy production, waste and water management, and building designs. Hammarby Sjöstad's energy platform is cutting edge even by Stockholm standards, which are among the world's highest. The energy use of buildings in Hammarby Sjöstad has been set at 60 kWh/year, a third less than for the city as a whole. All windows are triple glazed and walls are thoroughly insulated. Other conservation measures include extra heat insulation, energy-efficient windows, on-demand ventilation, individual metering of heating and hot water in apartments, electrically efficient installations, lighting control, solar panels, fuel cells, reduced water flow, and low-flush toilets.

The ecological feature of Hammarby Sjöstad that has garnered the most attention is the fully integrated closed loop eco-cycle model. This clever system recycles waste and maximizes the reuse of waste energy and materials for heating, transportation, cooking, and electricity. Hammarby Sjöstad's waste management/reuse involves the following:

• Glass, metals, and plastics are recycled.

• Combustible waste is incinerated and recycled as heat and electricity.

• Organic waste is composted and turned into soil or converted into biogas.

• All newspaper is recycled into new paper.

The three latter types of waste are dealt with through a stationary vacuum system for solid waste called the "ENVAC system." At each building, residents can deposit waste into vacuum tubes where it is transported to pick-up locations. This minimizes truck traffic through the development, thereby lowering emissions and allowing for narrower streets and less disruption from truck traffic. Waste is also converted into energy for district heating and cooling—in the form of bio-gas created from treated wastewater (produced in the wastewater treatment plant from digestion of organic waste

sludge) and the incineration of combustible waste. In addition, bio-gas is used to run the buses, and bio-gas cookers are installed in some 1,000 apartments. Solar hot water and solar PV cells are installed on many buildings. Solar panels provide 50 percent of the hot water needs of many buildings, although solar installations meet a small share of the development's energy needs due to the Nordic climate.

Also impressive is Hammarby Sjöstad's approach to water management. All stormwater, rainwater, and snowmelt is collected, purified locally through sand fiber, stormwater basins, and green roofs, and released in purified form into a lake. A preserved oak forest, ample green surfaces, and planted trees help collect rainwater to ensure cleaner air and provide a counterbalance to the dense urban landscape.

Impacts

Based on several environmental impact assessments, secondary data, and interviews, the environmental impacts of Hammarby Sjöstad's form of Green TOD are assessed below. According to the initial assessment, when Hammarby Sjöstad was roughly half built out, it had already achieved a 32 to 39 percent reduction in overall emissions and pollution (air, soil, and water), a 28 to 42 percent reduction in nonrenewable energy use, and a 33 to 38 percent reduction in ground-level ozone relative to comparison communities. Buildings and transportation accounted for most of the reduced environmental impacts.

The primary environmental benefit of improvements from Hammarby Sjöstad's buildings came from efficiencies in heating (i.e., recycled organic and combustible waste transformed into heat), use of water, and processing of wastewater. The project's reductions relative to conventional development were: (1) emissions and pollution (air, soil, and water)—40 to 46 percent; nonrenewable energy use—30 to 47 percent; and water consumption—41 to 46 percent. Similar to the rest of Stockholm, 95 percent of all waste produced by Hammarby Sjöstad's households is reclaimed.

On the transportation side of things, environmental benefits have accrued from Hammarby Sjöstad's relatively high share of nonmotorized (walking and bicycling) trips. In 2002, the project's modal splits were: public transport (52 percent), walking/cycling (27 percent), and private car (21 percent).[11] Non-car travel shares are thought to be considerably higher today, but even in 2002 they well exceeded that of comparison suburban neighborhoods of Stockholm with similar incomes (table 3). Residents' transit modal splits even exceed those of inner-city Stockholm. Also, 62 percent of Hammarby Sjöstad's households had a car in 2007, down from 66 percent in 2005 and in line with averages for the denser, core part of Stockholm city.[12] Studies show that residents' carbon footprint from transportation in 2002 was considerably lower than comparison communities: 438 versus 913 kg CO_2 equivalent/apartment/year.[13] This is in keeping with the goal of the city of Stockholm to become fossil-fuel free by 2050.

TABLE 3.
MODE SPLITS FOR JOURNEYS WITH DESTINATION IN STOCKHOLM COUNTY

	Inner City	Southern Suburbs	Western Suburbs	Hammarby Sjöstad
Car	17%	39%	43%	21%
Public Transport	36%	28%	23%	52%
Bike/Walk	47%	32%	34%	27%

Source: Grontmij (2008).

TABLE 4. GREEN TOD ATTRIBUTES OF RIESELFELD DISTRICT

Built Environment	GREEN TRANSPORTATION		GREEN URBANISM	
	Infrastructure	Programs and Policies	Energy	Open Space, Water and Stormwater

• Brownfield
 	
• Contiguous to edge of city
 	
• Former waste water leach field serving as greenbelt
 	
• High density along tramway
  ▪ 90% multi-family buildings
  ▪ 5 stories
 	
• Mixed use with ground-floor retail
	• TOD: main street is ⅔ mile tram corridor
	
	• Tram: 3 stops in district
	
	• 7-minute peak headway
	
	• 15–20 minutes to core
	
	• Extensive bike and pedestrian paths, access to coty center via separated bike paths
	
	• "Barrier-free" living, high permeability/connectivity
	
	• Uncontrolled shared space traffic system;
	  ▪ Shared 'play' streets, children have priority
	
	• No stop signs, right yield
		• Priority for trams, pedestrians, and bicycles
		
		• Car traffic limited:
		  ▪ Maximum traffic speed 30 kph
		  ▪ Traffic calming and narrow streets
		• Grid layout prevents cut-through traffic
		
		• Convenient bike parking/ storage
		
		• Park-and-ride facilities
		
		• Parking ratio; 1:1 in underground garages
			• Active and Passive Solar (architecture/orientation and photovoltaic)
			
			• Low-energy construction
			
			• District Healing
			
			• Combined heat and power plant (co-generation)
			
			• Energy saving measures
				• Stormwater management system
				  ▪ Rainwater collection
				  ▪ Maximum permeable surfaces
				
				• Purify run-off through soil filtration
				
				• Ample open space:
				  ▪ Inner courtyards
				  ▪ Parks
				  ▪ Playgrounds
				  ▪ Green medians
				  ▪ Borders large nature reserve with hiking trails

Another barometer of Hammarby Sjöstad's environmental benefits is the relatively healthy local economy—i.e., a higher median household income and lower unemployment rate relative to the city as a whole in 2006. Also, land prices and rents have risen more rapidly over the past decade than in most other parts of the Stockholm region. Today, Hammarby Sjöstad is considered to be a relatively desirable and thus more expensive place to live relative to the inner city and other "new towns/in town."

Overall, Hammarby Sjöstad has reduced its environmental impact by around one third relative to conventional suburban development in Stockholm. This percentage will likely increase over time, at least until Stockholm becomes carbon neutral and fossil free, currently targeted for mid-century.

Rieselfeld and Vauban Districts: Freiburg, Germany

The Rieselfeld and Vauban districts of the historic university town of Freiberg—Germany's greenest city—were conscientiously designed to push the envelope of sustainable urbanism. Both are peripheral redevelopment sites linked to central Freiburg via the region's tramway network. And both embody Freiburg's aim of becoming a "City of Short Distances" that allows "traffic avoidance" accomplished through mixed land-use patterns and near-ubiquitous public transit.

Rieselfeld and Vauban abide by Freiburg's obligatory low-energy building standard of 65 kWh/m2/year (twice as efficient as Germany's national energy standard). Both districts also generate heat and power through wood-chip-fueled cogeneration plants as well as active (e.g., photovoltaics) and passive solar energy (e.g., building orientation and architecture). Additionally, both developments have comprehensive stormwater management systems that collect rainwater, maximize permeable surfaces through provision of ample green space, parks, and playgrounds, and purify run-off through bioswales and other soil filtration systems.

Rieselfeld

Planned in the early 1990s, Rieselfeld—with a population of 9,100 residents living on 90 hectares—is today nearing completion (around 90 percent built out). The planned community, sitting on a former wastewater leach field, was designed and marketed specifically for ecologically minded families. The community boasts low-energy building construction, a district heating network powered by a combined heat and power plant, decentralized solar energy, and stormwater management. Rieselfeld's Green TOD features are summarized in table 4.

Rieselfeld can be described as "transit-led development" (TLD). A tramway extension to Rieselfeld opened in 1997, a year after the first families had moved in and when there were just 1,000 inhabitants. The presence of three tramway stations enabled urban growth to wrap itself around rail nodes. With seven-minute peak headways, residents can reach Freiburg's core within ten minutes.

TABLE 5. GREEN TOD ATTRIBUTES OF VAUBAN DISTRICT

| Built Environment | GREEN TRANSPORTATION | | GREEN URBANISM | |
	Infrastructure	Programs and Policies	Energy	Open Space, Water and Stormwater
• Brownfield 　▪ Former military barracks • Infill • Compact 　▪ 4 stories • Mixed use with ground-floor retail	• TOD: District organized around tram spine • Tram: 3 stops • 7-minute peak headway • Regional rail stop (Future) • 2 Buses • 10–15 minutes to city center by tram/bus/bike • Extensive bike and pedestrian paths; access to city center via separated bike paths • Network of off-street bike and pedestrian access to all parts of project	• Parking restricted: 　▪ High parking fees 　▪ Unbounded parking 　▪ 70% of units are "parking-free" 　▪ Access to parking in 2 shared garages on periphery • Auto restraints 　▪ 30 kph on main street 　▪ Limited access with very low speeds 5 kph 　▪ Street layout allows for very little car circulation • Bike priority: covered secure bike parking within 2 minutes of every residence • Car-sharing	• Low-energy building 65 kWh/m²/year standard, Voluntary; 55 kWh/m²/year; Passive houses: 15 kWh/m²/year • District Healing • Wood-chip fired combined heat and power station provides all energy • Solar —89 photovoltaic systems • Zero-energy Solar Village • One of largest passive house developments in Germany	• Bioswales, open-channel-trough system • Rainwater collection • Ample open space and permeable surfaces • Filtration of rainwater • Maintain existing tree coverage • Adjacent to creek biotope • Green roofs

Reiselfeld is also known for its "barrier-free" living environment, marked by high permeability and connectivity in its layout. Extensive bikeways and ped-ways— along with narrow streets that slow traffic, a grid pattern, and preferential treatments for trams, buses, pedestrians, and bicycles at intersections—have promoted sustainable mobility. The district has adopted an uncontrolled "shared space" traffic system that sets maximum car speed at 30 kilometers per hour and includes many shared "play" streets that give priority to children and pedestrians. Absent any stop signs, a right yield system is used at intersections. In addition, active living and physical fitness are promoted by a network of parks, playgrounds, and a natural reserve that surrounds the community.

Vauban

Situated on 40 hectares of land formerly used as a military barracks and inhabited by 5,000 residents, Vauban is arguably one of the greenest places in the world. The community is a product of a highly participatory grassroots process. A number of activists, feeling that the mobility and energy standards applied in Reiselfeld were insufficient, demanded that a car-free, ultra-low-energy district be built. Soon thereafter Vauban was born. The first residents formed a collective and occupied the former military barracks. Many still live there today.

Vauban's Green TOD attributes are summarized in table 5. The district features one of Germany's largest passive housing developments and a zero-energy solar village. Vauban's

cogeneration plant is fueled by a renewable source of refuse wood chips. There are also eighty-nine photovoltaic systems throughout the development. Due to its ambitious energy standards, the district performs 90 percent better than conventional construction in terms of energy use (Siegl, 2010). The combined heat and power plant runs at 90 percent efficiency compared to a conventional power plant. Additionally, all houses meet and many exceed Freiberg's energy standard of 65 kWh/year (including Vauban's numerous zero-energy houses and passive houses with solar, which actually produce more energy than they use).

In addition to its ecological design, Vauban is widely known for its car-restricted living (in contrast to Rieselfeld which averages 1.1 parking spaces per dwelling unit). Most of Vauban's streets ban cars and most housing units have no driveway or garage.[14] Cars on the main street are restricted to 30 kilometers per hour and all other streets are designed for very low-speed travel (5 kilometers per hour). Vauban was laid out so that all residents live within two minutes of a covered bike-sharing kiosk and five minutes of a tram.

With the district organized around a tramway spine that is nestled into the streetscape and seven-minute peak headways, transit has a certain omnipresence in Vauban.

Vauban's planners made sure that parking's environmental footprint was limited. All parking is unbundled from the price of housing units, and fees to purchase a space are quite high at €17,500 per space. Seventy percent of dwelling units are "parking-free," and what little parking that does exist is sited in two shared garages on the town's periphery.

Mobility Impacts

The environmental payoff of the pro-transit and bike-ped-friendly policies of Rieselfeld and Vauban are reflected in statistics. Both districts have low car use and ownership. As shown in table 5, Reiselfeld residents own fewer cars and use transit more than the typical Freiburg resident. Ninety percent of its residents buy a monthly transit pass. Because residents' travel was last surveyed in 2003, before the tramway had opened, it is difficult to provide an up-to-date account of experiences in Vauban.

However, other indicators suggest that Vauban has very low car use. Only 2.2 out of every 10 Vauban residents own a car (compared to 4.3 for Freiburg as a whole and 3.4 for Reiselfeld). Also, 57 percent of Vauban's adult residents sold a car upon moving to the district (statistics provided by Sustainability Office, City of Freiburg). It is notable that low car ownership was recorded in Vauban before its tram line opened. This very likely reflected the influences of "self selection"—i.e., the car-free ethic of new residents. However, other factors have weighed in as well, including the proactive promotion of other modes, the provision of a free universal transit pass to some households, and the availability of conveniently located car-sharing. Although recent modal split data are not available, the consensus view is that transit use has replaced many bike and walk trips.[15] Most of Vauban's residents buy a monthly transit pass, and half buy a German National Rail Pass. Moreover, 75 percent of car-free households buy the national rail pass, compared to 10 percent of Germans nationwide.[16]

Conclusion

Green TODs offer a form of urbanism and mobility that could confer appreciable environmental benefits. They emphasize pedestrian, cycling, and transit infrastructure over automobility. They mix land uses, which not only brings destinations closer but also creates an active, vibrant street life and interior spaces, instilling a sense of safety and security. And through building designs and resource management systems, they embrace minimal waste, low emissions, and, to the degree possible, energy self-sufficiency.

The case experiences reviewed in this paper highlight the potential benefits of Green TOD. While other places in Sweden (e.g., Mälmo) and Germany (e.g., the Kronsberg district of Hannover) have made strides in advancing green urbanism and transit-friendly development, places like Hammarby Sjöstad, Rieselfeld, and Vauban have successfully integrated both elements in their community designs. Perhaps the most ambitious version of Green TOD is now taking shape in the deserts of the United Arab Emirates: Masdar City, outside of Abu Dhabi. Besides being car-free and interlaced by rail at the surface level and personal-rapid transit (PRT) and freight-rapid-transit (FRT) below-ground, Masdar City is to be fully energy self-sufficient, courtesy of a massive solar farm on the project's edge. Additionally, all organic waste is to be converted into biomass, all construction materials are being

TABLE 6. MODAL SPLIT AND CAR OWNERSHIP STATISTICS

Mode of Travel	Rieselfeld (1999)*	Vauban (2003)**	Freiburg (1999)***	Region: Baden-Württemberg
Walk	16%	28% car-owning HH 33% car-free HH	23%	
Bike	28%	40% car-owning HHs 51% car-free HHs	27%	
Public Transport	25%	~4-11% (Before tram service commenced)	18%	
Car	31%	28% car-owning HHs 2% for car-free HHs	**Car** 26% **Carpool** 6%	
Car Ownership per 1000 residents (2008)	337	222	431	34*

*Broaddus (2009) ** Nobis and Welsch (2003). *** Schick (2009)

recycled, and over the long term the project is to become completely carbon neutral. Other communities should not necessarily seek to replicate the specific practices of these places but rather adapt principles of Green TOD to local circumstances and constraints.

Moving beyond the rhetoric to the reality of Green TODs will take money, time, and political leadership. The built-in structural forces that work against designing safe, resource-conserving, and pedestrian-friendly districts around transit stations are immense, particularly in countries like the United States. Barriers are most likely to come down through encouraging real-world examples, such as those reviewed in this paper.

One sensible way to help finance Green TODs is through value capture mechanisms. The degree to which Green TODs create benefits is reflected in land prices, as experienced in Hammarby Sjöstad. Indeed, land sales were the principal means by which early rail systems were financed in the U.S. and much of Europe (Bernick and Cervero, 1997). Today, Hong Kong recaptures the value-added from rail investments to help finance not only transit infrastructure but the armature of the surrounding community as well, including open spaces, sidewalks, and green corridors.[17]

Critics are apt to label Green TOD as "social engineering." In truth, many of those living in the suburbs of the United States are "engineered"—forced to drive to get from anywhere to everywhere, a result of segregated and low-density land-use patterns. Green TODs provide consumers with more choices around where to live and how to travel. Increased choices and variety is a good thing, especially given the increasingly diverse and plural make-up of households in America and other affluent societies. We suspect that, given the opportunity, more and more middle-class households will opt for Green TODs for lifestyle reasons.

ON MICRO-TRANSACTIONS
IN URBAN INFORMATICS

MALCOLM McCULLOUGH

Networked cities afford more participation. Much as eighteenth-century coffeehouses and newspapers generally created a new circuit for politics, so twenty-first-century media creates a new circuit for sustainability. A new layer of communications helps with recognizing, valuing, and governing resources.

Urban Informatics

Mobile, embedded, and social media have created a new basis in information technology. Locative media work best at street level. In an influential essay, "The Street as Platform," the blogger Dan Hill, also an engineer with Arup Associates, narrated nearly twenty examples of "clouds of data" surrounding spontaneous acts in everyday urban life. "This is a new kind of data, collective and individual, aggregated and discrete, open and closed, constantly logging impossibly detailed patterns of behaviour. The behaviour of the street."[1] To tag, to text, to navigate among both friends and amenities, it helps to not be driving a car. Urban computing adds to the advantages of the walkable city over automobile-abiding sprawl.

To know a city takes no new media, of course, but for a generation steeped in perpetual messaging, the next stage of growing up is to take social media to the streets. In many ways this is also the next stage of urbanism; many aspects of urban infrastructure are being layered with information technology. For instance: networked solar-powered digital parking meters for dynamic pricing to circumstances; tagged locations of local ethnic histories; ambient public displays of open-sourced air quality data. And of course the many resource streams of transit, retail goods, entertainment, and water and power that have long comprised the modern city now acquire interactivity, realtime status display, and small self-serve transactions. It becomes easier to know when your bus is coming. It seems normal enough to look at your phone to see where the nearest Zipcar might be (fig. 1).

All these are urban informatics, urban computing, situated technology, or ambient information. Whatever their name,

they have been recognized for some time as an alternative to disembodied cyberspace, which expression now seems dated. Urban informatics thus helps new urbanism or green urbanism seem less like romanticist throwbacks to less complex times. Instead, as information technology becomes pervasive, new design challenges arise, more non-technical disciplines must become involved, and this recasts some notions of commons.

Beyond Wayshowing

No technology, not even radio or television, has been adapted more widely and more quickly than handheld mobile computing, also known as cell phones. The implications of this connectivity for bottom-up enterprise and ad-hoc collective resource governance have only begun to be known. This seems especially so amid the chaos of the developing world's urban hypergrowth. The question of urban computing now attracts anthropologists, economists, political scientists, and environmental activists, not to mention architecture-trained electronic installation artists. The core of that question may be how information technology lets people tune in to their surroundings instead of tuning out into some distracting personal escape.

Among the design challenges of street-level media usage, perhaps the one most pertinent to sustainability concerns how communities assign value to resources. The word community has many different meanings and is abused by people interested only in market segments; it describes something of which people belong to—not just one person but many. But the idea of a resource community seems a clear enough instance: for example, the users of a local power co-generation facility.

The microtransactions and social connectedness typical of networking technology can reshape the respect and upkeep of some kinds of resources. The ad-hoc organizations that arise to accomplish this may complement usual partnerships of public and private players. According to the environmental activist Paul Hawken, who calls it "blessed unrest," mil-

	Organization	Depletion	Participation
Not a commons	Free enterprise	"Tragedy of the Commons" --free riding	Defense by owners
Physical commons	Designated area	Sustainable if well managed	Conflict resolution by members
Information commons	Networked access structure	Cornucopia: more use makes more of it	Thumbs up/down by millions
Ambient commons	Networked resource community	Undervaluation	Microtransactions by participants

FIG. I An everyday example of microtransaction for use of pooled resource: Zipcar.

lions of small local organizations exist to represent resources. As explored by the urban planner Nabeel Hamdi, for example in the book *Small Change*,[2] participating in such organizations proves quite important to the rise of the middle class in rapidly growing cities. In many of these cases, networking allows people to identify, meter, and monitor access to something of local value where big disinterested foreign money did not.

From the perspective of technology-building, these bottom-up phenomena present better opportunities to assist sustainable practices than the current corporate trend back toward proprietary media channels. (That was evident in the year 2010 in the Apple-Google deal that threatened net neutrality or the declaration by the influential *Wired* magazine that the Web is dead, at least as a near future horizon for wealth generation.[3]) If there is a word to describe how that top-down agenda regards locative media, it must be "wayshowing." Architects and planners may understand wayfinding, for their fields helped advance that concept half a century ago. Yet they may not notice how quicly current media practices have blended wayfinding and advertising into "wayshowing." Imagine a cognitive map (or view one on your phone) that includes only places where it is possible to spend money. Alas, in the short run there appears to be a move away from bottom-up aggregation toward top-down corporate push. Yet in the long run, the net has steadily proven itself worthy against attempts at enclosure and artificial scarcity. Instead it is best for expanding participation.

The Usability of Flows

Much use of the city consists of tapping into resources. Interaction design operates on fixtures and fittings to infrastructures. Pervasive computing lets this happen across a spectrum of physical scales, from the device, to the room, to the street, to the neighborhood; and it couples that spectrum to a more abstract scale of participation, from private to public, or from membership to mere lurking. Networked life becomes a series of acts to manage one's streams of data. Those might combine not only the feeds usually thought of as "media" but also social contacts, local politics, and physical resources. The latter involve not only the water and power that have long been governed as quasi-public utilities but also now flows of food, automobile usage, recycling, and more. Each of these flows behaves more like an information network connecting the individual citizen with local, regional, and global supply chains. For example, information technology makes it much more likely to know where your vegetables come from and easier to make choices about that. Thus the experience of networked cities becomes much more embodied and much less like the broadcast-era separation of passive consumers from one-way, one-to-many supplies, whether of fruit or films. In *Me++: The Cyborg Self and the Networked City*, William Mitchell famously characterized this neo-Joycean embodiment through boundaries and networks in the city: "Walls, fences, and skins divide; paths, pipes, and wires connect."[4]

More so than in architecture, interaction design puts usability first among its considerations. Usability begins from rote mechanical efficiency of the sort once studied by Taylorist industrial managers but quickly moves ahead into higher concerns of cognition. Embodied aspects of cognition prove particularly vital. Activity theory explains how people take cues from their surroundings to play situations (and to avoid having to memorize rules for everything). Embodied cognition allows for expertise and the delights of mastery. The sense of objects and contexts becomes part of the loop, so to speak, and not just a one-time input to mental process. This produces a quality of engagement quite different from sitting at a screen. One such delight is mastery of using a city. So despite how the world of Microsoft saw it, not all interfaces are for casual beginners. Indeed the arts of interface have long become much more aesthetic, especially with respect to the sense of context.

Situated technology exists in contrast to the placeless universal sameness of so much broadcast and web. Tangible and embedded interfaces create situations of use that gain aesthetic qualities through their materials and embodiment. Delight arises from engagement of otherwise latent sensibilities, for example in physical scale, touch, and orientation. This is an important instance of tacit knowledge. Principles of "embodied cognition" suggest that human capacity to use contexts, tools, and props as active components of skillful practices helps reduce excess of more rigidly codified representations. Experts do not follow rules so much as they play situations. This helps mitigate a sense of information overload. And that can feel restorative, sometimes aesthetically so. The pertinence of these cognitive principles in interaction design to the question of sustainable urbanism is the engagement that people feel in situated technology, how that may couple with engagement to place, and how that may be increased by participation in the place. For example, there has been a rise in historical tagging and storytelling. There are many more instances of do-it-yourself air quality monitoring. Public art installations visualize current states of open-sourced local resource data. Such activities give new form and meaning to ideas of an information commons, increasingly in relationship to more widely held ideas about other kinds of commons.

Embodied media have become a shared resource that requires good governance. Much as fifty years ago, when people discovered how to talk about "the environment," or fifteen years ago, when the rush to the World Wide Web spontaneously generated so many different visions of an "information commons," a new conversation is emerging, among otherwise separate disciplines, that gives identity to a shared cultural challenge. This new notion takes aspects from those two now dominant ones but increasingly appears distinct from either. Environmental yet not about the biosphere, informational yet not about the Internet, it still seeks a name more recognizable than "tangible media" or "urban computing."

Different Kinds of Commons

A persistent physical embodiment of some aspect of the information commons is difficult to explain in brief and seems much more like something people gradually come to notice. After all, few of urbanism's words are so loaded as "commons." Ideas of the commons challenge fundamental beliefs about markets, and so cut straight to the biggest debates about the Internet, not to mention the planet. Few ideas undermine resolve so quickly as the "tragedy of the commons," whose sharpest expression might be how "ruin is the destination toward which all men rush, each pursuing his own best interests . . ."[6] Few ideas distance the web from such concerns so quickly as the "comedy of the commons," that the more people use an information resource, the more valuable and sustainable it becomes. And especially in the West, few ideas create resentment more quickly than schemes for collective governance of anything.

Perhaps the best way past this conceptual impasse has been identified by the political economist and Nobel laureate Elinor Ostrom as "neither the market nor the state."[7] The commons is not a market, nor an opposition to markets, so much as a complementary form of production. The commons is not a state, and not communist, so much as a complementary form of governance. Whereas the market always wants more, and the state arbitrarily, often absurdly, declares where to stop, a commons builds a more intrinsic understanding of sufficiency.

The key to a more effective model is to encourage bottom-up arrangements between local participants in context. Neither the state nor the market, both operating too abstractly and remotely, is able to do this. This approach runs counter to the two more usual poles of thought regarding any commons: one, "the presumption that an external Leviathan is necessary to avoid tragedies of the commons"[8] (state), and two, the logic that since any commons will incur neglect, the only way to avert the tragedy is to privatize, i.e., to have no more commons (market). Through examples in governance of meadows, fisheries, and irrigation networks, Ostrom showed that "long enduring, self organized, and self governed" common pool resources do exist, and moreover that they depend on highly contextual agreements to do so. Whereas the top-down models of a less networked era too often assume "complete information, independent action, perfect symmetry of interests, no human errors, no norms of reciprocity, zero monitoring enforcement costs,"[9] the complex-systems models of more recent economic theory begin by questioning those assumptions. A commons can represent value that cannot be monetized or regulated. Yale economist Yochai Benkler has applied the idea of a commons to "commons-based peer production"[10] to describe what makes people willing to work without usual organizations, titles, or pay.

Ambient information now becomes essential to those models (fig. 2). Self-organizing, self-governing players—neither state nor market—depend on context to make sense of glutted and incomplete information in the worldwide effort to stabilize common pool resources. Economic theories of the long tail, the bottom of the pyramid, the wealth of networks, and blessed unrest generally champion the little guys, networked, using whatever information they can.

Upkeep

One of the most defining traits of ecosystems is the devotion of more energy (and apparent design sophistication) to stability than to expansion. The most sustainable arrangement is one where the most energy is devoted to upkeep. This means design for sustainability is about making places that people will want to take care of. That means aesthetics matter intrinsically; ugly is less sustainable. But more fundamentally still, it means that participation matters most of all. Top-down control is less sustainable. Access is key. And in networked cities, where an individual's belonging to place and community becomes multiple and by degree, access becomes what networks provide and regulate; and so access becomes more widespread. For example, information technology allows millions of customers to make choices about the sources and transmission of electric power, by means of options and surcharges at the monthly billing cycle. These are examples of microtransactions. Drastic increase in the number and context-sensitivity of transactions about the use of resources makes it possible to increase stakeholding, decrease waste, and identify and prevent free riding on those resources. Commons theory emphasizes microtransactions about access, use, and upkeep as the way to avert tragedy.

MOBILITY AS AN INFRASTRUCTURE OF DEMOCRACY[1]

RICHARD M. SOMMER

FIG.1 Interchange of Lincoln Highway and Pennsylvania Turnpike, as seen from the air, postcard, 1947.

Technologies exist, or are emerging, that will enable us to design and construct buildings in such a way that will use far less natural resources. Buildings aside, if we all chose to or were able to play out our lives in one, limited place like some electronically networked cyborg, we could very quickly and radically reduce our personal and collective energy footprint. But to engage architecture and urbanism from a fully ecological perspective means measuring environmental impacts, including carbon and nonrenewable resource usage in a more expanded context of social justice, economic opportunity, and human nature.

In societies aspiring toward modern forms of democracy, increasing mobility, in both geographic and socioeconomic terms, has become as critical to human emancipation as the more traditional liberal touchstones of civil liberty and equal representation. Concepts such as freedom and liberty have taken on competing meanings that pivot around enlighten-ment-inspired ideals of civil society and more individualistic, romantic notions of unlimited human potential. Breaking from their bonds, their heritage, and their communities to improve their station in life, modern people have almost always needed to move: across a city, from one city to another, or from one continent to another. This is not a uniquely modern phenomenon, but in recent history it has been accelerated by mechanical forms of locomotion and digital telecommunication.

The freedom of access that movement facilitates has been central to liberal notions of equal access and neoliberal notions of economic opportunity. The quintessential American figures of the pilgrim, the pioneer, and the beatnik all defined themselves by moving. Myth or no, this quest has been central to an understanding of "America" as a land of opportunity. This striking out is often related to a desire to own and privately control property—a mindset that has literally and figuratively driven the physical formation of modern societies like the United States.

Against this background, how are we to assess the ideas that most environmentalists, planners, and architects are proposing to achieve more sustainable, ecologically balanced forms of urbanity? There appears to be a remarkable degree of consensus among professionals, activists, and politicians that creating more compact and integrated urban agglomerations, with more efficient and public forms of transport to serve them, is the best bulwark against the coming environmental Armageddon. The experts argue that such reforms would both reduce environmental impacts and increase the potential for human collaboration and sociability.

However, do we all agree that a more compact yet ultimately less mobile form of city should be our goal? Almost half a century ago, Melvin Webber, in his essay "The Urban Place and the Non-Place Urban Realm," argued that modern forms of urbanity depend less on traditional places than the forms of mobility that are facilitated by modern technologies of virtual communication and physical transport.[2] He posed the rather obvious notion that the most successful individuals in advanced economies were those who could take most advantage of travel and communication technologies to create the most expansive social and economic networks. When I travel to conferences where sustainable architecture or urbanism is the ostensible subject, I always marvel at how many trains, planes, and automobiles have been taken to propel experts bent on saving the planet into one place only to hear the same individuals insist that everyone should, for example, walk or ride a bike to work (not to imply that this is a bad thing: those who can, should). Nevertheless, it would appear Weber's thesis has been borne out. By virtue of the World Wide Web, cell phones, cheap air travel, and (until recently) ever increasing levels of "automobilty," has not the relation between human community and place been under-

FIG. 3 Congress of Racial Equality "Freedom Riders" after being forced from a bus by a mob that stoned the bus, slashed the tires, and set it on fire. Anniston, Alabama, 1961.

going a constant and in many ways emancipating transformation for many of us?

Simply—but for brevity's sake, rather crudely—put, how do our current notions of ways to create a more ecological urbanism jibe with entrenched and deeply held cultural proclivities toward freedom of movement and association? Moreover, even if we can agree that a wholesale change in the organization and pattern of urban development is a worthy ecological and social goal, do we really think we can put the industrial genie that is the modern city (i.e., a highly disaggregated system of infrastructure provision and land development) back into a tidy green bottle? Are there other ways of understanding what it might mean to design a more mobile, democratic, and ecologically sound city?

There are questions and approaches being explored by particular designers and theorists today in which one can begin to recognize an important set of questions and debates that must be explored if we are to get beyond the seemingly narrow, formal solutions generally being proffered today. From the often neoliberal perspective that dominates in the

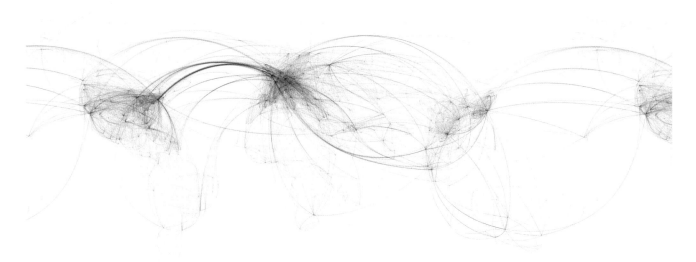

FIG. 2 Map of world airline routes, March 2009.

United States, some are asking how to effect change in the tastes and market-based choices of the middle-class population that is still understood as driving the making of the built environment. Taking the view that as the American middle-class consumer goes, so goes the many who still aspire to the American style of life, planners such as Andrés Duany have asked how we can effect change in the psyche of an American society that is still unable to reconcile the incompatibility of its romantic views of nature with urban life. Others, more active in environmental science and ecological modeling, are becoming essential partners in designing and redesigning the next cities and are already generating methods for composing and evaluating cities that defy many of

architecture and urban design's most cherished precepts. Others working in the vein of the late William Mitchell promise us that we can still have our highly mobile modern lives and fast-paced modern cities, if only we can redesign and reengineer our transport infrastructure to be more multiscaled, multifaceted, and digitally networked to real-time analysis of our patterns of movement. Ultimately, defining urban growth in terms that mean expanding social mobility and democratic access as much as, or more than, expanding built territories suggests a frank assessment of the agency and limits that design and technology have to "fix" the environment, as well as a corresponding confrontation with a changing and more fragile Nature.

PART 5: EVOLVING CITIES AND SUSTAINABLE COMMUNITIES

5.1

PROSPECTS FOR MEANINGFUL GLOBAL ENVIRONMENTAL GOVERNANCE

PETER M. HAAS

> Over the past few decades we have seen extensive significant international efforts to cope with the major threats to the global environment. In many respects this exercise of planetary stewardship has been impressive. However they are probably inadequate to address the full magnitude of the ecological challenge at hand, as many of the disturbing underlying destructive trends continue.
>
> — Speth, 2008

The question then is how best to improve global environmental governance. Two broad perspectives undergird an assessment of global environmental governance.[1] Liberal reformist approaches point to improvements to date and hope that these approaches can be replicated for dealing with other pressing global environmental issues—such as biodiversity or global warming—and that these approaches will galvanize a broader set of global systemic transformations as countries and populations are caught up in a dense network of environmental obligations which will lead them to accept more commitments as well as transform collective understandings about environmental threats in a more sustainable way.[2] More radical approaches are skeptical about these procedural aspirations and argue that changing fundamental practices by late modern industrial societies are unlikely to occur by stealth and require a direct assault.

Reformist Visions: How to Make the System Work Better

Much of the academic research on international environmental affairs in recent years has focused on environmental regimes and related institutions and processes. Out of this research has emerged a long list of reforms needed to improve and strengthen the current system.[3]

Effectiveness has been widely studied, as academics and policymakers have sought to identify factors that contributed to better international environmental cooperation and protection. Effective international arrangements are those that lead nations to make policy changes that further the goals of the arrangements, with the result that there are improvements in environmental quality. If we know what conditions and initiatives further the effectiveness and success of international regimes, then we will know where to invest for better results.

Examples of effective regimes, where the environment is confidently believed to be improved or on the path to improvement, include the stratospheric ozone regime; the European acid rain treaty; efforts to protect the North Sea, the Baltic Sea, and Antarctic living resources; the regulation of ocean dumping and marine pollution from ships; and, less clearly, the control of the endangered species trade.

Many of the factors leading to more effective regimes can be grouped under three headings: building the environment for *cooperation*, building national *capacity*, and building national *concern*.[4] Let's discuss each of the three C's.

Cooperative Environment

A number of factors can improve the context within which environmental negotiations are conducted and thus make it easier for states to reach meaningful agreements. For starters, the number of participants is important. A relatively small number of actors—whether private business corporations or nations at the negotiating table—makes it easier to identify culprits and to develop meaningful policies to mitigate the problems. The involvement of business stakeholders in negotiations can make the arrangements more effective in the end, but that is only feasible if small numbers are involved. A relatively small number of nations engaged in making decisions facilitates reaching agreement; achieving consensus with large numbers can be very difficult. Governments have grown accustomed to relying on caucuses and blocs of countries to reduce the difficulties created by large numbers of countries in the United Nations.

Continuing negotiations rather than one-shot sessions are better at generating meaningful compromises. Over time states grow more familiar with one another's positions and are also willing to make concessions at one meeting in the anticipation that those concessions may be reciprocated at future meetings. A high profile for negotiations also encourages breakthroughs and meaningful commitments that mid-level bureaucrats lack the authority to make. Thus, some conference of the parties meetings (COPs) and other meetings now include high-level ministerial sessions before or after the longer negotiations, at which such deals may be presented.

Voting rules are extremely important. Reaching consensus makes it difficult to achieve agreements with real bite—any government important to the outcome that wants to throw a wrench into the works can do so—yet consensus decision making is the norm in treaty negotiations since sovereignty requires that no nation be bound against its will. One way around these difficulties is for governments to agree to waive consensus-based decision making in certain situations. Progress has been made in this regard, and more is needed. As has happened with the Montreal Protocol on Substances that Deplete the Ozone Layer and the Stockholm Convention on Persistent Organic Pollutants, the COP can be empowered to make certain types of regulatory decisions that would not need to be ratified as separate treaties, and procedures can be introduced whereby a two-thirds supermajority, a double majority (a majority of both industrial and developing countries), or even a mere majority of the COP members could make decisions binding for all. Conceivably a COP could even delegate certain rulemaking or standard-setting powers to an expert body. The COP would limit itself to providing the broad policy framework and providing a check against abuse of discretion, much as Congress and the federal courts supervise decision making in U.S. regulatory agencies.

Well-designed treaties incorporate explicit provisions that encourage meaningful cooperation and compliance by parties. Three factors have been identified as critical: formal enforcement provisions, verification measures, and environmental monitoring. Each of these is likely to improve compliance as well as indirectly contribute to more ambitious regimes because nations are more confident that requirements will be widely respected and enforced. Formal enforcement provisions include economic sanctions against parties that are in violation and legal provisions for arbitration over disputes in interpretation or for enforcing sanctions. Curiously, few environmental treaties contain strong sanctions or compliance mechanisms. While most include legal language for arbitration, arbitration proceedings are rarely initiated. To the extent that environmental treaties are effective, it is through nations' own calculations of their self-interest, rather than through fears of consequences of noncompliance.

Verification is important to assure that parties are living up to their obligations. Most regimes include verification measures that collect information about parties' compliance. Nations are more likely to comply with their international obligations if infractions are promptly and accurately reported. Treaties vary widely in terms of who collects this information and how frequently. Since self-reporting can run the risk of nations misrepresenting their records, impar-

tial third parties can sometimes be used. For instance, after the Cold War ended it was discovered that the Soviets had been routinely lying about their whale catches and the amount of radioactive wastes they were dumping in the ocean. In practice most treaties rely on a complicated mix of verification arrangements.

Monitoring is also important for providing an accurate picture of conditions and trends. Robust monitoring programs encourage stronger treaties, because nations can ascertain if their efforts are having an impact and can develop new policies if new threats are identified or if earlier concerns are shown to be exaggerated.

Two features of the international organizations responsible for guiding environmental diplomacy may be significant. Horizontal linkages, or synergies, between international organizations can amplify the pressures on governments to improve their environmental performance within the environmental treaties administered by each organization. This is because nations that often interact with one another across a variety of environmental and other issues are also more likely to comply with obligations out of a need to maintain a broader reputation for being good international citizens. For instance, in the 1980s the United Kingdom suffered from its reputation as being the "dirty man of Europe." Seeking to shed this reputation led the UK to support a stronger acid rain regime than it had initially desired. The European Union is dense with horizontal linkages, so members are more likely to comply with EU directives. Similarly, EU members are more likely to comply with environmental treaties when those treaties become part of EU commitments.

Vertical linkages refer to broadly accepted international norms that can be applied to govern behavior in particular domains. Thus, if environmental issues are negotiated within the WTO, they will be subject to broader norms of promoting free trade and minimizing barriers to trade. If they are conducted under United Nations Environment Programme auspices, then norms of environmental protection and sustainable development will be accorded higher priority. For this reason promoting the paradigm of sustainable development may help improve the pursuit of environmental protection within organizations where the concept has been institutionalized.

Capacity

With any new law requiring serious efforts at implementation, new capacities must be built in and out of government. Capacity constraints are especially severe in most of the developing countries. There are various forms of capacity-increasing transfers that can be used to reward countries and support implementation and compliance: financial transfers, technology transfers, and knowledge transfers. Each can have a role in inducing countries to support and comply "with environmental treaties." Financial transfers provide money for improving compliance "with international obligations" and are particularly attractive to poorer developing countries. Technology transfers include sales and gifts of environmental technology and technical equipment for environmental monitoring. Knowledge transfers consist of training programs for government officials in environmental management, monitoring, and verification activities. Knowledge transfers also include environmental training programs for national scientists and even NCOs.

Concern

Heightened national concern can pressure governments to take stronger action. One key variable is the degree of domestic pressure. Effective regimes and organizations have included programs for building public concern, such as public education campaigns that include TV, radio, and other media. Public concern is also built when participation of national NGOs and scientists is enhanced. Building environmental norms at the international level can heighten national concern, as can publicizing monitoring results.

Analysts also point to an array of underlying conditions that make international environmental commitments more likely to be meaningfully addressed at home. Thus, attention by the international community has focused on capacity building as well as setting binding commitments for governments. Some of the major background conditions collectively embraced in the United Nations Millennium Development Goals[5] include:

• peace and stability
• favorable economic conditions and the absence of financial or other economic crises
• an open, democratic society and an independent, effective media presence
• a high level of public concern and active NGOs
• the presence of rule of law and a culture of compliance with international law
• the human and institutional capacities in government to participate meaningfully at all stages.

Current projects in the international community to expand the reformist agenda include:

• creating a World Environment Organization to support the environmental agenda internationally the way the WTO promotes free trade and the WHO promotes world health[6]
• corporate social responsibility and certification campaigns, such as the United Nations' Global Compact, intended to elevate the accountability of major companies for environmental protection, and other sustainability goals[7]
• broadened involvement of NGOs and other non-state actors through the expansion of global issue networks[8]

Alternative Visions: How to Change the System

Many observers argue that in order seriously to address global environmental threats, deeper changes must be undertaken that address the underlying causes of such problems, though they do not all agree on what the root causes are.[9] Some tend to see the causes of international environmental

decline as deriving from patterns of economic production and consumption, while others focus on structural factors having to do with economic inequality, an absence of political representation, and undeveloped environmental sensibilities among the majority of the world's population. Some of those urging these alternative approaches see them as important complements to environmental regimes; others see little hope for the regime approach and are disparaging regarding its prospects.

Despite a legacy of arguments about the environmental effects of rapid population growth, it now appears that population growth has stabilized everywhere in the world except for Africa. The environmental challenge is how to provide a sustainable life for a global population of 8 to 10 billion people, according to current UN estimates of the stable world population at mid-century.[10] Satisfying their needs involves changes in dominant technologies, consumption habits, and inequities of political power within and between societies.

Production Habits

A number of authors point to the need to accelerate the transition to lower energy-intensive and cleaner patterns of economic production. While energy consumption has been gradually delinked from economic growth in the major economies, the ecological footprint of modern industrial production remains unsustainable.[11]

Consumption Habits

A looming threat to sustainability comes from the consumption habits that accompany economic prosperity. The affluent societies consume vastly more than the world's poor, and the rapid transition of hundreds of millions of Indians and Chinese to middle class status raises serious challenges to ecological stability if they wish and choose to consume in the same manner as those in the industrialized world. Conversely, it is seemingly unethical to deny them the rights and living standards enjoyed elsewhere since the Industrial Revolution.

Power redistribution

Others relate environmental distress to the inability of those who are affected by environmental harm to act effectively on their own behalf. These authors question the reliance on large companies, and possibly on capitalism itself, to address the problems for which they are historically responsible.

In particular, a number of political analysts argue that only through greater empowerment of local political actors, and NGOs in international discussions, can the control over agendas and technologies by states and large corporations be avoided.[12]

Conclusion

Over the last thirty years, the international community's quest for planetary stewardship has encompassed a variety of intergovernmental, governmental, and civil society initiatives. The results are mixed and generally conceded to be inadequate. The disturbing trends in deterioration continue. A much stronger system of environmental regimes is essential; that is also widely conceded. Those most deeply concerned have looked beyond regimes and asked what else must be done.

We stand at a critical moment in Earth's history, a time when humanity must choose its future. As the world becomes increasingly interdependent and fragile, the future at once holds great peril and great promise. To move forward we must recognize that in the midst of a magnificent diversity of cultures and life forms, we are one human family and one Earth community with a common destiny. We must join together to bring forth a sustainable global society founded on respect for nature, universal human rights, economic justice, and a culture of peace. In the stirring words of the Earth Charter:

> Towards this end, it is imperative that we, the peoples of Earth, declare our responsibility to one another, to the greater community of life, and to future generations . . . The spirit of human solidarity and kinship with all life is strengthened when we live with reverence for the mystery of being, gratitude for the gift of life, and humility regarding the human place in nature.[13]

BUILDING COMMUNITY CAPACITY
FOR STRATEGIC SUSTAINABILITY

SEAN CONNELLY, MARK ROSELAND, SEAN MARKEY

"Near collapse," "crumbling," "looming crisis"—from tragic events such as the collapse of bridges and contamination of drinking water to the negative impacts on overall quality of life, infrastructure deficits continue to make headlines around the world. While these deficits represent an enormous challenge, they also provide a historic opportunity to replace our existing infrastructure and reshape our communities in a more sustainable manner.

Sustainability, sustainable development, and sustainable community development (SCD) are not new concepts.[1] Over 6,000 local governments from across the globe have committed to planning processes to make their communities more sustainable.[2] Many communities have incorporated sustainable development principles into their community vision statements and decision-making processes. However, translating high-level goals and objectives into tangible projects and actionable strategies has been more difficult.[3] In short, an *implementation gap* prevents communities from capitalizing on the many known and proven sustainable techniques and technologies that could significantly contribute to addressing our infrastructure deficit in a way that prepares urban communities for the challenges and opportunities of the coming decades.

In Canada, for example, the potential for sustainability planning will only accelerate with the commitments of successive federal governments to address the infrastructure deficit and related provincial agreements that link funding to integrated community sustainability plans.[4] Federal governments have made commitments of $13 billion over a ten-year period (2005–2014) for municipal investments in public transit, water and wastewater treatment, community energy systems, solid waste disposal, and road and bridge infrastructure from funding collected through gas taxes.[5] These gas tax agreements were designed to specifically link infrastructure investments and sustainability through the requirement for all recipient municipalities to complete or enhance existing integrated community sustainability plans by the end of the funding agreement (i.e., 2015). Given that municipalities are not required to develop sustainability plans prior to

accessing funding, that plans list conventional road and bridge repair as "sustainable" infrastructure, and that the recent economic stimulus package ($12 billion over two years) targets "shovel-ready" infrastructure projects, the influence of these programs on transforming Canadian communities toward sustainability is questionable. However, they do represent much-needed capital resources that can be used by communities to strategically rebuild their infrastructure in order to address the challenges and constraints that lie ahead.

The purpose of this paper is to better understand the implementation gap in SCD planning and to offer solutions and highlight best practices that will assist communities in overcoming common barriers associated with the planning process. Drawing upon a two-year Canadian research project, our research is grounded in the realities of the municipal condition through a focus on "strategic sustainability." Strategic sustainability is an approach to planning and implementation that allocates limited available resources with the greatest impact for sustainability. By thinking strategically about sustainability and making the connection to community infrastructure, communities will be able to identify the "quick wins" for sustainability in the short term while retaining and building support for broader and more complex solutions in the medium and long terms. In the following sections we present findings from a cross-section of case communities and synthesize lessons learned as opportunities for building the planning capacity and efficacy of communities. We focus particularly on leadership and governance decisions that enabled strategic sustainability action.

How Can Communities Be Strategic about Sustainability?

There is no shortage of actions that need to be taken to shift our communities toward sustainability. The challenge rests with identifying where to focus and where to start—hence our focus on strategic sustainability. Understanding how to capitalize on this opportunity was the focus of our research project, *Strategic Sustainability and Community Infrastructure*.[6] In this study, we looked at award-winning sustainability initiatives from across Canada to determine how these communities were able to overcome the planning-implementation gap and to use their limited resources in order to have the greatest sustainability impact. In the following sections, we provide brief descriptions of four case studies that were effective in bridging the planning-implementation gap and identify some of the key lessons that allowed these case study communities to use investments in community projects as catalysts for broader sustainability initiatives in their communities.

Craik, Saskatchewan—Sustainable Living Project

In 2000, the own of Craik, Saskatchewan, and the rural municipality of Craik joined forces to help establish a community-based sustainability project that would bring attention to the town and provide a model of sustainable living for other rural communities. Craik has a town population of approximately 400 people with an additional 300 people in the surrounding region (2006). From the time construction began for the Craik Eco-Centre in 2003, it has served as a focal point for outreach, education, and community action activities such as a seminar series and local ecological footprint campaigns. The Eco-Centre served as the starting point for the town's sustainability efforts in order to demonstrate the viability of energy-efficient and alternative approaches to construction, e.g., straw bale construction, alternative energy sources, and integrated environmental design (fig. 1). The Eco-Centre then served as a model for expanding the scale of the project to a full eco-village development on granted rural municipality land.

The motivation for the Craik Sustainable Living Project was concern regarding the overall viability of the town. Faced with the general decline of rural Saskatchewan, the community of Craik realized that something had to be done that would draw attention to the town in a positive sense and raise its profile relative to other rural communities. Rather than embarking on traditional economic development initiatives in competition with surrounding towns (i.e., free land,

FIG. 1 Craik Eco-Centre and straw-bale construction.

town marketing, and highway-oriented development), leaders in the community were convinced that sustainable community development provided the key to long-term stability and rural revitalization by making Craik a desirable place to live and as a means to promote the community for business and resident attraction. Sustainability was seen as a necessity because neither the town nor the rural municipality could afford to expand services. Craik was able to overcome the planning-implementation gap by relying on community leadership that was able to explain and accept the risks associated with sustainability (and also the risks of not responding); the leadership were able to galvanize interest around alternative approaches to addressing economic decline.

Rolling River First Nation, Manitoba—Comprehensive Community Plan

Rolling River First Nation is located in southern Manitoba and has a band population of 336 (2006). The Rolling River case study focused on the community's comprehensive community plan that was initiated in 1998. The plan is treated as a living document, constantly being modified to reflect changes in the community as new challenges and opportunities are identified. The main priorities of the plan are to promote economic development initiatives designed to create employment within the community and to generate revenue and reduce the reliance of the community on funding from Indian and Northern Affairs Canada. Some of the initiatives from the community plan that have been successfully implemented include a new health center, gas station, restaurant, video lottery terminal center, and new farms. Projects that are still underway include a modular home plant, community sawmill, and local wind energy project.

The challenge for the community is to identify what type of economic development initiatives to engage in and how to link existing capacity for economic development with the opportunities presented with the acquisition of new reserve status land. The overall long-term goals of the community are to achieve 95 percent employment through economic development initiatives that reflect the community's values to protect cultural and ecological integrity and involve community review and approval. The goal of the economic development plan and the capacity assessment is to meet the basic needs of community members through local self-reliance that links traditional culture and holistic thinking to the realities of the modern world. Bridging the planning-implementation gap in Rolling River was based on establishing community roundtables as the key decision-making venue for the community. The commitment to community engagement and participatory planning contributed to a strong sense of place that has been reinforced through cultures and traditions emphasizing collective responsibility; this contributed to addressing social, environmental, and economic concerns in the community.

Toronto, Ontario—Better Building Partnership (BBP)

Toronto is Canada's most populated city, containing over 2.5 million (2006). The initial motivation for the BBP can be traced back to 1988, when the city hosted an international conference on air quality and cities. At the time, Toronto was itself experiencing air quality problems such as smog. This spurred the city to commit to a 20 percent reduction in greenhouse gases from 1988 levels, making it the first city to make such commitments. This goal served as the "defining moment" that spurred future commitment from the city.

Toronto's Better Buildings Partnership (BBP) provided a practical example of implementation related to the city's CO2 emission reduction goals. This program aims to decrease greenhouse gas emissions and improve urban air quality through energy-efficiency retrofits to buildings in the industrial-commercial-institutional building sector. The program, launched in 1996, provides comprehensive energy retrofits to private and public buildings through lending schemes that allow building owners to payback retrofit costs through efficiency gains. BBP has "survived" eleven years within constitutional constraints of municipal financing and has made improvements to over 600 buildings, resulting in a reduction of 200,500 tons of CO2 annually, as well as $19 million in savings to building owners. As an example, the largest photovoltaic system in the country at Exhibition Place reduces greenhouse gas emissions by 115 tons per year and results in an annual savings of $10,000 in electricity costs. Bridging the planning-implementation gap relied on emphasizing the economic rationale and the institutional resources of the city to engage key actors around air quality and climate change. Public-sector leadership engaged key actors based on an approach to sustainability that emphasized the technological improvements that would both reduce energy consumption and generate financial savings.

Surrey, British Columbia—
East Clayton Neighbourhood Development

Surrey is British Columbia's second largest city with a population of approximately 394,000 (2006). The focus of the Surrey case study was the planning and development of a new neighborhood, East Clayton, achieved through the East Clayton Neighbourhood Concept Plan (NCP). Guided by seven sustainability principles, the main priorities of the East Clayton project were reductions in urban run-off through on-site infiltration techniques, and the application of neo-traditional urban design considerations such as rear lanes, higher densities, work-live zoning, integration of commercial and business zones in the neighborhood, and greenways (fig. 2). The city created the NCP through engagement with local property owners, citizens, and city staff in a series of design charrettes with the goal of introducing sustainability measures to the new neighborhood development through site design.

The East Clayton NCP arose from two sets of conditions: the need to develop new urban areas in response to population growth, and the need to develop East Clayton while protecting agricultural land and salmon-bearing habitats. East Clayton is located in an area of Surrey that contains farmland and salmon habitat, and the City of Surrey had already received threats of lawsuits from farmers who con-

tended that urban run-off from developments would cause damage to their lowland farms. These factors combined to provide the motivation to explore sustainable neighborhood design. Bridging the planning-implementation gap in East Clayton relied on public-sector leadership based on an incremental approach to sustainability; this leadership was based on high-level sustainability principles and innovative design standards that had proven successful elsewhere.

Building Community Capacity for Strategic Sustainability

We have identified a number of best practices that were effective in bridging the planning-implementation gap at various stages of the process. Further details and examples from our research can be found at the project Web site (http://www.sfu.ca/cscd/strategic_sustainability/index.html). While these best practices can be useful for other communities struggling to implement their sustainability initiatives, the key lesson is that there are a variety of options available for communities to bridge the planning-implementation gap at various stages of the planning process.

The key for achieving strategic sustainability is to understand the specific context of a given community and to assess which "bridges" will be most effective at a given stage of the planning-implementation process. Building capacity for greater community transformation toward sustainability requires community leadership and knowledge of options to manage the risks associated with departing from the status quo. These are areas where the public sector can play a critical role.

Much of the literature on sustainability planning is focused on local government leadership in terms of leading by example, aligning policies, and obtaining political and management support. In our case studies, leadership was critical. However, leadership was also thought of more broadly and extended beyond local government. Community leadership was critical for:
- setting the sustainability agenda
- engaging nontraditional partners
- promoting and motivating participation
- developing consensus around shared values and proactively engaging broader support
- pushing for innovation and challenging the status quo
- managing risk by creating shared ownership of sustainability initiatives

Again, the sustainability planning literature has stressed the ability to manage the complexity associated with sustainability initiatives as a critical factor for success. Each of our case studies recognized the complexity associated with sustainability and used information, education, and awareness strategically by:
- using best practices from elsewhere as "pretty good" solutions and the foundation for tangible demonstration projects

FIG. 2 Example of Surrey's live-work zoning.

- taking a pragmatic approach to research and technical information
- using demonstration projects to raise awareness, build capacity, and engage a broader cross-section of participants
- using knowledge of sustainability to link community problems with sustainability solutions

The overarching themes of leadership, knowledge, and awareness are interrelated and are critical throughout the planning-implementation process. It is leadership and awareness that allows for strategic decision making, problem solving, and the application of appropriate "bridges" at every stage of the planning-implementation process.

Conclusions

Far too often, sustainability is considered as a cost rather than as a critical investment. Spending on community infrastructure needs to be recognized as a significant long-term investment. SCD provides a framework for guiding those investments in a manner that will benefit communities for generations. Planning for sustainability must also be linked directly to planning for infrastructure; otherwise we risk re-creating unsustainable community development patterns and will miss the opportunity to reshape our communities to be prosperous, competitive, and resilient in the decades ahead.

While many municipalities and indigenous communities across the globe are facing an infrastructure crisis, there are a number of encouraging signals. Governments at all levels have recognized the reality of the infrastructure deficit. Many communities are addressing their infrastructure deficit by way of SCD and are either investing in green infrastructure or establishing innovative projects designed to reduce demand on existing infrastructure. These examples provide tangible evidence for other communities and real learning opportunities for how to shift status quo development toward SCD.

Our case studies demonstrate that sustainability initiatives often take place independent of official sustainability planning processes. This finding provides a cautionary tale with regard to the requirement for all Canadian communities to produce Integrated Community Sustainability Plans. These plans will assist communities in planning in a more integrated manner. However, in order to move from planning to implementation, communities need more than just plans—they need to build community capacity in the form of committed leadership, resources, and willingness to learn and adapt as they transition toward sustainable development. By thinking strategically about sustainability and making the connection to community infrastructure, communities will be able to identify the quick wins for sustainability in the short term while retaining and building support for broader and more complex solutions in the medium and long term.

THE NEIGHBOURHOOD UNIT

THE ANTITHESIS OF SUSTAINABLE URBANISM

PAUL MURRAIN

I was extremely proud to be in Charleston, South Carolina, in 1996 to be a signatory to the Charter of the New Urbanism. Both product and process were timely and brilliant and remain so. It comprises a gifted and committed group of people. Debates are intense within the movement, and I have been a party to one such debate for quite some time. I believe the issue to be one of the most fundamental elements of urbanism and arguably the biggest mistake made by this worthy group, namely the resurrection and promotion of the Neighbourhood Unit Diagram of 1929. Far from being the start of the solution, it was the start of the problem.

Clarence Perry and Friends

The infamous diagram appeared in the Regional Plan for New York. The name "Neighbourhood Unit" was telling. Clarence Perry was a sociologist planner who was strongly influenced by Charles Horton Cooley, a sociologist who held the view that society would be better for having people who cooperated closely and that this would correct the wayward nature of the population in a fast-growing urban environment. Others latched on to this and indeed saw the neighborhood as being a unit of control, a way to keep political and moral order.

The way it was designed effectively turned its back on the rest of the urban fabric. It was seen as an entity in itself rather than part of something greater. The elementary school was at the heart and indeed was the dictate of population and catchment, along with other functions that directed the population to worthy endeavors: the library, the church, the communal baths and washhouses. It was a determined effort at social control. The other temptations of the fast-growing city were pushed to the edges. Business and commerce, retail and general entertainment became peripheral to the "moral core."

And so, the neighborhood became a "unit." It had physical limits. It could be defined and easily drawn. Its contents

were simplistic and minimal. It was remarkably compelling for those who were essentially antiurban in so far as the city was profane, out of control, and a danger to civility. The best way to solve that problem was to defend against it by building an enclave keeping local activity isolated and separated from the wider "global" interactions of strangers.

In addition to this fundamental belief, another powerful rationale also contributed to this isolationist tendency—traffic. Even in the late 1920s it was becoming clear to the likes of Clarence Perry and others that private vehicles were on the increase and were to dominate movement for years to come. Perry was certainly ahead of his time in that regard.

FIG. 1 The Neighbourhood Unit. The Regional Plan for New York, 1929. Clarence Perry.

Hence, the "neighborhood unit" appeared to be the answer to all manner of professional bodies that would normally have little in common.

Main Street Blown Away

It does not take more than a momentary glance to see that Perry, in one fell swoop, removed one of the key spatial types in most civilizations, however varied different cultures may make it. Main Street disappeared. This is not a trivial matter. Main Street is crucial to the coming together of "local" and "global" citizens. It is where strangers meet other strangers in the company of locals, who in turn meet each other. Most Main Streets are local punctuations on global networks. That is why they are what they are. Some twenty-three years ago Carole Rifkind devoted a whole book to them, appropriately titled *Main Street: The Face Of Urban America*. Her summary description is one of deep resonance:

It was called Towne Street when it was a single wilderness road in New England, High Street in a southern New Jersey town, Broad Street in Pennsylvania, Market Street in Ohio, Grand Street in a brash Wyoming city, Broadway in California. But as Main Street it was uniquely American, a powerful symbol of shared experience, of common memory, of the challenge and the struggle of building a civilization. Through history, the name embraced a variety of urban forms—the thickened spine of a New England township, the central street in a neat grid, the city center at the junction of diagonal boulevards . . . Yet Main Street was always familiar, always recognizable as the heart and soul of village, town or city."[1]

To be clear, this does not mean that every neighborhood has a full-fledged Main Street. What it does mean is that a neighborhood focuses on the most integrated street in order to be the place where locals and strangers come together for mutual benefit at whatever scale. The exchange takes place here, in all its forms.

The Spread of the Disease

The "neighborhood unit" took over the planning of settlements with extraordinary speed and power. For those seeking to control something that appeared out of control, it was sublime. It proved to be the basic element of all twentieth-century new towns and new growth wherever the USA and the UK had influence. The worse the traffic became, the more segregated everyone wanted to be, safe in the misguided belief that there would be sufficient life and facilities in the heart of the neighborhood to justify and support the isolation.

Professor Bill Hillier summarizes it perfectly: " . . . a town of parts each spatially distinct with its own idiosyncratic layout, the ultimate embodiment of the belief that good local places can be designed 'free standing' then hierarchically combined to form an urban whole . . . towns as an assemblage of parts into a whole rather than wholes in which good parts arise."[2]

The "Neighbourhood edge"—
A Fundamental Error

It was crucial to Perry to give a neighborhood physical limits and thereby assert that it needed not just a center but also an edge: the need to defend. Having built the best wall he could, short of a castle, he cared little about what went on around the edges.

He called them "Main Highways," effectively giving them over to vehicles. Other than an awareness of the significance of retail at junctions supported by a few apartments, they are dismissed as being liveable places. This was manna from heaven for those who were charged with making more and more free-flowing space for the movement of vehicles.

Those with a social and community focus could have the middle, where the world was cozy. Those who needed to build roads could have the perimeter. The deal was done. The urban fabric had been carved up. It was so simple yet disastrous for the next seventy years.

Observe most city neighbourhoods: A center, yes, but where's the edge? And, how can you not live in your neighborhood?

Clearly edges exist in the city, be they major railway lines that separate, or inhospitable arterials, or sometimes topographical features. Edges become seams when the feature unites, as do great rivers because they bring more people to them than would otherwise be there. Sometimes these features coincide with the perception of a neighborhood edge. But to assert that every neighborhood needs a physically defined edge is crass in the extreme.

The number of key New Urbanism publications that state neighborhoods need well-defined edges boggles the mind. Clearly it is not necessary to have defined edges in order to have an efficient neighborhood. The two have nothing to do with each other. An edge in the sense of reinforcing separation is irrelevant and indeed totally subversive to the nature of a greater and more inclusive urbanism.

The twentieth-century New Town movement found itself utterly confused by this notion. The planners of the day were well aware that a neighborhood was many things to many people and drew diagrams expressing that awareness showing arrows going way beyond the defined edges of their neighborhood units. They then became utterly confused about where to put the center: In the center? On the edge to unite two neighborhoods? At the corners or at the midpoint of the superblock? There was utter confusion.

The UK new town of Milton Keynes illustrates this madness beyond belief. It did all of the above but was ultimately composed of "neighborhood units," having relinquished the perimeter roads to the traffic engineers. Each "neighborhood unit" was named to further signify the separate identity: the gentle face of determinism.

FIG. 2 City structure diagrams, from the Milton Keynes Development Corporation, 1977.

There Were Warnings

In *The New Town Story*, Frank Schaffer reminds us that back in the 1940s in the UK the Reith Committee on New Towns issued a warning that "the neighbourhood should not be thought of as a self contained community of which the inhabitants are more conscious than they are of the town as a whole."[3]

Schaffer reminds us that community life depends on identity of interest and desire to take part with others in enjoying that interest, and opportunity and enjoyment must be given. This is the essence of sustainability in that it must allow us to flourish as well as be environmental stewards. He concludes: "This cannot be confined to a planner's neighbourhood ring fence; and nobody would contemplate so organizing activity on a strictly geographical basis that a visitor from over the neighbourhood border felt like an interloper."[4]

New Urbanism rightly praises the genius that was Jane Jacobs, specifically her ability to observe how neighborhoods and their public spaces really work. New Urbanism claims her as their own. But how does that square with her vehement criticism of the "neighborhood unit," so central to the tenets of New Urbanism? In short, it does not.

She begins the relevant chapter in *The Death and Life of Great American Cities* by stating:

> It is fashionable to suppose that certain touchstones of the good life will create good neighborhoods—schools, parks, clean housing and the like. How easy life would be if this were so. How charming to control a complicated and ornery society by bestowing upon it rather simple physical goodies.[5]

She alludes to the demise of Main Street implicit in the Perry diagram too, pointing out the complete difference between that and the consolidated community facilities for a planned neighborhood, pointing out that with a Main Street model people keep crossing and recrossing from within and outside the neighborhood itself. She wisely advises, "we must first of all drop any ideal of neighborhoods as self contained or introverted units."[6]

This is an explicit condemnation of the Clarence Perry "neighborhood unit" and all that attends it. It is not a condemnation of neighborhoods as a crucial element of urban life. She reminds us that the vast majority of citizens care about the atmosphere of the streets and districts where they live, regardless of the choices beyond it. Neighborhoods are indeed crucial to the success of the everyday lives they lead. New Urbanism is right to remind us of that, but not Perry's interpretation.

Neighborhoods in New Urbanism

I speculate that as New Urbanism took on the bold, brave, and essential challenge of defeating suburban sprawl, the Neighborhood Unit did indeed rein in that amorphous mess after a fashion. It certainly allowed New Urbanism to major on walkable catchments and that is crucial. But you don't need Perry to do that. As Andrés Duany rightly points out in the brilliant compendium that is *The New Civic Art*, "Perry's diagram begins to break down the capillary network of thoroughfares into super blocks. *This represents the beginning of suburban sprawl*"[7] [emphasis added].

Yet it appears in the recently published and again remarkable Smart Growth Manual asserting that the Perry Neighbourhood Unit "clarified standards that have existed as long as humans have built cities."[8] Perry may indeed have understood the average walking distance, basing social and mixed uses around that metric, but it was not his real motivation. To isolate, truncate, and separate was—and these are most definitely *not* the standards that have existed as long as humans have built cities, quite the reverse.

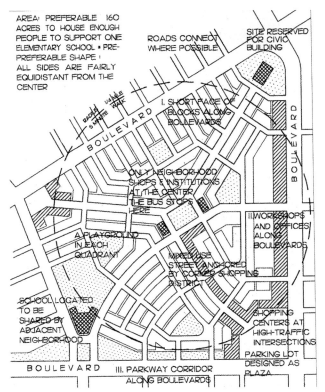

AREA: PREFERABLE 160 ACRES TO HOUSE ENOUGH PEOPLE TO SUPPORT ONE ELEMENTARY SCHOOL • PREFERABLE SHAPE : ALL SIDES ARE FAIRLY EQUIDISTANT FROM THE CENTER

ROADS CONNECT WHERE POSSIBLE

SITE RESERVED FOR CIVIC BUILDING

RADIUS - ¼ MILE VANNE 5 MINUTE WALK

BOULEVARD

BOULEVARD

I. SHORT FACE OF BLOCKS ALONG BOULEVARDS

ONLY NEIGHBORHOOD SHOPS & INSTITUTIONS AT THE CENTER THE BUS STOPS HERE

A PLAYGROUND IN EACH QUADRANT

II.WORKSHOPS AND OFFICES ALONG BOULEVARDS

MIXED USE STREET ANCHORED BY CORNER SHOPPING DISTRICT

SCHOOL LOCATED TO BE SHARED BY ADJACENT NEIGHBORHOOD

SHOPPING CENTERS AT HIGH-TRAFFIC INTERSECTIONS

PARKING LOT DESIGNED AS PLAZA

BOULEVARD   III. PARKWAY CORRIDOR ALONG BOULEVARDS

FIG. 3 "Diagram of an Urban Neighborhood," Congress for the New Urbanism, 1996.

To have a five- or six-minute walk from every home to daily needs results in a radius of roughly 400 yards. It is not an exact science but it is a very valuable anthropomorphic structuring principle. However, that is nothing whatsoever to do with Perry's neighborhood unit and is indeed made worse by giving it a physical edge.

Perry Modified

New Urbanism in several key publications has produced updated versions.

In the Charter of the New Urbanism,[9] implicitly, the peripheral roads are still demoted in the urban fabric, though they are given the designation "boulevard" and, if copied precisely, would be an undoubted improvement from Perry's designation. The urban response to these four "boulevards" varies. But clearly they are still regarded as a problem and remain to all intents and purposes arterials. There is an implied green buffer on one of them, almost half a mile of workshops and offices along another (for every neighborhood?), and the short face of residential blocks along a third. A classic sprawl shopping center sits at one corner, hardly the stuff of boulevards.

An undoubted improvement on Perry appears in the form of a reinstated Main Street but in a place where you would never ever find one in genuine urbanism. It is located there purely because of the assumption that all neighborhoods have to be surrounded by roads that are too heavily trafficked and pedestrian unfriendly.

What kind of urbanism is being promoted here if that is the condition surrounding every new neighborhood in our twenty-first-century vision of the good life? And why must we have "only neighbourhood shops and institutions at the centre"? In this regard it is identical to the apartheid proposed by Perry.

Around the periphery the diagram tells us "roads connect where possible." We saw exactly the same in the UK's New Towns. The traffic engineers simply said fine, it's not possible, and we walked away because we only cared about the local scale and willingly abandoned the citywide. It is as crucial to connect between neighborhoods as it is to connect

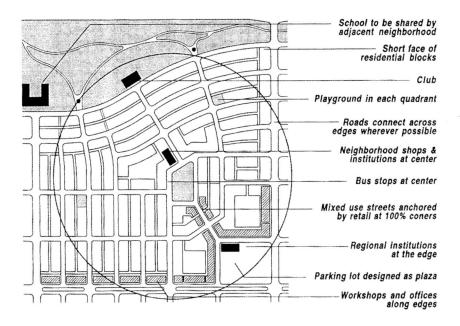

FIG. 4. From Duany, Plater-Zyberk, Alminana, 2003. *The New Civic Art: Elements of Town Planning.*

School to be shared by adjacent neighborhood

Short face of residential blocks

Club

Playground in each quadrant

Roads connect across edges wherever possible

Neighborhood shops & institutions at center

Bus stops at center

Mixed use streets anchored by retail at 100% coners

Regional institutions at the edge

Parking lot designed as plaza

Workshops and offices along edges

within them. How ridiculous to suggest otherwise. These modified diagrams pay lip service to getting that back.

This diagram is further modified in *The New Civic Art*.[10] Little has changed but space. Extensive facilities like schools have been placed on the periphery because of their size and because they are shared by an adjacent neighborhood, despite the totally implied lack of connectivity between the two. The internal permeability is undoubtedly improved but the connection from global to local toward the neighborhood center is far less direct and logical than its predecessor, guaranteeing yet more isolation.

Perry Goes "Green"

Sustainable Urbanism: Urban Design with Nature[11] is to be commended as essential reading for us all. Alas, when I come to the section on the neighborhood, I despair. Perry is taken as gospel and all the dangers to collective urbanism previously described are there to see. What the adoption of the inward looking Neighbourhood Unit allows here is the "greening" on at least three sides of every neighborhood, presumably ad infinitum!

Boulevards have become either Stormwater Boulevards, Transit Corridors, or Green Infrastructure Corridors. None of these global integrators are seemingly civilized enough to be local Main Streets. Yet a school is placed at the junction of four of them, focusing on an "energy efficient traffic circle"!

The transit corridor is to be welcomed, of course, and car-free multifamily dwellings front it. So again, why is this not the Main Street at the core of the neighborhood? The simplest of research as to where transit runs in great cities the world over reveals light rail and street cars running along the mixed use main streets of both city centers and peripheral neighborhood centers as a default condition wherever possible.

Light rail, of course, needs the greatest density possible to succeed, and yet New Urbanism constantly instructs new initiates to have a density decrease from center to edge. So presumably density is *decreasing* toward the school, the edge retail, and the transit? All the Perry modified diagrams fall into that density gradient trap because they have taken the center from where it logically wants to be and placed it "off pitch."

We then call them boulevards to somehow smooth over the cracks, thereby demanding the edges are the densest. In fact, there is a density *increase* from center to edge—confusion and contradiction reigns.

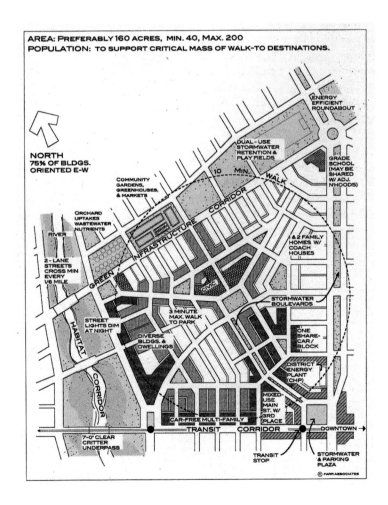

FIG. 5 "A Sustainable Neighborhood Unit," from Farr, *Sustainable Urbanism: Urban Design with Nature*.

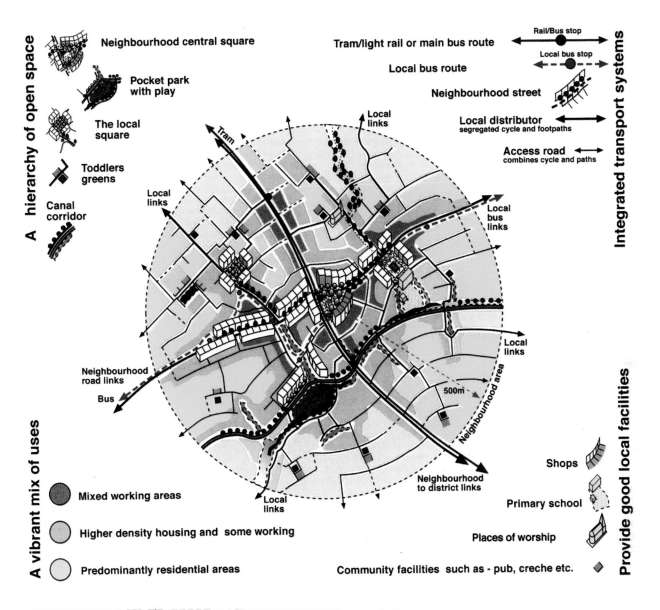

A hierarchy of open space

- Neighbourhood central square
- Pocket park with play
- The local square
- Toddlers greens
- Canal corridor

Integrated transport systems

- Rail/Bus stop
- Tram/light rail or main bus route
- Local bus stop
- Local bus route
- Neighbourhood street
- Local distributor
  segregated cycle and footpaths
- Access road
  combines cycle and paths

Tram

Local links

Local links

Local bus links

Local links

Local links

Neighbourhood road links

Bus

500m

Neighbourhood area

Local links

Neighbourhood to district links

A vibrant mix of uses

- Mixed working areas
- Higher density housing and some working
- Predominantly residential areas

Provide good local facilities

- Shops
- Primary school
- Places of worship
- Community facilities such as - pub, creche etc.

FIG. 6 The key components of a mixed-use urban neighborhood, from "Towards an Urban Renaissance," issued by the United Kingdom Urban Task Force in 1999.

FIG. 7 Diagram showing the sustainable growth of Harlow North, from Ropemaker Properties Ltd.

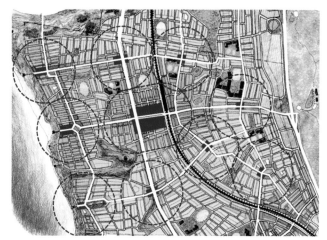

FIG. 8 "Jindalee Enquiry by Design," Western Australia Planning Commission, 1996.

True Urbanism

We all need diagrams that are rationalizations of complex issues to explain our positions, and there are others that exist in the New Urbanist lexicon but with nothing like the same exposure as the Perry series. The fundamental opponent to Perry and its derivatives respects and supports the walkable catchment. The distinction is fundamental to an urbanism that maximizes exchange. The neighborhoods focus on the main thoroughfares.

In the UK, the government has chosen to use this opposing model as the default, calling it "a mixed use integrated urban neighbourhood" (quite succinct for the British government!).[12]

In Australia it is called "a liveable neighbourhood."

These are not mere modifications to Perry, they are fundamentally and wholly different for the neighborhood itself and the wider urban structure. In the USA, it is called the "Australian model" for some utterly perverse reason. Put simply, it is Main Street, be it in the bustling city center or the quieter village or neighborhood. It is the diagram that simply explains urbanism for centuries.

If arterials have to exist in our new sustainable world (and why do they?), then they must be accommodated. That is wholly different from assuming and indeed proposing them on all sides of every neighborhood. If they are already in place, then let us make that point clear and attempt to fix them but not have as a *preferred option* in the creation of greenfield New Urbanism.

I take some comfort that in the last few years some New Urbanist practice in the USA eschews the "Neighbourhood Unit." If that is to continue, I welcome it. But we must stop promoting the 1929 "Neighbourhood Unit" and its variants in our publications. It is the antithesis of what we claim to believe.

WHY SUSTAINABLE NEIGHBORHOODS?

HARRISON FRAKER

Over the past forty years, since the first Earth Day in 1970 and the subsequent oil embargo in 1973, important work has focused on energy conservation in buildings. The research and development conducted on "super insulation," air infiltration, passive solar energy, shading, natural ventilation, daylighting, and energy-efficient lighting and appliances forms a solid foundation on which we now confront the challenges of climate change. Study after study has shown that when these strategies are designed and deployed wisely, they can save from 40 to 60 percent of energy consumption in typically constructed buildings. Indeed, these strategies constitute the first and most cost effective means of combating climate change.

Recent developments in technology have achieved even greater efficiencies in the area of lighting with LED, and in "smart buildings" with wireless lighting controls, occupancy sensors, and real time HVAC management systems. Materials research at the nano-technology scale and manufacturing breakthroughs in photovoltaic (PV) production are on the verge of making the wide-spread application of PVs on buildings cost effective. Even now, with limited tax subsidies and innovative third-party financing, PVs are cost effective in some markets (see California). With this trajectory in technical development, the idea of designing "zero carbon" buildings is a tantalizing goal for the not so distant future, especially given the well-known fact that buildings account for somewhere between 30 and 40 percent of our energy consumption.

Yet buildings have their challenges in achieving "zero carbon" operation. They are relatively small in scale, especially their individual flows of energy, water, and waste. They are further constrained by the particulars of their site and climate, and limited by their program of operation, which determines the size and timing of their energy demand. Furthermore, when considered as stand-alone design problems, important external energy flows on which they depend are not included in the problem solving. In some cases, these energy flows can be as large as the building energy consumption itself. The transportation energy (and CO_2 emissions) to get to them, the additional energy required to respond to the micro-climate effects ("heat island") of their material properties and required parking areas, and the energy required to build and operate the infrastructure (streets, water, sewer, power lines, etc.) are left out of the equation. From this perspective, while buildings remain the single biggest component in achieving a "zero carbon" future, there are larger system concerns that suggest that opportunities for creating sustainability need to be examined at a larger scale than just the building.

On the opposite end of the spectrum, sustainability is being pursued by the large-scale deployment of renewables in locations most favorable for capturing the natural resource: large wind farms in locations of high average annual wind speeds, large solar arrays in areas of high annual hourly solar radiation, and geothermal closest to geothermal sources. These large renewable strategies of energy supply are a natural for utilities because in many ways they are just another form of power plant. They are also similar in concept to hydroelectric generation, with which utilities have experience all over the world. However, they share some of the same problems of distribution. In many cases they are located at considerable distance from areas of demand, requiring significant investment in a new distribution system of power lines, relay stations, and new storage capacity because of the intermittency of supply. The challenges of capital cost, re-engineering the grid to accommodate the intermittency, and especially the approvals necessary to find an appropriate route for new power lines, not to mention their significant line losses, give reasons for pause. The location of large-scale renewables on remote sites may not be the most advantageous strategy or the right scale.

With the challenges of achieving sustainability and "zero carbon" operations at the relatively small building scale and the difficulties of deploying large-scale renewables in remote locations, neighborhoods (or intermediate to large-scale mixed-use development projects) offer intriguing advantages and opportunities. First, neighborhoods have a mix of uses, which makes it easier to balance loads and match the intermittent supply of renewables. Second, neighborhoods have larger flows of energy, water, and waste with which to work. Third, their design can influence transportation choices and reduce automobile use. Fourth, when designing at the neighborhood scale, the urban landscape can be brought into play to temper the climate, absorb carbon, clean stormwater and sewer effluent, provide biomass for energy, and even grow food. In these many ways, the neighborhood landscape becomes the "fifth infrastructure," beyond transportation, energy, water, and waste, because of all the ecological functions it performs. These flows, together with the urban landscape, create the opportunity for a more integrated whole-systems design approach to carbon reduction. If all of the energy can be generated locally and much of the waste processed on site, a further benefit of the neighborhood scale is that the cost and loss of efficiency in distribution infrastructure and transport can be avoided. Finally, neighborhood-scale development (from 1,000 to 10,000 units of housing) is a relatively typical form of development, both for private real estate developers and for cities doing urban renewal on underused or "brownfield" industrial sites all over the world. If neighborhoods can become their own micro-utility, supplying most, if not all, of their energy while treating and recycling their water and waste, there emerges a whole new form of sustainable development that is scaleable.

The case for sustainability at the neighborhood scale was first revealed to me in 2006 while conducting a graduate, interdisciplinary studio on transit-oriented neighborhoods for Tianjin, China. The Tianjin Urban Planning and Design Institute had asked students and faculty from the College of Environmental Design at UC Berkeley to develop principles and prototypes for transit-oriented development (TOD) on three sites along a new light rail system (LRT). Horrified by the chaos at many traffic intersections, caused by turning conflicts between the large number of pedestrians and bikes with cars, buses, and trucks, the students came up with an innovative street pattern at one of the sites to alleviate conflicts. They proposed a typical hierarchy of streets in the east-west direction, but in the north-south direction they alternated streets for vehicles with streets for pedestrians and bikes. The "tartan" grid of pedestrian/bike ways led to a system of interconnected parks created by preserving the landscape parade grounds of the military site. With its mature trees, the parks then provided landscaped pathways leading to the LRT stations. Neighborhood commercial, educational, and community facilities were located along the major routes to the stations. Because highest density housing and commercial office space was located within a five- to ten-minute walk of the stations, 70 percent of the 80,000 residents were located within a five- to ten-minute walk of public transit, and the rest within a seven-minute bike ride. By privileging pedestrian and bike access to public transit, not only was the innovative circulation system projected to reduce the need for daily car trips but the convenience of the land-use pattern was projected to reduce the total number of all trips. The overall scheme was projected to reduce the growth in CO_2 emissions from the use of new car ownership by as much as 60 percent.

In fulfilling the primary purpose of the studio by developing principles and prototypes for TOD, the students and faculty reduced a major contributor to CO_2 emission in the transportation sector. In an effort to achieve even further CO_2 reductions, they became fascinated with the idea of testing whether such a high-density neighborhood could also become resource self-sufficient or as close as possible to carbon neutral in its other operations. Could it generate all its own power, process its own waste, and recycle and reuse its water?

The effort to answer the question began with the fundamentals of conservation. Improved wall insulation and glazing, higher standards of air infiltration, and higher-efficiency lighting and appliances were proposed and modeled. These measures, combined with a modest passive solar direct gain system, reduced the heating load by 80 percent, and, appropriate shading and natural ventilation almost entirely eliminated the air conditioning load for the Tianjin climate (which is similar to Boston). The question became whether on site renewables could do the rest.

By deploying average-efficiency (15 percent) photovoltaic panels, equivalent to approximately 10 percent of the residential floor area (i.e., 10 square meters for a 100-square-meter unit), either as shading devices on the tall buildings or on the roofs of the surrounding four-to-six-story buildings, and by putting intermediate sized vertical axis wind machines (totaling 2 megawatts) on the tall buildings, it was discovered that these renewables could deliver approximately 70 to 80 percent of the remaining electric load. This left the waste streams as the last potential resource to close the gap of 20 to 30 percent in electric demand. Not knowing the research and development on waste-to-energy systems, the team had to explore unfamiliar territory to identify appropriate systems. Two potential systems were identified. One involved burning combustible garbage and wood chips to power an electric generator. The other involved converting the biomass in organic garbage, sludge, and green waste into biogas using an anaerobic digester and then powering a gas-fired electric generator. The latter was chosen as having the lowest CO_2 emissions and other air-pollution problems. Surprisingly, using conversion efficiency factors from the literature, calculations revealed that the potential energy in the neighborhood waste streams was capable of closing the 20 to 30 percent gap in electric load.

The discovery that a high-density, mixed-use, urban neighborhood in China could be close to zero carbon in its operation, using energy from its local climate, landscape, and waste flows, caught the imagination and funding from the Gordon and Betty Moore Foundation. As Gordon Moore commented, "If this works, it could transform how China builds." It has led to a four-year effort to develop and build a prototype, called the "EcoBlock," in both China and the Bay Area. The process is ongoing and has involved the collaboration between faculty and students at CED with Arup, Siemens, Cisco, additional foundations and multiple local design consultants, city planning agencies, utilities, and developers. Although the reasons are complex, not the least of which is the recent financial crisis, a prototype is yet to be built.

In the process of working on the "EcoBlock," a search was conducted to find any precedents for a similar whole-systems approach to neighborhood design and to discover if any performance data had been collected and reported. Not surprisingly, very few have been built and even fewer have collected performance data. Between eight and ten neighborhoods were identified as having aggressive goals for approaching "zero carbon" operation, integrated with goals for creating a high-quality built environment. Among those, in Sweden Bo01 in Malmö and Hammarby in Stockholm, and, in Germany, Kronsberg in Hannover and Vauban in Freiberg emerged as being the most instructive.

These neighborhoods fulfill basic criteria for sustainable design: 1) each is transit-oriented with an emphasis on walking and biking and convenient access to public transit (within five minutes), and 50 to 80 percent of all daily trips are by pedestrian, bike, or public transit; 2) all have aggressive conservation goals of approximately 100 kWh/m2-year for total energy use; 3) all employ local renewable energy strategies; 4) all are mixed use with a jobs-to-housing balance of at least 50 percent; 5) all have a net density of approximately thirty to forty units per acre and range in size from 1,200 to 8,000 housing units.

Beyond meeting basic sustainability criteria, the four neighborhoods together demonstrate the four possible strategies for generating energy from local renewable sources—wind, solar, geothermal, and waste—each with a different emphasis and combination. Bo01 uses local wind generation to power a geothermal ground and ocean water heat pump for heating and cooling. Hammarby has three different waste-to-energy systems: the first burns combustible garbage to power a local district heating and electric cogeneration plant, the second recovers heat from the sewage treatment system, and the third converts sludge to biogas for cooking (1,000 units) and to power local buses. Kronsberg has two large-scale wind machines (totaling 3.2 megawatts) which generate 50 percent of the electricity combined with a gas-fired heating and electric cogeneration plant, which provides the other 50 percent. Vauban has a local heating and electric cogeneration plant powered by waste wood chips from the city. It also has a section that demonstrates the most successful solar strategies, combining a model passive solar direct gain system for heating and a rooftop photovoltaic array for electricity, delivering more than 15 percent energy back to the city.

While all four neighborhoods demonstrate good energy conservation standards (see above), Kronsberg and Vauban have sections which meet the very aggressive "passive house" standard of 15 kWh/m2-year for heating. Together, the neighborhoods have employed all types of solar collection. Bo01 uses evacuated tube collectors to assist the district heating system. Hammarby uses flat plate panels and evacuated tubes to preheat domestic hot water. As a test case, Kronsberg combines a large solar hot water array with a large seasonal storage tank in order to capture summer solar energy to augment winter solar heating. All four neighborhoods have applied photovoltaic arrays to buildings. Hammarby has

vertical arrays on south-facing walls and Kronsberg on rooftops, primarily for demonstration purposes. Bo01 also has PVs for demonstration, while Vauban has a more aggressive deployment of PVs on the roofs of residential units and on large parking structures. All four neighborhoods have well-developed systems for solid waste collection, with Bo01 and Hammarby using an evacuated tube system. In addition, all four have developed on-site stormwater management systems that create significant landscape design features. On the other hand, none have employed local sewage treatment systems and recycling. Each relies entirely on the cities' central facilities for sewage treatment and on the cities' supply of potable water.

Of course, innovative strategies for sustainable neighborhoods do not occur on their own. By necessity they are the result of a development process. In these cases, the development process is shown to be as important in achieving the goals of sustainability as the logic, elegance, and cost effectiveness of any technical systems. All four projects offer important lessons to be learned about steps and dimensions of the development process which enabled the projects to achieve most of their sustainability goals.

These neighborhoods convincingly illustrate that zero carbon operation is achievable at the neighborhood scale. They also show that it is not just a matter of finding and applying the "right" technical systems and following the "right" development process, as important as these may be. It involves thinking of technical strategies and urban design as one, creating a high-quality built environment that fosters a vibrant experience. After all, no one wants to live inside a sustainability system diagram, where technical demands dominate. Such a system would reduce life to counting kilowatt hours. The challenge for designers is to learn how sustainability strategies can enhance the quality of the built environment and deepen the experience of peoples' everyday lives. How do concepts of urban design—the design of the streets, blocks, parks, and urban landscape—interact with strategies for sustainability? Are there conflicts? What, if any, trade-offs have been made?

On one level, the urban design, the principles of urban form for all four neighborhoods are similar. They assume a traditional plan of streets and blocks. Each plan is then modified to take advantage of the particular conditions of the site and landscape, including such features as lakes, shorelines, hills, orientation for sun and wind, and views. Different open space strategies for parks, recreation areas, courtyards, plazas, and urban landscape functions further enrich the form of each neighborhood. While quite traditional as an urban design framework, the subtle responses in the design of the blocks, the architecture, the streets, and especially of the urban landscape are where the neighborhoods come alive, suggesting further design strategies for sustainability.

Unknowingly, the "EcoBlock" concept advances the implications of these first-generation sustainable neighborhoods by integrating the urban landscape more completely into the whole-system operation. The landscape cleans sewage effluent using a "living machine" system, after the sludge has been removed and sent to the anaerobic digester. The area necessary to treat the effluent is easily accomplished within each block design. This enables the treated water to be collected and recycled at the block scale, eliminating the need for sewer lines and reducing the length of water supply lines. An extensive tree planting design strategy yields wood chips, which, along with other landscape clippings, adds fuel to the combustible solid-waste-to-energy system. The remaining waste from landscape planting and urban agriculture add to the supply of organic waste for the anaerobic digester. Thus the urban landscape becomes the cleaner of sewage effluent, local food for residents, and fuel for the energy systems, along with tempering the climate and cleaning and retaining stormwater, all while enhancing the experience of the public realm. The urban landscape helps to make up the difference in achieving zero carbon operation, which the buildings can not accomplish alone.

Ultimately, as Randall Thomas wrote, "sustainability is about poetry, optimism and delight. Energy, CO2, water and waste (while extremely important) are secondary. The unquantifiable is at least as important as the quantifiable; as Louis Kahn said, 'the measurable is only a servant of the unmeasurable' and ideally the two should be developed together."

Too often, however, urban design imperatives have been an excuse to ignore the empirical dimensions of sustainability. On the other hand, especially with the growing urgency of climate change, the empirical demands of sustainability can become ends in themselves, a moral imperative at the expense of design poetics. For "sustainability" to be sustainable, urban design must find a way to bring these two ways of thinking and making together into a compelling whole. The four case study neighborhoods and the "EcoBlock" designs described above indicate that a greater integration of waste systems and the urban landscape are the last pieces in the puzzle, the final secrets to achieving "zero carbon" operation. And the neighborhood is the scale that brings them into play. The challenge is to turn the whole into what Elizabeth Meyer has called "sustaining beauty."

LANDSCAPE URBANISM VS. LANDSCAPE DESIGN

THORBJÖRN ANDERSSON

The famous Nolli map, engraved in 1748, shows the public spaces of Rome as an accessible, structuring, open, and elaborate network giving shape to the city. Buildings exist as in-betweens in this web of public space and are depicted as closed, singular, and seemingly impenetrable. Public space is rendered light and transparent, buildings are black and solid. Urban life gets its definition by public space, but also by its counterpart, which is private life.

Planning or Design?

Since some ten years ago, the concept of *landscape urbanism* has caused discussion in the world of landscape architecture. As many emerging ideologies, it is the fruit of parallel and coinciding thinking among scholars and practicing landscape architects. As a term, "landscape urbanism" was coined by Charles Waldheim, presently chair at the Department of Landscape Architecture in the Graduate School of Design, at Harvard University. Others who have cooperated to form the concept are Alex Krieger and Mohsen Mostafavi of the same school, and James Corner, of the University of Pennsylvania.

More so in the United States than in Europe, there is great debate about landscape urbanism, which at times draws a dividing line between who is for and who is against. From the critical side, the arguments basically touch on three issues: (1) landscape urbanism contains little new thinking and is more a tuned-up version of the McHargian concepts from the 1970s; (2) landscape urbanism is hard to define and is more a brand than content; and (3) the breakthrough of landscape urbanism threatens to overtake the field from landscape design, especially at a classic design school such as the GSD at Harvard.

In Europe, the theory and thinking as well as the turmoil around landscape urbanism has not been as fraught as in the United States. Here, landscape architects have always been deeply involved in planning issues, much more than in the market-oriented United States. There has also been a clear tendency for quite some time for many European landscape architects to engage themselves professionally in a contextual understanding, in planning issues, and in urban politics and strategies instead of just on-site design. An influential office such as the Rotterdam-based West 8 has already for many years redirected their efforts toward urban design rather than the design of singular places. Clients have also adopted the tendency to move toward urban design, and today international competitions often deal with the reorganization of urban environments. A fairly recent example is the Toronto waterfront, a competition won by West 8, which aimed to restore former industrial land, arbitrarily laid out and now derelict, to meaningful content and intentional and new spatial relations.

A Short Academic Tradition

Landscape architecture has a relatively short history. In the public landscape, the professional field is no older than two hundred years. At the end of the eighteenth century, the first public park in Europe, Munich's Englischer Garten, was opened. Education within the field is, for the most part, equally without longstanding traditions. In my own country, Sweden, it was not until the 1960s when an educational program in landscape architecture with formal academic status was launched, and many countries still do not have such an academic program. Others introduced theirs fairly late, including countries with otherwise long cultural traditions, such as Italy, Spain, and Portugal. Switzerland, a country producing contemporary landscape architecture at a high level, has a school that offers a degree but not a master's program. Until only a decade ago, French landscape architects were referred to as *paysagistes*, without the suffix defining them as architects. In Africa, there are no such academic programs at all. In currently exploding China there are several, but their curriculum is hard to evaluate after European standards. And in Latin America there is still a lack of stability in the few programs that exist.

Olmsted and Green Urbanism

The oldest school for landscape architecture, at Harvard University, was founded well over one hundred years ago. An influential professor there during the early years was Frederick Law Olmsted Jr. His father, as we know, was the first to adopt the professional title *landscape architect* in his practice. Olmsted Sr.'s main contribution was twofold. First, he did considerable work to preserve the Yosemite Valley. The second contribution was to establish linked public spaces in American cities, resulting in contextual urban sequences that structured the cities and created green environs accessible for city dwellers, with Boston's so-called Emerald Necklace probably the most well-known example. When visiting Olmsted's work in, for instance, Boston, Rochester, and Buffalo, it becomes clear that it is the structure that forms the main quality. As design, the Olmsted parks are less significant and seemingly follow a formula, albeit one of trees, meadows, views, and water that has seldom proved wrong in landscape architecture. In the design, Olmsted seems to have relied on his partner, the Englishman Calvert Vaux. This is probably the case in other important work, such as New York's Central Park. In that sense, Olmsted himself can be said to have been more skilled in urban planning than in landscape design. This notion is important because from here we can already trace a centennial-long, and not always unproblematic, relationship between planning and design.

Postwar Planning: Ian McHarg and Restriction Planning

In spite of the fairly short tradition, the profession has gone through violent swings in search for a definition that is still hard to be exact about. During my own school days, landscape architecture was primarily a planning profession. As these were the last shivering days of modernism, and modernism was problem-oriented, our point of departure was to deliver solutions rather than coming up with ideas. Landscape architects at that time worked with functions rather than with aesthetic values. In the postwar years, Western Europe and the United States laid the foundation for their prosperous economies and steadily increased their living standard through the phenomena of consumerism. Natural resources were exploited in a ravenous way, without either knowledge or consideration to the sensitive natural balances that form the premise for the existence of life on earth.

This provoked many landscape architects, who took a political stand against the heavy exploitation of the landscape that we saw in the forests of Scandinavia, in the industrial Ruhr region in Germany, and in the fringes of American cities, where urban sprawl spread seemingly without control. From this political standpoint, landscape architects also became the architects of restriction. The profession more often aimed at saying "no" than "yes," and landscape archi-

tects became preservationists rather than visionaries. Possibly the most influential of landscape architects during these years was Ian McHarg, who realized that in a conflict between exploitation and preservation, exploitation would always win. McHarg's strategy aimed to avoid conflicts instead of going into them. His suggested method of superimposing layers of maps showing singular interests at least acknowledged nature as one factor among many. The overlay technique of maps permitted tracing of conflict-free zones, which was a survival strategy during years when nature and landscape were seen as merely assets for various kinds of industrial use.

While it is partly true that history repeats itself, it has to be added that when a tendency reoccurs in a new context and another era, the consequences and efforts can emerge very differently. Today's breakthrough for landscape urbanism bears resemblances to both Olmsted's green urbanism and Ian McHarg's planning methods. The zeitgeist, however, is quite different. During Olmsted's era, the ongoing industrial revolution caused severe health problems in the densely populated cities, where the workers spent most of their time in dusty, ill-lit factories. Access to the outdoors became a remedy for a population in bad physical shape. Olmsted's green urbanism was thus a matter of survival for mankind. McHarg's "design with nature" was instead a matter of survival for nature. Raw consumerism and galloping technology was a combination that meant a severe threat to ecological systems, which Rachel Carson's book *Silent Spring*, published in 1962, had shown.

The Promise of Landscape Urbanism

Landscape urbanism aims at reversing the modernist planning idiom. At its best, it supplies us with a tool and with arguments for a field that repeatedly has seen its mandate cut into smaller and smaller pieces. Maybe landscape urbanism can be seen as a matter of survival for the cities. The contemporary city seems to be positioned in a deadly crossfire between nostalgic New Urbanism, Koolhaasian Bigness, neo-liberal sprawl, and hardcore late-modernist segregated planning.

Landscape urbanism has a long trajectory, touching on Green Urbanism from the 1880s as well as the restriction planning in the 1970s, but today is heavily needed as an ideological input in order to reverse common interest from private to public. To me, landscape urbanism means taking public spaces as a point of departure instead of as building blocks. Landscape urbanism also means using landscape methods, including a process-oriented strategy, in urban design. And finally, landscape urbanism means reversing traditional planning ideology, which arranges buildings in urban patterns, leaving more or less arbitrary in-betweens, and instead considering open spaces as primary qualities, just like the Nolli map showed 250 years ago.

The goal of landscape urbanism, however, is to give enough space to the field of design. Landscape urbanism must not get blinded by its own ambition and should also acknowledge the potential of design. Rather, it must eliminate the prejudice that everything small belongs to design and that everything big belongs to planning. With such insights we could come to the conclusion that landscape urbanism may well include, or even be, design. Finally, my personal concern about landscape urbanism: by adopting it we must also be aware that by definition it leaves rural areas and nature outside our circle of interest. Nature, however, needs design, and also planning.

DESIGN IN THE NON-FORMAL CITY

INSIGHTS FROM LATIN AMERICA

CHRISTIAN WERTHMANN

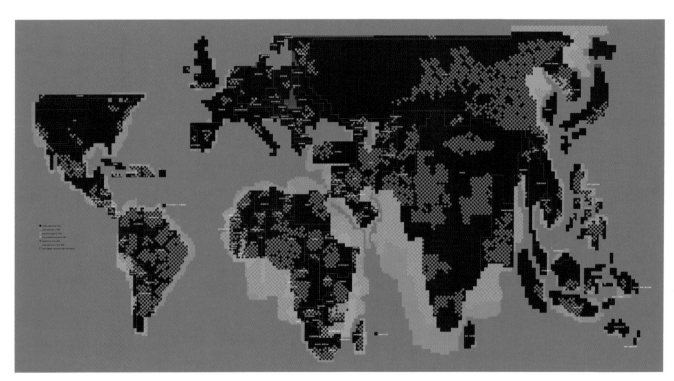

FIG. I This world map was created for the exhibition "Dirty Work: Transforming Landscape in the Non-formal Cities of the Americas" at the Harvard Graduate School of Design curated by Christian Werthmann and John Beardsley. The map is based on UN-habitat tabulations for global slum-households. Each square represents 250,000 residents. The squares are arranged by continent and country shape and do not reflect landmass, but population. Orange squares are slum households as of 2000. Light orange squares are projected slum households in 2020. Black squares are residents living in formal areas.

I recently asked a mother of two from Rocinha, one of the largest favelas of Rio de Janeiro, what her biggest problems are. It was not the lack of money, not the violence or flooding of the favela. It was noise; the constant din from neighboring houses and apartments, young kids partying well into the night, with their stereos on full blast, or couples arguing. Given the levels of violence and crime in Rio's favelas, it seemed to me at first like an unusual answer. An anthropologist who had lived in Rocinha for a year and a half was, however, not surprised by this proclamation.[1] He confirmed the great discrepancies between the problems favela residents themselves cite and the problems the outside world believes a favela would likely have. While outside parties generally view the favelas of Rio as dangerous, overcrowded, and unsanitary, the favela-dweller might see the favela as a fairly safe and inexpensive housing alternative with some inconveniences, such as noise; the biggest fear is police raids and gang wars, ending in deadly shootouts killing innocent bystanders. But still, most favela-dwellers in Rio are disinclined to move out. It is more the outside world that seems disruptive, with many favela-dwellers becoming nervous about turning into a victim of a crime themselves only when leaving the relative safety of their favela and venturing into areas of the so-called formal city, like world-famous areas such as the Copacabana.

What the Informal City Really Needs

This inverse condition of perception is just one of the many complex issues of informal cities. While discussion and efforts have increased in the last two decades to improve informal cities, all participants involved in non-formal city upgrading projects have had to encounter and contend with these perceptive fissures, not always with success. This is not an insignificant issue. When we as designers want to be involved in the improvement of the living condition of the one billion slum-dwellers on this planet, we ought to know which parts of this condition really need improvement. Obviously no general recipe can be found for the condition of one billion, as the informal city comes in as many variations as the formal city. There are massive differences between countries; even in each city every informal area has its own history, its own set of problems, its own legal framework, its own specific physical and ecological conditions and population composition. One of the few recurring lessons of upgrading projects all over the planet is that each informal settlement is unique; what works in one area does not necessarily work in the other. This uniqueness is actually quite familiar to designers who are trained to develop specific solutions for specific situations. So while we designers, accustomed to design by problem-solving, are well-equipped to work within the myriad permutations of settings in theory, we are nevertheless still in the initial stages of identifying optimal approaches for our involvement in reality and have not been able to fully judge the effects and limits of our interventions over longer periods of time. We are, however, able to postulate a few preliminary generalizations and to identify a handful of common mistakes to be avoided. Before I outline future challenges for our engagement with the informal city, I would like to discuss a few additional common misconceptions surrounding the topic. Here I relate my comments mostly to the Latin American context and the condition of non-formal cities in Brazil in particular.

Exclusion

There is the commonly held view that favela-dwellers are treated as second-class citizens, excluded from the services of the city, excluded from jobs and education. While partly true, this argument is not so simple. All residents of the so-called formal city are excluded from entering Rio's favelas. Unless they are in company with somebody well-connected to the favela, they will likely be expelled by druglords nervous about spies and the police. Most residents of formal Brazilian cities have actually never set foot in a favela. The accessible territory of the city shrinks even more for upper-class Brazilians. Many high-income Brazilians decide to live in heavily gated communities, drive in armored vehicles, and are reluctant to enter public space even in the formal parts of the city. Despite their wealth (or because of it) they are in fact excluded from large parts of the city. Exclusion is neither unilateral nor involuntary.

Urban Poverty

There is also a common perception that all the poor residents of the city live in the non-formal sections of the city. This does not prove true either. When talking about urban poverty one has to look at the whole city—formal as well as non-formal. Not all the residents living in favelas are the nation's poorest; often some of the poorest live well within the formal city. Some urban researchers point out that living conditions and poverty in overcrowded tenement housing (*cortiços*) in the formal city are worse than those of a favela, and get much less attention by both the media and the academy.[2] For example, there is a large population in São Paulo living as renters in moldy apartments, often housing fifteen to twenty people within 300 square feet. Toilets are broken and running water is dirty, that is if it runs at all. In contrast, the residents of the many favelas in Brazil own their homes by default and have basic infrastructure (public authorities have largely abstained from slum clearance policies in the recent past).

Informal versus Formal

The divisions between the formal and informal city are not as clear as one might think, and they blur yet more when one considers that a large, illegally built portion of Latin American cities was, in fact, planned by the private sector. It is a quite common procedure for developers to illegally occupy land, divide it into parcels, and sell it at a low cost to families who could never afford to buy a house or rent a decent apartment in the formal city. Once families have built their own houses, they still lack basic services as they find themselves in an official "no build" zone. After making themselves heard by the authorities, these areas are often retrofitted with electricity, water, sewage, and roads by the municipality (something that the developers actually count on). For example, from the estimated four million favela dwellers living in the São Paulo metropolitan area, approximately two million live within irregular subdivisions (*loteamentos irregulars* or *clandestinos*). The widespread appearance of these irregular subdivisions has led some researchers to claim that municipalities are quietly complicit in the procedure. By knowing that they cannot provide housing for all low-income citizens, they see irregular subdivisions as a better alternative than completely unplanned urbanization (these irregular subdivisions have at least some type of urban order that can be more easily retrofitted and integrated than the irregular layout of informal urbanization).[3] In the end, many Latin American cities consist of a patchwork of legal, semi-legal, and illegal developments. What might look like an informal neighbor-

FIG. 2 Cantinho do Cèu is a 30,000-resident favela on the largest water reservoir in São Paulo. Thirteen Harvard Graduate School of Design students under the direction of Christian Werthmann and Fernando de Mello Franco made proposals for the integration of socio-ecologic infrastructure.

hood may actually be planned by developers and tolerated (if not promoted) by cash-strapped municipalities. On the other hand, what might look like a formal city expansion might actually be the result of an informal process such as political corruption.

Formal = Legal, Informal = Illegal—True?

Given that 32 percent of the urban population in Latin America lives in illegal and semi-legal neighborhoods, one could rightfully claim that the legal framework and its executive branch was worse than ill-prepared for dealing with the massive urban migration of rural populations in the last century, a phenomenon that brought hundreds of thousands of poor people to large cities throughout Latin America as well as across the globe. Subsequently, many Latin American cities are now renegotiating land property rights. Some cities give out land titles, others hundred-year leases, transforming illegal squatters into law-abiding citizens overnight. The old formula that the formal areas of the city are legal and that the informal neighborhoods of the city are illegal cannot be sustained any longer in the face of this human crisis. New terms and land policies must be developed (and many legal reforms have been made in Latin America), but foremost our internal sense of order has to adjust to accepting the legality of squatting in the absence of better solutions.

Bottom-up Versus Top-down

There is a common differentiation between bottom-up and top-down approaches in the developing world. Bottom-up or grassroots approaches by individual designers, NGOs, or religious organizations are dominant in countries that still have slum clearance policies or neglectful and disorganized governments. Sometimes these organizations are the only help residents of the informal city will receive in the absence of state initiatives. Often there is a lack of coordination between the many agencies, making the combined long-term actions of private organizations less effective. In contrast, in countries with in situ upgrading policies, top-down approaches by municipal agencies promise the coordinated large-scale and multisector improvement of non-formal cities. The truly Democratic implementation of large top-down projects, though, has been rare.

Much has been written about the advantages and disadvantages of both approaches, but the general agreement today is that linking top-down to bottom-up appears to be most desirable. This linkage requires some rethinking by designers. In particular, designers dismissive of larger government programs in favor of small-scale approaches should not forget that many of the more successful larger programs such as Favela Bairro in Rio de Janeiro started out with small boutique-sized pilot programs.[4] Favela Bairro can actually be described as an assembly of small projects with the added bonus of being coordinated for the whole city. The genesis of Favela Bairro suggests that the difference between top-down and bottom-up is actually not so big. Rather than following ideology, designers have to insert themselves between bottom-up and top-down approaches, developing processes that can be scaled up or scaled down as necessary to fit to the particular governmental situation.

How to Go from There

As we are entering a phase in human history where half of our future urban growth will be informal, we as designers have to learn to effectively engage; otherwise we have failed as a profession. Even Western designers, who increasingly take part in global practice, will not escape the consequences of informality in their projects in the global South. Are we prepared to deal with informality when 90 percent of our design education concerns itself with the formal city?

Obviously, we have to build a global design culture that acknowledges all parts of the city and not predominantly the formal one. When working in the non-formal sector, it is very important that we understand some of the basic principles I have laid out before: the discrepancy of perception inside and outside of the informal city (since we are on the outside, we

have to learn to understand the inside as much as real understanding is a possibility); the multilateral condition of exclusion (it is not only the poor who are excluded—the whole city suffers); the pervasiveness of poverty throughout the city (disregarding formal and non-formal boundaries); the blurriness of formal and informal city distinctions; the acceptance of squatting as a justifiable act in the face of a global crisis; and the task of designing multi-scalar operations (the mode of implementation is equal in importance to the final built product, as is designing the operations needed for its continuance).

Informal City Upgrading in Latin America

These six observations can be derived from the decade-long experiences of Latin American designers and urban researchers who have engaged the non-formal sector. Great strides have been made during the last twenty years to improve living conditions in non-formal cities. Large upgrading projects have been undertaken by almost all major Latin American cities, most notably Favela Bairro in Rio de Janeiro, the Social Housing Agency in São Paulo (SEHAB), the PRIMED and PUI program in Medellin, and the innovative transportation and barrio upgrading pro-

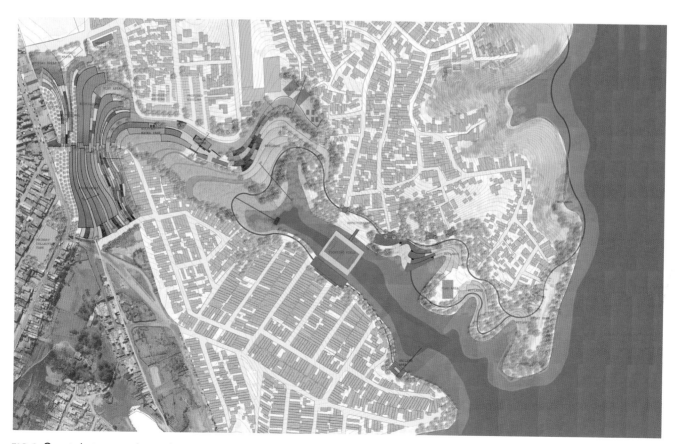

FIG. 3 One student proposed an-onsite sewage treatment plant using alternative methods of constructed wetlands with community agriculture integrated into the final cleaning stages, while recovering the eroded and polluted waterfront of the city. Her proposal combines ecological, economical, and recreational needs of the community while contributing to the recovery of the badly polluted watershed of the reservoir. All proposals were developed with the technical input of environmental engineers.

gram in Bogota. They all share the idea of upgrading the informal city with a minimal amount of displacement. Into the existing urban fabric they insert strategic interventions in the form of basic infrastructure (electricity, potable water, sewage); transportation elements (alleyways, stairs, bicycle paths, pedestrian promenades, streets, roads, bus systems, cable cars); social and educational infrastructure (day care centers, schools, libraries, hospitals, community centers, nurseries); and recreational and cultural infrastructure (parks, plazas, playgrounds , sport fields, sports centers, performance spaces, community gardens, river promenades). In all programs, the goal is the improved integration of informal cities into the city at large and to provide the informal city residents with equal access to social, recreational, and educational services. All programs focus on the creation of high-quality public spaces not only as a platform for the functions of daily life but also as a basic symbol of democracy.

The most successful programs have had a holistic approach with a good balance of physical interventions and social programs. The designers also had to learn about the limits of their physical interventions; while it may be nice for a poor community to be the beneficiary of a beautiful new soccer field, it is does not help much if the majority of the players on the field are illiterate and unemployed. It is certainly lovely when a new playground is erected for toddlers, but it is problematic when there are no day care programs that allow their young mothers to go to work or attend school. The fact that physical interventions have to be paired with targeted social programs makes the improvement of informal cities a multisector enterprise requiring the collaboration of many professions. In addition to designers and builders, cities must engage social workers, anthropologists, community organizers, engineers, lawyers, artists, educators, entrepreneurs, and businessmen, to name a few. The most important collaboration, however, is with the residents of the community. They cannot be treated as passive subjects of investigation, but rather should be treated as equal partners throughout the transformation process.

Crisis versus Opportunity:
Stigmatization, Unemployment, and Ecology

Visitors to informal cities that have undergone an upgrade can see how much has been improved. Where there were once dirt paths, flooded and muddy, there is now pavement and drainage. Residents living in perilous conditions have been resettled to safer areas. Children go to clean schools and have safe places to play. However, success is not universal. Despite the physical and educational improvements, the full acceptance of non-formal cities as natural parts of the larger city remains elusive. In the case of Rio de Janeiro, favela residents are still at a disadvantage when it comes time to finding a proper job.[5] Unemployment is sadly on the rise. Even when favelas have been upgraded, they remain a favela in the larger opinion of the population. The stigma of living in a favela cannot be erased in just ten years; it will take many generations until a once-poor and violent neighborhood is considered safe and sound.

Aside from the problems of continued stigmatization and unemployment, many of the upgrading projects display unduly timid approaches toward a better ecological integration of informal cities. In most cases the wasteful infrastructure systems of the formal city are imported into the non-formal context. In Brazil's large cities sewage is often transported over long distances and exported to other watersheds. Landfills are overflowing, and large agglomerations like São Paulo need to build new power plants in the Brazilian rainforest to keep up with electricity demands. Informal cities are increasingly connected to these large, centralized municipal systems creating new utility loads. One wonders if the informal city, which is characterized by a lack of infrastructure, can spawn a new type of infrastructure that is less wasteful of resources and does not export problems to the metropolis's hinterland. There are precedents such as the historic aquaculture sewage wetlands of Calcutta, the massive composting system initiated by Waste Concern in Dhaka or the agricultural gardens developed by Cidades Sem Fome in São Paulo that indicate a gentler type of infrastructure in poor urban areas. For more than thirty years designers in Europe and increasingly in North America have been developing and integrating decentralized infrastructure systems such as green roofs, stormwater and sewage treatment wetlands, urban farms, and solar applications into dense urban fabrics. Emergent theoretical frameworks such as Ecological Urbanism or Industrial Ecology offer fresh approaches to reading and modifying the modern city, deeply enmeshing cultural and ecological processes. As much as it is important to learn to engage with informal urbanism, for too long the non-formal city been treated as a problem on its own, separated from the formal city. The holistic integration of a more socially, economically, and ecologically beneficial infrastructure into the extremely dense urban fabric and the complicated social conditions of informal cities promises to bridge this gap and is one of the greatest contributions that the European–North American design profession can make to the problem of urban poverty.

PART 6: URBAN THEORY, CITY PLANNING, AND BEYOND

6.1   GLOBALIZATION, LOCAL POLITICS, AND, PLANNING FOR SUSTAINABILITY

SUSAN S. FAINSTEIN

Sustainability, in common discourse, usually refers to maintaining the physical environment for future generations. For example, Mayor Michael Bloomberg's plan for a sustainable New York City (plaNYC 2030) is stated entirely in relation to physical improvements. Goals are proposed in terms of reducing the city's carbon footprint, adding green space, reducing energy demands, etc. Its preamble states:

> Focusing on the five key dimensions of the city's environment—land, air, water, energy, and transportation—we have developed a plan that can become a model for cities in the 21st century. The combined impact of this plan will not only help ensure a higher quality of life for generations of New Yorkers to come; it will also contribute to a 30% reduction in global warming emissions.[1]

The plan makes no mention of the social environment in which this higher quality of life will transpire, nor does it express any intention of affecting social inequality.

Environment and Equity

Defining sustainability narrowly in terms of physical upgrading allows policy makers to avoid the conflicts involved in efforts to improve the social situation of relatively disadvantaged populations and to evade contradictions between environmental and social policy. Environmental improvements can be at odds with demands for equity, since provision of housing and services for low-income households may cause ecological stress.[2] Thus, homeowners often oppose new, high-density development that would accommodate low-income households on the grounds of environmental protection, arguing that increased densities result in loss of green space, destruction of trees, increased runoff, traffic congestion, shadowing of open spaces, etc. While such arguments are frequently rationalizations for excluding the unwanted, they have sufficient validity to indicate that trade-offs do exist between addressing social inequality and upgrading the physical milieu.

Advocates for the poor, nevertheless, have pressed for a definition of sustainability that goes beyond safeguarding the natural environment to include social sustainability, defined by improvements in the quality of life of poor people and minorities. The Brundtland Report, commissioned by the United Nations, is often cited in favor of this interpretation of sustainability; it famously states: "Sustainable development is development that meets the needs of the present without compromising the ability of future generations to meet their own needs."[3] The report's discussion of needs lays particular emphasis on the needs of the world's poor, and it argues that these should be given overriding priority.

The problem with such a broadening is that the term sustainability becomes an empty signifier, referring to anything that the proponent generally favors for whatever reason. David Harvey comments on "the incredible political diversity to which environmental-ecological opinion is prone," listing eight wildly different interpretations of achieving sustainability, ranging from authoritarianism to decentralized communitarianism.[4] He considers that despite its seeming progressivism, the Brundtland Report implies control by Western technocrats over vulnerable populations in developing countries.

An illustration of Harvey's argument concerning the varied political readings of ecological discourse is available in an excellent history of spatial policy in the United Kingdom entitled *Building Sustainable Communities*. Here Mike Raco defines sustainability in terms of labor mobility and absorption, contending that "sustainable communities" should be conceptualized in terms of a social policy that seeks to create competitive places and new forms of citizenship, thereby allowing individuals and communities to "act as both subjects and objects of policy."[5] Sustainability in this interpretation, which picks up on and critiques the British Labour Party's program for sustainable communities, becomes defined in terms of competitiveness and democracy, while physical ecology is not even mentioned. Moreover, since the drive for competitiveness by city governments generally involves subsidies to capital rather than benefits to the less well off, competitive advantage implies nothing about the quality of life of people who live in cities. Even though growth may be a prerequisite for increased social welfare, it does not necessarily produce improvements in well-being. Hence, the introduction of concerns over labor absorption adds yet another contradictory element to the definition of sustainability.

Rather than stretching the term sustainability to capture a vision of the good city, we are on firmer ground by regarding social equity and environmental protection as analytically separate. Improving the physical environment of disadvantaged groups, particularly in regard to reducing environmental hazards in poor neighborhoods and providing them with physical amenities, has usually been classified under the rubric environmental justice. As such, it is a desirable goal and may contribute to sustainability at the micro-scale, but it has relatively little to do with the quest for sustainability on the larger scale relative to reducing carbon dioxide in the atmosphere, developing sources of clean energy, preserving wetlands, etc. Social equity needs to be examined as an aim in itself; that there has been pressure to include it under the rubric of sustainability is primarily, as will be discussed below, a rhetorical ploy.

Globalization, Equity, and Environmental Management

The quest for social equity has become increasingly challenged by globalization, which, by intensifying the connectedness of places, creates both opportunities and difficulties for those demanding social justice. While this subject can be discussed on a worldwide scale—especially with regard to the dumping of hazardous materials in poor countries or efforts to limit emissions in developing countries—my focus here is on the interaction between globalization, local decision making, and its distributional effects. By exacerbating uneven development within metro areas as places compete with each other internationally and capital flows rapidly in and out of areas, globalization has led city governments to emphasize competitiveness at the expense of equity. This has led to huge public expenditures on sports stadiums, office developments, and festive marketplaces, while the concern with low-income communities that responded to earlier definitions of the urban crisis in terms of poverty has been largely abandoned.

At the same time the spread of certain, more benign approaches to urban development—green buildings, creative cities—has also been enhanced by globalization. Cities are competing not just for capital but for being identified with the provision of amenities. Moreover, environmental programs are rarely opposed by forces other than industry lobbyists countering pressures to regulate their clients' activities. Thus, we see tree-planting programs in Chicago and New York City, the development of sustainability plans in many cities, and the creation of new parks and playgrounds. At the local level politicians have found that developing park space, building bike lanes, and transforming streets into gathering places—as has been done in New York, where tables and chairs have been placed on traffic islands and streets have been narrowed—attracts huge amounts of popular support.

Richard Florida's argument in *The Rise of the Creative Class*[6] has been highly influential in causing civic leaders to believe that producing amenities and acquiring a reputation for greenness will enhance the position of cities in the global competition for investment by attracting entrepreneurial individuals who wish to live in attractive places. This strategy has a double-edged effect in relation to equity. On the one hand it results in better public spaces that are available to all; on the other it contributes to gentrification. There is the potential for such programs to contribute to both environmental improvement and social equity, but only if they are accompanied by public funding of programs to increase the supply of affordable housing and the provision of social services in tandem with the construction of amenities.

Globalization includes the flows of people and ideas as well as of capital. The ideal of sustainability has swept through schools of planning and architecture, which have become increasingly internationalized in their student bodies. As a result, when students graduate and return to their home countries, they bring with them concepts of green building types, transit-oriented development, adaptive reuse, and reduction of waste. These have been picked up by Middle Eastern potentates creating model new towns and Asian economic planners seeing future economic advantage in exporting green technologies. Ideals of equity, however, do not travel as easily, as their profitability is less obvious.

Usefulness of Rhetoric of Sustainability

While financial globalization has empowered capitalists and global telecommunication has raised the profile of right-wing bloggers, global networking has also permitted the development of coalitions on the left—e.g. the Right to the City and environmental justice movements. These movements, while linked by the Internet and the occasional conference, operate primarily on the local level. So far they have not reached a scale where they have had major impact on national decision making, but they have succeeded in affecting local politics in a number of cities. Using the rhetoric of sustainability can be of strategic importance to them, as it attracts allies who might be repelled by a program stated in class or racial terms.

For example, Elizabeth J. Mueller and Sarah Dooling report on the transformation of an airport site in Austin, Texas, into a planned neighborhood characterized by a dense core with retail, office, and residential uses, ample green space, pedestrian and transit orientation, and affordable housing.[7] The project was the result of years of lobbying by a community coalition that encompassed advocates for low-income groups but also developers and business leaders. Developers were attracted by the density levels allowed in the name of sustainability, and business leaders lent their support because of the general aura of progressiveness that the term connotes. It is unlikely that simply a demand for dense, affordable housing would have had similar appeal.

We see then that the political value of sustainability is such that its usage will persist. It is a quintessentially fuzzy concept that allows a variety of interests to claim it as its own. Its promulgation by the UN and its adoption by countries at all stages of development reflect its appeal. Doubtless as a result of its popularity we are seeing some progress toward reducing contributions to global warming, the provision of green space, and decreasing pollution. In specific cases, like Austin, its use may contribute to more equitable outcomes. On the whole, however, the ideal of sustainability is not likely to do much to mitigate conditions of inequality.

EVERYDAY AGRICULTURE

MARGARET CRAWFORD

Eating is an agricultural act.
— Wendell Berry

No part of everyday life is so universal yet so specific as the daily need to procure, prepare, and consume food. The need to eat is imposed by our bodies but economic, political, social, and cultural forces largely beyond our control shape what we eat. Recent critiques of the American food system, widely publicized through books, films, and news reports have drawn attention to its unsavory and even deadly aspects. Journalists such as Michael Pollan have demonstrated, often in horrifying detail, how agribusiness, fast food corporations, chemical companies, and government subsidies have produced cheap industrialized food that is not only of poor quality but often dangerously unhealthy. Partly in response to this situation, a new ethos of food production and consumption has emerged. Although stressing global awareness of the food chain and urging radical reform of federal food policies, at the local level this movement focuses on creating an alternative agricultural system to provide aware consumers with fresh local food. Food activists encourage shoppers to replace heavily processed foods and produce shipped from distant lands with ripe organic produce, responsibly raised meat, and breads and cheeses produced by traditional rather than industrial methods.

Although creating this new food culture is a national movement, Northern California functions as its de facto capital. This is partly the result of its favorable geography (fertile soil and a year-round growing season) and history (Japanese, Italian, and French immigrants who grew vegetables, planted vineyards, and opened restaurants). However, food historian Warren Belasco dates its more recent origins to the 1960s, seeing it as an offshoot of the counterculture that also thrived in the region. As part of an ethical rejection of mainstream institutions including supermarkets, hippies turned to "natural" foods such as whole grains, often as part of vegetarian and macrobiotic diets. The revolt against everything "plastic" led to a craft revival that included gardening, cooking, and the rediscovery of neglected foods such as buckwheat, soy products, and live acidophilus cultures.

This often melded with a local tradition of political activism. For example, in her 1971 bestseller, *Diet for a Small Planet*, Berkeley resident Frances Moore Lappé combined nutritional knowledge with global social awareness. The counterculture also pioneered nonprofit distribution channels and alternative retailing, such as co-ops and food "conspiracies," based on low prices and natural products. Shopping, cooking, and eating this way necessarily transformed daily lives, requiring time, focus, and expertise.

During the 1980s, as the '60s generation matured, the movement went in new directions. High-concept restaurants such as Berkeley's Chez Panisse and Oakland's Bay Wolf became famous for combining fresh, locally sourced ingredients with French cooking techniques, inventing what became known as California cuisine. Small-scale farms sprang up on the fringes of the Bay Area to provide them with the high-quality produce, meat, and dairy products their exacting standards demanded. A new generation of sophisticated market gardeners expanded the repertoire of available produce, reviving heirloom varieties and introducing European specialties. Former hippies tended goats and, after a few years, began producing cheeses comparable to those of France and Italy. Vineyards proliferated across the Napa and Sonoma valleys. By 2000, many farmers in the Central Valley, a stronghold of agribusiness, had converted to organic production.

Two Food Cultures

In the East Bay where I live, these changes have been surprisingly durable. The ethos of fresh, local, responsible food has trickled down into the nooks and crannies of most people's everyday lives. The large number of individuals, businesses, organizations, programs, events, and activities in the area devoted to transforming food systems and food cultures have been very effective. Fresh local produce, urban agriculture, and alternative marketing have created a kind of lower-case everyday urbanism here, visibly altering both space and time. Agriculture flourishes at two different scales: in small plots that dot urban areas, and in the regional belt of farms, wineries, orchards, and dairies that rings the San Francisco Bay, extending from Marin, Napa, and Sonoma counties on the north through the San Joaquin Valley on the east to the Salinas Valley on the south. In addition to possessing some of the most productive farmland in the world, they serve as the region's tourist hinterland, much of it organized around food. Since the seasons are not dramatically different, it is the changing availability of fruits and vegetables that marks the natural rhythm of the year. Immigrant cooks from all over the world creatively adapt their cuisines in response to these cycles. Our mild and sunny weather encourages people to eat outdoors.

At the same time, over the last thirty years, larger processes of economic and social restructuring have shaped the local food cultures into a strikingly uneven pattern of access and quality, even across such a small geographic area. Two adjacent cities, Berkeley and Oakland, dramatically reveal these disparities. Berkeley, a college town, once famous for radical politics, is now known for its food-oriented lifestyle, anchored by a plethora of successful restaurants and businesses. Oakland is a large city, with a significant percentage of poor and minority people. Its food scene reflects its varied neighborhoods, ranging from the affluent hills Fruitvale, a largely Latino neighborhood, to the "flats," shared by hipsters, African-Americans, and recent immigrants. The following survey of food culture and activism in these two places, although far from inclusive, is intended to communicate the extent and variety of this phenomenon as well as some of its possibilities and limits.

Berkeley

In Berkeley, fresh food is abundantly visible. The city's low-density landscape, where nearly every dwelling unit is surrounded by some green space, encourages fruit trees and gardens. Hidden behind fences, backyard farmers abound. They range from professors in the hills, seeking a balance

FIG.I The Monterey Market, Berkeley.

between mental and manual labor, to a resident of the less affluent flatlands, named Jim, who raises most of his food in his mini-farm, raising chickens, rabbits, and goats for meat and milk and cultivating an extensive vegetable garden and a fruit orchard. There are also popular community gardens, designed for apartment dwellers. If a tree or garden produces too much, there is a gleaner's organization ready to harvest the surplus and redistribute it to local schools and food banks. To encourage foraging, this group also provides Internet maps identifying sites where fruit falls into the public domain.

If they do not grow their own food, residents have access to a remarkable selection of produce and products grown or prepared nearby. They can easily avoid chain supermarkets since two locally owned food markets offer a broad range of high-quality food at reasonable prices. Operated by Japanese families whose roots in the produce business go back several generations, they depend on suppliers from adjacent agricultural counties. These markets inspire intense customer loyalty (as well as attracting regular shoppers from San Francisco and Marin). Heated debates about the comparative merits of the Berkeley Bowl or the Monterey Market have become a conversational staple at academic dinner parties. The Berkeley Bowl offers a vast selection, but the much smaller Monterey Market identifies its produce by the farm where it was grown. If that isn't fresh enough, the Berkeley Ecology Center operates year-round farmer's markets three times a week, featuring organic produce and drawing farmers from as far as two hundred miles away.

Berkeley's children are equally privileged. In 1996, Alice Waters established the Chez Panisse Foundation to focus on educating children about food. Her first initiative was the Edible Schoolyard, established at the Martin Luther King Junior Middle School. Transforming a parking lot into a flourishing garden, Waters developed a comprehensive food program, hiring specially trained teachers to help students plant, cultivate, harvest, cook, and eat a wide variety of foods. In addition to lessons integrated with classroom topics, students sit down and eat together, demonstrating Water's insistence on enjoyment as a key ingredient of food reform. The Edible Schoolyard has become a model for school gardens and programs across the country, although few of them are as comprehensive or as well funded.

The foundation also sponsors the School Lunch Initiative, a pilot program to upgrade public school lunches. It hired Ann Cooper, a chef and health advocate, to transform the Berkeley public school system's food service. Her changes, eliminating processed foods while introducing a wide variety of fresh foods, fruits, and vegetables, affected more than 10,000 students. My daughter, while a student at King Middle School, was an enthusiastic beneficiary of both programs, coming home with recipes and surprising requests for leafy green vegetables such as dinosaur kale. Although some critics dismiss these efforts as "feel-good" programs, a recent University of California study confirmed their real benefits, revealing that Edible Schoolyard participants demonstrated much more knowledge about food and the environment,

FIG. 2 The Edible Schoolyard.

selected healthier foods, and ate them with more pleasure than other students.

Many of the alternative institutions begun in the 1960s have disappeared, but some counterculture endeavors continue to thrive. The North Berkeley "Gourmet Ghetto" is home to juice, cheese, and pizza collectives. Over the last forty years, the Cheese Board expanded from a tiny storefront into an airy shop that now also sells its own bread and bakery products as well as housing an espresso bar. It spawned an even more popular spin-off, Cheese Board Pizza. Serving slices of a single daily type of vegetarian pizza for $2.50, it attracts lines out the door. Young customers, mostly UC Berkeley students, have created a new tradition of dining on the adjacent median strip. Occupying the grass, they eat their pizza slices directly across from Chez Panisse, where a meal for two costs upwards of a hundred dollars. Still completely worker owned and managed, the collective has recruited women and minorities to replace its aging members in order to maintain a democratic workplace. New socially aware business models are also appearing. Slow Money, a

fund headquartered in Berkeley, draws on a broad network of small investors to generate venture capital to invest in local food communities.

The easy availability of such high-quality food has nurtured an exacting population, reluctant to eat a hamburger without knowing exactly what farm the grass-fed beef came from and how the steer that provided it was raised. My local fish market not only specifies where its fish are caught but also documents the fishing method used in their capture. Taken too far, these standards can easily turn into elitism. Just across the Bay is the San Francisco Ferry Building, an urban marketplace famous for the high quality and prices of its farmers market. Even Carlo Petrini, the founder of the International Slow Food Movement, objected to this, calling the market "exclusive," its customers "either wealthy or very wealthy," and its vegetables "shown off like jewels." He considered this completely contrary to the populist origins of the Slow Food movement. In politically correct cities like Berkeley, an excessive concern with the provenance of foodstuffs has become a mark of what sociologist Pierre Bourdieu called "distinction," a method of demonstrating status not through wealth but through connoisseurship and ethical claims. This was recently satirized on the television show *Portlandia* (set in Portland, Oregon, another key site of food localism) as a locavore couple, not satisfied with the extensive information given to them about the free range chicken they were thinking of ordering (including its name), felt obliged to visit the farm where it was raised.

Oakland

Just over the border, in West Oakland, the situation is very different. West Oakland is a food desert, eight square miles without a single supermarket. The only local retail food outlets are fast-food restaurants and corner liquor stores that also sell high-cost processed snack food and some basic items like milk and bread. This situation is exacerbated by the

FIG. 3 Eating pizza on the grass.

FIG. 4 City Sicker Farms.

fact that, since more than a third of the area's population live under the poverty line, they have limited purchasing power and limited access to transportation. Unlike dense Berkeley, West Oakland is full of vacant land, abandoned as the warehousing and industries that formerly populated the area declined and moved away. During the last ten years, these conditions spurred food justice activists to work with neighborhood residents to create new sources of food and jobs.

In the absence of retail food markets, a number of nonprofit organizations and social enterprises are active in the area, each with its own specialized niche. Oakland Based Urban Gardens (OBUGS) partners with local schools to create school gardens and educational programs similar to those of the Edible Schoolyard. Mandela Marketplace, a worker-owned co-op, is a business incubator supporting local people entering food-based businesses. The People's Grocery, in spite of its name, is not a food store, but provides fresh and healthy food through multiple programs such as the Mobile Market, a distinctive red truck whose route stops at senior centers, schools, and parks to sell fresh produce and packaged staples at reasonable prices. At their headquarters, residents can buy bulk food at cost, pick up a weekly "Grub Box" of fruit and vegetables, or sign up for classes in cooking, business, and health. Former high-school teacher David Roach founded Mo' Better Food to reconnect urban African-Americans with their rural food traditions. The organization sponsors a farmers market featuring African-American farmers from the Central Valley.

After moving to West Oakland in the late 1990s, farming enthusiast Willow Rosenthal started City Slicker Farms to take advantage of the numerous vacant lots in the area. Hiring local residents and working with crews of volunteers, she transformed five lots into intensively cultivated gardens filled with rows of herbs and vegetable crops, fruit trees, beehives, and chicken coops. On a busy sidewalk, the farm operates a Saturday farm stand. Rather than selling their produce, which is currently prohibited by the city, they suggest three levels of "donations." "Free Spirit" is for those with minimal incomes, "Penny Pincher" for people who can pay something but not a lot, and "Sugar Momma/Daddy" for those who can pay enough to subsidize someone else. All of their farm plots produce more than 20,000 pounds of food a year. City Slickers Backyard Garden Program has helped residents plant more than a hundred gardens, providing them with free soil, seeds, compost, tools, and advice.

Answering skeptics who point out that these efforts only provide 20 percent of local food needs and are hard to maintain in a market economy, these groups argue that they produce much more than food. As community organizers, they

include education, youth programs, and political advocacy as part of their social justice mission. The People's Grocery has spun off another organization completely devoted to building community awareness about food and health. All of the organizations offer youth programs to provide training in agricultural and food-related jobs to local teenagers. Graduates of these programs staff many local food enterprises, such as the Mobile Market and the African American Farmers Market. City Slicker Farms offers workshops for local community members to learn about urban agriculture and health issues. All of them regularly bring neighborhood people together to eat, hosting dinners, barbeques, and food festivals. In 2009, these groups helped organize the HOPE Collaborative (Health for Oakland's People and Environment) a coalition of residents, nonprofits, and city agencies focusing on the city's health and food issues. The group has already convinced the City of Oakland to appoint a Food Policy Council to advise the city government. Establishing the goal of providing everyone in the city with access to healthy food, they are taking a comprehensive look at the city's food systems. Their policy recommendations include changing zoning to permit urban agriculture and removing restrictions on mobile food vending.

At the other end of the spectrum, Oakland is also home to a host of under-the-radar food producers. A surprising number of independently owned mini-farms exist, hidden in plain sight in urban areas. Unlike Berkeley, whose stringent regulations are enforced as much by vigilant neighbors as by city inspectors, Oakland's urban agriculture is relatively unfettered. Ten years ago, in the Ghost Town neighborhood on the fringes of downtown, aspiring writer Novella Carpenter borrowed a garbage-filled abandoned lot from her landlord to start a vegetable garden. After a while, she expanded to livestock, raising bees, chickens, ducks, and turkeys. She moved on to rabbits and pigs, feeding them with scraps from Chinatown dumpster-diving expeditions, then selling their meat to high-end restaurants. Although she operated without any licenses or permits, her mostly low-income neighbors not only tolerated but also often joined in her agricultural endeavors. After writing a best-selling memoir about her experiences, Carpenter was able to buy her 4500-square-foot lot, where she continues to farm and raise livestock.

Supporters of "outlaw" farmers and food processors are pioneering new forms of distribution. ForageSF, a group dedicated to encouraging wild foraging, also operates the Underground Market, a monthly event in Oakland, where backyard farmers and home kitchens can sell their products without health department oversight. To avoid liability problems, everyone attending must join the organization and sign a liability wavier. Founder Iso Rabins, a San Francisco resident, consulted Novella Carpenter to help him recruit East Bay vendors. Carpenter also operates her own unsanctioned pop-up farm stand to sell her own and other local farmers' products and is currently collaborating on a book about urban farming with Willow Rosenthal, an indication of the expanding informal food networks in the city.

Oakland also has a thriving food cart and truck scene. In

the last few years, the number of mobile vendors has grown almost exponentially, as gourmet chefs and purveyors of high-end snacks and fusion cuisine have joined the immigrant proprietors of "loncheros" and hot dog carts on the streets of the city. These new entrepreneurs bring culinary sophistication and marketing savvy (such as the use of Twitter) to what was formerly regarded as a marginal and questionable enterprise (trucks were known as "roach coaches"). The new popularity of street vending has served to legitimate all vendors, making them more accepted and more commercially viable. Although there are still many illegal vendors, support for legalizing food micro-enterprises has expanded. Economic development groups have opened nonprofit commercial kitchens to offer vendors the certified food preparation facilities and storage areas required by the Health department.

Events such as Oakland's annual Eat Real festival bring both kinds of vendors together in an attempt to bridge the social and economic gap between fast food and slow food. Eat Real, founded by Anya Fernald, is a social venture enterprise, a cause-driven business model that provides only limited profits. Although her mission is to revitalize regional food systems, she does this by promoting food craft and encouraging food entrepreurs. Eat Real, where all food is priced at five dollars or less, provides a showcase for their wares, attracting hordes of people from all over the city.

From Food to Urbanism

What does all of this have to do with urban design? From the upper-case Everyday Urbanist's perspective, everything. Rather than defining "sustainability" as a predetermined ideology or set of design imperatives, we approach the issue through studying and understanding already existing places, people, and practices like those described in this essay. Instead of demanding the transformation of the built environment or insisting that ordinary people change their preferences and habits, we look for specific circumstances that seem particularly promising. Oakland and Berkeley's food cultures both offer fertile ground for multiple urban interventions. None of the individuals, businesses, or organizations discussed here had urban planning or design as their goal. Yet by concentrating on producing crops, creating jobs, educating students, or selling or buying food, they inadvertently produced urbanism as a byproduct of their activities. Their

Everyday Urbanism of urban farms, school gardens, displays of fresh produce, fruit trees, backyard chickens, and people eating in public places contains powerful and evocative implications for urban transformation. But, in their current state, they are just the raw material for design. Enhanced, amplified, and orchestrated by everyday urban design, they have the potential to generate new and unique urban landscapes. By manipulating space and time, urban design can not only highlight the significant role these distinctive local food cultures play in their cities but also expand their users' daily experiences and economic potential.

The range of possible design interventions extends from a simple tweak to large-scale regional transformation. Urban farms and community gardens are a good example. Their changing cycles of plants and produce are beautiful, but the gardens themselves are all too often unsightly places with scraggly plants and funky garden sheds, surrounded by chain link fences. The predominant style is usually "retro hippy." With the addition of carefully considered hedges, fences, and entrances they could become showcases for their crops, public assets to the neighborhood, and green gathering spaces open to all. Even carefully maintained places like the Edible Schoolyard could use design help. It is currently a neighborhood oasis, pleasant to stroll through but nothing more. With the addition of a few terraces and seating areas, it could turn into a magical place, a public gathering spot for students, neighbors, and visitors. Students could host events here, building local support for the program by displaying their cooking and gardening skills.

Urban design could help Berkeley become more egalitarian. The concept of median dining could be extended to many of the city's many well-tended grassy spaces. If there isn't any cheap food nearby, the city can license food vendors to stop by at mealtimes. Design and planning could also increase West Oakland's commercial viability and visibility by introducing new food-based businesses. City Slickers' herb farm, for example, could open a tea café featuring their garden's products. This would publicize their program, increase demand for their herbs, and attract visitors into the area. At a larger scale, West Oakland could become a model for low-density inner cities, replacing devastation with an agrarian landscape. A green infrastructure connecting existing farm plots with school gardens and overgrown vacant lots would turn empty space into an asset rather than a problem. At the regional scale, a food guidebook would propose selected itineraries around the

FIG. 5 Novella Carpenter's GhostTown Farm.

FIG. 6 Eat Real Festival.

Bay's rural counties. Directing tourists to farms, restaurants, and local specialties, it uses agritourism to support farm economies.

Right now these are only ideas, but Everyday Agriculture can easily become more than just speculation. There are numerous potential clients. In addition to the individuals, businesses, nonprofits, and social enterprises identified above, local politicians and planners are becoming increasingly active in supporting urban agriculture and food economies. Based on an understanding of local practices, creating compelling visions of a food-producing city is the first step toward future urban transformation. These possibilities are necessarily grounded in reality, but they can have far-reaching consequences.

TOWARDS A SYSTEMS THEORY OF CITY DESIGN

JONATHAN BARNETT

Is it possible to write a mathematical formula or script that can generate a building, *algorithmic architecture*, or a city, *algorithmic urbanism*? Is it possible to write a set of rules, or set in motion a process, that will cause the design of a building—or the design of a city—to emerge the way the individual behaviors in a beehive or an ant colony self-organize to meet collective needs for survival? Many people are working on these issues, which promise to bring about fundamental changes in the relationships between the theory and the practice of designing buildings and cities. These theoretical investigations often begin with simple systems that can be reduced to computations, or with patterns produced by mathematical equations that appear to have analogies to observable characteristics of real cities. However, most such investigations are still a long way from dealing with the complexities that confront professional city designers or public officials responsible for urban growth and change.

What Can SimCity Tell Us about City Design Theory?

SimCity is a computer game created by Will Wright, who introduced the original version in 1989. It is primarily for a single player, the mayor, who has to map the construction of a city to satisfy requirements comparable to zoning and the delivery of municipal services while staying within a tax base comparable to a property tax. Later versions of the game introduced 3-D projections for buildings and landscape contours, underground levels for utilities and transit, and more nuanced distinctions among zones and the property taxes generated. A recent Web site for the game announces "our much-anticipated Rush-Hour expansion pack." SimCity also offers players the opportunity to destroy their city according to various disaster scenarios, and provides playful elements like newspapers and country clubs that recall another Will Wright computer game, The Sims, a simulation of personal lifetimes. The intention of SimCity is to engage the imagination in an entertaining way, not to solve real-life problems. Nevertheless, Sim City demonstrates that many of the elements that go into the creation of a city, such as zoning, property taxes, infrastructure, and transportation, are systems from which the whole city emerges. The simulation is cruder and more diagrammatic than a real city, but it is a strong indication that the design of real cities may one day be accomplished through understanding and defining systems.

Development Regulations as Systems

In the United States almost all local governments have zoning and subdivision ordinances. Zoning separates and locates land uses, and it also specifies how big a building in a particular zone may be, and sets requirements for where the building may be located on the property, how many off-street car spaces need to be provided, and how much of the property must be left as open space. Zoning can set height limits, or require setbacks on upper floors. Single-family houses are mapped in different zones from apartments, zones for stores and offices generally do not permit residences, and industry zones are carefully segregated from other activities.

The subdivision ordinance includes requirements for the layout of properties in accordance with the zoning and for the design, grading, and placement of streets, including minimum widths for street rights-of-way, the geometry of street corners, and the dimensions and other requirements for the paved roadway, sidewalks, and landscaping within the right-of-way. Subdivision regulations also deal with the grading of the whole property and requirements for stormwater retention, and may also specify areas that cannot be built on, such as where the land slopes at more than a specified number of degrees.

If the real-estate market is strong and the development regulations are strict, any developer seeking to maximize profit is likely to find that regulations closely determine what can be built. The regulations do not anticipate which properties will be built upon or in what order. But, over time, a built

TREND SCENARIO, 2005-2030-2050

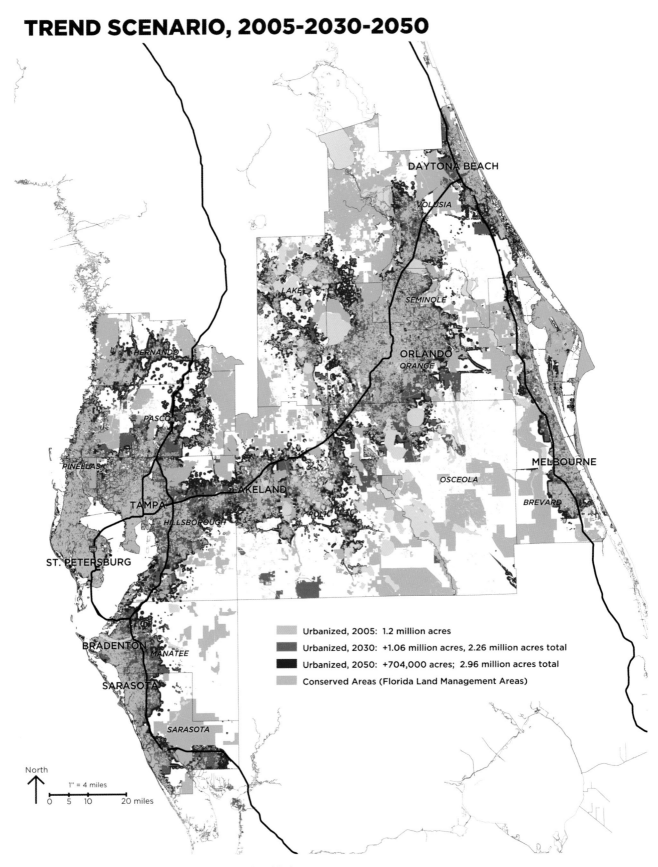

Urbanized, 2005: 1.2 million acres

Urbanized, 2030: +1.06 million acres, 2.26 million acres total

Urbanized, 2050: +704,000 acres; 2.96 million acres total

Conserved Areas (Florida Land Management Areas)

North

1" = 4 miles

0   5   10   20 miles

FIG. 1 A map developed in the Spatial Analyst extension of ArcGIS that projects current development policies for the thirteen-county Florida Super Region to 2050.

ALTERNATIVE SCENARIO, 2005-2030-2050

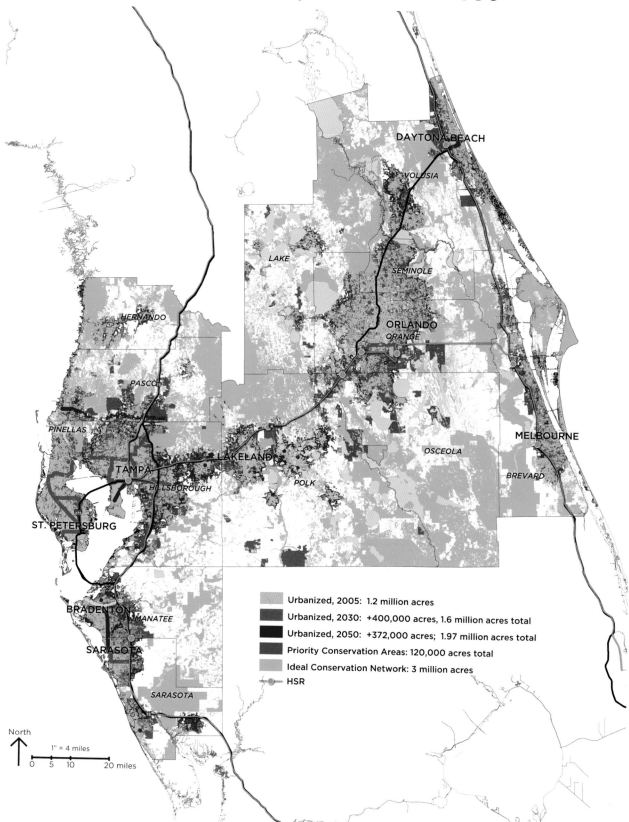

Urbanized, 2005: 1.2 million acres
Urbanized, 2030: +400,000 acres, 1.6 million acres total
Urbanized, 2050: +372,000 acres; 1.97 million acres total
Priority Conservation Areas: 120,000 acres total
Ideal Conservation Network: 3 million acres
HSR

North

1" = 4 miles
0 5 10   20 miles

FIG. 2 An alternative scenario. A high-speed rail system connects Tampa to Orlando and its airport, and then continues south to Miami. Local transit systems are put in place in both the Tampa and Orlando regions.

environment emerges through the activities of individual property owners acting for their own advantage on their own schedules. The form the built environment takes is strongly influenced by the regulations, which are a city-design script, although a primitive one.

These U.S. development regulations were created to protect adjacent property owners rather than to promote a positive concept of what a city or town should be. Understanding that codes are prescriptive as well as protective has led to the enactment of special zoning districts and form-based codes that permit a mix of uses and embody design concepts for future development. This has been an important improvement, but so far only small numbers of development regulations have been modified to be intentional city-design scripts.

Transportation and Land Development are Interacting Systems

For years transportation planners were amazed to discover that highways planned to accommodate traffic for the next fifteen or twenty years were jammed to capacity from the day they opened. Eventually, the planners figured out that the proposed highway, or highway widening, induced additional traffic beyond the demand measured at the time the highway was designed. Interchanges became the sites for office parks and shopping centers, and farmland could become residential because of the improved access. New development meant more traffic on the highway, which turned out to be part of a larger system of land-use and investment.

Critics of proposed rail transit systems who pointed out that the ridership was just not there to support a new line have been proved wrong. Relatively recent transit systems such as BART in San Francisco, DART in Dallas, and WMATA in Washington, D.C. are all reshaping their regions by inducing more intensive development around transit stations, which in turn induces more riders, who induce even more development. Arlington County, Virginia, is the textbook example where formerly automobile-based suburbs of Washington have become a series of urban centers along transit lines, including Rossyln, Courthouse, Clarendon, Ballston, Pentagon City, and Crystal City. Rail transit is more likely to induce development than bus lines, because rail is a permanent commitment, while a bus can easily be rerouted or discontinued. Historians of city-development know that cities grew outward along roads and highways, and that urban development followed trolley and rail lines. But public policies for transportation seldom recognize that the designs for highway and transit systems are scripts for the organization of future development.

Infrastructure Systems

You can live on a farm or in a multi-acre rural subdivision and rely on a well and a septic tank. The nearest road can be a long, unpaved driveway away. But you cannot have development at suburban or urban densities without water and sewer systems, and you cannot get from house to house without streets. Water and sewer sustems usually follow the street layouts, as do electricity, telephone, and cable services. The design of these infrastructure systems is also a script for the design of the city or suburb. In the United States, the arterial streets are planned by local governments; the local streets are provided by builders following the requirements of the subdivision ordinance. Water and sewer pipes are built in the street right-of-way; but the development cannot proceed at all unless the local utilities provide the necessary water supply and sewage treatment capacity. Utility companies and districts generally see themselves as serving growth, rather than shaping it. When capacity reaches its limit, the cost of enlarging the systems to provide for more development usually falls on the whole utility district, which means that residents of existing areas help subsidize new development by paying higher water and sewer charges. Urban expansion by building new utilities, as opposed to infill development to use existing utilities more efficiently, is seldom presented as a public policy choice.

The Natural Systems and Climate Change

Sewer systems are often shaped by the natural watershed for local rivers, because natural drainage in the region is determined by gravity and a gravity system is also the most economical way to design sewer pipes. However, many other infrastructure and grading decisions are made as if the land were flat and natural vegetation expendable. Ian McHarg forcefully articulated the need to understand the natural environment as a series of interrelated systems of water, terrain, and vegetation, and to make this understanding the basis for city design. The essence of McHarg's message, in his book *Design with Nature*, first published in 1969, was to preserve the natural environment as much as possible and to design development within nature rather than bulldoze hillsides to fill wetlands, put streams in culverts, and create erosion by clearing the trees and bushes that hold the soil in place. McHarg has been influential, but his message is still not fully accepted by the engineers and planners who make big decisions about roads, subdivision ordinances, and infrastructure systems.

McHarg saw the natural environment as an essentially stable equilibrium which, left to itself, would change only slowly. Today we have become aware that climate change is affecting natural systems. Sea levels are rising, putting the future of waterfront properties in question. Rising average temperatures are also affecting water supplies, increasing the likelihood of destructive storms and making forest fires more likely. It is becoming even more important to conserve the natural environment as much as possible and to keep development out of the path of future floods and fires.

Systems Design for the Florida Super Region

A recent research project that I directed at the University of Pennsylvania took a systems design approach to the thirteen-county Super Region comprising metropolitan Orlando and metropolitan Tampa in the central part of Florida. A first step was to look at the remaining undeveloped land, understand the natural drainage and other systems within it, and estimate the likelihood of changes in water levels and shorelines because of climate change. Then environmental priorities were mapped using the Spatial Analyst extension in ArcGIS to identify the land that most meets such criteria as preserving natural drainage basins, permitting the recharge of aquifers, providing contiguous land to preserve species, preserving high-value agricultural land, and keeping development away from shorelines at risk from sea-level rise. The computer program resolved these differing factors according to the weights assigned to them and created a map of what we called the Ideal Conservation Network. All the land mapped is important for conservation, but the land that the computer program identifies as satisfying the most conservation criteria deserves the highest priority for preservation from development.

Population in Florida has been growing rapidly, and the number of people in the Super Region is projected to double from 7.2 million to 14.4 million by mid-century. To accommodate this growth within the Ideal Conservation Network, the research project identified two scenarios for transportation, infrastructure, and development-regulation systems. The first projected current, automobile-based development trends up to 2050. The second scenario assumed development regulations and infrastructure and transportation planning were all directed towards making new development as compact and walkable as possible.

Development codes in Florida currently separate land uses and housing types, and the zoning and subdivision regulations are intended to implement low-density, auto-oriented development. Infrastructure policies support continued expansion of urbanized areas. The transportation system relies almost completely on highways for local travel and airplanes for long distances. Local access is by automobile or truck.

Figure 1 shows a map developed in the Spatial Analyst extension of ArcGIS that projects current development policies for the thirteen-county Florida Super Region to 2050. From 1.1 million urbanized acres in 2010, the urbanized area of the region extends to almost 3 million acres by 2050. Current development policies are so wasteful of land that while the population doubles, the amount of farm and open land that has to be urbanized triples, including more than 300,000 acres of the environmentally critical lands that make up the ideal conservation network.

Figure 2 maps an alternative scenario. A high-speed rail system connects Tampa to Orlando and its airport, and then continues south to Miami. Local transit systems are put in place in both the Tampa and Orlando regions. Development regulations are changed to permit higher-density and mixed-use development along transit corridors, although current development policies continue in areas not served by transit. Infrastructure policies are changed to favor more efficient use of existing systems through infill development rather than extending roads, water, and sewer services to new areas. In addition, proactive environmental protection measures conserve areas of the Ideal Conservation Network that otherwise would be developed. Under these assumptions, by 2050 only half as much additional land needs to be urbanized, about a million acres, and about 125,000 existing urbanized acres will have been redeveloped to higher densities along transit corridors. About 120,000 acres need to be acquired to preserve the Ideal Conservation Network, but only about a third as many of these environmentally critical areas are under pressure of development compared to the trend scenario.

This alternative scenario need not be fiction. The high-speed rail line has already been partially funded by the federal government, the transit lines are in official plans, and precedents exist in Florida for higher-density mixed uses along transit corridors. Florida has a strong program for acquiring land for conservation, although it has not always purchased the highest priority locations.

Mapping the consequences of the two scenarios dramatizes some important issues. High-speed rail and other transit are more important for facilitating efficient land use in the future than for the service they can offer riders on the day they begin operations. The efficiencies of land use are significant. If the cost of providing infrastructure to an acre of rural land is about $100,000 per acre, saving a million acres from development adds up to 100 billion dollars, which will buy a lot of trains and rails, pay for conservation land, and also pay for upgrading utilities in existing areas. More money is saved by not having to build the additional schools, police and fire stations, libraries, and other public investments that would accompany urbanizing another million acres. Thus the alternative scenario would actually save money while providing a far more desirable outcome.

Because the factors in the two alternative scenarios were fed into the Spatial Analyst extension of ArcGIS, it was not possible to know how the population would be distributed on the maps in accordance with the assumptions for each scenario until the computer program ran. So this design research was based both on an understanding of the constituent systems—natural, development code, transportation, infrastructure—and on a system of parameters that mimic development choices created with the aid of a computer program. It is systems city design at a very broad-brush regional scale, but within such a framework it would be possible to explore many more factors in much greater detail, using a comparable methodology.

SUSTAINABLE THEORY—SUSTAINABLE FORM

THE FUTURE OF URBAN DESIGN

ALEXANDER R. CUTHBERT

Introduction

The following chapter argues that for urban design to exist as a theoretically sustainable *field* it must move from its limited mainstream position as project design to one that encompasses urban form in its totality.[1] To do this it must embrace social rather than architectural theory as its point of origin. Since the inception of the architectural profession in London in 1834, *urban design* has been dominated by architects with ownership legitimated on the basis that they were the only individuals capable of conceptualizing the city. Even the birth of the Royal Town Planning Institute in London in 1913 had little effect on this monopoly, since architects also colonized the planning profession from the outset. For all practical purposes, architecture, urban design, and town planning constituted a single discipline—two professional bodies with the same cultural worldview and a shared region called urban design. What passed for theory permeated all three. But during the 1960s and early 1970s, urban planning went through a climacteric and was reinvented with an influx of urban geographers, social scientists, and economists. Within social science, urban theory and planning theory became conjoined albeit with an uneasy truce, and for the first time the term "urban" became replete with meaning.[2] For the new immigrants into planning, physical determinism was anathema and for very good reason, as many modernist urban design and planning projects had demonstrated. However, the same was not true of architecture, which remained blind to its own indiscretions and ideologically rooted to a mélange of aesthetics and technology within the new postmodernism. Hence an architectural definition of urban design not only prevailed, it was actually enhanced. At that point, urban design lost the evolutionary possibility of transformation and with it a sustainable theoretical field. So "theory" in urban design remained the domain of architecture where it has been embalmed for over fifty years.[3]

Therefore a massive hiatus remains— whether or not the mainstream view of urban design is theoretically sustainable.[4]

Clearly it is not. Urban theory as a whole has moved forward with the rapid advance of globalization, the Internet, new forms of imperialism, resource depletion, and climate change.[5] In contrast, mainstream theory in urban design remains divorced from the ideologies and forces affecting its own operation. It is also seriously isolated from sociospatial theory in urban geography and sociology, which holds the possibility of expanding and legitimating the field of urban design as a significant contributor. I have made an initial offering to correct this situation in a recent trilogy.[6] These texts are in large part motivated by the idea that we cannot generate a meaningful analytical field for urban design without invoking urban theory. *Ipso facto*, without *sustainable* theory in urban design, acceptable sustainable practices cannot be deployed.[7] In order to sketch out this argument more fully, I will concentrate on three related issues: (re)defining the field, the problematic of design, and the demands of ideology.

(Re)Defining the Field

In the absence of any coherent discourse in urban design, the floodgates were opened on a potentially endless deluge of definitions which have been continually recycled for half a century[8]; virtually none of these offerings actually defined anything, other than a few superficial properties of physical form and architectural practice. Almost all had a trivial relationship with any meaningful social reality yet were offered as self-evident truths. Examples are legion. José Luis Sert, credited (erroneously) with establishing the discipline of urban design in 1953, defined it as *project design*. In the 1960s, the iconic Reyner Banham noted that urban design dealt with situations "about half a mile square."[9] This was still being described as a "memorable" definition twenty years later.[10] Rowley lists many such definitions, portraying in great detail the sheer confusion and lack of purpose of the mainstream, i.e., "the words 'urban' and 'design' are slippery and problematic"; or "urban . . . now includes rural sites and settings"; or even "Trying to define urban design is like playing . . . the old parlour game, Twenty Questions."[11] Today, fifteen years later, we still find urban design being defined as a "*frame of mind*," "*a way of thinking*," "*large-scale architecture*," and "*an art of place making*" in a single edited book, *Urban Design*.[12] Structured for low or nonexistent levels of refutability, there is little possibility of any theoretical integrity emerging from the mainstream. Since substantial theory is dependent on an equally rigorous definition of the discipline, we can easily argue that debate has actually regressed over the last half century. As Michael Sorkin recently observed, the discipline has sunk to the point where all it does is "validate the grafting of a particular system of taste onto a limited set of organizational ideas."[13]

From this point two choices prevail. The first is to accept the fact that urban design and project design are actually the same thing. Many urban designers are comfortable with this idea. The second is to find it unsatisfactory and self-serving, demanding a better answer. But the sheer complexity of the problem this opens up is analogous to a situation we find in Bali where I now live most of the year. On the island, development is held in check by one simple rule—no buildings higher than a palm tree, roughly three to four stories. Development interests eager to rape more of the island than they have currently accomplished want to see this restriction lifted. What then would be the effect? Which considerations should be paramount? How many regulatory mechanisms would it take to replace this simple rule?

The Problematic of Design

Similarly, if urban design is not restricted to project design and is generalized to encompass the overall forms of building and space emerging from the processes of urbanization, in what manner do we explain the idea of the *designed* environment? One simple distinction is that theory in urban design requires it to be contained within an as yet unformulated but unified field of urban design. I would also suggest that the former is best limited to Sert's chosen terminology of *project design*—a process involved with the formal typologies of large-scale architectural projects. In the latter, the term "urban design," or what I prefer to call the *New Urban Design*, should be reserved for explanations of the formal properties of human settlements as a totality. In this context, project design exists as a small but significant component, and I have no wish to demean the contribution made to the built environment by many such projects. However, the New Urban Design does not engage merely with the atomized fragments of capitalist social and property relations, treating the remaining vastness of cities as "undesigned." Rather it encompasses the evolutionary dimension of urban form over millennia and the collective moral battle over the symbolic construction of social space. Urban design is embedded within, and produced by, urban development in its totality, not as isolated fragments within the architectural lexicon.[14] As I have noted elsewhere, legitimizing a new field for urban

design is a risky project: "But rather than reproducing ad nauseam the same tired and treadless definitions of urban design, the scaffolding of a unified field should be explored. If we fail it will have been to some purpose."[15]

Once conceptualized as a unified theoretical field, mainstream definitions become unnecessary, even counterproductive. But any catharsis implies the recognition that all prior efforts to define urban design have not actually defined very much. We are no longer trying to describe an object, but instead to explain an archaeology of causes and effects whose primary sedimentation is symbolic. Thirty years ago Manuel Castells, whom we are privileged to have with us in this volume, was arguably the first to locate urban design in a theoretically viable environment.[16] The idea of a *field* was implicit in his definition, where he used the concept of meaning as the organizing framework that linked urban design into a much broader set of social activities and concerns:

We call urban social change the redefinition of urban meaning. We call urban planning the negotiated adaptation of urban functions to a shared urban meaning. We call urban design the symbolic attempt to express an accepted urban meaning in certain urban forms.[17]

In so doing, Castells generalized the idea of *design* from ownership to evolution. So an entirely new horizon was proposed for a field of urban design through its absorption into the fabric of society. But the debate that this simple idea generates is life threatening to the mainstream community. The argument given to me by a colleague was that if the idea of design is extended to include *evolution*, in this case to urban form, a creator is implied and hence the concept of intelligent design is invoked. This challenged the most sacrosanct idea of project designers, that design is something that is individual, preconceived, authored, commissioned, owned, and controlled. Since design necessarily has these preceding qualities, the idea that *urban design* could apply to urban form in its entirety was sheer anathema. In this he was blind to four ideas. Firstly, even mainstream urban design recognizes that its history encompasses urban forms beginning with Çatal Hüyük and continuing over nine thousand years through Babylon, Chang'an, Knossos, Rome, Athens, Fez, Istanbul, Siena, Prague, and countless other masterpieces of urban design. How then can all of this human ingenuity and creativity be reduced in scope to project design? Second, it is project design that more closely models intelligent design, since it always emerges from a creator who is making conscious decisions as to how people should live. Third, the idea of transformation that is implicit to urban design does not exist in architecture in quite the same way. Projects are not designed to be transformed, and "evolution" lasts as long as it takes to build them. So each has a distinctly different approach to history. Fourth, the New Urban Design recognizes that its source lies within civil society, spatially manifest first and foremost in the public realm and not in private capital, as is the case with most project designs.[18] This fact also opens up key ideological issues such as the relationship between the state and private capital, with implications for both the public realm and project design, but more significantly for sustainable theory.

The Demands of Ideology

Ideology mitigates the relationship between idea and action and opens up a deeper understanding of the way we think and practice. Both forms of urban design can be differentiated from each other by the types of consciousness they bring to bear on theory/ideology. Since professions have a huge influence on practice and hence on project design, they will inevitably support private capital, and increasingly so within a neo-corporate state.[19] With practice dominating, we can argue that mainstream urban design could be described as a choreography of methods from which explanations of substance, i.e., of ideologies, are of little concern and are largely absent. Given the need for sustainable theory, such a position is hardly encouraging since we are entering a historical period where our own life form could easily be extinguished. Comprehending what we do is therefore of prime significance, and ideological practices lie at the core of this understanding. Hence the New Urban Design contains an increased capacity for interpretation as well as informed practice at all levels of engagement. For obvious reasons I can only briefly touch on this subject and refer readers to some classic writing.[20] The most famous is arguably that of Marx, who said that ideology comprised all non-economic institutions and hence was superstructural, or Gramsci, for whom ideology constituted a lived system of values. What then are the main ideologies urban designers now encounter?

Given differing types of consciousness, both forms of urban design will be differentially affected by ideologies that affect the design of cities. Globally, projects funded by private capital impose serious ideological constraints on symbolic representation, one clearly designed to reflect their own interests. Professional firms and corporations whose survival is based on fees are naturally reluctant to bite the hand that feeds them. So from the perspective of the New Urban Design, professionalism by its very nature is a profoundly ideological and political event, irretrievably connected into the mainstream of the capitalist system.[21] Other ideologies prevail which temper this monopoly somewhat. Most recently we have seen the rise of the Dark Mountain Project, an apocalyptic movement that attempts to resist the collapse of civilization using a Web-based equivalent of Castells's Urban Social Movements (1983). Also significant in addition to preexisting capitalism, professionalism, and Dark Mountain are sustainable development, natural capitalism, and the New Urbanism. Sustainable development, massively co-opted by private capital, is clearly unsustainable.

> Since it refers to the amount of abuse nature can withstand, rather than to how much it should be respected . . . true sustainable development relies at its core upon the supercession of the capitalist system as it is currently constructed.[22]

Any real possibility for enduring sustainable development has been co-opted by the private sector, where the social construction of nature as a provider of goods and services reflects the ideology of the neo-corporatist state. Within this system, urban design places heavy reliance on commodified, technological solutions to design problems, promoted in its most ideological form as Natural Capitalism.[23] Here we are asked to believe that preexisting capitalism will slowly morph into a more humane and greener form, making profit from waste and generating greater social equity. The sustainable design of cities, as well as a more democratic politic is therefore speculated as a logical outcome. How it does this with the existing apparatus of capital remaining unchanged is not explained. Given the financial Armageddon of 2008, such speculation seems utterly naïve. In urban design terms we can also posit that existing class, ethnic, and religious divisions cleaving society into its various spatial and formal typologies will be further polarized into those that can afford to access the new technologies and those who cannot. Many of these innovations are covered by Hawken, Lovins and Lovins,[24] Thomas,[25] Pitts,[26] and Keeler and Burke.[27] Inherent to this process however, is the assumption of state neo-corporatism and public-private partnerships, where the legal and bureaucratic apparatus of the state is co-opted in the interest of the private sector. Exemplary in this case is the rise of the surveillance state, in theory run by government but largely managed by private-sector interests.[28] The U.K. now has one CCTV camera for every fifteen citizens. Part and parcel of this process is the conscious reorientation of design principles from the spaces of community to the Benthamite spaces of surveillance and control. So traditional design utopias, part of every planner's repertoire, are perhaps better replaced by those of science fiction such as Paolo Bacigalupi's *The Windup Girl*, Catherynne Valente's *Palimpsest*, or China Miéville's *Perdido Street Station*, a raging critique of the contemporary police state and a globalizing world.

Of these ideologies, the one most understood and appreciated is that of the *New Urbanism*, a movement originating between 1970 and 1980.[29] By the year 2000 the movement had generated enough support to publish its own charter and can now rightfully claim to be a global movement. The debate it has generated neatly splits urban design into the two divisions under discussion. For project designers, the New Urbanism offers salvation through certainty, a formulaic response to the environment based on so called *theories* that claim Ian McHarg, Patrick Geddes, and Christopher Alexander as its alter egos. For the New Urban Design, sustainability demands a radical critique of theory for appropriate praxis to occur, one bypassed by the New Urbanism. Serious criticism has emerged of its basic philosophy, in particular its contribution to urban sprawl, escapism and nostalgia, fundamental "neotraditional" conservatism, a denial of the complexity of modern life, and its potential for race and hegemonic class fractions among other distinctions.[30] These examples raise substantial issues as to whether the New Urbanist approach and sustainable theory are contiguous events.

Conclusion—Sustainability and the Development: Design Homology

In forming the distinction between project design and the New Urban Design, the issue is raised as to whether or not the development of cities and the design of cities are homologous. Similarly, the relationship between evolution and design is clearly problematic, with the mainstream being unable to accept that the built environment is designed in its entirety, although not necessarily by architects or god. The answer to this hiatus largely determines whether a sustainable field can be established for the discipline. Contemporary social life is the current manifestation of successive modes of production and a long and arduous historical process. Considered as the progressive and increasing complexity of economic forms, development and design are inseparable phenomena, with a history of some nine millennia. The resultant geographic distribution of space exhibits infinite complexity in its material and symbolic organization. Similarly, over the last 500 years, the ideological structures of capitalism have also dictated an infinite variety of urban spaces and forms of building, all produced, let us say "designed," by human action of some kind, of which projects are one form within the multitude. So separating the design of cities from the form of cities seems, in the last instance, to be unsustainable.

THE FOURTH TYRANNY

MATTHEW CARMONA

In the UK until the mid-1990s, urban design quality was either given lip-service or actively excluded from the political agenda, resulting in open interprofessional conflict, substandard design outcomes, and (in the public sector) crude development standards as a substitute for design. This is a story that resonates around the world, and it has been argued that at the root of these problems are three tyrannies of practice—creative, market, and regulatory—which actively undermine positive engagement in design.[1] Today, in the context of the drive for sustainable development, these tyrannies are potentially joined by a fourth, emerging from a narrowly defined, technology-focused view of environmental sustainability. This, somewhat polemical, chapter starts by presenting the first three tyrannies, before turning to the issue of sustainable development and a potential fourth, technological tyranny.

The Tyranny Trinity

The built environment is a collective endeavor, influenced by a diversity of stakeholders, each with a role to play in shaping what we see and experience as the architecture, urban form, public space, and infrastructure that constitutes the urban environment. McGlynn argues that developers have the real power to shape the built environment though their ability to fund development.[2] The state has power over some aspects of design through its regulatory control, while designers have wide ranging responsibility but little real power. Instead, they gain their influence through their unique professional skill (to design) and via their professional/technical knowledge. The community has almost no power, or only indirectly through the right to complain to those with regulatory authority, whom (usually) they elect.

The idea of conflicting and varied power relationships, and the notion of multiple stakeholder aspirations, can each be understood in terms of the modes of praxis from which they emerge. Three distinct traditions are clear—creative, market-driven, and regulatory—each with a major impact on

the built environment as eventually experienced. At their worst, each can be characterized as a particular form of professional "tyranny," with the potential to impact negatively on the design quality of development proposals. The word tyranny is favored here because it epitomizes a single-minded pursuit of narrow ends in a manner that undermines, or oppresses, the aspirations of others. Though actual practice is not typically situated at such extremes, there is value in exploring these positions, which, it is contended, to greater or lesser degrees underpin all practice.

The Creative Tyranny

The first tyranny results from the fetishizing of design where the image rather than the inherent value—economic, social, or environmental—is of paramount concern, and where the freedom to pursue the creative process is valued above all else. Such agendas are most closely associated with the architectural profession, often under a guise of rejecting what is sometimes seen by architects as another tyranny, that of "context."

Perpetuated by the dominant model of architectural education, and by the continuing impact of modernism, many designers see all forms of regulation as limiting their freedom of self-expression.[3] Writing about what they see as the unwarranted restrictions of the drive for sustainability, for example, the group ManTowNHuman argue, "It is time to challenge . . . tawdry and compromised architecture . . . Instead we must seek a new sensibility . . . one that refuses to bow to preservation, regulation and mediation" and favors "discovery, experimentation, innovation."[4]

Lang, by contrast, questions the importance of creativity.[5] For him, the design professions place great esteem on what they see as "creative" designers, those individuals or companies able to challenge the status quo by producing schemes that depart from the norm in response to a perceived problem in the name of art, or simply to further careers: "Those observers who regard urban design as a fine art would argue for little or no outside interference into what an individual designer/artist does. The population simply has to live with the consequences." Analyzing fifty international urban design projects of the last fifty years, he argues that this "art defence" has often been used to justify design decisions that have later proved detrimental to the enjoyment of the city. To him, this is simply antisocial, a conclusion also reached by Worpole and Knox, who found that in focusing on the aesthetic qualities of public spaces, designers often ignored more fundamental factors about how spaces are used as social places.[6]

The Market Tyranny

The second tyranny reflects the argument that the market knows best, and what sells counts. In the UK, this argument has most frequently and most vociferously been made in relation to the speculative housing market, where builders have long campaigned for a free hand to use their standard housing designs and layouts on the basis that they know their market.[7]

In this market, producers are primarily concerned with their profitability and have typically (pre–credit crunch) built in a speculative market where demand exceeds supply. As such they have been able to produce the lowest quality development that will sell and, without too much delay, gain the necessary regulatory permissions. As Rowley has argued, they build "appropriate" rather than "sustainable" quality. Architects have often been cut out altogether from the process.[8]

Lang asks, "Who leads?", concluding that in capitalist countries, private corporations are the drivers of urban development.[9] Leinberger's analysis of real estate provision in the United States, for example, demonstrates how the built environment has been reduced to a range of simple, tradable real estate commodities[10]; while Wellings's instructive analysis of the British house building industry reveals that among builders it has been personal ambition, stock market position, and market share that have driven the agenda.[11] Thus issues such as design quality or sustainability are simply part of the context that needs to be negotiated: when it is in the interest of the corporation to do so, for example, if it returns higher profits[12];when relevant permissions are dependant on it; or when the particular site context requires it,[13] for example complex brownfield sites.[14]

The Regulatory Tyranny

For some, the regulatory tyranny can be analyzed (and challenged) in terms of the political economy it represents— namely, as an attempt to correct market failure. Van Doren, for example, argues that regulation is inherently costly and inefficient but difficult to change because of political support for it from "Bootleggers" (special interests who gain economically from the existence of regulation) and "Baptists" (those

who do not like the behavior of others and want government to restrict it).[15] He cites the work of regulatory economists who have generally come out against regulation, arguing that in most cases no market failure existed in the first place. While admitting that design regulation has not been subject to such analysis, Van Doren concludes it will inevitably create barriers to change and innovation.

Encapsulating these positions and, in the process, distorting the workings of a "natural" market might be the reactionary local politician proclaiming "we know what we like and we like what we know," or the unbending municipal technocrat determined that "rules is rules" and will be applied come-what-may. The tyranny also reflects McGlynn's concern that the state only has real power through the right to say no to development proposals via the series of overlapping regulatory regimes—planning permission, building permits, conservation controls, highways adoption, etc.—but that the power to make positive proposals is limited by it typically being the private sector that has access to resources, both financial resources (to deliver development) and skills (to design it).[16]

Regulatory processes themselves reflect one of two major types: either they are based on fixed legal frameworks with unquestioning administrative decision-making, or they are discretionary, where a distinction is drawn between law and policy, the latter enacted through "guiding" plans and professional and/or political decision-making.[17] Both forms of decision-making (reflecting the local politician/council technocrat positions above) contribute to the tyranny: the first because of its perceived arbitrary, inconsistent, and subjective nature; the second because of its lack of flexibility or inability to consider nonstandard approaches.[18] Moreover, the diversity of regulatory process and systems, and their often disjointed, uncoordinated, and even contradictory nature, adds to a perception that "a marathon of red tape needs to be run."[19]

A Zone of Conflict and Compromise

The three tyrannies discussed so far represent extremes, perhaps even caricatures, but arguably they also reflect realities that practitioners from whichever side of the tyranny trinity are repeatedly faced with during the development process. They result from profoundly different motivations, respectively: peer approval; profit; and a narrowly defined view of public interest. And they result from very different professional knowledge fields, respectively: design; management/ finance; and social/administrative expertise. Having long driven practice and debate in the UK,[20] the USA,[21] and throughout the world, the three tyrannies have perpetuated profound and ingrained stakeholder conflict within the development process,[22] leading to substandard development solutions based on conflict, compromise, and delay.[23]

At the heart of each is also a different and overriding imperative, respectively: to achieve an innovative design solution (within given constraints of site, budget, brief, etc.);

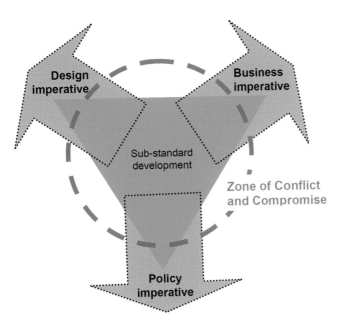

FIG. 1 Zone of conflict and compromise.

to make a good return on investment (in order to sustain a viable business); and to satisfy a broad range of public policy objectives. As these are often in opposition to each other, the result has tended toward a three-way tug of war, with the central ground stretched thinly within what can be characterized as a zone of conflict and compromise (fig. 1).

Sustainability and a Fourth Tyranny

If the first three tyrannies are long-standing and universal, a potential fourth also has long roots and has reemerged strongly in recent years as a response to the widely recognized sustainability imperative. Le Corbusier, at the advent of the modernist movement, famously celebrated how society might reap the benefits of new technology and industrialization. The car and the urban highway in particular were potent symbols of the new age.

> The cities will become part of the country: I shall live 30 miles from my office in one direction; my secretary will live thirty miles away from it too, in the other direction, under another pine tree. We shall both own cars. We shall use up tyres, wear out road surfaces and gears, consume oil and gasoline.

This "expansive" and "technological" view of the city (and its market-based incarnation, sprawl) is responsible for the high resource consumption of many Western cities and, increasingly, much of the still developing world. Cities were seen as machines for "logically" separating and ordering

human movement and activity rather than as places for people, a view still pervasive in much land use and transport planning today. The motivation was industrial (and aesthetic); the professional knowledge field, pseudo-scientific; and the imperative, human progress.

A New Technological Tyranny?

The use of the best technologies to address the city's problems is, one might argue, both appropriate and laudable. The danger comes when technology:

- is reduced to a mere surface wash, to an image of a technological solution without the content (e.g., solar panels on the roof of the latest airport terminal)
- becomes an end in itself
- is accepted and adopted without question

Each represents a particular danger in the context of today's drive for sustainable development. Focusing on the latter two, Lang has argued that sustainable approaches to urban design should first avoid the misconception that dealing with the environment is merely "an engineering problem" to be overcome by technology.[24] Post–credit crunch, however, governments around the world have increasingly seen sustainability as a new economic opportunity, and many are actively sponsoring the development of green technologies while companies fall over themselves to grab a piece of the action.

But our technological choices have sociological implications for the way we lead our lives.[25] For example, are we investing in technology in order to mitigate essentially unsustainable patterns of living, instead of facing up to the more basic and fundamental issues around place and lifestyle that over the long-term could deliver more profound change? If, for instance, we have more hybrid cars that use less fossil fuels, do we make the unspoken assumption that now it is okay to drive further, to build more roads, and to avoid the more difficult choices about how and where we live and the impact of this on the environment? Perhaps the most important question of all is: How can cities be made more sustainable by encouraging their citizens to live in more sustainable ways? This may or may not require technological solutions, but the provision of technology is certainly not the only answer, or necessarily the best starting point.

Taking the opposite view, from a technological determinist perspective, fundamental questions have arisen about whether the new sustainable imperative can be addressed within the "making places" tradition of urban design that now dominates practice and education.[26] The suggestion is that an entirely new orthodoxy is required, with resource reduction, rather than place-making, at its heart. For example, one of the most lauded "sustainable" developments, the Beddington Zero Energy Development (BedZED), in London, is based on a continuous structure of south-facing terraces that maximizes passive solar gain but deliberately

FIG. 2 Looking from one residential enclave to the next.

eschews its suburban context, in effect establishing itself as a self-contained zero-carbon enclave (fig. 2).

Other models are increasingly being put forward by high-profile architects that either see sustainable urban design as a return to object-architecture, for example Ken Yeang's "green" skyscrapers, or as technology-driven settlements on a "total design" model with designed lifestyles to match, such as Arup's proposed zero-carbon city in Dongtan, Shanghai. Foster and Partners' Masdar City in Abu Dhabi combines both, where the whole city is viewed as a single object in which technology enables residents to live carbon-neutral lives in the middle of a desert. These technology-driven, object-design models of sustainable urban form, which will undoubtedly prove seductive in architecture studios around the world, may fall into the trap of once again seeing the city solely as a technological and aesthetic design problem rather than as a place for people.

Such examples suggest a break with urban design as place-making, at least to the extent that form and impact rather than people and place are the priority. However, sustainable design precepts do not imply that concerns for place-making cannot also be met. Ritchie, for example, argues that we need to combine a concern for the changing climate with the need for more people to live in a more humane city environment.[27] Roger Evans Associates conclude, "There is a common misconception that a conflict exists between principles of good urban design . . . and an optimal approach to environmental sustainability."[28] On the contrary, they argue, it is perfectly possible to engage with street-based design while also achieving optimal thermal performance.

For Golany, wherever we live in the world we will need good urban design and modern technology combined to face the challenges that climate (and now climate change) will throw at us.[29] A failure to recognize this risks a new technological tyranny to join the other tyrannies already discussed, just as the modernists' love of the city as machine valued science and image over people and place and spawned the modernist city that proved so unsustainable in the past. As the doyenne of place-making, Jane Jacobs, has argued, "Le

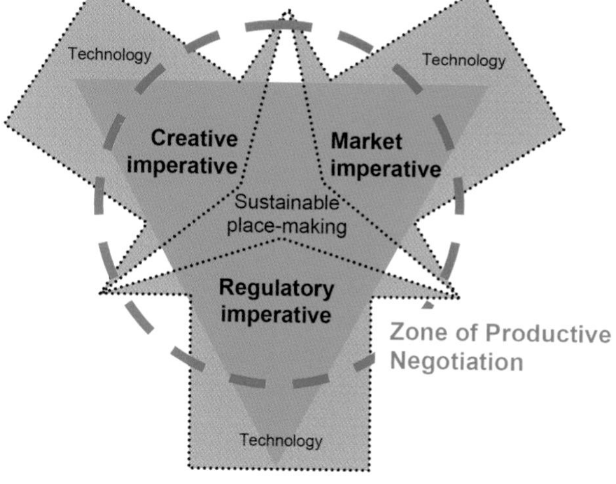

FIG. 3 Zone of productive negotiation.

Corbusier's dream city was like a wonderful mechanical toy, but as to how the city works, it tells nothing but lies."[30]

Conflict and Compromise to Productive Negotiation

The technological tyranny is perhaps different from the other three because technology is primarily a tool and an outcome of development rather than a mode of practice. It can be used by all players within the development process as a driver of creative design, as a means to secure market advantage, and as a basis for regulatory decision-making. Thus, although some players come from an inherently technological perspective (e.g., civil engineers), it is through creative, market, and regulatory processes that they achieve their ends.

Elsewhere, it has been argued that use of the right process-led tools, for example site-specific design codes, can help to bridge the gap between creative, market-driven, and regulatory modes of praxis.[31] In so doing they are not simply regulatory tools for the control of private interests by public ones, or even of some private interests (developers) by others (landowners), but also have the potential to be tools for guidance and consensus-building within a zone of productive negotiation (fig. 3). To be effective in this role, such tools require the involvement of, or at least a deep awareness of the aspirations of, all parties within the development process.

Sustainability might be used in a similar way, to bring players together in order to discuss and agree on common goals and overcome the conflict and compromise of the past (see fig. 1). Rather than representing a further tyranny via the pursuit of technology for technology's sake or technology as image, the goal of sustainable development should be seen as a new universal context for good urban design with the potential to focus all stakeholders toward an agreed goal rather than to extend conflict and compromise. In effect it could be the catalyst for all parties to engage in a fast-moving learning process with potentially profound impacts. Sustainable place-making must, however, be the goal. This will require new technologies, but these must serve people and place and not the other way around.

PART 7: SUSTAINABLE SPATIAL GEOGRAPHIES AND REGIONAL CITIES

7.1 # REGIONAL URBANIZATION AND THE TRANSFORMATION OF THE MODERN METROPOLIS

EDWARD W. SOJA

The modern metropolis is being progressively—and regressively—transformed, reflecting a fundamental change in the very nature of the urbanization process. In *Postmetropolis* (2000), I described this transformation rather vaguely as the "postmetropolitan transition," a movement beyond what we have known as a metropolitan mode of urban development to something quite different but not yet specifiable.[1] Today it is possible to describe the urban transformation more confidently and concretely as a *shift from metropolitan to regional urbanization*. This still ongoing paradigm shift in the urbanization process is perhaps the most profound in the history of the industrial capitalist city, yet it is not widely recognized. As I will try to explain here, however, I feel confident in predicting that regional urbanization will emerge over the next few decades as the central concept in urban studies.

Regional Urbanization

Regional urbanization as it is defined here has shaped the dominant trajectory of the urbanization process over the past thirty years. Rather than the simple combination of centripetal and centrifugal forces emanating from a single urban core that has shaped the formation of the modern metropolis over the past century—piling up high urban densities in the central city while sprawling low density suburbanization pushes ever outward into the nonurban periphery—a new dynamic has emerged, characterized by a marked leveling out of population densities between inner and outer cities, and an almost oxymoronic urbanization of suburbia, transforming the monocentric modern metropolis into polycentric regional networks of agglomerations that are called city regions or regional cities.

With the spread of regional urbanization, the sharp divide between urban and suburban areas and ways of life is becoming increasingly blurred. The once characteristic steep density gradient declining sharply around the city center is broadly flattening out, with central densities declining to varying degrees while densities in the suburban rings increase. The number of large urban nodes increases as urbanization and urban densities spread throughout the entire metropolitan region and occasionally well beyond it. Polycentric regional urbanization increasingly takes the form of an evolving network of cities as the city region stretches outward to connect with new hinterlands. Whereas we could once speak of the city as a system within a national system of cities, what is emerging now can be better described as regional city networks connecting into a hierarchical global web of city regions.

Regional urbanization and its associated formation of polycentric and networked city regions is leading to a growing erasure of the once clear distinction between urbanism and suburbanism as ways of life. This significantly different urbanization process is advancing at different rates in different city regions and is taking on a multiplicity of specific forms as regional urbanization processes interact with local contexts and cultures. This does not mean that traditional suburbanization has ceased but rather that it no longer dominates the urban growth process to the same degree it did in the past. I would add that this rising trajectory of regional urbanization is likely to continue well into the future, marking the end of the Metropolis Era. We have entered not just a new Urban Age, with the majority of the world's population now living in cities, but one that needs to be described as a Regional Urban Age.

Regional urbanization and the growth of polycentric megacity regions have evolved from many sources. In part, they build upon preexisting trends and in this sense represent continuities with the past development of the modern metropolis. To a larger degree, however, they are products of more recent developments and take on distinctively new and different features and characteristics. Particularly influential in shaping our understanding of regional urbanization has been the unprecedented diffusion of critical and/or analytical spatial perspectives across a wider spectrum of disciplinary fields than ever before. This transdisciplinary *spatial turn*, as some now call it, has reinvigorated urban and regional studies and stimulated the development of many new concepts and ideas in almost every field of knowledge, from archeology and theology to cultural studies and development economics.[2] This extended reach of spatial and regional thinking creates a much larger and more informed audience of scholars and policy makers aware of the significance of regions and regional thinking, and the meaning and implications of regional urbanization.

More specifically and directly, the concept of city regions has emerged from an extensive literature focusing on the profound restructuring of practically every aspect of modern life that has been taking place over the past forty years. In this sense, the growing importance of city regions can be traced back to the three major forces that have been shaping the reconfiguration of the modern world: the globalization of capital, labor, and culture; the formation of a New Economy variously labeled post-Fordist, flexible, global, and information-intensive; and the far-reaching revolution in information and communications technology. City regions are seen in this way as emergent forms of contemporary urbanization arising from the restructuring of the modern metropolis and the changing relationship between urbanization and industrialization processes. Rather than representing its termination, the city region is a new postmetropolitan phase in the development of the industrial capitalist city.

Inner vs. Outer Cities

Regional urbanization has had a different impact on the center and periphery of the modern metropolis. The core of many if not most of the world's major metropolitan regions, for example, has been experiencing some degree of "hollowing out" with the loss of population and jobs and reductions in overall density. This has led some to speak of the "suburbanization of the inner city" or "shrinking cities." In some cases, such as Detroit, this hollowing out has produced severe stagnation and desolate urban landscapes. In others, such as Osaka, the urban core of what was once the densest of major Japanese cities has been almost emptied of its resident population but is nevertheless vibrant and thriving. In still other cases, such as Los Angeles, New York, London, and Paris, the urban core has been refilled with migrant populations, maintaining if not increasing central densities while often instigating fierce conflicts and competition between immigrant and domestic populations.[3]

The experiences of the older central cities vary widely, creating great challenges to planners and policy makers over the unpredictable future of the downtown cores. This variation and unpredictability is closely related to the rise of city marketing and city branding, as "stressed" downtowns compete for investment, jobs, and tourist expenditures. Even when the region as a whole is thriving, the old downtowns seem to be suffering from neglect and decline, needing injections of revival juices such as those promised by the so called Bilbao effect or the development of the "creative industries." A major reason for this concern over the old centers has been

the urbanization of suburbia, signaled by the explosion of new terms such as edge cities, outer cities, exopolis, metroburbs, metroplex, postsuburbia.

While there are great variations in the old inner cities, suburbia and suburbanization nearly everywhere have been changing in roughly similar ways. Rather than continuing to sprawl ever outward in low-density developments, as was the case for most of the twentieth century, suburbia as we knew it is becoming denser, more economically and culturally heterogeneous, and, in short, increasingly urbanized. While this seemingly paradoxical urbanization of suburbia is a key driving force for regional urbanization, it does not mean that every part of old suburbia is urbanizing. Traditional suburban ways of life persist in every postmetropolis, and suburbanization continues in nearly all the world's city regions. What I am arguing here is that the rate of suburbanization has begun to decrease relative to the rate of regional urbanization, especially the still advancing urbanization of suburbia, and this trend toward polycentric densification is likely to continue in the future in almost every urban region on earth.

Los Angeles illustrates one of the most advanced cases of regional urbanization, and it is no surprise that both the terms city region and regional city have emerged most prominently in this area.[4] Once the epitome of the sprawling low-density metropolis, Greater Los Angeles, in a stunning reversal, passed Greater New York in 1990 as the densest urbanized or continuously built up area in the U.S. While the old inner urban core of Los Angeles lost around a million and a half black and white inhabitants and tens of thousands of Fordist manufacturing jobs in the 1970s and 1980s, more than five million migrants refilled the core, creating urban densities rivaling the densest areas of Manhattan. At the same time, in areas such as Orange County and the San Fernando Valley—paralleling what was happening in the better known Silicon Valley as well as Santa Clara County—new industrial employment complexes and polycentric outer cities took form, densifying what was once classic American suburbia.

What I am suggesting here is that in nearly every one of the five hundred largest megacity regions in the world, more than one hundred of which are in China alone, different forms of polycentric regional urbanization will become increasingly more prominent in the future compared to traditional forms of sprawling low-density suburbanization. This places a high premium on comparative studies of diverse inner and outer city experiences and elicits a deep questioning of many conventional urban concepts and theories. Because they typically mix together traditional and postmodern suburban built environments, the urbanized outer city complexes often do not look like conventional suburbs. They are denser, more compact, and reflect the location in surrounding areas of a greater number of job sites than so-called bedroom communities. Commuting patterns increasingly link suburban centers rather than connecting to the most prominent central city, as new urban complexes cluster together shopping centers, entertainment complexes, corporate offices, museums, and other typically urban attractions. They can no longer be viewed as traditional suburbs.

Most inner cities or old downtowns also no longer resemble what they once were, as some hollow out while others are filled with new immigrant populations introducing their cultures and cuisines into new enclaves and creating zones of increasing cultural diversity. More than ever before, central cities and their older downtowns have been absorbed into a global competition for investment, tourism (now the largest world industry), and general attention or image. This competition at the highest level involves attracting spectacular events such as Olympic games and World Expos, or architectural extravaganzas such as the Guggenheim Museum in Bilbao. Given the rising importance of the so-called cultural industries, urban and regional planners increasingly become city entrepreneurs, marketing and branding their central attractions for global consumption and thereby, it is hoped, effecting inner city regeneration while funds for alleviating poverty and improving social services are siphoned away.

This is particularly ironic since other features embedded in regional urbanization have been widening income gaps, growing inequality and poverty, and intensified forms of social and political polarization. In the U.S., the gap between rich and poor is greater than it has ever been, and it reaches its peak in Los Angeles and New York City, where the wealth gap is as large as it is in Karachi or Mexico City. Not only is wealth being concentrated to unparalleled degrees in a small number of globalized megacity regions, so too is poverty concentrating in what Mike Davis has described as a planet of slums.

The key point I am making is that long-established ways of interpreting metropolitan urbanization and suburbanization are becoming increasingly obsolete and ineffective in an era of polycentric regional urbanization. To meet contemporary demands and challenges, new approaches are needed, especially with regard to questions of urban citizenship, identity, and governance. It is this challenge that has led me to write *Seeking Spatial Justice*, an attempt to open up new strategies for coalition building and combining traditional social movements in the struggle to reduce injustice and increase democratic participation in the new and emphatically unjust geographies being created by the regional urbanization process.[5]

THE NEW RURALITY AND THE DIMINISHING URBAN-RURAL DICHOTOMY

MATS JOHANSSON AND HANS WESTLUND

The Urban-Rural Divide—Old and New Patterns

City and countryside have traditionally been regarded as antitheses. According to conventional wisdom, the urban economy was based on manufacturing and services, while the rural economy was based on agriculture and forestry. Urban culture was a modern, dynamic, innovative—but also dangerous—melting pot, whereas rural culture was traditional and static—but safe. Cities were also seen as polluters while the countryside was considered as an ecocycle system. The dichotomies go on and on.

In the knowledge economy of today, not much of this conventional wisdom holds. A historical transformation of urban-rural relations has happened. In all aspects mentioned above—economy, culture, and ecology—today's countryside is more or less a mirror of the city. The main difference between urban and rural that has remained is that of density and accessibility. It is no exaggeration to claim that we have entered a neo-urban era.

This means that throughout history, urban-rural relations have undergone a complete transformation. In preindustrial times, the mainly small cities performed limited services but were strongly dependent on products from their surrounding countrysides. The theories of Johann Heinrich von Thünen gave an explanation to the spatial variations of rural production under these conditions. According to him, the countryside's role was (briefly expressed) determined by the quantity, quality, and location of its natural resources.[1]

The agricultural and industrial revolutions changed the urban-rural relationships dramatically. An increasingly efficient agriculture was able to feed a growing share of nonagricultural population. This formed one of the prerequisites for urbanization. The other prerequisite was industrialization—the cities could provide work for the surplus rural population. A new urban-rural balance emerged in which the cities' consumption of rural goods increased with their size, and the countrysides' consumption of urban goods increased considerably.

The global knowledge economy of today represents still another phase of the relationship. Intercity exchange and trade, which grew during the industrial epoch, is now the predominate form of exchange on global as well as national levels, while the share of urban-rural trade has decreased with shrinking rural population shares. Even more significant is the "urbanization of countryside" in terms of industries and occupations, culture, and ways of living. If any rural peculiarity remains, it is the sparseness and low accessibility. Not just the "pure" countryside has lost population and activities. The lower levels of the urban hierarchies are also decreasing in a way that is similar to rural areas, except for the settlements and subcenters that are located in sufficient proximity of larger urban regions. In line with this development, the concept of countryside is transformed to often include urban settlements outside regional centers. On the other hand, even if we here write about the countryside, it should be observed that the various parts of *the* countryside are showing completely different developmental tendencies. Thus there is no single definition of rural areas and the conclusion is that there are *several* countrysides.

This development means that instead of being antitheses requiring different approaches and methods of studying, different types of policies, etc., cities and countryside constitute systems of nodes and resource flows with obvious similarities. Instead of opposites, they compose a continuum of varying densities. This has consequences both for research and for policies.

For research, it means that urban and rural issues not only can but often should be analyzed in the same analytical framework instead of being analyzed separately through different approaches and methods. This is especially important for rural issues, since they normally are influenced by external, urban matters. For policies, this can even mean that measures focusing solely on areas of a certain density might fail if the measures are formed without consideration of these areas' positions and dependencies in the "density hierarchy." This holds in particular for rural areas, since their development normally is not endogenous but indissoluble and connected to the cities' development.

The development outlined above can be described in the somewhat unfair terms of the countryside's transformation from nourishing to consuming. However, the important conclusion is that the countryside has lost its role as first predominate and later equal partner to the cities and is now more or less dependent on the cities' development and preferences. Where rural growth occurs, it is due to migration from nearby cities or urban preferences for certain rural products, e.g., certain tourism products. This means that while *regional* development can be based on certain endogenous resources and processes (as suggested in modern growth theory), *rural endogenous development*, independent of cities' resources and demand, can only occur in exceptional cases.

Up to the 1960s, industrialization and urbanization were the dominating processes on which research focused, and the decline of countryside was seen as inevitable. After Beale's 1975 discovery of a rural vitalization trend in migration in the United States, an extensive literature on *counterurbanization* and its causes has been published across the developed world. After the 1970s, the "population turnaround" seems to describe a wave pattern, where periods of counterurbanization have been followed by periods of urbanization.[2]

The New Rurality and the New Rural Economy

This "rural revival" has more and more been described in terms of the "new rurality" or the "new rural economy." The definitions of rural areas are thus manifold, resulting in differing development paths concerning their location and economic structure. The *new rurality* areas have more in common with urban and densely populated areas; they have taken advantage of the possibilities connected to the development toward the new rurality and are often regions characterized by accessibility, commuting, and growth. The new rurality is both an effect of the structural transformation of the rural areas and a renewal of people by in-migration— introducing people that often are urbanized in a behavioral or mental sense. Even if the rural areas still are rural, areas, ideas, jobs, and habits are more urban than the traditional rural values, and the prime driver behind this transformation is in-migration, with "mental urbanization" in rural areas being one consequence.

The New Rurality—A Middle-class Phenomenon?

That differing age groups show differing mobility patterns is a well-known fact. Young people and young adults have quite other preferences with regard to settlement than families or elderly people. For example, in Europe and Sweden it is obvious that the rural exodus is still valid for young people. This can be shown by the migratory flows for different cohorts but also that families with young children as well as young adults are overrepresented in the big cities.[3] The influence of the new rurality can be seen from the settlement patterns of the areas surrounding the metropolitan centers,

which have experienced an inflow of younger families. This is not the case in more remote localities where even families leave the rural areas.[4]

Another concept describing migration to rural areas close to the city is that of *rural gentrification*. A common feature in the literature on this concept is that the in-migrants belong to social groups with higher status than the original inhabitants. Also, a substantial literature dealing with the issues of counterurbanization has attempted to analyze the determinants of in-migration to rural areas at various spatial levels.[5] Westlund and Pichler[6] have studied factors behind rural population development in all non-metropolitan municipalities in Sweden for the periods 1990 through 1997 and 1998 through 2004. They found that rural population development was most positive in the metropolitan-adjacent municipalities. Socioeconomic variables, like the size of the local labor market, average real estate assessments, and average incomes, were among the strongest explanatory variables, beside the previous period's population change. It can be shown that the result has been a redistribution of people between rural and urban areas. Out-migration of young people from rural areas is a general phenomenon but the contrary is in many cases valid concerning families and elderly people, especially to rural areas in close proximity to big cities.[7] The preconditions for the new rurality seem, however, to be limited in the peripheral and deeper rural areas, which are still dominated by traditional activities and located far away from big cities, with bad infrastructure and low accessibility. The combination of low accessibility, few highly educated people, and an aging population is not a good precondition to take part in the new development trends that the new rurality implies.[8]

More commuting over longer distances has resulted in larger functional labor markets and regional enlargement, and the new rurality is a concept that is not associated with agriculture and the primary sector. Instead, it has more in common with the urban way of life, both in an economic and cultural sense. Instead of a convergent development process between different rural areas, a divergent or polarization process seems to be more relevant. Particularly in the United Kingdom and the United States, the development surrounding big cities has been described in terms of rural gentrification and "rurbanization," symbolizing a transformation of rural communities to (upper) middle-class communities with urban values and lifestyles.[9] This seems also be valid for the European Union, where according to the OECD terminology the "significantly urban areas" increased in population during the 1990s, while the "predominantly rural" areas still experienced population losses. This seems to be valid even during the first decade of the new century.[10]

Rural Areas and Attractiveness— Differing Locations, Differing Preconditions

The impact of in-migrants on new businesses and job creation in depopulating rural areas seems, however, to be less positive. In a study of two peripheral Scottish areas, Stockdale[11] found that relatively few in-migrants were self-employed and that those who were had businesses generally with no employees. The same results have been shown about the development in rural Sweden. In this case, much of the deviation in results between in-migrants and locals seems to be explained by tradition, social contacts, and age structure. Here a recent study shows that the rural out-migrants are younger than the in-migrants, who in turn are younger than the traditional inhabitants. It can also be mentioned that the "stayers" were more frequently working as self-employed entrepreneurs than the in-migrants, a fact that probably can be explained by the age structure and differing working traditions among in-migrants and locals, and the way in which the locals seem to be more frequently engaged in the agricultural sector.[12]

In Japan, similar tendencies can be found with rather clear features: the three major metropolitan regions, especially the Tokyo metropolitan region, have been magnets for people, enterprises, and urban activities. The peripheries, on the other hand, are faced with risks to their existence. Japanese society is aging rapidly. The megacities are expected to become "ultra-aged societies" in a few decades as the people of the baby-boomer generation after the last war join the aged class. But the inhabitants of the peripheral communities are getting younger, since the bulk of the baby-boomer generation has already left the regions. In a nutshell, many rural communities, especially in the west part of Japan, are being transformed from an *aged* society to a *post-aged* society. A post-aged society has some common features in a balanced cohort structure with a small population. The experimental policy initiatives to foster social capital among different generations will be central concerns for sustainable rural communities.

In the United States, development has been somewhat different as many peripherally located rural communities have experienced population growth. Green et al. connect this growth with a "shift in rural economies from extraction of natural resources to promotion of natural and cultural amenities."[13] Power defines amenities as location-specific public goods characteristics of a place that increases its attractiveness, giving the following examples: natural landscape features; climate; and social, cultural, and human-built environments.[14] Features of the local market economy, e.g., market size, job opportunities, and costs of living, are not treated as amenities.

Bolton coined the concept of *place surplu*s and defined it as the sum of consumer and producer surpluses of a spatially limited area.[15] Westlund points out that the reason for using the term place surplus is the notion that consumers' and producers' perceived utility varies in infinite combinations, and that places' capacity to fulfill all these preferences and needs varies.[16] In line with this reasoning, every individual and organization may be presumed to perceive a place surplus in certain places and "place break-even" and "place shortfall" in other places. In these terms, migration is a movement from a place with shortfall to a place with surplus in light of the preferences and needs of the individual.

A large part of the place surplus can be expressed in pure economic terms: wages and other incomes, costs and tax level, profits, etc. Another element of the place surplus consists of access to goods, services, amenities, inputs, and markets—which to a large extent can also be calculated in monetary terms relatively easily. The third element of the place surplus consists in the principle of the social network and the norms, values, and lifestyles which are connected to it—that is to say, the social capital of a place.

Research on locations' combinations of various characteristics and their potential matching of actors' preferences has a long tradition in the regional science literature.[17] Power lists a number of important characteristics of which each location has a unique combination.[18] Over time, both the supply of combinations of attributes and the demand for them change. The natural landscape, social and cultural attributes (such as social capital), and accessibility to markets are examples of characteristics that make a location attractive or not.

The attractiveness of a rural area or place is the result of a unique combination of supply factors, consisting of natural and man-made amenities and market factors. The "attractiveness supply" of places/areas does not only differ by their factor combinations (i.e., quality) but also by the quantity of each factor. Different actors respond to this supply in accordance with their demands. Actors' demands are results of complex functions in which the relative strength of preferences are determined by a large number of social and cultural factors (age, sex, family, education, income, profession, acquaintances, leisure interests, etc.). The unique supply of each place/area meets the unique supply of each actor. This means that the place surplus approach referred to above is useful in analyses of aggregates, but that attractiveness also can be analyzed at the micro level.

Rural Areas, Social Capital, and Renewal

A factor of special importance for rural development in the neo-urban era is social capital. The *social capita*l of rural areas has traditionally been built on traditional industries and activities. In order to develop in the current situation, when the countryside mainly is dependent on urban people's demand for dwelling or leisure, rural areas need to develop a social capital that combines tradition and neo-urbanism. Here the division of social capital in bonding and bridging component parts is useful.

Bonding social capital is necessary to keep a village or a place together, and people's attachment to a place is basically a positive factor. However, when such attachments are expressed in features like upholding outdated values, behavior, gender relations, or even xenophobia, these bonding factors play a negative role. From this perspective, the countryside needs to develop new forms of bridging social capitals, which can provide rural areas with new inflows of inhabitants, innovations, and entrepreneurship.

Differing localities are thus characterized by different kinds of social capital as a consequence of economic structure and development. Out-migration areas are often characterized by social cohesion founded on old ties among the non-movers ("stayers")—"bonding" social capital—while in-migration areas are characterized more by new constellations of social engagement and consequently also of new kinds of social capital—"bridging" social capital. The first types of communities are often homogenous, inflexible, and resistant to change. This can be contrasted to communities dominated by "bridging" social capital that instead are associated with heterogeneity and flexibility.[19]

This also means that the dividing line between newcomers and "stayers" is a threshold that hampers the establishment of new kinds of social capital in these kinds of localities. The difference can be seen, in a schematic way, as a consequence of 1) the necessity to work together in order to survive and hamper the development toward dying-out regions, while 2) in-migration areas might consist of more anonymous relations that will result in new social relations based on new firms, schools, and housing areas. The first case can be seen as a reactive action where well-established social capital is a cen-

tral ingredient, and "bonding" social capital is dominant. This kind of social capital has a tendency to exclude newcomers and then hamper new ideas to get a foothold in the community or the region.[20] In the latter case, new and more anonymous social capital will be created in order to solve common problems, and here the "bridging" social capital, or "bridging" links, ought to be the dominant kind of social capital.[21]

Concluding Remarks

With the emergence of the knowledge economy, urban-rural relations have entered a new stage in which urban norms and lifestyles are dominating. A worldwide city system has been formed, and rural areas' development is wholly dependent on how they are able to connect to this system. In the city-accessible countryside and rural areas that for various reasons are attractive for urban dwellers, a new rurality with urban overtones has appeared. The city has finally conquered the countryside.

MERGING LANDSCAPES, DIVERGING COMPETENCES

BOSSE BERGMAN

During the last decades, the metaphor "landscape" has taken an important place in the urban discourse, although with slightly different connotations in different cultural contexts. Analogous to other combinations of "scape"—as town- and cityscape, roadscape, mediascape, etc.—it has made it easier to challenge the obsolete dichotomies town-countryside and urban-rural, which in modified interpretations have even been reinforced in some normative discourses. For instance, it was not long ago that the notion "urban landscape" was used to discriminate suburban areas as not being authentically urban, while today many researchers choose the same terms to recognize whole city regions as urban.

Relying on this scape-talk, though with some hesitation due to its invitation to play with words, the purpose here is to comment on what I will call "traffical urban landscapes." Freeways, highways, and motorways probably at once come to mind, since they have indeed changed the urban landscape more substantially, creating new areas dependent on the visual and physical accessibility of road-bound sites. The dominant artery E4, which runs through Stockholm, the main reference for this article, has during slightly more than forty years experienced a development from nothing into a veritable corridor of office buildings and shopping- and service-facilities. Also, in several mid-sized cities in Sweden, national highways have given shape to such urban corridors, intensively used locally, but not yet recognized by planners as a kind of new main street.

While Swedish municipalities are still rather confused when handling these often unforeseen road-side developments—sooner wishing to move the roads further outwards than consider their possibilities—architects have seldom hesitated to explore the roadscapes, even if provocative analyses of Las Vegas undertaken in the late 1960s have always been far from a hit in Sweden. For more than a decade some Swedish municipalities—as in other parts of the world—have been busy working with the organization and rhythm of roadside sceneries. Mostly they rely on conventional spatial principles (landmarks, borders, porticos), thereby con-serving a traditional perception of urban space overall. However, today some of them have also begun to invest in spectacular arrangements which definitely "turn the roadside settings on" (roller-costers, transparent arena stands, ski-jumping slopes, water slides), though do not really change spatial relations beyond this visual dimension.

From the perspective of landscape, it is obvious that these road corridors, with their three main components—the road, the built-up areas, and the unexploited areas, have not only opened up for landscape planners but also paved the way for the practice today called "landscape urbanism." With more and more advocates, the latter has actually become a promising form of urbanism since it calls for the integration between traffic-, town-, and landscape planning into one and the same practice. It is even time to expand this triad of urban design and include the engineers of telecoms, energy, heating, water, and waste systems, since increasing demands for sustainability will increase the physical presence of technical structures in the urban landscape enormously: stockyards, wind power, tele-towers, and power stations (the latter are now built almost everywhere as expressive roadside landmarks).

However, bridging existing gaps between the four competences of urban design—traffic planning, architecture/town planning, landscape planning, and infrastructure planning, supported of course by many kinds of technicians, economists, and sociologists—cannot simply be done through professional collaboration and institutional adjustments. Practice, discourse, and academia still very much lean on their own education, cultural norms, and outlook. In Sweden, urban planners are considered the most influential group regarding ideas of how to build the city and, too simply of course, are identified with those responsible for (the politically decided plans of) the built-up areas. But they often show a tendency to join the earlier modernists in their beliefs in an ideal physical form for cities. Following the normally unquestioned idea of sustainable cities as being necessarily compact cities—moreover, often in traditional forms and patterns—the consequence is an effort to win the other competences for a common normative program through which, for instance,

TABLE 1: OVERVIEW OF MEASURES TAKEN FOR BIODIVERSITY CONSERVATION IN THE DUTCH TAX ADMINISTRATION OFFICE DESIGN

Measure	Aim	Type of measure
Adjustable groundwater drain between Sterrebos forest and office site	To keep the groundwater in the forest on the original level, thereby protecting the roots of the old trees in the Sterrebos forest from drowning or drought	Mitigation
Aerodynamic shape of the office building	To avoid or minimize heavy winds, often observed in direct surroundings of high (office) buildings; such a heavy wind could harm the old trees in the adjacent forest and its heron colony	Mitigation
Planting of new trees at the office site	To maintain existing migration routes for bats and birds across the office site, since some of the existing trees will be cut down because of construction activities	Compensation
Built-in wildlife space (5 × 3 × 2 meters) in the office building (on ground level)	To offer an extra reproduction site in the actual building for bats that currently live in the adjacent Sterrebos forest; some of those bat species prefer both forest trees as well as buildings as a suitable nesting place	Extra
Office green with habitat value	At the office site, in the so-called office garden that will surround the buildings, shrubs and trees will be planted; this vegetation will not only be chosen for its appearance and the enjoyment of people, but also for its habitat value for the birds, butterflies, and other animals that will visit the site in the future	Extra
External bat hibernation bunker	To financially contribute to the construction of a bat hibernation bunker in the direct surroundings of the office site; by doing so, the habitat value of the overall location (office site and Sterrebos forest) for bats will increase	Extra

national—and some even by international—biodiversity conservation laws.

Final design

A consortium of project developers, civil engineers, architects, landscape architects, and urban ecologists came up with the winning design for the office complex in Groningen (fig. 2). Key to the project's success concerning biodiversity conservation was the idea of creating extra values for plants and animals in the office complex design in addition to a basic set of mitigation measures (table 1).

The Process

As researchers in urban ecology, our interaction with architects, landscape architects, and project developers required a flexible attitude. In the conceptual phase, metaphors and inspiring pictures played a more important role than the functional approach that is typically used by (ecology) researchers. One metaphor we employed was the office complex as an old Mayan temple arising from the tropical jungle (the adjacent Sterrebos forest). This metaphor emphasizes the contrast between the building and its more natural, forested environment.

Building on this idea, the office complex and its "office garden" were then intended to act in way that is ecologically "complementary" to the natural context. How could the building offer something extra to its surroundings, thereby enlarging its sustainability level? In the end, the 5-meter-long and 3-meter-high "wildlife space" that will be constructed in the plinth of the building can be considered as such an ecological "added value." The collaboration was an exploration of one another's disciplines, searching for ways to come together and develop a common language and understanding.

Discussion

The Dutch Tax Administration building case shows how two disciplines, architecture and ecology, can enrich each other. The building, for all of its ecological gadgets, has an ecological narrative strongly related to the surrounding green context. Local biodiversity has been conserved as much as possible; moreover, additional habitats will be created in the office building complex and in its garden.

How can we scale up from this Dutch office complex case to conservation-inclusive architecture in general? More precisely, what principles can we develop to offer better guidelines for such practices? How can architects and urban planners make green statements including biodiversity conservation within their plans?

First, we would recommend that architects and urban planners with ambitions concerning "ecology" involve ecologists in their planning processes to integrate essential ecological insights into their urban design.

Second, as some of these insights can be applied universally, we would recommend that architects and urban planners consider the entire city environment, in addition to their specific planning, from the perspective of wild plants and animals. Consequently, we consider following these guidelines to be essential:

1. To integrate "biodiversity conservation" in the planning area, select species and habitats that are present in the wider surroundings.

Plant and animal species that may be found at particular spots in cities constitute part of larger (meta)populations on a regional scale. This is because individuals or small communities of plants and animals at a particular (urban) location are not able to survive on their own in the long run. Only if they are part of a larger, more regional community can the species survive at the particular (urban) spot. So, when considering biodiversity conservation in the design of the planning area, focus on species and habitats that are present in the wider surroundings.

2. Make sure selected plant and animal species are able to colonize the planning area.

Like humans, plants and animals find difficulties moving through the landscape. Especially for ground-dwelling animals, city environments with their roads and buildings can be real obstacle courses. In general, urban green networks are the best way to support the migration of species through cities, even for flying animals such as birds, bats, and butterflies. Therefore, for successful colonization of the planning area by the targeted plant and animal species, make sure that this area can be reached.

3. Create the right habitat conditions at the actual planning area.

Each species has its own habitat requirements, some species being more demanding than others. Often, the species that are most abundant in cities are habitat generalists, able to survive in a great range of urban biotopes. From a biodiversity conservation perspective, greater attention is required for less-common (urban) species. These plants and animals, often habitat specialists, can be supported only if their habitat requirements are strictly complied with.

About the role of buildings for biodiversity conservation: with specific measures, buildings can provide nesting, hibernation, and other habitat functions for wildlife. For example, BirdLife Netherlands has developed the "checklist for implementing biodiversity conservation measures in building design." This checklist offers clues to architects and project

FIG. 2 Final design of the Dutch Tax Administration office complex.

FIG. 3 Like the well-known Hanging Gardens of Babylon, this urban green design in the inner-city of Eindhoven, Netherlands, illustrates how highly built-up areas still can offer opportunities for conservation. The mix of plant species used at this location is selected on both visual quality and habitat suitability for bees, butterflies, and birds.

developers on how to integrate feasible conservation measures in their building designs.

All in all, these guidelines can be most effective with the help of urban ecological specialists collaborating with architects or urban planners. However, even then an essential prerequisite is still missing. "Ecological imagination" is essential. As we stated earlier, architecture often represents cultural identity including local and sustainable narratives, and those in turn may include biodiversity conservation. In the first stages of the architectural design and urban planning processes, creative impressions and strong narratives are of great importance. Meanwhile in (urban) ecology, the focus is on the functional level of urban ecosystems, networks, and ecological conditions. Ecology stands in a long tradition of intrinsic values; nature is a value in itself. So far, both clients and designers are directing relatively few resources, financial or creative, toward green statements that really conserve biodiversity. New buildings can include local biodiversity statements if ecologists dare to use their imagination, and architects broaden their scope on sustainable building to include biodiversity conservation.

CULTIVATING BUILT ENVIRONMENT

N. J. HABRAKEN

Metaphors to Work With

From the 1960s onward I have advocated adaptability in housing construction. The major reason for doing so was to reintroduce into the contemporary built environment what I have called the "natural relation,"[1] the age-old settlement process where inhabitation and built form were one. Sustainability in built environment has everything to do with that restoration.

The idea that built environment can be wasteful is peculiar to our times. For millennia humanity has produced shelter that could be highly complex and endure for centuries. No one has ever argued that such fabrics wasted available resources.

The constant aspect of historic urban fabrics was their organic quality. The term is justified because by a slow but continuous process of renewal, improvement, and adaptation of individual houses, they had a self-generating ability. Houses functioned like living cells of a larger organism. There the nominal social unit interacts without mediation with the smallest material unit recognizable as a changeable whole. House types never were architectural inventions but came to full bloom by that very interaction. House typology being self evident, acts of urban design were about providing context much in the way a gardener lays out the beds for plants to flower in.

Our contemporary built environment may look very different from past examples, but it is unlikely that humanity's settlement habits of more than five thousand years have suddenly evaporated. It is reasonable to assume that they have continued and that the degree in which that has happened may tell us something about the present-day environment's health.

Following up on that assumption, I will look at the present-day built environment by using the metaphors of "living cell" and "organism," with "living cell" denoting those instances where occupancy interacts immediately with its material envelope, and "organism" because a certain autonomy, a capacity for self organization, is found in all built environment, which we must accept as intrinsic to it. These terms provide a shorthand that can help us to understand age-old human settlement behavior and consider its continuation and interruption in the contemporary environment. This may help us to find out why we worry about sustainability in the first place.

Built Environment as Organism

A traveler flying at night from Washington, D.C., to Boston, a distance of some 400 miles, sees a pattern of lighted roads and buildings that never darkens and which, following the Eastern seaboard, stretches inland to the Appalachian mountains. There are spots where the network becomes vestigial, while other places are a blaze of light. As early as 1961, geographer Jean Gottmann named it Megalopolis.[2] From the air it appears as a giant weed on the surface of the earth with a life of its own, consuming energy and many other resources on a vast scale, day and night.

We know that today the world is replete with similar fields. The Mexican Federal District, the Nile delta triangle including Cairo and Alexandria, the Guangdong area opposite Hong Kong, and many others come to mind. They are at least as complex and energetic and uncontrollable in their growth.

The Living Cell: Change and Disappearance

The living cell is where human settlement most immediately assumes physical form and decides on the use of resources and the rhythm of the environment's metabolism. All infrastructures, particularly the many utility networks, serve to feed it. They also enable new innovations to reach that cell. Cells and infrastructure together make the organic whole.

In history, the house as living cell, under unified control, could encompass an extended family and might include servants and slaves. Spaces to work in were found as well:

spaces to do business, to sell merchandise, to process food, or to make handicrafts. Its contents represented a culture at its most intimate scale. As such, the living cell could be large as a Venetian Gothic palace, extensive like a family compound in eighteenth-century Beijing, or hierarchically ordered like an atrium house in Pompeii.

Today the house is still a living cell and still determines built fields that range from suburban sprawl including neighborhoods for well-to-do citizens to the "informal settlements" surrounding most of the world's megacities. Of those, the latter most faithfully continue the age-old process of human settlement where the house as living cell, for all its improvisational emergence and slow growth, harbors extended families and often combines domestic and work space. Informal settlement is now consuming materials like cement, glass, and bricks; elements like tiles, window frames, and doors; and all kinds of piping and wiring, bathroom and kitchen equipment, and more—partaking of the same nourishment for all other contemporary fabric.

The house, on the other hand, inhabited by the nuclear family, contains only one of many small social clusterings in need of a responsive envelope. Other social entities are found in the wide variety of work places, in retail stores, in the office of the therapist and consultant, the apartment building, and wherever else daily human interaction takes place. The diverse and tightly packed social activities found in the historic house have escaped the domestic realm and, having diversified and multiplied, are found all across contemporary fabric, promising a richer and more diverse interaction between inhabitation and physical form.

In contrast to this rich diversity of ever smaller but dynamic social clusters, the smallest material unit recognizable as a changeable whole in the environmental fabric is no longer just the single house but also the larger, sometimes very large, building. The result is an increasingly coarse fabric, unresponsive to inhabitation of any kind and at worst oppressively deterministic. The one-on-one interaction between material form and social entity, so naturally manifest in historic fabric, is no longer evident. Many social clusters do not inhabit a form that lives by their care and initiative, and which in turn stimulates and facilitates their actions. The living-cell-that-could-be has been weakened or has entirely disappeared. Inhabitation for both work and living can now be found as a nomadic activity in an environment that is no longer its product nor responsibility.

The Fine-grained Large Project

This lack of reciprocity between an increasingly diverse and dynamic social body and a less and less agile material environment is not just inconvenient. It complicates and slows down the metabolism that sustains built environment, and renders inhabitation passive and hence unproductive, leaving it incapable of stimulating innovation or of being stimulated by it. Only a fabric of living cells can be a truly self-generating system.

To be sure, pleading for the living cell is not a rejection of the large project, which is very much part of our world, is here to stay, and most likely will be larger and more common. The challenge is to make it accommodate the living cell, help the cell to take care of its own. Such a new way of restoring the "natural relationship" will produce what can be called the "fine-grained large project."

This challenge is intensified by the growing complexity of built form as such. Today's living cell, domestic or otherwise, must contain not only bathroom and kitchen equipment and replaceable partitioning, but also a host of conduits for sewage, water, electric power, data, ventilation, heating, and more. These utilities are distributed throughout habitable space to serve every room or workstation. Today's entities of inhabitation, so widely diverse and dispersed, may be small and singular compared to the closely packed historic household, but the envelope they want to animate is technically far more complex.

Before we look at this lack of reciprocity as another professional problem to be solved, we should pause and remember that the degrading or outright disappearance of the living cell had much to do with the modernist inclination to see all things environmental as a technical problem or, at least, a design problem, and with its belief in the economy of scale. Living cells cannot be designed or produced; we can only provide conditions by which they may come about. To meet today's environmental challenge, a strategy of cultivation is required, not a production program.

The Return of the Living Cell

If built environment is an organism, and as such has a certain autonomy, it can be expected to seek to remedy what is ailing it. And indeed, our present environment has been moving already in that direction almost unbeknownst to its observers and theorists. A gradual introduction of the living cell in parts of our environment where it could not be found previously can be noted.

For instance, the commercial office building across the world increasingly offers empty floors for the various occupant parties to have them fitted out by their own designers and fit-out contractors. There, inside the large built volume, a clear separation of the collective environment on the one hand and the small-scale act of inhabitation on the other hand, enables the living cell to return in a new way. In the same manner, an institutional client will expect a new office building to be able to respond to future mutations in the composition and location of work units. In the shopping mall, retail space is likewise left empty to be fitted out by specialized contractors familiar with the tenant retailer's house style.

So-called open residential projects have been done on an experimental basis for quite some time now,[3] but in the last decade or so the approach has entered the commercial world. Residential open building projects initiated for profit can be found in Japan, Finland, the Netherlands, and Switzerland, among other countries.[4]

When conditions are favorable, the living cell appears spontaneously. In Moskow, for instance, wealthy apartment owners would rip out the entire elaborately finished interior of their newly bought apartments to start again with their own designer. Appalled by this destruction of capital, developers, unaware of any international trend supporting such an approach, now routinely produce "empty" apartment buildings, selling available floor space and collective facilities.[5]

In hospital construction, the perennial need for partial and ad-hoc adaptation of space in response to the changing demands of work units has triggered debate in professional circles and has led to various innovations. The most advanced project so far is found in a new intensive care hospital for the city of Bern, where a radical separation of the so called primary system from the secondary system led to separate design competitions for each.[6]

All this leads to an awakening awareness of a new professional role implied in the design for the "fine-grained large project." This was perhaps first expressed when Professor Yoshitaka Utida , the leader of the design team for the pathbreaking NEXT21 residential "open building" project in Osaka, Japan,[7] declared that he did not want to create a "flexible building" but a "three dimensional urban fabric." True to this statement, he invited thirteen other architects to custom design the projct's eighteen dwelling units, occupying himself with the design of public spaces and infrastructure for the living cells to settle in.

A new professional attitude is also found in a Finnish company dedicated to helping developers to serve would-be apartment buyers in the custom design and specification of the fit-out of their units, and to oversee actual implementation.[8]

New Opportunities: Long-term Investment

Once this new perspective on urban fabric unfolds, it becomes possible to point out some opportunities worth exploration. The "base building," as it is already known in commercial development, now free from demands from individual inhabitation, can live a long time just as streets tend to live longer than houses. This allows for long-term investment which, in turn, makes higher initial investment feasible for internal public spaces and external architecture. Right now this approach is followed by a not-for-profit housing corporation in Amsterdam where an urban block containing seven such base buildings, here called "solids," each nine stories high, is under construction. Occupants renting the empty spaces are free to take care of their interior fit-out for any purpose that is not disruptive to the community. The extra investment in high-quality facades, an exterior arcade, and interior public spaces is expected to bring a profit in the long run.[9]

No doubt these initiatives will be regarded with skepticism by many. However, they are in tune with a law, passed by the Japanese congress in 2008, which encourages residential construction that can last up to two centuries. The law refers to detailed technical requirements in which subsystems are identified that must be replaceable to ensure the long life of the whole. Sometimes technical wear and tear force a shorter lifespan, while the presence of other subsystems is limited by user preferences. If a building meets those requirements of possible partial renewal, the owner will receive substantial tax reductions.[10] This is the first time that formal legal recognition is given to the dimension of time in housing policy. The practical result, of course, is that rendering a long life to what can endure and keeping adaptable what must respond to inhabitation makes the living cell possible again.

The Japanese law applies to all residential construction. Single-family houses as well will benefit if subsystems can be renewed and replaced with minimum disruption of more durable parts of the building. That is not now the case. The numerous utilities that have been added to buildings in modern times have led to a notorious entanglement of subsystems including piping and wiring. Although the freestanding house is the prototype living cell, this entanglement renders its metabolism suboptimal. Here as well, the new law's requirements will have a beneficial effect.

New Opportunities: A Fit-out Industry

Bundling user-related subsystems into a coherent "fit-out system" is one of the major objectives of the global residential open building movement, which advocates enabling the living cell. Where the "empty" base building provides space for the living cell to settle in, a dedicated fit-out system utilizes the full potential of that condition. As a composite of available subsystems, it is itself able to adopt the most efficient versions that enter the market. Experience has already shown that a dwelling unit can be fitted out by a team of two or three all-round installers in about three weeks time. The costs of such a fit-out is on par with the cost of the household's cars.

Developing a fit-out industry is not a matter of new manufacturing—the necessary hardware subsystems being already available—but it does require sophisticated logistics and software-supported preassembly and packaging. Well organized, such an industry will enable urban fabric to adapt smoothly and universally to more effective and less wasteful new technology.

The first initiatives to a dedicated fit-out system on a commercial basis have been taken in Japan as well. The NEXT Infill system company aims at serving new construction as well as renovation of existing stock. Its service is also used by a new breed of developers who buy old apartments that they entirely clean out and restore as new units for sale.[11]

A sustainable built environment needs a fit-out industry that has access to all parts of extant fabrics. Conversely, for a fit-out industry to reach full potential, existing stock must be made receptive to fit-out. Fit-out industry can also offer such conversion. Its effective emergence needs the support of a dedicated policy including legal and fiscal initiatives.

remains elusive in implementation. In short, mainstream understandings of sustainable urbanism reify ecological impacts and livability, but one must ask why there is not a carbon footprint score for social exclusion or equity. As we have emphasized here, spatial justice, seen through the lens of the JSP, brings the connectedness of the social, economic, and environmental to light.

Dale and Newman articulate sustainable urban development as a process that frequently benefits well-off populations "unless equity through affordability is deliberatively planned for, and funded with, strong political will and leadership."[32] How do urban planners design, plan for, and achieve a just environment, both in the natural and built/social sense? Many of the sustainability toolboxes in existence, such as that of New Urbanism, are successful in attaining mixed-use and transit-oriented development and livability for those who can afford to live in these communities.

The involvement of planners in both procedural and substantive spaces is essential. While the urban planner can help manage and resolve conflict as well as promote solutions,[33] the planner-as-facilitator may be inadequately suited to move communities toward sustainability. In a time period where the economic interests of potential developers (both retail and residential) as well as community members dictate the trajectory of communities, planners have a responsibility to educate all citizens (not just those in meeting attendance) on the long-term impacts of proposed developments, sustainable or not. To create just environments, to reimagine sustainable urbanism, we need to fundamentally rethink sustainability as well as the role of the planner. Fainstein has argued that Amsterdam is one ideal of the just city and suggested that in changing the popular dialogue of planners and policy makers to include just city rhetoric can in itself be a shift toward a more just city.[34] A truly integrated planning approach is necessary[35]; while some may call this new generation of planners advocates, the reality is that even an objective planner has the responsibility to advocate for those without a voice at the decision-making table, not simply to push the papers of an (under/mis)informed citizenry.

BEYOND THE BASICS

MODERN CITIES AS ENGINES OF ECONOMIC OPPORTUNITY AND SOCIAL PROGRESS

HENRY CISNEROS

Modern cities across the world are the current iterations of the gathering places where people over the millennia have performed the key social and economic functions of humankind. From the first gatherings of human beings in groups larger than nomadic tribes—for protection, for food production, for division of labor, for trade, for worship—came urban places. In the fertile crescent of the Middle East, including the great cities of Mesopotamia and Egypt, from China to India to Persia to Europe, the urban form evolved into the Greek polis and the Italian city-states, where the skills of diplomacy, arms, and politics made possible the arts of painting and literature, where trade abroad financed architecture and public works at home.

In the North Atlantic nations and in the New World, urban places have been the settings where great historical dynamics, such as representative democracy, industrialization, theories of capital, modern art forms, and scientific movements have been developed. In American history, urban places have been the building blocks of national progress and the settings where some of the epic themes of the American narrative have unfolded.

Among these themes is the quest for individual and family advancement in the economic and social hierarchy of society, the confluence of dreams and ambitions to improve one's lot in life. Because of the scale and intensity of the intersections they enable, cities often serve as platforms for advancing social and economic equity. The degree to which cities are successful as accelerators of equity depends on how they play their essential roles as the places where people work, learn, recreate, live, and govern themselves.

the Erie Canal into the interior. Later, Great Lakes shipping drew the industries to Cleveland, Buffalo, Detroit, Chicago, and Milwaukee during the first stirrings of industrialization and of the social restructuring that it would engender. It was work in the cities that preserved the Union, as armaments made in factories in Hartford, Lowell, Rochester, and Harrisburg overwhelmed the rural economy of the South.

After the Civil War, the iron horse opened the way to feed the nation from the stockyards of Chicago, Denver, Omaha, Fort Worth, and Kansas City, creating new industries and new wealth. In the West, clipper ships sailed to the Pacific and to Alaska from Seattle and San Francisco. In the East the industrial revolution matured in Toledo, Akron, Rockford, and Grand Rapids, each of which developed industrial specialization in particular products of importance to the country. The nation confronted union organizing battles, labor wage disputes, and exposés of working conditions. When World War II required an "arsenal of democracy," tanks rolled off the lines in Detroit, ships were launched from yards in Oakland, and airplanes flew out of Long Beach. The output from these cities created the jobs that broke the back of the Great Depression and built the foundation of the middle class that would support post-war prosperity.

Over the last decades, metropolitan areas that were little more than towns seventy years ago have become pillars of the national economy. Atlanta in communications, San Diego in the biosciences, and San Jose in technology, these became urban brainpower economies which clarified the new equation of economic equity: "High skills equals high wages; low skills equals low wages."

Work

A great nation sustains itself through work. From the labors of its people and from their productive capacities come national power and family advancement. In the American colonies, work included trade with England, based on shipbuilding and on transatlantic shipping from Boston. Waterborne commerce processed in New York City moved through

Learn

A great society helps its people learn and in so doing transforms their potential into national prosperity. That is what America did when it used the public schools of New York to transform the children of immigrants into students at the City Colleges of New York, and counted among these are a U.S. Secretary of State, Nobel Prize winners, Pulitzer Prize recipients, university presidents, financiers, doctors, and scientists. The legacy of the land-grant institutions may be rooted in rural places, but the nation has needed its city schools. The city public colleges created in Ohio, such as the universities of Cincinnati, Toledo, and Akron, paved the way for systems of community colleges all across the country. The great urban Catholic schools set as their mission the integration of immigrants: Marquette in Milwaukee, Villanova in Philadelphia, Fordham and St. John's in New York City, Loyola and DePaul in Chicago, and Xavier in New Orleans, which took on the special mission of preparing African-American students.

Today's urban anchor institutions are integral to the identities of entire metropolitan areas, such as Johns Hopkins in Baltimore; Tulane, carrying an extraordinary load in the revitalization of New Orleans; the University of Southern California, which has been an anchor for South Central Los Angeles since the civil disturbances there; and the University of Pittsburgh, driving the transformation of that city. In American history, education in the cities has helped the nation learn, and in so doing fueled the engine of social and economic equity.

Recreate

The greatest nations have places where people recreate, where they celebrate the national heritage and our human inheritance, where the human spirit is uplifted by the genius of the painter, the grace of the dancer, the athleticism of the ballplayer, the wisdom of the writer, the skill of a sculptor, and the inspiration of the preacher. Not only do gifted performers succeed on the basis of their art and not only are careers and creative industries financed, but societal barriers are surmounted and cross-cultural understandings are achieved.

In American history, urban places have been home to our churches, temples, museums, symphony halls, ballparks, convention venues, and conference centers. Imagine how much poorer our nation would be without the public museums in Washington, the Getty Center in Los Angeles, Central Park in New York, the Museum of Natural History in Chicago, Camden Yards in Baltimore, and the Calatrava-designed Museum of Art in Milwaukee. Our urban places give us identity and celebrate our common purpose.

Live

The greatest nations bring their people together to live, and out of the diverse masses are formed civil societies. In American history, the Lithuanians of Sinclair Lewis's *The Jungle* gathered in Chicago tenements as their first step toward Americanization. A half century later, African-American field-workers from Alabama and Mississippi provided the manpower for automobile plants and steelworks in Detroit and Chicago. And today those metropolitan areas' African American middle-class communities are among the largest in the nation.

Their routes of passage to life in the American middle class are the route of the Irish of Boston, the Poles of Detroit, the Slavs of Cleveland, the Jews of New York, the Germans of Milwaukee, the Swedes of Minneapolis, the Chinese of San Francisco, the Latinos of San Antonio, and the Vietnamese of Anaheim. Cities need a mix of housing types in order to function. Workers are needed near job centers, and higher income residents support private and public economies. The progression from tenements and public housing to boardrooms and City Hall is a well-documented staple of the urban narrative. In America the masonry and brick of urban housing have also provided the stepping-stones to a better life.

Governance

Great nations find the ways to govern themselves. In American history many of the most important processes of governance have played out in our urban areas. Governance in the sense of public competition for voice and for resources has often been raucous, rude, even brutish. From the self-serving efficiency of Tammany Hall to the grassroots common sense of Saul Alinksy in Back of the Yards Chicago, urban governance occurs in the streets, in the neighborhoods, at the polling places, and in the union halls.

Governance also means urban areas as the action end of state and federal programs: the WPA, decent housing after 1949, equal opportunity and voting rights from the Great Society, welfare reform in the Clinton Administration—all of these had to take hold in real places and for the majority of Americans those places were our metropolitan centers.

Cities embody these important roles—as places to work, learn, recreate, live and govern—and when they function as the points of convergence for these essential interactions of the society, they create the potential for the natural ambitions and aspirations of urban residents to be transformed into social and economic equity.

Social Justice and Economic Equity

The focus of this chapter is to explore how cities can go beyond merely the *potential* of social and economic equity. Our purpose is to explore how cities, by harnessing their inherent dynamics, and how city governments, by devising intentional strategies, can more assuredly serve as engines for advancing social justice and economic equity. To some degree those values can be advanced by the compelling urban dynamics of integration, of upward mobility, and of economic advancement which occur in the climate of transactions and of cultural interactions which cities make possible. But history and experience teach us that the natural evolution of these processes can be slow, uncertain, even brutal, and sometimes completely ineffective. As a result, societies that value social justice and economic equity have worked to advance them in more intentional ways.

Usually that work takes the form of national policies to guarantee civil rights, to provide safety nets of economic security, and to level the playing field of access to opportunity. In the United States such policies have included Social Security enacted during the Great Depression, the Civil Rights laws of the Great Society, and the recent passage of Health Insurance Reform during President Obama's administration. Federal housing programs, educational funding, labor protections, and public accommodations laws are further examples of federal actions.

The federal government acts principally by creating an umbrella of legal rights and by providing direct transfer payments to individuals, such as Social Security payments. These are profoundly important and establish the basic framework of a society in which rights and responsibilities and concepts of fairness and justice are recognized and respected. However, because so many of the actual dynamics of social justice and economic equity must necessarily occur in the physical places where people live, it follows that the reality of a just society must manifest itself in a nation's cities. It also follows that these values are most likely to be advanced at the city level when they are viewed as part of the purpose of a city, when they are recognized and respected as a purpose of the city's governance, and when they are addressed as the intentional strategy of city leadership.

Working Definitions of Equity

It might be helpful to consider for a moment some possible definitions of social and economic equity at the city level. One set of quantifiable definitions can be based on *economic statistics*, which measure indicators of prosperity, such as percentages of persons living in poverty, rates of minority poverty, or of income distribution, such as the Gini coefficient, which measures concentrations of income across percentiles of the population. Such measures of economic equity define the degree to which a city's jobs and incomes foster shared prosperity or perpetuate unequal economic status.

Other quantifiable statistics capture levels of shared prosperity in *spatial or geographic terms*. Comparative data across a city measured by census tracts, for example, reveal concentrations of poverty in specific neighborhoods, levels of educational attainment, and degrees of the segregation of racial and ethnic groups. Spatial patterns can document access to quality education, proximity to good jobs and commercial opportunities, the robustness of small business activities, and levels of public and private investments by area.

Less rigorously statistical but equally important in local decision-making are community understandings about longstanding histories of inclusiveness with regard to access to opportunity and to the educational resources that create pathways to opportunity. Cities generally have locally understood patterns concerning the *openness of opportunity*, as evidenced by the contour of white-collar and blue-collar jobs, segmentation of the local labor market, the quality of education in neighborhood public schools, and degrees of difficulty in accessing capital for small businesses or for home-related investments in specific neighborhoods.

Still another form of equity involves the climate of *tolerance and respect for cultural differences* and for shared leadership. Cities develop reputations over time for how well they include all sectors of the society in their cultural life and practical governance. Seattle is known as a city that has long evidenced nuanced and respectful attention to its multicultural origins and to the current composition of its residents. Other cities have to work to overcome legacies of bitter contention. Atlanta's leaders for example in the 1960s instituted regular "brown bag lunches" so that its white business executives and African-American community and church leaders could directly address the city's legacy of racial division. They advanced a progressive agenda under the slogan "a city too busy to hate," and by the 1990s not only had the city been led by several African-American mayors en route to its position as a global business center, but it hosted the successful 1996 Olympics, which continued Atlanta's transformation into a post-racial magnet for opportunity.

The art and science of harnessing the natural dynamics of a city and of steering the capacities of city government to explicitly advance an overarching strategy of social and economic equity are not well developed. It is possible, however, to define the general characteristics of social and economic equity that cities can hope to attain. The mission statement of the Local Initiatives Support Corporation, a national urban development intermediary, is as good an articulation of a definition as exists: "To build communities that offer the positive environments needed to ensure that all residents of varied income levels are provided the opportunities and tools to build assets, to participate in the benefits inuring to their communities, and to become part of the mainstream economy."

There are many other concepts one could employ to capture the values of social and economic equity—concepts such as fairness, justice, and equality—but the LISC mission statement concisely articulates both the values and the practical mechanisms for achieving them. It is grounded in the experiences of balancing equity ideals with the limits of political will and with the practical capabilities of institutions. In application it stresses putting people within reach of opportunity as opposed to guaranteeing outcomes. It stresses inclusion in the benefits of a quality community principally through fair participation in a robust economy.

In the American urban tradition, a community characterized by social and economic equity would be said to have open pathways to opportunity no matter a person's origins. Residents could reasonably hope to rise from the most poverty-stricken childhoods or from the penniless destitution of a recently arrived immigrant to a quality education and to the economic and reputational rewards of hard work. People could strive and sacrifice in the knowledge that rewards are fairly allocated for focused work, if not in the immediate generation, then for children and loved ones in the subsequent generation. In an equitable city these rewards would not be apportioned by inheritance or elitism or through patterns of segregation, favoritism, or unfair advantage. Cities can be the building blocks of the society that Dr. King prayed for when he dreamed that people would be judged not on "the color of their skin but on the content of their character." It would be an urban society in which higher education was accessible, jobs were available and characterized by career tracks to advancement, access to housing was fair and nondiscriminatory, capital was extended to "red-lined" neighborhoods, and decision-making was inclusive, open, and deliberate.

Such a city would reap the dividends of its quest for equity, including unleashed talents and enhanced productivity, ambitions sustained by attainable rewards, and an internally self-reinforcing consensus for progress. While it is clear that in any city there will be disagreements and contentiousness, in a city benefited by the dividends of equity the central currents of community momentum would include a culture of achievement, human capital investment, inclusive dialogue, and a

basis for common ground. Such a city would have a strong chance to advance by every measure of progress.

Strategic Understanding

Achieving such urban-based social and economic equity requires first certain strategic breakthroughs and then a framework for action. At the level of strategic understandings city leaders must first recognize that the basic functioning mechanisms of the city organism can be harnessed to broaden economic opportunity and to strengthen social equity. That requires a priori recognition that city government with its powers and resources can be an instrument for guiding that process. In subtle but important ways those understandings add up to a different way of guiding a city. Figure 1 presents

FIG 1. CONTRASTING CONCEPTS: TRADITIONAL URBAN GOVERNANCE AND EQUITY STRATEGIES

Traditional Concepts	Strategic Equity Concepts
• The city organism is an amalgam of its location and historical attributes, economic advantages, population dynamics, and amassed assets. It should function so as to enable efficient economic transactions and to foster an attractive quality of life. A city succeeds on the basis of how well it performs its economic purposes and of how its cultural attributes are converted into economic value. The resulting economic and social structure may or may not promote equity, but the city does provide a platform for potential upward mobility.	• A city through the mechanisms of its functioning has immense capacities to broaden and deepen economic opportunity. The challenge is to harness a city's relevant dynamics to enhance equity values. For example, the types of jobs that derive from a city's industry mix establish wage levels and determine the breadth of community prosperity, which in turn determines whether quality of life is broadly shared. Explicit public investments and services priorities can support equity goals.
• The traditional philosophy of local government administration would say that local governments are essentially instruments of efficiency. Local services ought to be offered with cost effectiveness as the principle criteria for decision-making, and local governments should be run like businesses and focus strictly on the outcomes of services delivery.	• Equity strategy would recognize that local governments are critical instruments by which we shape the quality of life in our communities. We shape the physical spaces in which our people live and we can apply the resources of local government to shape lives. This is a more goal-driven vision of the way local government can function and it is a more deterministic vision of the quality of communities that we can create.
• Traditional economic development suggests that the best way to approach the generation of economic opportunity is to enable businesses to prosper. While there is recognition of the jobs dimension, it puts first priority on the stated needs of business. In its least attentive form it becomes a philosophy that says that what is good for business should be good for the people of a community.	• The equity strategy approach to local economic development would say that the purpose of economic strategies is not to serve individual businesses or developers but rather to create the jobs that will raise incomes and broaden the middle class. Such an approach results in a different emphasis and brings purpose to economic decisions. If the purpose is to build a middle class from among people who are presently at the margins, economic development must create the broadest range of opportunities for as many residents of the community as possible.
• Among the most critical dimensions of urban development is the infrastructure of basic utilities: energy, transportation, communication, and water. Some would view those essentially as municipal business functions to be delivered with growth and expansion considerations foremost.	• The equity strategy approach would recognize that basic utilities are instruments for creating responsible sustainability, for shaping smart growth and land uses, and for creating the broadest range of opportunities. As we build for the future we are witnessing a tidal wave of new technologies which can apply modern infrastructure: ▪ Smart energy grids ▪ Internet applications to ▪ Alternative energy projects education ▪ Public transit ▪ Efficient vehicles ▪ Affordable, green homes ▪ Smart buildings ▪ Digital access ▪ Sustainable land use This new wave of infrastructure technologies can be used to rehabilitate urban cores, incentivize investment, and create new career track opportunities, as well as to reduce costs to consumers and provide relief to the most disadvantaged.

FIG. 2. ELEMENTS OF AN URBAN EQUITY STRATEGY CATEGORIZED BY CITY FUNCTIONS

MEASURES OF ECONOMIC AND SOCIAL EQUITY

	Economic Statistics	Spatial Patterns	Levels of Opportunity	Leadership and Cultural Inclusion
WORK	1. Focus economic development on jobs for urban residents 2. Develop promising economic sectors for job growth 3. Assist residents in wealth creation	4. Involve anchor institutions in urban revitalization and job creation	5. Enhance work skills for urban residents 6. Prepare for New Economy jobs	7. Address immigrant integration strategies
LEARN			1. Invest in public education – K-16 2. Introduce outside-the-box educational reforms 3. Engage anchor institutions in human capital development 4. Help children become ready for school through early childhood education 5. Train nontraditional workers for New Economy jobs 6. Use public libraries to provide after-school learning programs for students and parents 7. Extend academic rigor with after-school programs	8. Involve parents in strengthening their children's education
RECREATE				1. Engage cultural institutions in urban revitalization 2. Offer health, fitness, and recreational programs for all residents 3. Observe multicultural celebrations to encourage community pride and self-esteem
LIVE	1. Create a mix of affordable housing types 2. Prepare housing for older Americans who want to age in place	3. Transform deteriorated neighborhoods into safe, vibrant mixed-income communities 4. Prepare smart growth, sustainable land use policies 5. Link housing to public transportation 6. Recalibrate policing and security strategies 7. Focus land use and urban development policies to improve environmental outcomes		
GOVERN			1. Integrate community development corporations in a cohesive network of local services delivery and city governance	2. Engage neighborhood leadership in the formulation of city policies on a comprehensive and continuous basis

contrasts between traditional ways of thinking about cities and their governance, and between concepts that seek to optimize economic and social equity.

A Framework for Action

While figure 1 contrasts broad strategic concepts concerning the capabilities of cities themselves and of their governments to advance social and economic equity, it is important to determine precisely what concrete initiatives can put equity strategies into action. Figure 2 is an attempt to array a range of specific initiatives in a matrix that identifies each initiative by the kind of equity measure it is intended to advance and by the function of city life from which it originates. The result is a comprehensive framework of initiatives designed to harness the underlying functions and dynamics of a city to enhance social and economic equity. The most important aspect of the initiatives listed is that each one is currently being successfully executed in an American city. The fact that these initiatives are now underway removes them from the realm of speculation and theory, and underscores that they have the practical and operational potential to be replicated in cities across the nation. While no city is presently acting upon all the initiatives together at a citywide scale or with priority across the entire range, the framework taken as a whole would represent a coherent strategy to advance social and economic equity. The numbers assigned each initiative in figure 2 correspond with the initiative's place in the descriptions on the following pages.

A. Work

1. Focus economic development on good jobs for urban residents: Boston developed its Back Streets Business strategy to assist existing neighborhood businesses to add good-paying jobs within the reach of inner-city residents. Its stated mission is "to retain and grow Boston's viable industrial and commercial businesses and their diverse jobs base through the strategic use of land, workforce, and financial resources."[1]

2. Develop promising economic sectors for job growth: Cleveland has invested heavily in growing the medical devices industry in order to replace obsolete manufacturing jobs with new opportunities for area workers. Special emphasis has been placed on providing capital for medical device innovations that spin-off from the world-renowned Cleveland Clinic complex.[2]

3. Assist residents in wealth creation: San Francisco's Bank on San Francisco Program works to help San Francisco residents generate savings and convert income streams into net worth and wealth.[3]

4. Involve anchor institutions in urban revitalization and job creation: The University of Pennsylvania has cooperated closely with Philadelphia's city government and with neighborhood groups to utilize its jobs, contracts, construction spending, and expansion plans to revitalize its surrounding area.[4]

5. Enhance work skills for urban residents: San Antonio's Project Quest is a city-founded collaboration with neighbor-hood-based action groups, churches, and the community college system to reach deep into communities and train workers for new jobs.[5]

6. Prepare for New Economy jobs: Minneapolis has created networks to link area schools and universities with jobs in its targeted biosciences and technology industries.[6]

7. Address immigrant integration strategies: Houston's Neighborhood Centers, Inc., operates a network of seven neighborhood centers, four charter schools, two early childhood education centers, twenty-four Head Start centers, and twenty senior centers. From these community centers it seeks "to ensure that when people arrive in Houston—regardless of their origin or status, or whether they came to pursue a better life or to flee political oppression—they have the opportunity not simply to pursue the American Dream, but the human dream."[7]

B. Learn

1. Invest in public education K–16: The City of Denver, the Denver Public Schools, and private leaders are amassing a $200-million permanent endowment for need-based scholarships in fifteen public schools, nine charter schools, and three alternative schools. As one of the nation's largest city-led scholarship programs, it will support 4,000 students annually.[8]

2. Introduce outside-the-box educational reforms: Mayor Mike Bloomberg in New York City has committed city powers and raised public and private resources to enable wide-ranging educational reforms, which have resulted in steady gains in academic progress for students at all levels. The focus now is on replicating the best results in all of New York City's more than 1,600 public schools.[9]

3. Engage anchor institutions in human capital development: The University of Southern California has created the Neighborhood Action Initiative to bring disadvantaged students from nearby high schools to the university on a daily basis in order to prepare them for USC's rigorous admissions process, with approximately twenty students admitted from the NAI class every year.[10]

4. Help children become ready for school through early childhood education: The AVANCE program, which was founded in San Antonio and operates in fifteen cities, prepares children from the time their mothers are pregnant through the preschool years and reaches 27,000 parents and children.[11]

5. Train nontraditional workers for New Economy jobs: San Jose's city government has put special emphasis on its workforce and training programs to upgrade the skills of area workers in order that they can fill jobs in the city, considered one of the nation's most innovative economies because of its high-tech and biotech start-up firms.[12]

6. Use public libraries to provide after-school learning programs for students and parents: In Houston, Parents Alliance, Inc., uses neighborhood public schools after hours to offer computer education for children and parents, with a special focus on disadvantaged families in the poorest neighborhoods.[13]

7. Extend academic rigor with after-school programs: Miami's After-School All-Stars program has 4,000 children in 50 inner-city schools involved in an enhanced academic curriculum which is matched with character education and leadership training. It is part of the After-School All-Stars network that serves 80,000 children every day in over 450 schools in thirteen cities across the nation.[14]

8. Involve parents in strengthening their children's education: In Ft. Worth minority parents teamed up with the Industrial Areas Foundation to create Alliance Schools in order to help their children excel and to advocate for school resources and program improvements.[15]

C. Recreate

1 .Engage cultural institutions in urban revitalization: Newark's development of the New Jersey Performing Arts Center in its central business district has spurred arts-related economic activity and celebrated the multicultural and immigrant composition of the city. Its arts education program is the fourth largest in the nation and includes the Summer Youth Performance Workshop, the Young Artist Institute, and the "Passport to Culture" school program.[16]

2 .Offer health, fitness, and recreational programs for all residents: San Antonio's Sports for Life is a network of recreation and sports organizations which offer year-around fitness activities for persons over fifty years of age in order to extend the quality of life for older persons and to reduce medical costs.[17]

3. Observe multicultural celebrations to encourage community pride and self-esteem: Milwaukee's rich tradition of neighborhood ethnic festivals has been integrated into its city-wide arts and cultural agenda with the intent of unifying the city, promoting cross-cultural understanding, and strengthening participation in local governance.[18]

D. Live

1. Create a mix of affordable housing types: Chicago has organized its Housing Department to achieve Mayor Richard Daley's goals of ending chronic homelessness, renovating 25,000 units of public housing, and adding 48,000 units of affordable housing.[19]

2. Prepare housing for older Americans who want to age in place: Boston has developed a diverse variety of housing types which provide options for aging residents, including Web-based systems such as the Village Network, which extends public and private services and creates a virtual village.[20]

3. Transform deteriorated neighborhoods into safe, vibrant mixed-income communities: Atlanta has used the federal HOPE VI program for the renovation of public housing sites to transform all of its old public housing developments into mixed-income communities and has utilized the Section 8 program to integrate former residents into the mainstream economy.[21]

4. Prepare smart growth and sustainable land use policies: Austin, Texas, has created a "SMART" housing program which incentivizes builders to construct homes that are Safe, Mixed-income, Accessible, Reasonably-priced, and Transit-oriented.[22]

5. Link housing to public transportation: The Fruitvale project in Oakland, which includes workforce housing over retail stores adjacent to stations of the Bay Area Rapid Transit System, links neighborhood residents to jobs throughout the metropolitan area and places them within ten minutes travel time from downtown San Francisco.[23]

6. Recalibrate policing and security strategies: Minneapolis has instituted community policing strategies to reduce crime in inner-city neighborhoods and reduce unsafe environments on city streets, including designing new mixed-income communities using "defensible space" concepts for enhanced security.[24]

7. Focus land use and urban development policies to improve environmental outcomes: Seattle's city government has led a coalition of the nation's municipal leaders to enact local initiatives to combat global climate change and to take specific actions to assure environmental justice at the local level.[25]

E. Govern

1. Integrate community development corporations in a cohesive network of local services delivery and city governance: Boston relies heavily on a sophisticated group of community development corporations to deliver key public services such as early childhood education, elderly assistance, energy retrofitting, financial counseling, and skills training.[26]

2. Engage neighborhood leadership in the formulation of city policies on a comprehensive and continuous basis: Los Angeles changed its city charter to strengthen the role of neighborhood planning and involves community-based independent voices such as One LA in important decisions about programs and resources.[27]

Conclusion

Each of these initiatives builds upon a functional area of city life and devotes focused attention to the equity dimensions—to opportunity, inclusiveness, and economic uplift. To harness them together requires city leadership as well as public and private resources. Administered with accountability and managerial discipline they can generate substantial returns in the form of enhanced human capital, strengthened economic activity, and reduced social morbidities. If urban leaders would weave these kinds of initiatives into a cohesive management agenda—instead of the current reality of disparate, piecemeal, and disconnected equity programs—a new model of city governance would be introduced. It would for the first time in the long history of cities establish them as more than the dynamic places where people work, learn, recreate, live, and govern themselves. Our nation's cities would become the places where the social justice and economic equity ideals of our society are transformed into a life of promise for all.

PLANNING FOR A SILENT MINORITY

THE NEEDS OF CHILDREN FOR OUTDOOR PLAY, ACCESS TO NATURE, AND INDEPENDENT MOBILITY

CLARE COOPER MARCUS

FIG. 1 Clustered single family houses with shared outdoor space: Cononver Commons, Redmond, WA.

At the end of World War Two, Sweden was experiencing a critical labor shortage. New suburbs around the capital city were planned to be as child friendly as possible in order to encourage stay-at-home mothers back into the labor force. A transit system linked each suburban node to central Stockholm; shops and services around the transit stop provided for shopping before or after work; pedestrian and cycle paths splayed out like spokes of a wheel from the shopping/transit centers; paths for children's safe movements to school, day care, after-school care, and playgrounds wove through greenways, crossing over or under vehicular streets by bridges and tunnels. Cars took the long way round. Pedestrians were given priority.

At the same time, a quite opposite scenario was playing out in the United States. Highways and freeways shot out into the countryside from major metropolitan areas, promoted by the construction and automobile lobbies. Buying a car became necessary for commuting to work. An unspoken policy encouraged women to stay at home so that the jobs they had held during World War Two were available for returning veterans. The era of suburban sprawl had arrived. Subdivisions were built without sidewalks. Schools and parks were far apart, children's independent mobility was—and is—severely curtailed. Children were—and are—ferried around by school bus or the family car. Is it any wonder that children in the U.S. have a serious obesity problem, and those in Sweden and in other northern European countries do not?[1]

It is not only the problem of weight that has sprung from this often sedentary lifestyle. There is an alarming increase in the number of children diagnosed as having Attention Deficit Hyperactivity Disorder (ADHD) and the treatment of such with the drug Ritalin. Recent research at the University of Illinois indicates that even a short amount of time spent each day in (or looking at) green nature results in a reduction in levels of ADHD. If our children walked to school each day along tree-lined streets or through traffic-free greenways, the twin problems of rising rates of obesity and ADHD might begin to be addressed. Planning our residential areas *must* be seen not just as an architectural problem to be solved but as a public health issue of critical importance.

Compared to a generation ago, many fewer children travel independently between home and school. In 1969, 41 percent of U.S. children either walked or biked to school; by 2001, only 13 percent did, according to data from the National Household Travel Survey. Fewer and fewer children have free access to wild nature. Children learn by exploration, by manipulating the environment, picking up rocks, building secret "houses," examining leaves and bugs. If they have no opportunity to do this as children, they are much less likely as adults to have a concern for protecting the environment. Research has shown that those who become earth stewards as adults had free access to nature as well as one caring adult who encouraged this during their childhood.[2] If we neglect the imperative to provide children access to nature, where will the next generation of earth stewards come from?

Children's needs rarely receive the attention they deserve in current urban design practice, sustainable design literature, traffic-engineering directives, or in the philosophy and codes of new urbanism. Providing a scattering of parks—which might look good on a master plan—is not enough, especially if, once built, they resemble flat, green, mown deserts with little to attract or engage children's attention. It is time we gave as much attention to children—among our most vulnerable and least mobile citizens—as we have given to those with disabilities (in the enactment of the Americans with Disabilities Act) and to the demands of vehicular movement.

How often are children and youths themselves invited to be part of the design process? "Middle-age children (roughly between 6 and 12) are . . . capable of evaluating their surroundings and explaining their likes, dislikes, fears, and perceptions of physical barriers—and to make design proposals."[3] Asked what might be done to improve their

neighborhood, children have perceptive and practical suggestions such as calming traffic, improving maintenance, and providing more natural features, particularly trees.[4] Children complain about "not having enough to do," i.e., facilities and places to go. Ironically, children in more affluent suburbs are more likely to find their environment "boring" compared to those in the inner city. And then we wonder why so many turn to sedentary pursuits such as video games and TV for entertainment?

In spite of actions such as the 2005 Childstreet Conference and the resulting Delft Manifesto on a Child-Friendly Urban Environment,[5] planning philosophy regarding children still revolves around specific, bounded, equipped play spaces. While such a facility will be used and enjoyed, it is by no means sufficient to meet the developmental needs of growing children. As planners and designers, we need to ensure that future residential neighborhoods meet the needs of children for play, independent mobility, and access to nature as part of daily life. Any new residential development intended for families should include one or more of the following four essential child-friendly elements.

I. A cluster of dwellings (single-family homes, row houses, apartments, etc.) around a semi-private, vehicle-free green space, with traffic and parking relegated to the periphery.

These provide a green outlook and offer a safe play area within sight and calling distance of home, reducing parents' greatest fears: traffic and "stranger danger." Systematic studies of such spaces indicate that more than 80 percent of the users are likely to be children.[6]

This is neither a nostalgic throwback to the exclusive fenced squares of eighteenth-century London, nor support for contemporary gated communities, but consists of subtle site planning and landscape design measures ensuring that a group of dwellings all but encloses communally shared green space accessible to all who look onto it. Plenty of successful examples of this form of layout exist, both on greenfield sites and as in-fill developments. Thus, it is both surprising and saddening that in the many discussions of the need for community, places of meeting, "third places," and the like in the pages of *New Urbanism and Beyond*, no one sees fit to mention this obvious and successful solution. The grassroots planning of more than a hundred co-housing communities in North America have all embraced this form of site planning, which suggests that those seeking community have a much better sense of how built form will enhance face-to-face meeting and safe children's play than do many professional designers and planners. It is critical that we recognize there is a middle ground between public space—accessible to adults, and to children only if they are accompanied—and the private space of the home. This middle ground of shared or semiprivate space meets needs that neither public nor private space can fulfill.

"Alley Gating and Greening" is an interesting grassroots effort in Baltimore to reclaim and transform semiprivate space in the form of alleys in inner-city neighborhoods.[7] Formerly littered and subject to crime, alleys have been

FIG. 2 Apartments clustered around shared outdoor space for child and adult recreation close to home: The Gorbals, Glasgow, Scotland.

transformed into gated, attractive spaces by residents who want safe places for their children to play and for adults to gather—and even to garden. Residents insisted on gating because all the alleys so far reclaimed are in high crime areas. It remains to be seen whether the alleys in suburban, New Urbanist developments are some day reclaimed as non-vehicular, semiprivate play and gathering places in a similar manner.

2. A neighborhood plan where local streets end in cul-de-sacs that abut a greenway or local park.

While there is opposition to this form of neighborhood design from the proponents of New Urbanism (largely based on concerns for efficient traffic movement), the suggestion here is that *part* of any new residential development be developed either in this form, or in one of the other child-friendly proposals described in this essay, and that it be made clear that these areas are intended particularly for families with children.

There are a number of reasons why this form of layout is attractive and health-promoting for children and adults alike.

One, it enhances opportunities for play. One study comparing children's outdoor play behavior (other than in the back yard) in a traditional, grid pattern neighborhood with a more contemporary suburban neighborhood, found that cul-de-sacs were an important predictor of outdoor play for children aged six through twelve.[8] This was consistent with previous findings that children living on through-streets have fewer opportunities for outdoor play than children living on cul-de-sacs.[9] In a study of five Northern California towns, children living on cul-de-sacs played outside more often than those who did not, with 75 percent on cul-de-sacs being highly active versus 55 percent living on through-streets. One-third of parents on through-streets requested traffic calming measures versus zero percent on cul-de-sacs.[10] Considering the obesity epidemic, any planning measure that encourages childhood activity should be embraced. Two, a grid of walking and biking paths can be created by linking cul-de-sacs across greenways and connecting these to linear routes *along* greenways leading to local shops, schools, parks, etc. The health benefits of jogging and walking for adults and the fact that children's favorite activity is being "on the move" both account for the current popularity of linear parks and greenways versus the traditional square/rectangular neighborhood park. Mobility is not only important for a child's physical development but *independent* mobility—when a child is mature enough—is essential in promoting self-esteem, a sense of identity, and taking responsibility for oneself.[11]

Three, where greenways are created along stream valleys, drainage swales and ribbons of natural landscape—as they are in a number of successful U.S. new towns and master-planned communities[12]—they enhance wildlife habitat, exploratory play opportunities, and contact with nature as part of daily life.

Adopted in 1989 as the Open Space Element of the General Plan, the Davis, California, Greenway Plan has become the open space framework to guide the future growth of that city. The plan proposes fifty miles of bike and walking paths in a continuous loop through parks, trails, and natural areas without ever crossing a road. By 2007, it was 60 percent complete. In many places, cul-de-sacs abut this loop, permitting children safe and easy access from their homes onto this green amenity. The plan noted that despite a well-developed system of traditional parks, many were underused due to poor accessibility. The greenway system linking some of these parks has resulted in more use and greater user satisfaction. Clearly, it is time to affirm that the time-worn planning concept of "dropping" square plots of green into a master plan and assuming that will meet the needs for outdoor recreation just does not meet the needs of contemporary urbanites and their desire to be "on the move" for the physical and mental health of themselves and their children.

3. Woonerven (residential precincts) and home zones.

These are terms emanating from the Netherlands and the U.K. for streets with multiple traffic-calming components (speed bumps, bulb outs, planters, trees, play spaces, etc.) where pedestrians and cars share the street, which has no spe-

FIG. 3 Alley gating at Luzerne/Glover alley, Baltimore, MD, provides needed outdoor space for children and adults in this inner city neigborhood.

FIG. 4 Raised crosswalks slow traffic and houses face green pedestrian ways or "Living Courts" where paths wide enough for two tricycles or Big Wheels to pass provide safe play spaces for children close to home: Home Town, Aurora, IL.

cific sidewalk, and where the entries to the zone are clearly marked. Residents have auto access to their dwellings; through traffic is discouraged; speed limits are low. Initially created to curb speeding on grid-pattern streets in the Netherlands, this solution is now well established through guidelines and regulations in Germany, England, Denmark, Sweden, Switzerland, Japan, and Israel. Studies in Europe, Japan, Australia, and Israel have found reductions in traffic accidents, increased social interaction and play, and a high degree of satisfaction by residents.[13] One expert has noted: "Increased accessibility on all streets raises the likelihood of cut-through traffic and of speeds inappropriate to residential neighborhoods—the original impetus for abandoning the grid . . . more than sixty years ago."[14]

There are no fully developed residential precincts in the U.S. due to opposition from traffic engineers, road-building companies, and fire and police departments. Sadly, this may partially be a reflection of America's love affair with the car and—compared with other developed countries—its relative indifference to the needs of children. The United States is only one of two countries that has never ratified the U.N. Convention on the Rights of the Child—the other country being Somalia.

4. Every child should have daily access to an area of wild or semi-wild outdoor space whether in the open space in clustered housing, along a greenway, or in a green schoolyard.

With the growth of the "schoolyard greening" movement, it is increasingly recognized that outdoor space at school is not only a place for energetic recess play but also for interacting with nature and learning about ecological processes, gardening, and food production.[15] With limited land to add parks to existing urban neighborhoods and with the pressure from working parents to add after-school programs, such spaces can provide needed double duty.

When adults recall favorite places of their childhoods, most name outdoor locations, often involving natural features (trees, bushes, rocks, creeks, etc.) and playing with "loose parts" (leaves, twigs, seeds, earth).[16] It has been suggested that these represent an organized world for the child, empowering their "builders" and playing a unique role in empowering the self.[17]

It has also been argued that being outdoors could be viewed as a form of "preventive treatment" for a range of childhood mental, social, and physical health issues.[18] Playing outdoors together, children develop social skills necessary in adult life. It is possible that exposure to nature and "dirt" may train and boost a child's immune system, and lack of that exposure may go part way to explaining the dramatic growth in childhood asthma and other allergies.[19] When children in Swedish nursery schools were compared, those with access to woodland play in addition to standard play equipment scored better on fitness tests, were less likely to be absent due to illness, and less likely to bully than children with access only to standard equipment.

The Child Friendly Communities Alliance[20] is the first attempt to promote and eventually certify residential neighborhoods in terms of how well they meet the needs of children. The mission of this alliance is "to ensure that natural and social places essential to children's health will be included in new development and restored in existing neighborhoods and cities; and that barriers to children's mobility will be removed so that children can independently access nature and community life on a daily basis." The intention is to create and implement a voluntary Child-Friendly Standards and Certification Program for neighborhoods, with the participation of developers and municipal planners. The certification program will assign points for each aspect of the physical environment that makes a neighborhood child friendly. Four elements will inform the point system: There are places where children can interact with nature in a variety of ways; there are places where children can interact with the community in a variety of ways and learn essential social and conceptual skills; children have free range in their neighborhood and city, as appropriate to their age; the built environment stimulates children's cognitive and values development, health, and well-being in a variety of ways.

This is an excellent approach and hopefully given time it will be as influential in the promotion and development of child-friendly environments as have LEED and the Sustainable Site Initiative in promoting green building and sustainable planning. Child development is too valuable an asset to waste. While efficient vehicular movement and attractive street aesthetics are important, the codes and zoning regulations that promote them should not ignore the parallel, and potentially greater, importance of children's developmental needs. As Jan Gehl has succinctly and accurately written: "The formula must be: first *life*, then *spaces*, then *buildings*—*and* in said order, please."

HEALTHY AND JUST CITIES

JASON CORBURN

The modern professions of urban planning and public health emerged in the late nineteenth century with the common goal of improving health for city residents, particularly by arresting the spread of infectious diseases afflicting the poor. By the turn of the twentieth century, public health had shifted attention away from improving living conditions and urban environments to nonspecific interventions such as chlorinating drinking water as an attempt to eliminate bacterial pathogens. At this time urban planning began focusing largely on designing aesthetically pleasing and rational cities and moved away from an attention to health. By the end of the twentieth and the beginning of the twenty-first centuries, both urban public health and city planning had begun to return to their roots and began developing strategies to address persistent and increasing health inequities[1]—the avoidable disease, premature death, and unnecessary suffering afflicting the poor and people of color worldwide. The twenty-first century will be an urban century, as the world's population is increasingly living in expanding cities, and if it is to be a sustainable century, planners and others must find ways to promote greater health equity in cities.

The modern professions of urban planning and public health emerged in the late nineteenth century with the common goal of improving health for city residents, particularly by arresting the spread of infectious diseases afflicting the poor. By the turn of the twentieth century, public health had shifted attention away from improving living conditions and urban environments to nonspecific interventions such as chlorinating drinking water as an attempt to eliminate bacterial pathogens. At this time urban planning began focusing largely on designing aesthetically pleasing and rational cities and moved away from an attention to health. By the end of the twentieth and the beginning of the twenty-first centuries, both urban public health and city planning had begun to return to their roots and began developing strategies to address persistent and increasing health inequities[2]—the avoidable disease, premature death, and unnecessary suffering afflicting the poor and people of color worldwide. The twenty-first century will be an urban century, as the world's population is increasingly living in expanding cities, and if it is to be a sustainable century, planners and others must find ways to promote greater health equity in cities.

Urbanization and the planning practices and public policy decisions that shape cities are increasingly understood as powerful determinants of who gets sick, dies early, and suffers unnecessarily.[3] Importantly, urban health equity is not about access to health care; clinical interventions tend to treat illness after it occurs and send people back into the living and working conditions that created illness in the first place. The conditions that shape our health are called the *social determinants of health* and include much of the business of city planning—including policy decisions over housing affordability, transportation access, educational and employment opportunities, social services, and the quality of the urban environment.[4] This chapter suggests that sustainable cities will only be possible when planners and public policy makers commit to injecting health and social justice into urban governance, where both the substantive content of what contributes to human well-being—the physical and social qualities that promote urban health—and the decision-making processes and institutions that shape the distributions of these qualities across places and populations are improved.

Evidence of Urban Health Inequities: Learning from History

In 1977, doctors in Boston, Massachusetts, aimed to replicate the methods of Lemuel Shattuck, Massachusetts's first Sanitary Commissioner and author of the *Report of the Sanitary Commission of Massachusetts*, published in 1850. Shattuck's mid-nineteenth-century report found that the lowest life expectancy in Massachusetts was in the poorest districts of Boston, noting that "people who enjoy the greatest vital force, the highest degree of health . . . are the most wealthy." Shattuck's report mirrored one drafted by

Edwin Chadwick eight years earlier in England, a report on the sanitary conditions of the laboring populations of England that also documented a relationship between unhealthy living conditions, social class, and excess mortality. Both Shattuck and Chadwick emphasized that poor health in the nineteenth century was not due to lack of primary care or treatment, but from such preventable conditions as inadequate access to clean water and sanitation, filthy streets, overcrowded housing, low wages, lack of nutritious food, and—most importantly for both sanitarians—*a lack of public institutions and policies* geared toward improving living conditions and distributing basic health-promoting goods and services.[5] One of Shattuck's first recommendations in his sanitary study was to create the Massachusetts Board of Health, comprised of engineers, lawyers, physicians, chemists, and others.

The 1977 report, published in the New England Journal of Medicine, used data from the 1970s—not the 1840s— but found almost identical results as Shattuck; the areas in Massachusetts with the greatest excess mortality were the Boston neighborhoods of Roxbury and North Dorchester, communities with high poverty rates, a majority non-white population, poor housing conditions, and widespread "social instability."[6]

In 1990, another study aimed to build on this work and documented life expectancy in American cities with a focus on the Harlem neighborhood in New York City. This study highlighted that premature death for men in Harlem was double that of the general U.S. male population and 50 percent higher than the general U.S. African-American population, and that African-American men in Harlem were less likely to live to the age of sixty-five than men living in the slums of Bangladesh.[7] The authors only briefly speculated on the reasons behind these glaring mortality differences, but they did note that the causes were likely due to the social status of the neighborhood's largely impoverished African-American population, many of whom lived in dilapidated housing, experienced high unemployment and routine violence in their daily lives, and had a hard time accessing basic social services.

In 2009, 160 years after Shattuck's report, the Alameda County Health Department, in the San Francisco Bay Area, published a report entitled *Life and Death from Unnatural Causes: Health and Social Inequality in Alameda County*, noting:

> Compared with a White child in the Oakland Hills, an African American born in West Oakland is 1.5 times more likely to be born premature or with low birth weight, seven times more likely to be born into poverty, twice as likely to live in a home that is rented, and four times more likely to have parents with only a high school education or less . . . By fourth grade, this child is four times less likely to read at grade level and is likely to live in a neighborhood with twice the concentration of liquor stores and more fast food outlets . . . Born in West Oakland, this person can expect to die almost 15 years earlier than a White person born in the Oakland Hills.[8]

From Boston to New York to Oakland, from 1850 to 2009, these studies represent a snapshot of the preponderance of evidence that urban health inequities persist and the gaps in life expectancy and morbidity between the wealthy and those in poverty, whites and people of color, poor and well-off neighborhoods is not closing. This gap exists across urban areas of the U.S., Europe,[9] and countries of the global south.[10]

Healthy and Equitable Urban Governance

I suggest that moving toward urban health equity— not just documenting inequities— demands collaborative, multidisciplinary action. In other words, moving toward healthy and equitable cities will require new *healthy* and equitable *urban governance* strategies that are more than just governmental reform but are attentive to such political processes as:

- identifying and framing new policy issues
- generating appropriate standards of evidence
- constituting some social actors as "experts"
- adjudicating scientific uncertainty and different knowledge claims
- securing public accountability for decisions
- implementing and monitoring policies

Governance practices are, in short, the rules, norms, and processes for exercising power over collective actions and, when inattentive to social inequalities, often sort populations into unequal outcomes by upholding existing distributions of resources like political power, wealth, and knowledge. The next section of this chapter offers some suggestions for moving toward healthy and equitable urban governance in the twenty-first century.

The City as a Field Site, Not a Laboratory

During the late nineteenth century in the U.S., Progressive Era reformers viewed the city and its poorest places as action-research field sites, where planners, sanitarians, occupational health reformers, educators, community residents, and others worked collaboratively to investigate health problems and advocate for new policies and programs. For example, the women of Hull House, in Chicago, studied how neighborhood and workplace conditions influenced the well-being of urban immigrants, employed residents to survey streets in what became known as "shoe leather" epidemiology, and advocated for new workplace, housing, park, playground, and other urban social policy reforms. The settlement house workers' "field site" research tapped into the methodologies of the burgeoning Chicago School of sociology and collaborated with researchers such as John Dewey and Robert Park, but also documented living conditions in neighborhoods and stratified findings by race, ethnicity, and socio-economic status. Importantly, twenty-first-century urban health equity strategies should not romanticize the Progressive Era, since reformers often discriminated against African-Americans.

Instead, governance strategies should engage with the history of this era and recognize how it differed from a laboratory-like model of cities, where universal, non-specific strategies were developed with little attention to the history, culture, or politics of the people who lived in that place. Today health equity strategies will require a reframing of the core questions, from what makes some urban residents unhealthy to what historic and current practices and public policies have contributed to health inequities and what practice and policies might promote greater health equity in cities. Engaged scholarship, such as that promoted by community-based participatory action research is one strategy for ensuring that questions of health and equity are central to urban planning and policy making.[11]

Beyond the Built Environment: Healthy Places

Contemporary efforts to reconnect planning and public health have tended to define the issue as one of the "built environment" or "urban design" and health, with minimal attention given to the social and economic issues of racism, discrimination, and economic deprivation that are at the center of health inequities.[12] Much built environment and health research tends to define "place" using a limited set of static covariates in regression models, running the risk of being overly physically deterministic and missing the insights from sociology and other fields that places are co-produced; are given meaning by people, organizations, and institutions where physical and social characteristics are intimately related; and that these meanings get interpreted and redefined over time.[13] Quantitative, often technical proficiency conveys the false impression that analysis is not only rigorous but complete—in short, that it has taken account of all possible risks. Predictive methods tend in this way to downplay what falls outside their field of vision and to overstate whatever falls within.[14] Focusing on the broader category of healthy places must be central to new governance strategies.

Cumulative Vulnerabilities and Resistance

The cumulative vulnerabilities in places that influence disease and the assets in places that can enable populations to avoid risks must also be central to new analyses of healthy and equitable places. How policy issues are framed from the outset often impacts the quality of solutions; defined too narrowly or too broadly, public policy solutions will suffer from the same defects. For example, a chemical-testing policy focused on single chemicals cannot produce knowledge about the environmental health consequences of multiple exposures. The framing of the regulatory issue is more restrictive than the actual distribution of chemical-induced risks and is therefore incapable of delivering optimal management strategies. Similarly, a policy that frames urban health as primarily a function of individual behaviors, genet-ics, or access to clinical care may discourage policies that aim to address the social, economic, and environmental influences on well-being. In other words, planners and public health practitioners need to move away from current scientific and policy frames that tend to target one disease, lifestyle, or behavioral change, and explicitly reframe their work to address the cumulative impacts of physical, economic, and social disadvantage and the acts of resistance in communities.[15]

Housing and urban health offers an example of this reframing. Urban planning and public health have long recognized that housing quality and affordability is a key driver of health inequities.[16] However, less emphasis is placed on how racial residential segregation has had a cumulative heath effect on generations of people of color and what policy solutions can address the health impacts of segregation. Using a cumulative vulnerability frame means acknowledging the impacts of past and current housing and economic policies that promote residential segregation and neighborhood divestment (such as zoning ordinances, highway construction, planned shrinkage, and bank lending policies) and the combined health impacts of resulting poor physical conditions (e.g., dilapidated housing, toxic exposures, inadequate infrastructure) and social stressors (e.g., discrimination, crime/fear, poverty) in places.

Health Impact Assessment

One practical application of healthy and equitable urban governance might be the use of health impact assessment (HIA). HIA emerged in Europe, Canada, and Australia as a method to promote the consideration of health needs in non–health sector policies and respond to the lack of comprehensive health analyses within environmental impact assessment. Defining characteristics of HIA include prospective judgments about health impacts of social decisions based on available theory and evidence, a broad definition of health and health determinants, application to policy-making in diverse public sectors, engagement with decision-makers and stakeholders, and a commitment to transparency and democracy. For example, the San Francisco Department of Public Health (SFDPH) has used HIA to assess a proposed living wage ordinance, new housing proposals, and rezoning plans. During one HIA process, called the Eastern Neighborhoods Community Health Impact Assessment (ENCHIA), the SFDPH organized a participatory planning process that included over forty governmental and nongovernmental organizations for evaluating the positive and negative human health impacts from a proposed rezoning plan.[17] During the ENCHIA process, stakeholders collaboratively defined the elements of a healthy place, discussed how land use does or does not influence these elements, and investigated how a set of rezoning proposals and potential alternatives might influence the health of the largely low-income, immigrant communities of the Mission, South of Market, and Potrero Hill neighborhoods in San Francisco.[18]

Community Health Centers

Another concrete application of healthy and equitable urban governance is to revitalize national networks of community health centers. While not a new idea, many health centers have come to function largely as only ambulatory care providers. Yet early- and mid–twentieth-century community health centers were part of a broader movement to combine clinical care with other preventative social services and neighborhood planning.[19] Financed in the U.S. by federal matching grants through the Maternity and Infancy Protection Act (also known as the Sheppard-Towner Act), neighborhood health centers brought clinical and social services to poor neighborhoods and included block and occupational committees that allowed local residents and businesses to actively and directly participate in community health planning. Urban neighborhood health centers reemerged in the 1960s federal "War on Poverty" and were again federally funded, through the Office of Economic Opportunity. Sometimes called community-oriented primary care (COPC), health centers at their best integrate curative and preventive medical services, social and environmental change, and community organizing to build and maintain local political power.[20] From Durban, South Africa, to Manchester, England, to countless cities in the global south, community health centers have come and gone and faced opposition from the medical community, but now is the time to reinvent and reinterpret this good idea into urban health governance.

Monitoring and Ongoing Evaluation

Lemuel Shattuck, the nineteenth-century sanitarian from Massachusetts, was also a statistician. Shattuck's 1850 report noted above called for, among other things, new systematic "sanitary surveys" conducted regularly by local governments that counted more than births, deaths, and disease, but included the physical and social conditions of places—from the number of streets with drainage, garbage collection, and sidewalks to the homes with clean water, indoor sanitation, and adequate ventilation to family wages, education, and access to nutritious food. One of Shattuck's legacies is that disease surveillance is a core function of public health departments, but unfortunately the social, economic, and physical characteristics of places are rarely captured along with morbidity and mortality data. The WHO Healthy Cities Project has aimed to promote healthy urban and public policies, but less work has gone into developing robust monitoring and evaluation systems to answer the perennial question "What works and how do we know?" The WHO Healthy Cities Project has enrolled thousands of urban areas to develop "health development plans," but little is know about whether or how these plans and their implementation are impacting issues of health equity.[21] One monitoring tool that might assist in this effort is called the Healthy Development Measurement Tool (HDMT), which was developed in San Francisco through a collaborative public process and outlines the broad social indicators, land use development goals, and quantitative and qualitative data for healthy urban development.[22] The HDMT is now being used by health departments, planning agencies, and those concerned with "health in all policies" as one model for ongoing monitoring of the health equity impacts of urban policy decisions. A central component of the HDMT is to encourage learning-by-doing, so that monitoring informs practice, and interventions can adapt to new information, changing circumstances and policy goals.

Toward Just and Healthy Cities

This chapter has suggested that we cannot have sustainable cities without addressing existing urban health inequities. Reframing problems, new analytic methods, service delivery networks, and participatory processes of decision making are all necessary components of moving toward healthy and equitable urban governance. Processes and methods to elicit what the public wants and to use what is already known is as important as generating new knowledge. Urban governance must continually ask "What is the purpose; who will be hurt; who benefits; and how can we know?" To reorient urban governance toward health equity requires us to alleviate known causes of people's vulnerability to harm, to pay attention to the distribution of risks and benefits, and to reflect on the social factors that promote or discourage learning.

SPRAWL AND URBAN TYPES IN SUB-SAHARAN CITIES

DICK URBAN VESTBRO

To a large extent, the debate about urban sprawl is based on the experience in the United States and other industrialized countries. What about the situation in low-income countries? In Asia, Africa, and Latin America the rate of urbanization is considerably higher than in North America and Europe. In the former regions, the annual urban growth rate is 3.2 per cent as compared to 0.70 per cent in the developed countries. The urban population in middle- and low-income countries is estimated to increase five times over the next fifty years.[1] It is in the South where the new megacities are found, and here urban sprawl is becoming one of the most problematic issues. This paper discusses the issue of sprawl in sub-Saharan cities and focuses especially upon the potential for densification and the role of house and neighborhood types when addressing the problems of urban sprawl.

Definitions of Sprawl Relevant to Low-income Cities

One may ask whether definitions of urban sprawl, worked out on the basis of experiences in high-income countries, are relevant to the situation in low-income countres. One researcher who has discussed this question is the Ugandan architect Assumpta Nnaggenda-Musana. In her Ph.D. thesis she uses the Oliver Gillham's definition of sprawl from his book *The Limitless City: A Primer on the Urban Sprawl Debate* (2002). Summarizing several other researchers (mainly U.S.-based), Gillham identifies the following elements as part of urban sprawl:

- leapfrog development
- commercial strip development
- low density of the built environment
- large expanses of single-use development
- automobile dependency

By leapfrog development, Gillham refers to the fact that cities often jump over forests and farmlands when expand-

ing. The commercial strip phenomenon is defined as the development of huge arterial roads lined with shopping centers, gas stations, fast-food restaurants, parking lots, etc. Nnaggenda-Musana finds that leapfrog and commercial strip development are factors without relevance to the Ugandan situation, mainly because informal settlements expand without control by authorities. She finds that the functional separation typical of modernist planning is also a factor of little importance, although some elements of this type of planning remain from Uganda's colonial past. One part of the modernist doctrine is planning for the private car. The author finds that car dependency contributes to urban sprawl in Uganda's capital, Kampala, but the influence of this factor is limited by the fact that the vast majority of the population cannot afford cars.[2]

According to Nnaggenda-Musana, the most important factor contributing to urban sprawl in Kampala is the low density of the built environment. This is mainly due to the fact that the major part of the population lives in informal settlements dominated by detached, one-story, one-household units. Also, formally planned areas have low densities, as shown in the licentiate thesis of the same author.[3] A house type much favored by the colonialists was the bungalow—a separate, single-story, single-household dwelling built on a large plot. Smaller copies of this house type were built in Uganda and other British colonies for the indigenous population. These building types usually cover as little as 10 to 20 percent of the plot. It is estimated that the bungalow has had a strong ideological influence long after the downfall of colonialism.[4]

Measures of Density

Politicians, planners, and other decision-makers often refer to informal settlements and slums as congested, overcrowded, and dense. The true situation in these areas is seldom analyzed, however. Various measures of density are often confused.

FIG. 1 Khartoum, the capital of Sudan , is a city suffereing severely from urban sprawl. Greater Khartoum is estimated to have a population of 5.3 million, covering an area of 800 square kilometers (source: Eltayeb,. The average density is 163 persons per square kilometer (2004). This low figure is due to the fact that 92 percent of Khartoum's dwelling plots contain one-story developments of 300 to 500 square meters per plot and because much of urban land is used for roads.

FIG. 2 "Government quarters" in Kampala, built in the 1950s by the British colonial administration for African civil servants. Here only 20 percent of the land is covered by buildings.

For the purpose of understanding urban sprawl, it is important to use an appropriate definition of *physical* (building) *density*. This type of density is expressed in number of houses/apartments per hectare, or Floor Area Ratio (FAR). FAR is defined as the space covered by buildings multiplied by the number of floors of each building, divided by land area. It is easy to calculate the floor area of a group of buildings, but there is much confusion when it comes to the land by which the floor area is to be divided. Often the land is defined as the plot. This is far from adequate, since cities consist of many other types of land uses. Streets, parking spaces, playgrounds, sports fields, gardens, impediments, and other types of spaces outside the plots are to be included in the calculation if urban sprawl is to be properly understood. In order to assess what land to include, it is important to have an idea of what "belongs" to the respective urban types. The garden city idea implies, for instance, the existence of green open spaces adjacent to houses, while long distances between tall buildings are part of the modernist walk-up housing model. Half the street and open spaces belonging to each typology are to be included when assessing the land factor in FAR calculations.[5]

Often population density (expressed in number of people per hectare) is assumed to be related to building density. There is no such direct relationship, however. Population density depends to a large extent on overcrowding, expressed in the number of persons per habitable room, and this type of density depends mainly upon the income of households. It is possible to have high population density with fairly low building density and the other way round (for instance in New York, where rich people may live alone in very large apartments). The problem of overcrowding cannot be addressed by building more houses per land unit—unless densification leads to better access to jobs that provide higher incomes.

Sprawl in Low-income Cities

What is the problem of urban sprawl in low-income cities? To some extent, the consequences are the same as in industrial countries—for instance, the appropriation of valuable agricultural land, and the high infrastructural costs per unit (when such investments are made). In other respects, there are considerable differences. While sprawl generally leads to longer commuting distances, this factor is more severe in low-income cities because poor people cannot afford costs for transport to job opportunities. For survival, the urban poor need to be present where small-scale business may meet customers, or where temporary jobs are offered (often on a day-to-day basis). People living in informal settlements in fringe areas often cannot afford to travel to the city center, at least not if cities are large enough to require motorized transport.

With reference to the situation in South Africa—where urban densities are lower than in other African countries—Professor Dave Dewar from the School of Architecture and Planning at the University of Cape Town concludes that urban compaction is needed for the following reasons:

• Compaction may promote diversification and specialization, the motors of urban economic growth.

FIG. 3 Aerial photo of Hana Nasif with a floor area ratio of 0.2-0.7. Only a handful of buildings in this area are more than one story high.

• Movement on foot is the only mode of travel affordable to a growing majority of urban dwellers.

• When trying to solve the problems of public transport, compaction is necessary along continuous transportation routes.[6]

Dewar's analysis is available in one of the few books dealing with sprawl in low- and middle-income cities, namely the anthology *Compact Cities: Sustainable Urban Forms for Developing Countries*, edited by Mike Jenks and Rod Burgess (2000). The book provides a useful account of the situation in non-OECD countries. In his chapter about the compact city debate, Rod Burgess points out that compaction by reclaiming oversized spaces for cars or abandoned industrial sites is not feasible in low-income cities. He notes that low-income settlements have low residential densities but points out that these areas (whether formal or informal) are usually subject to continuous densification through squatting and self-help extensions "finely tuned to changes in household income and space requirements. Densification efforts should therefore be aimed at assisting this process and should focus on the upgrading and guided rationalization of urban space within these settlements."[7]

Strangely enough, very little attention is given to the role of house and neighborhood types in urban sprawl in the mentioned anthology. It is only in Claudio Acioly's chapter that figures for FAR are given and the role of urban types is discussed. In Cairo, the author finds that informal densification has led to streets only three meters wide lined with urban blocks consisting of six-story buildings covering plots up to 100 percent. It is concluded that this high density makes the environment unhealthy, since rooms lack daylight and ventilation, and since the air is polluted by adjacent heavy car traffic.[8]

The situation in Cairo stands in stark contrast to sub-Saharan Africa. Here many cities have densities far lower than that in Cairo. A study of Dar es Salaam by John Lupala shows, for instance, that FAR is as low as 0.4 to 0.6 in consolidated informal settlements areas, where the densification process has been going on for many decades. In younger informal settlements, FAR often ranges from 0.2 to 0.3. It is only in the central business and residential district of Kariakoo that one finds FARs as high as 1.5 to 2.2 in Dar es Salaam.[9]

The observations of Lupala are confirmed by studies of his colleague Huba Nguluma. Her study focuses on the development of house types in the consolidated informal settlement Hana Nasif (see fig. 4). The densification process has been stimulated by the fact that this area lies within walking distance from the city center. At the time of the fieldwork (2002), densities ranged from 0.2 to 0.7. The author shows that densification leads to a reduction of open spaces, which are frequently used for household activities and for socializing. She concludes that there is a need to promote multistory constructions in order to allow further densification while safeguarding spatial qualities such as daylight in rooms and air circulation both indoors and outdoors.[10]

Taking Nguluma's study as a starting point, two Swedish civil engineering students at the Royal Institute of Technology in Stockholm carried out a study in 2008 and 2009 on the possibility of introducing two-story constructions in low-income informal settlements in Dar es Salaam while keeping costs down through the use of self-educated craftsmen and local building materials. On the basis of a comprehensive survey of the construction sector in Tanzania and fieldwork in Hana Nasif, the students worked out a proposal for a two-story version of the urban Swahili type house. Walls are to be composed of interlocking bricks made of soil cement, a building material available at low cost in Dar es Salaam. This construction is easy to execute and demands less technical knowledge of workers. For the intermediate floor, composite slabs with reinforcement sheets were proposed. Since such sheets are imported, the researchers found that a shift to local production would be required in order to promote

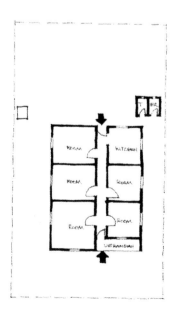
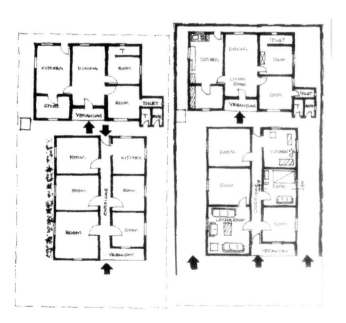

FIG. 4 An example of densification at plot level from 1975 to 2000 in Hana Nasif, Dar es Salaam. The urban Swahili type house with six rooms facing a corridor (usually with one household in each room) is gradually modified by additions of rooms and fences to the detriment of air circulation and usability of outdoor space.

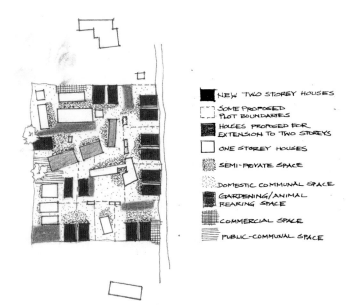

KEY:
- NEW TWO STOREY HOUSES
- SOME PROPOSED PLOT BOUNDARIES
- HOUSES PROPOSED FOR EXTENSION TO TWO STOREYS
- ONE STOREY HOUSES
- SEMI-PRIVATE SPACE
- DOMESTIC COMMUNAL SPACE
- GARDENING/ANIMAL REARING SPACE
- COMMERCIAL SPACE
- PUBLIC-COMMUNAL SPACE

FIG. 5 Proposed incremental upgrading of a cluster of houses in Mbuya, Kampala. Note the ample amount of open space between buildings, allowing for intensive household activities, socializing, and future extensions of houses.

community development. According to the authors, the FAR would increase to 0.55 if one third of the houses in Hana Nasif were two-story instead of one-story. Some two-story houses may replace buildings that now encroach upon streets and common areas.[11]

Densification and Upgrading in Kampala

Tanzania's neighbor Uganda is considerably less urbanized, but its capital, Kampala (accommodating a population of 1.4 million in 2008), nevertheless has problems with urban sprawl. Nnaggenda-Musana's study of residential densities in Kampala shows that FAR in informal settlements usually ranges from 0.1 to 0.3, while FAR in formally planned areas ranges from 0.05 (bungalows) to 0.8 (four-story walk-ups). In her calculations of FAR, Nnaggenda-Musana demarcates sections of land that contain between six and twenty buildings and divides the floor area of all buildings with the total piece of land selected. The fact that only 10 to 30 percent of urban land in most parts of the city is covered by buildings means that there is a great potential for densification. Such processes take place continuously, but no professional guid-

ance is given in a situation where the main feature of planning is "non-implementation."[12]

Nnaggenda-Musana's analysis shows that some of the existing house types are more appropriate for densification than others. She shows how densification can be combined with incremental and participative house upgrading, following the enabling model of planning. Houses of the lowest quality are to be replaced by new ones. She suggests that some of the new houses are designed to allow vertical extensions when residents can afford to build a second floor. The author shows how urban agriculture and home-based enterprise can be maintained—or added—during the densification process, even when FAR is trebled.[13]

Conclusions

In sub-Saharan cities, 60 to 85 percent of the population live in informal settlements. Virtually all buildings in these areas are detached one-story houses. The analysis above shows that land coverage usually ranges from 10 to 30 percent, which equals a Floor Area Ratio of between 0.1 and 0.3. The informal settlements are continuously being densified, a process without any type of professional guidance. If professionals would better understand the need for incremental upgrading and the possibility to promote compact house and neighborhood types, then densification can take place while maintaining basic spatial qualities such as functional outdoor spaces, air circulation inside and outside buildings, and daylight in rooms.

It is desirable to promote clusters of houses with groupings that are more land-efficient, plot dimensions that allow deeper blocks with few but accessible roads, house types with wall-to-wall design, and constructions that permit vertical extensions while still using local skills and simple building techniques. Nnaggenda-Musana's model for incremental upgrading shows that it is possible to increase densies three to five times and still maintain ample space between buildings for household chores, agriculture, and animal-rearing. If her model would be applied in all of Kampala's informal settlements, the capital could double or treble in population without encroaching at all upon agricultural land around the city. Alternatively, households may extend houses to reduce overcrowding (when incomes increase). Even after such densification, FAR would be less than one third or one quarter of normal inner city densities in Europe (where FAR is often 1.5 to 2.5).

PART 9: URBAN SHIFTS, NEW NETWORKS, GEOGRAPHIES

METROPOLITAN FORM

PETER BOSSELMANN

At the turn of the millennium, we learned that half of the world's 6.5 billion inhabitants lived in cities. We now know that by 2050 three quarters of the world's population, which will then reach 9 billion, will live in cities.[1] Urban living for the majority no longer means living in compact cities in the conventional sense but in conurbations, the term coined by Patrick Geddes (1854–1932) to describe an urbanized landscape with multiple centers, connected by corridors of movement, and represented by multiple political institutions and economic activities. But even Geddes's term could not quite describe the form of cities we will be living in. In 1995, the French sociologist François Ascher (1995) called the urbanized region *Métapolis* by going beyond the metropolitan scale to focus on interconnected networks composed of visible means of transport and invisible means of communication. Ascher argued that urban attributes are acquired by all those spaces which, whether they belong to the city or not, comply with the condition of the city by taxing its resources, work forces, and habitats to guarantee its daily functioning.[2] Others have also applied the inherently imprecise logic of city and non-city to the emerging form of dispersed cities,[3] especially to the porosity of many shrinking European, North American, and Japanese cities. As early as 1963, the American planner Melvin Webber in a follow-up paper to his "The Urban Place and the Non-Place Urban Realm" observed that urban settlements were no longer spatially discrete and physically bounded. "Now all Americans are coming to share very similar cultural traits; the physical boundaries of settlements are disappearing; and the networks of interdependence among various groups are becoming functionally intricate and spatially widespread."[4]

Rhetorically, Webber, like Asher almost forty years earlier, reminded us of futurist H. G. Wells, who predicted "the probable diffusion of cities" in his book *Anticipations* (1902) a few years after Ebenezer Howard wrote *To-Morrow: A Peaceful Path Real Reform*, later published as *Garden Cities of To-Morrow*, in 1902. Intellectually, the blurred distinction between cities and country had its origins over a century ago, but in schools of architecture and planning the centrality of the compact city has remained a central focus, for obvious reasons: the motivation for practicing urban design is grounded in the passion that professionals share for the social vitality of the compact city and, increasingly, for a commitment to a spatial form that does not overly tax the earth's nonrenewable resources. Critiques of American urban culture, starting with Jane Jacobs (1961) and including William H. Whyte (1988) plus a large number of contemporary professionals, continue to inspire us to design improvements to the compact city's overlapping mix of activities and to the experience of its public spaces. And with much success, though much more needs to be done to make life in the inner cities worthy of rediscovery by two generations of Americans who have moved away and grown up outside the compact city. But there is no denying that more citylike development occurred outside the compact cities. Even if more people would elect to live in inner-city neighborhoods, the extensive urbanized areas at the edge will not simply be abandoned but would need major design attention for social, environmental, and economic reasons.

Limits to Mobility

In North America the discussion about future metropolitan form was raised to a higher level of urgency when service sector office operations left the traditional core city locations during the early to mid-1980s. As the result of technological innovations to office operations and lower land values, the work force, in significant proportions, left high-rise towers in downtown areas and started to commute to suburban office parks. The consequences of the dispersed workplaces were discussed with much intensity, particularly in Anthony Downs's projections for the development of large U.S. metropolitan areas.[5] The low-density settlement patterns and low-density workplaces generated immense travel requirements. The chief components of Downs's vision depended upon: sizable areas of at least moderately dense housing and workplace development; populations encouraged to live closer to

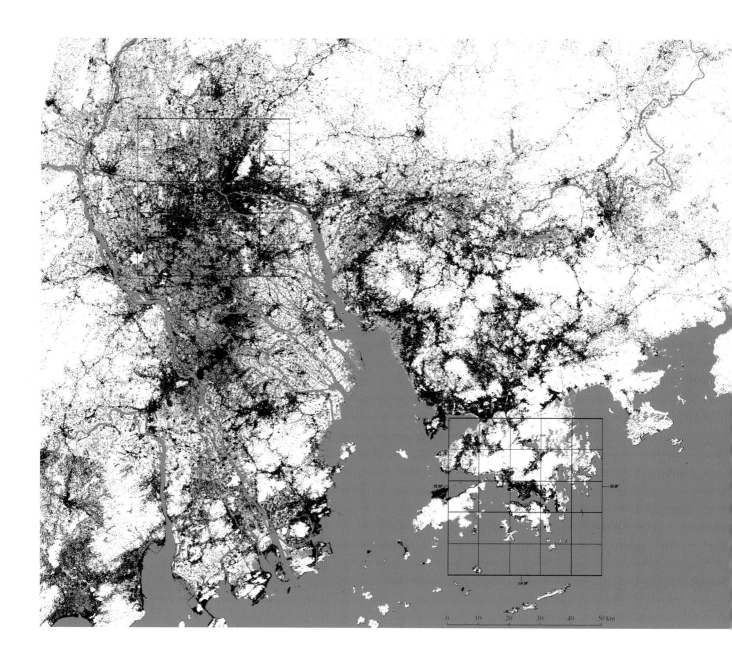

where they work; and local governments, while preserving their authority, working within a framework that compels them to act responsibly to meet area-wide needs. And lastly, Downs's vision takes a more realistic account of the collective cost of people's behavioral choices, for example, the need to charge drivers to pay for the use of the road system during times of congestion. The desire for mobility had met its limits, contrary to what Webber wrote back in 1963: "These changes now taking place in American society may well be compatible with—and call forth—metropolitan forms that are neither concentrated nor concentric nor contained. Sympathetic acceptance of this proposition might then lead us to new ways of seeing the metropolis, ways that are more sensitive to the environmental qualities that really matter."[6]

The effects of diffused settlement patterns on the environment have become a powerful motivation for a partial shift in focus from the compact cities to the repair of urban

regions: a gradual transformation of the urbanized landscape will be necessary for reasons chiefly related to what is broadly defined as the concern for greater sustainability. Specific to the form of cities, sustainability means the conservation of nonrenewable sources of energy and addressing the consequences of climate change, i.e., controlling carbon emissions. Society can no longer afford unbridled mobility, so important to the shape of urban regions in recent decades.

A second motivation for a shift in the attention of urban designers is the emergence of diffused urban forms in the rapidly urbanizing regions of India, the Middle East, and China. In stark contrast to existing compact urban form—even extremely compact informal settlements—the form of new urban expansion is intentionally much diffused. The stunning increases in urban populations will force professionals to reexamine the space-consuming standards and practices of land development, largely imported from the United States.

FIG. 1 The Pearl River Delta region in Southern China, where the historic cities of Guangzhou and Foshan (inside the gridded square on the upper left) are starting to connect into a continuously urbanized rim around the large delta that links these two cities to Dongguan and Shenzhen and southward toward Hong Kong (the gridded square in the lower center). From there, once a proposed new bridge is completed to Macao, the urban loop will connect back to Guangzhou via Zhuhai, Zhongshan, and Shunde. Together, these cities will form an urban rim, like the Randstad, in the Netherlands, but at unprecedented dimensions. The official population count for the Guangdong economic region, including Hong Kong and Macao, was approximately fifty million in 2002,[7] not including the floating population of industrial workers. The total population is conservatively estimated at eighty million.

FIG. 2 Three metropolitan areas with identical population sizes of 7 million shown at the same graphic scale: the San Francisco Bay Area, the Randstad, and Hong Kong.

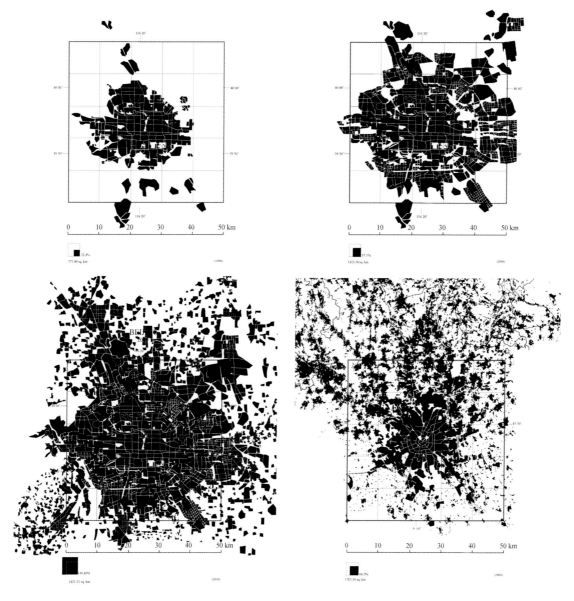

FIG. 3 The urban morphology of Beijing from 1990, 2005, and 2010, and the Milan metropolitan region in 2005 (Bosselmann/Moos).

For environmental, social, and economical reasons, limits to the consumption of land will rise to the same level of importance as consumption of energy because of their intrinsic relationships.

Urban Design Strategies for the Gradual Transformation of Urban Regions

Important differences remain between urbanized regions which have less to do with political, economic, or social geography than with local conditions. In a collection of fifty maps drawn at the same graphic scale to compare some of the largest metropolitan regions in the world, the easiest

observation one can make is that no two maps are the same.[8] Increasingly urbanized areas have similarities when seen at ground level, but when seen from space, satellite data shows distinct differences in form. Coastlines, lakeshores, rivers, and mountain ridges continue to define the shape of urbanized regions. At first, this observation appears obvious, but the fact that urban agglomerations were shaped by landforms (created chiefly by water) instills some optimism because a better understanding of the natural systems that existed before and that were altered by the growth of cities can inform the design of ongoing urban transformations.

Transformations of urban form will increasingly take into consideration the interrelated natural processes of climate, vegetation, landform, and water. Therefore, it is helpful to think of urbanized regions as metropolitan landscapes. California, as forerunner of sprawling urban agglomerations, has recently made attempts to set vehicle emission targets by reducing vehicle miles traveled. This has resulted in legislation to reduce greenhouse gasses and to develop renewable sources of energy.[9] For urban designers the implication of the laws is to make communities better connected to transit, to build at densities that support public transit, to reduce dependency on private cars, and to reduce distances to make possible alternative travel modes. The global financial crisis of 2008 brought the need for greenhouse gas reduction into sharper focus. First, the crisis resulted in diminished private equity in single-family properties, thus reducing the cherished ability for social upward mobility. Second, the growing public financial burden has prohibited communities from serving a dispersed population with their decentralized activities. These symptoms add up to a crisis mood that calls into question the resources available to solve very difficult and interconnected problems.

Space as a Resource

The three maps in figure 2 have in common the same population size. In 2005, the one hundred cities that form the San Francisco Bay Area had a population of seven million people; in the same year, the cities of the Randstad in the Netherlands also accommodated seven million inhabitants; and the city of Hong Kong that year had an equal population size. These three metropolitan areas are shown at the same graphic scale. A gridded square of 50 by 50 kilometers is superimposed onto each map that allows us to compute the land area covered by each metropolis. The geographic size of urbanization follows a morphological definition arrived from remote sensing of satellite data that depicts continuous urbanized areas, instead of the more customarily used government boundaries to depict size. The differences between the three maps are stunning: the cities around San Francisco cover 83.7 percent of a 50-square-kilometer area, the Randstad roughly half the surface area, or 42.7 percent, and

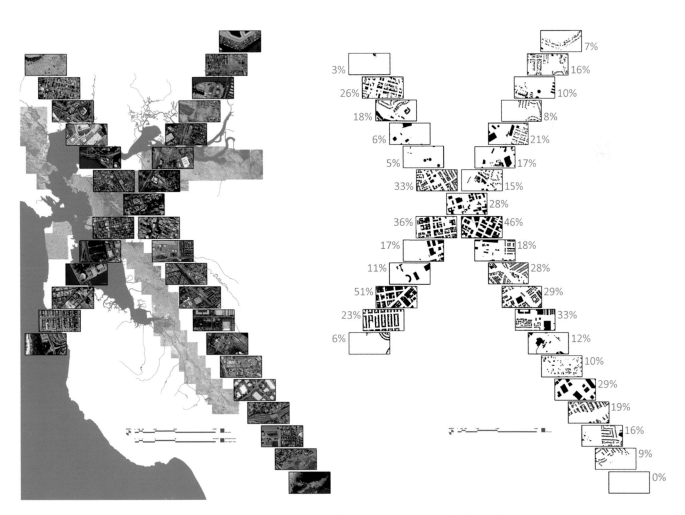

FIG. 4 Urban transects of the San Francisco Bay Area metropolitan region. The transects originate at the Campanile on the Berkeley University campus and project into the four cardinal directions. A total of thirty-two frames was taken every 5 miles (along the western transect, every 2.5 miles) to compute land-coverage by buildings (Bosselmann/Doyle).

Hong Kong only an astonishing 4.2 percent. If the people of the Randstad were to imagine what it might be like to live at Hong Kong densities, they would need to imagine what it might be like if all Randstad residents would live only in Delft, or the people of the San Francisco Bay Area would need to imagine that they would all live—not very congenially—in Sausalito, Tiburon, and in the southern portion of Marin County up to San Rafael.[10]

This is not to suggest that Hong Kong densities should be considered for future metropolitan form elsewhere. But the comparison highlights important differences in the way urban space is used. The Hong Kong example suggests the highest possible level of integration of workplaces with housing. The majority of people live and work in closely spaced high-rise structures. This results in high use of public transportation and walking as the chief mode of transport. The San Francisco Bay Area example suggests a low level of spatial integration between workplaces and housing. The population predominantly lives in freestanding single-family homes and uses private automobiles for long trips to work.[11] And the Randstad is twice as dense as the San Francisco Bay Area; urbanization covers only half the land compared to the Bay Area, and workplaces and housing are clustered into polycentric settlements with historic origins. As a result of the polycentric form, commute trips are shorter, and the flat terrain encourages public transport and especially bicycling. Randstad residents live predominantly in tightly spaced rowhouse configurations and, compared to the previous two examples, utilize a much wider range of housing types, and thus enjoy a greater choice of living conditions.

The comparison of urbanized metropolitan regions reveals a third observation: The highly populated and growing cities of India and China were still remarkably compact until the beginning of the new millennium. Over the course of the past decade, change has been dramatic. Looking at the maps of Beijing in figure 3, one can quickly conclude that Beijing has quadrupled in size between 1990 and 2005, a time period when the population nearly doubled from 6.7 million to 11.5 million inhabitants. But Beijing was still more compact compared to, for example, Milan's metropolitan area, which in 2005 covered 68.5 percent of a 50-square-kilometer area with approximately 7.4 million[12] inhabitants, compared to 11.5 million Beijing residents on 57.5 percent of the same size square. Beijing's population has grown further to 12.4 million by 2010,[13] but the continuously urbanized area of the Beijing urban agglomeration has increased to 137 percent of a 50-square-kilometer area.

While the maps give insight into natural systems that shaped urban regions, density, and compactness versus porosity of form, the representations do not readily allow us to conceive three-dimensional designs. A different kind of description of urban form is needed to guide design at the regional scale. One such method is a longitudinal sampling with reduced dimensionality. Borrowed from the natural sciences, the urban transect records the form of human habitats. In figure 4, transects explain the form of the San Francisco Bay Area metropolitan region. Frames are selected every five miles along cardinal directions. Various graphic conventions show in detail land coverage, land forms, and vegetation. All four transects result in a total of thirty-two frames, where each frame contains 50 acres. Such a model does not claim to show a truly representative account of land coverage for the entire region but a reconnaissance of land coverage in relation to settlement form: less than a third of all squares show compact settlements. These are the frames that display a land coverage of 30 percent or higher. The highest land coverage of 53 percent within a 50-acre frame was found in downtown San Francisco. Established inner-city neighborhoods generally have a land coverage of less than 30 percent, both in compact single and multifamily settings. In the San Francisco Bay Area, less than a third of the frames reach the 30 percent threshold. Areas with low land-coverage of 10 to 20 percent are the target for infill, and they make up the largest number of frames using this sampling method.

Changing the Way We Do Things

City design plays a limited but important role in addressing the gradual transformation of metropolitan form. In conclusion, I have grouped urban design's contribution under three headings:

"City design can demonstrate how to better integrate workplaces with places where people live." For functional reasons, most modern-day work and living could be integrated into adjacent structures, at times within the same structure. Office parks and financial districts should include housing, and neighborhoods could contain workplaces. Use-specific building typologies can be made more compatible, and workplace-related intrusions on housing can be minimized. The creative class can work where they live, and frequently do so already. Administrative and service activities do not need to be restricted to separate parts of the city or region. The obstacle is not zoning, as is commonly assumed. Community opposition is generally not an obstacle for including housing into commercial districts, but can be a strong obstacle for incorporating workplaces into neighborhoods. Local planning needs to address such opposition, which takes time. The main obstacles that make the integration of uses difficult are financing and land development practices. City design can develop better integration models, and should. The advantages are obvious, but not all people will be living close to places where they work. Households will continue to have varied and changing commuting patterns.

"Design can demonstrate that lowering automobile dependency does not result in a lower quality of life but that the opposite can be true." People move to metropolitan areas for a host of reasons. Access to a range of jobs is one of them. Designers can make public transit more attractive by improving connections between modes. For urban population to increase, city design must produce better-designed public spaces. More obvious and convenient transfer locations where additional services can be available would result.

Designers also can help to reduce distances and improve walkability by designing at a scale that is appropriate for the speed and interest of pedestrians and bicyclists.

"New housing types need to be designed at medium-high densities with amenities comparable to single-family living." Outside a few historically dense cities, like New York, San Francisco, and parts of Boston, multifamily housing in the U.S. suffers from a poverty of choices. For multifamily housing to be attractive, new models need to be developed that provide access to light from more than one orientation. Such models need to include private, if not sizeable, open space that can be personalized and thus be of significant importance for the well-being of a family or small group. The value of multifamily housing is greatly increased if apartments have their own private entrances via a porch, directly off the public sidewalk. The satisfaction of dwelling in the city is enhanced if family living is organized on two levels, or on a mezzanine. Higher density does not necessary imply high-rise development, but a range of housing types that allows for views of trees from upper floors, an easy walk to a nearby shopping area, and a public park and public transportation nearby.

What is described here is a form of city design that is aimed at building communities. But people and the communities they form do not exist in a vacuum. Some of us will agree that the reform of the metropolitan region cannot only follow the interpretation of sustainability as a response to environmental reasoning, but that such reforms need to be done by addressing L. C. Gercken's[14] concerns about the desire by a mobile society for social segregation by income and origin. Social dynamics might well be at the core when explaining the origins of the dispersed metropolitan regions.

ENVISIONING ECOLOGICAL CITIES

THE SCI-FI BASED SOLUTION TO CLIMATE CHANGE

MITCHELL JOACHIM

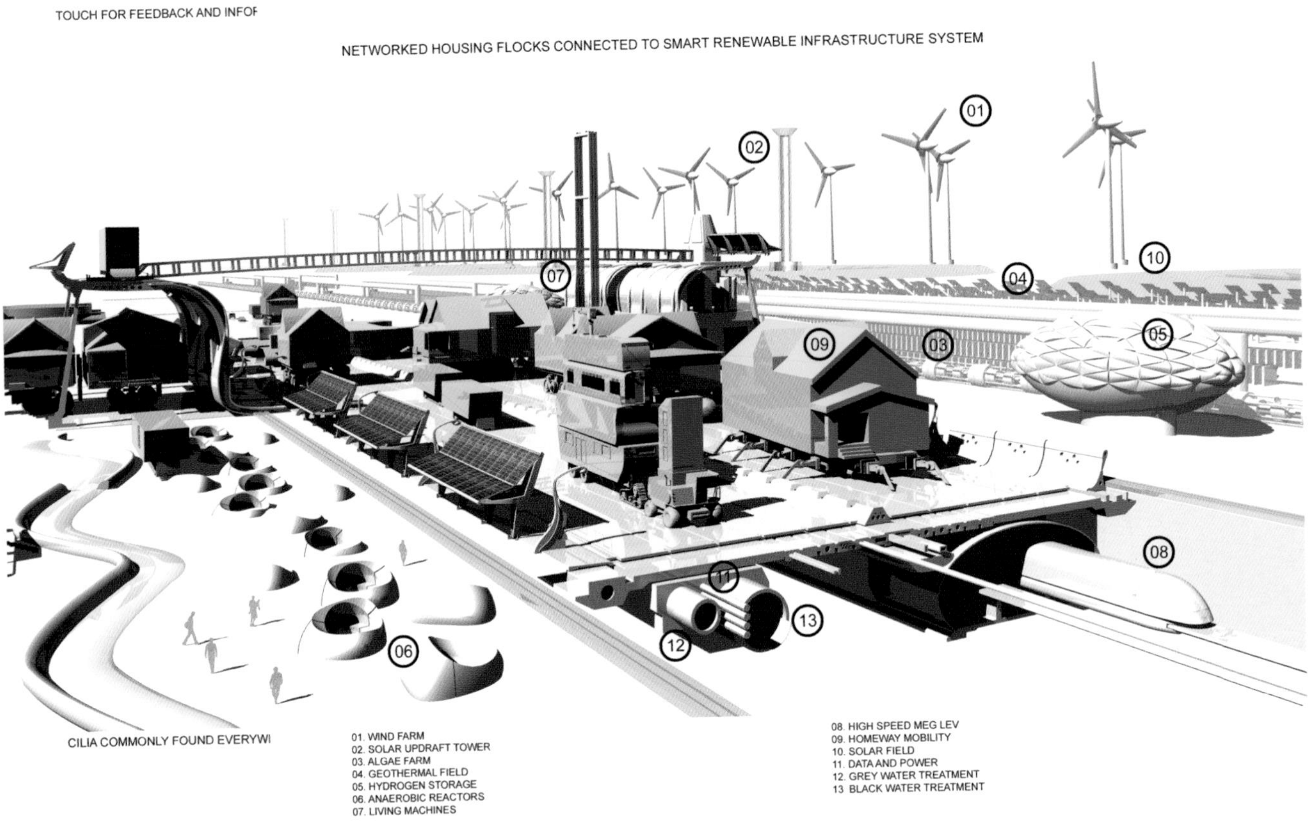

TOUCH FOR FEEDBACK AND INFOF

NETWORKED HOUSING FLOCKS CONNECTED TO SMART RENEWABLE INFRASTRUCTURE SYSTEM

CILIA COMMONLY FOUND EVERYWI

01. WIND FARM
02. SOLAR UPDRAFT TOWER
03. ALGAE FARM
04. GEOTHERMAL FIELD
05. HYDROGEN STORAGE
06. ANAEROBIC REACTORS
07. LIVING MACHINES

08. HIGH SPEED MEG LEV
09. HOMEWAY MOBILITY
10. SOLAR FIELD
11. DATA AND POWER
12. GREY WATER TREATMENT
13. BLACK WATER TREATMENT

FIG. I   From "Homeway: The Great Suburban Exodus."

How should urban design foresee new instrumentalist technologies for cities? For 150 years the innovation of the elevator has done more to influence urban design than most urban designers. Elevator systems had incredible success in the creation of compact and greener cities. Imagine what the advent of the jet pack will do for cities. Urban design is greatly altered by such devices. For instance, automobiles have defined limits in cities for almost a century. Unlike the elevator, however, the car has arguably caused more problems then it has solved. Perhaps it is time for urban design to rethink technologies to fit cities, not constrain them. As a wide-ranging discipline, it can effortlessly illuminate the technological potentials for cities. Urban design will successfully situate itself by the production of future macro-scaled scenarios predicated on innovative devices. Physicist and polymath Dr. Freeman Dyson has said the best way to comprehend our near urban future is to examine science fiction rather than economic forecasts.[1] In his experience, sci-fi is good for decades of technological projection. Economic forecasts, on the other hand, are only accurate within five to ten years maximum. Most of these predictive economic models are quantity based and fail to extrapolate the qualifiers associated with creativity. Sci-fi is a phenomenal way to chronicle our plausible urban future that should not be dismissed by urban designers.

Dyson is certain that the urban era of information will soon transition into "the age of domesticated biotechnology." In his novel, *Infinite in All Directions*, he writes, "Bio-tech offers us the chance to imitate nature's speed and flexibility." He envisions a realm of functional objects and art that humans will "grow" for personal use. According to a *New York Times* article on Dyson, he also believes that climate change is profoundly misstated: "He added the caveat that if CO2 levels soared too high, they could be soothed by the mass cultivation of specially bred 'carbon-eating trees.'"[2] He is not concerned with predicting the future but rather with expressing possibilities. These expressions are founded in line with societal desire as a kind of relevant optimism. Therefore Dyson measures the wants of civilization and advances our expectations.

At some level, urban design shares this position that promises a better tomorrow. Numerous practitioners and urbanists wish for clairvoyance. Alex Krieger describes the broadly defined vocation as more a scrupulous sensibility than an exclusive authority.[3] The profession is torn between many incompatible agendas: weighty theories and oversimplified applications, ivory towers and new urbanism, developer brands and radical ecologies, and vernacular forms and futurology. One of our chief directives at Terreform ONE and Terrefuge is the shrewd intersection between technology and urbanism, especially under the rubric of ecology. Our projects range from highlighting the possible effects of self-sufficient cities to studying flocks of jet packs. These ideations keep us thriving as urban design researchers. It is our supposition that the prospective ecological city is about extreme solutions to an extreme predicament. Our future fundamentally depends on the immensity our solutions envision.

Envisioning is by definition a view or concept which evolves beyond existing boundaries. This notion of foresight may be interpreted in many different ways, each foregrounding particular ideations and processes describing the next event. Here in America, we need these radical new visions to assist in solving our current global calamity. As of now, the earth's climate endures an unremitting state of trauma. We seek precise prescriptions that cover a wide scope to alter this massive dilemma. To paraphrase JFK, "If man created problems, man can solve them." We believe it is not to decipher our ecological issues but return to a system of perpetuity. This future vision unfolds a truly breathing interconnected metabolic urbanism. How does it reify from statistics to architectural form? What does the future look like for America's cities? How do technological devices affect these functions?

For a popular audience, the recent Disney sci-fi film *Wall-E* enabled society to anticipate one conceivable future. The film is set in a generic city that is completely buried in trash. Humans have abandoned life on earth for off-world dwelling, leaving one lone solar-powered robot to clear the rubbish. Part of the message of the film is that technology alone can not solve humanity's "affluenza," yet the film's powerful computer-generated visuals encourage us to confront our colossal wastefulness and rethink the city.

Wall-E inscribes a universal memo, "Dear future inhabitants of world cites, waste no longer has a place to go except home." Truly a masterpiece of foresight and visionary urbanism, and pure sci-fi, *Wall-E* unfurls new directions in prospective urbanity. This is a refinement where ecology is married to technology, a hypothesis of the socio-ecological city derived from plausible misuse. Here is where urban design finds credence: in a profession engaged in future-proofing the big problems with dangerously healthy ideations.

We foresee strategies for people to fit symbiotically into their natural surroundings. To achieve this, all things possible are considered. We design the scooters, cars, trains, blimps, as well as the streets, parks, open spaces, cultural districts, civic centers, and business hubs that comprise the future

FIG. 2 From "Homeway: The Great Suburban Exodus."

FIG. 3 From "Homeway: The Great Suburban Exodus."

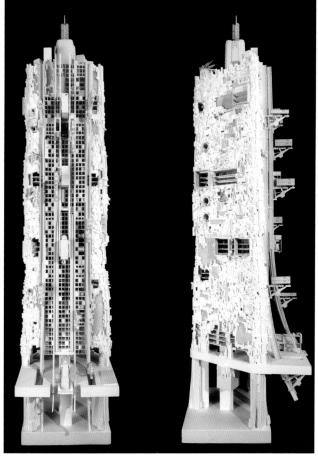

FIG.4 From "Rapid Re(f)use: Waste to Resource City 2120."

metropolis. For centuries cities have been designed to accommodate the theater of our human desires. We have joined the ranks of delivering a new sense of the city, one that privileges the play of nature over anthropocentric whims. We are constantly vying for a profound clairvoyant perspective. We desire to preview a likeness of our collective future yet untold.

Our foresight of ecological design is not only a philosophy that inspires visions of sustainability but also a focused scientific endeavor. The mission is to ascertain the consequences of fitting a project within our natural environment. Solutions are derived from numerous examples: living material habitats, climatic tall building clusters, and mobility technologies. These design iterations succeed as having activated ecology both as a productive symbol and an evolved artifact. Current research attempts to establish new forms of design knowledge and new processes of practice at the interface of design, computer science, structural engineering, and biology.

The Rapid Re(f)use City and Wall-E: 3-D Fabricated Positive Waste Ecologies

Imagine our colossal municipal landfills as sensible resource sheds to build our future urban and peri-urban spaces. Then what kind of effort is required to reuse their copious contents? Now that the bulk of humanity has chosen to settle in urbanized areas, waste management needs a radical revision.

For hundreds of years we designed cities to generate waste. It is time we design waste to generate our cities. This was the message we had been propounding for a few years and which had brought us and the design team at Terreform ONE to the attention of Disney. While we had been drawing up plans to transform our relation to waste, Disney's Imagineers had been working on a film around the same theme—*Wall-E*. How would fiction and reality mix? We wondered nervously as we headed to California to brainstorm with their team.

But first a little background. America is the lead creator of waste on the earth, making approximately 30 percent of the world's trash and tossing out 0.8 tons per U.S. citizen per year. At the risk of sounding ungracious, our American value system is out of balance. It seems value has devolved into rampant affluenza and megaproducts scaled for supersized franchise brands, big box retail outlets, jumbo-sized paraphernalia, etc., encapsulating a joint race for ubiquity and instantaneity in the U.S. mindset. Where does it all end up? Gertrude Stein cleverly pointed out that "away has gone away." The first step we must take is reduction, meaning a massive discontinuation of objects designed for obsolescence. Then we need a radical reuse plan. Our waste crisis is immense, so what is our call to action?

One illustration of this dilemma can be found in New York City. At the moment, New York is disposing of 38,000 tons of waste per day. Previously most of this discarded material ended up in Fresh Kills on Staten Island before operations were blocked. Manhattanites toss out enough

FIG. 5 From "Rapid Re(f)use: Waste to Resource City 2120."

paper products to fill a volume the size of the Empire State Building every two weeks. Our Rapid Re(f)use project strives to capture, reduce, and redesign New York's refuse. The initiative supposes an extended city reconstituted from its own waste materials. Our concept remakes the city by utilizing all the trash entombed in the Fresh Kills landfill. Theoretically our method should produce at minimum seven entirely new Manhattan Islands at full scale.

How does this work? Outsized automated 3-D printers are modified to rapidly process trash and complete this task within decades. These automatons are wholly based on existing techniques commonly found in industrial waste compaction devices. To accomplish this job, we deem nothing drastically new needs to be invented. Instead of machines that crush objects into cubes, devices can use adjustable jaws that will craft simple shapes into smart puzzle blocks for assembly. The blocks of refuse are predetermined using computational geometries to fit together to form domes, archways, lattices, windows, whatever patterns are needed. Different materials serve specified purposes: transparent plastic for fenestration, organic compounds for temporary scaffolds that decompose, metals for primary structures, etc. Eventually, the future city makes no distinction between waste and supply.

The idea of refuse city is not new. People are working on it using various platforms and utilizing their own needs and points of view. Now we are just starting to work together and realize that there are more of us out there; numbers make all the difference when it comes to being heard.

Often a fable or story comes from hopes that have not yet been realized. It's where things start. Every idea no matter how big or small started with something when someone imagined it. An hour north of the "happiest place on earth" is where the "happiest minds on earth" are housed. Think "think tank" with Mouse Ears. Here, people are assembled to imagine what they can while surrounded by the best resources and expertise. The Walt Disney Imagineering Headquarters is located on their Glendale campus but is coupled with the confidentiality of recovery rooms around the nation. Under an almost Wonkian code, one is ever reminded, "What you see and hear here, stays here." When you first walk in you get the sense that "big things" are brewing here, large brains at work on projects that are going to not just shape Tomorrowland at Disney but our Tomorrow.

We came to meet people with the finest imaginations on earth and talk shop about Tomorrow. Our Terreform ONE group had prepared a presentation that would unpack a comprehensive view of one version, our version, of the future,

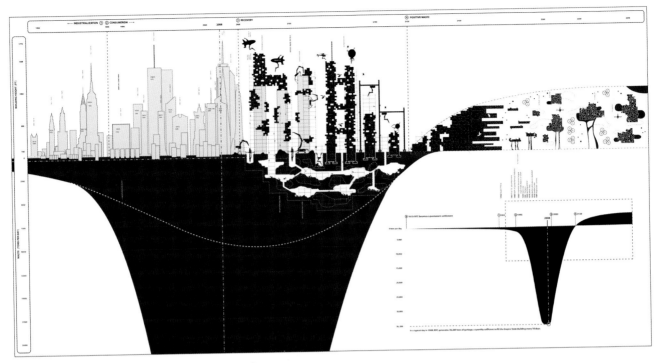

FIG.6 From "Rapid Re(f)use: Waste to Resource City 2120."

a world free of carbon loading in the atmosphere and abundant in self-sufficient lifestyles. As eco-savvy architects, we had meticulously crafted cities within the rubric of a socioecological domain. Everyone and everything in these urban ideations were "carborexic" to the hilt. We were rethinking the design of entire systems, from doorknobs to democracies.

Terreform ONE designs places for people to fit symbiotically into their natural surroundings. To achieve this, all things possible are considered. We design the scooters, cars, trains, blimps, as well as the streets, parks, open spaces, cultural districts, civic centers, business hubs, etc. that comprise the future metropolis. For centuries cities have been designed to accommodate the drama of our human will. Our sense of the city privileges the drama of nature over anthropocentric whims. We wanted the good people at Disney to preview a likeness of our collective future yet untold. Much to our chagrin they were light-years ahead, at least when it came to the topic of municipal wastes. At the time, we had a sketch of a new city composed of waste ordered by massive industrial 3-D printers. A cadre of our students had run through a number of iterations. All were schematic, but we inherently knew this was an exciting vector.

When Dr. Ben Schwegler, Chief Imagineer, pulled back the proverbial black curtain to reveal Wall-E, we were crestfallen. They beat us to it.

Wall-E is perfect—almost. He is a tightly packaged, solar powered, curious, obedient, evolved, robotic trash compaction and distribution device. His name is an acronym; Waste Allocation Load Lifter Earth Class. Left behind on earth by mankind, he toils with trillions of tons of nonrecycled inner-city trash. Not only is he a highly advanced rubbish manager, he is a mechanized new-fangled Mesopotamian architect. He piles ziggurats quicker than Hammurabi, and accomplishes all of this while remaining completely adorable. Not easy to do. Ceaselessly, he configures mountains of discarded material. Why pyramids of trash? Wall-E's daily perpetual feats seem almost futile. Disney omits exactly why he is programmed to pile refuse, and there's the rub.

We are in Hollywood, the top-shelf maker of make believe. It all looks perfect and "works" in the movies, but whether it is the amazing suit in *Ironman* or the perfectly art directed, "shabby" Wall-E, they just don't do in reality what we want to believe they do on the big screen. But, when it serves as inspiration and a jumping off point for teams to get to work on the real deal, then true magic can and does happen.

Collaborators at Terreform ONE were interested in exploring a deeper motivation for stacking refuse. In a fashion similar to the Disney film, what if the refuse was re-fabricated to become real urban spaces or buildings? How much new technology needs to be obtained to do so, or should we modify existing methods? If it is plausible to adapt the current machinery, how much material is available? At first look, any westernized sanitary landfill appears like an ample supply of building "nutrients." The heavy industrial technologies to compact cars into "lumber" or automatically sift/trommel through garbage are readily available. Other technologies are scalable to make the system articulate specific forms such as 3-D printing, an exhausted hackneyed capability that is mutable for grander tasks. That's where our city began . . .

Our city will be derived from trash, not ordinary trash but smart trash. We were inspired by Woody Allen. In his stand-up comedy days back in the 1960s, he used to tell a great parable about mechanical objects with attitude. He detailed the relationships he had with various household appliances, such as his blender, his toaster, and the quirkiness of their individual personalities. He met with them often to discuss problems and on occasion had to chastise them (he once hit his television set for poor signal display). One day in a New York elevator, the voice of an automated operator asked him, "Are you the guy that hit the television set?" and promptly bounced him up and down the building before dumping him in the basement. We don't expect all the systems in our future city to be perfect.

A significant factor in our city composed from smart refuse is post-tuning. Unitized devices will not immediately adapt. Integration into the city texture is a learning process. Things will need to talk or poll one another for useful information. After a time, the responses will become more attuned to the needs of the urban dweller. This city is made from trash, but each individual component is enhanced with a modicum of CPU power. Many short durational events will give these smart units the experiences they need to evolve.

Our final objective for this city is to establish a self-sufficient perpetual motion urbanism. Perpetual motion is said not to exist, yet. It defies the laws of thermodynamics and energy conservation. It claims that an apparatus can be created that produces more energy than it consumes. What if our city was like an instrument that produces more energy from renewable sources then it consumes? Or instead of a city like a single instrument, it is a city of a trillion instruments making more with less. In this case, nothing can be thrown away. Every bit is a vital piece of stored energy poised to be reused in a cyclical nutrient stream. It is a city without a tailpipe. It is a city that not only has zero impact but makes a positive contribution toward its natural surroundings. It is the highest standard we can conceive. JFK said, "If man created problems, man can solve them." We think it is not only about solving our ecological issues but returning to a system of perpetuity. This is the future for a truly breathing, interconnected, metabolic urbanism.

Cities have passed the age of industrialization and entered the age of recovery. After this great cleansing, we may transition into the grandest of orders: positive waste. Here is an order that captures our socioecological needs. Not utopia, but a philtopia, a place where everything is precious and nothing is disposed. And if the ideas come in a little louder while wearing Mouse Ears, so be it.

MARKET URBANISM

A PRELIMINARY OUTLINE
FOR AN ALTERNATIVE TO URBAN IDEOLOGY

ANDERS JERKER SÖDERLIND

Systematic proposals for solving urban problems, different "urbanisms," are in fact competing ideologies with structural resemblances to religion. Here I question the idea that cities and their inhabitants need an *ideology* to follow and be ruled by, from the "recipes" of the CIAM package to present New Urbanism schemes. Instead of urban ideologies based on values, I suggest a nonideological urbanism based on demand and designed to increase user-friendly urban solutions. The aim is to decrease the influence of self-appointed special interest groups, scientific worldviews, and architectural ideologies.

Market urbanism is not an urbanism of "capitalism," "developers," "profit making," or an argument for the abolishment of political decision making or regulations. An urbanism without urban ideology can be based on the general Western democratic market system itself, maximizing freedom of choice, the spirit of competition, and incentives to innovation. A strong argument for this is that cities themselves, as a rule, have come about as marketplaces, with an economic activity based on mutual gain and trade. A market situation can be defined as the voluntary and free interaction between a producer/supplier of something and the buyer/user of the same. The idea is that cities should develop based solely on *demand*, expressed as the collective expression of all individuals' aspirations and hopes (taking into account large differences in purchasing power, lifestyles, and priorities).

The opposite is a situation in which regulations based on ideas (right now, the modernist ideology) determine how cities develop. For me, as a believer in the ideology that modernism was a disastrous ideology, the present situation is the worst possible. But I do not think that I, or "we"—believing in a city that is more mixed-use, dense, attractive, walkable, etc.—will be successful if all we have to say is: "Our urban ideology is better than the other one. Let us decide for you." A stronger argument, at least in our Western society, is to base decisions on the foundations of the democratic market system itself.

Urban development is basically a political issue, tied to the distribution of power by one entity to another, tied to place and time. There is no such thing as an abstract "urban freedom." Urbanity is about creating borders and limitations that create advantages for some and disadvantages for others. A single building with a single use in fact excludes all other buildings and uses in a specific place. But to build cities according to the "will of the people" is extremely hard. Even defining what the people "want" is tricky. Should popular demand be defined by prices, popular vote, opinion polls, or what? Some professionals might find this a dangerous and populist position, as they themselves believe they "know" what people want or actually need. That position is close to the priest who has the right to interpret the wishes of a mysterious god, or the Marxist idea of the "objective interests of the proletariat" that only the self-appointed central committee can define. That is both a weak and unacceptable position.

The problem is that urban environments—more than most other products—are long-lasting, immobile, and expensive. It is easier to produce music, cars, and clothes that fulfill the users' wishes. The shorter time span of use, the less weight/volume, and the less costly something is, the easier it is for producers to adapt to change and diverse user demands and dreams. The main problem of today is that we have a growing number of urban recipes that compete for attention and followers. This "smorgasbord of urban ideologies" offers modernism, postmodernism, new urbanism, traditional urbanism, neomodernism, structuralism, everyday urbanism, new suburbanism, deconstructivism, critical regionalism, etc. They have two things in common: they are all formulated by the *producers* of urban products; and they all compete for popularity by trying to build a "church of believers" around themselves.

Political decision makers that at least formally act as the defenders of the "will of the people" today face an explosion of experts who all see themselves as the "true truth-sayers" on cities. This information inflation—*infoflation*—consists of a growing number of professionals and pressure groups that try to place their perspective as the "number one issue" on the urban agenda. All these wonderful new planning, analyz-

The INFOFLATION of urban perspectives

Every single question is important

Every perspective can be analyzed

Every aspect needs it's own regulation and process

And they all have their own group of experts, advocates and professions

Car traffic safety, noise disturbances, walkability, investment friendliness, orientation, resource consumption, openness for sunlight, air quality, crime prevention, adaptability, sewer systems, access for the handicapped, general attractivity, the public realm, rent levels, access for delivery of goods, greenery, parking, biological diversity, social exclusion, gender perspectives, children perspectives, adaptation to the elderly, taking care of the homelessness, shopping, economic diversity, night life quality, life cycle assessments, space syntax analysis, energy consumption, "queer perspective" (whatever that might be), cleaning, architectural adaptation, democracy, public participation and involvement in the planning process, exhaust levels, transportation of dangerous goods, police monitoring, sustainability of materials, public transportation, leasing contracts, refurbishment methods, antiquarian perspectives, noise emitting activities, play grounds, public manifestations and meeting places, water management, adaptation to the historic cityscape, preservation of the built heritage, signage, park management, street vendor contracts, fire prevention, street pattern, façade organization, tourism information, gentrification, advertisement, taxi permits, housing policy, restaurants, prostitution, offices, road crossings and signals, emergency eviction plans, congestion management, environmental justice…

FIG. I Every question represents an important perspective that could be used to analyze—and what is even more problematic, to criticize— a development proposal. Check lists, national polices, and international agreements—on issues from children safety to pollution, noise, and traffic safety—are all respectable and full of good intentions. But, as American writer Ayn Rand once put it: "Good intentions do not alter facts." And the fact is, that some of our most beloved and popular urban places—at least in Sweden—are illegal according to present planning practices and regulations.

FIG. 2 Medieval town of Strängnäs, situated along the shore line of Lake Mälaren is considered one of Sweden's more attractive and culturally significant urban places. If today nothing had ever been built on this spot, a new Strängnäs with the same layout would be illegal to develop. According to the regulation on "protection of shore lines," new development is not permitted closer to 100—or in some instances 300— meters from the water.

FIG. 3 The same goes for Sveavägen, one of the most urban main streets of Stockholm, with about 45,000 cars passing daily. Traffic safety, noise, and air quality regulations would ask for a traffic pattern with multilevel lanes, separate walking and bicycle lanes in tunnels or on elevated bridges, noise walls, and large safety distances between traffic and buildings.

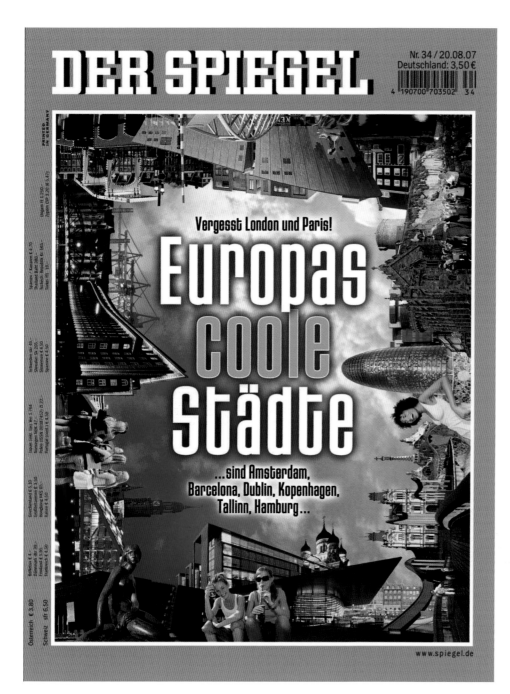

DER SPIEGEL

Nr. 34 / 20.08.07
Deutschland: 3,50 €

Vergesst London und Paris!

Europas coole Städte

...sind Amsterdam, Barcelona, Dublin, Kopenhagen, Tallinn, Hamburg...

www.spiegel.de

FIG. 4 (clockwise) German magazine *Der Spiegel* highlighting the "coolest" cities of Europe—most of them dense, mixed, with specific and different architecture, and open to different lifestyles. You could call them cities of freedom. The Tallinn Town Hall Square with traditional, historic urbanism and intimate human scale; and in the Gay Pride Parade in the Netherlands, an act called "The Pink Police" performs on a boat in one of the canals of Amsterdam, 2007.

ing, forecasting, decision making (etc.) tools have one thing in common: the wish to control and define the built environment before it is built. We inherited the idea of "beforehand programming" and "scientific planning" from the modernist movement. But all these urban axioms, truths, methods—and, thus, "urbanisms"—only reflect the wishes, the interests, and the ideologies of urban axiom builders themselves, not of the users of urban places, whom I here have called "the people."

The sad thing about urban ideology is that as soon as you apply for membership in any scientifically, morally, ecologically, politically, aesthetically, or otherwise value-based system of thought, your brain starts to shut out information that does not fit your ideology. This narrow-mindedness is more prevalent among experts than laymen. We may join a church and hope that our urban ideology will not be a repetition of the previous failed modernist vision. We may reinforce this ideology with tons of research and logic and computer programs (the more complicated and expensive, the better for the research budget).

The alternative would be to return to the basic Western democratic market system that is a result of Darwinian evolution, of trial and error, rather than of revolution and grand visions. This alternative has to develop a new balance between order and chaos, between regulation and freedom, between what I "know" as a planner and what the users actually want (or might want, once a new urban product has been invented). And in order to create a "freedom of choice situation" in urban development, "something" or "someone" has to create a basic "grid," a set of rules that prevents the dictatorship of the few, be they "public" or "private." This "market-inspired level playing field" also has to safeguard the freedom of weaker or smaller actors or ideas. This is not an argument for abstaining from knowledge and reading books. But it is an argument for an alternative to urban ideology. So let us try to build an urbanism not based on the ideas of the axiom producers themselves.

Let's start out fresh by considering the people, the various demands of the nonprofessionals, the user perspective, the market economy, the demand-supply perspective, Darwinism instead of intelligent design, the limitation of some freedoms as a way to create even greater freedoms, the division of church and state, the subsidiarity principle, the absolute freedom to invent and fail, the fact that organized "public opinion groups" do not express every opinion, the constitutional rights of the minorities, the expanding diversity of lifestyles, the freedoms of competition and thought. My contribution to the present "war of urbanisms" is labeled "Market Urbanism—Demand Based Urban Development."

Market Urbanism is a nonideological "ism" based on the demands of different actors. All planning and building activities have to fulfill two things only: the demand of today and the demand of tomorrow. As a result of the former, Market Urbanism implies an absolute demand for *pluralism*, characterized by a multitude of choices and real competition. As a result of the latter, Market Urbanism implies an absolute demand on *sustainability*, to safeguard the freedom of choice for future generations.

The first Golden Rule is: All solutions in architecture and urban planning are given the freedom to compete on equal terms, without regulatory support or prohibition. The second Golden Rule is: Solutions that are not appreciated by the consumers ("no one buys it") should have the freedom to fail and vanish, without subsidies or mercy. Marker Urbanism views architectural ideologies as scientists assess religious faiths—with an accepting, friendly, and disinterested smile.

The Twelve Commandments of Market Urbanism, Including Some Examples from the Swedish Situation

1. Never criticize demand

Never criticize popular demand. Beauty is in the eye of the beholder, not in the ambition of the producer, no matter how ambitious or educated. The definition of what is "modern" is solely what modern humans regard as attractive, nice, fantastic, practical, safe, rational; and makes our time on this planet a happy journey. If "old" and "traditional" architecture is more appreciated by the general public than "new" and "neomodernist" designs, then the "old" has to be defined as modern.

Example: Areas of high demand that are more popular and have a higher price curve define what is a modern urban environment. The producer can no longer say that "you may choose any color of this car as long as you choose black." The "company-defined quality" has to be replaced with the "consumer-defined quality." Listen to those you plan for. Do not preach or try to "educate" your customers. The communists tried this and they failed.

2. Always improve supply

Constantly improve and update the supply of urban products. Concepts such as "traditional," "preservation," or "adjustment to the local settings" may sound nice to some. Concepts such as "an architecture of our times," "inventive," or "original design" may sound nice to others. But these are all subjective and ideological categories. They are not quality categories (positive or negative). There used to be a "tradition" of thinking that held that the world was flat; Trofim Lysenko presented a truly "inventive" alternative to Darwinism, and both theories proved to be wrong. As is the case with wine, quality can only be judged by the user. And users of places and buildings have the right to demand better solutions than those of today and yesterday. Status quo is not an option. All progress breaks with traditions. But not everything "new" is a success. It has to be accepted by the users to become a "new tradition."

Example: The iPhone is an invention that has become popular. Largescale housing projects have not become popular. The only advantage of a "traditional" solution over an "inventive" one is that it has been tried before and can be judged, its popularity measured. Only popular traditions will have a market. But returning to history is only the last solution, if you cannot come up with something new that is better than the old stuff.

3. Increase diversity

Political decisions and regulations shall maximize the freedom of choice for all groups to implement their own life goals, business ideas, and dreams. Groups with limited resources generally have less freedom of choice. Demand-based planning therefore counteracts simplistic profit-max-imizing developments such as the privatization of public places, destruction of communal land, eradication of spontaneous and informal squatter settlements, and the like. To increase diversity and freedom of choice, it is important to plan both for the demand of the affluent and for the demand of the poor.

Example: Students often have little money but lots of time to party and study. Low-cost apartments are needed for car-free urban living close to bars and libraries. Make plans for student apartments on top of parking garages in city centers and on big retail boxes in shopping centers. This increases diversity, density, and social mix, and reduces the need for long-distance travel and new dispersed developments. If such projects are against "the regulations," then the regulations shall be replaced.

4. Balance the budget

The Brundtland Report of 1987 can be summarized in one sentence. "Thou shalt live on interest and yield, not on consumption of the capital stock." Present demand can only be met if it does not limit the freedom of future generations to demand what they want. Sustainability does not mean to "limit" our consumption but instead expand and share it in time and between generations.

Example: The green movement's idea of shifting the basis for taxation can balance the budget both in the long and the short term. Lower taxes on work (income) can be combined with higher taxes on energy, natural resources, and land (consumption). This gives incentives for energy efficiency, technological development, proximity, and hiring more people. Abolish all tax deductions for work-related travel and agricultural subsidies that only increase wasteful production and prevent free trade.

5. Power to the user

Local distribution of power and responsibility increases resource efficiency and leads to more place-adapted solutions, higher user satisfaction, shorter chains of command, and more democratic processes. Local ownership of real estate gives shorter and faster decision processes and better adaption of places compared to centralistic ownership patterns.

Example: Architectural competitions seldom involve the users. Therefore, architects may be advisrs to but never have a vote in a competition jury. Only users, clients, and politicians should make the urban decisions.

6. Defend the market

Rules are the opposite of chance and of dictatorship. Functioning markets are created by regulations that control the strongest and the most shortsighted actors. Rules can counteract monopoly and conformity and safeguard market access for nonestablished actors. Machiavelli's Prince detests rules. The invisible hand of Adam Smith demands it.

Example: The present system for investments in roads and rail favor lobbyism, with money distributed to those with the loudest voices. Instead, distribute state funds for road and rail proportionally to the size of population in each region.

7. Oppose monotheism

Ideal cities are bad. Centralized typified solutions and top down regulations for general use limit creativity, democracy, growth, and innovation. Place-related local regulations open up for higher levels of competition, as in the business sector. One size does not fit all! Apply the principle of subsidiarity on urban development. Decentralize place-making. But centralize the framework that shapes the general economic conditions (see point 12).

Example: Replace mandatory national regulations and guidelines with Consumer Product Information labels describing the quality of each urban area by local building codes. Replace present uniform noise regulations with local place-specific levels. Higher noise acceptance in urban areas can be combined with lower in the countryside. This makes it possible to build with more density than today. Also, liquidate present waterfront building limitations that prohibit developments close to the water, since people tend to like such places.

8. Globalized diversity

In a globalized world, the uniqueness of place is an important competition and identity asset. The twentieth-century idea of an "International Style" is antiquated. Deviating from the rule is a better marketing strategy than "following everyone else." Do not give "starchitects" *carte blanche* to design every place. That is good for their businesses and their brands, but it is catastrophic for the brand and the identity of the places themselves.

Example: Establish locally formulated regulations that limit architects' and developers' tendency to build identical projects everywhere. Create local building codes that force architects and planners to think differently instead of copying the latest project.

9. Form follows society

A modern urban development is in harmony with the technology, production system, lifestyles, and resources of its time. Modern means a balance between supply and demand of urban products. The built environment shall serve the different activities of society, not be part of an ideological package based on independent ideals. New technologies and lifestyles will generate new forms, expressions, and styles.

Example: Distribute more power and money to local

municipalities. With local real estate taxation, municipalities will gain from new developments, public-private partnership projects will be easier to manage, and local politicians will have more freedom and money to plan the community.

10. Plan for change

Urban evolution demands places in which non-preconceived solutions can grow and develop. Make plans for the unexpected and the unforeseen. All cities need an experimental field, a laboratory for the future.

Example: Establish centrally located "Experience Industry Areas" for the local service sector, repairs, minor industry, inventors, garage bands, bars, gyms, and other noisy but nice things. Regulations shall protect and serve these kinds of activities, which are often wiped out by rising real estate prices. At the legendary club Studio 54 in Manhattan, the doormen were instructed to maximize the diversity on the dance floor. Cities can also do this.

11. Increase proximity

The basic function of a city is to offer places for differences that are close to each other for mutual cooperation and reduced transport. Effective interfaces between different urban biotopes reduce time loss and increase what is called serendipity, the accidental discovery of something fortunate while looking for something else completely.

Example: Repair the geography of the twentieth century—based on functional separation, social segregation, and dead-end streets—with a new interface. Large open fields between suburban islands of only housing and workplaces can be connected with new urban parks and streets. Central Park in New York is a green and dense model to implement in the suburban desert.

12. Regulate with incentives

Sparse, sprawling, and dispersed suburban developments are hard to limit by regulations, especially if backed by money. A better method is to use the mechanisms of the market economy itself. Develop the "polluter pays" principle. Re-regulate the general economic framework so that transportation, production, and distribution have to carry their own costs, including those for the emission of CO_2 gases. National and international regulations shall establish economic incentives that improve resource efficiency.

Example: Replace state subsidies for highways with charge systems. Higher costs for transport favor dense and mixed development. Lower costs on work tend to lower unemployment. Focus on the economic framework, not on planning details, i.e., ecology and evolution, not ideology and revolution.

THE MARRIAGE OF ECONOMIC GROWTH AND SUSTAINABLE DEVELOPMENT

CHRISTOPHER B. LEINBERGER

Starting in the 1820s, accelerating in the nineteenth century, and coming to a crescendo in the mid-twentieth century, the industrial economy provided wealth for societies and households unlike the previous 10,000 years of the agricultural economy and the 6,000 years humans had previously been building cities. Per capita income was essentially flat for millennia before 1820 but, starting in Britain and the United States, a rapid increase in wealth occurred that was unprecedented in human history. As the industrial era peaked in about 1970 in the developed world, the average U.S. citizen earned thirteen times more in real dollar terms than his ancestor 150 years earlier.[1]

A new way of building the built environment accompanied the industrial economy, a way that had never been seen in human history. This new way of building human settlements was pioneered in the late nineteenth and early twentieth century but really took off after the Great Depression and the Second World War. That method, known as "drivable suburban," includes:

• extremely low-density development
• the nearly exclusive use of cars and trucks for all trips to and from home, shopping, and work
• the separation of different types of real estate (for-sale housing, apartments, retail, office, industrial, etc.)
• the separation of different income and racial groups from one another

As North Americans were "seeing the USA in their Chevrolet," they were making themselves wealthier. The real estate industry and the transportation system linking that real estate included the road builders, raw material providers, automobile companies, financial industry, insurance industry, oil industry, commercial bankers, and real estate developers. Directly and indirectly these industries provided at least 40 percent of the country's jobs and GDP. Drivable suburban development became the *de facto* domestic policy of the U.S. after the Second World War. This policy was reenforced by legal codes at the federal, state, and the local levels and massively subsidized by all levels of government directly (grants for infrastructure, particularly roads) and indirectly (mortgage tax deductibility and U.S. government guarantees for mortgages). North Americans in particular loved the freedom of the road, the privacy of suburbia, and the subsidies that allowed them to get what they wanted, all while putting a foundation under a booming economy.

The real estate industry by the 1970s had perfected drivable suburban development, which could be summarized by the nineteen standard product types. These were well-understood formulas for neighborhood retail centers, entry-level housing, walk-up apartments, office and industrial parks, etc. These standard products were easy to finance for initial development and were traded like Monopoly cards, and, most importantly, there was convenient, abundant, free parking. From 1970 until 2000, real estate and the infrastructure that supported it built more office, retail, and residential square footage than had been collectively built in the previous two hundred years in the United States. The financial industry also figured out how to get around the most difficult aspect of real estate over the millennia: how to easily, cheaply, and quickly sell and buy it. Through the use of stock-exchange-traded housing and commercial companies and the development of the secondary residential and commercial mortgage market, real estate became the fourth asset class on Wall Street, joining cash, bonds, and stock, during the 1990s.

The year 1970 marks not just the peak of the industrial era in the developed world, it marked a leveling off in worker earnings in the United States which was followed by the leveling off in other parts of the developed world, such as Japan and western Europe. Household incomes, as opposed to worker incomes, continued to increase due to a second wage earner going to work, and consumption continued to grow due to reduced savings and increased debt, but these trends began to run their course, paving the way for the Great Recession of 2008. The year 1970 marked the perfection of drivable suburban development in our metropolitan areas, which have over 80 percent of developed world population today. The result was a geometric increase in land use consumption compared to population growth in the U.S. In Europe and Japan the combination of less land and national government controls reduced that ratio, but land use still increased much more rapidly than population growth. For example, metropolitan Atlanta had a commuter shed of about 65 miles north to south in 1990 with 3.1 million in population. By 2000, it had a 110 miles commuter shed, a 38 percent increase in population (4.2 million) but over 200 percent increase in land area. Atlanta's land use consumption was over five times its population growth.

The industrial age and the drivable suburban development pattern it spawned created a dynamic the world had never seen before: as more growth and development took place, the quality of life and the environment was reduced. While wealth increased, industrial economic growth led to a desiccation of the environment that is only comparable to the mass extinctions of previous geologic eras. As Malcolm Cowley wrote in 1929 in *Harper's* magazine about growing up in central Pennsylvania at the nadir of the environmental destruction caused by industrialism, "There were no longer any deer in my country. The white pines, which once covered it, were reduced to a few weevil saplings. The trout had been poisoned by sawmills or sulfur from the mines." There was a trade-off during the industrial era; industrial growth meant environmental degradation and rising social problems. Industrial economic development was environmentally unsustainable even though it delivered unimagined wealth.

Real estate development followed the same principle; more drivable suburban growth eventually destroyed the early promise of suburbia—open space, the convenience of car commuting, and clean air. A new strip mall adjacent to a subdivision was not welcomed by residents since it degraded the very reasons they moved to suburbia. The over-development of the drivable suburban landscape generally provided the incentive to move further out to the ever-expanding fringe to start the process over again. Drivable suburban development became the personification of evil as movies portrayed real estate developers as the standard bad guys, along with Nazis, crooked politicians, and car dealers. In essence, industrial-era real estate has an underlying principle: *more is less*. More growth means lower quality of life, just as during the early industrial era before federal environmental regulation was forced upon industry. As the dangers of climate change came to the fore, research shows that over 70 percent of greenhouse gas emissions come from the built environment, 40 percent from our buildings, and 30 percent from the car-based transportation system. Drivable suburban development is environmentally unsustainable.

The more is less principle also led to the rise of neighborhood groups starting about 1970. Prior to 1970, few neighborhoods were organized. Today, virtually every North American neighborhood is organized . . . generally to fight real estate development. It is probably the largest democratic movement of the era. This is a rational reaction to the more is less principle and it has led to NIMBY (not in my backyard) opposition to nearly all growth, forcing growth further out to the fringe. If drivable suburban development could be stopped at a certain point, the promised benefits could be maintained; future growth would just have to be accommodated further out on the metropolitan fringe, as many counties and towns have demonstrated.

Just As We Got It Right, the Market Changes

As the industrial economy subsumed but did not completely obliterate the agricultural economy which preceded it, a new economic era is subsuming the industrial. The knowledge economy, whose workers are the "creative class," began to grow in the 1970s but really only began to change society and the built environment in the 1990s. The high-tech boom, followed by the crash, of the 1990s was the coming-out party for the knowledge economy. The mid-1990s was also the first sign that the market had changed in terms of what it was demanding for the development built environment.

The baby boomers, coming of age at the peak of the industrial age, were raised on popular television programs such as *Leave It to Beaver*, *The Dick Van Dyke Show*, and *The Brady Bunch*, all set in the suburbs. The Millennial generation, who are coming of age with the introduction of the knowledge economy, were raised on shows such as *Seinfeld*, *Friends*, and *Sex in the City*, all set in safe, exciting, walkable urban places. These different aspirations for how to live showed where the next phase of development was going. The redevelopment of many American downtowns in the mid-1990s was the first sign of this change on the ground. Now the transformation of the suburban landscape, particularly dead and dying strip malls and former suburban town centers, is demonstrating how broad and deep this new method of development is. It is actually a throwback to the pre-industrial city; the market is demanding "walkable urbanism," the way cities were built for thousands of years before the introduction of the automobile.

Walkable urbanism will act as an economic propellant similar to the one that turbocharged the economy in the mid- to late-twentieth century. It will provide a foundation under an economy that, as of this writing, is badly lagging every past recovery since World War II. There has been a structural change in how the built environment will be built just as there was a *structural* change sixty years ago. The pendulum that swung from building walkable urban cities in the nineteenth and early twentieth centuries to only building drivable suburban places over the past sixty years is swinging back.

In contrast, the real estate crash that started in 2006 was heavily concentrated on fringe drivable suburban housing development. This massive overbuilding drove down the mortgage industry and the banking industry and plunged the economy into the deepest recession since the 1930s. The subsequent bailout was unprecedented in size as well as in character—it is actually the bailout of drivable suburban sprawl. There are trillions of dollars invested in the wrong product in the wrong location, some of which are showing signs of becoming the next slums.

More Is Better

Building walkable urban places, whether in the center city or the suburbs, has demonstrated that as you build more restaurants, housing, and offices in a walkable urban manner the quality of life improves. More people are active on the street, which means there is more demand for new things to do; property values go up, as do property taxes; and a virtuous, upward spiral of value creation occurs. In essence, building the built environment no longer means *more is less* but *more is better*. Revived downtowns and former dead strip malls, occupying 10 to 20 percent of a jurisdiction's land mass, are in many cases producing more than half of public-sector revenues, effectively subsidizing bedroom communities. Walkable urban residential values in 2010 are the most expensive on a sales price per square foot or per square meter basis in most U.S. metropolitan areas versus comparable drivable suburban housing in well-to-do neighborhoods. Only ten years earlier, just the opposite was the case. This phenomenon is referred to as gentrification, either the most beloved or reviled word in the English language. Why? Rising real estate values mean that the poor and middle class cannot live in walkable urban places due to the supply shortage caused by the pent-up demand. That means society will have the obligation to replace the current affordable and workforce housing policy of "drive until you qualify" with a conscious strategy to build mixed-income communities.

The walkable urban future is built upon the emerging knowledge economy, which is far greener than the formerly dominant industrial economy. In the industrial economy, separating land uses made sense: Given a choice, who would want to live next to a noisy, polluting factory? Regional malls were disconnected from residential neighborhoods by hundreds of acres of surface parking lots, fronting eight-lane streets or freeways and turning their dumpster-lined backs on their residential neighbors. Today's walkable urban places make wonderful neighbors for the surrounding residential communities. Housing located in high-density suburban neighborhoods within walking distance to downtown centers see a 40 to 100 percent price premium on a price per square foot or per square meter basis compared to similar houses just beyond walking distance. Residents of such areas live in suburban splendor but can walk to great urbanism—the best of two worlds. The price premiums and numerous consumer research studies point out that it will probably take a generation to catch up with the pent-up demand since in a good year we add about 2 percent to the inventory of the built environment. The more is better principle means that for the first time in nearly two hundred years *sustainable development equals economic growth*. Places with high quality of life have become the most economically productive places in the economy. Self-reenforcing places engage in the virtuous upward cycle of value creation.

It also offers the opportunity for turning NIMBY into YIMBY, "yes in my backyard." Tysons Corner in Fairfax County, Virginia, outside of Washington, D.C., is the largest suburban commercial district in the U.S.: 44 million square feet (4.1 million square meters) of drivable suburban hell that is nearly universally loathed. The county approved a new master plan in 2010 allowing the total size to more than double, based upon the four new Metrorail stations and partially paid for by the property owners, and a commitment toward a walkable urban transformation. The surrounding neighborhood groups *supported* the plan because they want Tysons Corner to be like nearby Arlington County, which has seven rail transit–served, walkable urban places that replaced strip malls over the past twenty years. Arlington residents love the convenience and increased quality of life and property values. Their county gets 60 percent of its tax revenues from these seven places. Twenty years ago these abandoned strip malls were becoming slums.

It is probable that the next long-term economic trend, following the agricultural, industrial, and knowledge economies, is probably even more sustainable. The *experience* economy adds value by enriching citizens' lives through businesses, non-profits, and government. This was first seen when the tourism industry as eco-tourism, history-tourism, and cultural tourism provided far more depth and enrichment to the consumer, helping to make tourism the largest industry in the world. Here tourism occurs in a special environment, which tends to be either wilderness or a walkable urban place. No one has ever seen a television travel show or the travel section of a Sunday newspaper highlight a regional mall and suburban sprawl; it focuses on wilderness or great urbanism.

The transition to the experience economy will apply to all facets of everyday life. For example, the Apple store has taken the computer shopping experience to a whole new level. It is a combination of education, entertainment, and personal service, all in a high-design place. Many customers come back for education on a periodic basis, even weekly, and naturally end up buying more Apple products. Apple's announcement that it would enter the retail business was met with a great deal of skepticism. Disney, the master merchandiser, had just admitted their stores were underperforming, so what hope would Apple have? In the retail sector, a successful department store, like Nordstrom, earns $500 per square foot ($47 per square meter) annually. The highest-selling retailers tend to be jewelry stores (high-value, small products in small spaces), which can earn $1,500 per square foot ($140 per square meter). Apple stores earn $3,000 to $5,000 per square foot ($280 to $467 per square meter). They are not only in a different league, it is an entirely different game—a different economy. Since the stores' relatively highly educated staff are adding new value, Apple is investing in their employees with high-quality training and higher-than-average compensation.

The industrial economy trained low-paid manual laborers for more highly paid jobs requiring more highly skilled labor, fueling the growth of the middle class. The knowledge economy did the same thing for geeks. Richard Florida, the scholar who determined the role of the "creative class" in the knowledge economy, sees the "great reset" of the next economy taking place by the investment in service workers, who make up 78 percent of the workforce (compared to 2 percent in agriculture and 20 percent in industry). By making service jobs more creative in the experience economy, education and compensation will rise. Who knows how many currently low-paying businesses and organizations will be reinvented in the experience economy?

The experience economy will probably locate most of its assets and jobs in walkable urban places. Yes, the wilderness will have its role to play. But the bulk of the experience economy will be in small, medium, and large downtowns, suburban downtowns, transformed regional malls, and even a few greenfield places (e.g., Disney versions of walkable urban places). However, customers seem to want *authentic* experiences, not experiences manufactured, packaged, and helicoptered to a market-researched location. This desire for authenticity, particularly among the rising Millennial generation, means that places that invest in themselves, their parks, sidewalks, cleanliness, friendliness, their people, their educational system, will have an advantage in the marketplace. If you want to experience the wonder and excitement of downtown Savannah, midtown Manhattan, or Dupont Circle in Washington, you will have to visit, move your work there, or move your house there, spending money and bringing more self reinforcing value to the place. These places will offer the potential of transformative, maybe even self-actualizing, experiences.

The experience economy will be even more economically and environmentally sustainable than the knowledge economy; it might even be more socially equitable. Assuming green transportation on foot, bike, or public transit—which work best in walkable urban places—and high-density buildings—which are inherently more energy efficient (unintentionally sharing heat with your upstairs neighbor)—recent research is leading to the conclusion that energy usage and greenhouse gas emissions could drop from one-third to two-thirds the level of the drivable suburban way of living. Given that the built environment is the largest energy user and greenhouse gas emitter, the walkable urban experience economy would be the major means of addressing climate change, not to mention many other foreign policy, economic, and health challenges faced by the U.S. and the developed world today.

The possible result: Sustainable development equals economic growth.

CITY DESIGN FOR SUSTAINABLE CHANGE

JOHN LUND KRIKEN

The Challenge

At the beginning of the twenty-first century, our global environment is in serious trouble. Rapid population growth together with expanding rural-to-urban migrations are overwhelming both infrastructure capacity and job creation. Our very survival is threatened by the continuing loss of air quality, water quality, water quantity, valuable productive agricultural land, wildlife, and species habitats. The population grows larger and the per capita consumption of irreplaceable natural resources increases exponentially.

Solving this problem in a feasible, meaningful way seems overwhelming and beyond our collective human abilities. Images of doomed polar bears struggling to survive on diminishing ice contrasted by television advertisements for energy-efficient kitchen appliances illustrate the subject's profoundly frustrating irony. In reality, to even think about solving a problem of this scale and significance will require the moral and physical equivalent of a "world war" for global survival. The solutions, if and when they are addressed, will change almost everything.

Finding a Focus

It can be convincingly argued that this environmental crisis exists because of the damaging way humankind has settled on the land. This idea suggests to me that the city and its regional influences could become a very necessary geographic focus for achieving environmental sustainability. It is not defined by individual cities. In every part of the world, larger cities tend to cluster together, forming urban corridors. In America, the majority of the population, the greatest need for supporting infrastructure, and the greatest attraction for population growth are located in only six urban corridors (fig. 1):
1. Boston, Massachusetts, to Washington, D.C.
2. San Francisco to San Diego, California
3. Chicago, Illinois, to Pittsburgh, Pennsylvania
4. Kansas City, Missouri, to Houston, Texas
5. Atlanta, Georgia, to Miami, Florida
6. Seattle, Washington, to Portland, Oregon

These concentrations of population and economic activity are the primary consumers of nonrenewable natural resources as well as the primary sources of air, water, and land pollution.

To achieve sustainability, these corridors, together with similar urban corridors around the world, need to be comprehensively planned. This should be the first focus of the sustainable and livable design of cities. A plan for shared economic strength and shared environmental resources should provide new benefits and opportunities compared to the more limited planning within our man-made political boundaries. Rural land should not be a focus of this effort, except for environmentally damaging extractive industries or the protection of agricultural land, watersheds, and wildlife habitats.

Change as Opportunity

In 2009, for the first time in human history, more people lived in cities than in rural areas. This trend will continue. United Nations studies suggest that by 2030 two thirds of the world's population will live in cities, a staggering five billion people. By 2015 the world will be home to twenty-one megacities of over ten million people and sixty other cities of over five million. By 2030, America's population should double, from three hundred million to six hundred million people. This will have a huge impact on the growth and livability of American cities.

If there are no changes in the level of effort directed toward global sustainability and growth management, the environment war will be lost. On the other hand, given the necessary solutions are realized, this population growth could provide the opportunity to rebuild our cities to new

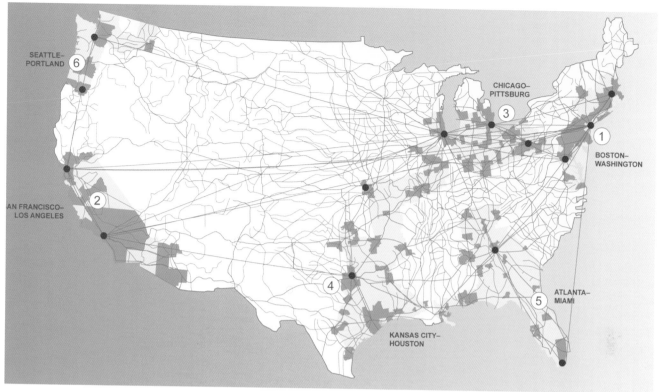

FIG. 1 America's six corridors of concentrated urban population.

Problem Solving

At the beginning of the twenty-first century, it is clear that our methods of problem solving have been inadequate. Problems are considered within the narrow boundaries of their subject. As a consequence, most solutions deal with symptoms, not with underlying causes.

If a road becomes congested the answer has been to make it wider. Alternatives such as multimodal transportation choices, flexible work hours, and concentrating work destinations are not considered. The problem should not be defined as road congestion. Rather it should be defined more broadly as accessibility.

I do not believe sustainable city design can ever come from statistical analysis, functional problem solving, or any particular decision-making process. These are too limited, too single purposed, and are the cause of many of our current problems. I would like to suggest that there are basic values that are common to successful and livable cities which I believe can be defined as principles to guide city design.

Sustainability and Livability Principles

The approach to sustainability has to be comprehensive. It can be based upon positive values or norms that are associated with existing sustainable and livable places. For the purpose of my city design work, I have determined nine values for what I call best practice principles.

Principle One: Sustainability
Committing to an Environmental Ethic

Principle Two: Accessibility
Facilitating Ease of Movement

Principle Three: Diversity
Maintaining Variety and Choice

Principle Four: Open Space
Regenerating Natural Systems to Make Cities Green

Principle Five: Compatibility
Maintaining Harmony and Balance

Principle Six: Incentives
Renewing Declining Cities/Rebuilding Brownfields

Principle Seven: Adaptability
Facilitating "Wholeness" and Positive Change

Principle Eight: Density
Designing Compact Cities with Appropriate Transit

Principle Nine: Identity
Creating/Preserving a Unique and Memorable Sense of Place

smart, sustainable, and livable standards. Preparation for this opportunity is essential.

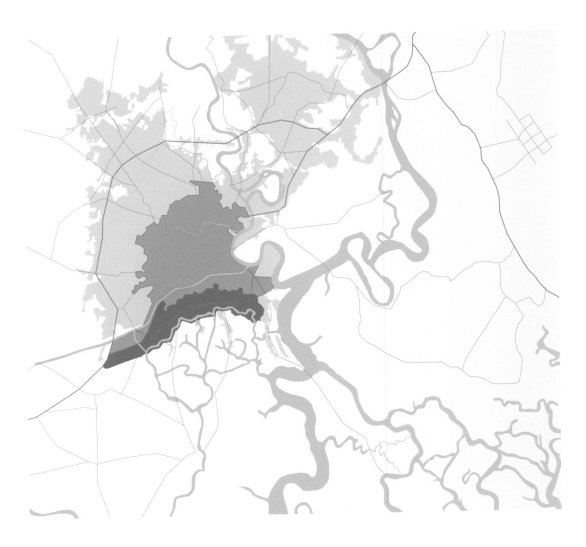

FIG. 2 Saigon South, Ho Chi Minh City expansion.

These are the terms of reference I use to describe city design for both domestic and international work. They are universally recognized and understood but always vary according to local culture, climate, and geography. They are not intended to advocate a particular design language. My hope is that they can promote contemporary city design, architecture, and landscape to its highest level. The only sustainability argument that may seem limiting to some designers is the need to return to a human and walkable scale. Sadly, this quality is often lost in today's city building because of the designer and developer's infatuation with gigantism and the quest for a singular image.

A Future City

If we were able to take a few snapshots of a future city that has been influenced according to the nine principles, how would it differ from cities of today?

Sustainability

The future cities do not spread out so much over surrounding open land. They have taken over the stewardship of their ecologically important land, air, and water. Land areas defined as Class A agricultural soil, watersheds, aquifer recharge areas, fish and wildlife habitats, migration corridors, forests, deserts, and areas of scenic value, to name a few, are now mapped and protected. If this land becomes necessary for other human uses, they would be carefully defined so that their ecological value would not be lost. By preplanned infrastructure improvements, new development is directed to nonecologically critical land within the region, to higher-density, transit-oriented development areas within existing cities, or to other urban corridor cities that are suffering economic decline. The new measures that guide sustainable development seek to eliminate the damaging patterns of our consumption for irreplaceable, nonrenewable natural resources.

Accessibility

It is easier to get around in the future city. Work destinations have become more concentrated so that transit can easily serve the home-to-work trip. Also, the population is denser, and transit is frequent and close to home. Not surprisingly, the highest density is located within a short walk to the transit stop. The private car is now nonpolluting, does not require nonrenewable fuel, is smaller in size, and is no longer the dominant means of travel. With less traffic, streets can remain narrow, and blocks are all small. Walking and bicycling are safe and comfortable. There are many ways to travel, and one can get anywhere in the city within thirty minutes (fig. 3).

Incentives

Some cities will not be as healthy as others. They may be experiencing economic decline, with diminishing jobs and population. The costly infrastructure and buildings of these cities should not be wasted. Nor should they need to be rebuilt elsewhere. As part of the urban corridor's responsibility for comprehensive planning, the future city will be provided with economic incentives and the necessary infrastructure to retain its population and attract new investments.

Compatibility

In the future city, new buildings will not try to outdo each other. Every building will no longer strive to be a "look at me" landmark. There will be an interest in the city's overall physical form and character. Where appropriate, landmarks are thoughtfully planned and carefully located. In the future city, the context buildings are understood to be as important as landmark buildings. Buildings that blend well with each other will define easily recognizable neighborhoods and will promote and maintain their distinctive sense of place.

Diversity

It is axiomatic that the best cities offer their citizens the most diverse choices that can be practically supported. Living in cities offers the maximum variety and choice for jobs, education, culture, recreation, and places to live and work. Yet in today's cities, large areas of land have been covered with identical uses in repetitive "cookie cutter" building types. They lack human scale and have no visual interest. The future city, by its design, offers a mix of uses as well as buildings and neighborhoods that are made to look and feel different from each other. It is easy to find your way around this city. Services and amenities are always close at hand.

Identity

It is difficult to identify special features or characteristics that distinguish one modern city from the next. The future city seeks to establish a unique and memorable sense of place to make every city different from other cities. A unique sense of place can be established by protecting and incorporating natural features such as rivers, harbors, lakes, forests, and hills (fig. 4). Cities in arid regions can gain unique identities by expressing its climate through a drought-resistant landscape, the design of exterior building walls that protect interior spaces from the sun's heat, or streets shaded by buildings and trees. Unique city identity can also come from preserving and renewing historic cultural institutions, buildings, and landscapes. Finally, identity can come from a unique, often large, and memorable structure that becomes

identified with a particular city. San Francisco's Golden Gate Bridge is a good example.

Adaptability

All cities are in a near constant state of change, by growth and sometimes by decline. The future city must anticipate this. When designing the future city, the approach must take into consideration how the city can renew and repair itself. The future city is organized by separate parcels so that parts can be changed without large-scale demolition or disruption. Adaptable cities are divisible. Adaptable cities also maintain a sense of completion for each stage of reconstruction.

Open Space

Open space is one of the most important elements of a city's livability and sustainability. Open space by landscape provides a green visual relief and balance to the urban hardscape. It also has important ecological benefits. Green consumes carbon, and through aspiration and shade it cools the air. It can provide food as well as clean water by biofiltration, and provide habitat for birds and other creatures, and it makes special places for civic gatherings and both active and passive recreation for humans. In the future city, open space must always expand with population growth to maintain this critical balance.

FIG. 3 San Francisco's Transbay Terminal high density mixed use development.

FIG. 4 Night view of the City of Islands, Saigon South.

Some Final Thoughts

For some, the emphasis on principles may seem like wishful thinking. How can sustainability be achieved given the almost universal appeal of the single-family suburban home with well-kept front lawns, private backyards, and access to the best schools? The answer is that there will always be people who choose low-density living, and the solution is more a matter of emphasis. In the future, cities must be made to attract more of the growing population, and what suburban growth does take place must be located in places and at a density that does no environmental harm.

No one believes that the making of sustainable and livable cities will be easy. But I believe a change in the way we think about cities and solve city problems is critical to finding the solution. Making cities sustainable and livable will take the equivalent effort of a global war for survival. It is not, as some would like to believe, a simple lifestyle choice.

PART 10: BEYOND URBANISM AND THE FUTURE OF GLOBALIZED CITIES

10.1

THREE MAJOR CONDITIONS OF MODERN/CONTEMPORARY URBANISM (THOUGHTS ON THE WORLD TRADE CENTER)

PETER EISENMAN

From Post Urbanism & ReUrbanism, *reproduced by permission from Peter Eisenman and* Michigan Debates on Urbanism, *series editor Doug Kelbaugh, vol. III edited by Roy Strickland, University of Michigan (New York: Arts Press, 2005).*

There are three major conditions in modern or contemporary urbanism. One is what I call the Arcadian impulse, which I think is represented by people like Leon Krier, Dimitri Porphyrios, Peterson/Littenberg, the New Urbanists, etc. I don't want to categorize them, but the general idea is a return to an idea of the city of the past, of the eighteenth and even nineteenth century.

The second I would call Utopian, which is that the world is never the same as the present and the future must always be better. Modernism was about the search for a Utopia. I think both of those positions in one way or another have been problematized by the failure of Modernism. But the idea that you can go backward in time is, in any case, possible.

The third position is what I call a realist or cynical position. It can be categorized by Rem Koolhaas's urban theories of junk space. Koolhaas's position is an extreme one, brought about both by the Arcadian and the Utopian. In one sense it is not cynical but nihilistic. However, the notion of the "project," whether it is an urban project or an architecture project, means some form of reflection on the status quo, i.e., a critical view. The nature of that reflection is what separates the Arcadian from the Utopian, even though they are both in one sense failed projects. Junk space, on the other hand, is not a project because it is not critical; it is what Massimo Cacciari calls nihilism fulfilled.

The difference in these reflections occurred in Rome in the late eighteenth century between Nolli and Piranesi's view of the urban condition. Nolli's idea was a way of looking at his present that was different than in the past. He was one of the first people to do figure/ground maps, and clearly the impetus of what one would call New Urbanism, or the Arcadian, deals with that moment in time when the Nolli map became an urban icon. The other icon is Piranesi's Campo Marzio map, which has no unified idea of what a city would be about. In fact it confounds the notion of the city as a linear narrative. It has no streets; it has no actual time because part of it is the Rome of the eighteenth century, and part of it is the imperial Rome of the first and second centuries. Part of the Piranesi map has monuments from the first and second centuries that are moved in different locations, part of it has monuments supposedly from a Rome that never existed. Thus, there is a condition of fiction as well as what I would call chance, the arbitrary, a mixing of reality and fiction into some arbitrary brew.

The difference between the Nolli map and the Piranesi map is significant; in fact, I could have done the lecture tonight with just those two images because they are what make a fundamental and important difference. For me, Piranesi was the beginning of the modem critical project, the project that suggested that there was no single time, that there was no single hierarchy or relationship between signs and their signifiers. This idea carried through from the Piranesi project to the present.

But there are three issues that define the critical project in our moment in time that are important. First is the notion of the metaphysics of presence, which is the dominant mode of discourse that has placed architecture in a situation in which it is seen to be static, stable, unified, rather than fragmentary, continuous, and complex.

It seems to me that 1968 was a watershed time, with Venturi's book *Complexity and Contradiction*, with Derrida's *Of Grammatology*, Tafuri's *Theories and History of Architecture*, Rossi's *The Architecture of the City*. All of them in one way or another attacked the notion of an historical and static notion of the city.

Architecture is supposed to be the locus of the metaphysics of presence. If we question that notion, if we are singular and autonomous because we are the only discipline that must place, and if we are to be critical, we must displace at the same time. Placing and displacing I call the becoming unmotivated of the metaphysics of presence. I think the relationship between signs and stable language has been questioned. What was called a transcendental signifier is no longer a believable notion. That would involve becoming unmotivated of the sign. This is a second project.

The third is the becoming unmotivated of the subject. The subject is still physically the same, but in terms of gender, in terms of color, in terms of ethnicity, in terms of psychology, we are all very different people. The life sciences, natural sciences, physics, mathematics—have changed enormously. We no longer have a mathematics of form as known through Rudolf Wittkower and Colin Rowe; we have a calculus of form. We have changed from the analogic models of a Frank Gehry to the digital models of a Greg Lynn. Those digital models are different from any previous models because they rely on a nonstable, nonstatic condition of origin. Today there is no single condition of origin. Whether they were Rowe's models, a semiological model, linguistic models, or diagrammatic models, they all relied on a stable condition of origin. The models called abstract machines, which people like Greg Lynn and others are working on, no longer require in their digital calculus a condition of wholeness to begin working.

The world has changed enormously. The tools available to us today are radically changed. Leatherbarrow talks about the notion of flow: The difference in flow today from the past is that flow is seen today as an integral part of matter. It is no longer separate from matter, and the conception of space and time as matter/flow as an integral proposition changes what is possible in the built environment.

Unfortunately, today architecture is not made up of those people who challenge the status quo. The only histories that we know, however, are histories that are made of those challenges. The rest return architecture to normalcy. The ebb and flow of things from Brunelleschi, Alberti, Bramante, Serlio, Palladio, Borromini, Piranesi, Rainaldi, down to the present, have always concerned the challenge to the status quo. Challenging the status quo means to have a critical project. It also means that criticality has to do with the possibility with what I would call an enfolded negativity. It is not just Utopian; it has to also contain its opposite, its shadow, both psychologically and in physical terms.

The difference between the Modernist project today and the Arcadian project lies in this area of an enfolded negativity. There is no enfolded negativity that I can see in the Arcadian project. The Modernist project still relies on the negativity that was first put forward by people like Walter Benjamin, Nietzsche, Adorno, Heidegger, and others. Much of contemporary science has been built on that skepticism, which incorporated the possibility of negativity into new research in mathematics, biology, physics, and other disciplines.

One of the most important things one can do as an architect is complexes of buildings on an increasingly large scale that probably approach urbanism. If matter is now animated with forces which are integral to matter, then the space between buildings can no longer be just left over. We can no longer have geometric mathematical formalism. Instead there will be calculus formalisms which deal with much more complex relationships between space, time, and buildings.

The shift from the analogic to the digital is the most important revolution that has occurred in architecture in a long time. When we have algorithms written for architects, about architecture in space and time, we are going to see very different things than are being produced by the Gehrys, the Hadids, and the Lynns today.

They are, like me, the endgame of what I call the society of the spectacle. The last blow to the society of the spectacle was 9/11 when reality overtook media. We could never make a science fiction film like that. When reality overtook media, you realize that being in New York near the event, the Heideggerian notion of being there, became more important than seeing it on media. For me, being there reestablished architecture and urbanism as an important condition of culture as we move forward.

A RETURN TO PLANNING?

ANTHONY GIDDENS

From The Politics of Climate Change *by Anthony Giddens.*
Reproduced by permission from Anthony Giddens and Polity Press 2009.

Key arguments of *The Politics of Climate Change* book are that the industrial nations must take the lead in addressing climate change and that the chances of success will depend a great deal upon government and the state. Whatever can be done through the state will in turn depend upon generating widespread political support from citizens, within the context of democratic rights and freedoms. I don't want to deny that reaching international agreements is essential, or that many other agencies, including NGOs and businesses, will play a fundamental role. However, for better or worse, the state retains many of the powers that have to be invoked if a serious impact on global warming is to be made.

What should the role of the state, as ensuring state, be? Its main function must be to act as a catalyst, as a facilitator, but certainly, as far as climate change and energy security are concerned, it has also to strive for guarantees. These are areas where solutions simply have to be found, and where there are timetables involved. If your living room is a mess, you can wait until you have time to clear it up. We can't do the same with emissions, as they pile up in the atmosphere and as oil and gas start to run out.

These are some of the tasks in which the state has to be prime actor. The state must:

• help us to think ahead: it is the responsibility of political leaders to introduce policies for the long term. For this shift in orientation to come about, there has to be a return to planning, in some guise or another. In case it isn't self-evident, thinking long term is not the same as setting targets for some distant date in the future and then sitting back and relaxing. "Rigorous" targets set two or three or more decades down the line might make government ministers feel good, but really there has to be an all-out concentration upon means. In the Soviet Union, five-, ten- and twenty-year targets were announced with a great deal of huffing and puffing. The results normally fell well short of expectations and new plans would then be instituted. Empty promises for the future won't do in the case of climate change, since the emissions in the atmosphere continue to mount. Planning, of course, isn't the sole prerogative of the state. Governments should encourage a shift toward long-term thinking among companies, third-sector groups, and individual citizens.

• manage climate change and energy risks in the context of other risks faced by contemporary societies: risk and opportunity are the two poles around which a great deal of social and economic policy now revolves. We face a future in which the past history of industrialism, as it were, is rapidly catching up with us, and major adjustments have to be made. However, the risks associated with climate change intersect with a variety of others, locally, nationally, and internationally.

• promote political and economic convergence as the main driving forces of climate change and energy policy. Both can and should be targets for the short and the longer term, and should form the foundation of forward planning. In the long term, a whole diversity of areas has to be considered, including preparing for the large-scale social and economic restructuring that a low-carbon economy inevitably will involve.

• make interventions into markets to institutionalize the "polluter pays" principle, thereby ensuring that markets work in favor of climate change policy rather than against it. In almost all developed countries at the moment, environmental costs remain largely externalized. I am dubious about how effective carbon markets as such will be, but there is a great deal that can be done to introduce full cost pricing, and therefore to allow market forces to become centered upon promoting environmental benefits. Government should act to reduce "negative externalities"—situations in which environmental costs are not brought into the marketplace—in order that markets can work to environmental ends.

• act to counter business interests which seek to block climate change initiatives: large-scale change is needed here, and at first blush this seems a tall order indeed. For business, especially big business, has a dominant role in contemporary societies. It is able to influence governments, even sometimes hold them to ransom, and also influence consumers through advertising and other means. When governments threaten regulation, businesses can simply announce that they will up sticks and move elsewhere—the so-called problem of "leakage." Yet couldn't all this be turned around and the power of business become deployed to climate change objectives? I believe it is possible, even in the short term, as long as governments act together with enlightened corporate leaders. Here again we see the key importance of economic convergence. Joint action can emerge from a confluence of interests; it doesn't have to come from a sudden burst of altruism on the part of business firms.

• keep climate change at the top of the political agenda: for most people, most of the time, global warming is not a worry that intrudes deeply into the routines of daily life. It can drift off the agenda as other concerns come to the fore, or as elections approach. There should be an agreement among competing political parties that climate change and energy policy will be sustained in spite of other differences and conflicts that exist. In addition, climate change should feature in the curriculum of all schools.

• develop an appropriate economic and fiscal framework for moving towards a low-carbon economy: subsidies are needed if new technologies are to thrive, since, in the beginning, they will be unable to compete with fossil fuels. I shall argue below that a holistic approach to carbon taxation is needed—it will not do just to think in terms of a handful of specific tax measures. The overall tax system needs continuous auditing in terms of its generic impact upon economic behavior and lifestyles.

• prepare to adapt to the consequences of climate change, which will now be felt in any case. Thinking ahead in this area is crucial—as in the case of mitigation, we can't just wait around to see what develops. We must try to anticipate exactly how and where the effects of global warming will be felt and act preemptively to counter or minimize them.

• integrate local, regional, national, and international aspects of climate change policy: without robust national programs, international agreements will not work. Conversely, however, international collaboration of one sort or another is a necessary condition for coping with climate change.

Is this all asking too much, given the fact that governments often find themselves hemmed in by the pressure of events of the day? The political theorist John Dryzek argues that the combination of capitalist markets, vested interests, and state bureaucracy means that government will be "thoroughly inept when it comes to ecology." He adds that "any redeeming features are to be found only in the possibilities they open up for their own transformation."[1] The first comment is too dismissive, but I agree with the thrust of the second. Responding to climate change will prompt and require innovation in government itself and in the relation between the state, markets, and civil society.

CITY FUTURES: PATHS THROUGH THE MAZE

PETER HALL

Where are cities going? Some observers have foreseen their disappearance as virtual communication renders the old face-to-face constraints irrelevant—but of this there is no evidence. On the contrary: the progressive shift from the manufacturing to the service-based economy, evident in advanced nations and cities for over a century, appears to entail ever greater exchange of precisely the kinds of high-level knowledge that can only be achieved in close physical proximity. Some others see the decline of Western cities as they lose competitive power in face of the dynamism of the vast urban agglomerations of China and the Indian sub-continent. That might be true of those industrial cities, of which Detroit is the archetype, which depended on precisely those industries where cheap Chinese and Indian labor, allied to the latest technology and industrial organization, now generate a flood of low-cost, high-quality manufactured products, from refrigerators to computers to cars, for export to the former manufacturing countries of the West. But it is categorically not true of the many dynamic cities and city regions, both in North America and Europe, which continue to generate new industries and services. Indeed, as these too are exported in their turn, AnnaLee Saxenian has shown that they develop close and symbiotic relationships with the recipient cities, thus forming extraordinary new forms of long-distance urban networking between such diverse megacity regions as the San Francisco Bay Area, Greater Taipei, and the Yangtze River Delta.

Understanding the Dynamics of Development: A Unified Theory

True, even boom cities can become bust cities within an astonishingly short time—as all too amply demonstrated by the vast tracts of unsellable and unlettable homes in cities as diverse as Greater Dublin, Madrid, and Phoenix. But this is a consquence of a quite extraordinary short phase of manic property investment and property speculation, which is by no means new: witness residential real estate development in Florida and California in the 1920s, or the orgy of office building in New York City at the end of that decade, culminating in the crash that in the 1930s left the Empire State Building as the Empty State Building. Likewise with the great eastern Asian property boom of the 1980s, where the Japanese urbanist Koicha Mera and World Bank economist Bertrand Renaud have traced the critical role played by speculative real estate investments by Japanese banks in the collapse of that country's bubble economy, from which it took ten years to recover. There is a similar story to be told about the role of subprime mortgages and over-ambitious commercial property investments in the first decade of the twenty-first century.

In all these phases of capitalist development, animal spirits in the banking industry, intervening injudiciously in real estate, play a critical role in intensifying a major boom just before its impending collapse. The Venezuelan economist Carlota Perez, in a remarkable book published in 2003, used a Schumpeterian framework to develop a thesis that over two hundred years the capitalist system has gone through five major so-called surges—a term she prefers to long waves—each marked by four phases: irruption (of a new technology), frenzy (wildly enthusiastic investment in the new product), synergy (a calming-down phase, in which the benefits diffuse), and maturity (when the process works itself out). Critically, at the end of each frenzy phase, finance capital became detached from production capital, resulting in wide excesses of hyperbole and outright fraud. And this culminated in a financial crash. She published this after the dot-com boom of 1995–2000 and the crash of 2000–2003, which precisely corresponded to her frenzy phase, but before the global financial implosion of 2007–2008, which provided perfect confirmation of her thesis.

Her comforting message was that each crash was followed by an age of expansion and affluence, such as the world experienced in the 1950s and 1960s. And we can glimpse its nature. In a book published in 1998, *Cities and*

Civilization, in the middle of the dot-com boom, I argued that we were indeed in yet another era of innovative activity, such as Mensch had predicted. This time one of the key drivers was the World Wide Web, invented by Tim Berners-Lee at CERN in Geneva in 1989, and commercialized by Mark Andreesen in California in 1994. It would, I argued, form a platform for the creation of many new novel service industries. The decade since then has duly seen the creation of thousands of such user-generated software creations: Google, Facebook, YouTube, Amazon, TripAdvisor, Second Life. The dot-com bust of 2000–2005 can now be seen as a very temporary pause in this process, which continues apace.

It is a critically important and very fundamental process, similar to previous Schumpeterian surges like the one that began in 1897 and generated the automobile and electrical and pharmaceutical industries, or the one that began in 1952 and generated the electronic and aerospace industries. But, just as past surges were marked by advances in more than one area, software is not the only innovation-driven industry we can identify in the current surge. Biotechnology, now producing massive commercial outcomes in the form of new drugs capable of tacking previously incurable conditions, was massively boosted by completion of the human genome mapping process in 2003. Here, innovation appears to come from new startup companies exploiting the latest scientific advance, companies which then invariably allow themselves to be bought out by existing pharmaceutical giants. But perhaps the most exciting new technological developments are coming in a totally new field of environmental engineering devoted to finding new ways of combating global warming. Here, Germany has taken a global lead. Nearly twenty years ago, at the start of the 1990s, it was one of the first countries to present a national timetable for reducing carbon dioxide. Germany's Renewable Energies Act came into force in 2000, introducing the groundbreaking idea of the feed-in tariff whereby consumers can generate their own green electricity and feed it into Germany's national grid; it has triggered a frenetic response. Already, 12 percent of all the electricity consumed in Germany comes from wind, solar, and water power. The government is backing the drive with three billion euros of additional spending over the next three years. Then, in 2007, Germany used its six-month status as EU president to push the EU into a commitment to cut CO2 emissions by 20 percent by 2020, to increase energy efficiency by 20 percent, and to raise the role of renewable energy by 20 percent: the "3 times 20" formula. Germany has pledged to do much better: a staggering 40-percent cut in CO2 emissions, from 880 million tons to 270 million tons.

For Germany, this is a logical policy. The country's economic rise, after unification in 1871, was based on applying top-quality scientific research to what were the high-technology industries of their day: electrical and electronic goods, optical products like microscopes and cameras, chemicals, cars—many of which, like the motor car, they actually invented. Now, Germany sees a real prospect of again achieving global technological leadership in new industries, creating yet another industrial revolution. It produces one third of all the solar cells and almost a half of all the wind turbines in the entire world. A German consultant, Torsten Henzelmann, claims that by 2020 this sector will be employing more people than mechanical engineering or the automotive industry.

There are other areas, apparently more prosaic in terms of technology, where another form of innovation—the discovery of new niche markets—will come into play. Tourism has been one of the most dynamic industries, globally, in the boom years of the last two decades, and, though its rate of growth has diminished sharply in the current recession, it is also likely to shift in its focus and geography. One evident trend has been that, as mass tourism grows and diversifies to more distant and more exotic locations, there is a parallel growth of more specialized travel to satisfy more informed and more sophisticated tastes. So-called ecotourism, to locations like the Galapagos Islands, provides an apt example—despite the evident contradiction in flying across the world to view unsullied natural habitats, with all the attendant strain on their ecosystems. Yet ecotourism can equally flourish closer to home, within Europe—and there, it is bolstered by the rapid development of the Europe-wide high-speed rail system, making it possible to travel half-way across the continent in half a day with a fraction of the environmental impact of flying.

A second niche service industry, already exhibiting phenomenal growth, is medical tourism. This is becoming a global industry, as clients from countries seek cheaper options in developing countries. *The Economist* magazine, in 2008, reported a prediction by the consultancy Deloitte that Americans traveling abroad for treatment will grow from 750,000 in 2007 to 6 million by 2010 and 10 million by 2012, bringing $21 billion per year to developing countries. Increasingly, in providing services as in making goods, the old adage "a good product delivered to the customer at the lowest price" will increasingly apply on a global scale.

However, to return to Perez, all this will involve building a new techno-economic paradigm: a total revolution in the way the world manages its business. The golden years of the postwar era rested on a firm foundation of public actions, remarkably similar in character from country to country, though differing in detail: in particular, the creation of new physical and social infrastructure (motorways, universities, hospitals) and the development of welfare systems to protect the basic living standards of ordinary people. Thus the system, as perceptive observers like Keynes had long ago observed, could not self-correct itself. We are just at the start of such an era; we cannot yet see clearly the outlines of the new techno-economic paradigm.

The Impact on Cities

We can begin to understand the urban impacts of these changes by looking at a very insightful analysis of European city types issued by the European Union's regional policy directorate in 2007. The analysts have divided the cities into thirteen types, combined them into three major groups, and arrayed them in terms of their performance (on the vertical scale) and population size (on the horizontal scale). It emerges that the really successful cities, on the top right corner, are those that are making the transition fastest to the knowledge economy, and conversely those on the bottom left are the old industrial cities that are to some extent failing to make the transition. This is shown by how the different kinds of cities are classified according performance on three separate indices: employment creation, qualified workers, and multimodal connectivity.

The analysis proceeds to explore the differences between the different groups. The first—a very interesting one—are the so-called *international hubs*: the big cities that top the league of growth. They are rich and growing; they include established capital cities such as London, Paris, and Madrid, which are comfortably well off but are showing local unemployment. A second category is the *established capitals*, whose performance is generally very strong, although slightly less so than the so-called knowledge hubs. Third are the so-called *reinvented capital*s, the Eastern European capitals: their populations are shrinking due to out-migration but their economies are growing and their performance, in the years since 2007, has been very strong.

The next major group in terms of performance are the *specialized service hubs*. First are the national service hubs: these are places like Hannover, Brno in the Czech Republic, Seville in Spain, or Utrecht in the Netherlands. They are doing reasonably well through having a strong administrative role, sometimes of course as provincial capitals as in the case of Hannover. The next category in this group of specialized poles are the so-called *transformation poles*: these are old industrial cities that are more or less successfully adapting to the New Economy. They are a very interesting group; they include a number of the bigger United Kingdom cities such as Glasgow and Birmingham and also cities like Lille in France or Torino, very successful recently, in Italy, or Pilsen in the Czech Republic. The third type are the so-called *gateway cities*, which are basically transport-based, often port cities like Antwerp, Marseille, Santander, Naples, Genoa, or Rotterdam. They are making a transition to the New Economy, but it very often takes the form of capital-intensive employment such as container ports that do not employ many people, so that these cities are actually often characterized by quite high rates of unemployment and a labor force somewhat lacking in qualifications. The next type is another group of specialized poles, the *modern industrial cities*: these are the really strong performers, the high-technology powerhouses of Europe. They are very often medium-sized or even quite small cities like Augsburg in Germany or Cork in Ireland or Tilburg in the Netherlands, together with one or two Eastern European cities like Poznan in Poland as well as Göteborg (Gothenburg) in Sweden.

The next group is an even more specialized group, the so-called *research centers* which are smaller cities with a very high gross domestic product per head, including such examples as Darmstadt in Germany or Karlsruhe near Bayern, Southern Germany, Grenoble in the French Alps or Eind-

hoven in Holland or—an outstanding example—Cambridge in England. These are among the most successful cities and yet they are quite small cities in what were previously rural agrarian areas away from the main industrial regions. Yet another category here are so-called *visitor centers*, tourist places like Verona in Italy or Krakow in Poland or Trier in Germany; these are cities that are highly specialized in tourist services. They have an average GDP per head with sometimes some problem of low-income population and seasonal employment.

The third major group consists of the so-called *regional poles*, and it is here that we begin to see some of Europe's problem cases. The first is a particularly problematic category of so-called deindustrialised cities: they include many UK cities—Sheffield is an example—and many smaller cities in northern England and Scotland and Wales, and also Belgian cities such as Charleroi or Liège, as well as a number of Eastern European cities including the new *Länder* of Germany such as Halle, or in Katowice in Poland. Often these are old coal mining or heavy industrial cities which are finding it difficult to make the transition to the new knowledge economy.

A second type in this group is the *regional market centers*, which play a key role in rural communities but sometimes suffer from weak connections to the rest of the world. They are generally found in ex-industrial areas—Erfurt in Germany, which of course is the *Land* capital of Thüringen, or Reims in the North-East of France, or Palermo in Sicily. They are performing reasonably well, but they are suffering from some problems. A related category, the so-called *regional public service centers*, are again smaller places in generally rural areas—Schwerin in Germany or Odense in Denmark or Lublin in Poland or Umeå in far northern Sweden. They have strong administrative growth for generally quite rural regions, but they are weaker in the market economy services. And another category here—highly specialized—are so-called *satellite towns* including British new towns, such as Stevenage, but also other places which are smaller cities close to larger ones, such as Gravesham in the Thames Gateway east of London or Worcester close to Birmingham in the West Midlands of England. Unlike the last three types, these are generally performing well because they are commuter towns that send workers into the neighboring big service city who then bring their salaries back home with them to spend, creating a kind of local economic base. That proves a fairly successful kind of formula and it is leading in some parts of Europe, as in southeastern England, to the growth of vast so-called megacity regions stretching up to approximately 160 kilometers from London and containing up to fifty of these smaller cities and towns, which are all in some sense subsidiary or tributary to London. The Randstad in the Netherlands is a similar example, and perhaps also the regions around Munich and Stuttgart and in particular Rhine-Main around Frankfurt. So, those are the main types distinguished in the 2007 Ecotec report on European city performance, which shows essentially that there are specialised places that are outstanding in making the transition to the new knowledge economy, contrasted with much less successful cities, generally smaller older industrial cities including a number in Eastern Europe, and in between a more mixed group of cities with moderately good economic performance, but some problems.

Different analyses of the performance of these city types show a consistent picture, which further confirms earlier work in the UK *State of the Cities* report issued by the UK Department for Communities and Local Government in 2006. The central issue is that some generally smaller cities are finding it easy to make the transition to the new economy, partly because, for instance, they have universities and strong research centers; at the other extreme, some cities are finding it difficult to make that transition because they have a heritage of old industries that have more or less disappeared, and their former workforces are insufficiently educated or insufficiently skilled to provide a support for the new service economy. Yet some larger cities, in particular the very biggest capital cities, are making the transition quite successfully in terms of knowledge-based service industries, such as financial services and the media, but are leaving some problems behind in the form of populations in some parts of those cities that are not equally making a transition to the New Economy.

That point is illustrated by a study produced in 1997 for the UK government, focusing on information exchange in the new knowledge economy, specifically in four sectors: first finance and business services; second power and influence (or command and control), meaning government and commercial headquarters; third creative and cultural industries; and fourth urban tourism. Each has a local component, a national component, and an international component. To take one obvious example—tourism—as a Londoner I go to the theater or to art galleries or museums to see new exhibitions, but I am sitting or standing there side-by-side with people from other parts of the UK and all over the world who come to visit these. The same principle applies to each of the other sectors. What is however even more interesting is that these four major sectors are highly synergistic with each other, and many of the key activities occur in the spaces between them. Thus, between tourism and the creative and cultural industries, there are theaters, galleries, and nightlife; between creative and cultural and command and control there are advertising and different kinds of public

relations and the media; between finance and business services there are legal services, commercial law, accountancy, and marketing, and between the power and influence sector and tourism we find restaurants, shops, exhibitions and conferences—and indeed, those activities fit in almost any of the gaps. Thus not just in London but in all successful cities these activities are simultaneously feeding into the main sectors and feeding off them in a very synergistic way. In the study we showed this for four major global cities: London, New York, Paris, and Tokyo. But the same principle applies to many smaller cities. In all, each of these sectors and the intervening activities simultaneously serve the local economy, the national economy, and the export economy in a highly successful way.

Thus one of the most interesting questions for public policy today is how far these synergistic relationships in the very biggest European capital cities—like London, Paris, Madrid, and Berlin—can spread downward and outward into the next level of cities and then the next level down from that, into the smaller cities—including those ex-industrial cities that often have the very biggest problems. The final point, however, is that much of this activity is face-to-face: you have to be there to be part of it. That is equally true if you come as a tourist or you work as a trader in a London bank or in the headquarters of a major corporation. During the spring of 2010, when the volcanic ash cloud shut down air travel, we discovered just how destructive the breakdown of physical communication, especially air transportation, could be. We still await the calculation of the economic loss the global economy suffered from that loss of face-to-face synergy—and that will illustrate a vital point about how cities work.

So the final point—relating to my earlier argument—is that we can export some of these activities from the big cities to smaller cities, we can create museums and galleries, and we can foster tourism in smaller cities outside the major capitals. To some extent we can move other media activities—in 2011 the BBC is moving an important part of its whole activity out of London to Manchester, and we shall see how well it works. But the paradox is that just as we do that, so more and more other activities in the big cities grow to take their place. This constitutes a process of constant refreshment, which means that the other cities can perhaps grow in these areas, but the really big cities tend to keep going on ahead of them.

GENERAL AGREEMENT ON ARCHITECTURE

ANDRÉS DUANY

The most intractable criticism of the New Urbanism is that its associated architecture is traditional in syntax. To the actual urban propositions as presented by the Charter of the New Urbanism there is usually little objection. But the modernist establishment is not inclined to compromise on anything as important as style, and so anathema has descended from the academies on *everything* New Urbanist

It need not be so. It is easy to explain what New Urbanist architecture is meant to be by quoting the applicable principles of the Charter:

19. A primary task of all urban architecture and landscape design is the physical definition of streets and public spaces as places of shared use.

20. Individual architectural projects should be seamlessly linked to their surroundings. This issue transcends style.

25. Civic buildings and public gathering places require important sites to reinforce community identity and the culture of democracy. They deserve distinctive form, because their role is different from that of other buildings and places that constitute the fabric of the city.

26. All buildings should provide their inhabitants with a clear sense of location, weather, and time. Natural methods of heating and cooling can be more resource-efficient than mechanical systems.

Admittedly, these principles do establish standards that curtail absolute freedom of expression, though none precludes modernist architecture, as Principle 20 makes explicit.

Why then, does traditional architecture predominate? There are several reasons: it offers a more cost-effective environmental performance (the "original green" argument); its conventional construction is more durable, mutable, forgiving, inexpensive, and easily obtained; it is culturally associated with most places that support pedestrian activity. But none of those are the *main reason*: traditional architecture

pervades New Urbanism because regular folk prefer it—and those folk constitute the middle class, of which there are currently 430 million worldwide and set to double each coming decade. It is they who drive around for everything, live large on the land, and entertain themselves with consumption in a public realm entirely dedicated to shopping. This lifestyle is the principal cause of climate change, so it is not a trivial issue.

The preference for traditional architecture was apparent from the inception, when Seaside's modernist buildings (yes, they exist) ended up as a small minority, a proportion that has recurred in most subsequent New Urbanist settlements. The preference manifests itself *wherever choice is available*, and, in the United States at least, the middle class has choice. Unlike the constrained markets of Europe, where the regular folk (and even the special folk) are pleased to secure any dwelling near their preferred location, in North America when someone does not like a particular design, there is another one readily available. This may be disheartening to modernist architects, but it cannot be for New Urbanists. However appealing it is to cultivate savvy upper-class *patrons*, or help out unquestioning underclass *victims*, those of us concerned with urbanism must deal with pesky *customers*. An urbanist does not have the opportunity to meet these customers—and to bring them along, like architects do clients by personal charm, intimidation, and other wiles, to an adequate level of sophistication. With customers, a building which does not "connect" will have them looking elsewhere soon enough. To operate, the New Urbanists cannot hold these middle-class folk "outside the discourse" as the academy does.

The New Urbanism is an urban reform movement—and that is quite ambitious enough. It has not taken on an agenda for architectural reform, and so modernists have not forgiven this failure to care desperately about what is most important to them. But it wasn't always that way. It is now usually forgotten that the first generation of New Urbanists were educated as modernists, and some of us were pretty good at it. Only when the urban agenda took over did modernism have to give way. Even after architecture became a secondary concern, the New Urbanists were accepted by the academy in the early years as interesting and insurgent outsiders (the record of teaching, awards, and publication is evidence). Only later, when the movement began to prevail, becoming the source of many architectural commissions, were the New Urbanists said to lack sophistication and perhaps solidarity by not directing the available work to modernists.

But we *did* so direct as much as was tolerated by the market. At Seaside alone there are modernist buildings by Walter Chatham, Deborah Berke, and Alexander Gorlin (about ten by these three), as well as buildings by Samuel Mockbee, Victoria Casasco, Scott Merrill, Machado and Silvetti, Aldo Rossi, and Steven Holl (his first large building). Many of these are first-rate (albeit "of their time," and so slightly musty today), and all were permitted within the Seaside code—that satanic instrument of Southern fascism.

The reason there are not more modernist buildings is simple: the customers did not want any more of them. Well before the confrontation at the sales office, the preference of the people becomes very clear in the charrette process when some firms present excellent renderings of modernist buildings. Unless they are mid-rise, they don't survive scrutiny. The house, it seems, must be traditional—and the house constitutes the great majority of North American urban fabric, even in those "urban" stalwarts Chicago, Boston, San Francisco, Vancouver, Washington, New York, and Toronto. Manhattan, as usual, is the blinding exception.

Is it too painful for architects already reeling from the concept of "customer" to propose that the New Urbanism might have conscripted traditional architecture in support of its urban reform agenda? But before I discuss that cynical possibility, I should make my own perhaps naïve reasoning explicit. I practice New Urbanism as a means to increase the sum of human happiness (the best blended metric) and I believe happiness is self-defined. It seems cruel to impose my architectural preference on the lives of others. If people prefer a certain style for their dear homes, I will argue their right to have it. This position is not unusual in the United States as it flows directly from the "right to life, liberty, and the pursuit of happiness," which happens to be the greatest marketing slogan ever devised. Other New Urbanists, I should make clear, practice with a preference for other agendas, among them the reduction of atmospheric pollution, responsible land use, social equity, better allocation of public funds, and so on.

Now, back to the reality of implementing urbanism: traditional architecture is sometimes deployed by New Urbanists as camouflage. Its familiarity (aka "revolting nostalgia") serves to ease the passage of such scary urban techniques as connected street networks, declensions of density, public transit, interspersed socioeconomic diversity, and commerce adjacent to dwellings. New Urbanists cannot deny themselves this powerful political tool for the sake of imposing an architecture that has for eighty years failed to become popular. We will not carry *that* old water bucket for the modernists.

But what of the well-intentioned ecological architects who are also modernists? Does that ethic not trump style?

Again, to take climate change seriously, modernists cannot avoid the middle class. The critical problem is *not*, as the Landscape Urbanists pretend, the hydrology of the land, to be salved by the application of an ornamental biophilia—the problem of climate change emanates from the hydrocarbon of the cars, and that is the concern of the New Urbanists. The academy's preferred client, the patron, may have a large carbon footprint individually, but there are too few, even in the aggregate, to matter. The academy's other clients, the hapless poor, already have minimal carbon footprints. There is no avoiding that it is the middle class in its overwhelming numbers that is causing the world's environmental crises. Any supposedly "green" architect who is unable to engage them will achieve next to nothing.

To overcome this division, we have in the past offered strategies for a rapprochement. One, by John Massengale, proposes a critical assessment that takes account of good, better, and best potential outcomes, explicitly acknowledging that the architectural playing field is not level, that buildings are to be judged within the limits of their circumstances. But if even the official AIA periodical, presumably representing all architects, is too snobbish to accept that distinction, imagine how it goes down with the elitists of the academy!

In the end it is not rational; it is a problem of simple prejudice. Modernist architecture no longer exists as a common set of positivistic propositions (that notion finally expired after the Case Study Houses). Rather, it is defined as the residue after the application of an arbitrary set of proscriptions: arches, columns with tops, moldings, symmetrically pitched roofs, brick, clapboard, latex paint, muntins, sash windows, and a few other perfectly harmless architectural elements are categorically banned! All else is allowed (think about this). This amounts to a suicide pact with society because it is precisely these banned elements which most easily connect with the middle class. And, really, what is the harm?

But never mind that! There is perhaps another strategy available: to develop a *tendenza*. A *tendenza* emerges when architects convene to resolve and agree on issues, resulting in shared syntax—enough so that the middle class can evolve a connoisseurship. It is not that the regular folk are terminally against modernism; it is just that they cannot be expected to understand the personal proposition of one architect and then be robust enough to withstand the whiplash of another's radically different conception. Where *tendenzas* have emerged, evidence shows that modernist architecture becomes locally popular. They have developed in Miami Beach in the 1930s, Southern California in the 1950s, Ticino in the 1960s, the Sea Ranch Coast in the 1970s, and in Austin during the 1990s. If such regional *tendenzas* were to again be consciously fostered, modernist architects might develop a middle-class patronage and thereby engage the campaign against suburban sprawl.

One more thing: Why does it behoove the New Urbanists to support modernists, when they are already so well served by traditional architects?[1] Why bother carrying this bucket now? Because it is now clear that the anathema of the academies is undermining the dissemination of our work. It cannot be that class after class of young, talented, and idealistic architects are deflected from their heroic destiny in ecology and taught instead to perform for the fickle opinion of a very few, possibly corrupt, critics.

The proposal made here, therefore, is that the rupture between the academy and the New Urbanism, based on a matter so trivial as the look of a building, can surely be overcome by method and by forbearance. A *tendenza* is one such method. One way to induce a *tendenza* is the local discussion of these propositions:

General Agreement on Architecture

In response to a global environment that can be seriously affected by the pattern of human settlement, we agree on the following five principles.

Social Responsibility

Good, plain, practical buildings must again become commonplace.

While architecture can express conditions, drawing critical attention to them, it can also improve them directly. To improve conditions directly is by far the more effective design strategy.

Contemporary buildings should be denied all implied dispensations. They should be held to as high a standard as were their predecessors. The means available today, after all, are greater not fewer.

It is irresponsible to impose untested or experimental housing designs on the poor. The likelihood of failure in such cases has proven to be very great, and the poor are powerless to escape its consequences. Architects should experiment, if at all, on conscious patrons of the arts.

Observation of the current situation should not result in the conclusion that the regular folk will accept only mediocrity.

Architects should participate in the political arena, guiding the built environment at the largest scale. It is risking failure to determine urban policy in the absence of those with knowledge of design.

Architects should participate in urbanism, which would otherwise be abandoned to the abstractions of zoning codes, traffic, and finance.

Architects, like attorneys, should dedicate a portion of their time without compensation to those who do not otherwise have access to design services.

Architects should harness those systems that make the best design available to the greatest number. Only what is produced in quantity is consequential.

Architects should engage the producers of manufactured housing, open-source products, and plan books, as these are the most efficient methods for achieving affordable housing. Their low quality is the result of being shunned by architects.

Composition

Architectural expression should assimilate cultural and climatic context no less than the will to form of the architect.

Buildings should respond to their context. If an existing context is not suitable, then it is proper to inaugurate one that is. While buildings should engage the character of their place, influence can travel along cultural and climatic belts to positive effect.

Private buildings should be visually recessive and collectively harmonious, lending themselves to the definition of the urban space. Civic buildings, however, should be individually expressive of the aspiration of the institutions they embody, and the inspiration of their architects.

Architecture should be responsive to the imperatives of economics and marketing while not being dominated by them. It is the role of architecture to civilize commerce.

Architects should also be gardeners and urbanists.

Architecture should engage engineering and sociology, though only as supporting disciplines.

Architecture is independent of politics. Buildings should be able to transcend their inaugural condition to become useful and beloved in subsequent circumstances. It is a falsification of history to consider a style intrinsic to this or that hegemony or liberation.

Graphic techniques should not determine the design of buildings. Computers should remain as labor-saving devices and not become determinants of form. Because something can be depicted does not mean that it should be constructed.

Buildings should incorporate authentic technical progress, but not for the sake of innovation. Mass production should affect the process of building, but it is not necessary that it determine the form.

Each building should be coherently composed. A building's visual complexity cannot be the surrogate of an absent urbanism. Authentic urban diversity results only from multiple buildings by many designers working in sequence.

Design controlled by known rules is preferable to the subjective opinions of review boards. Contrary to myth, without rules the default setting in North America is not innovation and excellence; it is kitsch.

Communication

The language of architecture should be in continual evolution, but not under the thrall of short fashion cycles. Architecture is not a consumer item.

Participation in a perennial avant-garde is an untenable pursuit that consumes those who attempt it and results in architects at the peak of their abilities being marginalized merely because their time of fame has passed.

Architecture should be practiced as a collective endeavor and not always as a means of brand differentiation in pursuit of the attention of critics.

Architects should not perform for the opinion of a very small number of critics—critics who are empowered only because they are recognized as such by architects. Those who do not possess the experience of building should not be granted undue influence on the reputation of those who do.

Architects should develop a direct voice in the periodicals, explaining their work themselves. (Architects should effect this demand by canceling their subscriptions to those publications that do not agree.)

Architects should endeavor to disseminate their work in the most popular media. How else will the people learn?

Architects should convene regionally to attempt to clarify and converge their thinking. One reason many regular folks remain so ignorant is that the withering individualism of buildings prevents them from developing connoisseurship.

Ecology

The architectural vernaculars of the world should be the subject of systematic study as a basis for ecological design.

The longevity of a building is crucial to its ecological performance. Construction technology should result in buildings that are both durable and mutable as required. This is usually achieved with conventional materials and time-tested detailing.

The assumption that only the high-tech offers green solutions is a fraud, as it results in unnecessary expense. The "original green" was exceptionally cost-effective, as in the past there was nothing to waste.

Old and new buildings should be assigned equal standing, as they provide parallel, persistent realities. Their evaluation should be pragmatic and not a function of chronology.

Additions and amendments to historic buildings must be allowed to be either harmonious or contrasting, as best determined by the architect.

Education

The design schools should accept the responsibility of teaching a body of knowledge, and not attempt to incite individualism. Students should be exposed to more than the few geniuses of each generation. Emulation of the exceptional does not provide an adequate model for professional training.

The wall between history and design must be torn down. The achievements of predecessors are the basis of all human progress.

Architectural history and theory should also include the masters of administration and development. Students who are not seduced by form-making might be inspired by such role models. Industry, government, and finance are sorely in need of their design abilities.

Apprenticeship should again be an available alternative to academic instruction. There has been no more effective method of learning architecture. Most of the finest buildings of all time were the result of apprenticeship, while most of the worst have been the result of architecture curricula. There is a lesson in that.

ECOLOGIES AND SCALES OF CITIES

SASKIA SASSEN[1]

Cities are a type of socioecological system that has an expanding range of articulations with nature's environment and ecologies. Today, most of these articulations are negative and produce environmental damage. Here I examine how we can begin to use these articulations to produce positive outcomes—outcomes that allow cities to contribute to environmental sustainability. The complex internal systems of cities and their multiscalar character in terms of geography, policy, society, economy, space, and time have a massive potential to effect a broad range of positive articulations with nature's ecologies.

Scaling

Many of the diverse issues affecting the environment can be conceived of analytically as questions of scale. Importantly, cities incorporate a range of scales at which a given ecological condition functions, and in that sense cities make legible the notion of scaling. For instance, one asphalted street in a village and a few buildings with air conditioners produce some heat emissions; thousands of such streets and buildings in a city produce a new socioecological condition—heat islands. This, in turn, implies that cities make the multiscalar aspect of ecological systems legible to residents of cities. The urban environment's capacity to make legible should be developed and strengthened because such legibility will become increasingly critical for policy matters concerning cities, as well as regions beyond urban areas.

Scaling is one way of handling what are now often seen as either/or conditions: local vs. global, markets vs. nonmarket mechanisms, green vs. brown environmentalism. I have found some of the analytic work on scaling being done among ecologists very illuminating in my efforts to conceptualize the city in this context.[2] Of particular relevance is the notion that complex systems are multiscalar systems as opposed to multilevel systems, and that the complexity resides precisely in the relations across scales. The ecological literature finds that tension among scales is a feature of complex ecological systems, a condition that would certainly seem to hold for cities. Let me illustrate by developing on the earlier mentioned case of how a few air-conditioned high-rise buildings merely add some harmful emissions whereas a city's downtown creates new ecological systems, such as heat islands, which then feed ozone holes at the planetary scale. Providing an air-conditioned hospital is likely to be experienced as a positive element in a neighborhood of a large city or in a small town: it would be difficult to see the negatives for the average resident. But the fact that at the level of the city it contributes to heat islands produces a tension between the advantage for that neighborhood and the damage to the larger environment, further accentuated by growing ozone holes.

This tension among the different scales forces the issue of environmental damage and the need to find and develop solutions at all levels. In brief, understanding how tensions among the multiple scales that might be operating in the context of the city enhances the analysis of environmental damages associated with urbanization. And it enhances our understanding of the ways in which cities are the source for solutions to such damages.

A crucial analytic operation involved here is giving spatiotemporal scaling to the object of study.[3] This also entails distinguishing the object of study from contextual variables, which in the case of cities might be population, economic base, etc. Executing such analytic operations would help us avoid the fallacy of holding "the city" guilty of environmental damage. Eliminating cities would not necessarily solve the environmental crisis.[4] We need to understand the functioning of and the possibilities for changing specific city-related systems: energy systems, economic systems, transportation systems, etc., which entail modes of resource use that are environmentally unsound. The fact that these various systems are amalgamated in urban formations is an analytically distinct condition from the systems involved.

The distinction between specific systems and background or contextual variables also helps us avoid the fallacy of seeing "the city" as a container, a bounded, closed unit. In my research on cities and globalization, I instead conceptualize the city as a multiscalar system through which multiple highly specialized cross-border economic circuits circulate. This idea can be applied to cities and the environmental dynamic by conceptualizing the city as a multiscalar system through which multiple specific socioecological circuits traverse. Rather than a closed system, cities are amalgamations of multiple "damage" circuits, "restoration" circuits, and policy circuits.

Changing the Valences

There is a set of specific issues raised by research on ecological systems that point to possibly fruitful analytic strategies to understand cities and urbanization processes both in terms of environmental conditions and in terms of policy. One of the reasons this may be helpful is that we are still struggling to understand and situate various types of environmental dynamics in the context of cities, and wondering how to engage policy. When it comes to remedial policy and cleaning up environmental damage, there is greater clarity in understanding what needs to be done.

But understanding the city as a broader system poses enormous difficulties precisely because of the multiple scales that are constitutive of the city, both as a system of distributed capabilities and as a political-economic and judicial-administrative system. That is to say, the individual household or firm or government office can recycle waste, but cannot effectively address the broader issue of the excess consumption of scarce resources; the international agreement can call for global measures to reduce greenhouse emission levels, but depends on individual countries and individual cities and individual households and firms to implement many of the necessary steps; and the national government can mandate environmental standards, but it depends on systems of economic power and systems of wealth production.[5]

A key analytic step is to decide which of the many scaled ecological, social, economic, and policy processes are needed to explain a specific environmental condition (whether negative or positive) and design a specific action or response. Another analytic step is to factor in the temporal scales or frames of various urban conditions and dynamics: cycles of the built environment, of the economy, the life of infrastructures, and of certain types of investment instruments. The damage produced by a car's unclean motor spewing fumes is immediate, and promptly visible; but when the car is not on, it is, strictly speaking, not producing damage. The damage produced by a building's outside walls does not stop—it is constant and relentless, and it is not as legible as a fuming car's motor. The combination of these two steps helps us deconstruct a given situation and to locate its constitutive conditions in a broader grid of spatial, temporal, and administrative scales.

The connection between spatial and temporal scales evident in ecological processes may prove analytically useful

to approach some of these questions in the case of cities. What may be found to be negative at a small spatial scale, or a short time frame, may emerge as positive at a larger scale or longer time frame. For a given set of disturbances, different spatio-temporal scales may elicit different responses from ecosystems. Using an illustration from ecology, we can say that individual forest plots might come and go but the forest cover of a region overall can remain relatively constant.

This raises a question as to whether a city needs a larger system in place that can neutralize the impact on the overall city system of major disturbances inside the city. One outcome of the research by ecologists in this domain is that movement across scales brings about change, which is the key process in multiscalar systems: it is not only a question of bigger or smaller, but rather that the phenomenon itself changes. Biological processes are good examples: the pest that is experienced as pure damage at one scale becomes the food for another species that is experienced as benevolent at that scale. In the case of cities we can return to the aforementioned example of buildings and heat islands as one illustration. This multiscalar dynamic also allows us to recognize that an unstable system at a given scale can be a condition for stability at a lower or higher scale.

We can extend this process of changing valence to other features of systems: bottom-up control turns into top-down control; competition becomes less important. This also is suggestive for thinking about cities as the solution to many types of environmental damage: What are the scales at which we can understand the city as contributing solutions to the environmental crisis?

An important issue raised by scaling in ecological research is the frequent confusion between levels and scales: what is sometimes presented as a change of scales is actually a translation between levels. A change of scale results in new interactions and relationships, and often a different organization. Level, on the other hand, is a relative position in a hierarchically organized system. Thus, a change in levels entails a change in a quantity or size rather than the forming of a different entity; in some cases an expanded quantity or size can indeed become a different scale, as in the case cited below of an illness that spreads to vast numbers of people becoming an epidemic.

Conclusion: The Capacity to Escalate

Relating some of these analytic distinctions to the case of cities suggests that one way of thinking of the city as multiscalar is to note that some of its features, notably density, alter the nature of an event. The individual occurrence, e.g., a high-rise building, is distinct from the aggregate outcome, e.g., density. It is not merely a sum of the individual occurrences, i.e., a greater quantity of occurrences. It is a different event.

The city contains both occurrences and aggregate outcomes. It can thus be described as instantiating a broad range of environmental damage that may involve very different scales and origins yet get constituted in urban terms. For instance, CO_2 emissions produced on the micro-scale of vehicles and coal burning by individual households becomes extensive air pollution that covers the whole city, with effects that go beyond CO_2 emissions *per se*. Air and waterborne microbes materialize as diseases at the scale of the household and the individual body and become epidemics thriving on the multiplier effects of urban density and capable of destabilizing operations of firms whose machines have no intrinsic susceptibility to the disease but which are dependent on humans who might be infected.

A second way in which the city is multiscalar is in the geography of the environmental damages it produces.[6] Some of it is atmospheric; some of it internal to the built environment of the city, as might be the case with much sewage or disease; and some of it is in distant locations around the globe, as with deforestation. The case of ozone holes is one of the most serious instances of scale-up: the damage is produced at the micro-scale of cars, households, factories, buildings, but its full impact becomes visible and measurable over the poles, where there are no cars and buildings.

A third way in which the city can be seen as multi-scalar is that its demand for resources can entail a geography of extraction and processing that spans the globe, though it does so in the form of a collection of confined individual sites, albeit sites distributed worldwide. This worldwide geography of extraction instantiates in particular and specific forms, such as furniture, jewelry, machinery, fuel . . . all inside the city. The city is one moment—the strategic moment—in this global geography of extraction, and it is different from that geography itself. A fourth way in which the city is multiscalar is that it instantiates a variety of policy levels. It is one of the key sites where a very broad range of policies—supranational, national, regional, and local—materialize in specific procedures, regulations, penalties, forms of compliance, and types of violations.[7] These specific outcomes are different from the actual policies as they get designed and implemented at other levels of government.

It is also important to factor in the possibility of conflicts in and between spatial scales. Environmentalists can operate at broad spatial and temporal scales, observing the effects of local activities on macro-level conditions such as global warming, acid rain formation. and global despoliation of the resource base. Environmentalists with a managerial approach often have to operate in very short time frames and confined levels of operation, pursuing clean ups and remedial measures for a particular locality, remedial measures that may do little to affect the broader condition involved. Indeed, they may diminish the sense of urgency about larger issues of resource consumption and thereby delay much-needed responses. On the other hand, economists or companies will tend to emphasize maximizing returns on a particular site over a specific period of time.

RESTORATIVE URBANISM
FROM SUSTAINABILITY TO PROSPERITY

NAN ELLIN

A significant shift has been underway globally, emerging from broad-based sustainability efforts that have contributed to enhance the quality of our places in recent decades. Thanks to these great strides, we are now taking the next step, with a yet smaller ecological footprint, by moving beyond sustainability to prosperity. While sustainability is certainly an improvement over declining, better still is flourishing, thriving, and prospering. How are we moving in this direction and how might we accelerate that movement?

Recognizing Gifts

"That flowing imagination which founded the city in the first place can be re-found. It is planted in our midst always ready to flower—if we begin, not with the "problem" of what needs to be changed, or moved, or built, or demolished, but begin with what already is here, still stands and sings of its soul, still holds the sparks of the mind that initiated it."

— James Hillman

The point of departure for the prosperity paradigm is recognizing assets, environmental as well as cultural. This approach begins by identifying the data—the givens, or gifts—in contrast to the prevailing tendency of the last century to begin with problems or deficits. That tendency is demonstrated, for instance, by Abraham Maslow's hierarchy of needs, introduced in 1943 (fig. 1). Maslow's analysis implies people have deficits that need to be filled, often by experts, rather than intrinsic qualities and abilities that can be developed.

What if instead of focusing on deficits, we focus on assets? What if we thought in terms of a hierarchy of the gifts (fig. 2)? From "Fuels" at the base (sun, water, food, fossil fuels, and other sources of energy) and "Tools" above (knowledge and skills), this model would imply that we can extract "Jewels."

Replacing needs with gifts shifts attention to assets rather than deficits. Instead of inciting helplessness, it inspires capacity-building, channeling energy to proaction and away from futile complaining. Identifying gifts builds confidence and morale in individuals as well as groups, spilling over into other arenas. In the process, weaknesses often become strengths, and the greatest problems may become the greatest solutions. At the same time, a perception of scarcity is supplanted by one of abundance, converting a zero-sum economy with a limitless one and competition into collaboration.[1]

In contrast, focusing attention on lack tends to demoralize rather than empower. As a result, it may contribute to blaming rather than assuming responsibility, and consequently erode prosperity due to resulting denial, deflection, and distraction.[2] For instance, fear leads to gates, which lead to more fear and more gates. Alternatively, focusing on what we value and want allows us to build upon existing strengths and spiral up. The virtuous cycle—or spiral—replaces the vicious one. Robert Kennedy famously evinced these divergent attitudes, saying, "There are those who look at things the way they are, and ask why . . . I dream of things that never were and ask, why not?"

In sum, the sustainability paradigm has been informed by scientific/modern convention that begins with a critique by identifying a need or problem, proposes a solution, establishes goals, and attempts to implement them. In contrast, the prosperity model begins by recognizing assets, connects them, and adds energy to the system through catalytic interventions that respect the whole, including a self-adjusting feedback mechanism to monitor and effect change. Addressing problems from a larger context that engages more people with an attitude of respect, this approach becomes yet another gift, offering tools for extracting jewels.

Realigning Urban Design

IIn urban design, this shift is manifest in a range of efforts, which I describe cumulatively as "restorative urbanism." Practitioners of restorative urbanism understand the human

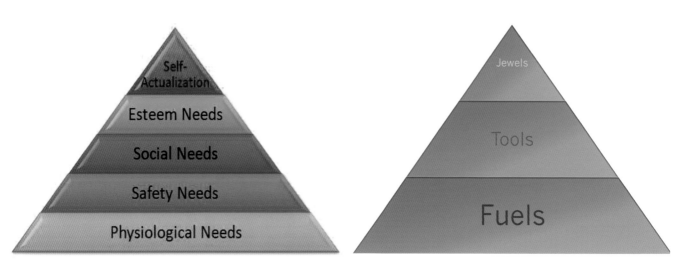

FIG. 1 Abraham Maslow's Hierarchy of Needs (1943).

FIG. 2 Hierarchy of Gifts.

FIG. 3 The Shift from sustainability to prosperity in urban design.

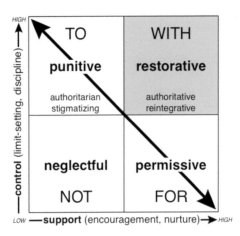

FIG. 4 Restorative justice.

habitat as part of nature rather than regarding cities and buildings as machines. Accordingly, practitioners of restorative urbanism aspire to local and global prosperity, rather than aiming principally for power, prestige, and profits (fig. 3).

The shift is evident in small and larger changes in training, practice, and representation of work. In teaching, for instance, we are seeing a move away from the "critique" (or "crit"), where teachers identify deficits in students' work, to "conversations" where students and teachers mutually discuss the work in a two-way learning process characterized by "appreciative inquiry."[3] Practitioners (architects, planners, and landscape architects) are increasingly developing and applying tools for stakeholder-based urban design, becoming catalysts and co-creators, rather than all-knowing experts, a process that deeply inflects the product. As practitioners conceive, describe, and present work, an evolved contextualism has emerged whereby geography, history, culture, experiential qualities, and postoccupancy evaluations are primary generators of form. Renderings express this evolved contextualism, a welcome departure from the conventional pristine architectural rendering devoid of people, often from a bird's-eye view as though the viewer is peering down upon a model. In contrast to the expert or artist working largely in isolation, the restorative urbanist is a co-creator, collaborating with client-communities and a team. These are just a few of the many ways in which the shift has been occurring.

Restorative urbanism might take cues from restorative justice, which aims to repair harm done to people and relationships rather than punish offenders, a movement that has proven successful and spread throughout the world over the last few decades. Restorative justice moves beyond the "punitive-permissive" continuum, inserting it into a larger matrix along the axes of support and control, thereby adding neglectful as well as restorative approaches (fig. 4). The restorative approach employs high control over wrongdoing while supporting and valuing the intrinsic worth of the wrongdoer.

Restorative urbanism can also learn from organizational learning and change. C. Otto Scharmer and Peter Block, leaders in this field, both emphasize the importance of shifting the focus from problems to possibilities. Problem-solv-

ing, maintains Scharmer, is about making improvements on the past, while possibility-finding focuses on the future. According to Block, "The context that restores community is one of possibility, generosity, and gifts, rather than one of problem solving, fear, and retribution. A new context acknowledges that we have all the capacity, expertise, and resources that an alternative future requires. Communities are human systems given form by conversations that build relatedness . . . Conversations that focus on stories about the past become a limitation to the community; ones that are teaching parables and focus on the future restore community" (29). We create this new context, Block maintains, by shifting from blaming others to taking responsibility, from retributive to restorative practices.[4]

The language of restoration and prosperity is spoken widely by environmentalists. Paul Hawken, environmentalist as well as entrepreneur, called for a shift to prosperity through a "restoration economy" in 1993. A restoration economy, he explained, builds upon and works with ecosystems, restoring natural (including human) capital as vital economic foundations and shifting investment decisions from short-term returns to longer-term returns that include costs of natural resources, unemployment, health issues, and so forth. Hawken maintains, "Humans want to flourish and prosper . . . and they will eventually reject any system of conservation that interferes with these desires. [Prosperity] will only come about through the accumulated effects of daily acts of billions of eager participants" (1993: xv).[5] Environmentalist Bill McKibben similarly advocates a shift from "growth" as the paramount economic ideal to the pursuit of prosperity (2007).

Restoring Urbanism

Just as a good manager builds on existing strengths of an organization, so good urbanism builds upon existing strengths of a place. Restorative urbanism begins by engaging communities to identify such assets and consider how best to leverage them, whether they are buildings, neighborhoods, businesses, cultural institutions, natural landscapes, or creative and intellectual capital. In this way, it sets a generative and dynamic self-adjusting feedback mechanism into motion, whereby communities build creatively upon their strengths, in the process often converting their greatest problems into their greatest solutions. Restorative urbanism also recognizes exemplary practices from which to learn and upon which to build.

The first step involves identifying what a community values and assuring its preservation. Recognizing these assets and capacities inflects the process, invariably leading to a consideration of what would be of greater value with minor adjustments. After identifying and protecting what is valued and enhancing what is underperforming, restorative urbanism addresses what may be missing and should be added, all informed by effective community involvement. When this process is applied, transformations are inspired by the

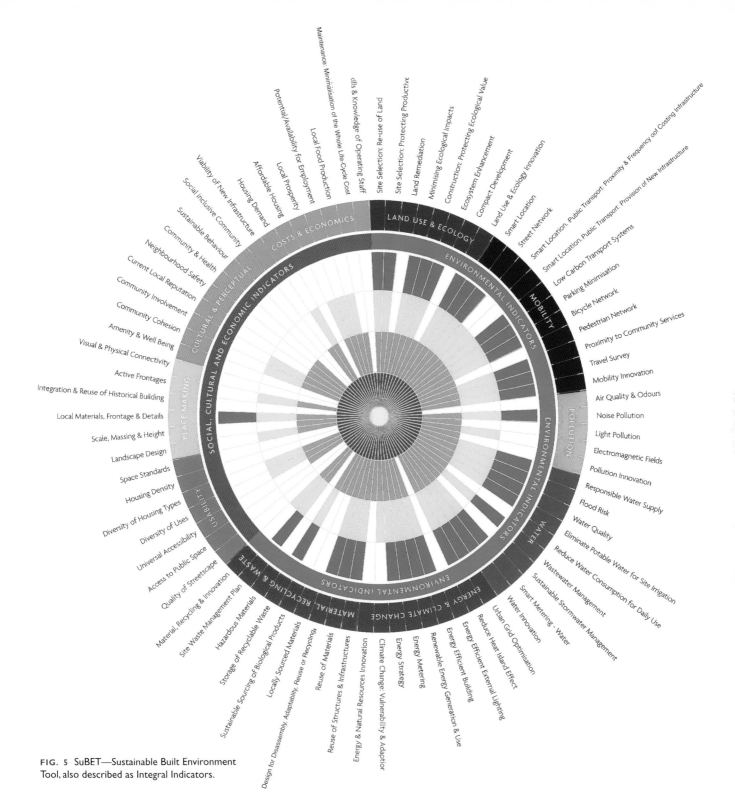

FIG. 5 SuBET—Sustainable Built Environment Tool, also described as Integral Indicators.

"DNA" of a place, allowing for unique and meaningful expressions to unfold.

Conventional urban intervention has proceeded in the reverse order, considering first what is needed, but too often at the expense of what is valued. In many instances over the last century, urban designers have even opted to begin with a *tabula rasa*, or clean slate, by razing what was already there or finding pristine land upon which to erect master plans. The sustainability paradigm extends these conventions to produce high control–low support (punitive) approaches. For instance, urban growth boundaries, which create a noose around the city, say "don't go," rather than inviting participation in making a great city along targeted areas throughout the urban network. Many sustainability indicators, such as LEED, do not adequately acknowledge site and cultural specificity or dynamism, thereby failing to respond to local conditions and adapt over time. Restorative sustainability indicators, such as SuBET (fig. 5) account for specificity and are adaptive.

Restorative urbanism veers away from the clean slate as well as master planning, which, in its focus on controlling everything, ironically tends to generate fragmented cities without soul or character. Instead, restorative urbanism

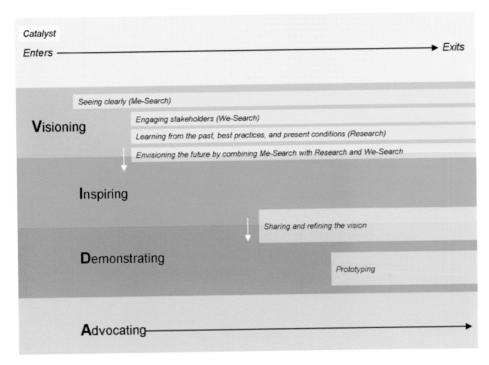

Catalyst
Enters ———————————————————→ Exits

Visioning
Seeing clearly (Me-Search)
Engaging stakeholders (We-Search)
Learning from the past, best practices, and present conditions (Research)
Envisioning the future by combining Me-Search with Research and We-Search

Inspiring

Sharing and refining the vision

Demonstrating

Prototyping

Advocating ———————————————————→

FIG. 6 The VIDA process.

determines where there is energy, both physical and social, in the larger system, and where it is lacking. It can thus perform "urban acupuncture," skillfully inserting interventions into the urban organism that clear blockages and liberate energy to catalyze additional growth and change.[6] Setting the self-adjusting feedback mechanism into place, this process activates underutilized resources and *attracts* new ones.

To practice restorative urbanism, I have developed a process called VIDA, Spanish for "life," because it brings vitality to places, an acronym for Visioning, Inspiring, Demonstrating, and Advocating (fig. 6).[7]

Countering the tendency to begin with problem-finding, VIDA applies two kinds of vision: the ability to see things clearly and a vision for a better future. These are acquired through *me-search*, *re-search*, and *we-search*. Me-search entails listening to our intuitions, preconceptions, and biases. Re-search investigates the past, best practices elsewhere, and current conditions. And we-search involves listening to others and carefully observing places to build relationships, identify assets, and consider how best to leverage them. Combining all three enables us to "co-create" (Scharmer) and paint a vision of what could be while inspiring all to implement the vision through collectively sharing the possibilities. Demonstration begins with painting this picture to/with others, and evolves through prototyping, turning the possibilities into realities. Advocating takes place during the entire VIDA process by communicating the vision to appropriate audiences through writing, presenting, and convening public programs. Depending on the project, demonstration and advocacy may involve public scholarship, scholarly writing, branding, and/or development of a business plan including funding sources, management, impact assessments, and long-term environmental, economic, and quality-of-life projections.

The VIDA process becomes yet another asset, in addition to the product of the process. As Peter Block explains, the community collaboration to support urban revitalization effects a "collective transformation," bringing together the knowledge of many to support something new, and to maintain or transform it accordingly (2008). Thanks to this collective transformation, the successful VIDA process is catalytic, effecting significant and ongoing change, eventually without the initial stewards, who may then move on to catalyze other projects.

Recurring Themes

Designing for prosperity, simply put, finds and builds upon the gifts of a given place and community. Recurrent themes of this work are slow, flow, low, and local:

Slow: The Slow City Movement and Incremental Urbanism

Flow: An evolved contextualism finds existing flows, follows them, and/or unblocks them (urban acupuncture)

Low: The most simple, elegant, and efficient design for living is often low-tech, such as swales instead of sewers

Local: Grow, Eat, and Shop Local

Restorative urban practices contribute to support existing local businesses and incentivize new creative entrepreneurship while also providing an attractive place for national and global businesses to establish themselves. They build upon cultural assets, supporting the rich cultural diversity of our communities, including expressive arts and culture (entrepreneurial creatives). And they showcase environmental assets, along with our ability to reclaim and enhance them, often featuring connected public space systems and integrating more nature into the city.

Restorative practices favor an "integral urbanism" which privileges adjacencies of uses and people, allowing relationships among them to develop and flourish (Ellin, 2006). Rather than separate functions and control people—the guiding ethos of modern urbanism—this approach works toward integration, inclusion, and dynamism. Bringing together functions that the twentieth century city separated (living, working, circulating, creating, and recreating), integral urbanism integrates buildings with nature, center with periphery, local character with global forces, the various professions involved with urban growth and development, and people of different ethnicities, incomes, ages, and abilities. Aiming to heal the wounds inflicted upon the landscape by the modern and postmodern eras, integral urbanism engages in a range of restorative efforts incorporating five qualities: hybridity, connectivity, porosity, authenticity, and vulnerability.

Hybridity and *connectivity* bring activities and people together at all scales. While modern urbanism espoused the separation of functions, integral urbanism reaffirms their symbiotic nature by combining and linking them. These various integrations can be accomplished through cross-programming buildings and regional plans—spatially (plan and section) as well as temporally. Examples of cross-programming include the office building with basketball court and day care center, the intergenerational community building (combining day care, teenage community center, adult education, and senior center), the public school/community center, the integrated parking structure (into office buildings and retail centers), the movie theater/restaurant, and the urban plaza by day/movie theater by night.

Transposing this concept onto the larger scale can increase density of activity without necessarily increasing building density, translating into reduced commuting, greater convenience, preservation of the natural environment, increase in quality public space, and greater social interaction. The outcome is new hybrid typologies and morphologies that pool human and natural resources for the benefit of all. This approach activates places by creating thresholds, or places of intensity, where diversity thrives. By increasing density of activity and perhaps building mass, these thresholds weave connections between and among people, places, and experiences.

Porosity preserves the integrity of what is brought together while allowing mutual access through permeable membranes, as opposed to the modernist attempt to dismantle boundaries or the postmodernist fortification. *Authenticity* involves actively engaging and drawing inspiration from actual social and physical conditions with an ethic of care, respect, and honesty. Like all healthy organisms, the "authenti-city" is always growing and evolving according to new needs, thanks to a self-adjusting feedback loop that measures and monitors success and failure. Finally, *vulnerability* calls upon us to relinquish control, listen deeply, value process as well as product, and reintegrate space with time.

An integral urbanism allows greater self-determination and empowerment because it brings people together in a quality public realm and allows more time and energy to develop visions and implement them. By enabling efficiencies and synergies, integral urbanism allows greater conservation and less waste, more quality time, and less distrust, paranoia, and fear. In other words, convergences in space and time (of people, activities, businesses, and so forth) generate new hybrids. These hybrids, in turn, allow for new convergences and the process continues. As Jane Jacobs points out in *The Nature of Economies*, this is, in fact, the definition of development (2000).

While the modern paradigm discouraged convergences, restorative practices encourage them. Just as ecosystem resilience relies upon ecodiversity of a place, prosperous places conserve energy (including human) and other resources while decreasing social isolation, thereby empowering people to envision alternatives and implement change most responsively and creatively.

Re Generation

Restorative practices are possible everywhere and increasingly apparent. Indeed, the upward spiral toward prosperity is occurring at all scales, from the wastebasket to the watershed. It is part of what Paul Hawken describes as a worldwide "movement with no name" that will prevail because it is not based on ideology, but on the identification of what is humane, behaving like an immune system (2007). These practices seek to restore connections that have been severed over the last century between body and soul, people and nature, and amongst people. The strength and resilience of relationships and communities rely upon trust, but urban fragmentation during the second half of the twentieth century challenged trust, allowing an "architecture of fear" to occupy the void.[8] Restorative urbanism rebuilds community by cultivating relationships through a process that engages and builds mutually supportive networks of people.[9] The trust upon which relationships and communities rely ensues.

The prosperity paradigm is enabling us to address some of the knotty problems of twentieth-century urbanism such as: How can we accommodate urban growth without harming the natural environment? How can we guide urban growth so that today's solutions do not become tomorrow's problems? How can we contribute to creating places that support humanity so we can thrive, not simply survive? And, how can we plant seeds today that will leave a legacy of urban health and well-being for our children and theirs?

Looking back, we might regard the 1960s as the We generation extolling peace and love, the seventies the Me generation striving for self-awareness and self-actualization, the eighties the Whee generation pursuing materialism and escapism, and the 1990s the Whoa generation, placing a self-imposed brake upon the rapid changes which were wreaking havoc upon our landscapes and our well-being. Looking ahead, this new millennium has been spawning the Re generation, with a clear-eyed vision of a more prosperous future along with the courage and conviction to Re-build our towns and cities, Re-vitalize our communities, and Re-align design with the goal of supporting humanity through Re-storative practices.

HOW THE CITY LOST ITS SOUL

SHARON ZUKIN

Published in Playboy, *April 2010.*

FIG. 1 The street that began the preservation of SoHo in 1973 when the cast-iron facades of dilapidated nineteenth-century factory buildings on Greene Street were designated historic landmarks.

When I was seventeen and left my parents' house in Philadelphia for a college dorm in upper Manhattan, I found a cultural melting pot that fed my fantasies of urban life. Crowds on every street! Stores on every block! Neon nights, makeshift clubs, poets and writers hanging out in dingy cafés! Times Square was a crazy theater of the absurd; in the East Village hippies were running wild and because the drinking age at that time was only eighteen, you could indulge your desire for alcohol without breaking the law (foreign beers!). The city offered space for us to be different—and to make common cause with others who wanted to be different too.

This was no less true for earlier generations of cultural migrants. From the actress-protagonist in *Sister Carrie* to Ayn Rand's architect-hero Howard Roark, fictional characters of the early 1900s came to the big city—Carrie to Chicago, Roark to New York—to pursue their dreams. Langston Hughes, Zora Neale Hurston and W. E. B. Du Bois could only create new forms of literary and political expression in Harlem. During the 1950s, first in San Francisco and then in New York, the Beat generation took advantage of the city's sexual freedoms. Thelonious Monk and other great musicians jammed all night at the jazz loft on Sixth Avenue and invented bebop at the Five Spot downtown. Bob Dylan fled Minnesota to be with other folksters in Greenwich Village.

Artists who came to New York City when I moved there in the 1960s gave us storefront galleries and "happenings" in SoHo. Punk rockers sharpened our sense of irony at CBGB on the Bowery and Max's Kansas City near Union Square. Andy Warhol and then the East Village artists showed us that New York was the place for endless self-creation. Though many experiments, especially with drugs, turned out to be lethal for those who indulged, the whole experience taught us that Cities = Art, and Art = Life.

When did the city lose this feeling? Was it Reaganism or AIDS, as the musical *Rent* suggested, that took the Shangri-La of Avenue A out of our grasp?

New Yorkers saw the city tighten up in the 1980s, when homeless people were chased out of town and hippies were replaced by yuppies. You saw it getting more expensive during the dot-com boom of the 1990s, when working-class families who had lived in your neighborhood for years were replaced by young investment bankers, college students doubling up in railroad flats, and recent art school graduates. You felt the mood shift after 9/11, when our elected leaders' preoccupations turned to shopping and security.

Money made a big difference. With capital flowing like Cristal, real estate investors, many of them headquartered overseas, colonized the city with corporate entertainment venues and upscale condos. Mayors oversaw the crafting of a wholesome public relations image to attract smug suburbanites and uptight foreign visitors fearful of the city's graffiti, dirt, and crime. Within a few years, sleazy districts were Disneyfied. The old Times Square sprouted a Disney store and theater, as well as a Hello Kitty shop, an ESPN Zone and the new corporate headquarters of both Condé Nast and NASDAQ.

It wasn't just Mayor Rudolph Giuliani who did us in, though his name became synonymous with New York's repressive revival during the 1990s. More focused, zero-tolerance policing drove down crime rates; the AIDS and crack epidemics abated. Many dangerous urban areas—where people had gone "slumming" over the years in opium dens, jazz clubs, and dive bars—were pacified by arrests followed by imprisonment, most often for sales of illegal drugs. Dicey neighborhoods were gentrified by affluent homebuyers and stabilized by community organizations that took charge of affordable housing.

New York City has lost its soul, but it's really just a microcosm of what is happening everywhere. It's a cleaner, safer place than it was only thirty years ago, but it has lost the air of freedom that over the years lured so many migrants to escape the boredom and conformity of mainstream culture. The city's unique constellation of raunch and glitz is gone.

There are still dive bars and expensive restaurants, factory ruins and desolate piers, illicit marketplaces for drugs and sex. But the city as we knew it has been homogenized, suburbanized, and domesticated, one latte at a time.

At the same time, travel and technology changed the way consumers cater to their vices. Today you can fly to Vegas for the weekend almost as easily as driving downtown and watch porn privately on the Internet instead of going to an adult video store. Video games absorb youthful energies that used to be spent prowling the city's darker corners for excitement.

Some critics look at the new upscale neighborhoods and blame gentrification. Local officials lusting after investment dollars praise revitalization. Tourists on family vacations call it fun. If you're a longtime city dweller, though, you're in denial. You still ♥ New York, Los Angeles, or Chicago, but you see downtown turning into an urban shopping mall, private guards patrolling local business districts, and—despite the current economic recession—housing prices continuing to soar into the stratosphere. Cities are both too expensive and too predictable to enjoy.

New York has led the way to the cleaner, safer city. The East Village punk scene is dead, Harlem and other black neighborhoods are gaining white residents for the first time in years, and the indie music clubs of Williamsburg, the area that made Brooklyn "cool," are threatened by rising rents and new condo towers (thanks to stalled financial markets, most of these are in remission). The city's first IKEA store has been improbably implanted on the site of a derelict shipyard on the Brooklyn waterfront. Zones that were made toxic by industry and crime grow Whole Foods Markets, trendy restaurants, and bars that wouldn't be out of place in any college town.

These areas are now too expensive to support the mix of social classes and ethnic groups that drew earlier generations. Both the ghetto and the grunge are gone.

It's not all bad. New York's murder rate is lower than it has been in more than forty years; the subways are no longer marred by graffiti. Parks run by private business improvement districts offer farmers' markets, free movies, and the opportunity for cocktails with picnics on the grass. Neighbors harvest tomatoes in community gardens.

But these don't replace the old, authentic city with its bohemian districts where you could nurse a cup of coffee or hang out in an art gallery for hours, the gritty warehouses used for raves and edgy performances, the specialized little shops without a corporate logo. Both the creative city and the city of neighborhoods are gone. There is no space where we can flaunt our difference from the mainstream.

NOTES

PART I. SUSTAINABLE URBANISM, CLIMATE CHANGE, AND RESILIENCE

1.1. PETER CALTHORPE
Urbanism and Climate Change

Notes

1 Author's analysis of data from the World Resources Institute, "US GHG Emissions Flow Chart," http://cait.wri.org/figures.php ?page=/US-FlowChart (accessed April 1, 2010).

2 Information about the assumptions, methodology, and results of the Vision California study and modeling tools can be found at www.visioncalifornia.org.

3 California Department of Finance, "Population Projections by Race," State of California, http://www.dof.ca.gov/research/demographic/reports/projections/p-3/ (accessed February 12, 2010).

4 Natural Resources Conservation Service, "National Resources Inventory 2003 Annual NRI," U.S. Department of Agriculture, http://www.nrcs.usda.gov/technical/NRI/ (accessed February 12, 2010).

5 San Francisco bay estimate based on William Emerson Ritter and *Charles Atwood Kofoid, eds., University of California Publications in Zoology* 14 (Berkeley: University of California Press, 1918), 22; agricultural data from Economic Research Service, "Western Irrigated Agriculture," U.S. Department of Agriculture, http://www.ers.usda.gov/Data/WesternIrrigation/ (accessed April 1, 2010).

6 Research and Innovative Technology Administration, "Table 5-3: Highway Vehicle-Miles Traveled (VMT)," Bureau of Transportation Statistics, http://www.bts.gov/publications/state_transportation_statistics/state_transportation_statistics_2006/html/table_05_03.html (accessed February 12, 2010).

7 Bureau of Transportation Statistics, "National Transportation Statistics 2009" (Washington, D.C.: U.S. Department of Transportation, 2009), table 2-1. The fatality rate per mile traveled is assumed to hold consistent from 2009 until 2050. Hospital costs data from National Highway Traffic Safety Administration, "The Economic Impact of Motor Vehicle Crashes 2000" (Washington, D.C.: U.S. Department of Transportation, 2002), 60.

8 U.S. Environmental Protection Agency (EPA), "National Air Quality: Status and Trends through 2007" (Research Triangle Park, N.C.: EPA, 2008).

9 David R. Bassett Jr. et al., "Walking, Cycling, and Obesity Rates in Europe, North America, and Australia," *Journal of Physical Activity and Health 5* (2008): 795–814.

1.2. PETER NEWMAN, TIMOTHY BEATLEY, AND HEATHER BOYER
Resilient Cities

References

Beatley, T. (2005), *Native to Nowhere*, Washington, D.C.: Island Press.

Beatley, T., and K. Manning (1997), *The Ecology of Place*, Washington, D.C.: Island Press.

Beatley T. (2010), *Biophilic Cities*, Washington, D.C.: Island Press.

Benedict, M., and E, MacMahon (2006) *Green Infrastructure: Linking Landscapes and Communities*, Washington, D.C.: Island Press.

City of Hannover (1998), *Hannover Kronsberg: Model for a Sustainable New Urban Development*, Hannover.

Halweil, B., and D. Nierenberg (2007), "Farming Cities," in O'Meara, M. (ed.), *State of the World, 2007*, Washington, D.C.: Worldwatch Institute.

Hardoy, J., D. Mitlin, and D. Satterthwaite (2001), *Environmental Problems in an Urbanising World*, London: Earthscan.

Hargrove, C., and M. Smith (2006), *The Natural Advantage of Nations*, London: Earthscan.

Hawkens, P., A. Lovins, and H. Lovins (1999), *Natural Capitalism: The Next Industrial Revolution*, London: Earthscan.

Lerch, D. (2007), *Post Carbon Cities: Planning for Energy and Climate Uncertainty*, Portland, Ore.: Post Carbon.

Newman, P., and I. Jennings (2008), *Cities as Sustainable Ecosystems*, Washington, D.C.: Island Press.

Newman, P., and J. Kenworthy (1999), *Sustainability and Cities: Overcoming Automobile Dependence*, Washington, D.C.: Island Press.

Newman, P., T. Beatley, and H. Boyer (2009), *Resilient Cities:*

Responding to Peak Oil and Climate Change, Washington, D.C.: Island Press.

Newman, P., and J. Scheurer (2010), "The Knowledge Arc Light Rail," Parsons Brinckerhoff–Curtin University Sustainability Policy Discussion Paper, Curtin University, Perth.

Newman, P. (2010), *Resilient Cities and Application to Singapore, Environment and Urbanization Asia*, forthcoming.

Putnam, R. (1993), Making Democracy Work: Civic Traditions of Modern Italy, New York: Princeton Architectural Press.

Sawin, J .L., and K. Hughes (2007), "Energizing Cities" in *State of the World*, 2007, Washington, D.C.: Worldwatch Institute.

Scheurer, J., and P. Newman (2008), *Vauban: A Case Study in Public Community Partnerships*, Case Study for United Nations Global Review of Human Settlements, and at www.sustainability .curtin.edu.au.

Walker, B., D. Salt, and W. Reid (2006), *Resilience Thinking: Sustaining Ecosystems and People in a Changing World*, Washington, D.C.: Island Press.

Went, A., W. James, and P. Newman (2008), *Renewable Transport: Integrating Electric Vehicles, Smart Grids, and Renewable Energy*, Parsons Brinckerhoff–Curtin University Sustainability Policy Discussion Paper, www.sustainability. curtin.edu.au/renewable transport.

Notes

1 Walker and Salt, 2006.
2 Newman, Beatley, and Boyer, 2009.
3 City of Hannover, 1998; Scheurer and Newman, 2008.
4 Lerch, 2007.
5 Benedict and McMahon, 2006.
6 Went, James and Newman, 2008.
7 Sawin and Hughes, 2007.
8 Beatley, 2010.
9 Newman, 2010.
10 Halweil and Nierenberg, 2007.
11 Hawkens et al., 1999; Hargrove and Smith, 2006.
12 McDonaugh and Braungart, 2002.
13 Newman and Jennings, 2008.
14 Newman, Beatley, and Boyer, 2009.
15 UN Habitat, 2008.
16 Hardoy et al., 2001.
17 Putnam, 1993.
18 Beatley and Manning, 1997; Beatley, 2005.
19 Newman and Kenworthy, 1999.
20 Newman and Scheurer, 2010.
21 Newman, Beatley, and Boyer, 2009.

1.3. LAWRENCE J. VALE
Interrogating Urban Resilience

Notes

1 Lawrence J. Vale and Thomas J. Campanella, eds., *The Resilient City: How Modern Cities Recover from Disaster* (New York: Oxford University Press, 2005); Steward Pickett, Mary Cadenasso, and J. Morgan Grove, "Resilient Cities: Meaning, Metaphor, and Models for Integrating the Ecological, Socio-economic, and Planning Realms," *Landscape and Urban Planning* 69, 4 (2004), 369–84; Peter Newman, Timothy Beatley, and Heather Boyer, *Resilient Cities: Responding to Peak Oil* *and Climate Change* (Washington, D.C.: Island Press, 2009); Brian Walker and David Salt, *Resilience Thinking: Sustaining Ecosystems and People in a Changing World* (Washington, D.C.: Island Press, 2006); Erik Hollnagel, David D. Woods, and Nancy Leveson, eds., *Resilience Engineering: Concepts and Precepts* (Aldershot, England: Ashgate, 2006); Kenneth R. Ginzburg and the American Academy of Pediatrics, *A Parent's Guide to Building Resilience in Children and Teens* (Elk Grove Village, Illinois: American Academy of Pediatrics, 2006).

2 Yossi Sheffi, *The Resilient Enterprise: Overcoming Vulnerability for Competitive Advantage* (Cambridge, Mass.: MIT Press, 2007); Liisa Välikangas, *The Resilient Organization: How Adaptive Cultures Thrive Even When Strategy Fails* (New York: McGraw-Hill, 2010); William J. Mitchell and Anthony M. Townsend, "Cyborg Agonistes: Trauma and Reconstruction in the Digital Electronic Era," in Vale and Campanella, eds., *The Resilient City*.

3 Ted Steinberg, *Acts of God The Unnatural History of Natural Disaster in America* (New York: Oxford University Press, 2006); Chester Hartman and Gregory Squires, *There Is No Such Thing as a Natural Disaster: Race, Class and Katrina* (New York: Routledge, 2006).

1.4. STEFFEN LEHMANN
Green Urbanism: Formulating a Series of Holistic Principles

References

Brundtland, Gro H. (1987): *The Brundtland Report: Our Common Future* (UN Report, published); Oxford University Press, New York.

Club of Rome (1972): *The Limits of Growth, first report to the Club of Rome*; MIT Press, Cambridge, Mass.

Lehmann, Steffen (2005): *Towards a Sustainable City Centre: Integrating Ecologically Sustainable Development Principles into Urban Renewal*; in *Journal of Green Building* 1, 3, College Publishing, Virginia.

Lehmann, Steffen (2010): *The Principles of Green Urbanism: Transforming the City for Sustainability*; Earthscan, London.

McHarg, Ian (1969): *Design with Nature*; Doubleday, New York.

Wheeler, Stephen M., and Timothy Beatley (2004; 2nd ed. 2009): *The Sustainable Urban Development Reader*; Routledge, London.

Notes

1 McHarg, 1969; Brundtland, 1987; Wheeler and Beatley, 2004; Lehmann, 2005.

1.5. PETER DROEGE
From Renewable Cities to Regenerating Regions: Fire, the First Element of Sustainable Urbanism

References

Carlisle, N., 2009, "Closing the Planning Gap: Moving to Renewable Communities," in Droege, P., ed., *One Hundred Per Cent Renewable—Energy Autonomy in Action*, Earthscan.

Davis, M., 2007, *Planet of Slums*, Verso.

Genske et al., 2009, "Urban Energy Potentials—A Step Towards the Use of 100% Renewable Energies," in Droege, P., ed., 2009. *One Hundred Per Cent Renewable—Energy Autonomy in Action*, Earthscan.

Hansen, J., et al., 2008, "Target Atmospheric CO2: Where Should Humanity Aim?", *Open Atmospheric Science Journal 2*.

Lenzen, M., C. Dey, and C. Hamilton, 2003, "Climate Change," in Hensher, D. A., and K. J. Button, eds., *Handbook of Transport and the Environment*, Elsevier.

Lenzen, M., et al., 2008, "Direct versus Embodied Energy—The Need for Urban Lifestyle Transitions," in Droege, P., ed., 2008, *Urban Energy Transition*, Elsevier.

Peter, S., and H. Lehmann, 2004, *Das deutsche Ausbaupotential erneuerbarer Energien im Stromsektor*, Institute for Sustainable Solutions and Innovations (ISUSI)/Eurosolar.

Puig, J., 2008, *Barcelona and the Power of Solar Ordinances*, in Droege, P., ed., *Urban Energy Transition*, Elsevier.

Schindler, J., and Werner Zittel, 2008, *Crude Oil—The Supply Outlook*, Ludwig-Bölkow-Systemtechnik.

Schuster, J. M., J. de Monchaux, and C. A. Riley II, eds., 1997, *Preserving the Built Heritage: Tools for Implementation*, University of New England.

Delaware Sustainable Energy Utility Web site (http://www.seu-de.org/), 2009.

Von Carlowitz, H. C., 1713, *Sylvicultura Oeconomica, oder haußwirthliche Nachricht und Naturmäßige Anweisung zur Wilden Baum-Zucht*, Johann Friedrich Braun.

Notes

1 Quotes from Carl Sagan and Stephen Hawking collected on http://350orbust.wordpress.com, July 23, 2010.
2 Schindler and Zittel, 2008.
3 Lenzen et al., 2003.
4 Hansen, 2008.
5 Chinese tradition sees wood and metal in place of air and aether/space.
6 Von Carlowitz, 1613.
7 Lenzen et al., 2008.
8 Davis, 2006.
9 Carlisle, 2009.
10 Puig, 2008.
11 www.seu-de.org.
12 www.wildpoldsried.de.
13 See also "Sustainable and Renewable Energy Installations" at www.cfsd.org.uk.
14 Genske et al., 2009.
15 Martinot, 2009.

PART 2. BEYOND NEW URBANISM

2.2. STEPHEN MARSHALL
Sustainable Urbanism in Evolution

Notes

1 See, for example, Le Corbusier's *Ville Contemporaine* (1922).
2 The core evolutionary argument is fully set out in Marshall,

S. (2009), *Cities Design and Evolution*. London and New York: Routledge.
3 Alexander, C. (1966), "A City Is Not a Tree," in *Design*, no. 206, 46–55.
4 Steadman, P. (2007), *The Evolution of Designs*, 2nd edition. London and New York: Routledge; Ziman, J., ed. (2000), *Technological Innovation as an Evolutionary Process*. Cambridge: Cambridge University Press.
5 Marshall, S. (2009), *Cities, Design, and Evolution*.
6 See, for example, Johnson, S. (2001), *Emergence: The Connected Lives of Ants, Brains, Cities, and Software*. London: Penguin; Batty, M. (2005) *Cities and Complexity*. Cambridge, Mass.: MIT Press.
7 Marshall, S. (2010), "Sustainability in Transition," in *Urban Design and Planning*, Proceedings of the Institution of Civil Engineers, no. 163, 93–94.
8 Marshall, S. (2005), *Streets and Patterns*. London and New York: Spon Press; Marshall, S., ed. (2011), *Urban Coding and Planning*. New York: Routledge.

PART 3. EMERGING TOOLS OF URBAN DESIGN SUSTAINABILITY

3.1. CHARLES C. BOHL, ELIZABETH PLATER-ZYBERK, DAVID BRAIN, AND ANDREA GOLLIN
Community Design Charrettes: An Essential Methodology for Civic Engagement in the Community Design Process

Notes

1 Quareshi, 2005.
2 Fieldstone Alliance and Partners for Livable Communities, 2006.
3 Congress for the New Urbanism, 2002.

3.3. SANDY SORLIEN AND EMILY TALEN
Out of Place: Context-Based Codes and the Transect

Notes

1 Duany, Andrés. 2002. "An Introduction to the Special Issue: The Transect." *Journal of Urban Design* 7, 3: 251–60.
2 Bassett, Edward M. 1922. *Zoning*. New York: National Muncipal League, Technical Pamphlet Series No. 5., National Muncipal Review Supplement, 315.
3 Logan, Thomas Harvey. 1972. *The Invention of Zoning in the Emerging Planning Profession of Late-Nineteenth-Century Germany*. Chapel Hill: University of North Carolina Doctoral Dissertation.
4 Ibid.
5 Williams, Frank B. 1914. *Building Regulation by Districts: The Lesson of Berlin*. New York: National Housing Association, 2.
6 Williams, Frank B. 1922. *The Law of City Planning and Zoning*. New York: The MacMillan Company, 251.
7 Civic Development Department. 1929. *Zoning: A Statement of Principles and Procedure*. Washington, D.C.: Chamber of Commerce of the United States.
8 New York City Board of Estimate and Apportionment.

1916. *Final Report of the Commission on Building Districts and Restrictions.* New York: Board of Estimate and Apportionment, Committee on the City Plan, chapter IV, 25, 26.

9   Gries, John M., and James Ford, editors. 1931. *Planning for Residential Districts.* Washington, D.C.: The President's Conference on Home Building and Home Ownership, 32.

10 Williams, Norman. 1956. "The Evolution of Zoning." *The American Journal of Economics and Sociology* 15, 3: 259.

11 Power, Garrett. 1989. "The Advent of Zoning." *Planning Perspectives* 4: 7.

12 www.transect.org.

13 www.phillywatersheds.org/what_were_doing/documents_and_data/cso_long_term_control_plan/.

14 Kellert, Stephen R., ed. 1993. The Biophilia Hypothesis. Island Press.

15 www.epa.gov/compliance/monitoring/programs/cwa/csos.html.

16 www.epa.gov/smartgrowth/pdf/dover.pdf.

17 http://en.wikipedia.org/wiki/Landscape_urbanism.

18 www.brown.edu/Research/EnvStudies_Theses/summit/Briefing_Papers/Greenspace_Openspace/Urban_Trees.html.

19 www.completestreets.org.

3.6. EUGENIO MORELLO AND CARLA RATTI
From Evaluation to Design of the Urban Form
through Assessment of Environmental Indicators

References

Carneiro, C., E. Morello, and G. Desthieux (2009). "Assessment of Solar Irradiance on the Urban Fabric for the Production of Renewable Energy Using LIDAR Data and Image Processing Techniques." In M. Sester, L. Bernard, and V. Paelke, *Advances in GIScience* (Lecture Notes in Geoinformation and Cartography ed., 83–110). Berlin: Springer.

Carneiro, C., E. Morello, C. Ratti, and F. Golay (2008). "Solar Radiation over the Urban Texture: LIDAR Data and Image Processing Techniques for Environmental Analysis at City Scale." In J. Lee and S. Zlatanova, *3D Geo-information Sciences* (Lecture Notes in Geoinformation and Cartography ed., 319–40). Berlin: Springer.

Martin, L., and L. March, L., eds. (1972). *Urban Space and Structures.* London: Cambridge University Press.

Morello, E., V. Gori, C. Balocco, and C. Ratti (2009). "Sustainable Urban Block Design through Passive Architecture: A Tool that Uses Urban Geometry Optimization to Compute Energy Savings." *Proceedings of the 26th International Conference on Passive and Low Energy Architecture.* Quebec City.

Morello, E., and C. Ratti (2007). "Raster Cities: Image Processing Techniques for Environmental Urban Analysis." In K. Thwaites, S. *Porta, and O. Romice, Urban Sustainability through Environmental Design: Approaches to Time-People-Place Responsive Urban Spaces* (119–22). London: Spon Press.

Morello, E., and C. Ratti (2009a). "SunScapes: 'Solar Envelopes' and the Analysis of Urban DEMs." *Computers, Environment, and Urban Systems* 33 (1), 26–34.

Morello, E., and C. Ratti (2009b). "A Digital Image of the City: 3-D Isovists in Lynch's Urban Analysis." *Environment and Planning B: Planning and Design* 36 (5), 837–53.

Ratti, C. (2001). *Urban Analysis for Environmental Prediction.* Unpublished Ph.D. dissertation, Cambridge: University of Cambridge.

Ratti, C., and P. Richens (2004). "Raster Analysis of Urban Form." *Environment and Planning B: Planning and Design* 31 (2), 297–309.

Ratti, C., N. Baker, and K. Steemers (2005). "Energy Consumption and Urban Texture." *Energy and Buildings* 37 (7), 762–76.

Notes

1   Ratti, 2001; Ratti and Richens, 2004; Ratti, Baker, and Steemers, 2005.

2   Morello and Ratti, 2007.

3   Ratti, Baker, and Steemers, 2005; Morello, Gori, Balocco, and Ratti, 2009.

4   Morello and Ratti, 2009a.

5   Carneiro, Morello, Ratti, and Golay, 2008; Carneiro, Morello, and Desthieux, 2009.

6   Morello and Ratti, 2009b.

PART 4. SYSTEMIC MOBILITY, STRUCTURAL ECOLOGY, AND INFORMATICS

4.1. STEPHEN GRAHAM AND SIMON MARVIN
Urbanism in the Anthropocene: Eco-emergency, Resource Securitization,
and Premium Ecological Enclaves

References

Dalby, S. (2007), "Anthropocene Geopolitics: Globalisation, Empire, Environment, and Critique," *Geography Compass* 1 (1), 103–18.

Graham, S. (2010), *Cities Under Siege: The New Military Urbanism.* Verso.

Harvey, D. (2008), "Right to the City," *New Left Review* 53 (September–October).

Hodson, M., and S. Marvin (2010), *World Cities and Climate Change: Producing Urban Ecological Security.* Open University Press.

Luke, T. W. (2003), "Codes, Collectivities, and Commodities: Rethinking Global Cities as Megalogistical Spaces," in Krause, L., and P. Petro (eds), *Global Cities: Cinema, Architecture, and Urbanism in a Digital Age.* Rutgers University Press.

Luke, T. W., (2008), "Climatologies as Social Critique: The Social Construction/Creation of Global Warming, Global Dimming, and Global Cooling," in S. Vanderheiden (ed.), *Political Theory and Global Climate Change.* MIT press.

Zalasiewicz, J., M. Williams, A. Smith, et al. (2008), "Are We Now Living in the Anthropocene," *GSA Today* 18 (2), 4–8.

Notes

1   Graham, 2010; Hodson and Marvin, 2010.

2   Zalasiewicwz et al., 2008.

3   Dalby, 2007.

4   Luke, 2003.

5   Luke, 2008.

4.2. WILLIAM R. BLACK AND BRADLEY W. LANE
The Role of Transit in the Development
of Urban Areas of the United States

References

APTA 2010 Public Transportation Fact Book, 61st Edition. Washington, D.C.: American Public Transportation Association.

Black, W. R. (2003), *Transportation: A Geographical Analysis*. New York: Guilford Press.

Black, W. R. (2010), *Sustainable Transportation: Problems and Solutions*. New York: Guilford Press.

Boarnet, M. G., and R. Crane (2001), *Travel by Design: The Influence of Urban Form on Travel*. New York: Oxford University Press.

Cervero, R., and R. Gorham (1995), "Commuting in Transit versus Auto Oriented Neighborhoods," *Journal of the American Planning Association*, 61 (2), 210–25.

Cervero, R. (1998), *The Transit Metropolis: A Global Inquiry*. Washington, D.C.: Island Press.

Hass-Klau, C., G. Crampton, R. Benjari, (2004), *Economic Impact of Light Rail: The Results of Fifteen Urban Areas in France, Germany, UK, and North America*. Brighton: Environmental and Transport Planning.

Lane. B. W. (2008), "Significant Characteristics of the Urban Rail Renaissance: A Discriminant Analysis," *Transportation Research Part A: Policy and Practice* 42 (2), 279–95.

Lane, B. W. (2010), "TAZ-level Variation in Work Trip Mode Choice between 1990 and 2000 and the Presence of Rail Transit," *Journal of Geographical Systems*, DOI 10.1007/s10109-010-0110-z.

Loukaitou-Sideris, A., T. and Banerjee (2000), "The Blue Line Blues: Why the Vision of a Transit Village May Not Materialize Despite Impressive Growth in Transit Ridership," *Journal of Urban Design*, 5 (2), 101–25.

Smerk, G. M. (1979), "The Development of Public Transportation and the City," in G. E. Gray and L. A. Hoel (eds.), *Public Transportation: Planning, Operations and Management*. Englewood Cliffs, N.J.: Prentice-Hall.

Notes

1 See Smerk, 1979; and Black, 2003.
2 Black, 2010.
3 Lane, 2008.
4 APTA, 2010.
5 For example, Cervero, 1998; Hass-Klau et al., 2004.
6 For example, Lane, 2010.
7 Loukaitou-Sideris and Banerjee, 2000.
8 Hass-Klau et al., 2004.
9 For example, Cervero and Gorham, 1995; Boarnet and Crane, 2001.
10 Hass-Klau et al., 2004.

4.3. ROBERT CERVERO AND CATHERINE SULLIVAN
Green TODs

References

Beatley, T. (2000), *Green Urbanism: Learning from European Cities*. Washington, D.C.: Island Press.

Bernick, M., and R. Cervero (1997), *Transit Villages in the 21st Century*. New York: McGraw-Hill.

Bertolini, L. (1996), "Nodes and Places: Complexities of Railway Station Redevelopment," *European Planning Studies*, 4 (3), 331–45.

Broaddus, A. (2009), "A Tale of Two Eco-Suburbs in Freiburg, Germany: Parking Provisions and Car Use," *Transportation Research Record* (forthcoming).

Center for TOD, TOD 101. 2008. Washington, D.C.: Federal Transit Administration.

Cerfontaine, C. (2007), "The Vauban District in Freiburg in Brisgau: Living in a Holiday Destination, *PTI* September/October, 30–33.

Cervero, R. (1998), *The Transit Metropolis: A Global Inquiry*. Washington, D.C.: Island Press.

Cervero, R. (2007), "Transit Oriented Development's Ridership Bonus: A Product of Self Selection and Public Policies," *Environment and Planning* A, 39, 2068–85.

Cervero, R. (2008), "Transit-Oriented Development in America: Strategies, Issues, Policy Directions," in *New Urbanism and Beyond: Designing Cities for the Future*, T. Haas, ed. New York: Rizzoli, 124–29.

Cervero, R., A. Golub, and B. Nee (2007), "City Car Share: Longer-Term Travel-Demand and Car Ownership Impacts," *Transportation Research Record* 199, 70–80.

Cervero, R., and J. Murakami (2009), "Rail + Property Development in Hong Kong: Experiences and Extensions," *Urban Studies* 46 (10), 2019–43.

Cervero, R., A. Adkins, and C. Sullivan (2010), "Are Suburban TODs Over-parked?", *Journal of Public Transportation* 13 (2), 47–70.

Daisa, J. (2004), "Traffic, Parking, and Transit Oriented Development," *The New Transit Town: Best Practices in Transit-Oriented Development*, Dittmar, H., and G. Ohland, eds. Washington, D.C.: Island Press, 114–29.

Ewing, R., and R. Cervero (2010), "The Built Environment and Travel: A Meta-Analysis," *Journal of the American Planning Association*.

FWTM (Management and Marketing), City of Freiburg, *Quartier Vauban: A Guided Tour.*

Grontmij, A. B. (2008), *Report Summary—Follow Up of Environmental Impact in Hammarby Sjöstad*. Stockholm.

Melia, S. (2007), *On the Road to Sustainability: Transportation and Carfree Living in Freiburg*. Faculty of the Built Environment, UWE Bristol.

Newman, P., T. Beatley, and H. Boyer (2009), *Resilient Cities: Responding to Peak Oil and Climate Change*. Washington, D.C.: Island Press.

Nobis, C., and J. Welsch (2003), "Mobility Management at District Level: The Impact of Car-reduced Districts on Mobility Behavior," 7th European Conference on Mobility Management, Karlstad, Sweden, May.

Renne, J. (2009), "From Transit-adjacent to Transit-oriented Development," *Local Environment* 14 (1), 1–15.

Rieselfeld Projekt Group (2007), "The New District of Rieselfeld." City of Feiburg in Breisgau.

Rietveld, P. (2000), "Non-motorized Modes in Transport Systems: A Multimodal Chain Perspective for The Netherlands," *Transportation Research* D (5), 31–36.

Rietveld, P., V. Daniel (2004), "Determinants of Bicycle Use: Do Municipal Policies Matter?", *Transportation Research* A (39), 531–50.

Scheurer, J. (2001), *Urban Ecology, Innovations in Housing Policy and the Future of Cities: Towards Sustainability in Neighbourhood Communities*. Freemantle, Australia:

Murdoch University, Institute for Sustainability and Technology Policy.

Schick, P. (2009), "Urban Development and Transportation Planning in Freiburg im Breisgau." Freiburg: unpublished report.

Siegl, K. (2010), "The New District of Freiburg-Rieselfeld: A Case Study of Successful, Sustainable Urban Development." Freiburg in Breisgau.

Sustainability Office, City of Freiburg (2009), *Freiburg: Green City*. Freiburg im Breisgau.

U.S. Environmental Protection Agency (2010), Inventory of U.S. Greenhouse Gas Emissions and Sinks: 1990–2008. Washington, D.C.: U.S. Environmental Protection Agency, EPA 430-R-10-006.

Notes

1 Cervero, 2008; Renne, 2009.
2 Beatley, 2000; Newman et al., 2009.
3 Diasa, 2004.
4 Cervero, 1998; Bertolini,1996.
5 Cervero, 2007; Ewing and Cervero, 2010.
6 Cervero et al., 2007.
7 Rietveld, 2000; Rietveld and Daniels, 2004.
8 Cervero, 2007; Ewing and Cervero, 2010; Cervero et al., 2007.
9 This estimate is based on assigning 32 percent of end-use carbon emissions from fossil fuel consumption of urban residents to the surface transportation sector and 22 percent to domestic household consumption, such as for electricity power generation, heating, and cooling. These represent pro-rata estimates of carbon dioxide emissions by end-use sector in the U.S. in 2008, as recorded by U.S. Environmental Protection Agency (2010). Carbon dioxide represented 85 percent of human-induced (anthropogenic) greenhouse gas emissions in the U.S. that year. Other savings would accrue that are not explicitly accounted for in these calculations of end-use emissions, such as reduced transportation costs from shipping and marketing food that, as a form of food security, is instead grown in community gardens.
10 Cervero, 1998.
11 Grontmij, 2008.
12 Ibid.
13 Grontmij, 2008.
14 Nobis and Welsch, 2003.
15 Siegl, 2010.
16 Nobis and Welsch, 2003.
17 Cervero and Murakami, 2009.

4.4. MALCOLM MCCULLOUGH
On Micro-Transactions in Urban Informatics

Notes

1 Hill, Dan (2008), "The Street as Platform," www.cityofsound .com.
2 Hamdi, Nabeel (2004). London: Earthscan.
3 Anderson, Chris (2010), "The Web is Dead, Long Live the Internet," 17 August 2010.
4 Mitchell, William (2003), *Me++: The Cyborg Self and the Networked City*. Cambridge, Mass.: MIT Press.
5 Clark, Andy (1997), *Being There: Putting Brain, Body, and World Together Again*. Cambridge, Mass.: MIT Press.

6 Hardin, Garrett (1968), "The Tragedy of the Commons," *Science* 162 (3859).
7 Ostrom, Elinor (1990), *Governing the Commons: The Evolution of Institutions for Collective Action*. Cambridge: Cambridge University Press.
8 Ostrom, *Governing the Commons*, 9.
9 Ostrom, *Governing the Commons*, 214.
10 Benkler, Yochai (2006), *The Wealth of Networks: How Social Production Transforms Markets and Freedom*. New Haven: Yale University Press.

4.5. RICHARD M. SOMMER
Mobility as an Infrastructure of Democracy

Notes

1 An earlier version of this essay was first published as "Mobility, Infrastructure, and Society," in *Ecological Urbanism*, Moshen Mostafavi and Gareth Doherty, eds. (Lars Muller Publishers, 2009).
2 Melvyn Webber, "The Urban Place and the Non-Place Urban Realm," in *Explorations into Urban Structure*, edited by Melvin Webber, John Dyckman, Donald Foley, Albert Guttenberg, William Wheaton, and Catherine Bauer Whurster (Philadelphia: University of Pennsylvania Press, 1964).

PART 5: EVOLVING CITIES AND SUSTAINABLE COMMUNITIES

5.1. PETER M. HAAS
Prospects for Meaningful Global Environmental Governance

References

Bank, T. W. (2010), Development and Climate Change. Washington D.C.: The World Bank.

Benner, T., et al. (2005), "Multisectoral Networks in Global Governance: Towards a Pluralistic System of Accountability," *Global Governance and Public Accountability*, D. Held and M. Koenig-Archibugi, eds. Malden, Mass.: Blackwell, 67–86.

Biermann, F. B., ed. (2005), *A World Environment Organization: Solution or Threat for Effective International Environmental Governance?* Aldershot: Ashgate.

Brown, L. R. (2003), *Plan B: Rescuing a Planet under stress and a Civilization in Trouble*. New York: Norton.

Cashore, B. A., et al. (2004), *Governing Through Markets: Forest Certification and the Emergence of Non-State Authority*. New Haven: Yale University Press.

Choucri, N. (1993), *Global Accord*. Cambridge, Mass.: MIT Press.

Clapp, J., and P. Dauvergne (2005), *Paths to a Green World*. Cambridge, Mass.: MIT Press.

Ehrlich, P., and A. Ehrlich (2004), *One with Ninevah: Politics, Consumption, and the Human Future*. Washington, D.C., Island Press.

Esty, D. C., and M. H. Ivanova, eds. (2002), *Global Environmental Governance*. New Haven: Yale School of Forestry and Environmental Studies.

Florini, A. M., ed. (2000), *The Third Force*. Washington, D.C.: Carnegie Endowment for International Peace.

Haas, P. (2004), "Addressing the Global Governance Deficit," *Global Environmental Politics* 11 (4), 1–19.

Haas, P. M. (2002), "Constructing Environmental Security from Resource Scarcity," *Global Enviornmental Politics* 2 (1), 1–19.

Haas, P. M., (2007), "Promoting Knowledge Based International Governance for Sustainable Development," *Participation for Sustainability in Trade*, S. Thoyer and B. Martimort-Asso, eds. Brookfield, Vt.: Ashgate.

Haas, P. M., et al., eds. (1993), *Institutions for the Earth*. Cambridge, Mass.: MIT Press.

Hawken, P., et al. (1999), *Natural Capitalism*. Boston: Little Brown.

Kaldor, M. (2003), *Global Civil Society*. Cambridge, Polity Press.

Lipschutz, R. D. (2004), *Global Environmental Politics*. Washington, D.C.: CQ Press.

Najam, A., et al. (2006), *Global Environmental Governance: A Reform Agenda*, IISD.

Pacala, S., and R. Socolow (2004), "Stabilization Wedges," *Science* 305 (5698): 968–72.

Raskin, P., et al., eds. (2002), *Great Transition*. Boston: Stockholm Environment Institute.

Reinicke, W. H., and F. Deng (2000), *Critical Choices*. Cambridge: Cambridge Univeristy Press.

Rischard, J.-F. (2002), *High Noon*. New York: Basic Books.

Smil, V. (2003), *Energy at the Crossroads*. Cambridge, Mass.: MIT Press.

Speth, J. G. (2004), *Red Sky at Morning*. New Haven: Yale University Press.

Speth, J. G. (2008), *The Bridge at the Edge of the World*. New Haven: Yale University Press.

Speth, J. G., and P. M. Haas (2006), *Global Environmental Governance*. Washington, D.C.: Island Press.

Victor, D. G., et al., eds. (1988). *The Implementation and Effectiveness of International Environmental Commitments*. Cambridge, Mass.: MIT Press.

Vogel, D. (2005), *The Market for Virtue*. Washington, D.C.: Brookings.

Wapner, P. (1995), "Politics Beyond the State," *World Politics* 47, 411–40.

Wapner, P. (1996), *Environmental Activism and World Civic Politics*. Albany: SUNY Press.

Weiss, E. B., and H. K. Jacobson (1998), *Engaging Countries: Strengthening Compliance with International Accords*. Cambridge, Mass.: MIT Press.

Weizsacker, E. V., et al. (2009), *Factor Five: Transforming the Global Economy through 80% Improvements in Resource Productivity*. London: Earthscan.

Notes

1   Haas, 2002; Clapp and Dauvergne, 2005; Speth, 2008.
2   Haas, 2007.
3   Victor et al., 1988; Choucri, 1993; Haas et al., 1993; Weiss and Jacobson, 1998.
4   Haas et al., 1993.
5   www.un.org/millenniumgoals.
6   Esty and Ivanova, 2002; Haas, 2004; Biermann, 2005; Najam et al., 2006.
7   Cashore, 2004; Vogel, 2005.

8   Wapner, 1996; Florini, 2000; Reinicke and Deng, 2000; Benner et al., 2005.
9   Hawken et al., 1999; Raskin et al., 2002; Rischard 2002; Brown, 2003; Ehrlich and Ehrlich, 2004; Speth, 2004.
10   http://esa.un.org/unpp/p2k0data.asp.
11   Hawken et al., 1999; Smil, 2003; Pacala and Socolow, 2004; Weizsacker et al., 2009; Bank, 2010.
12   Wapner, 1995; Kaldor, 2003; Lipschutz, 2004.
13   www.earthcharter.org.

5.2. SEAN CONNELLY, MARK ROSELAND, SEAN MARKEY
Building Community Capacity for Strategic Sustainability

Acknowledgments

We would like to thank our community partners for their participation and contribution to the research. This article is based on the research project "Strategic Sustainability and Community Infrastructure" conducted by Simon Fraser University's Centre for Sustainable Community Development in partnership with the Centre for Indigenous Environmental Resources and ICLEI-Local Governments for Sustainability. Funding for the research was provided by Infrastructure Canada's Peer Review Research Strategy. The views expressed herein do not necessarily represent the views of the government of Canada.

Notes

1   See, for example, Roseland, M. (2005), *Toward Sustainable Communities: Resources for Citizens and Their Governments*. Gabriola Island, B.C.: New Society Publishers.
2   ICLEI (2002), Local Agenda 21 Survey. UNDESA. Accessed March 28, 2010: http://www.iclei.org/documents/Global/final _document.pdf.
3   See, for example, Dale, A. (2001), *At the Edge: Sustainable Development in the 21st Century*. Vancouver: UBC Press; Parkinson, S., and M. Roseland (2002), "Leaders of the Pack: An Analysis of the Canadian 'Sustainable Communities' 2000 Municipal Competition," Local Environment 7 (4), 411–29; Gahin, R., V. Veleva, and M. Hart (2003), "Do Indicators Help Create Sustainable Communities?", Local Environment 8 (6), 661–66.
4.   Federation of Canadian Municipalities (2007), *Losing Ground: Canada's Cities and Communities at the Tipping Point*. Ottawa: Federation of Canadian Municipalities.
5   Infrastructure Canada (2010), *Canada's Economic Action Plan: Immediate Action to Build Infrastructure*. Accessed December 6, 2009, http://www.buildingcanada-chantierscanada.gc.ca/index-eng.html.
6   See project website www.sfu.ca/cscd/strategic_sustainability for more details.

5.3. PAUL MURRAIN
The Neighbourhood Unit: The Antithesis of Sustainable Urbanism

Notes

1   Rifkind, C. (1977), *Main Street: The Face of Urban America*. New York: Harper and Row, xi.
2   Hillier, B. (1992), "Look Back To London," in *The Architects Journal*, April 15, 42–46.

3 Schaffer, F. (1970), *The New Town Story*. London: Paladin, 71.

4 Ibid., 72.

5 Jacobs, J. (1961), *The Death and Life of Great American Cities*. London: Pelican Books, 123.

6 Ibid., 124.

7 Duany, A. M., E. Plater-Zyberk, and R. Alminana (2003), *The New Civic Art: Elements of Town Planning*. New York: Rizzoli, 88.

8 Duany, A. M., J. Speck, and M. Lydon (2010), *The Smart Growth* Manual. New York: McGraw Hill, 61.

9 Congress of the New Urbanism (2000), *Charter of The New Urbanism*. New York: McGraw Hill, 76.

10 Duany, A. M, E. Plater-Zyberk, and R. Alminana, op. cit., 84.

11 Farr, D. (2008), *Sustainable Urbanism: Urban Design with Nature*.

12 Urban Task Force (1999), *Towards an Urban Renaissance*. London: UK Government Office of the Deputy Prime Minister.

5.6. CHRISTIAN WERTHMANN
Design in the Non-formal City: Insights from Latin America

Notes

1 Moises Lino da Silva, verbal conversation.

2 Regina Meyer, verbal conversation.

3 It is ironic that the extralegal subdivisions follow the much-acclaimed Sites and Services approach propagated by John Turner and the World Bank in the 1960s. There the strategy was to provide settlers with properties and basic infrastructure to build their own houses, with the decisive difference of incorporating the new areas into the legal framework of city planning.

4 Conde, Luiz Paulo, and Sérgio Magalhães (2004), *Favela-bairro, uma outra história da cidade do rio de janeiro: 1993/2000 uma ação urbanizadora para o rio de janeiro*. Rio de Janeiro: ViverCidades.

5 Janice Perlman (2010), *Favela: Four Decades of Living on the Edge in Rio de Janeiro*, Oxford: Oxford University Press.

PART 6: URBAN THEORY, CITY PLANNING, AND BEYOND

6.1. SUSAN S. FAINSTEIN
Globalization, Local Politics, and Planning for Sustainability

Notes

1 PlaNYC, http://www.ci.nyc.ny.us/html/planyc2030/html/plan/plan.shtml.

2 See Scott Campbell, "Green Cities, Growing Cities, Just Cities? Urban Planning and the Contradictions of Sustainable Development." In *Readings in Planning Theory*, edited by Scott Campbell and Susan S. Fainstein, 435–58 (Oxford: Blackwell, 2003).

3 UN, "Our Common Future," http://www.un-documents.net/ocf-02.htm (1987).

4 David Harvey, *Justice, Nature, and the Geography of Difference* (Oxford: Blackwell, 1996), 177 and 177–82.

5 Mike Raco, *Building Sustainable Communities: Spatial Policy and Labour Mobility in Post-War Britain* (Bristol: Policy Press, 2007), 16.

6 Richard L. Florida, *The Rise of the Creative Class* (New York: Basic Books, 2002).

7 Elizabeth J. Mueller and Sarah Dooling, "Investing in Community: Struggling for Community Benefits in Austin, Texas." Paper presented at the annual meeting of the Association of Collegiate Schools of Planning, Minneapolis, October 2010.

6.4. ALEXANDER R. CUTHBERT
Sustainable Theory—Sustainable Form: The Future of Urban Design

References

Bacigalupi, P. 2010: *The Windup Girl*. San Francisco. Nightshadebooks.

Banham, R. 1976: *Megastructure: Urban Futures of the Recent Past*. London: Thames and Hudson.

Bentley, I. 1976: "What Is Urban Design?—Towards a Definition." *Urban Design Forum 1*. Oxford: Oxford Polytechnic.

Bourdieu, P. 1977: *Outline of a Theory of Practice*. Cambridge: Cambridge University Press.

Bogard, W. 1996: *The Simulation of Surveillance: Hypercontrol in Telematic Societies*. Cambridge: Cambridge University Press.

Burton, E., and M. Jencks. 2000: *Achieving Sustainable Urban Form*. London: Spon.

Castells, M. 1977: *The Urban Question: A Marxist Approach*. London: Edwin Arnold.

Castells, M. 1983: *The City and The Grassroots: A Cross-Cultural Theory of Urban Social Movements*. Berkeley: University of California Press.

Castells, M. 1996: *The Rise of the Network Society*. Oxford: Blackwell.

Castells, M. 1997: *The Power of Identity*. Oxford: Blackwell.

Castells, M. 1998: *End of Millennium*. Oxford: Blackwell.

Cullen, G. 1961: *Townscape*. London: The Architectural Press.

Cuthbert, A. R. 1995: "Surveillance, Private Interest and the Public Domain in Hong Kong." *Cities* 12 (5), 293–311.

Cuthbert, A. R. (ed.). 2003: *Designing Cities*. Oxford: Blackwell.

Cuthbert, A. R. 2006: *The Form of Cities*. Oxford: Blackwell.

Cuthbert, A. R. 2007: "Urban Design: Requiem for an Era—Review and Critique of the Last 50 Years." *Urban Design International* 12 (4), 177–226.

Cuthbert, A. R. 2010: "Whose Urban Design?". *Journal of Urban Design* 15 (3), 443–48.

Cuthbert, A. R. 2010: *Understanding Cities*. (London: Routledge).

Donald, J., and S. Hall. 1987: *Politics and Ideology*. Milton Keynes: The Open University Press.

Ellis, C. 2002: "The New Urbanism: Critiques and Rebuttals." *Journal of Urban Design* 7 (3), 261–91.

Freidson, E. 1994: *Professionalism Reborn: Theory, Prophecy and Policy*. Cambridge: Polity.

Gosling, D. 1984: "Definitions of Urban Design." *Architectural Design* 54 (1/2), 16–25.

Gosling, D., and B. Maitland. 1984: *Concepts of Urban Design*. London: Academy.

Gouldner, A. 1979: *The Future of Intellectuals and the Rise of the New Class*. New York: Seabury Press.

Gramsci, A. 1971: *Selections from Prison Notebooks*. New York: International Publishers.

Harvey, D. 1989: *The Condition of Postmodernity*. Oxford: Blackwell.

Harvey, D. 2000: *Spaces of Hope*. Edinburgh: Edinburgh University Press.

Harvey, D. 2003: *The New Imperialism*. Oxford University Press: Oxford.

Harvey, D. 2006: *Spaces of Global Capitalism*. London: Verso.

Haas, T. 2008: *New Urbanism and Beyond: Designing Cities for the Future*. New York: Rizzoli.

Hawken, P., A. Lovins, and L. Lovins. 1999: *Natural Capitalism: The Next Industrial Revolution*. London: Earthscan.

Isaacs, R. 2000: "The Urban Picturesque: An Aesthetic Experience of Urban Pedestrian Places." *The Journal of Urban Design* 5 (2), 145–80.

J.U.D. 2002: *Journal of Urban Design* 7 (3).

Katz, P. 1994: *The New Urbanism: Towards an Architecture of Community*. New York: McGraw Hill.

Keeler, M., and B. Burke. 2009: *Fundamentals of Integrated Design for Sustainable Building*. Hoboken, N.J.: Wiley.

King, R. J. 1996: *Emancipating Space: Geography, Architecture and Urban Design*. New York: Guilford Press.

Krieger, A., and W. S. Saunders (eds.). 2009: *Urban Design*. Minneapolis: University of Minnesota Press.

Larrain, G. 1982: *The Concept of Ideology*. London: Hutcheson.

Lash, S., and S. Urry. 1994: *Economies of Signs and Space*. London: Sage.

Low, S., and N. Smith. 2006: *The Politics of Public Space*. Abingdon: Taylor and Francis.

Lynch, K. 1960: *Image of the City*, Cambridge, Mass.: MIT Press.

Lynch, K. 1981: *A Theory of Good City Form*. Cambridge, Mass: The MIT Press.

Marshall, N.G. 2000: *Into the Third Milennium: Neocorporatism, the State, and the Urban Planning Profession*. Doctoral Thesis. University of New South Wales, Faculty of the Built Environment.

Mieville, C. 2010: *The City and the City*. New York: Ballantine Books.

Mieville, C. 2000: *Perdido St. Station*. New York: Random House.

Pitts, A. C. 2004: *Planning and Design Strategies for Sustainability and Profit*. Oxford: Elsevier.

Punter, J. 1996: "Urban Design Theory in Planning Practice: The British Perspective." *Built Environment* 22 (4), 263–77.

Rowley, A. 1994: "Definitions of Urban Design." *Planning Practice and Research* 9 (3),179–97.

Schurch, T. W. 1999: "Reconsidering Urban Design: Thoughts about Its Definition and Status as a Field or Profession." *Journal of Urban Design* 4 (1), 5–28.

Scott, A. 2000: *The Cultural Economy of Cities*. London: Sage.

Sorkin, M. 2009: "The Ends of Urban Design." In A. Krieger and W. S. Saunders (eds.) 2009: *Urban Design*. Minneapolis: University of Minnesota Press, 155–83.

Therborn, G. 1982: *The Ideology of Power and the Power of Ideology*. London: Verso.

Thomas, R. 2005: *Sustainable Urban Design*. Abingdon: Spon.

Trancik, R. 1986: *Finding Lost Space: Theories of Urban Design*. New York: Van Nostrand Reinhold.

Valente, C. 2010: *Palimpsest*. New York. Bantam Books.

Notes

1 Bourdieu, 1977.
2 Castells, 1977.
3 Cuthbert, 2007.
4 Cullen, 1961; Lynch, 1981; Gosling and Maitland, 1984; Trancik, 1986; Schurch, 1999; Isaacs, 2000; Krieger and Saunders, 2009.
5 Castells, 1977, 1996, 1997, 1998; Scott, 2000; Harvey, 1989, 2003; Lash and Urry, 1994.
6 Cuthbert, 2003, 2006, 2010.
7 Burton and Jencks, 2000.
8 Bentley, 1976; Gosling, 1984; Rowley, 1994; Punter, 1996.
9 Banham, 1976, 130.
10 Gosling and Maitland, 1984, 7.
11 Rowley, 1994, 181.
12 Krieger and Saunders, 2009.
13 Ibid., 168.
14 Rowe and Koetter, 1978.
15 Cuthbert, 2010, 447.
16 See also King, 1996.
17 Castells, 1983, 304.
18 Low and Smith, 2006.
19 Harvey, 2003, 2006.
20 Gramsci, 1971; Therborn, 1980; Larrain, 1982; Donald and Hall, 1987.
21 Gouldner, 1979; Friedson, 1994; Marshall, 2000.
22 Cuthbert, 2006, 150.
23 Hawkin, Lovins, and Lovins, 1999.
24 Ibid.
25 Thomas, 2003.
26 Pitts, 2004.
27 Keeler and Burke, 2009.
28 Cuthbert, 1995; Bogard, 1996; Harvey, 2000.
29 Katz, 1994; Haas, 2008; J.U.D., 2002.
30 Ellis, 2002.

6.5. MATTHEW CARMONA
The Fourth Tyranny

References

Bentley, I. (1999): *Urban Transformations: Power, People, and Urban Design*. London, Routledge.

Commission for Architecture and the Built Environment (CABE; 2007): *Housing Audit: Assessing the Design Quality of New Housing in the East Midlands, West Midlands, and the South West*. London: CABE.

Carmona, M. (1998): "Design Control: Bridging the Professional Divide—Part 1: A New Framework." *Journal of Urban Design* 3 (2), 175–200.

Carmona, M. (2001): *Housing Design Quality: Through Policy, Guidance, and Review*. London: Spon.

Carmona, M. (2009a): "Design Coding and the Creative, Market, and Regulatory Tyrannies of Practice." *Urban Studies* 46 (12), 2643–67.

Carmona, M. (2009b): "Sustainable Urban Design: Definitions and Delivery." *International Journal for Sustainable Development* 12 (1), 48–77.

Carmona, M., C. de Magalhaes, M. Edwards (2001): *The Value of Urban Design*. London: Thomas Telford.

Carmona M., S. Carmona, and N. Gallent (2003a): *Delivering New Homes: Processes, Planners, and Providers*. London:

Routledge.

Carmona, M., T. Heath, T. Oc, and S. Tiesdell (2003b): *Public Places, Urban Spaces: The Dimensions of Urban Design.* Oxford: Architectural Press.

Cullingworth, B. (1999): *British Planning: 50 Years of Urban and Regional Policy.* London: Athlone Press.

Ellis, C. (2002): "The New Urbanism: Critiques and Rebuttals." Journal of Urban Design 7 (3), 261–91.

Golany, G. (1996): "Urban Design Morphology and Thermal Performance." *Atmospheric Environment* 30 (3), 455–65.

Heriot-Watt University, School of the Built Environment (2007): *Design at the Heart of House-Building.* Edinburgh, The Scottish Government.

Imrie, R., and E. Street (2006): "The Attitudes of Architects Towards Planning Regulation and Control." In *The Codification and Regulation of Architects' Practices.* London, Kings College London.

Jacobs, J. (1994): *The Death and Life of Great American Cities.* London: Penguin Books.

Lang, J. (2005): *Urban Design: A Typology of Procedures and Products.* Oxford: Architectural Press.

Le Corbusier (1927): *Towards a New Architecture* (reprint, 1970). London: Architectural Press.

Leinberger, C. (2008): *The Option of Urbanism: Investing in a New American Dream.* Washington, D.C.: Island Press.

Mantownhuman (2008): *Manifesto: Towards a New Humanism in Architecture*, www.mantownhuman.org.

McGlynn, S. (1993): "Reviewing the Rhetoric." *In Making Better Places: Urban Design Now.* Hayward, R., and S. McGlynn (eds.). Oxford: Architectural Press.

Moore, S., and C. Wilson (2009): "Contested Construction of Green Building Codes in North America: The Case of the Alley Flat Initiative." *Urban Studies* 46 (12), 2617–41.

Reade, E. (1987): *British Town and Country Planning.* Milton Keynes: Open University Press.

Ritchie, A. (2009): "Summary." In Ritchie and Thomas (eds.), *Sustainable Urban Design: An Environmental Approach.* Second Edition. London: Taylor and Francis, 92–94.

Roger Evans Associates (2007): *Delivering Quality Places: Urban Design Compendium 2.* London: English Partnerships & The Housing Corporation.

Rowley, A. (1998): "Private-Property Decision Makers and the Quality of Urban Design." *Journal of Urban Design* 3 (2), 151–73.

Tiesdell, S., and D. Adams (2004): *Design Matters: Major House Builders and the Design Challenge of Brownfield Development Contexts.*

Van Doren, P. (2005): "The Political Economy of Urban Design Standards." In E. Ben-Joseph and T. Szold (eds.), *Regulating Place: Standards and the Shaping of Urban America.* London: Routledge, 45–66.

Walters, D. (2007): *Designing Community: Charrettes, Masterplans, and Form-based Codes.* Oxford, Architectural Press.

Wellings, F. (2006): *British Housebuilders: History & Analysis.* Oxford, Blackwell Publishing.

Worpole, K., and K. Knox (2007): *The Social Value of Public Spaces.* York: Joseph Rowntree Foundation.

Notes
1   Carmona, 2009a.
2   McGlynn, 1993.
3   Walters, 2007, 96.

4   Mantownhuman, 2008, 3.
5   Lang, 2005, 384–85.
6   Worpole and Knox, 2007, 13.
7   Carmona, 2001, 105–9.
8   Rowley, 1998, 172.
9   Lang, 2005, 381.
10   Leinberger, 2008.
11   Wellings, 2006.
12   Carmona et al., 2001.
13   Heriot-Watt University, 2007, 3.
14   Tiesdell and Adams, 2004, 25.
15   Van Doren, 2005, 45, 64.
16   McGlynn, 1993.
17   Reade, 1987, 11.
18   Booth, in Cullingworth, 1999, 43.
19   Imrie and Street, 2006, 7.
20   Carmona, 1998.
21   Ellis, 2002, 262.
22   See Carmona et al., 2003a.
23   CABE, 2007.
24   Lang, 1994.
25   Moore and Wilson, 2009, 2618.
26   Carmona et al., 2003b, 7.
27   In Ritchie and Thomas, 2009, 92.
28   Roger Evans Associates, 2007, 72.
29   Golany, 1996, 464.
30   Jacobs, 1994, 33.
31   Carmona, 2009a.

PART 7: SUSTAINABLE SPATIAL GEOGRAPHIES AND REGIONAL CITIES

7.1. EDWARD W. SOJA
Regional Urbanization and the Transformation of the Modern Metropolis

References

"Regional Urbanization and the End of the Metropolis Era," in Gary Bridge and Sophie Watson, eds., *Companion to the City.* New York and London: Routledge (forthcoming, 2011).

"From Metropolitan to Regional Urbanization," in A. Loukaitou-Sideris and Tridip Banerjee, eds., *Companion to Urban Design.* New York and London: Routledge (forthcoming 2011).

"Regional Urbanization and the Future of Megacities," in Steef Buijs, Wendy Tan, and Deusari Tunas, eds., *Megacities: Exploring a Sustainable Future.* Rotterdam: 010 Publishers, 2010: 57–76.

Notes

1   Edward W. Soja (2000), *Postmetropolis: Critical Studies of Cities and Regions.* Oxford and Malden: Blackwell Publishers.
2   "Taking Space Personally," in Barney Warf and Santa Arias, eds. (2008), *The Spatial Turn: Interdisciplinary Perspectives.* New York and London: Routledge, 11–35.
3   Interesting comparisons can be made, I am sure, of the different trajectories taken by the inner cores of Chinese cities,

such as Beijing, Shanghai, and Guangzhou, especially now that the fastest urban growth rates have shifted to interior regions from the coast.

4   Allen J. Scott, ed. (2001), *Global City-Regions: Trends Theory Policy*. Oxford: Oxford University Press; see also Peter Calthorpe and William Fulton (2001), *The Regional City: Planning for the End of Sprawl*. Washington and London: Island Press.

5   *Seeking Spatial Justice*. Minneapolis: University of Minnesota Press, 2010.

7.2. MATS JOHANSSON AND HANS WESTLUND
The New Rurality and the Diminishing Urban-Rural Dichotomy

References

Agnitsch, K., J. L. Flora, and V. Ryan (2006). "Bonding and Bridging Social Capital: The Interactive Effects on Community Action." *The Journal of the Community Development Society* 37 (1), 36–51.

Beale, C. L. (1975). "The Revival of Population Growth in Non-metropolitan America, Economic Research Service," publication 605, U.S. Department of Agriculture, Washington, D.C.

Bolton, R. (2002). "Place Surplus, Exit, Voice, and Loyalty." In B. Johansson, C. Karlsson, and R. Stough (eds.). *Regional Policies and Comparative Advantage*. Cheltenham: Edward Elgar.

Copus, A. K., et al. (2006). *Study on Employment in Rural Areas*. A study Commisioned by Eurpean Commission, Directorate General for Agriculture. Edinburgh: Scottish Agricultural College.

Copus, A. K., and M. Johansson (2010). *Relationships between Demographic Change and Economic Restructuring in Rural Europe at the Beginning of the 21st Century*. Paper presented at the European population conference, Vienna, September 1–4, 2010

Cross, D. F. W (1990). *Counterurbanization in England and Wales*. Newcastle Upon Tyne: Avebur.

Eliasson, K., M. Johansson, and H. Westlund (2010). "Labour Market Aspects of the 'New Rurality': Employment, Commuting and Entrepreneurship in Rural Sweden." In H. Westlund and K. Kobayashi (eds.), *Social Capital and Development Trends in Rural Areas*, Vol. 5. Jönköping: RUREG, Jönköping International Business School.

ESPON 1.1.1. (2005). *Potentials for Polycentric Development in Europe*. Final report. Luxembourg: ESPON 2004, www.espon.eu.

Fuguitt, G. V, and C. L. Beale (1996). "Recent Trends in Nonmetropolitan Migration: Toward a New Turnaround?". *Growth and Change* 27, 56–174.

Grabner, G. (1993). "The Weakness of Strong Ties: The Lock-In of Regional Development in Ruhr Area." In G. Grabner (ed.), *The Embedded Firm: On Socioeconomics Economics of Industrial Networks*. London: Routledge.

Grabner, G., and D. Stark (1997). "Organising Diversity: Evoluéuinary Theory, Network Analysis, and Post-socialism." In G. Grabner and D. Stark (eds.), *Restructuring Networks in Post-socialism: Legacies, Linkages, and Localities*. Oxford: Oxford University Press.

Green, G. P., S. C. Deller, and D. W. Marcouiller (2005). Intro-

duction. *Amenities and Rural Development*. Theory: Methods and Public Policy. Cheltenham: Edward Elgar.

Hall, P. (1991). "Structural Transformation in the Regions of the United Kingdom." In L. Rodwin and H. Sazanami (eds.), *Industrial and Regional Transformation: The Experience of Western Europe*. New York: United Nations.

Johansson, M. (2009). *Migration and Settlement Patterns among Young People and Families in Swedish Rural and Urban Areas*. Paper presented at the sixth workshop on social capital and development trends in the Japanese and Swedish countryside. Ishigaki Island, Japan, July 1–2, 2009.

Kontuly, T. (1998). "Contrasting the counterurbanization experience in European nations." In P. Boyle and K. Halfacree (eds.), *Migration into Rural Areas: Theories and Issues*. Chichester: John Wiley & Sons, 61–78.

Lancaster, K. (1971). *Consumer Demand: A New Approach*. New York: Columbia University Press.

Phillips, M. (2005). "Differential Productions of Rural Gentrification: Illustrations from North and South Norfolk." *Geoforum* 36, 477–94.

Portes, A., and P. Landolt (1996). "The Downside of Social Capital." *The American Prospect* 94, 18–21.

Power, T. M. (2005). "The Supply and Demand for Natural Amenities: An Overview of Theory and Concepts." In G. P. Green, S. C. Deller, and D. W. Marcouiller (eds.), *Amenities and Rural Development*. Cheltenham: Edward Elgar.

Putnam, R. (2000). *Bowling Alone: The Collapse and Revival of America's Civic Community*. New York: Simon and Schuster.

Roback, J. (1988). "Wages, Rents, and Amenities: Differences among Workers and Regions." *Economic Inquiry* 26, 23–41.

Stockdale, A. (2006). "Migration: Pre-requisite for Rural Economic Regeneration?". *Journal of Rural Studies* 22, 354–66.

Tiebout, C. (1956). "A Pure Theory of Local Expenditure." *Journal of Political Economy* 64, 416–24.

Ullman, E. L. (1955). "Amenities as a Factor in Regional Growth." *Geographic Review* 44, 119–32.

Von Thünen, J. H. (1826). *Der isolierte Staat in Beziehung auf Landwirtschaft und Nationalökonomie*. Hamburg: Perthes.

Westlund (2002). "An Unplanned Green Wave: Settlement Patterns in Sweden During the 1990s." *Environment and Planning* 34, 1395–1410.

Westlund (2006). *Social Capital in the Knowledge Economy: Theory and Empirics*. Berlin, Heidelberg, New York: Springer.

Westlund, H., and W. Pichler (2006). "Settlement Patterns on the Swedish Countryside in the Emerging Knowledge Society." In K. Ito et al. (eds.), *Social Capital and Development Trends in Rural Areas Vol. 2*. Kyoto: MARG, Kyoto University.

Wolcock, M. (1998). "Social Capital and Economic Development: Towards a Theoretical Synthesis and Policy Framework." *Theory and Society* 27.

Notes

1   Von Thünen, 1826.
2   Fuguitt and Beale, 1996.
3   ESPON 1.1.1, 2005.
4   Johansson, 2009.
5   See Kontuly, 1998, and Westlund, 2002, for overviews.

6   Westlund, 2002; Westlund and Pichler, 2006.
7   Ibid.; Johansson, 2009.
8   Eliasson, Johansson, and Westlund, 2010.
9   See, for example, Hall, 1991; Cross, 1990; Phillips, 2005.
10 Copus et. al., 2006; Copus and Johansson, 2010.
11 Stockdale, 2006.
12 Eliasson, Johansson, and Westlund, 2010.
13 Green et al., 2005.
14 Power, 2005.
15 Bolton, 2002.
16 Westlund, 2005.
17 For example, Ullman, 1955; Tiebout, 1956; Lancaster, 1971; Roback, 1988.
18 Power, 2005.
19 See, for example, Grabner, 1993; Garbner and Stark, 1997; Wolcock, 1998; Putnam, 2000; Westlund, 2006; Agnatsch et. al., 2006.
20 Portes and Landholt, 1996.
21 Wolcock, 1998; Putnam, 2000; Agnatsch et. al., 2006.

7.4. WIM TIMMERMANS AND ROBBERT SNEP
Bridging the Gap between Architecture and Biodiversity Conservation: A Step beyond "Greening" Buildings

References
Castells, M. 1996. *The Rise of the Network Society*. Cambridge: Blackwell Publishers.

Evans, G. 2003. "Hard Branding the Cultural City: From Prado to Prada." *Internat J Urban Regional Res* 27 (2): 417–40.

Haken, H., and J. Portugali. 2003. "The Face of the City Is Its Information." *J Environ Psychology* 23: 385–408.

Heckmann, K. E., P. N. Manley, and M.D. Schlesinger. 2008. "Ecological Integrity of Remnant Forests along an Urban Gradient in the Sierra Nevada." *Forest Ecol Management* 255 (7): 2453–66.

Hong, S. K., I. J. Song, and J. Wu. 2007. "Fengshui Theory in Urban Landscape Planning." *Urban Ecosystems* 10: 221–37.

Houben, F. 2001. *Compositie, Contrast, Complexiteit*. Rotterdam: NAi Publishers.

Kretser, H. E., P. J. Sullivan, and B. J. Knuth. 2008. "Housing Density as an Indicator of Spatial Patterns of Reported Human-Wildlife Interactions in Northern New York." *Landsc Urban Plann* 84 (3–4): 282–92.

Kong, L. 2007. "Cultural Icons and Urban Development in Asia: Economic Imperative, National Identity, and Global City Status." *Political Geography* 26: 383–404.

Kooijman, D. 2000. "The Office Building: Between Globalization and Local Identity." *Environ Plann* 27: 827–42.

Lynch, K. 1981. *Good City Form*. Cambridge, Mass.: MIT Press.

Mak, M. Y., and S. T. Ng. 2005. "The Art and Science of Feng Shui—A Study on Architects' Perception." *Building and Environment* 40: 427–34.

McHarg, I. 1971. *Design with Nature*. New York: Doubleday.

McKinney, M., J. L. Lockwood. 1999. "Biotic Homogenization: A Few Winners Replacing Many Losers in the Next Mass Extinction." *TREE* 14 (11): 450–53.

McNeill, D. 2005. "In Search of the Global Architect: The Case of Norman Foster (and Partners)." *Internat J Urban Regional Res* 29 (3): 501–15.

Miller, J. R., R. J. Hobbs. 2002. "Conservation Where People Live and Work." *Conserv Biol* 16: 330–37.

MVRDV. 2006. *FARMAX*. Rotterdam: 010 Publishers.

Pejchar, L., P. M. Morgan, M. R. Caldwell, C. Palmer, and G. C. Daily. 2007. "Evaluating the Potential for Conservation Development: Biophysical, Economic, and Institutional Perspectives." *Conserv Biol* 21: 69–78.

Ren, X. 2008. "Architecture as Branding—Mega Project Developments in Beijing." *Built Environ* 34: 517–31.

Snep, R. P. H., and P. Opdam. 2010. "Integrating Nature Values in Urban Planning and Design. In K. Gaston (ed), *Urban Ecology*. Cambridge: Cambridge University Press: 261–86.

Sudjic, D. 2005. *The Edifere Complex: How the Rich and Powerful Shape the World*. London: Penguin.

Timmermans. 2001. *Nature and the City*. Best, Netherlands: Aeneas Publishers.

Throgmorton, J. A. 2003. "Planning as Persuasive Storytelling in a Global Scale Web of Relationships." *Plann Theory* 2: 125–50.

Tjallingii, S. P. 1996. *Ecological Conditions, Strategies, and Structures in Environmental Planning*. Dissertation. IBN Scientific Contributions 2. Wageningen University, The Netherlands.

Turner, W. R. , T. Nakamura, and M. Dinetti. 2004. "Global Urbanization and the Separation of Humans from Nature." *Bioscience* 54: 585–90.

Uprichard, E., and R. Byrne. 2006. "Representing Complex Places: A Narrative Approach." *Environ Planning* A (38): 665–76.

Notes
1   Turner et al., 2004.
2   McKinney and Lockwood, 1999.
3   Miller and Hobbs, 2004.
4   Snep and Opdam, 2010.
5   Mak and Ng, 2005; Hong et al., 2008.
6   Tjallingii, 2001; Zhang et al., 2008.
7   Pejchar et al., 2007; Heckmann et al., 2008; Kretser et al., 2008.
8   Ren, n.d.; Evans, 2003; Kong, 2007.
9   Sudjic, 1993; McNeill, 2005.
10 Kooijman, 2000.
11 Castells, 1996.
12 Haken and Portugali, 2003; Uprichard and Byrne, 2006.
13 Throgmorton, 2003.
14 Timmermans, 2001.

7.5. N. J. HABRAKEN
Cultivating Built Environment

Notes
1   Habraken, *Supports: An Alternative to Mass Housing*, Urban International Press, U.K. Edited by Jonathan Teicher, reprint of the 1972 English edition.
2   Jean Gottmann, *Megalopolis*, The Urbanized Northeastern Seaboard of the United States, The Twentieth Century Fund, New York, 1961.
3   Stephen Kendall and Jonathan Teicher, *Residential Open Building*, Spon, 2000.
4   For projects of the last decade see the booklet by Prof. Jia Beishi at the Open Building website: http://www.open-building.org/archives/booklet2_small.pdf.
5   See: Project Russia 20, *The Free Plan: Russia's Shell-and-*

Core Apartment Buildings, Bart Goldhoorn, editor, A-Fond publishers, 2001.

6   The INO project, Bern, Switzerland, Client: Office of Properties and Buildings of the Canton Bern, Giorgio Macchi, director.

7   For English language documentation of the Next21 project: *GA Japan* 6, Jan/Feb 1994; *Domus* 891, October 1999.

8   MOOR Ltd., a subsidiary of the Tocoman Group Ltd. Helsinki: www.moor.fi.

9   The IJburg "Solids" Project, by housing corporation Stadgenoot, Frank Bijdendijk, Director, Baumschlager Eberle, architects. http://www.Solids.nl.

10   The " Act for Promotion of Long-Life Quality Housing." Source: Prof. Kazunobu Minami, *The New Japanese Housing Law to Promote the Longer Life of Housing*. Paper, presented at the Open Building conference in Bilbao, Spain, 2010.

11   From an unpublished report by architect Shinichi Chikazumi, Tokyo.

PART 8: JUST ENVIRONMENTS AND STRUCTURE OF PLACES

8.1. JULIAN AGYEMAN AND JESSE MCENTEE
Reimagining Sustainable Urbanism

References

Agyeman, J. 2005, "Sustainable Communities and the Challenge of Environmental Justice," New York: New York University Press.

Agyeman, J., R. D. Bullard, and B. Evans. 2003, "Joined-up Thinking: Bringing Together Sustainability, Environmental Justice, and Equity," in *Just Sustainabilities: Development in an Unequal World*. Cambridge, Mass.: MIT Press.

Alkon, A. 2008, "Paradise or Pavement: The Social Constructions of the Environment in Two Urban Farmers' Markets and Their Implications for Environmental Justice and Sustainability," *Local Environment*, vol. 13, no. 3, pp. 271–89.

Antipode, 2003. Special issue: Urban Political Ecology, Justice and the Politics of Scale. Vol. 35, no. 5, pp. 839–1042.

Beatley, T. 2000, "Green Urbanism: Learning from European Cities," Island Press: Washington, D.C.

Campbell, S. 1996, "Green Cities, Growing Cities, Just Cities? Urban Planning and the Contradictions of Sustainable Development," *Journal of the American Planning Association*, vol. 62, no. 3, pp. 296–312.

Centner, R. 2009, "Conflictive Sustainability Landscapes: The Neoliberal Quagmire of Urban Environmental Planning in Buenos Aires," *Local Environment*, vol. 14, no. 2, pp. 173–92.

CLF Chapter One, 2007. Coalition for a Livable Future, "Chapter One: Regional Equity." The Regional Equity Atlas.

Crossa, V. 2010, "Disruption Yet Community Reconstitution: Subverting the Privitization of Latin American Plazas." *Geojournal*, in press.

Dale, A., andL. L. Newman. 2009, "Sustainable Development for Some: Green Urban Development and Affordability," *Local Environment*, vol. 14, no. 7, pp. 669–81.

Dikeç, M. 2001, "Justice and the Spatial Imagination," *Environment and Planning A*, vol. 33, pp. 1785–1805.

Dooling, S. 2009, "Ecological Gentrification: A Research Agenda Exploring Justice in the City," *International Journal of Urban and Regional Research*, vol. 33, no. 3, pp. 621–39.

Executive Order 12898: Federal Actions To Address Environmental Justice in Minority Populations and Low-Income Populations," 1994, Federal Register, vol. 59, no. 32.

Fainstein, S. 2005, "Cities and Diversity: Should We Want It? Can We Plan For It?", *Urban Affairs Review*, vol. 41, no. 1, pp. 3–19.

Fainstein, S. S. 2006, "Planning and the Just City." Columbia University: Conference on Searching for the Just City, GSAPP, Farr, 2007, p. 42.

Fisher, A., and R. Gottlieb. 1996, "Community Food Security and Environmental Justice: Searching for a Common Discourse," *Agriculture and Human Values*, vol. 3, no. 3, pp. 23–32.

Harvey, D. 1996, *Justice, Nature & the Geography of Difference*, Blackwell: Cambridge.

Harvey, D. 1973, *Social Justice and the City*, The Johns Hopkins University Press: Baltimore.

Heynen, N. 2003, "The Scalar Production of Injustice within the Urban Forest," *Anitpode*, vol. 35, no. 5, pp. 980–998.

Low, N., and B. Gleeson. 1998, *Justice, Society, and Nature: An Exploration of Political Ecology*, Routledge: London.

Low, S., D. Taplin, and S. Scheld. 2005, *Rethinking Urban Parks: Public Space and Cultural Diversity*, University of Texas Press, Austin.

Maroko, A. R., J. A. Maantay, N. L. Sohler, K. L. Grady, and P. S. Arno. 2009, "The Complexities of Measuring Access to Parks and Physical Activity Sites in New York City: A Quantitative and Qualitative Approach," *International Journal of Health Geographics*, vol. 8, no. 1, art. no. 34.

Metro Regional Government, 2010. *Welcome to Metro*. Available at: http://www.oregonmetro.gov/.

Pavel, M.P. 2009, "Breakthrough Communities: Sustainability and Justice in the Next American Metropolis," MIT Press, Cambridge, Mass.

Pirie, G. H. 1983, "On Spatial Justice," *Environment and Planning A*, vol. 15, pp. 465–73.

Rotmans, J., M. van Asselt, and P. Vellinga. 2000, "An Integrated Planning Tool for Sustainable Cities," *Environmental Impact Assessment Review*, vol. 20, pp. 265–76.

Scholsberg, D. 2007, *Defining Environmental Justice: Theories, Movements and Nature*, Oxford University Press, Oxford.

Sherriff, G. 2009, "Towards Healthy Local Food: Issues in Achieving Just Sustainability," *Local Environment*, vol. 14, no. 1, pp. 73–92.

Soja, E. 2000, *Postmetropolis: Critical Studies of Cities and Regions*, Blackwell, Malden, Mass.

Soja, E. 2010, *Seeking Spatial Justice*, University of Minnesota Press, Minneapolis, Minn.

Swyngedouw, E., and N. Heynen. 2003, "Urban Political Ecology, Justice, and the Politics of Scale," vol. 35, no. 5, pp. 898–918.

Wakefield, A. 2000, "Situational Crime Prevention in Mass Private Property," in *Ethical and Social Perspectives on Situational Crime Prevention* (ed. A. von Hirsch, D. Garland, and A. Wakefield), pp. 125–46, Hart Publishing, Portland, Ore.

World Commission on Environment and Development 1987, "Our Common Future," Oxford University Press, Oxford.

Notes

1 Farr, 2007, 42.
2 Beatley, 2000, 5.
3 World Commission on Environment and Development, 1987, 43.
4 Insofar as we can call it the natural environment in an anthropogenic system.
5 Heynen, 2003.
6 Agyeman et al., 2003, 6.
7 Fisher and Gottlieb, 1996.
8 Low and Gleeson, 1998, 1.
9 Swyngedouw and Heynen, 2003, 910.
10 A political ecology approach has acknowledged the importance of process in urban environmental justice. For examples, see special issue of *Antipode*: "Urban Political Ecology, Justice, and the Politics of Scale" (2003).
11 Agyeman et al., 2003.
12 Ibid.
13 Agyeman, 2005.
14 Agyeman et al., 2003, 2.
15 Alkon, 2008.
16 Sherriff, 2009.
17 Centner, 2009.
18 Pearsall and Pierce, 2010.
19 Pavel, 2009.
20 Schlosberg, 2007.
21 Harvey, 1973.
22 Harvey, 1996, 210, 212.
23 Dikeç, 2001.
24 Ibid., 1792.
25 Harvey, 1996, 340.
26 See, for example, Maroko et al., 2009; Low et al., 2005; Dooling, 2009.
27 Wakefield, 2000.
28 Crossa, 2010.
29 Soja, 2000; 2010.
30 For example, Metro Regional Government, 2010.
31 CLF Chapter One, 2007.
32 Dale and Newman, 2009.
33 Campbell, 1996.
34 Fainstein, 2006.
35 Rotmans et al., 2000.

8.2. HENRY CISNEROS
Beyond the Basics: Modern Cities as Engines of Economic Opportunity and Social Progress

Notes

1 City of Boston, Backstreet; http://www.bostonredevelopmentauthority.org/backstreets.
2 BioEnterprise.
3 San Francisco's Treasurer's Office.
4 Judith Rodin, *The University and Urban Revival: Out of the Ivory Tower and into the Streets*, University of Pennsylvania Press, 2007.
5 Aspen Institute, *Project Quest: A Case Study of a Sectoral Employment Development Approach*, 2001.
6 Metropolitan Business Planning Initiative, *Accelerate: A Minneapolis Saint Paul Regional Prospectus for Stimulating the Entrepreneurial Ecosystem.*
7 Neighborhood Centers Inc.: Houston; http://www.neighborhood-centers.org.
8 Denver Scholarship Foundation; http://www.denverscholarship.org.
9 New York City School System; http://schools.nyc.gov/aboutus/schools/childrenfirst.html.
10 Neighborhood Action Initiative, University of Southern California; http://www.usc.edu/ext-relations/nai/index.html.
11 "The Avance Model"; http://www.avance.org/why-avance/model/.
12 Community and Economic Development Committee Work plan; http://www.sanjose.gov/clerk/CEO.
13 Parents Alliance; http://www.parentalliance.org.
14 Annual report, 2008–2009, After-School All-Stars; www.afterschoolallstars.org.
15 Dennis Shirley, "Community Organizing for Parental Engagement," in Robert H. Wilson, *Public Policy and Community*, University of Texas Press, Austin.
16 New Jersey Performing Arts Center, Newark New Jersey; http://www.njpac.org.
17 Sports for Life, San Antonio Jewish Community Center; http://www.jccsanantonio.org.
18 Office of the Mayor, City of Milwaukee; www.visitmilwaukee.org.
19 Joint Center for Housing Studies, *Our Communities, Our Homes: Pathways to Housing and Homeownership in American Cities*, Harvard University.
20 United Villages, Cambridge, Mass.; http://www.unitedvillages.com.
21 Rene Glover, "The Atlanta Blueprint: Transforming Public Housing Citywide," in *From Despair to Hope: Hope VI and the New Promise of Public Housing in America's Cities*, Brookings Institution Press, Washington, D.C., 2009.
22 Office of the City Manager, Austin, Texas; www.ci.austin.tx.us/ahfc/smart.htm.
23 Unity Council of Oakland, Oakland CA.; http://www.unitycouncil.org/html/ftv.html.
24 "A Case Study of Minneapolis, Minnesota," in Bill Geller and Lisa Belsky, *Building Our Way Out of Crime: The Transformative Power of Police-Community Developer Partnerships.*
25 Seattle Climate Action-Now; http://www.seattlegov/html/citizen/climate/html.
26 Paul Grogan and Tony Proscio, *Comeback Cities: A Blueprint for Urban Neighborhood Revival*, Westview Press, 2000, pages 96–101.
27 "Paul Krekorian Proposes Reforms to Neighborhood Council System," in *The Planning Report*, Los Angeles, California.

8.3. CLARE COOPER MARCUS
Planning for a Silent Minority: The Needs of Children for Outdoor Play, Access to Nature, and Independent Mobility

References

Ben-Joseph, E. 1995. "Changing the Residential Street Scene: Adapting the Shared Street (*Woonerf*) Concept to the

Suburban Environment." *Journal of the American Planning Association* 61(4): 512.

Chawla, L. 1986. "The Ecology of Environmental Memory." *Children's Environments Quarterly*, Winter, 34–42.

Chawla, L. 2006. "Learning to Love the Natural World Enough to Protect It." *Barn* 2: 57–78.

Chawla, L., and K. Malone. 2003. "Neighborhood Quality in Children's Eyes." In *Children in the City: Home, Neighborhood, and Community*, edited by P. Christensen and M. O'Brien. London: RoutledgeFalmer.

Check, E. 2004. "Link from Hygiene to Allergies Gains Support." *Nature* 25 (428): 354.

Cobb, Edith. 1977. *The Ecology of Imagination in Childhood.* Dallas: Spring Publications.

Cooper Marcus, C. 1974. "Children's Play Behavior in a Low-Rise, Inner City Housing Development." In *Childhood City*, edited by R. Moore and D. Carson. Stroudsberg, Pa.: Dowden, Hutchinson, and Ross.

Cooper Marcus, C. 1978. "Remembrances of Landscapes Past." *Landscape* 22 (3).

Cooper Marcus, C. 1993. "Postoccupancy Evaluation of Cherry Hill, Petaluma, CA." Berkeley: University of California, Berkeley.

Cooper Marcus, C., and W. Sarkissian. 1986. *Housing as If People Mattered: Site Guidelines for Medium-Density Family Housing.* Berkeley: University of California Press.

Danks, S. 2010. *Asphalt to Ecosystems: Design Ideas for Schoolyard Transformation.* Oakland: New Village Press.

Dowdell, J. A. 2010. "Gated for Community's Sake: Baltimore Alleys Become Gathering Grounds." *Landscape Architecture Magazine* 100 (11).

Eberstadt, M. 1999. "Why Ritalin Rules." *Policy Review* 94, April–May.

Eubank-Ahrens, B. 1991. "A Closer Look at the Users of Woonerven." In *Public Streets for Public Use*, edited by A. Vernez-Moudon. New York: Columbia University Press.

Gause, J., ed. 2002. *Great Planned Communities.* Washington, D.C.: Urban Land Institute.

Gehl, J. 2008. "Lively, Attractive and Safe Cities—But How?". In *New Urbanism and Beyond: Designing Cities for the Future*, edited by Tigran Haas. New York: Rizzoli.

Handy, S., et al. 2007. "Cul-de-sacs and Children's Outdoor Play: Quantitative and Qualitative Evidence," presented at Active Living Research conference, San Diego.

Handy, S., et al. 2008. "Neighborhood Design and Children's Outdoor Play: Evidence from Northern California." *Children, Youth, and Environments* 18 (2). Available from www.colorado.edu/journals/cye.

Kegerreis, S. 1993. "Independent Mobility and Children's Mental and Emotional Development." In *Children, Transport, and the Quality of Life*, edited by M. Hillman. London: Policy Studies Institute.

Moore, R. 1980. "Collaborating with Young People to Assess their Landscape Values." *Ekistics* 281: 128 –35.

Moore, R., and C. Cooper Marcus. 2008. "Healthy Planet, Healthy Childhood: Designing Nature into Daily Spaces of Childhood." In *Biophilic Design: The Theory, Science, and Practice of Bringing Buildings to Life*, edited by S. R. Kellert, J. H. Heerwagen, and M. L. Mador. New York: John Wiley and Sons.

Moore, R., and D. Young. 1978. "Childhood Outdoors: Toward a Social Ecology of the Landscape." In *Human Behavior and Environment*, edited by I. Altman and J. Wohlwill. New York: Plenum Press.

Morrow, V. 2003. "Improving the Neighborhood for Children: Possibilities and Limitations of 'Social Capital' Discourses." In *Children in the City: Home, Neighborhood, and Community*, edited by P. Christensen and M. O'Brien. London: RoutledgeFalmer.

Noschis, K. 1992. "Child Development Theory and Planning for Neighborhood Play." *Children's Environments* 9 (2): 3–9.

O'Brien, M. 2003. "Regenerating Children's Neighbourhoods: What Do Children Want?". In *Children in the City: Home, Neighborhood, and Community*, edited by P. Christensen and M. O'Brien. London: RoutledgeFalmer.

Rigby, N., and P. James. 2003. *Obesity in Europe.* London: International Obesity Task Force.

Sobel, D. 1990. "A Place in the World: Adult Memories of Childhood's Special Places." *Children's Environments Quarterly* 7 (4): 13–17.

Veitch, J., et al. 2006. "Where Do Children Usually Play? A Qualitative Study of Parents' Perceptions of Influences on Children's Active Free Play." *Health and Place* 12 (4).

Notes

1. Rigby and James, 2003.
2. Chawla, 2006.
3. Moore, 2008, 154.
4. Chawla and Malone, 2003; O'Brien, 2003; Morrow, 2003.
5. www.urban.nl/childstreet2005/programme.htm.
6. Cooper Marcus, 1974, 1993; Moore and Young, 1978; Cooper Marcus and Sarkissian, 1986.
7. See www.communitygreens.org.
8. Handy et al., 2008.
9. Veitch et al., 2006. For more detail and case studies of clustered housing see Moore and Cooper Marcus, 2008.
10. Handy et al., 2007.
11. Kegerreis, 1993; Noschis, 1992.
12. Gause, 2002.
13. Eubank-Ahrens, 1991.
14. Ben-Joseph, 1995.
15. Danks, 2010.
16. Cobb, 1977; Cooper Marcus, 1978; Chawla, 1986.
17. Sobel, 1990.
18. Moore and Cooper Marcus, 2008.
19. Check, 2004.
20. See www.childfriendlycommunities.org.

8.4. JASON CORBURN
Healthy and Just Cities / 225

References

Alameda County. 2009. "Life and Death from Unnatural Causes: Health and Social Inequity in Alameda County." www.acphd.org/AXBYCZ/.../unnatural_causes_exec_summ.pdf.

Chadwick, E. 1842. *Report on the Sanitary Condition of the Labouring Population of Great Britain.* Ed. and intro., M. W. Flinn. Edinburgh: University Press, 1965.

CSDH. 2008. "Closing the Gap in a Generation: Health Equity through Action on the Social Determinants of Health." Final Report of the Commission on Social Determinants of

Health. Geneva: World Health Organization.

Corburn, J. 2005. *Street Science: Community Knowledge and Environmental Health Justice.* Cambridge, Mass.: The MIT Press.

Corburn, J. 2009. *Toward the Healthy City: People, Places, and the Politics of Urban Planning.* Cambridge, Mass.: The MIT Press.

Cummins, S., S. Curtis., et al. 2007. "Understanding and Representing 'Place' in Health Research: A Relational Approach." *Social Science and Medicine* 65: 1825–38.

De Leeuw, E. 2009. "Evidence for Healthy Cities: Reflections on Practice, Method, and Theory." *Health Promotion International* 24: i19–i36.

Equality and Human Rights Commission (EHRC). 2010. "How Fair is Britain?". http://www.equalityhumanrights.com/key-projects/triennial-review/.

Geiger, H. J. 1984. "Community Health Centers: Health Care as an Instrument of Social Change." In V. W. Sidel and R. Sidel, eds. *Reforming Medicine: Lessons from the Last Quarter Century.* New York: Pantheon Books.

Geronimus, A. T., and J. P. Thompson. 2004. "To Denigrate, Ignore, or Disrupt: Racial Inequality in Health and the Impact of a Policy-Induced Breakdown of African American Communities." *Du Bois Review: Social Science Research on Race* 1 (2): 247–79.

Jackson, R. 2003. "The Impact of the Built Environment on Health: An Emerging Field." *American Journal of Public Health* 93: 1382–84.

Jenkins, C. D., R. W. Tuthill, S. I. Tannenbaum, and C. R. Kirby. 1977. *New England Journal of Medicine* 296:1354–56.

Harpham, T., S. Burton, and I. Blue. 2001. "Healthy City Projects in Developing Countries: The First Evaluation." *Health Promotion International* 16 (2): 111–25.

Harpham, T. 2009. "Urban Health in Developing Countries: What Do We Know and Where Do We Go?". *Health and Place* 15: 107–16.

Krieger, J., and D. L. Higgins. 2002. "Housing and Health: Time Again for Public Health Action." *American Journal of Public Health* 92: 758–68.

McCord, C., and H. P. Freeman. 1990. "Excess Mortality in Harlem." *New England Journal of Medicine* 322: 173–77.

Rosen, G. 1971. "The First Neighborhood Health Center Movement—Its Rise and Fall." *American Journal of Public Health* 61: 1620–37.

Shattuck, L. 1850. *Report of the Sanitary Commission of Massachusetts, 1850.* Reprint: 1948, Cambridge, Mass.: Harvard University Press.

Vlahov, D., N. Freudenberg, F. Proietti, D. Ompad, et al. 2007. "Urban as a Determinant of Health." *J Urban Health* 84 (Suppl. 1): 16–26.

World Health Organization (WHO). 2009. "The Social Determinants of Health." http://www.who.int/social_determinants/en/.

World Health Organization (WHO). 2010. "Urban Planning Essential for Public Health." http://www.who.int/mediacentre/news/releases/2010/urban_health_20100407/en/index.html.

Notes

1 The World Health Organization (WHO) emphatically noted in a 2008 publication, *Closing the Gap in a Generation: Health Equity through Action on the Social Determinants of Health,* that: "Where systematic differences in health are judged to be avoidable by reasonable action they are, quite simply, unfair. It is this that we label health inequity. Putting right these inequities—the huge and remediable differences in health between and within countries—is a matter of social justice. Reducing health inequities is, for the Commission on Social Determinants of Health (hereafter, the Commission), an ethical imperative. Social injustice is killing people on a grand scale" (CSDH 2008: 1).

2 WHO, 2010; Vlahov et al., 2007.

3 WHO, 2009.

4 Shattuck, 1850; Chadwick, 1842.

5 Jenkins et al., 1977.

6 McCord and Freeman, 1990.

7 Alameda County, 2009, 2.

8 For example, in 2010, Britain's Equality and Human Rights Commission released a report called "How fair Is Britain?", which emphasized that geography, race, and class matter for health; men and women from the highest social classes and wealthiest neighborhoods live up to seven years longer than those from lower socio-economic groups, and Black Caribbean and Pakistani babies are twice as likely to die in their first year as Bangladeshi or White British babies (EHRC 2010).

9 Harpham, 2009.

10 Corburn, 2005.

11 Jackson, 2003.

12 Cummins et al., 2007.

13 Corburn, 2005.

14 Corburn, 2009.

15 Krieger and Higgins, 2002.

16 Geronimus and Thompson, 2004.

17 http://www.sfdph.org/phes/ENCHIA.htm.

18 Corburn, 2009.

19 Rosen, 1971.

20 Geiger, 1984.

21 De Leeuw, 2009; Harpham et al., 2001.

22 www.thehdmt.org.

8.5. DICK URBAN VESTBRO
Sprawl and Urban Types in Sub-Saharan Cities

References

Acioly, Claudio (2000): "Can Urban Management Deliver the Sustainable City? Guided Densification in Brazil versus Informal Compactness in Egypt," pp. 127–40 in Mike Jenks and Rod Burgess (eds): *Compact Cities: Sustainable Urban Forms for Developing Countries,* London and New York: Spon Press.

Burgess, Rod (2000): "The Compact City Debate. A Global Perspective", p 9-24 in Jenks, Mike & Rod Burgess (eds): *Compact Cities: Sustainable Urban Forms for Developing Countries,* London and New York: Spon Press.

Dewar, David (2000): "The Relevance of the Compact City Approach: The Management of Urban Growth in South African Cities," pp. 209–18 in Mike Jenks and Rod Burgess (eds): *Compact Cities: Sustainable Urban Forms for Developing Countries,* London and New York: Spon Press.

Eltayeb, Galal Eldin (undated): *The Case of Khartoum, Sudan,* Department of Geography, University of Khartoum.

Gillham, Oliver (2002): *The Limitless City: A Primer on the Urban Sprawl Debate*, Connecticut: Island Press.

King, Anthony (1984): *The Bungalow: The Production of a Global Culture*, London: Routledge and Kegan Paul.

Kruse, Hanna, and Lotta Torstensson (2010): *Vertical Extensions of the Urban Swahili House: A Proposal for a Standardised Two-storey Construction*, master's thesis in Civil Engineering and Urban Mana¬gement, Royal Institute of Technology, Stockholm.

Lupala, John (2002): *Urban Types In Rapidly Urbanizing Cities: Analysis of Formal and Informal Settlements in Dar es Salam, Tanzania*, Ph. D. thesis, Royal Institute of Technology, Stockholm.

Nguluma, Huba (2003): *Housing Themselves: Transformations, Modernisation, and Spatial Qualities in Informal Settlements in Dar es Salam, Tanzania*, Ph. D. thesis, Royal Institute of Technology, Stockholm.

Nnaggenda-Musana, Assumpta (2004): *Sprawl and the City: House Types in the Formal and Informal Settlements of Kampala*, Ph. D. thesis, Royal Institute of Technology, Stockholm.

Nnaggenda-Musana, Assumpta (2008): *Housing Clusters for Densification within an Upgrading Strategy: The Case of Kampala, Uganda*, Stockholm: the Royal Institute of Technology.

Rådberg, Johan (1996): "Towards a Theory of Sustainability and Urban Quality: A New Method for Typological Classification," pp. 384–92 in Madi Gray (ed): *Evolving Environmental Ideals: Changing Ways of Life, Values, and Design Practices*, Book of Proceedings of the 14th Conference of the International Association of People-Environment Studies, Royal Institute of Technology, Stockholm.

"Sudan Post-Conflict Environmental Assessment," *Sudan Vision*, December, 24 2008.

Notes

1   Burgess, 2000.
2   Nnaggenda-Musana, 2008.
3   Nnaggenda-Musana, 2004.
4   King, 1984; Nnaggenda-Musana, 2004.
5   Rådberg, 1996.
6   Dewar, 2000, 212–13 (text shortened by Vestbro).
7   Burgess, 2000, 18.
8   Acioly, 2000, 129.
9   Lupala, 2002.
10 Nguluma, 2003.
11 Kruse and Torstensson, 2010.
12 Nnaggenda-Musana, 2004; 2008.
13 Nnaggenda-Musana, 2008.

PART 9: URBAN SHIFTS, NEW NETWORKS, GEOGRAPHIES

9.1. PETER BOSSELMANN
Metropolitan Form

References

Ascher, Francois. 1995: *Mètapolis, ou, L'avenir des villes*, Paris: Editions O. Jacob.

Bosselmann, Peter. 2008: *Urban Transformation: Understanding City Design and Form*, Washington, D.C.: Island Press.

Downs, Anthony. 1989: *The Need for a New Vision for the Development of Large U.S. Metropolitan Areas*, Washington, D.C.: Brookings Institution.

Geddes, Patrick. 1915: *Cities in Evolution: An Introduction to the Town Planning Movement and to the Study of Civics*, London: Williams and Norgate.

Gercken, L. G. 1994: *Planning Commissioners Journal* 15, p. 10.

Gehl, Jan. 2010: *Cities for People*, Washington, D.C.: Island Press.

Howard, Ebenezer. 1898: From *Tomorrow: The Peaceful Path to Real Reform*, in *Ebenezer Howard*, eds. Peter Geoffrey Hall, Dennis Hardy, Colin Ward; London and New York: Routledge, 2003.

Jacobs, Jane. 1961: *The Death and Life of Great American Cities*, Random House: New York.

Secchi, Bernardo. 2005: *La città del ventesimo secolo*, Rome: Laterza.

Sieverts, Thomas. 2003: *Cities without Cities*, London: Spon.

Webber, Melvin. 1963, "Order in Diversity: Community without Propinquity," in *Cities and Space: The Future Use of Urban Land*, ed. Lowdon Wingo; Baltimore: John Hopkins Press, p. 24.

Wells, H. G. 1902: From *Anticipations*, in *H. G. Wells*, Harry Wellington Laidler; New York: Vanguard Press, 1927.

Whyte, William H. 1988: *City: The Rediscovery of the Center*, New York; Doubleday.

Notes

1   See http: www.eurostat.Europa.eu.
2   See http: www.Atributosurbanos.es/en/terms/metapolis/.
3   Secchi, Bernardo, 2005; Sieverts, Thomas, 2003.
4   Melvin Webber 1963, "Order in Diversity: Community without Propinquity," in Lowdon Wingo, ed., *Cities and Space: The Future Use of Urban Land*, Baltimore: Johns Hopkins Press, p. 24.
5   Anthony Downs, 1989, "The Need for a New Vision For the Development of Large US Metropolitan Areas," Brookings Institution for Solomon Brothers Inc.
6   Webber, 1962, p. 26.
7   See http://www. theGPRD.com.
8   Peter Bosselmann, 2008, *Urban Transformations*, Washington, D.C.: Island Press.
9   California state assembly bill AB 32, the "Global Warming Solutions Act," signed into law in 2006, set a 2010 greenhouse gas emission reduction goal into law, followed in October of 2008 by senate bill SB375, which demonstrates how to implement the emission reduction goals.
10 Bosselmann, 2008, ibid.
11 The city of San Francisco by itself is a notable exception. Here close to 50 percent of all work-related trips are conducted by public transit, bike, walking. or carpool. Across the Bay Area that number amounts to less than 5 percent.
12 *OECD Territorial Review*, 2006, p. 32, fig. 19.
13 See http://esa.un.org/wup2009/unup/. The UN population estimates for urban agglomerations in China do not include the substantial floating populations that migrate from rural areas. Actual populations are higher.
14 The exact Gerckens quote reads as follows: "Virtually every American problem, real, imagined or sociopsychopathic was solved by physical isolation and segregation, whether race,

illness, illegal behavior or undesired contact with persons of lower income, spatial segregation was the answer."

9.2. MITCHELL JOACHIM
Envisioning Ecological Cities:
The Sci-Fi-Based Solution to Climate Change

References
Dawidoff, Nicholas. 2009. "The Civil Heretic," *New York Times* (March 25, 2009).
Dyson, Freeman. 1988. *Infinite in All Directions*. New York: HarperCollins.
Krieger, Alex, and William S. Saunders (eds.). 2009. *Urban Design*. Minneapolis: University of Minnesota Press, 2009.

Notes
1 Dyson, 1988.
2 Dawidoff, 2009.
3 Krieger and Saunders, 2009.

9.4. CHRISTOPHER B. LEINBERGER
The Marriage of Economic Growth and Sustainable Development

Note
1 William J. Bernstein, *Contours of the World Economy 1–2030 A.D.*, table A.7.

PART 10. BEYOND URBANISM AND THE FUTURE OF GLOBALIZED CITIES

10.2. ANTHONY GIDDENS
A Return to Planning?

Note
1 John Dryzek, "Ecology and Discursive Democracy," in Martin O'Connor, *Is Capitalism Sustainable?* (New York: Guilford Press, 1994), 176–7.

10.3. PETER HALL
City Futures: Paths Through the Maze

References
European Union, Regional Policy (2007). *State of European Cities Report: Adding Value to the European Urban Audit.* By ECOTEC Research and Consulting Ltd, in cooperation with NordRegio and Eurofutures. Brussels: European Union DGH Regio.
G.B. Department for Communities and Local Government (2006). *State of the English Cities: The Competitive Economic Performance of English Cities.* By Parkinson, M., et al. London: DCLG.
Mera, K., and B. Renaud, eds. (2000). *Asia's Financial Crisis and the Role of Real Estate.* Armonk, N.Y.: M. E. Sharpe.
Perez, C. (2002). *Technological Revolutions and Financial Capital: The Dynamics of Bubbles and Golden Ages.* Cheltenham: Edward Elgar.

10.4. ANDRÉS DUANY
General Agreement on Architecture

Note
1 The quality of hundreds of houses in only the Florida resorts of Seaside, Rosemary, Alys, and Windsor is so high that ideological opponents of New Urbanism should avoid first-hand experience, as it is difficult, having actually visited them, to maintain the misconceptions so necessary for their polemic.

10.5. SASKIA SASSEN
Ecologies and Scales of Cities / 273

References
Beddoe, R., R. Costanza, J. Farley, E. Garza, J. Kent, I. Kubiszewski, L. Martinez, T. McCowen, K. Murphy, N. Myers, Z. Ogden, K. Stapleton, and J. Woodward (2009). "Overcoming Systemic Roadblocks to Sustainability: The evolutionary Redesign of Worldviews, Institutions, and Technologies." PNAS 106 (8).
Daly, H. E. (1977). *Steady-State Economics: The Economics of Biophysical Equilibrium and Moral Growth.* San Francisco: W. H. Freeman and Company.
Daly, H.E., and J. Farley (2003). *Ecological Economics: Principles and Applications.* Washington, D.C.: Island Press.
Dietz, T., E. A. Rosa, and R. York (2009). "Environmentally Efficient Well-being: Rethinking Sustainability as the Relationship between Human Well-being and Environmental Impacts. *Human Ecology Review* 16 (1).
Environment and Urbanization. 2007. "Special Issue: Reducing the Risk to Cities from Disasters and Climate Change." Vol, 19, No.1. Retrieved from http://eau.sagepub.com/content/vol19/issue1/.
Etsy, D. C., and M. Ivanova (2005). "Globalisation and Environmental Protection: A Global Governance Perspective." In F. Wijen et al. (eds.), *A Handbook of Globalisation and Environmental Policy: National Government Interventions in a Global Arena.* Cheltenham: Edward Elgar.
Girardet, H. (2008). *Cities People Planet: Urban Development and Climate Change* (2nd ed.). Amsterdam: John Wiley & Sons.
Gund Institute for Ecological Economics, University of Vermont. 2009. http://www.uvm.edu/giee/.
Gupta, A. K. (2004). *WIPO-UNEP Study on the Role of Intellectual Property Rights in the Sharing of Benefits Arising From the Use of Biological Resources and Associated Traditional Knowledge.* Geneva: World Intellectual Property Organization and United Nations Environmental Programme.
Low, N. P., and B. Gleeson, eds. (2001). *Governing for the Environment: Global Problems, Ethics, and Democracy.* Basingstroke: Palgrave.
Mgbeogi, I. (2006). *Biopiracy: Patents, Plants, and Indigenous Knowledge.* Vancouver: University of British Columbia Press.
Morello-Frosch, R., M. Pastor, J. Sadd, and S. Shonkoff (2009). *The Climate Gap: Inequalities in How Climate Change*

Hurts Americans and How to Close the Gap. Los Angeles: USC Program for Environmental and Regional Equity. Retrieved from http://college.usc.edu/geography/ESPE/documents/The_Climate_Gap_Full_Report_FINAL.pdf.

Porter, J., R. Costanza, H. Sandhu, L. Sigsgaard, and S. Wratten (2009). "The Value of Producing Food, Energy, and Ecosystem Services within an Agro-ecosystem." *Ambio* 38 (4).

Redclift, M. (2009). "The Environment and Carbon Dependence: Landscapes of Sustainability and Materiality." *Current Sociology* 57 (3), 369–87.

Rees, W. E. (1992). "Ecological Footprints and Appropriated Carrying Capacity: What Urban Economics Leaves Out." *Environment and Urbanization* 4 (2), 121.

Rees, W. E. (2006). "Ecological Footprints and Bio-Capacity: Essential Elements in Sustainability Assessment." In J. Dewulf and H. Van Langenhove (eds.), *Renewables-Based Technology: Sustainability Assessment*. Chichester: John Wiley and Sons, 143–58.

Reuveny, R. (2008). "Ecomigration and Violent Conflict: Case Studies and Public Policy Implications." *Human Ecology* 36, 1–13.

Sassen, S. (2005). "The Ecology of Global Economic Power: Changing Investment Practices to Promote Environmental Sustainability." *Journal of International Affairs* 58 (2), 11–33.

Sassen, S., ed. (2006). *Human Settlement and the Environment. EOLSS Encyclopedia of the Environment* 14. Oxford: EOLSS and Unesco.

Sassen, S. (2001). *The Global City* (2nd ed.). Princeton, N.J.: Princeton University Press.

Sassen, S. (2008). *Territory, Authority, Rights: From Medieval to Global Assemblages*. Princeton, N.J.: Princeton University Press.

Satterthwaite, D., S. Huq, M. Pelling, H. Reid, and P. Romero Lankao (2007). "Adapting to Climate Change in Urban Areas: The Possibilities and Constraints in Low- and Middle-income Nations." Human Settlements Discussion Paper Series, London: IIED; http://www.iied.org/pubs/pdfs/10549IIED.pdf.

Schulze, P.C. (1994). "Cost-benefit Analyses and Environmental Policy." *Ecological Economics* 9 (3), 197–99.

Van Veenhuizen, R. and G. Danso (2007). *Profitability and Sustainability of Urban and Peri-urban Agriculture*. Rome: Food and Agriculture Organization of the United Nations. Retrieved from http://www.ruaf.org/sites/default/files/2838.pdf.

Warner, K., C. Ehrhart, A. de Sherbinin, S. Adamo, S., and T. Chai-Onn (2009). *In Search of Shelter: Mapping the Effects of Climate Change on Human Migration and Displacement*. CARE International. Retrieved from http://www.ehs.unu.edu/file.php?id=621.

Notes

1   Saskia Sassen is the Robert S. Lynd Professor of Sociology and co-directs The Committee on Global Thought, Columbia University (www.saskiasassen.com). Her new books are *Territory, Authority, Rights: From Medieval to Global Assemblages* (Princeton University Press, 2008) and *A Sociology of Globalization* (W. W.Norton, 2007). Forthcoming is the fourth fully updated edition of *Cities in a World Economy* (Sage, 2011). She organized a five-year project on sustainable human settlement with a network of researchers and activists in over thirty countries; it is published as one of the volumes of the *Encyclopedia of Life Support Systems* (Oxford: EOLSS Publishers).

2   For example, Dietz et al., 2009.

3   Sassen, 2005; for an application see, for example, Porter et al., 2009.

4   For the impact of environmental destruction on generating refugee flows, often directed to cities, see, for example, Warner et.al. (2009) and Reuveny (2008). For the differences in impacts on the rich and poor in cities, see, for example, Morello-Frosch et al. (2009) and *Environment and Urbanization* (2007). For the development of urban agriculture as a major response see, for example Van Veenhuizen and Danso (2007).

5   Some kinds of international agreements are crucial, for instance, when they set enforceable limits on each national society's consumption of scarce resources and their use of the rest of the world as a global sink for their wastes. I find other such agreements problematic, notably the one for carbon trading, which has negative incentives: firms need not change their practices insofar as they can pay others to take on their pollution, which could mean no absolute reduction in pollution.

6   Girardet, 2009; Rees, 2006.

7   Satterthwaite et al., 2007; Low and Gleeson, 2001; Etsy and Ivanova, 2006.

10.6. NAN ELLIN
Restorative Urbanism: From Sustainability to Prosperity

References

Alexander, Christopher (1987). *A New Theory of Urban Design*. New York: Oxford University Press.

Al Waer, Husam. and Hilson Moran (2010). "Sustainable Innovation of the Year" (competition submission).

Block, Peter (2008). *Community: The Structure of Belonging*. Berrett-Koehler.

Cooperrider, David L., and Diana Whitney (2005). *Appreciative Inquiry: A Positive Revolution in Change*. Berrett-Koehler Publishers.

De Sola-Morales, Manuel (2004). "The Strategy of Urban Acupuncture," presented at Structure Fabric and Topography Conference," Nanjing University.

Ellin, Nan (2010). "The Tao of Urbanism," *What We See: Advancing the Observations of Jane Jacobs*, Stephen A. Goldsmith and Lynne Elizabeth, eds., New Village Press and Center for the Living City.

Ellin, Nan (2006). *Integral Urbanism*, Routledge.

Ellin, Nan (1999). *Postmodern Urbanism*, Princeton Architectural Press.

Ellin, Nan, ed. (1997). *Architecture of Fear*, Princeton Architectural Press.

Frampton, Kenneth (1999). "Seven Points for the Millennium: An Untimely Manifesto," *Architectural Record*, p. 15.

Hawken, Paul (2007). *Blessed Unrest: How the Largest Movement in the World Came into Being and Why No One Saw It Coming*, Viking Press.

Hawken, Paul (1993). *The Ecology of Commerce*.

Hawken, Paul, Amory Lovins, and Hunter Lovins (1997). *Natural Capitalism: Creating the Next Industrial Revolution*.

Hillman, James (2003). "City," in *City and Soul*, Spring Publications.

Jacobs, Jane (2000). *The Nature of Economies*, Modern Library.

Kim, W. Chan, and Renée Mauborgne (2005). *Blue Ocean Strategy: How to Create Uncontested Market Space and Make Competition Irrelevant*, Harvard Business Press.

Koh, Jusuch, and Anemone Beck (2007). "Landscape Is What; Landscape Is How: On a Landscape/Ecological Approach to Contemporary Urbanism," MS.

Landry, Charles (2000). *Creative City*.

Lerner, J. (2003). *Acupunctura Urbana*, Editora Record.

Nordström, Kjell, and Jonas Ridderstråle (1999). *Funky Business: Talent Makes Capital Dance*, Pearson Education.

McKnight, John, and John Kretzmann (1996). *Building Community from the Inside Out*.

Scharmer, C. Otto (2007). *Theory U: Leading from the Future as It Emerges*, Society for Organizational Learning.

Stavros, Jacqueline, and Gina Hinrichs (2009). *The Thin Book of SOAR: Building Strengths-Based Strategy*.

Notes

1   Such transformation is being advocated in today's corporate business world. In *Funky Business*, Kjell Nordström and Jonas Ridderstråle of the Stockholm School of Economics proclaim: "Competitive Strategy is the route to nowhere" (1999). And in *Blue Ocean Strategy*, W. Chan Kim and Renée Mauborgne similarly contend that companies need to go beyond competing by creating new opportunities, or what they call "blue oceans" (2005).

2   Ellin, 1997, 1999.

3   See Cooperrider and Whitney.

4   The shift to this new model is illustrated by a shift in organizational management from the SWOT (strengths, weaknesses, opportunities and threats) analysis to SOAR (strengths, opportunities, aspirations and results); see Stavros and Hinrichs.

5   This theme was further developed in Paul Hawken, Amory Lovins, and Hunter Lovins, 1997.

6   This term has been applied by Frampton, Lerner, de Sola-Morales, Ellin (2006), and Koh and Beck.

7   VIDA draws from community-building and organizational learning approaches, particularly Asset-Based Community Development (McKnight and Kretzmann, 1996), the Creative City (Landry, 2000), Theory U (Scharmer, 2007), and the work of Peter Block (2008).

8   See Ellin, 1997.

9   This approach towards healing places was advocated by Christopher Alexander, 1987.

CONTRIBUTORS

SUSTAINABLE URBANISM AND BEYOND

TIGRAN HAAS is the Associate Professor of Urban Planning and Design at the School of Architecture and the Built Environment at KTH—Royal Institute of Technology in Stockholm, Sweden.

PART 1. SUSTAINABLE URBANISM, CLIMATE CHANGE, AND RESILIENCE

PETER CALTHORPE is a San Francisco–based architect, urban designer, and urban planner. He is the principal of Calthorpe Associates and a cofounding member of the Congress for New Urbanism.

PETER NEWMAN is an environmental scientist, author, and educator based in Perth, Western Australia. He is currently the Professor of Sustainability at Curtin University.

TIMOTHY BEATLEY is the Teresa Heinz Professor of Sustainable Communities, in the Department of Urban and Environmental Planning, School of Architecture at the University of Virginia.

HEATHER BOYER is senior editor at Island Press and 2005 Loeb Fellow at the Harvard Graduate School of Design.

LAWRENCE VALE is the Ford Professor of Urban Design and Planning at the Department of Urban Studies and Planning, Massachusetts Institute of Technology.

STEFFEN LEHMANN is the Director of the Zero Waste SA Research Centre for Sustainable Design and Behavior (sd+b) and is the Professor of Sustainable Design in the School of Art, Architecture, and Design at the University of South Australia.

PETER DROEGE is the Professor of Sustainable Spatial Development at the Institute of Architecture and Planning, University of Liechtenstein, and is the President of Eurosolar.

RAYMOND L. GINDROZ is a cofounder and principal emeritus of Urban Design Associates (UDA) and a Senior Fellow of the HRH Prince's Foundation in London.

HARALD KEGLER is the Professor of City Planning at the Laboratory for Regional Planning in Bauhaus-University Weimar, Dessau, and the Chair of Council for European Urbanism.

MICHAEL MEHAFFY is an educator, researcher, author, public speaker, and strategic planning consultant and the President of the urban development consultancy Structura Naturalis Inc.

PART 2. BEYOND NEW URBANISM

STEFANOS POLYZOIDES is the principal of Moule & Polyzoides Architects and Urbanists and he is a cofounder of the Congress for the New Urbanism.

STEPHEN MARSHALL is the Senior Lecturer, Reader in Transport Planning and Urban Design and the Director for Ph.D. Town Planning at the Bartlett School of Planning University College London.

DOUG FARR is an American architect and urban planner, director of Farr Associates Architecture and Urban Design, Inc., and the inaugural chair of the LEED for Neighborhood Development committee.

VICTOR DOVER serves as principal-in-charge of Dover, Kohl & Partners—Town Planning, and is the current Chair and cofounder of the Congress for the New Urbanism.

JOSEPH KOHL was among the founders who established Dover, Kohl & Partners—Town Planning and he is a cofounder of the Congress for the New Urbanism.

JEFF SPECK is a city planner and architectural designer who was the Director of Design at the National Endowment for the Arts and Director of Town Planning at Duany Plater-Zyberk and Co.

DHIRU THADANI is a consultant, architect, urbanist, and educator and the former Principal and Director of Urban Design and Town Planning at Ayers/Saint/Gross, Washington, D.C.

PART 3. EMERGING TOOLS OF URBAN DESIGN SUSTAINABILITY

ELIZABETH PLATER-ZYBERK is the Distinguished Professor of Architecture and Urbanism and the Dean at the School of Architecture, University of Miami, Principal of Duany Plater-Zyberk & Company, and cofounder of the Congress for the New Urbanism.

CHARLES C. BOHL is a Research Associate Professor and director of the Knight Program in Community Building at the University of Miami's School of Architecture.

DAVID BRAIN is the Professor of Sociology at the New College of Florida.

ANDREA GOLLIN is the Publications Manager of New Urbanism Online, the CNU Daily News, and a freelance writer in Miami.

TORBJORN EINARSSON, an architect and urban designer, is principal of Arken SE Arkitekter AB.

SANDY SORLEIN is a fine-art photographer and educator, SmartCode and Charrette Consultant.

EMILY TALEN is the Professor of Geography and Urban Planning at the School of Geographical Sciences, Arizona State University, Tempe.

PATRICK CONDON is a professional city planner and Professor at the University of British Columbia, School of Architecture and Landscape Architecture.

JACKIE TEED is a landscape architect and Senior Manager at the Design Centre for Sustainability, University of British Columbia.

CHRIS BUTTERS is an architect, consultant, and co-principal of GAIA International, Oslo, Norway.

CARLO RATTI is an Associate Professor of the Practice and Director, Senseable City Laboratory, MIT Boston, and Partner of CarloRatti Associati—Walter Nicolino & Carlo Ratti, Architecture Design Office.

EUGENIO MORELLO is the Professor of urban design at the Polytechnic of Milan and consultant in architecture and urban design at the Human Space Lab, Milan.

PART 4. SYSTEMIC MOBILITY, STRUCTURAL ECOLOGY, AND INFORMATICS

SIMON MARVIN is Professor of Sustainable Urban and Regional Development and Co-Director of SURF—The Centre for Sustainable Urban and Regional Futures at the University of Salford, Manchester.

STEPHEN GRAHAM is the Professor of Cities and Society at the Global Urban Research Unit and is based in Newcastle University's School of Architecture, Planning, and Landscape.

WILLIAM R. BLACK is the Professor Emeritus, Department of Geography, Indiana University, Bloomington.

BRADLEY W. LANE is the Assistant Professor at the University of Texas at El Paso, Institute for Policy and Economic Development.

ROBERT B. CERVERO is the Professor of City and Regional Planning; Director, University of California Transportation Center; Director, Institute of Urban and Regional Development at UC Berkeley.

CATHERINE SULLIVAN is a Graduate Researcher, Department of City and Regional Planning at UC Berkeley.

MALCOLM MCCULLOUGH is an Associate Professor of Architecture at Taubman College of Architecture and Urban Planning at the University of Michigan.

RICHARD SOMMER is the Dean and Professor of Architecture and Urbanism at Daniels Faculty of Architecture, Landscape, and Design, University of Toronto.

PART 5: EVOLVING CITIES AND SUSTAINABLE COMMUNITIES

PETER M. HAAS is a professor of Political Science at the University of Massachusetts, Amherst, and the Karl Deutsch Visiting Professor at the Wissenschaftszentrum Berlin.

MARK ROSELAND is the Director, Centre for Sustainable Community Development, and Professor, School of Resource and Environmental Management, Simon Fraser University, B.C., Canada.

SEAN CONNELLY is a senior researcher at the Center for Sustainable Community Development, Simon Fraser University, B.C., Canada.

SEAN MARKEY is an Assistant Professor in the Explorations in Arts and Social Science program at Simon Fraser University, B.C., Canada.

PAUL MURRAIN, an architect, urban design practitioner, and landscape architect, is Visiting INTBAU Professor and Scholar at the University of Greenwich, U.K.

HARRISON S. FRAKER is the former Dean and Professor of Architecture and Urban Design at the College of Environmental Design (CED) at the University of California, Berkeley.

THORBJÖRN ANDERSSON is a landscape architect at SWECO FFNS Architects and Guest Consulting Professor at Swedish

University of Agricultural Sciences SLU, Landscape Architecture.

CHRISTIAN WERTHMANN is an Associate Professor and Program Director at the Department of Landscape Architecture, Graduate School of Design, Harvard University.

PART 6: URBAN THEORY, CITY PLANNING, AND BEYOND

SUSAN FAINSTEIN is the Professor of Urban Planning, Department of Urban Planning and Design, Graduate School of Design, Harvard University, Boston

MARGARET CRAWFORD is the Professor of Architecture and Urbanism at the College of Environmental Design (CED) at the University of California, Berkeley.

JONATHAN BARNETT, architect and planner, is a professor of practice in city and regional planning, and director of the Urban Design Program at the University of Pennsylvania.

ALEXANDER CUTHBERT is Emeritus Professor of Planning and Urban Development at the University of New South Wales in Sydney.

MATTHEW CARMONA is the Professor of Planning and Urban Design and the Head of the Bartlett School of Planning in London.

PART 7: SUSTAINABLE SPATIAL GEOGRAPHIES AND REGIONAL CITIES

EDWARD SOJA is the Distinguished Professor of Urban Planning at the UCLA School of Public Affairs and Visiting Professor at the London School of Economics.

HANS WESTLUND is the Visiting Professor of Regional Science and Social Capital at the School of Architecture and the Built Environment at KTH—Royal Institute of Technology in Stockholm, Sweden.

MATS JOHANSSON is the Associate Professor of Regional Science and Planning at the School of Architecture and the Built Environment at KTH—Royal Institute of Technology in Stockholm, Sweden.

BOSSE BERGMAN is an Urban Historian and Associate Professor Emeritus at the School of Architecture and the Built Environment at KTH—Royal Institute of Technology in Stockholm, Sweden.

WIM J. TIMMERMANS is a Senior Research Fellow at Alterra, Research Institute for Our Green Living Environment, Wageningen University & Research Centre, Team Urban and Regional Development, Associate Professor at Van Hall Larenstein, University of Applied Sciences, Landscape Architecture, The Netherlands.

ROBBERT SNEP is a Senior Research Scientist, Alterra, Research Institute for Our Green Living Environment, Green Metropolises Research Program, Wageningen University & Research Centre, Team Urban and Regional Development, The Netherlands.

N. JOHN HABRAKEN is a Dutch architect, educator, and theorist and Professor Emeritus at the Department of Architecture at the Massachusetts Institute of Technology.

PART 8: JUST ENVIRONMENTS AND STRUCTURE OF PLACES

JULIAN AGYEMAN is an environmental social scientist and the Professor and Chair of Urban and Environmental Policy and Planning at Tufts University.

JESSE MCENTEE is a Research Fellow at the ESRC Centre for Business Relationships, Accountability, Sustainability, and Society, Cardiff University, and Principal of McEntee Research & Consulting Company.

HENRY G CISNEROS, a former mayor, a politician, and a businessman, served as the tenth Secretary of Housing and Urban Development in the administration of President Bill Clinton.

CLARE COOPER MARCUS is the Professor Emerita of Architecture and Landscape Architecture at the College of Environmental Design (CED) at the University of California, Berkeley.

JASON CORBURN is the Associate Professor of City and Regional Planning at the College of Environmental Design (CED) at the University of California, Berkeley.

DICK URBAN VESTBRO is the Professor Emeritus of Built Environment Analysis at the School of Architecture and the Built Environment at KTH—Royal Institute of Technology in Stockholm, Sweden.

PART 9: URBAN SHIFTS, NEW NETWORKS, GEOGRAPHIES

PETER C. BOSSELMANN is a Professor of Urban Design in Architecture, City and Regional Planning, and Landscape Architecture, College of Environmental Design (CED) at the University of California, Berkeley.

MITCHELL JOACHIM is a leader in ecological design and urbanism. He is a Co-Founder at Planetary ONE [Open Network Ecology] and Terreform ONE [Open Network Ecology]. Mitchell is an Associate Professor at NYU and the European Graduate School, Switzerland.

ANDERS J. SÖDERLIND is a journalist, architect, researcher, urbanist, and blogger. He is the director of the City in Cooperation Organization (Citysamverkan) in Stockholm, Sweden.

CHRISTOPHER B. LEINBERGER is a metropolitan land strategist and developer. He is the Visiting Fellow, Metropolitan Policy Program, The Brookings Institution, and Professor of

Practice in Urban and Regional Planning, Taubman College, University of Michigan, Ann Arbor.

JOHN KRIKEN is a city planner and urban designer and the founder of Skidmore, Owings & Merrill's San Francisco–based Urban Design and Planning Studio and an Adjunct Professor at University of California, Berkeley, College of Environmental Design.

PART 10. BEYOND URBANISM AND THE FUTURE OF GLOBALIZED CITIES

PETER EISENMAN is an American architect of global renown. Founder of the Institute of Architecture and Urban Studies and Founder and Principal of Eisenman Architects, he is also an educator and the Charles Gwathmey Professor in Practice at the Yale School of Architecture.

ANTHONY GIDDENS, Baron Giddens, serves as Emeritus Professor at the London School of Economics and is considered to be one of the most prominent modern contributors in the field of sociology.

SIR PETER HAL is Professor of Planning and Regeneration at the Bartlett School of Architecture and Planning, University College London, and Senior Research Fellow at the Young Foundation (formerly the Institute of Community Studies).

ANDRÉS DUANY is an architect, writer, and urbanist, Principal of Duany Plater-Zyberk & Company, and the cofounder of the Congress for the New Urbanism.

SASKIA SASSEN is the Robert S. Lynd Professor of Sociology at Columbia University, New York, and the Centennial Visiting Professor at the London School of Economics.

NAN ELLIN is the Chair and Professor of city and metropolitan planning at the University of Utah, College of Architecture and Planning.

SHARON ZUKIN is the Professor of Sociology at Brooklyn College, New York, and the City University Graduate Center, and Visiting Professor, University of Amsterdam.

ACKNOWLEDGMENTS

I am especially grateful to the authors in the book, all of whom have exhibited great patience and commitment in bringing this project to life and kindly providing their latest thoughts and ideas on the subject in the framework provided. I am also privileged to have had the honor in moderating this new amazing group of individuals. I thought this can only happen once, but as they say: *Never say never*. (Who knows, there might be even a third time around!) Every author and editor owes intellectual debt to and draws upon the ideas, thoughts, and insights of many before him. I have been influenced and inspired by many who have stimulated, perplexed, and challenged me throughout my career, not least from a large number of the contributors assembled here. I am also grateful to one of the authors for giving me a nickname: "the Bob Geldof of Urban Design." It was surely an exclusive privilege to moderate this special "Live (Green) Urban Design Aid."

As it was the case with *New Urbanism and Beyond*, I am deeply indebted to the co-founders of the New Urbanism movement, Andrés Duany and Peter Calthorpe, for continuous support and guidance. Throughout the last two decades they have been an intellectual inspiration for me. I am very privileged to know them. Without them the New Urbanism and Beyond Summer Conference, Course, and Debates in Stockholm, October 2004, would have never materialized and therefore the idea and inspiration to put together the first and even this follow-up book (whose structures were the result of my research) would have never seen the proper light of day. As was the case with its predecessor, *Sustainable Urbanism and Beyond: Rethinking Cities for the Future* also got its initial inspiration from a conference: The Council for European Urbanism and Congress for New Urbanism Conference on Climate Change and Urban Design, held in Oslo, Norway, in September 2008. Michael Mehaffy, Audun Engh, and Harald Kegler deserve kudos for pulling that one off!

At Rizzoli, thanks to David Morton for his continuing foresight and urban vision in believing that this new extraordinary group of ladies and gentleman could be assembled yet again in one place, and to Douglas Curran and Ron Broadhurst for patience and support during the long and tedious work of seeing this second book through and bringing this whole project to a successful end. Thanks are due to all the editors, expert reviewers, and various professionals that offered their valuable comments and suggestions during the way and at the near end. Also, to Stephen Fournier (New Urbanism and Beyond) and to Helen Runting (Sustainable Urbanism and Beyond), huge thanks for the fine language brush strokes, sensitivity, and proper word suggesitons. And, as the usual disclaimer goes, all errors of omission are mine, and mine only.

The research that led to this book was partly made possible by the support of the Axel and Margaret Ax:son Johnson Foundation, The Swedish Research Council (Formas), and the Riksbyggen Anniversary Fond ("The Good City"). I am especially indebted to Peter Elmlund, Urban City Research at the Ax:son Johnson Foundation, for providing initial seed money and long-term vision for the whole "Urbanism and Beyond" project; Louise Nyström, Göran Cars, Douglas Kelbaugh, Manuel Castells, Saskia Sassen, Michael Mehaffy, William J. Mitchell, and Robert Cervero for offering intellectual guidance and mentorship. I owe particular debt and gratitude to my U.S. hosts, William J. Mitchell, Cynthia Wilkes, Anne Beamish, and Kent Larsen, Massachusetts Institute of Technology, Media Lab; and Robert Cervero, Peter Bosselmann, and Vicky Garcia, CED, University of California, Berkeley. It was during those visits that this project was envisioned, created, and executed. Special thanks goes to Dr. Federico Cinquepalmi, Ministry of Education, Universities, and Research, Italy, and my EU research colleagues at the Sapienza—Università di Roma. I am also grateful for the intellectual and professional sustenance at my home base, School of Architecture and the Built Environment at KTH—The Royal Institute of Technology in Stockholm, Sweden. And special acknowledgment goes to Joel Garreau.

Finally, this is a suitable occasion to remember the late Professor William J. Mitchell, a visionary architect and urbanist with a truly Renaissance mind who inspired many.

INDEX

Page numbers in *italics* refer to illustrations.

A

Abu Dhabi, UAE, 187
Acconci, Vito, *8*
Acioly, Claudio, 231
Adelaide, Australia, 127
Adickes, Franz, 100
Africa, sub-Saharan, 229–32
African Americans, health inequities among, 226
Agrarian Urbanism, 102
agribusiness, 169
agriculture, 15, 192
    locally-sourced movement in, 28, 35, 169–74
    "outlaw," 172
    urban, 26, 28, 84, 126, 170–73
    see also farmland
Agyeman, Julian, 208–11
AIA, 89
AIA Committee on the Environment (COTE), 62
AIDS, 283
air conditioning, *see* heating/cooling (HVAC) systems
air pollution, air quality, 15, 16, 28, 102, 146, 275
    see also carbon (CO_2) emissions; greenhouse gas emissions
Alameda County Health Department, 226
Alexander, Christopher, 50, 58, 182
Alexandria, Egypt, 204
Allen, Woody, 245
"Alley Gating and Greening," 220–21, *222*
American Society of Heating, Refrigerating, and Air-Conditioning Engineers (ASHRAE), 65
Amsterdam, Netherlands, 35, 211, *248*
Andersson, Åke E., 10
Andersson, Thorbjörn, 159–61
Andreesen, Mark, 266
Andrew, Hurricane, 86–87
Anthropocene Era, 120–22
Anticipations (Wells), 233
Antwerp, Belgium, 52–53
Apple, 254

ArcGIS, 176, 179
architects, architecture:
    as collective endeavor, 271
    communication by, 271–72
    ecology and, 199–203, 272
    social responsibility of, 271
Architecture of the City, The (Rossi), 261
Arlington County, Va., 71–72, *73*, 178, 254
Arup Associates, 112
Ascher, François, 233
Atlanta, Ga., 124, 214, 253
Attention Deficit Hyperactivity Disorder (ADHD), 220
Aurora, Ill., *223*
Austin, Tex., 168
Australia, 19, 93
authenticity, 281
automobile industry, development and, 220
automobiles:
    dependency on, 9, 14, 16, 21, 27, 67, 79, 123–25, 156, 179, 220, 229, 238
    development and, 252–53
    Le Corbusier and, 51–52, 186
    rail lines vs., 80, 120, 219
    restricting use of, 131–32
    sharing of, 127, *128*, 132

B

Bacigalupi, Paolo, 182
Baker, Nick, 118
Baltimore, Md., 124, 220–21, *222*
Banham, Reyner, 180
Barcelona, Spain, 18, 53
Barnett, Jonathan, 175–79
BART (San Francisco), 178
batteries, 19
Bauhaus, 44
Baumeister, Richard, 100
Bay Wolf, 169
Beatley, Timothy, 18–21
Beddington Zero Energy Development (BedZED), 19, 186–87
Beijing, 236, 238
Belasco, Warren, 169

Benfield, Kaid, 64
Benkler, Yochai, 135
Bergman, Bosse, 196–98
Berkeley, Calif., 169, 170–71, *172*, 173
Berkeley Bowl, 170
Berkeley Ecology Center, 170
Bern, Switzerland, 206
Berners-Lee, Tim, 266
Berry, Wendell, 169
Better Building Partnership (BBP), 145–46
bicycling, 27, 48, 67, 124, 126, 127, 129, 130, 132, 157, 238, 239, 259
bike-sharing, 127, *128*
Bilbao effect, 190
biodiversity, 18, 26, 140, 199–203
bio-gas, 20, 128, 129
biomass energy, 19, 25–26, 32
biophilia, 50, 102
biotechnology, 266
Blaabaerstein (Nesodden, Norway), *111*
Black, William R., 123–25
Black Death, 46
black water, 19, 26
Block, Peter, 278, 280
Bloomberg, Michael, 167
Bochum, *43*, 45, *45*
Bogota, Colombia, 165–66
Bogunovich, Dushko, 9
Bohl, Charles C., 86–90
Bosselmann, Peter, 233–39
Boston, Mass., 160, 225–26
Bourdieu, Pierre, 171
Boyer, Heather, 18–21
Brain, David, 86–90
Brazil, 163, 166
Bristol, UK, 210
British Columbia, University of, 106
brownfields, rebuilding of, 257
Brundtland Report, 115, 167, 250
Buddhism, 31
Buffalo, N.Y., 124
buffer zones, 92
building codes, 64–65, 81, 84–85
    see also zoning codes
building materials:
    locally-sourced, 27, 63

Florida, 86–87, 179
Florida, Richard, 168, 254–55
Florida Public Officials Design, 90
Florida Super Region, *176, 177,* 179
food:
    globalization and, 31
    locally-sourced, 28, 35, 169–74
    security of, 28
ForageSF, 172
forest conservation, 26
46th & Hiawatha Station Area
        (Minneapolis), 64
Foshan, China, 235
fossil fuels:
    dependence on, 10, 21, 25, 31, 32, 33, 129
    zero reliance on, 32
    see also specific fuels
Fraker, Harrison, 155–58
Franco, Fernando de Mello, *164*
Frankfurt, Germany, 100
Freedom Riders, *138*
Freiburg, Germany, 18, 20, *113,* 127–28,
        130–32, 157
French National Library, 200
Fresh Kills landfill, 242–43
Fuller, Richard Buckminster, 15, 30, 62
"Functional City, The," 51
functions and activities, integration of, 281
future, unpredictability of, 60–61

G

Garden Cities of To-Morrow (Howard), 233
gardens:
    community, *see* agriculture, urban
    rooftop, 28, *63,* 166
GATEPAC, 53
Gay Parade, 248
Geddes, Patrick, 115, 182, 233
Gehl, Jan, 95, 224
Gehry, Frank, 262
gentrification, 210, 282–83
    of rural areas, 193
geothermal energy, 25–26, 32, 155, 157
Gercken, L. C., 239
Germany, 43, 45, 99, 126, 157, 160
    history of zoning in, 100
    renewable energy in, 34, 130–32, 266
Giddens, Anthony, 263–64
Gillham, Oliver, 229
Gindroz, Ray, 36–42
Giuliani, Rudolph, 283
globalization, 31, 120, 180, 190
    diversity and, 250
    local decision making and, 168
global warming, 140, 178, 266
Gollin, Andrea, 86–90
Gordon and Betty Moore Foundation, 156
Gottmann, Jean, 204
government, governance, 29, 33, 213
    cities and, 213, 218
    environmental, 140–43
    health equity and, 226
    as master developers, 70–71
Graham, Stephen, 120–22
Grand Avenue Vision Plan and Master Plan,
        88

Grant Park (Chicago), *82*
gray water, 19, 26
Graz, Austria, 8
Green Building Council, U.S., 89
green buildings, 14, 26–27, 84, 127, 155,
        200
    LEED criteria for, 62–64, *63, 64,* 90,
        112, 279
green cities, 19–20, 257, 259
greenhouse gas emissions, 15, 27, 32, 128,
        129, 146, 237, 253, 274
    see also carbon (CO2) emissions
green infrastructure (GI), 102
green jobs, 121
green technologies, 10, 12, 14
Green Urbanism, *see* sustainable urbanism
greenways, 221–22
Groningen, Netherlands, 35, 200–203
Guangdong, China, 204
Guangzhou, China, 235
Guggenheim Museum, Bilbao, 191

H

Haas, Peter M., 140–43
Haas, Tigran, 9–13
habitat:
    conservation of, 14
    destruction of, 48, 120
Habraken, N. J., 204–7
Hall, Peter, 265–68
Hamburg, Germany, 100
Hamdi, Nabeel, 134
Hamlet, N.Y., 209
Hammarby Sjöstad (Stockholm), 20,
        127–30, *128,* 132, 157
Hana Nasif (Dar es Salaam), 231–32
handheld mobile computing, 133
Hannover, 18, 132, 157
Hannover World Expo, 200
Harlem (New York, N.Y.), 226
Harvard University, 160
Harvey, David, 167, 209
Hawken, Paul, 133–34, 278, 281
health equity, 225–28
health impact assessment (HIA), 227
Healthy Development Measurement Tool
        (HDMT), 228
heating/cooling (HVAC) systems, 19, 126,
        129, 155
    district-based, 130
    waste streams and, 128
heat island effect, 26, 126, 127, 155,
        273
heat pumps, 32
Henzelmann, Torsten, 266
hierarchy of gifts, *276, 277*
hierarchy of needs, *276, 277*
Hill, Dan, 133
Hillier, Bill, 149
Hillman, James, 276
Hindu tradition, 31
Ho Chi Minh City, Vietnam, *258*
homogenization, biodiversity and, 199
Hong Kong, 132, 204, 235, 237–38
Hoover, Herbert, 101
HOPE Collaborative, 172

housing:
    affordable, 14, 28, 79, 81–83, *83*
    choice and, 16, *57*
    cities and, 213, 218
    cluster, *111,* 219, 220–21, *221,* 232
    evolution of, 204–5
    health inequity and, 227
    integration of workplace with, 238
    as living cells, 204–7
    modernism and, 51–57
    multifamily, 239
    open-space design for, 205–6
    single-family homes, 124, 125
Housing and Urban Development
        Department, U.S. (HUD), 65, 87
Howard, Ebenezer, 233
Hull House, 226
hybridity, 281
hydroelectric energy, 25–26, 155

I

Ideal Conservation Network, 179
ideology, urban design and, 182, 246, 249
immigrants, in rural areas, 193–95
incentives, as regulatory tools, 33, 251
India, 234, 238, 265
induced demand, 80
industrial age, 120, 160
    built environment and, 252–53
    environmental degradation and, 253
Industrial Ecology, 166
industrialized nations, 30
industry, 15
inequality, social and economic, 167, 191
Infinite in All Directions (Dyson), 241
information commons, 135
information technology, 190
infrastructure, 10, 14, 79, 178, 196
    car-based, 21, 47–48
    decentralized, 166
    energy policy and, 33–34
    green (GI), 102
    in non-formal cities, 166
    as parkland, *63*
    regional, *56*
    "shovel-ready" projects for, 144
Institute for Transportation Engineers (ITE),
        68
Intergovernmental Panel on Climate Change,
        44
Intermodal Surface Transportation Efficiency
        Act (1991), 125
International Slow Food Movement, 171
Internet, 180
Interstate Highway Act (1956), 125
Israel, 84

J

Jacobs, Jane, 16–17, 48–49, *49,* 50, 74, 150,
        188, 233, 281
Japan, 31, 194, 206
Jenks, Mike, 231
Joachim, Mitchell, 240–45
Johansson, Mats, 192–95